The Normativity of Formal Orders and Procedures in Antiquity: A Comparison of Mathematical and Legal Systems

Die Normativität formaler Ordnungen und Prozeduren in der Antike: Mathematische und rechtliche Regelsysteme im Vergleich

Edited by Daliah Bawanypeck,
Annette Imhausen, Guido Pfeifer

Kārum – Emporion – Forum

Beiträge zur Wirtschafts-, Rechts- und Sozialgeschichte des östlichen Mittelmeerraums und Altvorderasiens

Band 4

Herausgegeben von
Angelika Lohwasser, Hans Neumann und Kai Ruffing

Ugarit Verlag

Edited by Daliah Bawanypeck,
Annette Imhausen, Guido Pfeifer

The Normativity of Formal Orders and Procedures in Antiquity: A Comparison of Mathematical and Legal Systems

Die Normativität formaler Ordnungen und Prozeduren in der Antike: Mathematische und rechtliche Regelsysteme im Vergleich

2021
Ugarit-Verlag
Münster

Edited by Daliah Bawanypeck, Annette Imhausen, Guido Pfeifer

The Normativity of Formal Orders and Procedures in Antiquity:
A Comparison of Mathematical and Legal Systems

Die Normativität formaler Ordnungen und Prozeduren in der Antike:
Mathematische und rechtliche Regelsysteme im Vergleich

Kārum – Emporion – Forum 4

www.ugarit-verlag.com

Printed in Germany

ISBN: 978-3-86835-284-9

Printed on acid-free paper

Table of Contents

Introduction 1

Law and Order in Ancient Mesopotamia:
Legal Codes and Mathematical Problems
Jim Ritter 7

Mathematische Anleihen in altmesopotamischen Rechtssammlungen
Guido Pfeifer 47

Zu den formalen Gliederungsprinzipien und sprachlichen Ausdrucksformen früher keilschriftlicher Rechtssammlungen unter dem Gesichtspunkt ihrer normativen Intentionen
Das Beispiel Codex Ur-Namma (§§ 1–43)
Hans Neumann 61

Zur Frage von Ausdruck und Normgültigkeit mathematischer Regeln in Mesopotamien
Hagan Brunke 83

Hethitische Landschenkungsurkunden:
Normative Ausgestaltung und praktische Geltung königlicher Schenkungsverfügungen
Daliah Bawanypeck 107

Normative Structures in Texts from the Contexts of Mathematics, Justice, and Law in Pharaonic Egypt
Annette Imhausen 141

How to Express Normativity in Demotic.
The Mathematical and Legal Manuals in Context
Mark Depauw 167

Normative Texts in Ptolemaic Egypt
Katelijn Vandorpe and Valérie Wyns 181

On the Authority of Normative Texts.
Inscriptional Law and Mathematical Literature in Ancient Greece
Markus Asper 197

Überlegungen zu den Klagen strengen Rechts – *certum* und *incertum* als Leistungsgegenstand
Peter Gröschler 221

Al-Shāfiʿī und Kelsen:
Bestimmtheit, Wahrscheinlichkeit und Fehler(bewusstsein) in der formalen Rechtsordnung
Nahed Samour 253

Indices 281

Introduction

The present volume is the result of the project "The Normativity of Formal Orders and Procedures in Antiquity – A Comparison of Mathematical and Legal Systems", carried out in two Workshops held within the framework of the former cluster of excellence "Normative Orders" at the Goethe-University during 2015 and 2016. The project was originally planned as part of a diachronic overview covering periods from antiquity to modern times. Its point of departure was the observation that systems of legal norms (constitutions, law collections, legal handbooks etc.) and mathematical systems (expressed for example as compilations of definitions and theorems) both represent formal orders. Their value in certain legal and scientific theory perspectives is based on a high degree of internal coherence, which can enable deductive derivations and, in their application to concrete problems, provide unambiguous decisions (problem solutions). On both sides, the existence of a formal order is characterized by certain superordinate norms (meta-norms), which guide the construction and application of the respective system of rules. At first glance, the orientation towards such meta-norms, which underline a formal understanding of legal and mathematical orders and procedures, is a characteristic feature of a specifically *modern* understanding of law and mathematics, formulated and founded in the first decades of the 20th century in the context of scientific and cultural modernity by representatives of the disciplines like Hans Kelsen and David Hilbert.[1] However - and this was the starting point of the present project in this context - when looking at very early stages of written legal and mathematical systems and procedures, it is apparent that the establishment of formal orders in these two (and indeed other) areas was a historically early achievement of at least some (if not all) written cultures.[2] Therefore, the formation, but also the historical and cultural variation of those meta-norms that relate to the construction and application of formal orders and procedures in law and mathematics should be understood as a historical process *de longe durée*. The present volume presents studies of the beginnings of this process.[3]

The individual contributions include studies of Egyptian and Mesopotamian sources as well as studies of sources from the Graeco-Roman world and one contribution from a medieval islamicate context. The contributions that focus on Egypt and Mesopotamia, which presumably yielded the earliest attestations of

---

[1] Kelsen, 1934 and Hilbert, 1899.

[2] For examples from a variety of disciplines cf. Bawanypeck / Imhausen, 2014. On normativity and scientific disciplines see also Renn, 2014.

[3] Research on the later periods of this process was not carried out within the framework of the cluster of excellence *Normative Orders*. However, there are some earlier publications that take steps in this direction for later periods, e.g. Radbruch, 1989 and Stephanitz, 1970. Earlier contributions that focus on the relation between mathematical and legal texts for Mesopotamian and ancient Greek examples can be found in Asper, 2001 and 2005; Cuomo, 2000 and Ritter, 2004.

written mathematical and legal texts, illustrate that despite some formal similarities (e.g. the usage of written procedures) some of the underlying concepts as well as the design of individual documents are strikingly different. Mesopotamia and Egypt are the most ancient cultures who developed systems for writing and number notation, which were then used by a literate and numerate group of people to administer the country for their respective rulers. Writing as well as numeracy were fundamental in securing and governing the royal claim to the resources of the country. In the further development of both cultures, they were also employed in the creation of formal systems to structure the respective societies by fixing specific information in writing and thus enabling the establishment of enduring normative orders. Egypt, as well as Mesopotamia used structured lists and collections of paradigmatic individual cases in establishing bodies of knowledge.[4] These early formal systems express explicitly and implicitly elements of the normative orders that they are based on, e.g. by setting fixed numerical values to allow royal control of the amount of work that was expected to be delivered from a specific individual in a set time.[5] Collections of paradigmatic examples indicate concrete procedures how to deal with a specific case. These procedures can be used to reconstruct elements and characteristic aspects of a normative order that they were based on. Two prominent corpora of such procedures are mathematical problem texts (extant from roughly contemporary times in Egypt and Mesopotamia) and law collections/codes (attested first in Mesopotamia and from later periods in Egypt as well). A direct comparison between sources from the context of mathematics and a source from a legal context in Mesopotamia from a formal point of view is explicated in the contribution of Jim Ritter. Mark Depauw analyses expressions of normativity in demotic mathematical and legal texts. The chapter by Markus Asper compares mathematical and legal sources from ancient Greece with regard to their textual technologies of authority and trust. The authority of Mesopotamian mathematical texts with regard to their normative character is studied by Hagan Brunke. Daliah Bawanypeck analyses the formal normativity found in royal Hittite land grants.

Regarding sources from Egypt and Mesopotamia (as well as the Hittite sources), which were not as influential as the Greco-Roman tradition for the development of normative and scientific orders in the Western world, allows a different approach to study the creation of formal orders in mathematical and judicial contexts. They force us to reflect on concepts familiar to us, such as coherence and abstraction. At first glance, it seems that the compilations of mathematical problems or legal cases seem to have been consciously designed neither for consistency nor for completeness. Above all, the processing of older templates can make the law collections appear inconsistent, while the mathematical texts at least compile related procedures that build on each other. The degree of formalization of the texts (the mathematical collections lack the symbolism we are familiar with) and the degree of abstraction of the law collections also appear inconsistent,

[4] Cf. for Egypt Deicher / Maroko, 2015. For Mesopotamia, a large corpus of lists is available online, cf. http://oracc.museum.upenn.edu/dcclt/index.html (access August 24, 2020). For studies of these lists see e.g. Edzard, 2007; Veldhuis, 1997.

[5] Cf. Imhausen, 2013.

mainly thanks to their casuistic, sometimes seemingly random structure. However, the assumption of coherence in the scholarly treatment of the sources makes these texts accessible on a level beyond pure description, while at the same time avoiding levelling differences with other formalization possibilities. The fact that the character of the law collections is still disputed and even their normative power is doubted with good reason, because no explicit references can be found in the records of the contemporary legal practice, makes them a particularly interesting object of research.[6] The study of ancient oriental and Egyptian citation or general reference practice can receive new impulses here. Thus, the contribution of Hans Neumann aims to explain the sequence found in the codex Ur-Namma and Jim Ritter analyses the structure found in the codex Ḫammurapi. Textual normative elements from Ptolemaic Egypt are studied by Katelijn Vandorpe and Valérie Wyns.

In any case, the sources from the fields of mathematics and law provide procedures in the cultural areas under consideration which, if applied, enable unambiguous results – whether these procedures were actually used or not is another problem. Thus, the legal and mathematical procedures share another feature with regard to their normativity. In order to solve a mathematical problem, the respective procedure (assuming it is correct) must be followed precisely – there is no (or very little) room for creative variation, and there is not much chance of unexpected things happening (unlike, for example the carrying out of a medical procedure, in which the reaction of the patient to the treatment cannot be predicted with certainty). One might imagine the wish for a similar certainty in the carrying out of legal procedures. In order to avoid arbitrariness which presumably would lead to injustice, the procedures here, too, are meant to lead in identical cases to identical results. The discussion in the legal system that arises should only concern the identity of the cases under dispute. However, also an originally coherent system of legal remedies can be challenged in terms of ensuring justice as presented in the examination of claims on *certum* and *incertum* by Peter Gröschler. A related connection that links the legal procedures to mathematics arises from the attempt to avoid arbitrariness, namely the mapping of numeric values to specify consequences of legal procedures. These numeric values indicate what has been set (usually by the ruler) as just.[7] In the Egyptian sources, the relation between fixed numerical values (and their correct application) and the demand for justice appears explicitly within the teachings as is documented in the contribution by Annette Imhausen. Apart from this usage of numerical values, a variety of other mathematical content can also be found within legal documents as Guido Pfeifer demonstrates in his analysis of the Codex Ḫammurapi.

The contributions in the volume are loosely structured according to regional and chronological criteria. While some of the earlier sources from Mesopotamia and Egypt are contemporary, the Mesopotamian contributions of our volume do not include the later material bridging the gap to ancient Greece. Therefore, the volume begins with the contributions concerning Mesopotamia, followed by those

[6] For an overview of the literature on the possible roles of law codes cf. Jackson, 2008, 69–113 and 257–276.

[7] On justice in Mesopotamia cf. Pfeifer, 2012.

of ancient Egypt, which focus on earlier material (i.e. sources from the Middle and New Kingdoms) as well as Demotic material from Graeco Roman times. These are followed by the chapters that study Greek and Roman material. The volume ends with the contribution by Nahed Samour, which bridges the gap to one of the actors from the Modern period mentioned initially.

The editors are well aware of the fact that this volume is not perfectly coherent and cannot offer solutions to all problems deriving from the sources. But the interdisciplinary cooperation of scholars from rather distant fields has dispatched the individual studies without any doubt. Furthermore, they would like to express their gratitude to all contributors as well as to Charlotte Berg for their support in redacting the texts of this volume.

References

Asper, Markus, 2001. "Stoicheia und Gesetze. Spekulationen zur Entstehung mathematischer Textformen in Griechenland." In: Jochen Althoff / Bernhard Herzhoff / Georg Wöhrle (eds.) *Antike Naturwissenschaft und ihre Rezeption* 11. Trier: Wissenschaftlicher Verlag Trier, 73–106.

— 2004. "Law and Logic. Towards an Archaeology of Greek Abstract Reason". *Annali dell'università degli studi di Napoli "l'orientale"* 26, 73–94.

Bawanypeck, Daliah / Annette Imhausen (eds.), 2014. *Traditions of Written Knowledge in Ancient Egypt and Mesopotamia* (Alter Orient und Altes Testament 403). Münster: Ugarit Verlag.

Cuomo, Serafina, 2000. "Divide and rule: Frontinus and Roman land-surveying". *Studies in History and Philosophy of Science Part A* 31, 189–202.

Deicher, Susanne / Erik Maroko (eds.), 2015. *Die Liste. Ordnungen von Dingen und Menschen in Ägypten* (Ancient Egyptian design, contemporary design history and anthropology of design 1). Berlin: Kadmos.

Edzard, Dietz-Otto, 2007. "Die altmesopotamischen lexikalischen Listen – verkannte Kunstwerke?". In: Claus Wilcke (ed.) *Das geistige Erfassen der Welt im Alten Orient. Sprache, Religion Kultur und Gesellschaft.* Wiesbaden: Harrassowitz, 17–26.

Hilbert, David, 1899. *Grundlagen der Geometrie.* Leipzig: Teubner.

Imhausen, Annette, 2013. "Experten und die Umsetzung normativer Ordnungen im Alten Ägypten: Theorie und historisch fassbare Praxis". In: Andreas Fahrmeir / Annette Imhausen (eds.) *Die Vielfalt Normativer Ordnungen. Konflikte und Dynamik in historischer und ethnologischer Perspektive* (Normative Orders 8). Frankfurt: Campus, 49–78.

Jackson, Samuel A., 2008. *A Comparison of Ancient Near Eastern Law Collections Prior to the First Millenium B. C.* (Gorgias Studies in the Ancient Near East 4). Piscataway, NJ: Gorgias Press.

Kelsen, Hans, 1934. *Reine Rechtslehre: Einleitung in die rechtswissenschaftliche Problematik.* Leipzig / Wien: Deuticke.

Pfeifer, Guido, 2012. "Gerechtigkeit aus der Perspektive der altorientalischen Rechtsgeschichte". In: Markus Witte (ed.) *Gerechtigkeit.* Tübingen: Mohr Siebeck.

Radbruch, Knut, 1989. "Recht und Mathematik". In: Knut Radbruch (ed.) *Mathematik in den Geisteswissenschaften.* Göttingen: Vandenhoeck & Ruprecht.

Renn, Jürgen, 2014. "The Globalization of Knowledge in History and its Normative Challenges". *Rechtsgeschichte – Legal History* 22, 52–60.

Ritter, Jim, 2004. "Reading Strasbourg 368: A Thricetold Tale". In: Karine Chemla (ed.) *History of Science, History of Text* (Boston Studies in the Philosophy of Science 238). Dordrecht: Kluwer Academic Publishers, 177–200.

Stephanitz, Dieter, 1970. *Exakte Wissenschaft und Recht. Der Einfluss von Naturwissenschaft und Mathematik auf Rechtsdenken und Rechtswissenschaft in zweieinhalb Jahrtausenden. Ein historischer Grundriss* (Münsterische Beiträge zu Rechts- und Staatswissenschaft 15). Berlin: De Gruyter.

Veldhuis, Niek, 1997. *Elementary education at Nippur: the lists of trees and wooden objects*. Dissertation, Groningen.

Law and Order in Ancient Mesopotamia: Legal Codes and Mathematical Problems

Jim Ritter

Abstract ... 7
1 The Ḫammurapi law code ... 9
1.1 Sequential structures ... 15
1.1.1 The use of the preterite in the consequent ... 16
1.1.2 Three-tense and two-tense sequences ... 17
1.1.3 Preterite – Durative sequences ... 18
1.2 Branching structures ... 19
1.2.1 Simple conditional branching ... 19
1.2.2 Multiple conditional branchings I – parallel ... 22
1.2.3 Multiple conditional branchings II – sequential ... 25
1.2.4 The functional role of branchings ... 27
1.3 Legal conclusions ... 28
2 A comparison with mathematical problem texts ... 29
3 Telling an electronic computer what to do ... 37
Abbrevations and references ... 43

Abstract

If one were asked to spontaneously name a norm-centered domain in human society it is probable that the field of law would be the immediate response. The formulation and administration of justice, the establishment of rules of licit and illicit behavior, the rewards and punishments associated with the one and the other; all these posit a constructed network of institutions, personnel and social practices. In the context of a vanished civilization like that of Ancient Mesopotamia, our only access to this network is through the texts which were produced as a part of these activities and through which its contours are more or less reconstructible by us.

If the accurate identification of such texts could be guaranteed a priori, the process of reconstruction would be comparatively straightforward. But since the point of the establishment of a corpus is precisely to explore the nature of the domain, the ability to choose which texts do or do not fall into the 'correct' corpus is precisely the sticking point. For if we do not initially know enough about the field to choose the texts correctly, how can we construct the corpus of texts needed to establish the field's nature? More specifically here, how can we understand the functioning of norms in Mesopotamian society if we do not know what were the norm-laden practices of that society?

In the face of such a difficulty, I would like to propose another, minimalist approach, in which as small a number as possible of assumptions are made as to category. This cannot in itself decide the question of how norms were established but will hopefully act as a prolegomenon to this. We shall base our analysis on the formal aspects of texts, with particular attention to the question of verbal forms, as a means of determining the contours of those classes of texts in the Mesopotamian tradition which enjoyed a special relationship with respect to the use of norms.[1]

When, in the Old Babylonian period at the beginning of the second millennium BCE, Akkadian language texts came to replace to a large extent the Sumerian-language texts which had dominated the written record until then, there appeared a class of texts which shared a number of formal characteristics, characteristics completely absent from other kinds of texts. These texts pertain to a variety of subjects, at first glance quite unrelated: they include mathematics, medicine, jurisprudence and divination, a class of domains I have called that of 'rational practice'. More specifically, not all the texts in a given domain share this formal structure. For example, only those mathematical texts which present a problem to be resolved and then give a detailed solution to this problem possess it, mathematical tables and numerical calculations do not. Similarly for medical texts; only those which concern case studies, in which a group of symptoms is described or a disease named, followed by a step-by-step procedure for its cure, show this particular organization. Further, legal texts which present case law, normally called 'law codes' – specific violations of norms with precisely described actions to be followed in the attribution of guilt and selection of punishment – share exactly this same structure. Of these classes of documents involving a normed discourse, we shall restrict ourselves here to just two: '*law*', as represented by the legal codes and '*order*', embodied in the mathematical texts; in which two different kinds of norms are present. Law codes present *ethical* norms, rules for correct behavior in society, implicitly specified in the negative through specifying punishment for violations of them. Mathematical problem texts on the other hand deal with what might be called *prescriptive* norms in which the solution of a problem involves the correct ordering of a set of arithmetic or other operations. Here we shall consider these two rational practices only in that culture in which they first came into being, Old Babylonian Mesopotamia.

Since we shall be approaching these texts from a formal, linguistic point of view, as a prerequisite some understanding of something of the Akkadian verbal system is necessary.[2] The Akkadian verb, like that of most other Semitic languages, consists of a basic consonantal skeleton ('stem' or 'root'), usually triconsonantal, which can undergo two kinds of independent variation: 1°, one involving consonantal changes to the stem itself ('stem derivation'): duplication of one of the consonants and/or adding an infixed *-t-* or *-tan-*, and which principally provides lexical nuance,[3] and 2°, one involving variation of the vowels

[1] This approach has proven useful in other ancient norm-laden domains such as mathematics (Ritter, 2004; Imhausen, 2003) and medicine (Ritter, 2009).

[2] The standard grammatical reference for Akkadian is von Soden, 1995; see also Kouwenberg, 2010.

[3] These nuances can include giving an intensified or reflexive or repetitive, etc., coloration to the basic verbal activity. In some cases, these derived stems can acquire a level of autonomy which essentially creates a new verb.

together with possible prefixes and suffixes ('verbal form'), indicating temporal and modal differences.[4] Central to our investigation here is the second of these variations, and in particular, the three conjugation classes which fix the temporal situation of the action described, corresponding most closely to the 'tense' of the English verb.

It will be the second of these axes, and the three associated Akkadian 'tenses' – the preterite, the durative and the perfect – which lie at the center of all the analysis which follows.

We turn now to the first object of our study, the text inscribed on the 'Stela of Ḫammurapi'.

1. The Ḫammurapi law code

As mentioned above, only the 'law codes' of the Old Babylonian period present the specific grammatical form typical of rational practices. None of the other texts which treat the formulation and administration of justice – records of court cases, contracts, wills, etc. – employ this structure. It is therefore the formal, grammatical and logical study of examples of this class of texts that will interest us here.

Of the Akkadian-language law codes of the Old Babylonian period, the longest and best-preserved text is that of the 'Codex Ḫammurapi', a collection of laws[5] dating to the early period of the reign of that king, around 1750 BCE. They are inscribed on all sides of a basalt stela, some two and a quarter meters high. [6] The upper part of the front of the stela is marked by a bas-relief of the sun-god Šamaš presenting the laws to King Ḫammurapi of Babylon. The bottom part was partially erased by the Elamite king Šutruk-Naḫḫunte in the 12th century BCE, when it was captured as war booty and transported to his capital at Susa in Iran, probably preparatory to an inscription by that king that was never incised.

---

[4] These consist of 1° finite forms: besides the three 'tenses', this class includes the stative conjugation and the imperative/precative forms; and 2° non-finite forms: infinitive and participles.

[5] Whether the various entries of the stela were seen as 'laws' in the modern sense has been a subject of long-standing debate; see e.g. Bottéro, 1982; Renger, 1994 and Westbrook, 2003, as well as the contributions of Hans Neumann and Guido Pfeifer in this volume. Our purpose in this chapter does not depend on the exact social function of this text; thus, for simplicity, we shall, from now on, merely refer to each entry on the stela as a 'law' and use the standard siglum, '§', for their numeration.

[6] For detailed photographs of the stela, see the *editio princeps*, Scheil, 1902. The best hand copy of the stela, together with that of contemporaneous and later copies of parts of the Codex on tablets, is to be found in Bergmann, 1953; a transliteration of all sources is in Borger, 2006, 1–50. An excellent recent transcription and English translation is Roth, 1997, 71–142.

Figure 1. The Stela of Ḫammurapi
(Musée du Louvre, S^b 8).

The laws, together with a lengthy prologue and epilogue, are written in archaizing cuneiform characters, quite different from the ordinary Old Babylonian horizontally oriented script, as used on the thousands of clay tablets from the period. The stela thus, as is typical of most Mesopotamian monumental inscriptions up until the middle of the second millennium BCE, is inscribed using the sign forms of some 500 years earlier.

The signs are in the ancient orientation, i.e., turned 90° clockwise with respect to the horizontal orientation that had become standard starting at the end of the third millennium. Each phrase is contained in a ruled rectangular case, to be read from top to bottom in each case, the cases themselves reading from right to left.[7]

[7] There are however some differences with the original cuneiform writing style. One of the most immediately obvious, as can be seen in the photograph in figure 2, is that in the Codex, the horizontal wedges are written from right to left, as can be seen by the fact that the head of the wedge is on the right, whereas in the third millennium inscriptions, the head is on the left. This distinction suggests that the signs were conceived by Old Babylonian scribes as ordinary horizontal signs having undergone a 90° rotation.

As an example of this, we present here the first law on the stela, with the order of reading the cases indicated by the number below each:

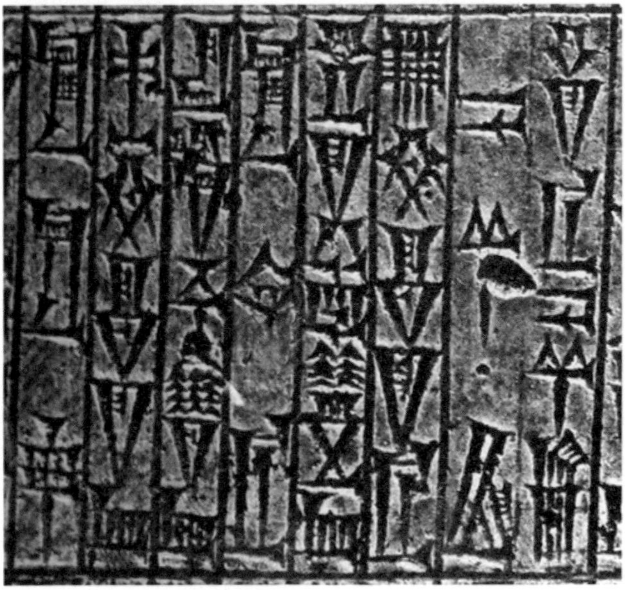

7 6 5 4 3 2 1

Figure 2. Photograph of the start of the section containing laws on the Stela of Ḫammurapi (Musée du Louvre, S^b 8: V 26–32). The image is taken from Scheil 1902, plate XXII.

It will be observed in the photograph that the vertical lines separating the cases and their phrases from one another are all of the same nature, something that is true on the entire stela; there is no indication in the text of the end of one law and the beginning of another. The division of the stela's text into 282 separate laws is in fact a modern editorial decision, based on an analysis of content; it was established by Vincent Scheil in his *editio princeps* of 1902 and accepted without essential change by all later editors.[8] Furthermore, as is visible in figure 1, about 15% of the original inscription is missing, erased in antiquity; some of these missing laws we still possess, since selections of the corpus were copied on clay tablets during the Old Babylonian period and later (some 50 tablets and fragments are extant).

It is the purpose of this section to explore the procedural schemas used in this text; in doing so we shall see that this analysis leads naturally to a *regrouping* of the laws that is arguably closer to their original contours as conceived by their Babylonian authors. Since our analysis depends on grammatical structure, in what

[8] It has become standard however, on the one hand, to split up each of Scheil's §§ 133, 171 and 176 into two separate parts, and on the other, to combine his §§ 242, 243 into one single 'law', producing a modern total of 284 'laws'. But note that this is not universally the case, e.g. Roth, 1997 does not split up § 171 whereas Richardson, 2000 and Borger, 2006 do.

follows we shall deal only with fully complete laws, with no missing verbal clauses. Our corpus will consist then of the 225 complete laws on the stela.[9]

Returning to our first text, § 1, we present the transcription of the Akkadian divided as in the original, with each line of our transcription corresponding to a single case, and provided with a facing literal English translation:

1	*šumma awīlum awīlam*	If a man a(nother) man
2	*ubbirma*	he has accused and
3	*nērtam elīšu*	murder against him
4	*iddīma*	he has charged but
5	*lā uktīnšu*	he will not have proven the case against him,
6	*mubbiršu*	his accuser
7	*iddâk*	shall be killed.

or, in a translation following English rather than Akkadian syntax:

> If a man has accused a(nother) man and he has charged murder against him but he will not have proven the case against him, his accuser shall be killed.

We note that the law states a 'problem' – false accusation in a capital case – and then prescribes a course of action to 'solve' this – the putting to death of the perjurer. Formally speaking, the laws possess a standardized *conditional* form ('if … then'),[10] with an explicit initial 'if' (*šumma*) followed by the problem, and an implicit 'then' with the procedure to be followed in the case – "**If** a man has (falsely) accused another … (**then**) the accuser shall be killed." The bipartite nature of a conditional sentence is faithfully reflected verbally by a bipartite distribution of Akkadian tenses. The first half or *premise* of the conditional uses only verbs in the preterite (*ubbir*, *iddi*) and perfect (*uktīn*) tenses, while the second half or *consequent* employs only the durative tense (*iddâk*).[11] Moreover the distribution of the two tenses of the premise are such that the verbs in the preterite come first, with the final verb in the perfect. This is not coincidental, it is true for *all* the laws in the Codex, or at least all that use all three tenses. We shall be looking at this question in some detail in what follows.

From the point of view of the *content* of the law, each of the tenses plays a specific role in the law. The preterite and perfect tenses indicate the events and actions which have led to the necessity of judgement being passed; the distinction between the two residing in the *general*, *contextual* nature of the preterite chain, whereas the perfect tense serves to indicate the *particular* circumstance or circumstances which determine the actions to be taken.[12] Actions expressed by

---

[9] Though three of the laws erased from the stela are extant and essentially complete on tablet copies (gap §§ t, z. and cc in the nomenclature of Roth, 1997), we shall not consider them here as they lack the context of neighboring laws, necessary in our approach.

[10] The expression 'casuistic' is often used in the Assyriological literature for this form. I prefer to avoid the modern pejorative and theological overtones of this term and take 'conditional' from the terminology of logic and programming. For a detailed study of the grammar of the conditional in Akkadian, see Cohen, 2012.

[11] Note that normal Assyriological nomenclature follows traditional grammatical (ultimately classical Greek) usage: the premise is called the *protasis* and the consequent the *apodosis*.

[12] Note that there is no claim here that the Akkadian perfect performs this role *outside* of legal codes. This is a much more complex question into which, as it has no bearing on the

verbs in the consequent are exclusively in the durative tense and this tense is employed only there.[13]

We need to address not only the question of the verbal nature of each individual clause in a law but also the question of how it is connected to other clauses in that law; in other words, how information flows within the law from clause to clause. Now the Akkadian language possesses an enclitic particle *-ma* which, postfixed to a verb, indicates just such an interclausal connection. It can generally be translated 'and' or 'and then' but it can also indicate contrast, with a translation 'but' or 'yet'. It occurs in our example, § 1, after the preterite verbs *ubbir* (*ubbir-ma*) and *iddi* (*iddīma*) but not after the perfect verb *uktīn*, which marks the passage from the premise to the consequent of the conditional sentence. In this context it should be pointed out that, as can be seen from the dual column Akkadian–English version above, Akkadian has a sentence structure of the SOV (subject–object–verb) kind; thus all clauses are verb final and the verbal particle *-ma* is literally the linking element between clauses.

We shall be using a particular typographic coding in the presentation of the laws we shall be examining in order to bring out these grammatical points in a clearer way. The premise will be set out with the preterite verb(s) on one line and the perfect verb(s) on the following line; then will come the consequent and its durative verb(s). Furthermore, in the translation only, we shall separate the premise from the consequent by the use of a dash '–' at the end of the former. These verbs (and the suffix *-ma*) will be typographically coded, using the following conventions:

Akkadian	**English**	**Typography**
preterite	**present perfect simple** ('has ...ed')	**boldface**
PERFECT	FUTURE II SIMPLE ('will have ...ed')	SMALL CAPITALS
durative	*future I simple* ('shall ...')	roman/*italic*[14]
-*ma*	'and', 'then', 'but', etc.	underline

discussion here, we shall not enter. A good point of departure for such an investigation is to be found in Loesov, 2004–2005.

[13] There is one exception – the use of a subjunctive form of the preterite – to this exclusivity of the durative in the consequent but, as we shall see, this preterite plays a totally different structural role from that of the verbs we will be discussing.

[14] The fact that roman type is used for the Akkadian durative while italic type is used for the corresponding English future I simple is just due to the convention that the Akkadian transcription be in italics and the English translation in roman font, thus requiring the different conventions to mark the verb form in the two cases.
Moreover, since only the third person is used in the law codes, it would be more technically correct to translate 'will ...' for the simple future in these texts. But in British and American legal practice, 'shall', because of its modal force, is used systematically in official texts as auxiliary in the third person future and it is this convention that we shall follow here.

For clarity, the *-ma* enclitic suffix will be written separated from the verb by a hyphen in the Akkadian text (as will all pronominal and ventive verbal suffixes). All this yields then the following for § 1:

§ 1 *šumma awīlum awīlam* **ubbir**-*ma nērtam elīšu* **iddī**-*ma*
lā UKTĪN-*šu*
mubbiršu iddâk

If a man **has accused** a(nother) man and he **has charged** murder against him but
he WILL not HAVE PROVEN THE CASE against him –
his accuser *shall be killed.*

By employing a particular visualization tool – the 'flow diagram' – we can make all this even more intuitively clear and, more importantly, we can go further by using it; we shall be able to follow the way in which the laws are constructed and how information flows within each individual law, and to some extent between laws. 'Flow diagrams' are schema which were invented at the very beginning of the computer age to deal with precisely the same kind of problems appearing in the new field of programming.[15] We shall resume each clause in a law in a few words (and without tense indication) and enclose this in a rectangle – one with rounded corners for each clause in the premise and with square corners for each clause in the consequent. We shall further distinguish clauses in the premise which involve a verb in the perfect from those with verbs in the preterite by shading the inside of the rectangle in the former case.

Resuming these rules in the following list, we then represent § 1 as a flow diagram:

 (rectangle with rounded corners) = clause in the premise with verb in the preterite

 (shaded rectangle with rounded corners) = clause in the premise with verb in the perfect

 (rectangle with square corners) = clause in the consequent with verb in the durative

→ (horizontal arrow) = use of *-ma* as enclitic linking particle between clauses

[15] They were introduced at the start of the very first document on programming: Goldstine / von Neumann, 1947–1948, volume I, p. 4. See section 3 below.

§ 1

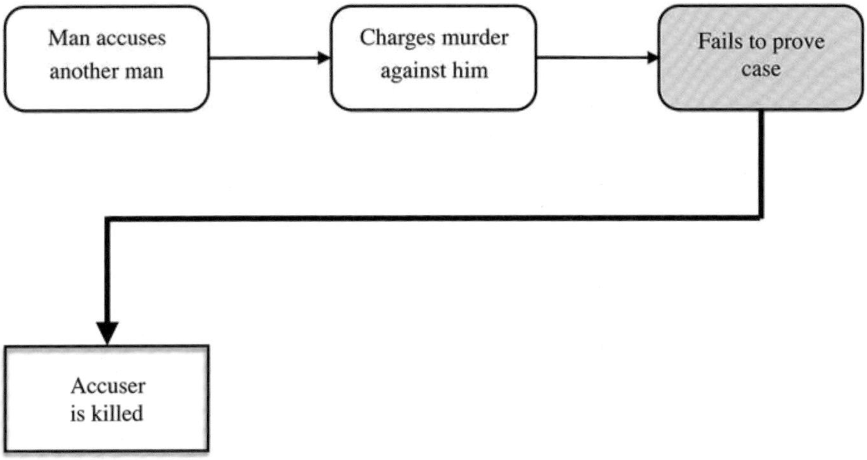

The passage from the premise, with its preterite- and perfect-tense verbs, to the consequent, and the use of the durative tense, appears visually in the flow diagram as a change from one *level* to another, symbolized by a thick black *vertical* arrow, here from the (last) verb in the preterite–perfect tense series to the (first) verb in the durative. It underscores, in this two-level diagram, the visual correspondent to the functional and grammatical bipartite nature of the conditional sentence embodying a law, the passage from the descriptive to the normative. In view of the rigid identity of the premise of a law with the upper chain (Level 1) of preterite and perfect verbs, we shall use the two terms ('premise' and 'Level 1') interchangeably; equally so for the term 'consequent' and its equivalent lower chain ('Level 2') of verbs in the durative.

1.1 Sequential structures

The kind of linear sequence of verbs we see in § 1 is typical of a large number of laws in the Codex; we shall call such a linear structure a *sequential* law. As we shall see when we turn to other examples, there is no inherent limit to the number of preterite, perfect or durative verbs in their respective chains; subject only to the rule that, in the premise, the perfect verbs follow those in the preterite. Thus the generalized flow diagram for a sequential law is the two-level schema:

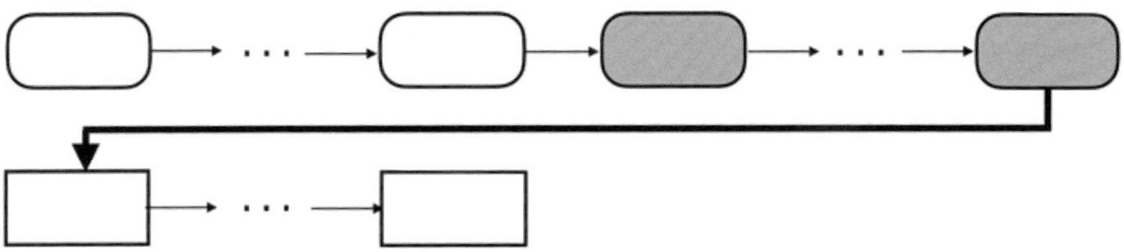

1.1.1 The use of the preterite in the consequent

In the Codex, there is one exception to the rule that the preterite is a tense that only occurs in the premise of a conditional. There are a large number of laws in which a preterite verb is to found in the consequent, among the durative-tense verbs. However, in all such cases the role played by the preterite verb is completely distinct from that played by the verbs we have been investigating here; these consequent preterites are always in a *subordinate clause* – and as such marked by their being in the Akkadian subjunctive mood (suffix *-u*) – where they serve to *delimit* a preceding noun, pronoun, noun phrase or verb, never to indicate an action. In fact, this preterite + subjunctive combination can appear in either of the two parts of the conditional. To illustrate this we take the example of § 107, dealing with the dispute between a merchant and his trading agent over whether or not the latter has repaid a loan to the former:[16]

§ 107 *šumma tamkārum kaspam šamallâm* **iqīp**-*ma*
šamallum mimma ša tamkārum ***iddinu***-*šum ana tamkārišu* UTTĒR
tamkārum mimma ša šamallûm ***iddinu***-*šum* ITTAKIR-*šu*
šamallûm šū ina maḫar ilim u sībī tamkāram ukân-*ma tamkārum aššum šamallâšu* ***ikkiru*** *mimma ša* ***ilqû*** *adi 6-šu ana šamallêm* inaddin ***ikkiru*** *mimma ša* ***ilqû*** *adi 6-šu ana šamallêm* inaddin

If a merchant **has entrusted** silver to a trading agent and then
the trading agent WILL HAVE RETURNED to his merchant everything that the merchant ***had given*** him (but) the merchant WILL HAVE DENIED (receiving) everything that the trading agent ***had given*** him –
that trading agent *shall prove* the charges before the god and wit nesses against the merchant, and because he ***had denied*** the account of his trading agent, the merchant *shall give* to the trading agent sixfold the amount that he ***had taken***.

Here the subjunctivized preterites have been marked typographically by the use of ***boldface italic*** and translated in the English ***past perfect simple*** ('had …ed'). In the premise, each of the two uses of 'had given' (*iddinu*) serve to explicate the sense of the 'everything' (*mimma*) associated with each of the two perfect-tense verbs. In the consequent, where the preterites in the subjunctive are both associated with the durative-tense verb 'shall give' (*inaddin*), one of them – 'had denied' (*ikkiru*) – provides a justification for the act of restitution while the other – 'had taken' (*ilqû*) – explains the sense of the 'amount' (*šamellûm*) that must be restituted.

These subjunctive-mood preterites, although finite verbs, play then a very different functional role from that of the finite verbs marking the presentation of the problem or its resolution. Though, for the sake of clarity, we shall continue to mark them in our transcriptions and translations, they will not be further discussed here nor will they appear in the flow diagrams.

---

[16] Note in this example the use of a *pair* of verbs in the perfect. As mentioned in section 2.1 the number of perfect verbs in a premise, like the number of preterite verbs, can be as many as are required.

1.1.2 Three-tense and two-tense sequences

In the absence of physical demarcations between successive laws on the stela itself, the first editors of the Codex started from the supposition that all laws begin with an 'if' (*šumma*) section (premise) of the conditional form. It was assumed then that, normally, each law would begin with an initial *šumma* and extend until the next *šumma*. Of the 225 complete laws as currently constituted in the modern editions, 198 satisfy this condition, that is, consist of a *single* conditional with its prefixed *šumma*, corresponding to a purely sequential procedure. For reasons of content, however, in 27 cases the editors grouped together two or more successive conditionals in a single law: 20 with two conditionals and 7 with three or more. The 'if' of the first conditional, that which marks the start of the law, we shall call an *initial šumma*, each later 'if' in a single multi-conditional law we shall call an *internal šumma*.

Taking first the 198 complete laws possessing a purely sequential form as presently constituted, their verbal chains are organized as follows:

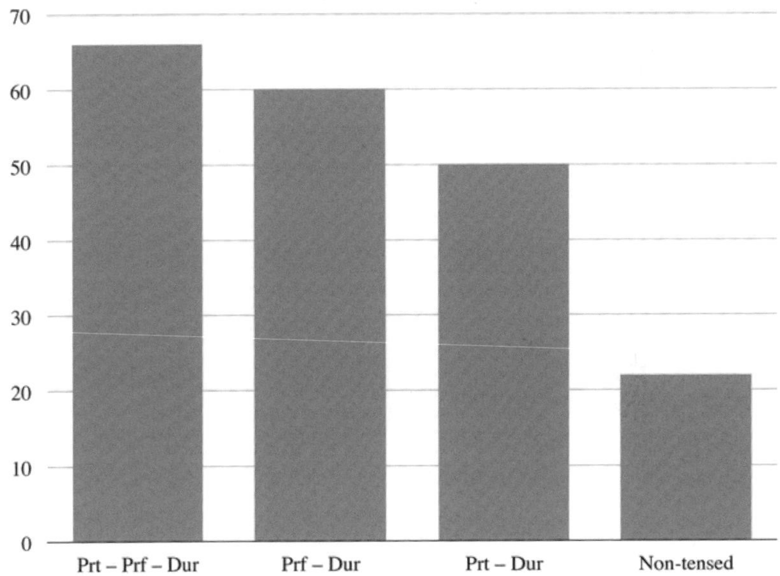

Figure 3. Graph of the nature of the verbal chains in simple sequential laws.

Of these, 66 have the full Preterite – Perfect – Durative (Prt – Prf – Dur) sequence, 60 have a Perfect – Durative (Prf – Dur) order (without any preterites) and 50 have a Preterite – Durative (Prt – Dur) order (without perfects). The remaining 22 laws I have classed as 'non-tensed' in the sense that each involves at least one nominal clause or stative verb, both these being verbal forms which take their 'tense' coloration from the surrounding finite 'tensed' verbs if any, and thus cannot be unambiguously put into any one of the three preceding categories. Since they cannot provide independent evidence for tense order we shall not consider this last category of 22 laws any further here.

We have dealt above (Section 1.1) with the laws presenting the full Prt – Prf – Dur sequence; they make up the standard sequential class. Now we need to consider the other two, seemingly 'incomplete', classes; we turn first to the Prt – Dur case.

1.1.3 Preterite – Durative sequences

A particularly simple example of this case is given by § 59. In a long series of laws treating the penalties incurred in an agricultural setting, and situated between the various infractions involving a shepherd and those involving a gardener, this law stands alone in concerning the felling of a tree in an orchard without the permission of the owner:

§ 59 *šumma awīlum balum bēl kirîm ina kirī awīlim iṣam* **ikkis**
½ *mana kaspam* išaqqal

If a man, without permission from the owner of the orchard, **has cut down** a tree in the orchard of a(nother) man –
he *shall pay* ½ mana of silver.

with the simple corresponding flow diagram:

§ 59

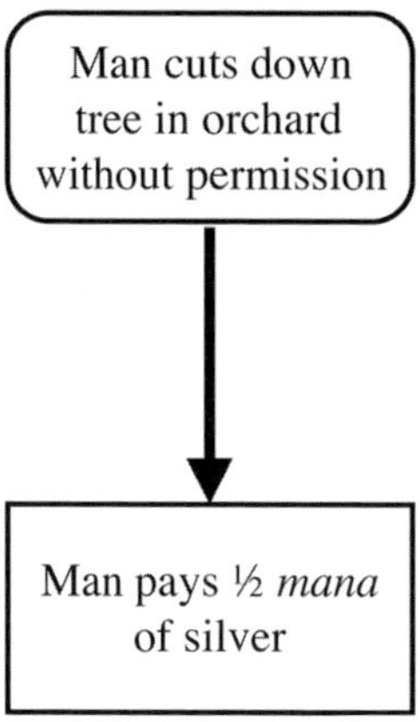

Level 1 consists of (a single) preterite verb with no following perfect. The reason is clear. The act of felling a tree on another's property without permission is the whole of the infraction; no mitigating or exacerbating circumstances are foreseen and there is thus no need for a verb in the perfect tense to present such a situation. It turns out then that the existence of verbs in the perfect tense on Level 1 is optional, and simply depends on the nature of the offense. There is thus no real reason to treat this case as being any different structurally from the full Prt – Prf – Dur case; so that from this point of view there are in total 66 + 50 = 116 complete sequential laws (roughly half the 225), those presenting a standard Prt – (Prf) – Dur sequence.[17]

[17] As we shall see in the next subsection, there are not infrequent cases in which a return to level-1 preterites is possible within a single (non-sequential) law. The

The remaining case – that of the two-verb Prf – Dur sequence – turns out to be a much more complex and interesting situation. It is to this remaining case that we now turn.

1.2 Branching structures

1.2.1 Simple conditional branching

What is the purpose of a Prf – Dur sequence without the preterite? To explore this question, we look at a typical example, § 23:

§ 23 *šumma ḫabbātum lā* ITTAṢBAT
awīlum ḫabtum mimmâšu ḫalqam maḫar ilim ubār-*ma ālum urabiānum ša ina erṣetišunu u paṭṭišunu ḫubtum* ***iḫḫabtu*** *mimmâšu ḫalqam* iriabbū-*šum*

If the robber WILL not HAVE BEEN SEIZED –
the robbed man *shall establish* the extent of his lost property before the god and then the city and the governor, in whose territory and district the robbery ***had been committed***, *shall replac*e his lost property for him.

The nature of the incompleteness in the sequence here gives a clue to where to look for an explanation; the absence of an immediate referent for the 'robber' (*ḫabbātum*) in the premise suggests that we look at what precedes this law in the Codex:

§ 22 *šumma awīlum ḫubtam* **iḫbut**-*ma*
ITTAṢBAT
awīlum šū iddâk

If a man **has committed** a robbery and then
he WILL HAVE BEEN SEIZED –
that man *shall be killed.*

where we now find a complete Prt – Prf – Dur sequence, treating exactly the same subject as § 23 with the difference that the preterite announces the concrete fact of the existence of a robbery and the perfect verb here is the non-negative variant of that occurring in the following law. In short, §§ 22–23 form in fact a *single* law which *share* a preterite and present a *binary* choice in the perfect, leading to two distinct durative-verb proceedings.

§ 22–23 *šumma awīlum ḫubtam* **iḫbut**-*ma*
ITTAṢBAT
awīlum šū iddâk

šumma ḫabbātum lā ITTAṢBAT
awīlum ḫabtum mimmâšu ḫalqam maḫar ilim ubār-*ma ālum u rabiānum ša ina erṣetišunu u paṭṭišunu ḫubtum* ***iḫḫabtu*** *mimmâšu ḫalqam* iriabbū-*šum*

number 116 is thus in fact an upper limit to the number of possible independent laws in the Codex.

> If a man **has committed** a robbery <u>and then</u>
> he WILL HAVE BEEN SEIZED –
> that man *shall be killed*;
>
> if the robber WILL not HAVE BEEN SEIZED –
> the robbed man *shall establish* the extent of his lost property before the god <u>and then</u> the city and the governor, in whose territory and district the robbery ***had been committed***, *shall replace* his lost property for him.

Now legal texts often privilege binary pairs (guilty/innocent is an obvious example), so it is not surprising that such a binary pair exists in the Codex. The procedure splits on a dichotomy: the robber has either been seized or has not, and the procedure to be followed depends on the relevant state of affairs. Now just such binary yes/no divisions are ubiquitous in modern computer programming where they have their own name: 'conditional branching', and their own notation in flow diagrams: their symbol is a lozenge <>, within which is placed the choice determining the split. We adopt both the name and the notation here, adding for our purposes a contour and shading of the lozenge adapted to the verbal form employed:

§ 22–23

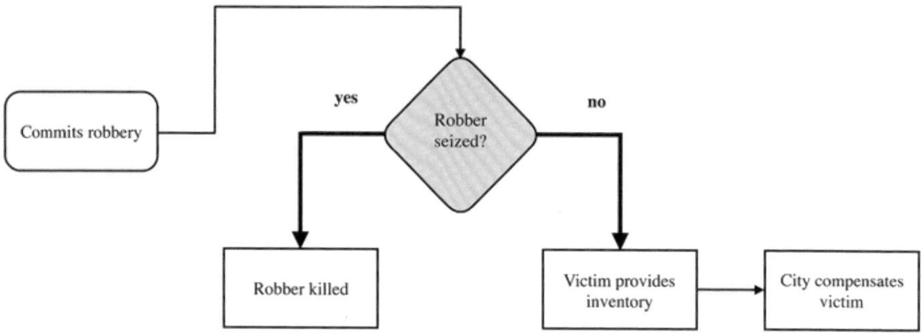

The question underlying the binary verbal opposition 'has been/has not been seized' is summarized in the lozenge and the two verbal forms replaced by the corresponding 'yes/no'. It should be noted that for branching in the Codex, the perfect, as here, is generally the operative tense since such options, for the most part, form precisely the pertinent circumstance of the legal problem and thus determine the procedure to be followed.

In the laws containing conditional branchings, the transition from Level 1 to Level 2 is not irreversible. It can be the case that, once a triggering circumstance (perfect-tense verb) is launched that there is an intermediate procedure (durative-tense verbs) that is necessary, leading in turn to a further trigger (another perfect-tense verb), taking the form of a conditional branching. Such a situation occurs in § 2 of the Codex.[18]

[18] This law is one of the 27 mentioned above in Section 1.2, already containing internal *šumma* in the standard editions.

§ 2 *šumma awīlum kišpī eli awīlim* **iddī**-*<u>ma</u>*
lā UKTĪN-*šu*
ša elīšu kišpū nadû ana nārim illak *nāram* išalli-*am*-*<u>ma</u>*

šumma nārum IKTAŠAS-*su*
mubbiršu bīssu itabbal

šumma awīlam šuāti nārum ŪTEBBIBAŠ-*šū*-*<u>ma</u>* IŠTALMAM
ša elīšu kišpī ***iddû*** iddâk *ša nāram* ***išliam*** *bīt mubbirišu* itabbal

If a man **has charged** sorcery against a(nother) man <u>but</u>
he WILL not HAVE PROVEN THE CASE against him –
he against whom sorcery is charged *shall go* to the River; he *shall plunge* into the River <u>and</u>

if the River WILL HAVE MASTERED him –
his accuser *shall carry off* his household;

if that man, the River WILL HAVE PURIFIED him <u>and</u> he WILL HAVE COME OUT SAFELY –
he who ***had charged*** him with sorcery *shall be killed*; he who ***had plunged*** into the River *shall carry off* the household of his accuser.

Here an accusation of witchcraft which the accuser does not succeed in proving (first perfect-tense trigger) requires a River Ordeal – the accused leaps into the divine Euphrates and the gods determine his guilt, he drowns, or his innocence, he succeeds in reaching the bank – and, on the basis of this (perfect-tense) conditional branching, one of the protagonists inherits the household goods of the other. The flow diagram appears then as follows:

§ 2

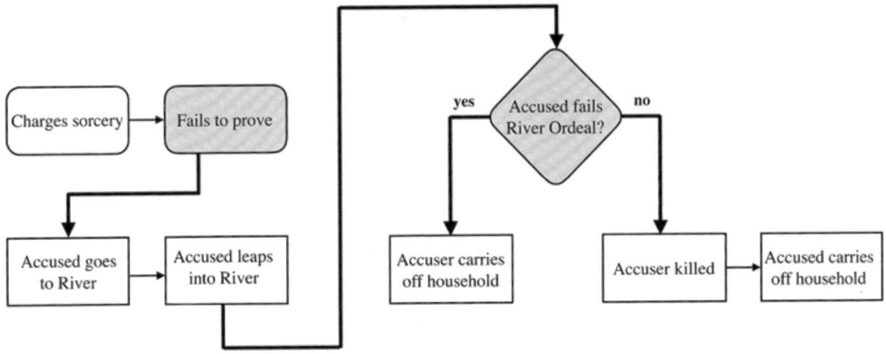

Here the thick vertical arrows indicate: 1° a transition from Level 1 to Level 2 at the point where the accuser fails to prove his charge and an Ordeal must be prepared, 2° a *return transition* from Level 2 to Level 1 after the River Ordeal has been prepared and the ordeal starts, and 3° a second and final transition from Level 1 to Level 2 with the procedure to be followed in each of the two possible outcomes. The possibility of passing from one level to another in both senses opens up the option of having *intermediate* procedures within any given law.

1.2.2 Multiple conditional branchings I – parallel

Though explicit yes/no branchings comprise a large part of the consecutive Prf – Dur sequences, there are cases which do not seem to present such simple dichotomies. An example is to be found in the Prf – Dur sequence law § 18:

§ 18 *šumma wardum šū bēlšu lā* IZZAKAR
ana ekallim ireddī-*šu warkassu* ipparras-*ma ana bēlišu* utarrū-*šu*

If that slave WILL HAVE REFUSED TO IDENTIFY his owner –
he *shall lead* him off to the palace, his circumstances *shall be investigated* and they *shall return* him to his owner.

The absence of a preterite at the beginning of the level-1 chain and the presence of the apparently referenceless demonstrative 'that' (*šū*), referring to the slave, both again point to the preceding law as making up an integral part of § 18.

§ 17 *šumma awīlum lū wardam lū amtam ḫalqam ina ṣērim* **iṣbat**-*ma*
ana bēlišu IRTEDĪ-*aš-šu*
2 šiqil kaspam bēl wardim inaddiš-*šum*

If a man **has seized** a fugitive slave or slave woman in the open country and
he WILL HAVE LED him back to his owner –
the slave owner *shall give* him 2 *šiqil* of silver.

§ 18 *šumma wardum šū bēlšu* lā IZZAKAR
ana ekallim ireddī-šu warkassu ipparras-*ma ana bēlišu* utarrū-*šu*

If that slave WILL HAVE REFUSED TO IDENTIFY his owner –
he *shall lead* him *off* to the palace, his circumstances *shall be investigated* and they *shall return* him to his owner.

This, like §§ 22–23, is to be read as a single Prt – Prf – Dur sequential form with a secondary, internal *šumma.* But now though the determining perfect verbs are indeed alternately positive and negated forms, they are not such of the same verb (*irtedī* from *redûm* 'to lead' and *izzakar* from *zakārum* 'to identify'):

§ 17–18 *šumma awīlum lū wardam lū amtam ḫalqam ina ṣērim* **iṣbat**-*ma*
ana bēlišu IRTEDĪ-*aš-šu*
2 šiqil kaspam bēl wardim inaddiš-*šum*

šumma wardum šū bēlšu lā IZZAKAR
ana ekallim ireddī-šu warkassu ipparras-*ma ana bēlišu* utarrū-*šu*

If a man **has seized** a fugitive slave or slave woman in the open country and
he WILL HAVE LED him back to his owner–
the slave owner *shall give* him 2 *šiqil* of silver;

if that slave WILL HAVE REFUSED TO IDENTIFY his owner –
he *shall lead* him off to the palace, his circumstances *shall be investigated* and they *shall return* him to his owner.

But in fact this block of laws extends beyond § 18; the following §§ 19–20 treat the same subject and share the same absence of a preterite verb, hence implicitly referring back to the last occurring preterite, that in § 17.[19] The group of 4 laws §§ 17–20 form then a single law and should be written and understood as follows:

§ 17+ *šumma awīlum lū wardam lū amtam ḫalqam ina ṣērim* **iṣbat**-*ma*
ana bēlišu IRTEDĪ-*aš-šu*
2 šiqil kaspam bēl wardim inaddiš-*šum*

šumma wardum šū bēlšu lā IZZAKAR
ana ekallim ireddī-*šu warkassu* ipparras-*ma ana bēlišu* utarrū-*šu*

šumma wardam šuāti ina bītisu IKTALĀ-*šu warka wardum ina qātišu* ITTAṢBAT
awīlum šū iddâk

šumma wardum lā ina qāt ṣābitānišu IḪTALIQ
awīlum šū ana bēl wardim nīš ilim izakkar-*ma* ūtaššar

If a man **has seized** a fugitive slave or slave woman in the open country and
he WILL HAVE LED him back to his owner –
the slave owner *shall give* him 2 *šiqil* of silver;

if that slave WILL HAVE REFUSED to identify his owner –
he *shall lead* him off to the palace (and) his circumstances *shall be investigated* and they *shall return* him to his owner;
if he WILL HAVE DETAINED that slave in his own house (and) the slave WILL HAVE BEEN DISCOVERED in his possession –
that man *shall be killed*;

if the slave WILL HAVE ESCAPED the custody of his captor –
that man *shall swear* an oath by the god to the owner of the slave and he *shall be released.*

where we have numbered the laws §§ 17–20 as a single law, represented by § 17+ with four distinct perfect verbs. We can now write out the complete flow diagram as a *multiple parallel branching*, in this case quadripartite:[20]

[19] The block ends with § 20 since the following law, § 21, begins with a preterite and treats of a quite different matter.
[20] The complexity of this schema and the constraints of space in a printed book obliges us to renounce a presentation of these flow diagrams in the correct two-level form. In these cases we shall rely on the thick arrow and the contrast of rounded vs non-rounded rectangle forms, both indicating level change, to signal the transition from Level 1 to Level 2.

§ 17+ (= §§ 17–20) (A)

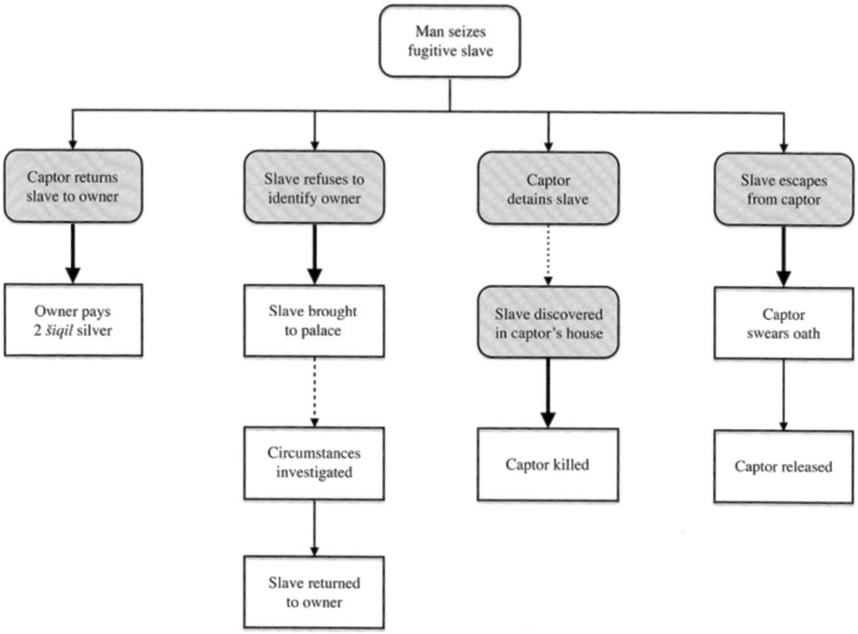

The idea of this single law is that, given the general situation of the seizure of a runaway slave, the following judicial action depends on – and is triggered by – a choice among different options, expressed by verbs in the perfect tense. If the captor returns the slave to his owner, all is well and he is given a monetary reward by the owner. If he cannot return the slave because the latter refuses to name his owner, the state intervenes and determines the rightful owner. If the captor does not return the slave because he desires to unlawfully keep him and the slave is discovered in the captor's house, this theft by the captor is punished by death. Finally, if he cannot return the slave because the slave has escaped from his custody, a sworn oath to this effect is to be made and the captor is then absolved of all responsibility in the affair. Only one of the four options adumbrated can be the case and the four cases are clearly deemed to be exhaustive of all possible relevant situations.

This is then a case of a four-part conditional branching in which all four possibilities are treated on an equal footing. Yet though it is true that all four verbs in the perfect are distinct, they fall into a natural dichotomous pairing. In the first two cases the choice is based on an identification of the owner by the slave: he either presumably does so (and the captor can then lead him back to his owner) or explicitly refuses to do so (and thus the captor cannot, though of good faith, return him). In the final two cases, the question is posed whether the slave has or has not escaped from the possession of the captor: if he has escaped, the captor is blameless; if he has not escaped, and it is the captor's intention to retain him (evidenced by the fact that the slave is discovered in the captor's house, *in flagrante delicto*), then the captor pays the capital penalty for his theft. From this point of view one may consider the law as treating two *parallel conditional branchings*, as shown in the following flow diagram:

§ 17+ (= §§ 17–20) (B)

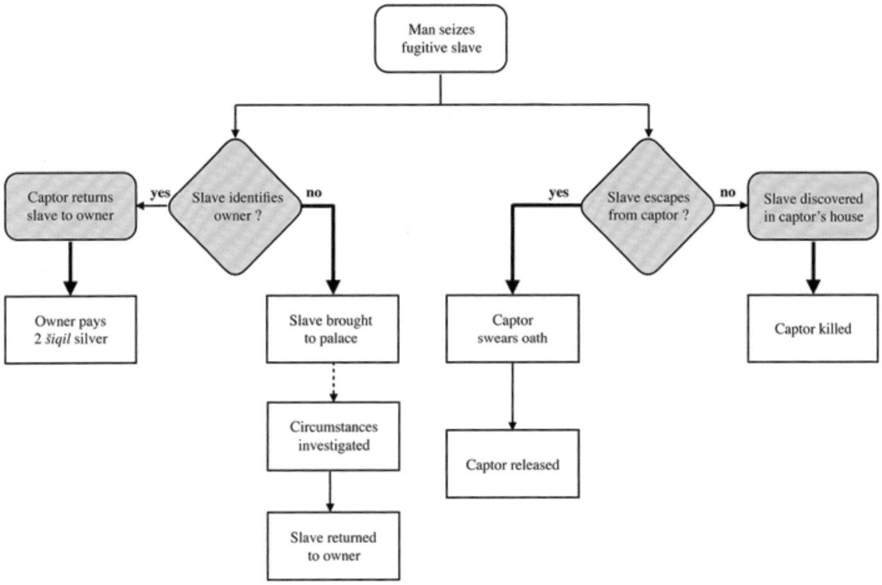

Whatever be the answer to the question of an ultimately dichotomous nature of parallel structures in Old Babylonian jurisprudence, parallel branching indicates that the space of possible pertinent circumstances divides into two or more disjoint subspaces: here in §§ 17–20, there are two subspaces, defined, one by the identification of the rightful owner and the other by the intention of the captor to return the slave.

There are a number of blocks of laws like these four: other examples include §§ 60–63, §§ 191–192, §§ 229–232, §§ 253–256 and others besides.[21] Taking seriously the union of these blocks as representing just a single law with internal *šumma*, we must exclude many of the 60 apparent Prf – Dur sequences from the collection of 'simple sequential laws' and reclassify them as a considerably smaller group of non-sequential branching structures. In every case, each choice (generally in the Akkadian perfect, as here)[22] is introduced by an internal *šumma* and followed by the procedure for that case, using the Akkadian durative tense.

1.2.3 Multiple conditional branchings II – sequential

Deciding whether or not binary branchings always underlie the organization of multiple branchings would require a systematic review of the entire Codex Ḫammurapi. But there are a few laws which suggest the existence of another kind of branching typology, one where a law contains multiple cases of an internal *šumma*

[21] In connection with the question treated above, whether *multiple* conditional branchings are invariably concatenations of *binary* branchings, it may be noted that there seem to be only *even* numbers of internal *šumma* in the CḪ, i.e., multiples of 2.

[22] One occasionally finds the preterite or even the durative used for the branching verb.

with binary branchings, but in which the branchings are not parallel as above, but rather *sequential*, a series of choices to be made one *after* the other. I offer § 32 as an example:[23]

§ 32 *šumma lū rēdûm ū lū bā'irum ša ina ḫarrān šarrim* **turru** *tamkārum* **ipṭur**-*aš-šu-ma*
ālšu UŠTAKŠID-*aš-šu*

šumma ina bītišu ša paṭārim ibašši
šûma ramanšu ipaṭṭar

šumma ina bītišu ša paṭārišu lā ibašši
ina bīt ili ālisu ippaṭṭar

šumma ina bīt ili alisu ša paṭārišu lā ibašši
ekallum ipaṭṭar-*šu eqelšu kirāšu ū bissu ana ipṭerišu ul* innaddin

If a merchant **has paid the ransom** for a *rēdûm*-soldier or a *bā'irum*-soldier who ***had returned*** from a royal expedition and
he (the merchant) WILL HAVE ENABLED him (the soldier) TO REACH his city,

if there exists (silver for) ransoming him in his (the soldier's) house –
he himself *shall pay* (back) *the ransom*;

if there does not exist any (silver for) ransoming him in his house –
it *shall be paid* (back) by the temple in his city;

if there does not exist any (silver for) ransoming him in the temple in his city –
the palace *shall pay* (back) for him (and) neither his field, his orchard, nor his house *shall be given* for his ransom price.

The sequence begins with an initial *šumma*, introducing the level-1 presentation of the problem, with a preterite for the general situation – the payment of a ransom by a merchant for a captured soldier on an official military expedition – followed by a level-1 perfect – that the merchant has made it possible for the soldier to reach his home. There then follow three internal *šumma*, treating the circumstances under which the merchant will be reimbursed for his advance of the ransom. The repayment is first to be sought from the soldier himself and then, in case of inability to pay, from the temple of his home town and finally, if this too fails, from the palace.

Examining how the text treats this tripartite division from a formal point of view, we note that the first two internal *šumma* form a typical binary branching, the positive branch with the first internal *šumma*, then the negative with the second, centered on the soldier and posing the question of the existence of silver for the repayment of the merchant. The third *šumma* then poses only the negative part of the same question for the city temple, since its positive branch is

[23] This law, like § 2 treated above in Section 2.1, is one of the 27 published laws with internal *šumma* in the standard editions.

coterminous with the negative branch of the preceding question concerning the soldier.[24]

There is some difficulty in fixing the tense of the verb involved in the branching in this law. In all three cases of the internal *šumma*, the verb used to describe the ability or inability to pay is *ibašši* (durative tense of the G-stem *bašûm*, 'to exist'). But *bašûm* is a defective verb which, in the G-stem, has no perfect and whose preterite is quite rare.[25] There is thus no way to determine whether the tense involved for this verb is intended as really the durative – or the preterite or perfect. As the tense is undetermined we do not mark the Akkadian verb in any way and we translate using the English present (tense-neutral in our conventions). In the associated flow diagram we color the branching lozenge half white (Prt) and half gray (Prf) to indicate this temporal ambiguity.

§ 32

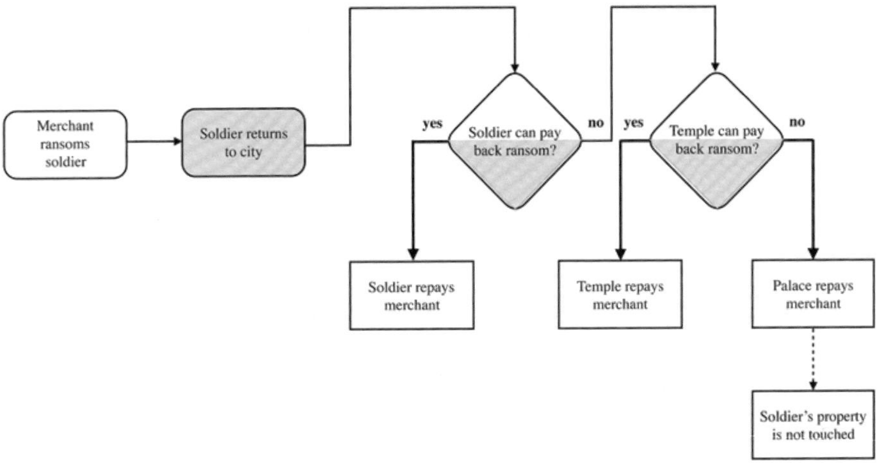

Given then the general situation of the return of a ransomed soldier to his city, the question arises as to the means of repayment to the merchant payer of the ransom. The priority goes to the soldier himself (and his family); he must reimburse if possible; if not, the second in order is his city temple. Only if this latter cannot reimburse either, will the palace do so. Note the implicit hierarchization of responsibility from local to global, family to state. This brings a sequential ordering of dichotomous choices following a pre-established order.

1.2.4 The functional role of branchings

As the preceding examples have shown, a branching, either parallel or sequential, comes into play when for a given general situation the procedure to be followed depends on which of a number of possible specific circumstances is applicable;

[24] That this is a standard structure for sequential binary branchings is reinforced by a similarly structured situation in the Old Babylonian medical text HS 1883, see Ritter, 2010, 368–369.

[25] Moreover even where it occurs as a durative or preterite it has generally, as here, stative and thus non-temporally fixed meaning.

that is, the domain of possible *cases* is to be examined, the applicable one chosen, and the corresponding procedure followed. In short, branchings are equivalent to case divisions. Moreover, for the branching to be unambiguous the case divisions must be *disjoint*, that is, they must divide up (at least part of) the space of all possible circumstances into non-overlapping subsets of cases, though such a subdivision need not be *exhaustive*. In the case of a simple dichotomous parallel division (like § 2) the division covers the only two possible cases supposed and thus is exhaustive, while in a multiple parallel branching (such as §§ 17–20) more possibilities are explored though in this case there is no indication that they are intended to cover the entire domain of all possible situations. A sequential branching comes into play where there exists a pre-established *ordering* of cases with the branchings taking place successively, starting from the most highly prioritized case.[26]

1.3 Legal conclusions

Two-level verbal chains, with preterite verbs on Level 1 and durative verbs comprising Level 2 – and, in a unique feature of jurisprudential texts in the rational-practice domain, perfect-tense verbs as closure of the first level; pure sequential and parallel and sequential branching structures; these are the main aspects of the underlying formal structure of the Codex Ḫammurapi. To what extent does such a formal analysis aid us in going further toward an understanding of the sense of the Code?

1. On an organizational level, the formal structure analysis tells us that the contour of a rational-practice text goes generally from preterite to preterite – and not, as has become standard in Assyriological practice, from *šumma* to *šumma*.[27] Of course the two will coincide for a purely sequential law. But if there is branching, as in the case of jurisprudence (and medicine[28]), there will be at least one internal *šumma* and the standard decomposition will generally miss this. In particular, the number of laws in the Codex Ḫammurapi must be significantly decreased, since the 60 'laws' with apparent Prf – Dur sequences are, by this argument, in fact fragments of laws, and the total number of laws must be reduced by approximately this number.

2. Step-by-step descriptions of actions to be carried out, the possibility of branching, that is the choice of one or another way of going forward depending on the specifics of the result of one of the steps: these form part of the tool box available to the ancient Babylonians in the very restricted class of rational-practice texts. Now it is striking that, as will be seen in Section 3, precisely these criteria were developed as the defining criteria of what must constitute a programming language at the very start of the development of computers.

---

[26] The use of branching in Old Babylonian law codes is related to the modern logical and jurisprudential concept of 'subsumption'. For more on this question see the discussion and bibliography in the chapter by Markus Asper in this volume.

[27] Furthermore, this new rule is equally valid for mathematics, a rational-practice domain which, as we shall see, generally does not use *šumma*.

[28] For branching in Old Babylonian medical texts, see Ritter, 2009, 88–89.

Are these tools then inevitable to any attempt to structure information flow in an algorithmic way? Or are there radically different options available to control such flows; the choices made in second millennium BCE Babylonia only coincidentally conforming to those made four thousand years later?

3. Returning to our original questions about norm-laden practices: a formal analysis can separate out subgroups of a genre, it cannot itself explain why and in what way one subgroup bears this specific form. The rational-practice structure we have explored here is applicable to the one other known Akkadian-language law code of the Old Babylonian period, that carrying the modern title of 'Laws of Ešnunna'.[29] But this structure is not found in any other juridical text of the period. Now, if there is any class of legal texts which carry a normative charge, it is certainly the law codes. Not only do they explicitly present normative behavior – or rather the punishment meted out to non-normative infractions – but both in the prologue to the Codex Ḫammurapi:

> When the god Marduk commanded me to provide just ways for the people of the land (in order to attain) appropriate behavior, I established truth and justice as the declaration of the land, I enhanced the well-being of the people.

and in its epilogue:

> May this stela reveal for (any future king) the traditions, the proper conduct, the judgments of the land that I rendered, the verdicts of the land that I gave and may he, too, provide just ways for all humankind in his care. May he render their judgments, may he give their verdicts, may he eradicate the wicked and the evil from his land, may he enhance the wellbeing of his people.[30]

Ḫammurapi makes explicit claims that the laws contained are indeed *awāt mīšarim* 'pronouncements of justice', just ways, normative behavior. But as we have already mentioned, other legal documents, such as court proceedings, contracts, land grants, etc., have a completely different structure, as do indeed the prologue and epilogue of the Codex Ḫammurapi itself.[31] If legal texts in general carry a normative charge, what specificity of that charge determines the boundary between the rational-practice (law code) subclass and the others?

2. A comparison with mathematical problem texts

To what extent are the algorithmic tools used in the construction of the normative domain of law codes unique to that domain? Of the other Old Babylonian rational practices, that whose texts most clearly parallel the law codes, from both a formal

---

[29] As well as, at least partially, to later codes of law from Mesopotamia. But just what changes in later periods would require a complete diachronic study. For the laws of Ešnunna, see Roth, 1997, 57–70.

[30] The translation of the text from the prologue (S^b 8: VI 14–24) and from the epilogue (S^b 8: XLVIII 59–94) is taken from Roth, 1997 (80–81 and 135 respectively).

[31] For examples of these various classes of documents see e.g. Pritchard, 1969; Joannès, 2000; Janowski / Wilhelm, 2004; as well as the study of Akkadian-language land donations from Ḫatti in the chapter by Daliah Bawanypeck in this volume.

and a normatively charged point of view, is mathematics. Not, as already mentioned, all mathematical texts, but precisely that class of solved problems (of which some 500 are known today) in which a problem is posed and its step-by-step solution is explicitly given, that is, just those mathematical texts which communicate a 'correctly ordered' form of action. And the way in which these solved-problem texts do that reveals an illuminating comparison with the law codes.

Because I have discussed the mathematical texts at some length elsewhere I shall very briefly outline the salient points of their analysis here.[32] We shall be taking our examples from an Old Babylonian solved-problem collection BM 13901 which originally contained some 24 solved problems concerning squares, organized, as will become clear, systematically and pedagogically.

Figure 4. Obverse of an Old Babylonian mathematical solved-problem text (British Museum 13901).
Photograph courtesy of the British Museum.

[32] For more details on this approach the reader is referred to Ritter, 2017. For more detail on the specific problems dealt with in this short Section, see Ritter, 2010, 353–360; for a different approach to another problem on the same tablet, see the chapter by Hagan Brunke in this volume.

In our discussion of the mathematical problem-texts we shall be using much the same conventions as we have employed in the law section, the sole exception being that the Akkadian enclitic particle *-ma* will be translated by a dash '–', not by the English words 'and' or 'but'.

The first problem on this tablet, BM 13901: # 1,[33] reads as follows:

BM 13901: # 1 *eqlam u mitḫartī* **akmur**-*ma 45*
1 wāṣitam tašakkan
bāmat 1 teḫeppe
30 u 30 tuštakkal
15 ana 45 tuṣṣab-*ma 1*
1 basûm
30 ša ***tuštākilu*** *libba 1* tanassaḫ-*ma 30 mitḫartum*

I **have added** the surface and my side – 45.

You *will set down* 1, the *wāṣitum*.
You *will fractionalize* the half of 1: (30).
You *will square-multiply*[34] 30 by 30: (15).
You *will add* 15 to 45 – 1.
1 is (its) square root.
You *will subtract* 30, that you ***had square-multiplied*** from 1 – 30 is the side of the square.

Now, structurally speaking, the mathematical problem here has strong points of similarity with the nearly contemporaneous Code of Ḫammurapi. Like the latter, the mathematical text presents a problem to be resolved followed by the solution itself. Moreover the presentation of the problem, like the premises in the Code, is in the preterite tense while the solution procedure employs the durative. Indeed, even the use of a subjunctivized preterite in the consequent parallels its similar use in the CḪ, namely as a way of identifying a term (a noun in legal codes, a number in mathematical texts) as something that has been introduced earlier in the procedure.[35]

Nonetheless there are three evident points of difference with the law codes, differences which are common to all the mathematical problem text corpus:

1° the conditional formulation of the problem is lacking – there is no *šumma*.[36]

---

[33] We shall use the symbol # *N* to mark the *N*th problem on a multi-problem tablet, such as BM 13901.

[34] There are two Akkadian verbs 'to multiply': *našûm* and *šutākalum*. The first is the ordinary multiplication which takes any two numerical arguments (X, Y), returning $X \times Y$, while the second, which I translate by 'square-multiply', generally takes either a *single* argument (X) or else generally, as here, two *identical* arguments, (X, X), and, in either case, returns X^2; it is thus more nearly equivalent to the English 'to square'.

[35] We shall not be pursuing here this issue of the subjunctivized preterite in the consequence of mathematical problem texts; the interested reader can see more detail in Ritter, 2017.

[36] Though no conditional forms are to be found on this tablet, there are in fact more than 50 mathematical problems (some 10 % of the total) which use either an initial or an internal *šumma*, or both.

2° there is no use of the perfect tense.
3° the solution algorithm of the problem is couched in the second person not the third.

Indeed, this last point, the change in person, allows something in mathematical texts that the law codes do not: the use of the imperative mood for verbs in the consequent as a possible alternative to the durative. Though only the durative is used in our particular tablet, BM 13901, the imperative is found in the solution part of many other problem texts, often in parallel with the durative.

Nonetheless, on the structural level, the similarities are much more important than the differences and we can thus apply the same rules and conventions as we have used up to now for creating legal-code flow diagrams to cover the case of mathematical texts, such as our Problem # 1 above.

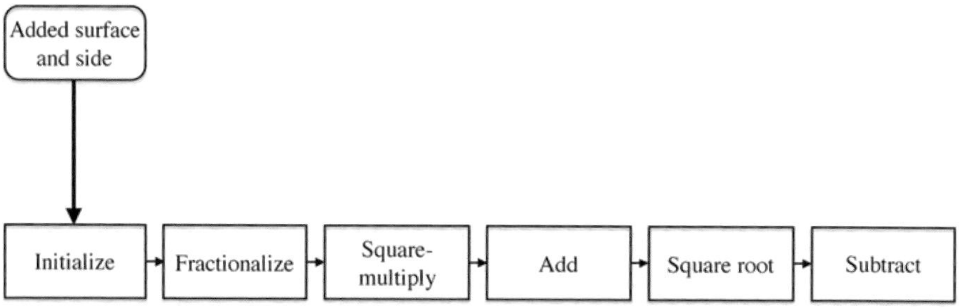

Problem # 1 uses a straightforward sequential algorithm. Indeed, unlike the Codex Ḫammurapi, *no* Old Babylonian mathematical solved-problem text possesses a branching structure; all are simple sequential procedures. Moreover the range of actions used in these texts is very restricted compared to the variety present in the law codes, consisting of a half-dozen or so *arithmetic operations* (addition, subtraction, …) and an equally small number of *control operations* (initialization, storage, …). Though structurally much simpler on this level, the limited array of operations in the mathematical texts permits a codification and symbolic representation of them which facilitates a deeper analysis of their formal structure. We can use this symbolic representation of both arithmetic and control commands to rewrite the Babylonian problem in a modernized and compact form. In the example above:

	Text # 1	**Symbolic algorithm # 1**
	I have added the surface and my side – 45.	Datum = 45
1	You will set down 1, the wāṣitum.	← 1
2	You will fractionalize the half of 1: (30).	½ (1) = 30
3	You will square-multiply 30 by 30: (15).	30 ⊠ 30 = 15
4	You will add 15 to 45 – 1.	15 ∔ 45 = 1
5	1 is (its) square root.	√1 = 1
6	You will subtract 30…from 1 – 30.	1 – 30 = 30

Note that the details of the textual formulation have been simplified to concentrate on the operation sequence and step numbers introduced for each operation in the solution. Steps **2** through **6** are arithmetical operations with standard modern notation (the only non-standard one, *square-multiplication*, is represented by $\boxtimes$), while Step **1** is a command operation, *initialization*, symbolized by $\leftarrow$.

This **symbolic algorithm** can be further abstracted to show the source of the numbers appearing in specific numerical example and thus reveal the logical *information flow* in the algorithm. One attributes to each numerical value in the solution algorithm one of the following symbols:

1° for a value obtained as a result in a preceding step, the step number **N** from which it comes;
2° for a value used which derives from the *i*'th datum of the problem, the symbol $\mathbf{D}_i$;
3° for a constant (such as the 1 in Step **1**), the constant itself in normal roman typeface.

In this way an **abstract algorithm** is obtained:

	Symbolic algorithm # 1	**Abstract algorithm # 1**
	Surface + Side = 45	**D**
1	$\leftarrow 1$	$\leftarrow 1$
2	½ (1) = 30	½ (**1**)
3	$30 \boxtimes 30 = 15$	$\mathbf{2} \boxtimes \mathbf{2}$
4	$15 \dotplus 45 = 1$	$\mathbf{3} \dotplus \mathbf{D}$
5	$\sqrt{1} = 1$	$\sqrt{\mathbf{4}}$
6	$1 - 30 = 30$	$\mathbf{5} - \mathbf{2}$

In the abstract algorithm one can see the flow of information required to find the side of a square for any choice of the numerical value of the sum of the area and the side of that square. This underlying pattern represents one of the fundamental algorithmic patterns used in the other problems of the tablet as can be seen by a comparison of their underlying abstract algorithms. The second problem, for instance, reveals itself as a simple variant of the first. The problem presented is that of the difference between the area and a side of a square with the same implicit problem of determining the side of the square. The abstract algorithms of problems ## 1 and 2 are here presented side by side:

	Abstract algorithm # 1	**Abstract algorithm # 2**
	I have *added* the surface and my side…D.	I have *subtracted* my side from the surface…D.
	D	**D**
1	$\leftarrow 1$	$\leftarrow 1$
2	½ (**1**)	½ (**1**)
3	$\mathbf{2} \boxtimes \mathbf{2}$	$\mathbf{2} \boxtimes \mathbf{2}$
4	$\mathbf{3} \dotplus \mathbf{D}$	$\mathbf{3} \dotplus \mathbf{D}$
5	$\sqrt{\mathbf{4}}$	$\sqrt{\mathbf{4}}$
6	$\mathbf{5} - \mathbf{2}$	$\mathbf{5} + \mathbf{2}$

with the sole difference between the two algorithms residing in the substitution of an addition in the place of the original subtraction in the last step.

The third problem, Problem # 3, shows a further complexification of the mathematical problem:[37]

BM 13901: # 3 *šalušti eqlim* **assuḫ**-<u>*ma*</u> *šalušti mitḫartim ana libbi eqlim* **ūṣib**-<u>*ma*</u> *20*
1 wāṣitam tašakkan
šalušti 1 wāṣitam 20 tanassaḫ-<u>*ma*</u>
40 ana 20 tanašši
13 20 talappat
bāmat 20 šaluštim ša ***tassulu*** teḫeppe
10 u 10 tuštakkal
1 40 ana 13 20 tuṣṣab *15*
30 basûm
10 ša ***tuštākilu*** *ina libbi 30* tanassaḫ-<u>*ma*</u> *20*
1/40-šu 1 30 ana 20 tanaššī-<u>*ma*</u> *30 mitḫartum*

I **have subtracted** a third of the surface <u>and then</u> I **have added** a third of the side to the surface – 20.
You *will set down* 1, the *wāṣitum*.
You *will subtract* a third of 1, the *wāṣitum*, (that is) 20 – 40).
You *will multiply* 40 by 20: (13 20).
You *will write down* 13 20.
You *will fractionalize* the half of 20, the third that you ***had subtracted***: (10).
You *will square-multiply* 10 by 10: (1 40).
You *will add* 1 40 to 13 20: 15.
30 is (its) square root.
You *will subtract* 10, that you ***had square-multiplied***, from 30 – 20.
You *will multiply* its 1/40, (that is) 1 30, by 20 – 30 is the side of the square.

Here are the symbolic and abstract rewritings of the third algorithm side by side:

	Symbolic algorithm # 3	**Abstract algorithm # 3**
	$A - ⅓ A + ⅓ S = 20$: $\mathbf{D}_1$ (⅓), $\mathbf{D}_2$ (⅓); $\mathbf{D}_0$ (20)	$\mathbf{D}_1$, $\mathbf{D}_2$; $\mathbf{D}_0$
1	← 1	← 1
2	⅓ (1) = 20	$\mathbf{D}_1$ **(1)**
3	1 – 20 = 40	**1 – 2**
4	40 × 20 = 13 20	**3** × $\mathbf{D}_0$

[37] As can be seen in the photograph of the tablet, Problem #3 is partially destroyed. However, the extant numerical data and verbal forms as well as parallel problems on other tablets makes the restoration almost completely certain and indeed the version given here and due to François Thureau-Dangin (Thureau-Dangin, 1936) has been accepted by all later commentators.

5	13 20 $\rightarrow$	**4** $\rightarrow$
6	$\frac{1}{2}(20) = 10$	$\frac{1}{2}(\mathbf{D_2})$
7	$10 \boxtimes 10 = 1\ 40$	$\mathbf{6 \boxtimes 6}$
8	$1\ 40 + 13\ 20 = 15$	$\mathbf{7 + 5}$
9	$\sqrt{15} = 30$	$\sqrt{\mathbf{8}}$
10	$30 - 10 = 20$	$\mathbf{9 - 6}$
11	$40^{-1} = 1\ 30$	$\mathbf{3}^{-1}$
12	$1\ 30 \times 20 = 30$	$\mathbf{11 \times 10}$

New here are the arithmetic commands for 'multiplication' ($\times$) in Step **4** and square-multiplication (multiplication of a number by itself, $\boxtimes$) in Step **12** and, finally, inverse ($^{-1}$) in Step **11**, while a new command operation, 'storage' ($\rightarrow$), is used in Step **5**, a command to save for later use the result of the preceding Step **4**. That is, the storage command marks the end of a sub-algorithm, indicating that the following steps are independent of what precedes and that the result stored will be used later on in the solution algorithm (here in Step **8**).

But going down to the abstract-algorithm level shows that there is a close relationship between this longer solution algorithm and the shorter earlier algorithms. Here are the third and the first algorithms side by side:

	Abstract algorithm # 3	**Abstract algorithm # 1**
	$\mathbf{D_1, D_2; D_0}$	**D**
1	$\leftarrow 1$	$\leftarrow 1$
2	$\mathbf{D_1 (1)}$	$\frac{1}{2}(\mathbf{1})$
3	$\mathbf{1 - 2}$	$\mathbf{2 \boxtimes 2}$
4	$\mathbf{3 \times D_0}$	$\mathbf{3 + D}$
5	**4** $\rightarrow$	$\sqrt{\mathbf{4}}$
6	$\frac{1}{2}(\mathbf{D_2})$	$\mathbf{5 - 2}$
7	$\mathbf{6 \boxtimes 6}$	
8	$\mathbf{7 + 5}$	
9	$\sqrt{\mathbf{8}}$	
10	$\mathbf{9 - 6}$	
11	$\mathbf{3}^{-1}$	
12	$\mathbf{11 \times 10}$	

Though at first glance these two algorithms seem to have little in common, yet one should note that the steps in Problem #3, from that following the storage of an intermediate result in Step **5** up to that preceding the inverse operation of Step **11**, are *identical* both in the sequence of operations and in the relative relations of the arguments entering into those operations with Steps **2**–**6** in Problem # 1. That is, it is as though the main algorithm of Problem # 1 had been inserted bodily into Problem # 3 as Steps **6**–**10**, using the (explicitly stored) result of Step **5** as the 'datum'. We can represent this state of affairs in a modified version of the preceding diagram, where now the boundaries of the separate sub-algorithms are marked by dashed lines for the explicitly indicated boundary (storage command in Step **5**) and dotted lines for an implicit change of sub-algorithm (following the embedded sub-algorithm, Steps **6** to **10**), while the embedded sub-algorithm itself is put against a shaded background.

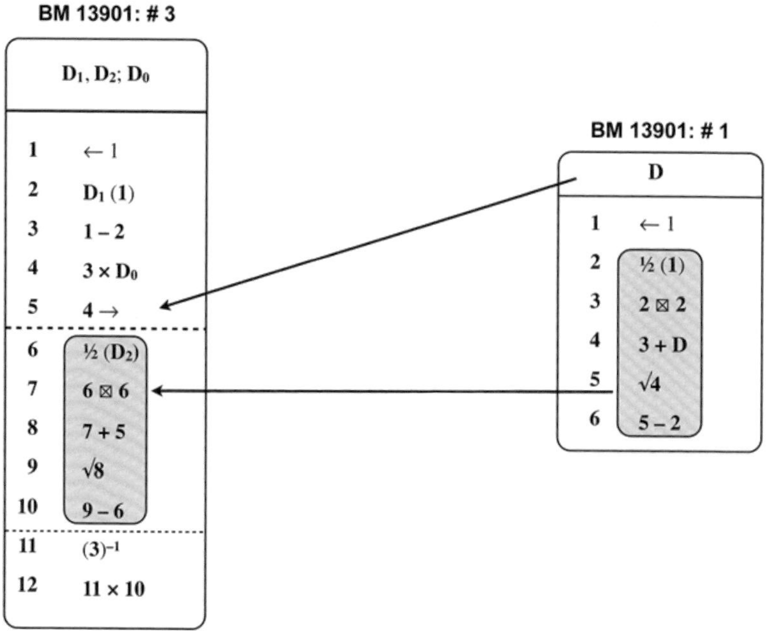

From this point of view, Steps **1**–**5** of Problem # 3 act as a preparation of a suitable 'datum' to be used in the third step – Step **8** in Problem # 3 (corresponding to Step **4** in Problem # 1). The value to be used is calculated in Step **4** of Problem # 3 and then stored (Step **5**), since it will only be called into use three steps later.

This '*embedding*' of a sub-algorithm as an essential operative part of a larger algorithm is something that becomes clearly visible for us in the mathematical texts because of the simplicity and clarity acquired at the abstract-algorithmic level of their solutions.[38] Many of the other extant problems on this tablet embed one or the other of the subalgorithms introduced by Problems # 1 and # 2, and a number of other Old Babylonian mathematical problem texts do as well. One might well imagine a library of such useful sub-algorithm modules being developed and available for use where necessary in the construction of solution algorithms.

But embedding is not the only novelty introduced into this deeper abstract level of the fundamental two-level algorithmic form. To take one other example, one might consider the use of *parallel* sub-algorithms,[39] in which two or more chains of autonomous and independent calculations are laid out, generally introduced by "set down N twice" or "set down N_1 and N_2", where N, N_1 and N_2 are numbers. In the first case different suites of operations or different numerical values are to be applied to the two copies of the number, while in the second case an identical or two distinct suites of operations are assigned to the two different numbers. Though no doubt calculated sequentially by an individual scribe, the two (or more) parallel computations are conceptually distinguished as autonomous, such that they might

[38] The question as to whether such embeddings operate in the legal codes is open, requiring a more fine-grained and detailed analysis of the constituent parts of the procedures.

[39] For a discussion of this point see Ritter, 2004 and Ritter, 2010.

be handled by two scribes working independently. In any case the symmetry among the multiple branches of the parallel sub-algorithms is a pedagogic aide.

On the other hand, as has been already stated, branching, so powerful and versatile a tool in the Codex Ḫammurapi – and used also in medicine and divination among the rational practice texts – plays no role whatsoever in Old Babylonian mathematical solved-problem texts. But this is not to say that branching was not available in a mathematical context if it was needed. The mathematized rational-practice domain of astronomy grew to maturity in Mesopotamia a millennium after the Old Babylonian period. In its procedural texts, besides arithmetic operations it uses branching, both parallel and sequential.[40]

Looking at the legal and the mathematical texts from the formal point of view adopted in this chapter, one is struck by their underlying fundamental similarity: both share the same two-level division – the presentation of a problem using essentially the preterite tense, while the solution procedure that follows constitutes a distinct level and is couched in some form of the durative (the indicative always in the legal and often in the mathematical texts, which last also often employ the imperative at this second level). The connective role of the enclitic particle *-ma* and the referencing function of the subjunctivized preterite in the procedural second level are also current in both. The differences, such as branching in the case of the legal codes and embedding in the mathematical texts, seem contingent in comparison; one could easily imagine each being useful in the other corpus – as is clear from the existence of branching in the late first-millennium astronomical texts. From a historical point of view the question this raises is why do these differences exist in the Old-Babylonian case? Are we face to face with a 'tool-box' of available tools – branching, embedding, parallelism, … – which can be freely chosen at will or is their presence or absence in any given rational-practice domain a result of specific historical development in early second-millennium Mesopotamian culture?

A possible reply can be sought in a recontexualization of the issue, displacing our questions to a conceptually similar though historically very different context; that confronting the very first people faced with the problem of how to tell a machine, whose basic function is to order and transform data, how to do just that in order to resolve a given problem; that is to create a 'lawful' set of commands which will determine the specific 'order' of operations in an electronic computer as a solution to a problem.[41] We thus skip four thousand years and ten thousand kilometers for our final look at law and order.

3. Telling an electronic computer what to do

The question of the extent to which the procedural/algorithmic characteristics of the Mesopotamian legal codes and mathematical texts are inherent to the genre or specific to the Old Babylonian context can be helpfully addressed by examining a quite different historical period; that of the modern (re)discovery of

---

[40] For the first-millennium astronomical procedure texts, see Ossendrijver, 2012 and Ossendrijver, 2017.

[41] The French word for computer, '*ordinateur*' captures better than the English, this aspect of an electronic computer.

the algorithm in the context of the invention of the idea of programming with the advent of the electronic digital computer. Since the American side of this story is currently better documented than others we shall be looking at the development in that country.

During the Second World War, the principal center in the United States for the development of automatic calculation was the Army Ballistic Research Laboratory at the Aberdeen Proving Ground in Maryland, in conjunction with the Moore School of Electrical Engineering at the University of Pennsylvania in Philadelphia. Under the direction of J. Presper Eckert and John Mauchly at the latter site, the first electronic computer, the ENIAC, was designed, built and used in the context of this collaboration, and the history of this and the immediately following machines has been told in some detail.[42] The emphasis in the literature has been principally on the hardware architecture of the machines and on the organization of the teams which produced them, but what interests us here is rather the ways which were developed to *program* the first computers, to direct them how to go about solving the mathematical problems for which they were created.

Among the few firsthand accounts of this question one of the most interesting is that of a semi-outsider, the young Martin Schwarzschild, who was later to become a well-known astrophysicist and one of the pioneers in the application of computers to the field of astronomy. Having joined the Army during the Second World War, he was first assigned to the Aberdeen Proving Ground for a short time in early 1943 before being transferred to Army intelligence. In January 1944, before leaving for Italy, Schwarzschild passed briefly again through Aberdeen. During his first visit, he had observed how a very strong group there in applied mathematics, theoretical physics and astrophysics (including Oswald Veblen, Theodore von Kármán, Isidore Rabi, Henry Norris Russell, Subrahmanyan Chandrasekhar) had faced major difficulties in trying to figure out just how to present mathematical problems to the ENIAC, then still under construction at the Moore School. But, on his return visit, Schwarzschild was told that the impasse had been resolved thanks to the input of the mathematician John von Neumann. Describing the new situation, Schwarzschild (1986, 7–8) remarked in a 1986 interview:

> That was for me an entirely unbelievable experience because some time in between [my two visits] von Neumann got involved in a very effective way and the obvious answer to all our muddled questions was there. I had no contacts with von Neumann himself that I can remember, but all the people in the laboratory told me how one now, according to von Neumann, looked at the problems, and it was so obvious and was so simple.
>
> (…) And it was so incredibly striking because it was all so simple. I mean, there was no more question the moment you were once told. You could understand everything. And you immediately saw how you would write down sequences of statements to solve any particular problem that you ever had done.

[42] The standard general history of early computers is Goldstine, 1972; for the ENIAC in particular one may refer to Burks / Burks, 1981.

That solution was the algorithm: the 'list of something of the order of a dozen commands that a machine ought to be able to understand and then you could code in any convenient way' (Schwarzschild, 1986, 8). Far from being something recipe-like and trivial, it was something that had escaped some of the finest mathematical minds of the mid-twentieth century, something 'obvious' and 'simple' only after the key had been found by von Neumann, arguably the ablest mathematical talent of that period.[43]

However, the applicability of this new algorithmic approach to the practical programming of the ENIAC machine was severely limited, since instructions for any problem had to be entered by changing the wiring of the machine itself. The idea of treating (both the command and the arithmetical) instructions on how to solve a problem on the same footing as the numerical data of a problem was part and parcel of this new thinking on programmation, but ENIAC was not the machine in which this could be put into effect without a radical redesign.

Figure 5. Inauguration of one of the first stored-program, parallel-processor electronic computers at the Institute for Advanced Studies, Princeton, New Jersey on 22 August 1952.
Left to right: Julian Bigelow, Hermann Goldstine, Robert Oppenheimer, John von Neumann.
Alan Richards photographer. From the Shelby White and Leon Levy Archives Center, Institute for Advanced Study, Princeton, NJ, USA.

[43] On an early example of programming the ENIAC and a discussion of the problems, see Bullynck / De Mol, 2010.

At the end of the war, the scientific director of Aberdeen, Oswald Veblen, and von Neumann returned to the Institute for Advanced Studies (IAS) and launched the project of designing and building a digital computer for the Institute, one which would integrate the new algorithmic and storable conceptions of programming from the start. Von Neumann would head the team and, with Hermann Goldstine from the ENIAC project, would create the programs, while the electrical engineer and pioneer cybernetician, Julian Bigelow, from mathematician Norbert Wiener's wartime team at MIT, would oversee the hardware side (Dyson, 2012). The project was launched in 1946, though the machine was not operational until August 22, 1952 when it was inaugurated at the Institute with the three members of the team and the Institute director, Robert Oppenheimer:

But the main ideas were in place at the start in 1946 with the circulation of the first volume of the series *Report on the Mathematical and Logical Aspects of an Electronic Computing Instrument*, entitled *Preliminary Discussion of the Logical Design of an Electronic Computing Instrument* (Burks / Goldstine / von Neumann, 1946). Over the following two years, von Neumann and Goldstine would circulate the various parts of the second volume of the series, subtitled *Planning and Coding of Problems for an Electronic Computing Instrument* (Goldstine / von Neumann, 1947–1948), the first programming manual, laying down the basic guidelines of the new field and detailing the new approach and methods.

Beside the invention of the flow diagram that we have used throughout this chapter, the *Report* introduced the idea of a short list of arithmetic instructions necessary for calculating and, on an equal footing, a short list of commands to direct the flow of these instructions. The basic principles were first laid down in the introductory volume in which the list of the fundamental operating features necessary for a computer were first publicly announced:[44]

> 3.2. There must certainly be instructions for performing the fundamental arithmetical operations. …
>
> 3.3. It must be possible to transfer data from the memory to the arithmetic organ and back again. …
>
> 3.4. It is clear that one must be able to get numbers from any part of the memory at any time. The treatment in the case of orders can, however, be more methodical since one can at least partially arrange the control instructions in a linear sequence. Consequently the control organ will be so constructed that it will normally proceed from place *n* in the memory to place (*n* + 1) for its next instruction.
>
> 3.5. … We must, in most cases, give two parallel trains of orders preceded by an instruction as to which routine is to be followed. (…) Consequently we introduce an order (the conditional transfer order) which will … cause the proper one of two routines to be executed. (Burks / Goldstine / von Neumann, 1946, 5–6)

---

[44] The first item, 3.1, simply states that, from formal considerations, such a code must exist but that "the really decisive considerations from the present point of view, in selecting a code, are more of a practical nature." (Burks / Goldstine / von Neumann, 1946, 5). And here follow the points quoted above.

It is interesting to compare this modern list with the structures we have seen embodied in the algorithms used in the legal codes and mathematical problem texts of the Old Babylonian period, nearly four millennia earlier. Understanding 'fundamental arithmetical operations' to be just that in the mathematical texts and 'standard judicial actions' in the legal codes, the first principle (3.2) is fulfilled in both domains. The second (3.3) makes reference to the control commands of storage and recall, both being explicitly used in the mathematical texts.[45] The standard linear command order envisaged in the third principle (3.4) is certainly in use in both the Old Babylonian domains treated here. The fourth and final conception – the 'conditional transfer order' (branching command) – plays, as we have seen, a preeminent role in the law code while being absent from the Old Babylonian mathematical texts. Indeed, as Martin Schwarzschild later recalled, this was the most important concept of all:

> I think the greatest contribution at this step was the breaking down of logical requirements into that very short list of necessary commands, of which I think that conditional transfers may be in some sense the biggest invention. (Schwarzschild, 1986, 8)

It was this idea that really gave the algorithmic approach the capacity to go beyond a simple sequential structure and had already been put forward in the first volume of the *Report*. We have seen the power and sophistication that such a concept permits in our study of the Codex Ḫammurapi.

But even if mathematical texts – of the Old Babylonian period at least – seem not to have used the branching tool, there was another that they did employ, one that was foreseen by the twentieth-century inventors of programming as being essential to the future development of their newly-created field: the possibility of the creation of sub-algorithms that could be used, in modular fashion, wherever needed in problems of a given sort. Since 'routine' was the term used by the computer science pioneers for algorithm or program, these sub-algorithms were called 'subroutines', as first laid out in the third volume of the *Report*:

> 12.2 … We wish to develop here methods that will permit us to use the coded sequence of a problem, when that problem occurs as part of a more complicated one, as a single entity, as a whole, and avoid the need for recoding it each time when it occurs as a part in a new context, i.e., in a new problem. …
>
> 12.3 We call the coded sequence of a problem a *routine*, and one which is formed with the purpose of possible substitution into other routines, a *subroutine*. As mentioned above, we envisage that a properly organized automatic, high speed establishment will include an extensive collection of such subroutines … . The character of the problems which can thus be disposed of in advance by means of such subroutines will vary over a very wide spectrum – indeed a much wider one than is now generally appreciated. (Goldstine / von Neumann 1948, volume III, p. 2)

[45] The possible existence of such operations in the law codes I feel is probable but this would require a full analysis of the CḪ.

As it turned out, this idea of a generally accessible subroutine library, though dominant during a certain time, was ultimately replaced by the development and use of high-level programming languages.

What are we to make of the similitudes between the principles we have deduced from the formal structure of the Old Babylonian legal and mathematical texts and those created and stated by the pioneers of programming? It would seem that, faced with a new technological creation – the electronic computer – and the subsequent need to make explicit the calculations and ordering involved in resolving a mathematical problem for that new instrument, they were forced to step outside the standard mathematical approach and conventions of the previous three centuries and create a new procedural, algorithmic method. The essential parts of that method were considered to be: a limited number of simple commands, the possibility of testing the status of the procedure at any moment and then modifying the continuance of the algorithm according to the results of that test, and the facility of developing small stand-alone algorithms which could be inserted when needed in larger procedures.

All these considerations, conceived by the programming pioneers of the mid 1940s, had already been brought into play by the creators of the Mesopotamian rational-practice tradition sometime in the transition from the third millennium to the second millennium BCE. Previously, throughout the third millennium, scribes had been faced with the challenge of learning how to employ and extend a new tool – writing – that permitted the setting down in a permanent and autonomously transmittable form the stockage of information and the oral and hands-on knowledge transmission that had heretofore been the only available methods. By the end of the third millennium a number of types of text had been created, starting with economic records and later extending to literary works.[46] But generalized problem-solving such as is involved for example in mathematics, legal codes and medical practice seems to have been first put into writing only at the end of this period. The solution found to this challenge was the two-level procedure form that we have traced here in the Old Babylonian legal codes and mathematical solved-problem texts.

The two cases just discussed concern the formulation and structure of rule-making in the context of technological innovation. But this is only part of the story since rule-making can also arise in other situations. Even in the Mesopotamian context, the number and choice of rational-practice domains varied over time. Harp tuning, glass production, mathematical astronomy, all acquired procedural texts at different times in Mesopotamia and, in the first two cases at least, seem to have used such texts only for a limited time. Other early societies – Egypt, China, India – also developed written rational-practice procedural texts but not always in the same domains. More distinctively, other historical periods and cultures have witnessed the making explicit of the norms of certain intellectual and social practices for quite other reasons than technological. One example would be the Renaissance and the following Early Modern Period in Europe,

[46] For the early history of writing in Mesopotamia see Nissen / Damerow / Englund, 1993; the specific socio-technological interactions between writing and numbers during the third millennium are treated in Ritter, 2001.

with the development of a genre of *reductio ad artem*[47] of different practices, previously insufficiently or undocumented in writing.[48] Such making explicit of the norms articulated in a tacit savoir-faire occurred here for reasons connected to the changing social status of the practitioners. This is not to say that the Mesopotamian case was not also driven by or associated with such sociological changes. One such change, obvious but not necessarily determinant for our question, was the linguistic transition in the written texts from their domination by Southern Mesopotamian-based Sumerian language groups to that of more northerly Akkadian speakers.

Whatever the reasons for the creation of this new procedural class of texts in early Mesopotamia, it is striking that their principal application is to be found in the 'law' of legal texts and the 'order' of mathematics. Both these norm-based domains – though the type of norm is different in the two – generated a clearly typical step-by-step procedural way of committing their practices to writing. The particular tools they employed in these areas largely coincided though each used at least one specific tool not to be found in the other. Yet later examples show that the authors of such texts, in any domain, could draw on any of a large group of generally available conceptual tools. The use of procedural structures clearly demarcates a small group of 'rational practice' domains that enjoyed a special relation to Mesopotamian norms, a group which contained legal codes and mathematical solved-problem texts as exemplary members.

Abbrevations and references

BM = Museum siglum of the British Museum, London.
CḪ = Codex Ḫammurapi.
HS 1883 = Köcher, Franz, 1963, *Die babylonisch-assyrische Medizin in Texten und Untersuchungen*. Berlin: De Gruyter, volume III, no. 393.
S^b = Museum siglum Louvre (Susiane).

Bergmann, Eugen, 1953. *Codex Ḫammurabi. Textus Primigenesis* (Scripta Pontificii Instituti Biblici 51). Rome: Pontificio Istituto Biblico. (3rd edition).

Borger, Rykle, 2006. *Babylonisch-Assyrische Lesestücke.* Heft I: *Die Texte in Umschrift*. Rome: Pontificio Istituto Biblico. (3rd revised edition).

Bottéro, Jean, 1982. "Le code de Hammurabi". *Annali della Scuola normale superiore di Pisa, Classe di Lettere e Filosofia* III/xii: 4, 409–444. [English translation in Bottéro 1992, 156–184].

— 1992. *Mesopotamia. Writing, Reasoning, and the Gods* (translated by Zainab Bahrani and Marc Van De Mieroop). Chicago: University of Chicago Press.

---

47 "Reduction to an art" was the Renaissance expression, the phrase being attributed to the Roman author and lawyer/politician Marcus Tullius Cicero. The term actually appears in Cicero as "*ad artem redigi*" (*De oratore*: I XL 186, Sutton / Rackham, 1948, I XLI 186), while a lost book of Cicero's was entitled *De iure civili in artem redigendo* (Rolfe, 1927, I XXII 7). In both cases Cicero's 'reducing' concerns the field of law.

48 The question of the nature and consequences of this '*reductio ad artem*' has been treated in detail by various authors in Glatigny / Vérin, 2008. Such a social analysis remains to be applied to Antiquity.

Bullynck, Maarten / Liesbeth De Mol, 2010. "Setting-Up Early Computer Programs: D. H. Lehmer's ENIAC Computation". *Archive for Mathematical Logic* 49, 123–146.

Burks, Arthur W. / Alice R. Burks, 1981. "The ENIAC: First General-Purpose Electronic Computer". *Annals of the History of Computing* 3, 310–399.

Burks, Arthur W. / Herman H. Goldstine / John von Neumann, 1946. *Report on the Mathematical and Logical Aspects of an Electronic Computing Instrument. Part I: Preliminary Discussion of the Logical Design of an Electronic Computing Instrument.* Princeton: Institute for Advanced Study.

Cohen, Eran, 2012. *Conditional Structures in Mesopotamian Old Babylonian* (Languages of the Ancient Near East 4). Winona Lake: Eisenbrauns.

Dyson, George, 2012. *Turing's Cathedral: The Origins of the Digital Universe.* New York: Pantheon Books.

Glatigny, Pascal Dubourg / Hélène Vérin (eds.), 2008. *Réduire en art: la technologie de la Renaissance aux Lumières.* Paris: Éditions de la Maison des sciences de l'homme.

Goldstine, Herman H., 1972. *The Computer: From Pascal to von Neumann.* Princeton: Princeton University Press.

Goldstine, Herman H. / John von Neumann, 1947–1948. *Report on the Mathematical and Logical Aspects of an Electronic Computing Instrument. Part II: Planning and Coding of Problems for an Electronic Computing Instrument.* Princeton: Institute for Advanced Study. (3 volumes).

Imhausen, Annette, 2003. *Ägyptische Algorithmen. Eine Untersuchung zu den mittelägyptischen mathematischen Aufgabentexten* (Ägyptologische Abhandlungen 65). Wiesbaden: Harrassowitz.

Janowski, Bernd / Gernot Wilhelm (eds.), 2004. *Texte zum Rechts- und Wirtschaftsleben* (Texte aus der Umwelt des Alten Testaments. Neue Folge 1). Gütersloh: Gütersloher Verlagshaus.

Joannès, Francis, 2000. *Rendre la justice en Mésopotamie. Archives judiciaires du Proche-Orient ancien (IIIe–Ier millénaires avant J.-C.).* St.-Denis: Presses Universitaires de Vincennes.

Kouwenberg, Norbertus J. C., 2010. *The Akkadian Verb and Its Semitic Background.* Winona Lake: Eisenbrauns.

Loesov, Sergey, 2004–2005. "T-Perfect in Old Babylonian: The Debate and a Thesis". In: Leonid E. Kogan (ed.) *Babel und Bibel.* Winona Lake: Eisenbrauns. Volume 1 (2004), 53–181; volume 2 (2005), 713–717.

Nissen, Hans J. / Peter Damerow / Robert K. Englund, 1993. *Archaic Bookkeeping. Early Writing and Techniques of Economic Administration in the Ancient Near East* (translated by Paul Larsen). Chicago: University of Chicago Press.

Ossendrijver, Mathieu, 2012. *Babylonian Mathematical Astronomy: Procedure Texts.* New York: Springer.

— 2017. "Translating Babylonian Astronomical Diaries and Procedure Texts". In: Annette Imhausen / Tanja Pommerening (eds.) *Translating Writings of Early Scholars in the Ancient Near East, Egypt, Greece, and Rome* (Beiträge zur Altertumskunde 344). Berlin / New York: De Gruyter, 125–171.

Pritchard, James B., 1969. "Legal Texts". In: James B. Pritchard (ed.) *Ancient Near Eastern Texts Relating to the Old Testament*. Princeton: Princeton University Press, 159–223, 521–549. (3rd edition).

Renger, Johannes, 1994. "Noch einmal: Was war der 'Kodex' Hammurapi – ein erlassenes Gesetz oder ein Rechtsbuch?". In: Hans-Joachim Gehrke (ed.) *Rechtskodifizierung und soziale Normen im interkulturellen Vergleich*. Tübingen: Gunter Narr, 27–58.

Richardson, Mervyn E. J., 2000. *Hammurabi's Laws. Text, Translation and Glossary* (The Biblical Seminar 73; Semitic Texts and Studies 2). Sheffield: Sheffield Academic Press. [Reprinted: 2008. London: T&T Clark International].

Ritter, Jim, 2001. "Les Nombres et l'Écriture". In: Yves Michaud (ed.) *Université de tous les Savoirs. Tome IV: Qu'est-ce que l'Univers?* Paris: Odile Jacob, 114–129.

— 2004. "Reading Strasbourg 368: A Thricetold Tale". In: Karine Chemla (ed.) *History of Science, History of Text* (Boston Studies in the Philosophy of Science 238). Dordrecht: Kluwer Academic Publishers, 177–200.

— 2009. "Science and Reason in Ancient Mesopotamia". In Xavier Faivre / Brigitte Lion / Cécile Michel (eds.) *Et il y eut un esprit dans l'Homme. Jean Bottéro et la Mésopotamie*. Paris: De Boccard, 83–103.

— 2010. "Translating Rational-Practice Texts". In: Annette Imhausen / Tanja Pommerening (eds.) *Writings of Early Scholars in the Ancient Near East, Egypt, Rome, and Greece: Translating Ancient Scientific Texts* (Beiträge zur Altertumskunde 286). Berlin: De Gruyter, 349–383.

— 2017. "Translating Babylonian Mathematical Problem Texts". In: Annette Imhausen / Tanja Pommerening (eds.) *Translating Writings of Early Scholars in the Ancient Near East, Egypt, Greece, And Rome* (Beiträge zur Altertumskunde 344). Berlin / New York: De Gruyter, 75–123.

Rolfe, John C. (trans. and ed.), 1927. *Gellius. Attic Nights*, volume 1 (Loeb Classical Library 195). Cambridge, MA: Harvard University Press.

Roth, Martha T., 1997. *Law Collections from Mesopotamia and Asia Minor* (Writings from the Ancient World 6). Atlanta: Scholar's Press. (2nd edition).

Scheil, Vincent, 1902. "Code des Lois (droit privé) de Hammurabi roi de Babylone vers l'an 2000 avant Jésus-Christ". In: Vincent Scheil (ed.) *Textes élamites-sémitiques. Deuxième série.* (Mémoires de la Délégation en Perse 4). Paris: Ernest Leroux, 11–162, plates iii–ix.

Schwarzschild, Martin, 1986. *An Interview with Martin Schwarzschild* (Interviewer: William Aspray). Minneapolis: Charles Babbage Institute, Center for the History of Information Processing, University of Minnesota.

von Soden, Wolfram, 1995. *Grundriss der akkadischen Grammatik* (Analecta Orientalia 33), together with Werner R. Meyer. Roma: Editrice Pontificio Istituto Biblica. (3rd edition).

Sutton, Edward / Harris Rackham (trans. and eds.), 1948. *Cicero, On the Orator*, volume 1 (Loeb Classical Library 348). Cambridge, MA: Harvard University Press.

Thureau-Dangin, François, 1936. "L'équation du deuxième degré dans la mathématique babylonienne d'après une tablette inédite du Brisitish Museum". *Revue d'Assyriologie et d'Archéologie Orientale* 33, 27–48.

Westbrook, Raymond. 2003. "The Character of Ancient Near Eastern Law." In: Raymond Westbrook (ed.) *A History of Ancient Near Eastern Law.* Volume 1 (Handbuch der Orientalistik, Abteilung I Band 72). Leiden / Boston: Brill, 1–90.

Mathematische Anleihen in altmesopotamischen Rechtssammlungen

Guido Pfeifer

Abstract ... 47
1 Einleitung ... 47
1.1 Mathematik und Recht im é-dub-ba-a ... 48
1.2 Gegenstand und Methode: Die Spitze des Eisbergs ... 48
2 Mathematik im Codex Ḫammurapi ... 49
2.1 Mathematische Aspekte in den Rechtssätzen ... 49
2.1.1 Überblick ... 49
2.1.2 Einzelne Aspekte ... 54
2.2.3 Praktische Mathematik ... 55
2.2 Systematik ... 56
2.3 Komposition ... 57
3 Konsistenz und Kohärenz des Codex Ḫammurapi als Regelsystem ... 58
4 Ergebnisse ... 58
Abkürzungs- und Literaturverzeichnis ... 59

Abstract

Der gemeinsame „Sitz im Leben" von Mathematik und Recht in Form der Schreiberausbildung legt nahe, dass über den Bildungshorizont der Akteure dieser beiden Regelsysteme Charakteristika des einen für das jeweils andere System Einfluss gewonnen haben. Am Beispiel der Rechtssammlung Ḫammurapis von Babylon lässt sich eine nicht unerhebliche Zahl von Aspekten verifizieren, die vor allem der praktizierten Mathematik zuzuordnen sind. Daraus und aus der normativen Adressierung potenzieller Anwender ergeben sich Implikationen für den Anwendungs- und Geltungsanspruch der Rechtssammlung, während spezifische mathematische Einflüsse auf Systematik und Komposition des Texts zurückhaltender zu beurteilen sind.

1. Einleitung

Die übergeordnete Fragestellung des in diesem Band dokumentierten Projekts „Die Normativität formaler Strukturen" zielt auf den Vergleich mathematischer und rechtlicher Regelsysteme. Dem liegt die Annahme zugrunde, dass Mathematik und Recht als formale Ordnungen vergleichbar sind, etwa hinsichtlich ihrer jeweiligen inneren Kohärenz, ihrer Eignung zur Lösung konkreter Probleme oder ihrer jeweilige Prägung durch den Rekurs auf Meta-Normen, aber auch im Hinblick auf ihre historisch frühe Entstehung, zumal in den Schriftkulturen des Altertums.[1] Daher

[1] Siehe die Einleitung zu diesem Band, S. 1.

mag es grundsätzlich nahe liegend erscheinen, Recht und Mathematik zunächst als parallele Phänomene auf die genannten Charakteristika hin zu untersuchen und – in einem zweiten Schritt – auf der Grundlage der erzielten Ergebnisse miteinander zu vergleichen.

1.1 Mathematik und Recht im é-dub-ba-a

Die nachfolgende Untersuchung mathematischer Anleihen in altmesopotamischen Rechtssammlungen modifiziert diesen Blickwinkel und seine methodischen Implikationen, indem den genannten Grundannahmen eine weitere hinzugefügt wird: Für die Geschichte der Schriftkultur wie auch des Rechts des Alten Zweistromlands darf es heute wohl als *communis opinio* gelten, dass der Entstehungskontext der so genannten Rechtssammlungen und zugleich ihr „Sitz im Leben" in der Schreiberausbildung zu sehen ist. Im é-dub-ba-a, im „Haus, in dem die Tafeln zugeteilt werden", zählten neben anderen Wissensgebieten sowohl Metrologie und Mathematik als auch juristische Terminologie bereits zum Elementarunterricht.[2] Vor diesem Hintergrund kann für die Rechtssammlungen vorausgesetzt werden, dass ihre Verfasser zumindest im Rahmen ihrer Allgemeinbildung auch über mathematische Grundkenntnisse verfügten. Insoweit ist jedenfalls die Möglichkeit eröffnet, dass dieser Bildungshorizont auch in die Redaktion der Rechtssammlungen Eingang gefunden und deren Gestaltung – in welcher Art und Weise auch immer – beeinflusst hat. Die Untersuchung zielt also gerade nicht auf einen Vergleich der beiden Regelsysteme, sondern auf den Zusammenhang im Kontext ihrer Entstehung, man könnte auch an eine Art genetischer Verwandtschaft denken. Soweit ein signifikanter Zusammenhang überhaupt feststellbar sein sollte, könnten sich daraus aber weitere Modifikationen einer Reihe von Aspekten ergeben, denen sich die rechtshistorische Forschung zu den Rechtssammlungen gewidmet hat und die etwa das Verhältnis dieser Texte zur rechtlichen Praxis betreffen, insbesondere, was die Genese der „Codizes", aber auch ihren Geltungsanspruch anbelangt.[3] Abstraktionsfähigkeit und Normativität mögen schlagwortartig die Modalitäten umschreiben, an die in diesem Zusammenhang zu denken wäre. Sie sind uns angesichts der überlieferungsbedingt fehlenden Möglichkeit zu einer theoretischen Kontextualisierung der Texte, etwa anhand von Motiven oder dergleichen, ansonsten kaum zugänglich. Simplifizierend kann der hier gewählte Ansatz demnach in der Frage zusammengefasst werden: „Wieviel Mathematik steckt in den ‚Codizes' und was bedeutet das für das Recht?"

1.2 Gegenstand und Methode: Die Spitze des Eisbergs

Vor der eigentlichen Betrachtung erscheinen indes noch einige Bemerkungen zum konkreten Untersuchungsgegenstand und zur Vorgehensweise angebracht. Der genannte Hintergrund der Schreiberausbildung betrifft bekanntermaßen nicht

---

[2] Waetzold / Cavigneaux, 2009–2011, 301 f.

[3] Letzteres zählt zweifellos zu den „Dauerbrennern" der Rechtsgeschichte des Alten Orients; dazu im Überblick Jackson, 2008, 69–113 und 257–276; zur Bewertung der Diskussion Wilcke, 2007, 213 f.

allein die Rechtssammlungen als eine von mehreren literarischen Gattungen von Rechtstexten in der keilschriftlichen Überlieferung. Lexikalische Listen etwa und vor allem Vertragsurkunden sowie Prozessdokumente stehen gleichermaßen in diesem Kontext und würden sich daher in gleicher Weise als Gegenstand der Analyse eignen.[4] Wenn sich die nachfolgenden Überlegungen gleichwohl auf die Rechtssammlungen konzentrieren, hat das in erster Linie pragmatische Gründe. Die damit einhergehende gattungsmäßige Beschränkung, die einen überschaubaren Textkorpus zur Verfügung stellt, lässt sich aber auch sachlich begründen, wenn man den Rechtssammlungen im Hinblick auf rechtliche Regelsysteme einen besonders hohen Grad an Repräsentanz zubilligt. Bildhaft gesprochen mag man sie als „Spitze des Eisbergs" verstehen, was jedenfalls die Überlieferungslage annähernd verdeutlicht.[5] Die Untersuchung in einem weiteren Schritt auf die Rechtssammlung Ḫammurapis von Babylon zu konzentrieren, erscheint nicht nur mit Blick auf die rechtshistorische Prominenz dieses Texts vertretbar, sondern auch, weil die altbabylonische Überlieferung den umfangreichsten Korpus an mathematischen Texten bereitstellt[6], und damit die oben thematisierte Schnittstelle mathematischen und juristischen Fachwissens auf einer vergleichsweise günstigen Quellenbasis verortet werden kann.

Die gewählte methodische Herangehensweise ist denkbar schlicht und konzentriert sich auf den unmittelbaren Textbefund. Am Anfang steht eine statistische Auswertung mathematischer Aspekte in der Rechtssammlung Ḫammurapis.[7] Als solche werden im Wesentlichen verstanden Zahlen und Bruchteile, Maße, die Grundrechenarten und daraus abgeleitete Rechenoperationen sowie geometrische Figuren im weitesten Sinne. Daneben soll die Frage nach einer etwaigen Systematik sowie nach weiteren strukturellen Elementen des Codex aufgegriffen werden, bevor die Aspekte von Konsistenz und Kohärenz der Rechtssammlung als rechtliches Regelsystem zur Sprache kommen.

2. Mathematik im Codex Ḫammurapi

2.1 Mathematische Aspekte in den Rechtssätzen

2.1.1 Überblick

Ein erster Überblick über die Rechtssätze des Codex Ḫammurapi anhand der Tabelle 1 zeigt, dass sich mathematische Aspekte praktisch über die gesamte Rechtssammlung verteilen und sich also nicht von vorneherein auf bestimmte Regelungsmaterien beschränken. Allerdings lassen sich unschwer gewisse Schwerpunkte ausmachen, etwa beim Bußkatalog der §§ 198 ff. oder bei den Tarifen der §§ 257 ff. und der §§ 268 ff. CḪ.

[4] Dazu jetzt auch Pfeifer, 2018, 6 sowie 8.
[5] Pfeifer, 2010, 81.
[6] Friberg, 1987–1990, 580 f.
[7] Siehe im Folgenden Tabellen 1 und 2.

Tabelle 1: Zahlen, Rechenoperationen, geometrische Figuren, Maße, Gewichte u.ä. im Codex Ḫammurapi

CḪ	Inhalt	Mathematischer Aspekt
Prolog	Festigung der Grundrisszeichnungen von Kiš	Geometrie (Praxis)
§ 1	Analoge Talion bei nicht bewiesener Anschuldigung des Mordes	Symmetrie
§ 2	Analoge Talion bei nicht bewiesener Anschuldigung der Zauberei	Symmetrie
§§ 3 f.	Analoge Talion bei falscher Zeugenaussage	Symmetrie
§ 5	Zwölffacher Ersatz des Streitwerts als Sanktion des geänderten Rechtsspruchs	Multiplikation
§ 8	Dreißig-/Zehnfacher Ersatz als Sanktion des Palastdiebstahls	Multiplikation
§ 12	Fünffacher Ersatz als Sanktion bei Eviktion	Multiplikation
§ 13	Analoge Talion bei betrügerischer Eviktion	Symmetrie
§ 17	2 Šekel Silber als „Belohnung" für Rückführung flüchtiger Sklaven	Zahlenbetrag/Gewicht
§ 24	1 Mine Silber als Sanktion für Raub mit Todesfolge	Zahlenbetrag/Gewicht
§ 29	Übertragung von 1/3 Feld an die Mutter des Sohnes eines verhinderten Lehnspflichtigen	Bruchteil
§§ 42 f.	Sanktion der Nichtbebauung eines gepachteten Grundstücks mit entsprechendem Ertrag des Nachbargrundstücks	Relation
§ 44	Sanktion der Nichtbebauung gepachteten Brachlands mit 3.000 l Gerste pro 64.800 qm Fläche	Proportionalität/Hohlmaß/Flächenmaß
§ 46	Ertragsteilung zwischen Eigentümer und Pächter entsprechend vertraglicher Feldteilung	Division/Relation
§ 51	Rückerstattung eines Silberdarlehens in Getreide oder Sesam nach Wertverhältnis	Umrechnung von Wertmessern
§ 54	Erlösteilung aus Personenverkauf statt Schadensersatz	Division
§ 55	Schadensersatz in Entsprechung zum Ertrag des Nachbargrundstücks	Relation
§§ 56–58	Schadensersatz mit 3.000 l Gerste pro 64.800 qm Fläche	Proportionalität/Hohlmaß/Flächenmaß
§ 59	1/2 Mine Silber als Sanktion für unbefugtes Baumfällen	Bruchteil/Gewicht
§ 60	Teilung eines auf Brache angelegten Baumgartens	Division
§ 61	Anrechnung von Brache auf Baumgartenanteil	Subtraktion
§ 62	Feldabgabe entsprechend Nachbargrundstück	Relation

CḪ	Inhalt	Mathematischer Aspekt
§ 63	Schadensersatz mit 3.000 l Gerste pro 64.800 qm Fläche	Proportionalität/Hohlmaß/Flächenmaß
§ 64	Ertragsteilung im Verhältnis 2:1	Division
§ 65	Baumgartenabgabe gemäß Nachbargrundstück	Relation
§ a	Entsprechung zwischen Silberdarlehen und Dattelertrag	Umrechnung von Wertmessern
§§ t f.	Darlehenszinssätze (33 1/3 %, 20 %)	Zinsrechnung (Proportionalität)/ Gewicht/Hohlmaß
§ w	Duplum als Sanktion	Multiplikation
§ x	Betrügerische Verwendung von Gewichten und Maßen	Gewicht/Hohlmaß
§ cc	Gewinn- und Verlustteilung bei Gesellschaft	Division
§ 100	Zinsen in Entsprechung zu Gewinn und Zeit	(zeitl.) Proportionalität
§ 101	Duplum als Sanktion	Multiplikation
§ 106	Dreifacher Ersatz als Sanktion	Multiplikation
§ 107	Sechsfacher Ersatz als Sanktion	Multiplikation
§ 108	Betrügerische Umrechnung	Gewicht/Umrechnung von Wertmessern
§ 111	5 l Getreide als Leihgebühr	Zahlenbetrag/ Hohlmaß
§ 112	Fünffacher Ersatz als Sanktion	Multiplikation
§ 114	1/3 Mine Silber als Sanktion	Bruchteil/Gewicht
§ 116	Talion (Todesstrafe); 1/3 Mine Silber als Sanktion	Symmetrie/Zahlenbetrag/Gewicht
§ 120	Duplum als Sanktion	Multiplikation
§ 121	5 l pro 300 l Getreide als Mietzins p.a. für Speicher	(zeitl.) Proportionalität/Hohlmaß
§ 124	Duplum als Sanktion	Multiplikation
§ 126	Duplum als Sanktion	Multiplikation
§ 137	Anteilsabfindung bei Scheidung	Division
§ 138	Entschädigung in Entsprechung zu Brautpreis und Mitgift bei Scheidung	Relation
§§ 139 f.	1 (bzw. 1/2) Mine Silber als Scheidegeld	Zahlenbetrag/Bruchteil/Gewicht
§ 156	1/2 Mine Abfindung der Schwiegertochter	Bruchteil/Gewicht
§§ 160 f.	Duplum als Sanktion	Multiplikation
§§ 163 f.	Verrechnung von Mitgift und Brautpreis	Subtraktion
§ 165	Bevorzugung des Erbsohns bei Erbteilung	Subtraktion/Division
§ 166	Berücksichtigung künftigen Brautpreises bei Erbteilung	Division/Addition

CḪ	Inhalt	Mathematischer Aspekt
§ 167	Erbteilung unter Söhnen verschiedener Mütter	Division
§ 173	Mitgift-(erb-)teilung durch Kinder verschiedener Väter	Division
§ 176 (a/b)	Nachlassteilung zwischen Eigentümer und Ehefrau eines Sklaven	Division
§§ 180 –182	Erbteilung nach dem Vater zugunsten mitgiftloser Priesterinnen	Division/Bruchteil
§ 184	Mitgiftbestellung durch Brüder entsprechend dem Vatersvermögen	Relation
§ 191	Abfindung des Ziehkindes durch Drittel der Erbschaft	Division/Bruchteil
§ 196 f.	Talion bei Körperverletzung	Symmetrie
§ 198	1 Mine Silber als Sanktion	Zahlenbetrag/Gewicht
§ 199	Hälfte des Kaufpreises als Sanktion	Relation/Bruchteil
§ 201	1/2 Mine Silber als Sanktion	Bruchteil/Gewicht
§ 202	60 Peitschenschläge als Sanktion	Zahlenbetrag
§ 203	1 Mine Silber als Sanktion	Zahlenbetrag/Gewicht
§ 204	10 Šekel Silber als Sanktion	Zahlenbetrag/Gewicht
§ 207	1/2 Mine Silber als Sanktion	Bruchteil/Gewicht
§ 208	1/3 Mine Silber als Sanktion	Bruchteil/Gewicht
§ 209	10 Sekel Silber als Sanktion	Zahlenbetrag/Gewicht
§ 211	5 Šekel Silber als Sanktion	Zahlenbetrag/Gewicht
§ 212	1/2 Mine Silber als Sanktion	Bruchteil/Gewicht
§ 213	2 Šekel Silber als Sanktion	Zahlenbetrag/Gewicht
§ 214	1/3 Mine Silber als Sanktion	Bruchteil/Gewicht
§ 215	10 Šekel Silber als Sanktion	Zahlenbetrag/Gewicht
§ 216	5 Šekel Silber als Sanktion	Zahlenbetrag/Gewicht
§ 217	2 Sekel Silber als Sanktion	Zahlenbetrag/Gewicht
§ 220	Hälfte des Kaufpreises als Sanktion	Relation/Bruchteil
§ 221	5 Šekel Silber als Sanktion	Zahlenbetrag/Gewicht
§ 222	3 Šekel Silber als Sanktion	Zahlenbetrag/Gewicht
§ 223	2 Šekel Silber als Sanktion	Zahlenbetrag/Gewicht
§ 224	1/6 des Kaufpreises als Lohn des Tierarztes	Relation/Bruchteil
§ 225	1/4 des Kaufpreises als Schadensersatz	Relation/Bruchteil
§ 228	2 Šekel Silber pro 36 Ellen Hausgrundstück als Werklohn	Proportionalität/ Gewicht/Flächenmaß
§§ 229 f.	Talion als Sanktion	Symmetrie
§§ 231 f.	Ersatz eines Sklaven o.ä.	Symmetrie
§ 234	2 Šekel Silber als Werklohn für Schiff von 18.000 l Fassungsvermögen	Zahlenbetrag/ Gewicht/Hohlmaß
§§ 236 f.	Ersatz von Schiff oder Waren	Symmetrie
§ 238	Hälfte des Kaufpreises als Sanktion	Relation/Bruchteil
§ 239	1.800 l Getreide p.a. als Schiffsmiete	Zahlenbetrag/Hohlmaß/ zeitl. Proportionalität

CḪ	Inhalt	Mathematischer Aspekt
§ 240	Ersatz von Schiff oder Waren	Symmetrie
§ 241	1/3 Mine Silber als Sanktion	Bruchteil/Gewicht
§ 242	1.200 l Getreide p.a. als Miete für ein Rind	Zahlenbetrag/Hohlmaß/ (zeitl.) Proportionalität
§ 243	900 l Getreide p.a. als Miete für Qabla-Rind	Zahlenbetrag/Hohlmaß/ (zeitl.) Proportionalität
§§ 245 f.	Ersatz Rind um Rind	Symmetrie
§ 247	Hälfte des Kaufpreises als Sanktion	Relation/Bruchteil
§ 248	1/4 des Kaufpreises als Sanktion	Relation/Bruchteil
§ 251	1/2 Mine Silber als Sanktion	Bruchteil/Gewicht
§ 254	Duplum als Sanktion	Multiplikation
§ 255	Schadensersatz mit 18.000 l Getreide pro 64.800 qm Fläche	Proportionalität/ Flächenmaß
§ 257	2.400 l Getreide p.a. als Miete für einen Landwirt	Zahlenbetrag/Hohlmaß/ (zeitl.) Proportionalität
§ 258	1.800 l Getreide p.a. als Miete für einen Rinderknecht	Zahlenbetrag/Hohlmaß/ (zeitl.) Proportionalität
§ 259	5 Šekel Silber als Sanktion	Zahlenbetrag/Gewicht
§ 260	3 Šekel Silber als Sanktion	Zahlenbetrag/Gewicht
§ 261	2.400 l Getreide p.a. als Miete für einen Hirten	Zahlenbetrag/Hohlmaß/ (zeitl.) Proportionalität
§ 263	Ersatz Rind um Rind, Schaf um Schaf	Symmetrie
§ 265	Zehnfaches als Sanktion	Multiplikation
§ 268	2 l Getreide als Miete für Rind zum Dreschen	Zahlenbetrag/ Hohlmaß
§ 269	1 l Getreide als Miete für Esel zum Dreschen	Zahlenbetrag/ Hohlmaß
§ 270	1 l Getreide als Miete für Bock zum Dreschen	Zahlenbetrag/ Hohlmaß
§ 271	3 Scheffel Getreide p.d. als Miete für Gespann	Zahlenbetrag/Hohlmaß/ (zeitl.) Proportionalität
§ 272	4 l Getreide p.d. als Miete für Wagen	Zahlenbetrag/Hohlmaß/ (zeitl.) Proportionalität
§ 273	6 bzw. 5 Gran Silber p.d. als Miete für Mietling	Zahlenbetrag/Hohlmaß/ (zeitl.) Proportionalität
§ 274	5 bzw. x Gran Silber als Miete für diverse Handwerker	Zahlenbetrag/Hohlmaß/ (zeitl.) Proportionalität
§ 275	3 Gran Silber p.d. als Miete für Langschiff	Zahlenbetrag/Hohlmaß/ (zeitl.) Proportionalität
§ 276	2 1/2 Gran Silber p.d. als Miete für Ruderschiff	Zahlenbetrag/Hohlmaß/ (zeitl.) Proportionalität
§ 277	1/6 Šekel Silber p.d. als Miete für Schiff von 18.000 l Fassungsvermögen	Zahlenbetrag/Hohlmaß/ (zeitl.) Proportionalität
Epilog	Reihung der göttlichen Verfluchungen	Hierarchie der Ordinalzahlen als Hintergrund

Anhand der quantitativen Auswertung des Auftretens mathematischer Aspekte in den Rechtssätzen[8], wie sie in Tabelle 2 erfasst ist, ergibt sich ein Gesamtanteil von etwa 45 %.

Mathematischer Aspekt	**Auftreten absolut**	**Prozentual zu allen Normen**	**Prozentual zu allen mathematischen Aspekten**
Gesamt	129	45,03 %	100,00 %
Zahlenbetrag	37	13,12 %	28,68 %
Bruchteil	24	8,51 %	18,60 %
Hohlmaß	22	7,80 %	17,05 %
Gewicht	40	14,18 %	31,00 %
Flächenmaß	7	2,48 %	5,42 %
Addition	1	0,35 %	0,77 %
Subtraktion	4	1,41 %	3,10 %
Multiplikation	15	5,31 %	11,62 %
Division	16	5,67 %	12,40 %
Proportionalität (einschl. Zins)	22	7,80 %	17,05 %
Symmetrie	18	6,38 %	13,95 %
Relation	15	5,31 %	11,62 %
Umrechnung	3	1,06 %	2,32 %

Tabelle 2: Quantitativer Anteil mathematischer Aspekte im Normenteil des Codex Ḫammurapi (282 Paragraphen)

2.1.2 Einzelne Aspekte

Das Bild gewinnt aber durch die Differenzierung der quantitativen Anteile einzelner Aspekte durchaus noch an Kontur, zumal wenn man sie in Relation zur Gesamtzahl der Rechtssätze sowie zu den mathematischen Aspekten insgesamt setzt. So gehören absolute Zahlenwerte und Bruchteile zu den häufigsten Aspekten[9]. Sie treten nahezu durchweg in Verbindung mit Maßeinheiten, vor allem Gewichten und Hohlmaßen auf. Lediglich § 202 CḪ enthält einen Zahlenwert ohne Maßeinheit (Anzahl von Peitschenhieben). In den §§ 29, 180–182 sowie 191 findet sich jeweils eine Bruchteilsangabe ohne Maßeinheit; diese Fälle betreffen die Teilung von Vermögensgegenständen (Feld, Nachlass), die betreffenden Bruchteilsangaben könnten insofern auch als Rechenoperation in Form einer Division mit fixiertem Ergebnis verstanden werden. Ohne Maßeinheit stehen auch die Bruchteilsangaben in den §§ 199, 220, 224, 225, 238, 247 und 248 CḪ, die sich allesamt auf den Kaufpreis einer Sache beziehen.

[8] Zugrunde gelegt ist hier die Zahl von 282 Rechtssätzen bzw. Paragraphen, wie sie der Zählung der gängigen Editionen entspricht, etwa bei Roth, 1997, 71 ff. und 132. Dabei steht die Willkür der modernen Paragrapheneinteilung außer Frage; eingehend dazu Oelsner, 2012; vgl. auch Jim Ritter in diesem Band, S. 11 ff. Die Bestimmung eines prozentualen Anteils bezogen auf „alle" Normen ist insoweit natürlich bedingt aussagekräftig.

[9] Zu den Zahlenwerten und Maßeinheiten in der Hethitischen Rechtssammlung siehe Daliah Bawanypeck in diesem Band, S. 114 f.

Die ebenfalls zahlreichen Maßeinheiten wiederum betreffen fast ausnahmslos Gewichte und Hohlmaße, mit denen Mengen der Wertmesser Silber und Getreide angegeben werden. Lediglich § x CḪ thematisiert Gewicht und Hohlmaß als solches, und in den §§ 234 und 277 CḪ dient das Hohlmaß zur Angabe des Fassungsvermögens eines Schiffes. Die Angabe bestimmter Quantitäten der Wertmesser Silber und Getreide betrifft entweder Buß- bzw. Ersatzleistungen oder Miet- und Lohntarife, die hinsichtlich ihrer Höhe eine beachtliche Variationsbreite aufweisen[10].

Die Grundrechenarten zeigen ein zweigeteiltes Bild: Während Addition und Subtraktion eher sporadisch verwendet werden und zwar bei der Anrechnung bzw. Verrechnung bestimmter Beträge (§166, §§ 61, 163–165 CḪ), treten Multiplikation und Division deutlich häufiger auf. Multiplikationen kennzeichnen stets eine Sanktion in Form eines Vielfachen eines Sachwerts; Divisionen betreffen die Teilung von Erträgen oder von Vermögensmassen, vor allem Nachlass- bzw. Erbteilungen. Als abgeleitete Rechenoperationen können betrachtet werden die durchaus zahlreichen Umschreibungen eines Betrags durch die Angabe eines proportionalen Verhältnisses und die eher seltenen Umrechnungen. Proportionale Verhältnisse werden eingesetzt im speziellen Fall von Zinsen und im Übrigen ausnahmslos in Verbindungen mit den Wertmessern Silber und Getreide für die Angabe von Ersatzleistungen oder von Miet- und Lohnbeträgen. In letzteren Fällen wird nahezu immer ein Verhältnis zwischen einem bestimmten Betrag und einem Zeitfaktor gebildet. Umrechnungen werden in insgesamt drei Fällen als solche genannt (§ 51, § a und § 108 CḪ), nicht aber anhand von konkreten Zahlenbeträgen durchgeführt.

Als geometrische Figur lässt sich lediglich die Symmetrie ausmachen, wenn man diese in der Sanktion der Talion erkennen will. Als weiteren mathematischen Aspekt kann man schließlich Relationen ansehen, d.h. die Angabe von Beträgen mittels Verweisung auf eine bestimmte Vermögensquantität (so in den §§ 42, 43, 46, 55, 62 und 65 CḪ auf Grundstücke, in den 138 und 184 CḪ auf Mitgift und Brautpreis bzw. auf das Vermögen einer Person insgesamt) oder durch Verweis auf einen Betrag, in diesen Fällen ausnahmslos in Form eines Bruchteils des Kaufpreises einer Sache.

2.1.3 Praktische Mathematik

Will man diese statistischen Befunde zusammenfassen, so kann man wohl sagen, dass die in den Rechtssätzen erkennbaren mathematischen Aspekte durchweg die praktische Anwendung von Mathematik im Lebensalltag betreffen. Insoweit bestehen durchaus Überschneidungen mit dem altbabylonischen Korpus mathematischer Texte, der eine beträchtliche Zahl von Übungstexten vergleichbaren Inhalts aufweist; Erwähnung verdienen hier insbesondere Tarife und Preise, Zinsen sowie Vermögensteilungen.[11] Was die Rechtssätze anbelangt, fällt zudem in

[10] In diesen Zusammenhang gehören natürlich auch die Wertäquivalenzen in den §§ 1–14 der Gesetze von Ešnunna, Roth, 1997, 59–61. Zu den Wertäquivalenzen in administrativen Texten siehe Hagan Brunke in diesem Band, S. 86 f.

[11] Dazu Friberg, 1987–1990, 569 f.

struktureller Hinsicht auf, dass bis auf zwei Ausnahmen die mathematischen Aspekte nur auf der Seite der Rechtsfolgen auftreten; lediglich § x[12] und § 108 CḪ thematisieren sie auch als Tatbestände bei der betrügerischen Verwendung von Maßen und der betrügerischen Umrechnung von Wertmessern. Von besonderem Interesse sind diejenigen Rechtssätze, die auf Rechenoperationen zurückgreifen, aber deren Ergebnis offen lassen, also insbesondere Multiplikationen, Divisionen und Proportionalrechnung: Sie setzen nämlich für die Konkretisierung der Rechtsfolge voraus, dass die Rechenoperation zutreffend durchgeführt werden kann, mit anderen Worten, das der Rechtsanwender tatsächlich „rechnen" kann.[13]

Für die übergeordnete Fragestellung ist der Erkenntniswert der statistischen Analyse sicherlich limitiert: Sowohl das Recht als auch die Mathematik stellen nicht lediglich abstrakte Regelsysteme dar, sondern weisen zugleich auch applikativen Charakter auf, ja dürften bei der praktischen Anwendung ihren Ausgangspunkt genommen haben. Ein Einfluss der Mathematik auf die Gestaltung des Rechts lässt sich auf dieser Ebene der Betrachtung zwar nicht ohne weiteres nachvollziehen, auch wenn konkrete vergleichende Textanalysen – etwa im Sinne Jim Ritters[14] – solches nahe legen. Der gemeinsame Sitz im Leben – und zwar nicht nur in den Schreiberschulen – scheint jedoch eine gewisse argumentative Kraft im Hinblick auf die Frage nach dem Geltungsanspruch des Regelsystems Recht in Gestalt der Rechtssammlungen zu besitzen: Warum sollte dieser nämlich, wenn er für die Mathematik schlechterdings nicht in Zweifel zu ziehen ist, nicht auch für das Recht zutreffen?

2.2 Systematik

Verlässt man die Ebene praktizierter Mathematik (im praktizierten Recht) und zieht man darüber hinausgehende Verbindungen zwischen den Regelsystemen Recht und Mathematik in Betracht, die sich in den Rechtssammlungen manifestieren könnten, evoziert das unmittelbar die Frage nach einer etwaigen Systematik dieser Texte. Gerade der Codex Ḫammurapi war insoweit – fast schon naturgemäß – immer wieder Gegenstand einschlägiger Untersuchungen.[15] Die größte Akzeptanz haben dabei die entsprechenden Arbeiten Herbert Petschows erzielt, auf die hier Bezug genommen werden kann[16]: In Anlehnung an Benno Landsbergers Postulat einer Eigenbegrifflichkeit der babylonischen Welt[17] sind es für Petschow

---

[12] Zählung nach Roth, 1997, 98.

[13] Dabei mag man sich an die Sentenz „iudex non calculat" erinnert fühlen, die in einer spöttischen Verwendung Juristen unterstellt, dass sie das Rechnen nicht beherrschen. Die eigentliche Bedeutung der Redewendung zielt indes darauf, dass das Rechnen nicht Aufgabe des Richters ist, und offensichtliche Rechenfehler im Urteil auch ohne Berufung berichtigt werden können – vgl. D. 49,8,1,1 oder heute § 319 ZPO –, oder auch im übertragenen Sinne darauf, dass der Richter nicht durch das Zusammenrechnen der Argumente zur Entscheidung gelangt, sondern durch deren Abwägung; siehe zu alldem Liebs, 2007, 114. Dieser Aspekt verdiente durchaus einer eigenen Betrachtung, zumal im Hinblick auf die Semantik metaphorischer Stilmittel.

[14] Ritter, 2004.

[15] Siehe Neumann, 2011, 164 mit Fn. 33.

[16] Petschow, 1965, 1984 und 1986.

[17] Landsberger, 1926.

Gesichtspunkte, die mit den zeitgenössischen Denk- und Ordnungsschemata konform gehen, welche den Codex Ḫammurapi systematisch gestalten. Dazu zählen äußere Lebensbereiche und (wiederum) praktische Zweckmäßigkeit, Chronologie, soziale Stellung und Häufigkeit der Fälle, aber auch Muster wie Fall und Gegenfall, schlichte gedankliche Assoziation und Attraktion verschiedener Materien, bis hin zur Differenzierung von vertraglichen und außervertraglichen Rechtsgrundlagen. Der Rechtshistoriker kann mit Petschow diese Ansätze als Manifestationen „juristisch-theoretische[r] Reflexion“[18] bzw. „juristisch-dogmatische[r] Gedankenführung“[19] oder kurz als „Rechtswissenschaft“ *avant la lettre* werten. Genauso gut lässt sich an ihnen aber auch ein allgemeines wissenschaftliches Denken ablesen.[20] Allein eine spezifisch mathematische Prägung der auf diese Weise fassbaren Systematik ist auch hier nicht ohne weiteres identifizierbar – ein Umstand, der nicht zuletzt der Tatsache geschuldet ist, dass die mathematischen Regelsysteme Mesopotamiens selbst noch erhebliche Forschungsdesiderate aufwerfen.[21]

2.3 Komposition

Ähnlich verhält es sich auch mit anderen strukturellen Elementen, die etwa die Komposition des Textes insgesamt betreffen. Hierbei ist insbesondere an die Rahmung des eigentlichen Normenteils mit den Rechtssätzen durch einen Prolog und einen Epilog zu denken.[22] Zwar weisen auch die älteren Rechtssammlungen der neusumerischen Zeit ähnliche Elemente auf, allerdings nicht vergleichbar elaboriert wie der Codex Ḫammurapi.[23] Das Ende des Prologs des CḪ, die Rechtssätze als solche sowie der Anfang des Epilogs lassen sich als eine syntaktische Einheit verstehen (*inūmišu* … §§ 1–282 … *dīnāt mīšarim* – „damals (waren) … §§ 1–282 … Rechtssprüche der Gerechtigkeit“).[24] Dadurch wird bewirkt, dass der Normenteil mit den in Prolog und Epilog enthaltenen Bildern und Topoi, namentlich der göttlichen Herrschaftslegitimation und der Realisierung von Gerechtigkeit durch den Herrscher, unmittelbar kontextualisiert wird.[25] Ob sich diese auffällige literarische Gestaltung allerdings auch unter mathematischen Gesichtspunkten interpretieren lässt, etwa als Prozedur im Sinne Jim Ritters[26], erscheint fraglich. Letztlich erscheinen auf dieser Ebene der Betrachtung fachliche Spezifika zu wenig greifbar, als dass sich die Frage nach einem möglichen Einfluss auch nur ernsthaft stellen ließe. Gleichwohl lohnt sich der Blick auf derartige Phänomene, da sich an ihnen jedenfalls die Fähigkeit zu einer reflektierten formalen Gestaltung ablesen lässt, die nicht notwendigerweise mit einem spezifischen Inhalt in Verbindung stehen muss.

---

[18] Petschow, 1965, 172.
[19] Petschow, 1986, 20.
[20] Pfeifer, 2011.
[21] Dazu auch der Beitrag von Hagan Brunke in diesem Band.
[22] Grundlegend dazu Ries, 1983, 18–30.
[23] Siehe Ries, 1983, 8–18.
[24] Eingehend Lang, 2008, 56–60.
[25] Pfeifer, 2012a, 21; zur Verbindung von Mathematik und Gerechtigkeit auch Daliah Bawanypeck in diesem Band, S. 115–117.
[26] Ritter, 2004.

3. Konsistenz und Kohärenz des Codex Ḫammurapi als Regelsystem

Zuletzt seien kurz die Aspekte Konsistenz und Kohärenz angesprochen und damit gleichsam die Gretchenfrage im Hinblick auf den Codex als einem rechtlichem Regelsystem der altmesopotamischen Kultur. Bemerkenswert erscheint, dass gerade in diesem Zusammenhang der Text selbst uns ausnahmsweise Informationen bietet, die sich auf einer Metaebene verorten und als normative Anweisung verstehen lassen. Die Adressierung des Rechtssuchenden im Epilog, der aufgefordert wird, vor die Königsstatue zu treten und die Inschrift zu lesen, um daraus die Lösung seines Rechtsfalls zu ersehen[27], deutet darauf hin, dass die Rechtssammlung von ihren Urhebern als konsistentes und kohärentes Regelwerk betrachtet wurde und seine Anwendung bei der Entscheidung konkreter Probleme zumindest intendiert war. Freilich steht außer Frage, dass diese Perspektive weder modernen Ansprüchen an ein rechtliches Regelsystem[28], im Idealfall eine abschließende Kodifikation, gerecht wird, noch im zeitgenössischen Kontext des ausnehmend gut dokumentierten Rechtsalltags auch nur annähernd diese Funktion erfüllen konnte. Dafür sind der inhaltlich fragmentarische Charakter der Rechtssammlung, ihre Abhängigkeit von ungeschriebenen Rechtsgewohnheiten[29] und eine ganze Reihe von Widersprüchen zur überlieferten Rechtspraxis der Zeit zu manifest. Auch finden sich gerade in diesem Abschnitt des Epilogs keinerlei Anklänge an ein auch nur entfernt mathematisches Verständnis des Texts, so dass mögliche Einflüsse insoweit eher fern liegend erscheinen.

4. Ergebnisse

Als Ergebnisse lassen sich folgende Befunde zusammenfassen:

Die Rechtssätze des Codex Ḫammurapi weisen eine nicht geringe Anzahl von mathematischen Aspekten auf. Unter ihnen überwiegen Zahlen und metrische Einheiten, die zur Bezifferung von Leistungen dienen. Alternativ werden zum gleichen Zweck aber auch Rechenoperationen eingesetzt, deren Ergebnis offen bleibt, und die daher die Fähigkeit zur korrekten Durchführung der Rechenoperationen voraussetzen.

Die genannten mathematischen Aspekte in den Rechtssätzen sind ausschließlich auf der Ebene praktizierter Mathematik zu verorten. Inhaltlich können Überschneidungen mit mathematischen Übungstexten der altbabylonischen Zeit identifiziert werden. Daran lässt sich eine nachhaltige Verankerung der Regelsysteme Mathematik und Recht im Alltagsleben ablesen, sowohl was ihre Genese wie auch ihre Anwendungsorientiertheit anbelangt.

Die erkennbaren systematischen Ansätze bei der Abfassung der Rechtssammlung lassen in gewisser Weise Anfänge einer spezifisch juristischen Reflexion erkennen, können aber gleichermaßen als Ausprägungen allgemeinen wissenschaftlichen

---

[27] KH XLVIII 3–19, vgl. Roth, 1997, 134. In diesem Zusammenhang sind freilich auch die Aspekte von Monumentalität und Publizität von erheblicher Bedeutung; dazu Markus Asper in diesem Band, S. 200 f.

[28] Etwa im Sinne Luhmanns, siehe Luhmann, 1995. Zu Regelcharakter und Geltungsanspruch siehe auch Hagan Brunke in diesem Band, S. 85 f.

[29] Dazu Pfeifer, 2012b.

Denkens verstanden werden. Ein spezifisch mathematischer Einfluss ist jedoch nicht erkennbar. Dies trifft auch auf die Komposition des gesamten Textes zu.

Im Epilog kann die Adressierung des Rechtssuchenden als normative Anweisung auf einer Metaebene gedeutet werden, die ein Verständnis des Textes als konsistentes und kohärentes Regelwerk indiziert, dessen tatsächliche Anwendung zumindest intendiert war.

Mathematik spielt im Recht des Codex Ḫammurapi eine gewisse Rolle, aber ganz offenbar nicht die entscheidende.

Abkürzungs- und Literaturverzeichnis

CḪ = Codex Ḫammurapi
D. = Digesta
p.a. = per annum
p.d. = per diem
u.ä. = und ähnlich
ZPO = Zivilprozessordnung

Friberg, Jöran, 1987–1990. „Mathematik". In: Dietz Otto Edzard (Hg.) *Reallexikon der Assyriologie und Vorderasiatischen Archäologie* 7. Berlin / New York: De Gruyter, 531–585.

Jackson, Samuel A., 2008. *A Comparison of Ancient Near Eastern Law Collections Prior to the First Millennium B.C.* (Gorgias Studies in the Ancient Near East 4). Piscataway, NJ: Gorgias Press.

Landsberger, Benno, 1926. „Die Eigenbegrifflichkeit der babylonischen Welt". *Islamica* 2, 355–372. (Nachdruck 1965, 2. Auflage 1974).

Lang, Martin, 2008. „Zum Begriff von menschlicher und göttlicher Gerechtigkeit in den Prologen der altorientalischen Codices", in: Heinz Barta / Robert Rollinger / Martin Lang (Hg.), *Recht und Religion. Menschliche und göttliche Gerechtigkeitsvorstellungen in den antiken Welten* (Philippika 24). Wiesbaden: Harrassowitz, 49–71.

Liebs, Detlef, 2007. *Lateinische Rechtsregeln und Rechtssprichwörter.* München: C.H. Beck. 7. Auflage.

Luhmann, Niklas, 1995. *Das Recht der Gesellschaft.* Frankfurt am Main: Suhrkamp.

Neumann, Hans, 2011. „Bemerkungen zu einigen Aspekten babylonischen Rechtsdenkens im Spannungsfeld von Theorie und Praxis". In: Eva Cancik-Kirschbaum / Margarete van Ess / Joachim Marzahn (Hg.), *Babylon. Wissenskultur in Orient und Okzident* (Topoi – Berliner Studien der Alten Welt 1). Berlin: De Gruyter, 159–170.

Oelsner, Joachim, 2012. „Zur Einteilung des Kodex Ḫammu-rāpi im Altertum". *Zeitschrift für Altorientalische und Biblische Rechtsgeschichte* 18, 79–125.

Petschow, Herbert, 1965. „Zur Systematik und Gesetzestechnik im Codex Hammurapi". *Zeitschrift für Assyriologie und Vorderasiatische Archäologie* 57, 146–172.

— 1984. „Die §§ 45 und 46 des Codex Hammurapi. Ein Beitrag zum altbabylonischen Bodenpachtrecht und zum Problem: Was ist der Codex Hammurapi?". *Zeitschrift für Assyriologie und Vorderasiatische Archäologie* 74, 181–212.

— 1986. „Beiträge zum Codex Ḫammurapi“. *Zeitschrift für Assyriologie und Vorderasiatische Archäologie* 76, 17–75.

Pfeifer, Guido, 2010. „Rechtsgewohnheiten in der Perspektive der altorientalischen Rechtsgeschichte“. *Rechtsgeschichte* 17, 81–83.

— 2011. „Vom Wissen und Schaffen des Rechts im Alten Orient“, *Rechts-geschichte* 19, 263–266.

— 2012a. „Gerechtigkeit aus der Perspektive der altorientalischen Rechtsgeschichte“. In: Markus Witte (Hg.) *Gerechtigkeit* (Themen der Theologie 6). Tübingen: Mohr Siebeck, 15–35.

— 2012b. „Gewohnheitsrecht oder Rechtsgewohnheit(en) in altbabylonischer Zeit oder Was war die Grundlage des „Codex“ Ḫammurabi?“. *Zeitschrift für Altorientalische und Biblische Rechtsgeschichte* 18, 127–132.

— 2018. „Das Recht im Kontext normativer Ordnungen der Welt des Alten Orients“. *Zeitschrift der Savigny-Stiftung für Rechtsgeschichte: Romanistische Abteilung* 135, 1–20.

Ries, Gerhard, 1983. *Prolog und Epilog in Gesetzen des Altertums* (Münchener Beiträge zur Papyrusforschung und antiken Rechtsgeschichte 76). München: C.H. Beck.

Ritter, Jim, 2004. „Reading Strasbourg 368: A Thricetold Tale“. In: Karine Chemla (Hg.) *History of Science, History of Text* (Boston Studies in the Philosophy of Science 238). Dordrecht: Kluwer Academic Publishers, 177–200.

Roth, Martha T., 1997. *Law Collections from Mesopotamia and Asia Minor* (Writings from the Ancient World 6). Atlanta: Scholar’s Press. (2. Auflage).

Waetzold, Hartmut / Antoine Cavigneaux (2009–2011): „Schule“. In: Michael P. Streck (Hg.) *Reallexikon der Assyriologie und Vorderasiatischen Archäologie* 12. Berlin / New York: De Gruyter, 294–309.

Wilcke, Claus, 2007. „Das Recht: Grundlage des sozialen und politischen Diskurses im alten Orient“. In: Claus Wilcke (Hg.) *Das geistige Erfassen der Welt im alten Orient. Sprache, Religion, Kultur und Gesellschaft.* Wiesbaden: Harrassowitz, 209–244.

Zu den formalen Gliederungsprinzipien und sprachlichen Ausdrucksformen früher keilschriftlicher Rechtssammlungen unter dem Gesichtspunkt ihrer normativen Intentionen
Das Beispiel Codex Ur-Namma (§§ 1–43)

Hans Neumann

Abstract ... 61
1 Die Gesetze des Ur-Namma und ihre rechtshistorische Bedeutung ... 61
2 Gliederungs- und Formulierungsprinzipien ... 64
3 §§ 1–3 ... 67
4 §§ 4–5 ... 68
5 §§ 6–8 ... 68
6 §§ 9–11, 12–14, 15 und 16 ... 70
7 §§ 17–36 ... 72
7.1 §§ 17–26 ... 72
7.2 §§ 27–29 ... 72
7.3 §§ 30–31/32 ... 73
7.4 §§ 33–36 ... 73
8 §§ 37–38 ... 74
9 §§ 39–41 und 42–43 ... 74
10 Schlussbemerkung ... 75
Abkürzungs- und Literaturverzeichnis ... 75

Abstract

Die sumerische Gesetzessammlung des Königs Ur-Namma von Ur (21. Jahrhundert v. Chr.) ist in Teilen durch mehrere altbabylonische Abschriften des frühen 2. Jahrtausends v. Chr. überliefert. Das zur Verfügung stehende Material erlaubt für eine Reihe von Tatbeständen und Sachzusammenhängen eine Analyse der Gliederungs- und Formulierungsprinzipien. Diese werden unter dem Gesichtspunkt ihrer Bedeutung für die Norm(durch)setzung anhand der §§ 1–43 vorgestellt und diskutiert. Dabei geht es um die Kennzeichnung des Zusammenhangs von (zeitbedingtem) logisch-juristischem Denken (mit dem entsprechenden Erfahrungshintergrund), der Regelhaftigkeit des Stils und der auf spezifische Wirkung in der Praxis zielenden Intention.

1. Die Gesetze des Ur-Namma und ihre rechtshistorische Bedeutung

Spricht man von keilschriftlich überlieferten Gesetzen bzw. Rechtssammlungen des Alten Orients, dann dominiert in der öffentlichen und auch weiteren akademischen Wahrnehmung zunächst der in akkadischer, d.h. in babylonischer Sprache überlieferte sog. Codex Ḫammu-rāpi aus dem 18. Jahrhundert v. Chr. Das ist auch nicht verwunderlich, handelt es sich doch bei der Rechtssammlung des Königs Ḫammu-rāpi von Babylon (1792–1750 v. Chr.)[1] aus altbabylonischer Zeit zweifellos um die bedeutendste Rechtssammlung des alten Mesopotamien. Als einzige babylonische Gesetzessammlung ist der Codex Ḫammu-rāpi (CḪ) uns nicht nur durch Auszüge bietende (fragmentarische) Tontafelabschriften[2] und Stelenfragmente,[3] sondern auch durch eine den fast vollständigen Rechtstext (nach moderner, auf der formalen Stilisierung der Rechtssätze basierender Zählung 282 Paragraphen) sowie Prolog und Epilog enthaltende authentische Inschrift erhalten geblieben, die sich – wie allgemein bekannt – auf der berühmten, in Susa in Elam gefundenen, heute im Louvre aufbewahrten, etwa 2,25 m hohen Dioritstele befindet.[4] Sie war ursprünglich wahrscheinlich an einem offiziellen Ort in Babylonien aufgestellt.[5] Die überlieferten Fragmente von weiteren Stelen deuten darauf hin, dass man den Gesetzestext darüber hinaus auch in anderen Städten des Reiches der sog. I. Dynastie von Babylon öffentlich aufgestellt hatte.[6] Die Überlieferung auf Tontafeln über fast 1500 Jahre hinweg verdeutlicht die große literarische und rechtsgeschichtliche Bedeutung der Rechtssammlung, die dazu führte, dass Teile des Codex Ḫammu-rāpi immer wieder zu Lehrzwecken (nicht zuletzt mit Blick auf den praktischen juristischen Gebrauch) bzw. aus literarhistorischen Gründen abgeschrieben und tradiert worden sind.[7]

Dabei ist es wichtig zu betonen, dass der Codex Ḫammu-rāpi Vorgänger und auch Vorbilder hatte, und zwar sowohl in akkadischer als auch in sumerischer Sprache. Neben weiteren Rechtssammlungen der frühaltbabylonischen Zeit[8] handelt es sich dabei um die sumerische Gesetzessammlung des Königs Ur-Namma von Ur[9] aus dem 21. Jahrhundert v. Chr. Zwar ist der sog. Codex Ur-Namma (CU) nur fragmentarisch in späteren altbabylonischen Abschriften aus Nippur, Ur und Sippar und sowie auf einem unlängst von Miguel Civil edierten,

---

[1] Zu Ḫammu-rāpi von Babylon und seiner historischen Bedeutung vgl. in monographischer Form Klengel, 1991; Charpin, 2003; Van De Mieroop, 2005; zusammenfassend (mit Literatur) Neumann, 2014, 50–54 und Michalowski / Streck 2016–2018.

[2] Zu den aus Babylonien und Assyrien stammenden Tontafeln des 2. und 1. Jahrtausends v. Chr. vgl. jetzt Oelsner, 2012, 99–108, der „aus den etwa 60 Fragmenten rund 40 Abschriften auf Tontafeln" rekonstruiert (ebenda 80); vgl. zusätzlich die Bemerkungen bei Bartelmus, 2016, 70 und 162 sowie Jiménez, 2014.

[3] Zu den 8 Steinfragmenten weiterer Stelen vgl. die Angaben bei Oelsner, 2012, 81 mit Anmerkung 10 (mit Literatur; zusätzlich jetzt auch Thomas, 2016, 296 f.), 99.

[4] Vgl. Roth, 1995, 71–142; Oelsner, 2012, 80.

[5] Zur Diskussion stehen Sippar und Babylon; vgl. dazu Ries, 1983, 27 mit Anmerkung 122; Van De Mieroop, 2011, 306 mit Anmerkung 2 f.

[6] Vgl. Petschow, 1957–1971, 256b.

[7] Vgl. in diesem Zusammenhang auch Neumann, 2004; Hurowitz, 2005, 501–506.

[8] Vgl. hier vor allem den sumerischsprachigen Codex Lipit-Eštar (CL) aus dem 20. Jahrhundert v. Chr. und den sog. Codex Ešnunna (CE) in akkadischer Sprache aus dem 18. Jahrhundert v. Chr. Zum CL vgl. zuletzt Wilcke, 2014, 573–605 (mit Literatur); zum CE vgl. Roth, 1995, 57–70 (Text) und 251 (Literatur und Quellen).

[9] Zu Ur-Namma (2110–2093 v. Chr. [vgl. Sallaberger / Schrakamp, 2015, 302]), den Begründer der sog. III. Dynastie von Ur, vgl. zuletzt zusammenfassend (mit Literatur) Sallaberger, 2014–2016.

gleichfalls aus (früh-)altbabylonischer Zeit stammenden Zylinder der Schøyen Collection[10] überliefert,[11] jedoch besteht kein Grund, an der Authentizität der sumerischsprachigen Rechtssammlung zu zweifeln, die gewiss auf den Text eines Steinmonuments bzw. mehrerer Stelen/Statuen des Ur-Namma zurückgeht.[12] Erhalten sind nach moderner, gleichfalls auf der formalen Stilisierung der Rechtssätze basierender Einteilung ca. 90 Paragraphen sowie Teile des Prologs und die als Epilog den Text abschließende Fluchformel (gerichtet gegen eine spätere Tilgung der Inschrift). Allerdings lässt sich der Gesamtumfang des Gesetzeswerkes nach wie vor nicht rekonstruieren. Im Prolog des Codex Ur-Namma scheint mit Claus Wilcke eine Passage darauf hinzudeuten, dass anlässlich der Errichtung der Stele mit dem Gesetzestext, also wohl doch anlässlich seiner öffentlichen Proklamation, Opferfeste an den Ufern von Euphrat und Tigris begangen wurden.[13] Dabei dürften die verschiedenen Tontafelabschriften ein Indiz dafür sein, dass die altbabylonische Texttradition auf mehrere derartige, an unterschiedlichen Orten aufgestellte Stelen zurückgeht.

Während die Bedeutung der keilschriftlichen Rechtssammlungen, und hier insbesondere die des Ḫammu-rāpi, aber auch die des Ur-Namma, für unsere Kenntnis altorientalischer Rechtsvorstellungen in der assyriologischen wissenschaftlichen Literatur unbestritten ist, so gilt dies allerdings nicht bezüglich der Frage, als was die Rechtssammlungen denn nun eigentlich zu gelten haben: Handelt es sich hier tatsächlich um (erlassene) Gesetze oder waren sie eher Produkte babylonischer Gelehrsamkeit, die – aus dem Curriculum der Schreiberausbildung erwachsen – aus einem bestimmten, in erster Linie propagandistischen, aber eben nicht legislativen Grund verschriftet auf Stelen präsentiert wurden. Eine Entscheidung dieser Frage ist für das Problem eines (auch von mir) angenommenen normativen Charakters der besagten Rechtssammlungen jedoch von eminenter Bedeutung.

Ohne dies hier nun im Einzelnen wissenschaftshistorisch nachvollziehen und inhaltlich im Detail diskutieren zu können,[14] sei an dieser Stelle die (meines Erachtens richtige) Auffassung von Claus Wilcke wiedergegeben, der anhand

---

[10] Zum Text aus der Schøyen Collection (MS 2064) vgl. Civil, 2011; dazu jetzt ausführlich Wilcke, 2014, 455–573. Civil, 2011, 223 datiert den Schøyen-Text in die Ur III-Zeit, wobei „linguistic considerations suggest that may have been written in Umma", während für Wilcke, 2014, 459 der Text „in den letzten Jahren der Ur III-Zeit (oder vielleicht in den allerersten der Isin-Zeit), d.h. um das Jahr 2000 v. Chr.", entstanden ist (vgl. auch ebenda 457 mit Anmerkung 4; Wilcke, 2013, 173 Anmerkung 3 „Ur III-zeitlich"). Meines Erachtens spricht eine Reihe von Indizien für eine Datierung des Textes in die (früh-) altbabylonische Zeit, worauf an anderer Stelle eingegangen werden soll.

[11] Zu den Quellen im Einzelnen vgl. Wilcke, 2014, 459 f. Das seinerzeit von Wilcke, 2002, 291 Anmerkung 4 (und Civil, 2011, 223) noch als möglicher Textvertreter aus Kiš notierte Fragment AO 10638 „gehört zu einer anderen Sammlung von Gesetzen" (Wilcke, 2014, 551 Anmerkung 238; vgl. auch ebenda 458).

[12] Vgl. bereits Wilcke, 2002, 292; im vorliegenden Zusammenhang vertiefend jetzt Wilcke, 2013.

[13] Wilcke, 2002, 298; Wilcke, 2014, 533.

[14] Ein Hinweis auf die den Diskussionsstand in wesentlichen Teilen zusammenfassende Studie von Renger, 1994, sowie auf die ergänzend bei Neumann, 2004, 73 Anmerkung 6 zitierte Literatur mag hier genügen.

des Textes von Pro- und Epilog des Codex Ḫammu-rāpi nochmals klargestellt hatte, „dass die Stele … dem Wissen um das geltende, vom König autorisierte Recht dienen“ sollte, während sie „dem Ruhm des Herrschers (selbst) … nur mittelbar“ diente. Die im Epilog formulierten Wünsche an den künftigen Herrscher wie auch der folgende Fluch lassen klar die „intendierte Geltung der Gesetze“ erkennen: „Nicht das Denkmal wird hier der Pflege des künftigen Herrschers anvertraut, auch nicht die in es gemeißelte Inschrift – … – sondern das in ihr aufgezeichnete Recht“.[15] Auch legen zeitgenössische altbabylonische Kopien von Teilen des Codex Ḫammurapi sehr wohl nahe, dass man Abschriften auch für den praktischen juristischen Gebrauch angefertigt hatte. Nach allem, was wir wissen, kann man ohne weiteres feststellen, dass die Rechtssammlungen in der Mehrzahl der Fälle – darunter eben auch der Codex Ur-Namma – als Beispiele für Gesetzgebungsakte im Sinne staatlicher Willenskundgebung gewertet werden dürfen, zumal man hinsichtlich des Begriffsinhalts von „Gesetz“ keine modernrechtlichen Maßstäbe anlegen kann, da dieser stets von dem konkreten historischen und politisch-sozialen Umfeld abhängig war, in dem Rechtsprechung und Gesetzgebung jeweils erfolgten.[16] Wie der Codex Ḫammu-rāpi zeigt auch der Codex Ur-Namma eine „gewollte Regelhaftigkeit, also Allgemeinheit, Normativität“, als „Regelung an eine abstrakt bestimmbare Personenmehrzahl (ge)-richtet“ und auch „eine abstrakt bestimmbare Vielzahl von Fällen“ betreffend.[17] Damit waren die Rechtssammlungen nicht nur einfach Produkte babylonischer Gelehrsamkeit, die in erster Linie aus propagandistischen, aber eben nicht legislativen Gründen verschriftet auf Stelen präsentiert worden sind, sondern sind sehr wohl gleichfalls als Zeugnisse der juristischen Praxis in jener Zeit anzusehen.[18]

2. Gliederungs- und Formulierungsprinzipien

Das durch die bereits erwähnten Abschriften des Codex Ur-Namma aus altbabylonischer Zeit aus dem frühen 2. Jahrtausend v. Chr. zur Verfügung stehende Material erlaubt nun für eine Reihe von Tatbeständen und Sachzusammenhängen eine Analyse der Gliederungs- und Formulierungsprinzipien, insbesondere auch unter dem Gesichtspunkt ihrer Bedeutung für die Norm(durch)setzung. Kennzeichnend ist hier ein feststellbarer Zusammenhang von logisch-juristischem Denken (mit dem entsprechenden praktischen und intellektuellen Erfahrungshintergrund), der Regelhaftigkeit des Stils und der auf spezifische Wirkung in der Praxis zielenden Intention.

---

[15] Wilcke, 2007, 213 f.

[16] Zu den im vorliegenden Zusammenhang zu beachtenden materiellen Grundlagen und geistig-weltanschaulichen Implikationen altmesopotamischer Gesetzgebung und Rechtsprechung vgl. Neumann, 2006.

[17] Willoweit, 1987, 127 Anmerkung 16; vgl. auch Neumann, 2004, 73 f. mit Anmerkung 7 f.

[18] Zur intendierten Geltung der Gesetze des Ur-Namma vgl. jetzt ausführlich Wilcke, 2014, 490–519; zur grundsätzlichen rechtspolitischen Bedeutung des Codex Ur-Namma im Rahmen der territorialstaatlichen Entwicklung Mesopotamiens in der zweiten Hälfte des 3. Jahrtausends v. Chr. vgl. die Bemerkungen bei Neumann, 2014, 42 mit Anmerkung 61 f. (Literatur).

Grundlage und Ausgangspunkt einer derartigen Analyse ist immer noch die meisterhafte Studie von Herbert Petschow „Zur Systematik und Gesetzestechnik im Codex Hammurabi“ aus dem Jahr 1965, in der es – mit Bezug auf ältere Bemühungen – gelang nachzuweisen, dass die „Haupteinteilung des Rechtsstoffes [des Codex Ḫammu-rāpi] und teilweise auch die Untergliederungen nicht nach modernen juristisch-wissenschaftlichen Gesichtspunkten“,[19] sondern „nach einem dem Denken der Zeit gemäßen Ordnungsprinzip“ erfolgten.[20] Petschow erkannte hier spezifische Anordnungsprinzipien, so etwa „nach chronologischen Gesichtspunkten, also nach der tatsächlichen oder möglichen Abfolge der Ereignisse; nach der sachlichen Bedeutung der geregelten Materie oder nach der sozialen Stellung der betroffenen Personen oder der Wertigkeit der Gegenstände; nach der Häufigkeit der Fälle; als Gegenüberstellung von Fall und Gegenfall; in möglichst einheitlicher Reihenfolge bei sachlich oder rechtlich gleichartigen Tatbeständen, wenn nicht andere Gesichtspunkte – z.B. die Überleitung auf ein neues Thema – entgegenstehen“.[21] Hinzu kommen Einschübe bzw. Anhänge, „die durch – teils zeitgemäß übliche – Gedankenassoziationen und Attraktion verursacht sind“.[22] Drei Jahre später, im Jahre 1968, versuchte Petschow, sich der „‚Systematik‘ in den [gleichfalls altbabylonischen] Gesetzen von Eschnunna“ in akkadischer Sprache zu nähern, wobei er sich sehr wohl bewusst war, dass diese „auch wegen ihres erheblich geringeren Umfangs gegenüber dem CH nicht von vornherein ein in jeder Beziehung gleiches Ergebnis versprechen“.[23] Auch hier erkannte er „eine Reihenfolge vom Höher- zum Geringerwertigen, nach der zu erwartenden Häufigkeit der Fälle oder nach chronologischer Ordnung“, verbunden mit der „Erscheinung der Attraktion, verursacht durch gewisse Stichworte oder Gedankenassoziationen“.[24]

Ähnliche „Gesichtspunkte, Gedankengänge und ‚Prinzipien‘“ lassen sich nun auch – zumindest in Teilen – für den ca. 90 Paragraphen bzw. Paragraphenfragmente enthaltenden Text des Codex Ur-Namma ermitteln,[25] wobei es natürlich zeit- und intentionsbedingte Eigenheiten zu beachten gilt. Inhaltlich behandeln die erhaltenen Paragraphen Mord bzw. Tötung und Raub, Freiheitsberaubung, Rechtsfälle, die mit der Heirat von Sklaven zusammenhängen, Vergewaltigung und Ehebruch, Ehescheidung, Witwenrecht, falsche Bezichtigung einer Ehefrau des außerehelichen Geschlechtsverkehrs, Nichterfüllung der Eheabsprache, Sklavenflucht, Körperverletzung, Sklavenrecht, falsches Zeugnis, Rechtsfälle im Zusammenhang mit Feldern, Erbrecht, Fragen der Haftung von Hauseigentümern, Hirten und Depositaren, Tariffestsetzungen sowie kredit-, pacht-, kauf- und mietrechtliche Bestimmungen und anderes mehr.[26]

---

[19] Petschow, 1965a, 170.

[20] Petschow, 1968a, 3 f.

[21] Petschow, 1965a, 170 f.

[22] Petschow, 1965a, 171; vgl. auch die nochmals zusammenfassende Einschätzung von Petschow, 1986, 19–21.

[23] Petschow, 1968b, 132.

[24] Petschow, 1968b, 142 f.; vgl. auch Eichler, 1987; Otto, 1989. Vgl. im vorliegenden Zusammenhang auch Otto, 2012, der sich aus alttestamentlicher Sicht zum Teil kritisch zu den von Petschow formulierten Thesen äußert.

[25] Vgl. im vorliegenden Zusammenhang auch die Ausführungen von Petschow, 1968a, 2–12.

[26] Vgl. die Übersicht bei Wilcke, 2014, 485 f.; Sallaberger, 2014–2016, 427.

Äußerlich zunächst auffällig ist die durchgängige Regelhaftigkeit des Stils, wenn man sich die Formulierung der Rechtssätze im Codex Ur-Namma anschaut: Die fast ausschließliche Stilform ist hier die sog. konditionale Form, d.h., die zu regelnden Tatbestände werden als Bedingungssatz mit „wenn" eingeleitet (sumerisch tukumbi, deckungsgleich mit dem [späteren] akkadischen *šumma* und hethitischen *takku*), woraus sich die in einem Hauptsatz formulierten Rechtsfolgen ergeben. Singulär findet im Zusammenhang mit den Preis- und Tarifvorschriften das Gebot Anwendung.[27] Die konditionale Form mit Protasis und Apodosis – das Kausalverhältnis zwischen Vergehen und Sanktion in normativer Weise kennzeichnend – entspricht exakt der Formulierung in den akkadischen Omina wie auch in den medizinisch-diagnostischen Texten, was nicht nur eine formale Nähe zwischen diesen Quellengruppen, sondern wegen der ihnen unter religiös-weltanschaulichen Gesichtspunkten zugrundeliegenden Vorstellung einer durch Kausalität charakterisierten „Gesetzmäßigkeit des Weltgefüges" durchaus eine Sinngleichheit dokumentiert.[28] Damit einher geht die Regelhaftigkeit der internen grammatikalischen Struktur vor allem in Bezug auf die Verben in der Tatbestands- und Sanktionsformulierung. So werden die Tatbestände in der Regel mit der sumerischen *ḫamṭu*-Form wiedergegeben, der in der Sanktionsformulierung die *marû*-Form des jeweiligen Verbums folgt.[29] Dies entspricht der Regelhaftigkeit in Konditionalsätzen im Sinne einer *consecutio temporum*, hier zudem die unabdingbare, *normativ formulierte Folge* eines Vergehens kennzeichnend.[30]

Die in entsprechender Weise formulierten Paragraphen lassen sich – soweit auf Grund der spezifischen Überlieferung erkennbar – in ihrer Anordnung zunächst in verschiedene Gruppen einteilen, basierend vor allem auf Sachzusammenhängen, wobei es sich hier sowohl um Einzelparagraphen als auch um mehrere Paragraphen zu einem Thema handeln kann. In letzterem Fall werden die Themen nach bestimmten Prinzipien bzw. Assoziationen spezifiziert. Die Gliederung erfolgt in der Regel vom Höher- zum Geringerwertigen, wobei die gruppenübergreifenden Anschlüsse bzw. Übergänge nicht selten zeitgemäßen Wort- bzw. Gedankenassoziationen geschuldet sind. Dies lässt sich vornehmlich anhand jener Paragraphengruppen des Codex Ur-Namma zeigen, die über einen größeren Bereich hinweg kaum Lücken im Text aufweisen und damit zweifelsfrei auch als zusammengehörig zu charakterisieren sind. Dies trifft vor allem auf die ersten 43 Paragraphen zu,[31] so dass sich die folgenden Bemerkungen paradigmatisch auf diese konzentrieren.[32]

---

[27] Zu den in altorientalischen Rechtssammlungen gebräuchlichen Stilformen vgl. Petschow, 1965b.

[28] Vgl. Maul, 1997, 704; Maul, 2003–2005, 46.

[29] Vgl. dazu im Einzelnen, auch zu den (begründeten) Abweichungen Wilcke, 2014, 476–484.

[30] Zu den religiös-weltanschaulichen Implikationen dieser Formulierungen in den Gesetzestexten vgl. auch Neumann, 2006, 36 (mit Literatur).

[31] Vgl. im vorliegenden Zusammenhang auch Wilcke, 2014, 486–489; vgl. dazu im Einzelnen die Diskussion im Folgenden.

[32] Für die weiteren, hier nicht behandelten Paragraphen des bislang vorliegenden Textes des Codex Ur-Namma vgl. Wilcke, 2014, 489 f.

3. §§ 1–3

Als ersten zu ahndenden Tatbestand (§ 1) nennt der Codex Ur-Namma die Tötung = Ermordung eines Menschen, die mit dem Tode bedroht wurde.[33] Es folgt § 2: „Wenn jemand einen Raub begangen hat, (dann) wird man ihn töten". Die in letzterem Fall verwendete sumerische Verbalkonstruktion sa-gaz-šè – ak „rauben, einen Raub begehen"[34] deutet auf einen schweren, höchstwahrscheinlich mit Todesfolge für den Geschädigten begangenen Raub hin, was – die Sanktion einschließend – den Anschluss an § 1 erklärt.[35] Dass die als Kapitaldelikt mit der Todesstrafe zu ahndende Tötung eines Menschen explizit als erster Tatbestand in den Gesetzen des Ur-Namma auftaucht, ist von Herbert Petschow zu Recht damit begründet worden, dass es sich hier um ein „Primärdelikt" handelt.[36]

Der Raub zieht assoziativ § 3 nach sich,[37] in dem es heißt: „Wenn jemand eine (ungerechtfertigte) Freiheitsberaubung vorgenommen hat, (dann) wird dieser Mann im ‚Gefängnis' sitzen (und) 15 Sekel Silber wird er darwägen". Die Inhaftnahme des Täters in einer Örtlichkeit namens en-nu[ĝ] „Gefängnis"[38] ist zunächst einmal mit Blick auf die Tat „Freiheitsberaubung" (hier ohne Rechtsgrund) als Strafandrohung gemäß des *ius talionis* zu verstehen,[39] dem die Vermögensleistung beigeordnet ist. Man könnte dabei nun zum Einen vermuten, dass die (im Sinne der Talion) angeordnete Haft sich auf eine vorläufige Festnahme bzw. Untersuchungshaft bezog, d.h., der Täter wurde (zunächst) in Ge-

---

[33] Vgl. Neumann, 2012, 165 mit Anmerkung 15.

[34] Vgl. PSD A3 102 f.; Civil, 2011, 253; Attinger, 2005, 245 („faire le bandit, agir en bandit" = „dévaliser"). Die Kasuspostposition -šè ist in der Umschrift bei Wilcke, 2014, 534 ausgefallen.

[35] Vgl. Neumann, 2012, 165 mit Anmerkung 16, wo auch auf die abweichende Auffassung von Wilcke, 1992, 54 und Wilcke, 2002, 311 hinsichtlich des Strafvollzugs in § 2 („so wird er [= der Geschädigte] ihn totschlagen/töten") gegenüber dem in § 1 („so wird dieser Mensch totgeschlagen/getötet werden") hingewiesen wird. Wilcke, 2014, 534 mit Anmerkung 127 bekräftigt dies nochmals, indem er von der Intransitivität der Verbform ì-gaz-e-dam in § 1 ausgehend „eine umschreibende Übersetzung" der Sanktion befürwortet: „wird dieser Mensch durch Hinrichtung sterben"; vgl. auch ebenda 517 Anmerkung 89 „Tötung durch Hinrichtung (gaz)". Vgl. in diesem Zusammenhang bereits Civil, 1993, 78 Anmerkung 20, der gaz in entsprechenden Zusammenhängen mit „to execute" wiedergibt (vgl. auch Civil, 2011, 246 „he will be executed").

[36] Vgl. Petschow, 1984, 189 f. Anmerkung 13. Ähnliches lässt sich auch an dem ersten Paragraphen des über 300 Jahre jüngeren Codex Ḫammu-rāpi zeigen; vgl. dazu im Einzelnen (mit Literatur) Neumann, 2012, 165 f.

[37] Nach Wilcke, 2014, 488 beginnt „das Korpus der Gesetze … mit dem Schutz der Grundwerte der Gesellschaft: Leben, Eigentum und Freiheit (§ 1–3)". Es ist jedoch zu bezweifeln, dass sich die altorientalischen Rechtssammlungen an dem Wertekanon des modernen Rechtsstaates orientierten. Für Roth, 2019, 887 behandeln §§ 1–3 „homicide and other serious violations of the civic order", wobei „these serve to underscore the king's (that is, the state authority's) right to intervene in such cases, removing them from the realm of self-help".

[38] Zu den Termini für Haftörtlichkeiten vgl. Neumann / Paulus, 2011–2013, 201b (mit Literatur).

[39] Vgl. Wilcke, 2014, 535 Anmerkung 130 „Inhaftnahme ohne rechtlichen Grund (wird) unter eine spiegelnde Strafe gestellt".

wahrsam genommen und musste (dann) die Strafsumme zahlen.[40] Oder aber es handelt sich hier tatsächlich um eine Strafanordnung in dem Sinne, wie Claus Wilcke sie thematisiert hatte. Er ging von einem zusätzlich zu zahlenden Betrag aus und fasst die Sanktion dementsprechend auf: „dieser Mensch (wird) im Gefängnis leben; er wird 15 Sekel Silber abwiegen".[41]

4. §§ 4–5

Die Freiheitsberaubung intendierte gewiss den Anschluss der §§ 4 und 5, die sich mit Sklaven beschäftigen,[42] und zwar – mit entsprechenden Rechtsfolgen – deren Ehe betreffend, zunächst auf die Heirat von Sklaven untereinander bezogen (§ 4),[43] folgend dann die Heirat eines Sklaven und einer freien Frau (§ 5).[44] In letzterem Fall werden die besonderen status- und erbrechtlichen Konsequenzen thematisiert.[45] D.h., der juristisch und sozial einfachere Fall (Heirat von Sklaven untereinander) attrahiert – vor allem in Bezug auf das Personen- und Erbrecht – den komplizierteren Fall der Ehe eines Sklaven mit einer freien Frau.

5. §§ 6–8

Das Stichwort „Ehe" führt dem Denken der Zeit gemäß zu den §§ 6–8,[46] beginnend mit der (vollendeten) und mit dem Tode bedrohten Vergewaltigung einer Ehefrau, „die (noch) nicht entjungfert ist" (§ 6): „Wenn der Ehefrau eines Mannes,[47] die (noch) nicht entjungfert ist, jemand Gewalt angetan und sie defloriert

---

[40] Vgl. in diesem Sinne Neumann / Paulus, 2011–2013, 201.

[41] Vgl. Wilcke, 2002, mit Anmerkung 82; vgl. jetzt auch Wilcke, 2014, 535 mit Anmerkung 130, wo betont wird, dass „der Text … nicht erkennen (lässt), ob Straf-Haft des Schuldigen (im öffentlichen Interesse) und Bußzahlung (an den Geschädigten) addiert wurden oder die Buße die Strafe ersetzen konnte"; vgl. im vorliegenden Zusammenhang auch Reid, 2015, 595.

[42] Das verbindende Stichwort dürfte hier die „(begründete/rechtmäßige) Unfreiheit" sein. Nach Wilcke, 2014, 488 ist in §§ 4–5 „die mögliche Überschreitung der Klassengrenze Freier || Sklave in der Ehe und durch Freilassung" das Thema, was aber nicht den Anschluss an § 3 erklärt.

[43] Vgl. Wilcke, 2014, 491–495 und 535 mit Anmerkung 132 mit der Bemerkung, dass „der Paragraph … die Sklavin und ihre Ehe (schützt)", indem ihr Ehemann – ein Sklave – nach erfolgter Freilassung „nicht aus dem Haus entlassen werden darf" (dagegen sieht Reid, 2017, 14 mit Anmerkung 29 die Sklavin als diejenige an, die „will not leave the household", was mit Wilcke, 2014, 535 Anmerkung 132 allerdings weniger wahrscheinlich ist); etwas anders Neumann, 1989, 230 („wohl um den Verlust der im Sklavenstand verbleibenden Frau des ehemaligen Sklaven zu verhindern") mit Anmerkung 67 f. (Literatur zu den verschiedenen Interpretationsmöglichkeiten); vgl. auch Neumann, 2018, 112.

[44] Vgl. Wilcke, 2014, 535 f.

[45] Vgl. Wilcke, 2014, 495–498; vgl. auch Neumann, 1989, 232 mit Anmerkung 78–86; Reid, 2014, 14 (mit weiterer Literatur); Neumann, 2018, 112 f.

[46] In diesem Sinne auch Wilcke, 2014, 488: „das Thema Ehe schlägt die Brücke zu § 6–8, dem Schutz der Integrität der Ehe, d.h., der Rechte des Ehemannes und Hausherrn". CU §§ 6–8 waren zuletzt Gegenstand einer Studie von Roth, 2019.

[47] Roth, 2019, 882 sieht in ĝuruš „(junger) Mann" hier den „man of any chronological age whose father is still alive and thus who has not yet set up an independent household" und übersetzt den Terminus im vorliegenden Kontext daher als „dependent male", was aber nicht zwingend, meines Erachtens sogar eher unwahrscheinlich ist.

hat, (dann) wird man diesen Mann töten".[48] Als Kapitaldelikt galt nach § 7 assoziativ auch der Ehebruch, wobei die Todesstrafe hier nur für die Ehebrecherin galt[49]: „Wenn die Ehefrau eines Mannes[50] freiwillig einem (anderen) Mann gefolgt ist und er in ihrem Schoß gelegen hat, (dann) wird man diese Frau töten; diesen Mann (= den Beischläfer) wird man freilassen".[51] Die Straffreiheit für den Mann erklärt sich aus der Tatsache, dass die Ehefrau „freiwillig", d.h. aus eigener Initiative sich dem Liebhaber hingegeben hatte[52] und dieser somit nicht vermuten konnte, dass seine Geliebte eine Ehefrau war.[53] Im Gegensatz zur gewaltsamen Defloration einer jungfräulichen (freien) Ehefrau galt dagegen die Vergewaltigung einer jungfräulichen Sklavin nicht als Kapitaldelikt, sondern wurde mit einer Vermögensstrafe geahndet (§ 8): „Wenn der Sklavin eines Mannes, die (noch) nicht entjungfert ist, jemand Gewalt angetan und sie defloriert hat, dann wird er (= der Vergewaltiger) 5 Sekel Silber darwägen".[54] Die Strafsumme entsprach dem durchschnittlichen Kaufpreis einer Sklavin in neusumerischer Zeit.[55] Das hier deutlich werdende Anordnungsprinzip ist durch die Reihenfolge vom Höher- zum Geringerwertigen charakterisiert: Zunächst geht es um den erzwungenen Beischlaf der freien Ehefrau, dem der freiwillige ehebrecherische als Gegenfall nachgeordnet wird, um mit der Vergewaltigung der sozial unter der freien Frau stehenden Sklavin abzuschließen.[56]

---

[48] Vgl. Neumann, 2012, 166 mit Anmerkung 23; Wilcke, 2014, 498–501 und 536, Neumann, 2018, 120 f.

[49] Vgl. Wilcke, 2014, 500 Anmerkung 75.

[50] Vgl. oben Anmerkung 47.

[51] Vgl. Neumann, 2012, 166 mit Anmerkung 24; Wilcke, 2014, 498 f. und 536; Stol, 2016, 240 f. mit Anmerkung 31.

[52] Die davon abweichende Annahme von Roth, 2019, 883–885, dass die Begrifflichkeiten ní-te-a-ni-ta (Exemplar S_I; zur vorliegenden Schreibung vgl. Wilcke, 2014, 537 Anmerkung 144) bzw. me-te-ni-ta (Exemplar U = U. 7739[+]7740) nicht die Freiwilligkeit der Aktion, sondern eher den Status der Frau als jemanden „‚who acts for herself', ‚living on her own', ‚dependent on her own resources', or simply ‚independent'", kennzeichnen würden, erschließt sich mir aus sprachlichen und sachlichen Gründen nicht. Für Roth, 2019, 886 f. und 892 ist der Liebhaber der alleinige Akteur in der Protasis, so dass sie als Begründung für die der Frau angedrohten Todesstrafe annimmt, dass „although she has been ‚pursued' by the offender, the fact that she was not sexually abstinent was deemed an audacious flaunting of norms and punishable" (Roth, 2019, 892). Das Abheben auf eine angebliche Promiskuität der Frau scheint mir im vorliegenden Zusammenhang jedoch sehr gewagt und nicht wirklich beweisbar zu sein.

[53] Vgl. in diesem Sinne bereits Neumann, 2004, 86 mit Anmerkung 79; vgl. auch Wilcke, 2014, 499 f. mit Anmerkung 75 (Die hier von Wilcke monierte Annahme von Petschow, 1968a, 4 f. und Neumann, 2012, 166, dass für die Ahndung des Ehebruchs ein [im Text nicht genanntes] Ergreifen der Ehebrecher *in flagranti delicto* Wahrscheinlichkeit besitzt, ist aus sachlichen Erwägungen heraus keineswegs abwegig. „Zeugenaussagen" und „das Fehlen von Spuren von Gewaltanwendung" allein hätten für eine Verurteilung wohl nicht gereicht, sondern wohl CU § 14 zur Anwendung gebracht. Dazu siehe weiter unten mit Anmerkung 67 f.

[54] Vgl. Neumann, 2012, 166 f. mit Anmerkung 28; Wilcke, 2014, 537 mit Anmerkung 150.

[55] Vgl. Neumann, 2012, 167 Anmerkung 29; Neumann, 2018, 119 f.

[56] Zum Problem der divergierenden Abfolge (§§ 6, 8, 7 statt [6], 7, 8) in dem Exemplar Si 277 = S_I vgl. Wilcke, 2014, 466, wonach hier die „Fälle von Vergewaltigung jung-

6. §§ 9–11, 12–14, 15 und 16

Dem Stichwort „Ehefrau“ ist der Anschluss der §§ 9–11, die Ehescheidung (und Konkubinat) betreffend, geschuldet,[57] auch hier unter sozialem und juristischem Aspekt vom Höher- zum Geringerwertigen gegliedert. Verließ der Ehemann ohne ersichtlichen Grund seine Ehefrau, so hatte er nach § 9 eine Mine Silber als Scheidegeld zu zahlen. War die geschiedene Ehefrau vormals eine Witwe, so betrug die Höhe des Scheidegeldes nur eine halbe Mine Silber (§ 10).[58] Voraussetzung für die Zahlung eines Scheidegeldes war jedoch der beeidete Ehekontrakt. Fehlte dieser, dann konnte die Ehefrau – zumindest im Falle einer vormaligen Witwenschaft – ohne eine Entschädigung verstoßen werden, was § 11 ausdrücklich für den geschlechtlichen Verkehr bzw. das Zusammenleben mit einer Witwe ohne (schriftlichen) Ehevertrag vermerkt.[59] Bereits Benno Landsberger wie auch Claus Wilcke sahen letzteres als Beleg für das Vorliegen eines Konkubinats.[60] Das ausdrücklich vermerkte Fehlen eines (schriftlichen) Ehekontrakts veranlasste auch Herbert Petschow, den hier geschilderten Fall als „ein Konkubinat oder höchstens … (als) eine Ehe minderen Rechts“ zu bezeichnen.[61]

Der fragmentarische § 12 betrifft – im Anschluss an das Konkubinat[62] – den geschlechtlichen Verkehr bzw. das Zusammenleben mit einer Priesterin mit unklaren Rechtsfolgen,[63] was aber eindeutig zwei Delikte nach sich zieht, die das (rituell aufgeladene) Flussordal als Beweismittel vorschreiben: Zauberei[64] und (angeschuldigter, jedoch nicht durch Augenschein bewiesener) Ehebruch. So sah der Codex Ur-Namma im Falle einer falschen Anschuldigung wegen Zauberei[65] für den Beschuldigenden nach Ordalbeweis eine Geldbuße in Höhe von 2/3 Minen Silber vor (§ 13).[66] Wurde dagegen die Ehefrau des Ehebruchs beschuldigt, offensichtlich ohne dass man sie bei ihrem verwerflichen Tun ange-

---

fräulicher Opfer zusammen(gestellt)“ worden sind, während die anderen Exemplare „nach sozialer Klassenzugehörigkeit (trennen) und … das Gemeinsame in einer bestehenden Ehe und in der Todesstrafe für die schuldige Person“ sehen. Vgl. im vorliegenden Zusammenhang auch Roth, 2019, 888 mit Anmerkung 31.

[57] Vgl. Wilcke, 2014, 488; Roth, 2019, 888.

[58] Vgl. Wilcke, 2014, 538.

[59] Vgl. Wilcke, 2014, 538 f.

[60] Vgl. Landsberger, 1968, 89; Wilcke, 1985, 303.

[61] Petschow, 1968a, 7.

[62] Vgl. in diesem Sinne Wilcke, 2014, 488.

[63] Wilcke, 2014, 539 liest das Verb in der Apodosis ì-bíl-i-dè-eš und übersetzt je nach Exemplar „[der Mann und] diese Frau / die ereš-diĝir-Priesterin und dieser Mann werden brennen“; vgl. ebenda 517: „Feuertod für Bruch des Sexual-Tabus der ereš-diĝir-Priesterin für beide Partner“.

[64] Dass nach Wilcke, 2014, 488 „das Sexualtabu der ehelosen Priesterin (§ 12) … und der Schutz vor Hexerei (§ 13) … zu den Grundwerten“ zu zählen sind, scheint mir terminologisch und sachlich sehr modern gedacht zu sein.

[65] Anders Roth, 2019, 889 („accusation … remains unclear“) mit Anmerkung 33.

[66] Vgl. Lang, 2012, 42 f.; Neumann, 2012, 170 mit Anmerkung 63; Wilcke, 2014, 539–541. Die von Letzterem (ebenda 539) vorgenommene Ergänzung im Exemplar X (MS 2064) III 15’ [nam-tag] dugud-bi [ḫé$^{?}$-Í]L$^{?}$-[e] „und die entsprechende schwere Strafe wird er erleiden“ ist unsicher.

troffen hatte,[67] dann erhielt sie nach erwiesener Unschuld durch Ordalbeweis vom Anschuldiger 1/3 Mine Silber (§ 14).[68]

Mit § 15 folgt eine fragmentarische Bestimmung zu einer Besonderheit des Eherechts, betreffend die Nichteinhaltung der (bindenden) Eheabsprache seitens des Brautvaters.[69] Möglicherweise ist dieser Paragraph noch dem Thema „Ehe" bzw. „Ehefrau" geschuldet.[70] Für Claus Wilcke könnte im vorliegenden Zusammenhang auch „an üble Nachrede als Ursache des Geschehens gedacht" worden sein,[71] was dann die Verbindung zu den vorherigen Anschuldigungsparagraphen erklären würde. Der folgende § 16 zur Sklavenflucht[72] darf vielleicht als nachgeordneter Einschub zum Thema „Sklave" gelten, bevor mit den §§ 17–36 dann das neue Thema „Körperverletzung" behandelt wird.[73]

---

[67] So ausdrücklich mit Petschow, 1968a, 8; damit ist § 14 beweistechnisch als Gegenstück zu § 7 zu betrachten; siehe oben mit Anmerkung 53.

[68] Vgl. im vorliegenden Sinne (mit Literatur) Neumann, 2012, 166 mit Anmerkung 26 f. Anders (ebenda 166 Anmerkung 26 thematisiert) Wilcke, 2002, 315 mit Anmerkung 93, der den Beischläfer als Beschuldigten sieht, so dass dieser zum Ordal geschickt wurde (ebenso Civil, 2011, 247, und erneut Wilcke, 2014, 541 mit Anmerkung 173). Nach seiner Auffassung sei der Beschuldigte – wie in § 13 geschrieben – in einem, in § 14 allerdings nicht geschriebenen (Wilcke, 2002, 315 Anmerkung 93: „ich nehme Tilgung des [in § 13 genannten] Dativs an"), lú-ra zu sehen. Den Komitativ dam-ĝuruš-a-da in der Protasis übersetzt er mit „bei der Ehefrau eines Mannes (im Schoße gelegen zu haben), ..." Dies scheint mir aber keineswegs eindeutig zu sein. Zwar ist es richtig, dass der Komitativ beim Verbum lá „bezichtigen", der sich auf den Bezichtigten bezieht, in den ansonsten in geringer Zahl vorliegenden Belegen seine Entsprechung im Dativ (oder Direktiv) beim Nomen (= Bezichtigten) hat (vgl. Edzard, 1968, 159 zu Zeile 6), jedoch liegt dieses Rektionsverhältnis in § 14 eindeutig nicht vor (eine Tilgung des Dativs ausgerechnet hier anzunehmen, würde bedeuten, dass der Mann als Beischläfer vom Gesetzgeber/Autor automatisch als potentieller Täter angesehen wurde, was meines Erachtens wenig wahrscheinlich ist). Das einzig sinnvolle Rektionsverhältnis im vorliegenden Fall sehe ich – ohne eine Tilgung bemühen zu müssen – in der Komitativentsprechung von Verbum und Nomen, d.h., dass der/die Bezichtigte im Komitativ steht, also die „Ehefrau eines Mannes". Daraus ergibt sich dann auch das Ordal für die Beschuldigte (und zwar auf Grund der Tatsache, dass sie eben nicht *in flagranti delicto* ertappt wurde), was rechtshistorisch auch einen Sinn ergibt; vgl. Petschow, 1968a, 8 Anmerkung 23; Roth, 2019, 889 Anmerkung 34. Der Vorwurf, „Neumanns [und anderer – H.N.] Annahme ..., der CU sehe ‚das Flussordal für die beschuldigte Ehefrau vor', entbehrt jeglicher Grundlage im Text" (Wilcke, 2014, 541 Anmerkung 173), geht daher ins Leere.

[69] Vgl. Wilcke, 2014, 542.

[70] Für Wilcke, 2014, 488 knüpft „mit der ‚Ehe in der Schwebe' ... § 15 an § 6 an und schließt einen Kreis".

[71] Wilcke, 2002, 302.

[72] Vgl. Wilcke, 2014, 542 mit den Bemerkungen ebenda 503–505; zum Problem der Paragraphenzählung vgl. ebenda 469.

[73] Vgl. Wilcke, 2014, 488: „Der schuldrechtliche Anspruch aus § 15 kann die Verbindung zum Anspruch dessen, der einen über die Stadtgrenze hinaus entkommenden Sklaven zurückbringt, auf Vergütung (§ 16') herstellen und die Entschädigungen und Strafen für Körperverletzung (§ 17'–36') attrahiert haben".

7. §§ 17–36

7.1 §§ 17–26

Die Verletzung der körperlichen Integrität wurde mit der Zahlung von Geldbußen bestraft, wie die §§ 17–21 sowie 23 und 24 zeigen.[74] Die Prügelstrafe findet sich im vorliegenden Zusammenhang in § 22, wonach jemand, der (mit Vorsatz) den anderen schwer am Kopf verletzt hat, 180 Peitschenschläge zu erwarten hatte,[75] und in § 26, in dem es heißt: „Wenn ein Sklave einen Freien (oder Freigelassenen)[76] geschlagen hat, (dann) wird man ihn 60 mal mit einem Lederriemen schlagen".[77] Schlägt dagegen ein Freier (oder Freigelassener) einen Sklaven, so wurde dem Angreifer nach § 25 das Haar halbseitig geschoren und er wurde dann öffentlich in der Stadt herumgeführt.[78] Letztere Tatbestände folgen in ihrer Anordnung dem sozialen Prinzip, und zwar mit Blick auf den Angreifer/Täter: In § 25 ist dies ein Freier (oder Freigelassener), in § 26 ein Sklave.[79]

7.2 §§ 27–29

Im Rahmen des Themas „Körperverletzung" folgen mit den §§ 27–29 Bestimmungen, die sich aus dem Tod des angegriffenen Opfers ergaben, d.h. die Paragraphen stehen in einem unmittelbaren Zusammenhang mit dem in den §§ 25 und 26 geschilderten Tatvorwurf der Schlägerei, die ja letztlich zum Tode von Beteiligten führen konnte. § 27 bestimmte möglicherweise die Übergabe der Ehefrau (des Sklaven als Täter?) als Sklavin? (verbunden mit einer an ihr vollzogenen diffamierenden/entehrenden Strafe?) an die geschädigte Seite (= Familie des Opfers, das ein Freier war?).[80] Im Falle, dass der Täter, ein Freier, (nach dem zum Tode führenden Schlagen eines Sklaven) nicht in der Lage war, (dem Eigentümer des Sklaven) eine Sklavin (géme) zur Verfügung zu stellen, hatte er eine Zahlung von 10 Sekel Silber zu leisten (§ 28). War der Täter mittellos, entfiel die Zahlung (§ 29).[81]

---

[74] Vgl. Wilcke, 2014, 542–545.

[75] Vgl. die einleuchtende Interpretation bei Wilcke, 2014, 544 mit Anmerkung 191.

[76] Vgl. die ausführliche Diskussion zu dumu-gi$_7$ von Wilcke, 2014, 522–526, der in Auseinandersetzung insbesondere mit Westbrook, 2003, („freedman") für eine Deutung dieses Begriffs als Bezeichnung für den/die „freie(n) Bürger(in)" plädiert.

[77] So mit Wilcke, 2014, 545 mit Anmerkung 203 (Vertauschen der Protasen).

[78] Vgl. Wilcke, 2014, 545.

[79] In Bezug auf die Gruppe der §§ 17–22 verweist Wilcke, 2014, 488 darauf, sie „mit ihrer auf vorhandenen/fehlenden Vorsatz weisenden Differenzierung nach Taten mit Faust oder Waffe deutlich juristische Reflexion" zeigt.

[80] Vgl. Wilcke, 2014, 546 mit Anmerkung 205–207; nach ebenda 503 soll es sich bei der Ehefrau des Täters eher um die des für die Tat des Sklaven haftenden Eigentümers gehandelt haben, die als Strafe darüber hinaus „eine öffentliche? Vergewaltigung" zu erdulden hatte (ebenda 518: „Versklavung und sexuelle Demütigung der Ehefrau des [Eigentümers des] Täters"). Der Text bleibt aber nach wie vor schwierig zu deuten und bedarf weiterer Diskussion.

[81] Vgl. Wilcke, 2014, 546.

7.3 §§ 30–31/32

Das Stichwort géme „Sklavin“ (in § 28) attrahiert die §§ 30 f. (und vielleicht § 32).[82] Die hier vermerkte Strafandrohung, den Mund mit einem Liter Salz eingerieben zu bekommen, galt demjenigen, der „zur Sklavin eines Mannes, die wie ihre Herrin gemacht worden ist, einen Fluch gesprochen hat“.[83] Dies ist als eine (mehr oder weniger symbolische) „spiegelnde“ Strafe mit entsprechendem abschreckenden Charakter zu verstehen.[84] Hintergrund dieser und der folgenden, nur fragmentarisch erhaltenen Bestimmung (§ 31)[85] war wohl der Schutz einer in ihrem sozialen Status veränderten Sklavin vor Anfeindungen bzw. – in letzterem Fall § 31 – vor der Verletzung ihrer körperlichen Integrität. Hintergrund könnte die Möglichkeit sein, dass die Sklavin von ihrem Herrn zu seiner zweiten Frau gemacht worden ist, ohne dass in diesem Fall die erste Frau verstoßen wurde, da man sonst die Herrin (nin) nicht ausdrücklich genannt hätte. Der Grund für eine Zweitehe bei gleichzeitigem Fortbestehen der ersten ehelichen Verbindung, also für eine legale Bigamie, könnte z.B. in einer unheilbaren Krankheit der ersten Ehefrau bestanden haben, wie dies durch zeitgenössische Urkunden belegt ist. Zur Verschaffung von Kindern erhob daher der Ehemann seine Sklavin in den Stand einer zweiten Ehefrau, was gesellschaftlich auch akzeptiert war, so dass deren Integrität hier geschützt wurde.[86]

7.4 §§ 33–36

Abgeschlossen wird das Thema Körperverletzung mit den §§ 33-36, das Verlieren der Leibesfrucht nach vorheriger körperlicher Attacke auf die Frau betreffend. Gemäß § 34 drohte – an die Protasis von § 33 anschließend – nach Schlagen[87] einer (freien) schwangeren Frau mit Todesfolge (für die Frau) dem entsprechenden Angreifer die Todesstrafe. Das Verlieren der Leibesfrucht allein wurde dagegen mit einer Geldbuße in Höhe von einer halben Mine Silber geahndet (§ 33). Sozial und damit juristisch abgestuft war im Falle, dass das Opfer eine Sklavin war, eine niedrigere (je nach Überlieferung 10 bzw. 5 Sekel) Silber für den Abgang der Leibesfrucht zu zahlen (§ 35), bei Versterben der geschlage-

[82] Von § 32 sind nur wenige Zeichenspuren erhalten; vgl. Civil, 2011, 240; Wilcke, 2014, 547.

[83] Zur entsprechenden Übersetzung der Protasis vgl. bereits Wilcke, 1969, 182 (ebenda Anmerkung 463 „nach mündlicher Anregung A. Falkensteins“); Römer, 1982, 22; Wilcke, 2002, 319 f.; Neumann, 2012, 171 Anmerkung 67; zuletzt Wilcke, 2014, 546; Stol, 2016, 168.

[84] Vgl. Neumann / Paulus, 2011–2013, 200.

[85] Vgl. Neumann, 2012, 171 Anmerkung 68; Wilcke, 2014, 547.

[86] Vgl. dazu bereits die ausführliche Begründung bei Neumann, 1987, 135 f. (vgl. in diesem Sinne auch Attinger, 1993, 449 [ex. 214]), von Wilcke, 2014, 546 f. Anmerkung 208 übersehen. Vgl. im vorliegenden Zusammenhang auch Lafont, 1999, 315–319.

[87] Wilcke, 2002, 318 liest am Anfang von § 33 (UM 55–21–71 I$^{!}$1’) tuk[umbi á-su]ḫ „wenn (jemand) [mit dem Ellenbo]gen …“, mit der Schlussfolgerung (Wilcke, 2014, 547 Anmerkung 210), dass „der Stoß mit dem Ellenbogen … das Anrempeln als Ursache einer Fehlgeburt“ formuliert. Die Ergänzung bleibt allerdings unsicher, so dass bislang einzig das Verbum ra „schlagen (mit$^{?}$)“ in den §§ 33 und 35 zur Charakterisierung der Attacke zur Verfügung steht (im Anschluss an § 31 [und § 32$^{?}$]?).

nen Sklavin hatte der Angreifer „Haupt für Haupt“, d.h. eine Sklavin (dem Eigentümer) zu geben (§ 36).[88] In beiden Fällen handelt es sich um Schadenersatzleistungen, die in erster Linie den jeweiligen Verlust des Sklaveneigentümers zu kompensieren hatten. Letztere Tatbestände werden in sozialer Abstufung nach den Angriffen auf die freie Frau genannt.

8. §§ 37–38

An die Körperverletzungsparagraphen schließen sich mit §§ 37 und 38 Bestimmungen prozessrechtlicher Natur an, dem Denken der Zeit gemäß ausschnittsweise auf die Zeugenschaft vor Gericht bezogen. So drohte dem vor Gericht (gewiss in einem Vermögensstreit) erwiesenermaßen (uneidlich) falsch aussagenden Zeugen eine Geldstrafe (§ 37).[89] Verweigerte ein Zeuge (dabei) vor Gericht den Beweiseid,[90] dann hatte er eine Strafe in Höhe des Wertes des Prozessgegenstandes zu entrichten (§ 38).[91] Bereits Herbert Petschow hob im Zusammenhang mit § 38 darauf ab, dass es hier um jenen Zeugen geht, „der zwar zunächst als Zeuge auftritt, dann aber den Zeugeneid über die zuerst uneidlich gemachte Aussage verweigert.“ Dieser hatte dann den Wert des Prozessgegenstandes zu ersetzen, was darauf hindeutet, „dass den Gegenstand der Bestimmung nicht Kapitalprozesse, sondern Streitigkeiten mit nur vermögensrechtlichen Folgen bildeten.“[92]

9. §§ 39–41 und 42–43

Damit ist die Intention dieser Paragraphen klar: Sie leiten zu einem neuen Themenfeld im Codex Ur-namma über: Rechtsfälle im Zusammenhang mit Vermögensschädigungen, hier bezogen auf den Feldbesitz.[93] So haben die §§ 39–41 fahrlässige Schädigungen, Vernachlässigung der Bebauungspflicht bzw. unrechtmäßige Bearbeitung eines fremden Feldes durch einen Unbefugten zum Gegenstand.[94] Konkret bestand Schadenersatzpflicht für denjenigen, der (fahrlässig) das kultivierte Feld eines anderen überflutet[95] bzw. als Pächter sein Pachtfeld unbebaut gelassen hat (§§ 40 und 41). Bei unrechtmäßiger Bearbei-

[88] Zu §§ 33–36 vgl. im Einzelnen Wilcke, 2014, 547 f.

[89] Vgl. Neumann, 1996, 261 f. Anmerkung 44 f.; Neumann, 2012, 170 Anmerkung 64 (mit Literatur); Wilcke, 2014, 548 mit Anmerkung 217; vgl. auch die Bemerkungen zur Sache ebenda 505–507.

[90] Sallaberger, 2015, 190 sieht in nam-érim-ta gur „vom Eid zurückkehren“ eine Formulierung für den Tatbestand des Meineids, was aber nicht zutrifft. Die Phrase kennzeichnet die „Eidverweigerung“; vgl. dazu Falkenstein, 1956, 67 mit Anmerkung 6; vgl. auch Edzard, 1976, 91 („vor einem assertorischen Eid zaudern“); Wilcke, 2014, 549 („vom Beweiseid zurückscheuen“).

[91] Vgl. Lafont / Westbrook, 2003, 196; Neumann, 2012, 170 Anmerkung 65 (mit Literatur); Wilcke, 2014, 548 f.

[92] Petschow, 1973, 20; vgl. auch Leemans, 1970, 65 f.

[93] Vgl. im vorliegenden Zusammenhang auch Wilcke, 2014, 488 f.

[94] Zu den Felderparagraphen vgl. im Einzelnen Petschow, 1968a, 10 f. mit Anmerkung 32; Klíma 1979, 27 f.; Wilcke, 1999, 338 f.; Wilcke, 2002, 320 f.; Wilcke, 2014, 549 f. Zu den Tatbeständen vgl. auch Neumann, 1993, 227 f.

[95] Vgl. dazu auch Neumann, 2017, 33 f.; George / Spada, 2019, 84.

tung eines fremden Feldes durch einen Unbefugten ging letzterer (erst) nach einem (vom Eigentümer angestrengten und für den Bearbeiter im Ergebnis ungünstigen) Prozess sämtlicher Aufwendungen (ersatzlos) verlustig (§ 39).[96] Es folgen mit §§ 42 f. Bestimmungen zur Feldpacht (Bewässerungsabgabe, Pachtzins, Arbeitermiete).[97]

10. Schlussbemerkung

Will man die Anordnungsprinzipien und die interne Struktur der Gesetzesbestimmungen abschließend werten, dann wird deutlich, dass sie ähnlichen Vorstellungen folgen, wie sie insbesondere von Herbert Petschow in Bezug auf den Codex Ḫammu-rāpi und den Codex Ešnunna herausgearbeitet worden sind. Natürlich erreicht der Codex Ur-Namma in dieser Hinsicht nicht das Niveau des paradigmatisch über mehr als 1000 Jahre Wirkungsmacht entfaltenden Codex Ḫammu-rāpi, jedoch konnten die Redaktoren des letzteren bereits auf die intellektuellen und praktischen Erfahrungen der Ur III-Zeit zurückgreifen. Hinsichtlich letzterer wird zudem deutlich, dass die Bestimmungen des Codex Ur-Namma gleichermaßen auf Ausgleich einer Rechtsverletzung durch Sühne (zwecks Wiederherstellung von Gerechtigkeit)[98] und durch seinen abschreckenden Charakter auf Kriminalprävention gerichtet war. Dabei griff man gewiss auf bereits bestehende, möglicherweise regional differenzierte Rechtsregeln zurück, die man nicht zuletzt unter dem Gesichtspunkt der Rechtsvereinheitlichung unter dem Dynastiebegründer Ur-Namma zu kompilieren und weiterzuentwickeln suchte. Dies wirft – neben anderem, was hier nicht ausgeführt werden kann – ein bezeichnendes Licht auf das Niveau des methodischen und systematischen Rechtsdenkens bereits in der hier in Rede stehenden Ur III-Zeit im 21. Jahrhundert v. Chr.

Abkürzungs- und Literaturverzeichnis

AO = Museumssigel Louvre (Antiquités orientales).
CE = Codex Ešnunna.
CḪ = Codex Ḫammu-rāpi.
CU = Codex Ur-Namma.
MS = Sigel der Sammlung Schøyen.
PSD = The Sumerian Dictionary of the University Museum of the University of Pennsylvania. Philadelphia: Babylonian Section of the University Museum, 1984 ff.

[96] Zu CU § 39 vgl. zuletzt Badamchi, 2017.

[97] Vgl. dazu im Einzelnen Wilcke, 2014, 550 f., auch mit Anmerkung 238 (Bemerkungen zur darauf folgenden Lücke im Text, in der Claus Wilcke „Gesetze über Entgelt und Haftung für gemietete Rinder nach Art der im Anfangsunterricht in den altbabylonischen Schulen als Lehrmaterial dienenden ‚Ox Laws'" vermutet. Damit könnte der Anschluss zu § b1 hergestellt sein [Zugtiermiete]); vgl. auch ebenda 489, wonach „die Haftung für fremdes Eigentum (Pacht und Zugtiermiete § 42'–b1) … die Brücke zu der des Depositars für Verluste an in seinem Haushalt hinterlegtem fremdem Eigentum (§ b4–5) + Tarif für Depositum (§ b6)" schlägt, unterbrochen von Bestimmungen zum Erbrecht von Töchtern (§ b2–3).

[98] Vgl. im vorliegenden Zusammenhang auch Neumann, 2008.

Si = Tontafeln aus Sippar in den Sammlungen der Archäologischen Museen (Istanbul).
U. = Tontafeln aus Ur in den Museen London, Philadelphia und Baghdad.
UM = Tafelsigel University Museum, Philadelphia.

Attinger, Pascal, 1993. *Eléments de linguistique sumérienne. La construction de du₁₁/e/di « dire »* (Orbis Biblicus et Orientalis Sonderband). Fribourg Suisse / Göttingen: Editions Universitaires / Vandenhoeck & Ruprecht.

— 2005. „A propos de AK « faire »". *Zeitschrift für Assyriologie und Vorderasiatische Archäologie* 95, 46–64, 208–275.

Badamchi, Hossein, 2017. „Usurpation of Agricultural Land and Codex Ur-Namma, 39". *Akkadica* 138, 181–188.

Bartelmus, Alexandra, 2016. *Fragmente einer großen Sprache. Sumerisch im Kontext der Schreiberausbildung des kassitenzeitlichen Babylonien* (Untersuchungen zur Assyriologie und Vorderasiatischen Archäologie 12). Boston / Berlin: De Gruyter. (2 Bände).

Charpin, Dominique, 2003. *Hammu-rabi de Babylone*. Paris: Presses Universitaires de France.

Civil, Miguel, 1993. „On Mesopotamian Jails and Their Lady Warden". In: Mark E. Cohen / Daniel C. Snell / David B. Weisberg (Hg.) *The Tablet and the Scroll. Near Eastern Studies in Honor of William W. Hallo*. Bethesda: CDL Press, 72–78.

— 2011. „The Law Collection of Ur-Namma". In: Andrew R. George (Hg.) *Cuneiform Royal Inscriptions and Related Texts in the Schøyen Collection* (Cornell University Studies in Assyriology and Sumerology 17). Bethesda: CDL Press, 221–286.

Edzard, Dietz Otto, 1968. *Sumerische Rechtsurkunden des III. Jahrtausends aus der Zeit vor der III. Dynastie von Ur* (Abhandlung der Bayerischen Akademie der Wissenschaften. Philosophisch-historische Klasse NF 67). München: Verlag der Bayerischen Akademie der Wissenschaften.

— 1976. „Zum sumerischen Eid". In: Stephen J. Lieberman (Hg.) *Sumerological Studies in Honor of Thorkild Jacobsen on His Seventieth Birthday June 7, 1974* (Assyriological Studies 20). Chicago / London: The University of Chicago Press, 63–98.

Eichler, Barry L., 1987. „Literary Structure in the Laws of Eshnunna". In: Francesca Rochberg-Halton (Hg.) *Language, Literature, and History: Philological and Historical Studies Presented to Erica Reiner* (American Oriental Series 67). New Haven: American Oriental Society, 71–84.

Falkenstein, Adam, 1956. *Die neusumerischen Gerichtsurkunden. Erster Teil: Einleitung und systematische Darstellung* (Abhandlung der Bayerischen Akademie der Wissenschaften. Philosophisch-historische Klasse NF 39). München: Verlag der Bayerischen Akademie der Wissenschaften.

George, Andrew R. / Gabriella Spada, 2019. *Old Babylonian Texts in the Schøyen Collection*. Part 2: *School Letters, Model Contracts, and Related Texts* (Cornell University Studies in Assyriology and Sumerology 43). University Park: Eisenbrauns.

Hurowitz, Victor A., 2005. „Hammurabi in Mesopotamian Tradition“. In: Yitchak Sefati et al. (Hg.) *An Experienced Scribe Who Neglects Nothing. Ancient Near Eastern Studies in Honor of Jacob Klein*. Bethesda: CDL Press, 497–532.

Jiménez, Enrique, 2014. „On the Commentary to the *Code of Hammurapi* and the Babylonian God of Ordeals“. Nouvelles Assyriologiques Brèves et Utilitaires 2014/4, 132 f. (no. 84).

Klengel, Horst, 1991. *König Hammurapi und der Alltag Babylons*. Zürich: Artemis & Winkler.

Klíma, Josef, 1979. „Landwirtschaftliche Regelungen in den vorhammurapischen Gesetzen“. *Archív Orientální* 47, 21–32.

Lafont, Bertrand / Raymond Westbrook, 2003. „Neo-Sumerian Period (Ur III)“. In: Raymond Westbrook (Hg.) *A History of Ancient Near Eastern Law*. Volume I (Handbuch der Orientalistik, Abteilung I Band 72). Leiden / Boston: Brill, 183–226.

Lafont, Sophie, 1999. *Femmes, Droit et Justice dans l'Antiquité orientale. Contribution à l'étude du droit pénal au Proche-Orient ancien* (Orbis Biblicus et Orientalis 165). Fribourg Suisse / Göttingen: Editions Universitaires / Vandenhoeck & Ruprecht.

Landsberger, Benno, 1968. „Jungfräulichkeit: ein Beitrag zum Thema ‚Beilager und Eheschließung‘ (mit einem Anhang: Neue Lesungen und Deutungen im Gesetzbuch von Ešnunna)“. In: Johan A. Ankum / Robert Feenstra / Wilhelmus F. Leemans (Hg.) *Symbolae iuridicae et historicae Martino David dedicatae. Tomus alter: iura orientis antiqui*. Leiden: E.J. Brill, 41–105.

Lang, Martin, 2012. „Von der Unordnung der Zauberei und von der Ordnung des Rechts: ratio legis und ‚Sitz im Leben‘ eines lange bezeugten Tatbestandes“. *Zeitschrift für Altorientalische und Biblische Rechtsgeschichte* 18, 37–61.

Leemans, Wilhelmus F., 1970. „Le faux témoin“. *Revue d'Assyriologie et d'Archéologie orientale* 64, 63–66.

Maul, Stefan M., 1997. „Divination I. Mesopotamien“. In: Hubert Cancik / Helmuth Schneider (Hg.) *Der Neue Pauly. Enzyklopädie der Antike* 3. Stuttgart / Weimar: Verlag J.B. Metzler, 703–706.

— 2003–2005. „Omina und Orakel. A. Mesopotamien“. In: Dietz Otto Edzard (Hg.) *Reallexikon der Assyriologie und Vorderasiatischen Archäologie* 10. Berlin / New York: De Gruyter, 45–88.

Michalowski, Piotr / Michael P. Streck, 2016–2018. „Hammurapi. Fifth king of the First Dyn. of Babylon, 1792-1750 (middle chronology)“. In: Michael P. Streck (Hg.) *Reallexikon der Assyriologie und Vorderasiatischen Archäologie* 15. Berlin / New York: De Gruyter, 380–390.

Neumann, Hans, 1987. „Bemerkungen zu Ehe, Konkubinat und Bigamie in neusumerischer Zeit“. In: Jean-Marie Durand (Hg.) *La Femme dans le Proche-Orient Antique. Compte Rendu de la XXXIIIe Rencontre Assyriologique Internationale (Paris, 7-10 juillet 1986)*. Paris: Editions Recherche sur les Civilisations, 131–137.

— 1989. „Bemerkungen zur Freilassung von Sklaven im alten Mesopotamien gegen Ende des 3. Jahrtausends v.u.Z.“. *Altorientalische Forschungen* 16, 220–233.

— 1993. „Zum Problem der privaten Feldpacht in neusumerischer Zeit“. In: Julia Zabłocka / Stefan Zawadzki (Hg.) *Šulmu IV. Everyday Life in Ancient Near East. Papers Presented at the International Conference, Poznań, 19-22 September, 1989*. Poznań: Adam Mickiewicz University Press, 223–233.

— 1996. „Zum privaten Werkvertrag im Rahmen der neusumerischen handwerklichen Produktion“. *Altorientalische Forschungen* 23, 254–264.

— 2004. „Prozeßführung im Edubba'a. Zu einigen Aspekten der Aneignung juristischer Kenntnisse im Rahmen des Curriculums babylonischer Schreiberausbildung“. *Zeitschrift für Altorientalische und Biblische Rechtsgeschichte* 10, 71–92.

— 2006. „Schuld und Sühne. Zu den religiös-weltanschaulichen Grundlagen und Implikationen altmesopotamischer Gesetzgebung und Rechtsprechung“. In: Joachim Hengstl / Ulrich Sick (Hg.) *Recht gestern und heute. Festschrift zum 85. Geburtstag von Richard Haase* (Philippika 13). Wiesbaden: Harrassowitz, 27–43.

— 2008. „Göttliche Gerechtigkeit und menschliche Verantwortung im alten Mesopotamien im Spannungsfeld von Norm(durch)setzung und narrativer Formulierung“. In: Heinz Barta / Robert Rollinger / Martin Lang (Hg.) *Recht und Religion. Menschliche und göttliche Gerechtigkeitsvorstellungen in den antiken Welten* (Philippika 24). Wiesbaden: Harrassowitz, 37–48.

— 2012. „Todes- und Körperstrafe versus Versklavung und Geldbuße. Überlegungen zur mesopotamischen Strafrechtspraxis im 3. und frühen 2. Jt. v. Chr.“. In: Robert Rollinger / Martin Lang / Heinz Barta (Hg.) *Strafe und Strafrecht in den antiken Welten. Unter Berücksichtigung von Todesstrafe, Hinrichtung und peinlicher Befragung* (Philippika 51). Wiesbaden: Harrassowitz, 163–179.

— 2014. „Altorientalische ‚Imperien‘ des 3. und frühen 2. Jahrtausends v. Chr. Historische Voraussetzungen und sozioökonomische Grundlagen“. In: Michael Gehler / Robert Rollinger (Hg.) *Imperien und Reiche in der Weltgeschichte. Epochenübergreifende und globalhistorische Vergleiche, Teil I: Imperien des Altertums, Mittelalterliche und frühneuzeitliche Imperien*. Wiesbaden: Harrassowitz, 33–64.

— 2017. „Zum außergerichtlichen Vergleich in Mesopotamien in der Zeit der Wende vom 3. zum 2. Jahrtausend v. Chr.“. In: Guido Pfeifer / Nadine Grotkamp (Hg.) *Außergerichtliche Konfliktlösung in der Antike. Beispiele aus drei Jahrtausenden* (Global Perspectives on Legal History 9). Frankfurt a. M.: Max Planck Institute for European Legal History, 27–42.

— 2018. „Eherechtliche Bestimmungen und Sexualdelikte im Sklavenrecht des alten Mesopotamien (spätes 3. und frühes 2. Jt. v. Chr.)“. In: Irmtraud Fischer / Daniela Feichtinger (Hg.) *Sexualität und Sklaverei* (Alter Orient und Altes Testament 456). Münster: Ugarit-Verlag, 109–122.

Neumann, Hans / Susanne Paulus, 2011–2013. „Strafe (im Strafrecht). A. In Mesopotamien“. In: Michael P. Streck (Hg.) *Reallexikon der Assyriologie und Vorderasiatischen Archäologie* 13, Berlin / New York: De Gruyter, 197–203.

Oelsner, Joachim, 2012. „Zur Einteilung des Kodex Ḫammu-rāpi im Altertum“. *Zeitschrift für Altorientalische und Biblische Rechtsgeschichte* 18, 79–125.

Otto, Eckart, 1989. *Rechtsgeschichte der Redaktionen im Kodex Ešnunna und im ‚Bundesbuch'. Eine redaktionsgeschichtliche und rechtsvergleichende Studie zu altbabylonischen und altisraelitischen Rechtsüberlieferungen* (Orbis Biblicus et Orientalis 85). Freiburg Schweiz / Göttingen: Universitätsverlag / Vandenhoeck & Ruprecht.

— 2012. „Nach welchen Gesichtspunkten wurden Rechtssätze in keilschriftlichen und biblischen Rechtssammlungen zusammengestellt? Zur Redaktionsgeschichte keilschriftlicher und biblischer Rechtssatzsammlungen". *Zeitschrift für Altorientalische und Biblische Rechtsgeschichte* 18, 63–77.

Petschow, Herbert, 1957–1971. „Gesetze. 6. Der Codex Ḫammurabi (CH)". In: Ernst Weidner / Wolfram von Soden (Hg.) *Reallexikon der Assyriologie und Vorderasiatischen Archäologie* 3, Berlin / New York: De Gruyter, 255–269.

— 1965a. „Zur Systematik und Gesetzestechnik im Codex Hammurabi". *Zeitschrift für Assyriologie und Vorderasiatische Archäologie* 57, 146–172.

— 1965b. „Zu den Stilformen antiker Gesetze und Rechtssammlungen". *Zeitschrift der Savigny-Stiftung für Rechtsgeschichte (Romanistische Abteilung)* 82, 24–38.

— 1968a. „Neufunde zu keilschriftlichen Rechtssammlungen". *Zeitschrift der Savigny-Stiftung für Rechtsgeschichte (Romanistische Abteilung)* 85, 1–29.

— 1968b. „Zur ‚Systematik' in den Gesetzen von Eschnunna". In: Johan A. Ankum / Robert Feenstra / Wilhelmus F. Leemans (Hg.) *Symbolae iuridicae et historicae Martino David dedicatae. Tomus alter: iura orientis antiqui.* Leiden: E.J. Brill, 131–143.

— 1973. „Altorientalische Parallelen zur spätrömischen calumnia". *Zeitschrift der Savigny-Stiftung für Rechtsgeschichte (Romanistische Abteilung)* 90, 14–35.

— 1984. „Die §§ 45 und 46 des Codex Ḫammurapi. Ein Beitrag zum altbabylonischen Bodenpachtrecht und zum Problem: Was ist der Codex Ḫammurapi?". *Zeitschrift für Assyriologie und Vorderasiatische Archäologie* 74, 181–212.

— 1986. „Beiträge zum Codex Ḫammurapi". *Zeitschrift für Assyriologie und Vorderasiatische Archäologie* 76, 17–75.

Reid, J. Nicholas, 2015. „Runaways and Fugitive-Catchers during the Third Dynasty of Ur". *Journal of the Economic and Social History of the Orient* 58, 576–605.

— 2017. „The Children of Slaves in Early Mesopotamian Laws and Edicts". *Revue d'Assyriologie et d'Archéologie orientale* 111, 9–23.

Renger, Johannes, 1994. „Noch einmal: Was war der ‚Kodex' Ḫammurapi – ein erlassenes Gesetz oder ein Rechtsbuch?". In: Hans-Joachim Gehrke (Hg.) *Rechtskodifizierung und soziale Normen im interkulturellen Vergleich* (ScriptOralia 66). Tübingen: Gunter Narr Verlag, 27–59.

Ries, Gerhard, 1983. *Prolog und Epilog in Gesetzen des Altertums* (Münchener Beiträge zur Papyrusforschung und antiken Rechtsgeschichte 76). München: C.H. Beck'sche Verlagsbuchhandlung.

Römer, Willem H. Ph., 1982. „Aus den Gesetzen des Königs Urnammu von Ur". In: Otto Kaiser (Hg.) *Rechtsbücher* (Texte aus der Umwelt des Alten Testaments I/1). Gütersloh: Gütersloher Verlagshaus, 17–23.

Roth, Martha T., 1995. *Law Collections from Mesopotamia and Asia Minor* (SBL Writings from the Ancient World 6). Atlanta: Scholars Press.

— 2019. „Seductress or Victim? Another Look at Laws of Ur-Namma §§ 6–8“. In: Grégory Chambon / Michaël Guichard / Anne-Isabelle Langlois (Hg.) *De l'Argile au Numérique. Mélanges assyriologiques en l'honneur de Dominique Charpin* (Publications de l'Institut du Proche-Orient Ancien du Collège de France 3). Leuven: Peeters, 879–892.

Sallaberger, Walther, 2014–2016. „Ur-Namma“. In: Michael P. Streck (Hg.) *Reallexikon der Assyriologie und Vorderasiatischen Archäologie* 14. Berlin / New York: De Gruyter, 422–431.

— 2015. „Sumerische und altbabylonische Eidesformeln in lexikalischer und kulturhistorischer Perspektive“. In: Heinz Barta / Martin Lang / Robert Rollinger (Hg.) *Prozessrecht und Eid. Recht und Rechtsfindung in antiken Kulturen.* Teil I (Philippika 86, 1). Wiesbaden: Harrassowitz, 179–192.

Sallaberger, Walther / Ingo Schrakamp, 2015. „Conclusion“. In: Walther Sallaberger / Ingo Schrakamp (Hg.) *History & Philology* (ARCANE III). Turnhout: Brepols, 297–304.

Stol, Marten, 2016. *Women in the Ancient Near East.* Boston / Berlin: De Gruyter.

Thomas, Ariane (Hg.), 2016. *L'histoire commence en Mésopotamie.* Lens / Gand: Musée du Louvre-Lens / Snoeck Publishers.

Van De Mieroop, Marc, 2005. *King Hammurabi of Babylon. A Biography.* Malden / Oxford / Carlton: Blackwell Publishing.

— 2011: „Hammurabi's self-presentation“. *Orientalia* 80, 305–338.

Westbrook, Raymond, 2003. „A Sumerian Freedman“. In: Walther Sallaberger / Konrad Volk / Annette Zgoll (Hg.) *Literatur, Politik und Recht in Mesopotamien. Festschrift für Claus Wilcke* (Orientalia, Biblica et Christiana 14). Wiesbaden: Harrassowitz, 333–339.

Wilcke, Claus, 1969. *Das Lugalbandaepos.* Wiesbaden: Otto Harrassowitz.

— 1985. „Familiengründung im alten Babylonien“. In: Ernst W. Müller (Hg.) *Geschlechtsreife und Legitimation zur Zeugung.* Freiburg / München: Verlag Karl Alber, 213–317.

— 1992. „Diebe, Räuber und Mörder“. In: Volkert Haas (Hg.) *Außenseiter und Randgruppen. Beiträge zu einer Sozialgeschichte des Alten Orients* (Xenia 32). Konstanz: Universitätsverlag, 53–78.

— 1999. „Flurschäden, verursacht durch Hochwasser, Unwetter, Militär, Tiere und schuldhaftes Verhalten zur Zeit der 3. Dynastie von Ur“. In: Horst Klengel / Johannes Renger (Hg.) *Landwirtschaft im Alten Orient. Ausgewählte Vorträge der XLI. Rencontre Assyriologique Internationale, Berlin, 4.-8.7.1994* (Berliner Beiträge zum Vorderen Orient 18). Berlin: Dietrich Reimer Verlag, 301–339.

— 2002. „Der Kodex Urnamma (CU): Versuch einer Rekonstruktion“. In: Tzvi Abusch (Hg.) *Riches Hidden in Secret Places. Ancient Near Eastern Studies in Memory of Thorkild Jacobsen.* Winona Lake: Eisenbrauns, 291–333.

— 2007. „Das Recht: Grundlage des sozialen und politischen Diskurses im Alten Orient“. In: Claus Wilcke (Hg.) *Das geistige Erfassen der Welt im Alten Orient. Sprache, Religion, Kultur und Gesellschaft.* Wiesbaden: Harrassowitz, 209–244.

— 2013. „Dieser Ur-Namma hier … Eine auf die Darstellung weisende Statueninschrift.“ *Revue d'Assyriologie et d'Archéologie orientale* 107, 173–186.

— 2014. „Gesetze in sumerischer Sprache“. In: Natalia Koslova / Ekaterina Vizirova / Gábor Zólyomi (Hg.) *Studies in Sumerian Language and Literature. Festschrift für Joachim Krecher* (Orientalia et Classica LVI / Babel und Bibel 8). Winona Lake: Eisenbrauns, 455–616.

Willoweit, Dietmar, 1987. „Gesetzgebung und Recht im Übergang vom Spätmittelalter zum frühneuzeitlichen Obrigkeitsstaat“. In: Okko Behrends / Christoph Link (Hg.) *Zum römischen und neuzeitlichen Gesetzesbegriff. 1. Symposion der Kommission „Die Funktion des Gesetzes in Geschichte und Gegenwart“ vom 26. und 27. April 1985* (Abhandlungen der Akademie der Wissenschaften in Göttingen. Philologisch-historische Klasse. 3. Folge Nr. 157). Göttingen: Vandenhoeck & Ruprecht, 123–149.

Zur Frage von Ausdruck und Normgültigkeit mathematischer Regeln in Mesopotamien[1]

Hagan Brunke

Abstract 83
1 Allgemeines 83
  1.1 Textevidenz 84
  1.2 Mathematische Regeln 88
2 Manifestation und Gültigkeitsanspruch 90
3 Beispiel: Quadratische Gleichungssysteme 94
4 Anhang: Vier Quadrate 101
Abkürzungs- und Literaturverzeichnis 104

Abstract

Es besteht ein Zusammenhang zwischen dem Grad an Fundamentalität einer mathematischen Regel, der Explizitheit ihres Aufscheinens im Textbefund, und ihrem Maß an Normgültigkeit: Je weniger grundlegend eine Regel ist, desto expliziter ist sie formuliert; je komplexer sie ist, desto weniger zwingend ist sie. Entsprechend sind die Algorithmen in den Aufgabentexten eher Möglichkeiten denn Vorschriften. Illustriert wird dieser Umstand anhand eines Beispiels zweier gänzlich verschiedener Lösungsverfahren für dieselbe Aufgabe auf derselben Sammeltafel.

1. Allgemeines

Um mathematische Regelsysteme mit anderen Regelsystemen, beispielsweise rechtlichen, vergleichen zu können, ist zunächst zu klären, was unter einer mathematischen Regel verstanden werden soll. Das bedeutet zum einen die Frage, was

---

[1] Diese Studie entstand während meiner Förderung durch das Exzellenzcluster 264 TOPOI „The Formation and Transformation of Space and Knowledge in Ancient Civilisations". Der Beitrag ist in leicht modifizierter Form auch erschienen in: *Cuneiform Digital Library Preprints* 11, 18.12.2017 (http://cdli.ucla.edu/?q=cuneiform-digital-library-preprints). Die Transliteration der Originaltexte erfolgt kursiv für Akkadisch (z.B. *mi-it-har-tum*) und im Fettdruck für Sumerisch (z.B. **a-ša$_3$**). Tiefgestellte Zahlen (z.B. in *lib$_3$* oder **ša$_3$**) dienen der Differenzierung von Homophonen. Die Ziffern zur Notation der sexagesimal dargestellten Zahlen in den babylonischen mathematischen Keilschrifttexten werden durchgehend zweistellig geschrieben (00, 01, 02, …, 58, 59) und durch einen kleinen Zwischenraum voneinander getrennt, z.B. 08 20 für $8 \cdot 60 + 20$ (= 500 in dezimaler Notation). Dabei wird 00 der Übersichtlichkeit wegen verwendet, z.B. 05 00 für $5 \cdot 60$ $(+ 0 \cdot 1)$, obwohl „Null" in der Keilschrift nicht notiert wird. Das Symbol „▲" steht für ein „sexagesimales Komma", das es ebenfalls nicht gibt, z.B. 01 ▲ 25 für $1 + 25 \cdot \frac{1}{60}$.

im altorientalischen Kontext überhaupt als „mathematisch" gelten soll, insbesondere also, welche Textgattungen zu betrachten sind. Und zum anderen, welche Typen von mathematischen Regeln es gibt.

1.1 Textevidenz

„*Mathematische Texte*". In der Altorientalistik und der altorientalischen Wissenschaftsgeschichte ist der Begriff „mathematischer Text"[2] weniger über den mehr oder weniger mathematischen Inhalt definiert, sondern ganz praktisch über die Zugehörigkeit zu einem der folgenden Textformate:[3]
(a) Aufgabentexte („problem texts")[4],
(b) arithmetische und metrologische Tabellentexte[5],

---

[2] Für einen allgemeinen Überblick zur Mesopotamischen Mathematik und zu den Textformaten siehe z.B. Vogel, 1959; Neugebauer, 1969 und Friberg, 1987–90; für umfangreiche und erschöpfende Detailstudien MKT I–III; Neugebauer / Sachs, 1945; Høyrup, 2002 und Friberg, 2007; und speziell zum Thema der gesellschaftlichen Verortung der Mathematik in Mesopotamien und ihres „Sitzes im Leben" Robson, 2008. Für Verzeichnisse publizierter mathematischer Texte mit Bibliographie siehe Nemet-Nejat, 1993, 251–290 und Robson, 2008, 299–342.

[3] Vgl. Nemet-Nejat, 1993, 17–25.

[4] Es handelt sich um mathematische Aufgabenstellungen, teilweise mit und teilweise ohne Angabe des Lösungswegs. Erstere finden sich sowohl einzeln (d.h. eine Tafel mit nur einer einzigen Aufgabe) wie auch zu mehreren, in der Regel inhaltlich sortiert und nach Schwierigkeitsgrad angeordnet, auf Sammeltafeln. Ein Beispiel für eine solche Sammeltafel ist BM 13901 (vgl. Fußnote 33), von der zwei Aufgaben in Abschnitt 3 behandelt werden.

[5] Arithmetische Tabellentexte sind Multiplikations- und Reziprokentabellen, Tabellen von Potenzen, Wurzeln, Logarithmen etc.; bei metrologischen Tabellentexten handelt es sich um Listen von Längen-, Flächen- und Gewichtsmaßen als Kombinationen von Maßzahl und Maßeinheit, gegebenenfalls mit Umrechnung in ein sexagesimales Äquivalentsystem. Zu diesen Texten siehe Neugebauer, MKT I, 3–94; Friberg, 2007, 45–126 und zuletzt Proust, 2007. Zwei Beispiele:

1. *Reziprokentabellen* geben die Kehrwerte ganzer Zahlen, z.B. MLC 1670 (Clay, 1923, Text 37) mit der allgemeinen Struktur (01) **igi**-*n*-**ĝal₂-bi**(-**am₃**)) $\frac{1}{n}$ „01: der *n*-te Teil davon ist) $\frac{1}{n}$":

01		$\frac{2}{3}$	**-bi**	40	**-am₃**
		šu-ri-a	**-bi**	30	
igi	03	**ĝal₂**	**-bi**	20	
igi	04	**ĝal₂**	**-bi**	15	
igi	05	**ĝal₂**	**-bi**	12	
igi	06	**ĝal₂**	**-bi**	10	
igi	08	**ĝal₂**	**-bi**	07 30	
igi	09	**ĝal₂**	**-bi**	06 40	

(**šu-ri-a** = „Hälfte"). Als Werte für *n* stehen genau die sexagesimal-regulären Zahlen (das sind solche, deren Kehrwerte eine endliche Sexagesimalbruchentwicklung besitzen). Einträge für sexagesimal-irreguläre Werte von *n* (7; 11; 13; 14; 17; …) fehlen; in älteren Textvertretern (z.B. Ist.T 7375, Delaporte, 1911, 131) sind auch diese Werte für *n* gelistet und mit dem Hinweis **nu** „nicht" versehen, z.B. 29 **igi nu** „29: Inverses (existiert) nicht".

2. *Quadratwurzeltabellen* listen die Quadratwurzeln von Quadratzahlen (1, 4, 9, 16 etc.), z.B. im Format n^2-**e** *n* **ib₂-sa₂** „aus n^2 ist *n* die Quadratwurzel":

(c) Koeffizientenlisten[6]. Diesen Texten, die im Zusammenhang mit der Schreiberausbildung stehen und die deshalb in der Regel als „Schultexte" angesprochen werden, stehen solche gegenüber, die die Anwendung der/des in diesen Texten vermittelten Kenntnisse/Wissens/Praktiken in der Praxis dokumentieren. Es sind das vor allem *administrative Texte* („Wirtschaftsurkunden"). Gerade im Zusammenhang mit der Frage nach Regelcharakter und Normgültigkeit erweist sich die Beschränkung auf die eben angeführten, in der Fachliteratur als „mathematisch" bezeichneten Texte als hinderlich. Zum einen, weil in ihnen viele solche praxisbezogenen, in administrativen Texten allgegenwärtigen (impliziten) Regeln fehlen. Zum anderen, weil sich der Regelcharakter von etwas und weiter die Normgültigkeit der Regel nicht bereits aus seinem bloßen Geltungs*anspruch* ergibt, sondern erst durch seine allgemeine *Anerkennung als Regel* (also durch Anerkennung dieses Anspruchs) und weiter durch deren Anerkennung als Norm, die wiederum sich in der tatsächlichen und möglichst ausschließlichen Verwendung in

---

	01-e	01	**ib$_2$-sa$_2$**	15	00-e	30	**ib$_2$-sa$_2$**
	04-e	02	**ib$_2$-sa$_2$**	16	01-e	31	**ib$_2$-sa$_2$**
	09-e	03	**ib$_2$-sa$_2$**	17	04-e	32	**ib$_2$-sa$_2$**
		.			.		
		.			.		
		.			.		
13	04-e	28	**ib$_2$-sa$_2$**				
14	01-e	29	**ib$_2$-sa$_2$**				

Textvertreter sind z.B. HS 226 (Hilprecht, 1906, Text 28) und CBS 14233 Rs. (Legrain, 1922, Text 22).

[6] Koeffizientenlisten sind Sammlungen geometrischer, physikalischer oder technischer Konstanten, Arbeits- bzw. Leistungsparameter etc. Geometrische Konstanten sind beispielsweise Werte für $\sqrt{2}$ (Länge der Diagonale eines Einheitsquadrats), das Verhältnis des Kreisumfangs zum Kreisdurchmesser (entsprechend unserem π), das Verhältnis der Kreisfläche zum Quadrat des Kreisumfangs (entsprechend unserem $\frac{1}{4}\pi$) etc.; physikalisch-technische Konstanten beschreiben z.B. quantitative Materialeigenschaften etc. Das Akkadische Wort für „Koeffizient" ist *igigubbû* (< sumerisch **igi-gub**[**-ba**] „[fest]gesetzter Bruchteil o.ä."). Zu diesen Texten siehe Robson, 1999. Als Beispiele seien Ausschnitte aus den altbabylonischen Koeffizientenlisten TMS 3 (Bruins / Rutten, 1961, Text 3) angeführt; zur Interpretation der Koeffizienten siehe Robson, 1999, 34–40:

2)	05	**igi-gub**	*ša$_3$*	**gur$_2$**	Koeffizient des Kreises
3)	20	**dal**	*ša$_3$*	**gur$_2$**	Durchmesser des Kreises
4)	10	*pi-ir-ku*	*ša$_3$*	**gur$_2$**	Radius des Kreises
7)	15	**igi-gub**	*ša$_3$*	*us$_2$-qa-ri*	Koeffizient des Halbkreises
8)	40	**dal**	*ša$_3$*	*us$_2$-qa-ri*	Durchmesser des Halbkreises
9)	20	*pi-ir-ku*	*ša$_3$*	*us$_2$-qa-ri*	Radius des Halbkreises

und A 3553 (Kilmer, 1960, Text A); zur Interpretation der Koeffizienten siehe Robson, 1999, 125–129:

18)		01	12	**igi-gub**	**urudu**	Koeffizient (von) Kupfer
19)		01	20	**igi-gub**	**zabar**	Koeffizient (von) Bronze
20)	01	20	21	**igi-gub**	AN.NA	Koeffizient (von) Zinn
21)		01	36	**igi-gub**	**ku$_3$-babbar**	Koeffizient (von) Silber
22)		01	48	**igi-gub**	**ku$_3$-sig$_{17}$**	Koeffizient (von) Gold

der Praxis manifestiert.[7] Soweit die administrativen Texte die praktische Anwendung mathematischer Regeln (insbesondere z.B. die Verwendung technischer Konstanten und Leistungsparameter) reflektieren, sollen sie deshalb im Rahmen dieser Betrachtungen ebenfalls als „mathematisch" angesehen und berücksichtigt werden. Das betrifft insbesondere das umfangreiche Corpus der neusumerischen[8] administrativen Texte. Zwei Beispiele werden kurz vorgestellt: Feldpläne und Wertäquivalenzen.

Feldpläne. Diese Urkunden dokumentieren Erfassung und Berechnung von landwirtschaftlich genutzten Feldflächen, deren Längenausdehnung bis zu mehrere Kilometer betragen hat. Diese Texte sind impliziter Reflex der Grundregel (siehe unten) der Additivität des Maßes (vgl. Fußnote 17), der zufolge der Inhalt eines Flächenstücks berechnet werden kann, indem man das Flächenstück in Teilflächenstücke zerlegt, deren Inhalte berechnet und die Ergebnisse addiert. Das allgemeine, standardisierte Muster dieser Texte ist das Folgende:[9] Zunächst wird das Feld durch eine aus annähernd rechtwinklig-trapezförmigen Vierecken zusammengesetzte Figur (sum. **temen** „Basis") in seinem Innern approximiert (die Basis kann an einzelnen Stellen über das eigentliche Feld hinausragen, in welchem Fall die überstehenden Teile nachträglich abgezogen werden). Der über die Basis hinausragende Rest der Feldfläche (sum. **bar** „Äußeres"), wird in einfach zu berechnende Flächenstücke, nämlich (annähernd) rechtwinklige Dreiecke und Trapeze zerlegt. Die Kantenlängen der so entstehenden Teilfiguren werden entlang der Kanten angeschrieben, die daraus berechneten Flächeninhalte im Innern der Basis bzw. (für die Teilstücke des Außenbereichs) außerhalb der Feldfigur, mit Schreibrichtung von innen nach außen. Die Flächeninhalte der Teilstücke, aus denen die Basis zusammengesetzt ist, werden nach einem speziellen Verfahren zweimal berechnet (einmal „richtig herum" und einmal „auf dem Kopf stehend" angeschrieben) und anschließend gemittelt.[10] Ein Beispiel zeigt Brunke 2017, S. 15, Abbildung 1.[11]

Wertäquivalenzen. Ein charakteristisches Merkmal der Verwaltung administrativer Haushalte (z.B. Palast, Tempel) ist die Verwendung von Bezugsgrößen-Äquivalenten zur Erfassung des Gesamtwertes großer Mengen ein- oder ausgelieferter Waren. Bei diesen Waren handelt es sich häufig um Getreide, Getreidefolgeprodukte und diverse daraus erzeugte Lebensmittel, die Bezugsgröße ist dann hauptsächlich Gerste. Jedes Produkt hat einen festen, über die Zeit konstanten Gerste-

---

[7] Dies ist analog zu rechtlichen Regeln, die erst durch ihren Niederschlag in den Dokumenten der rechtlichen *Praxis*, also z.B. in Prozessurkunden, als geltende Norm offenbar werden.

[8] Zeit der Dritten Dynastie von Ur („Ur III-Zeit"), 21. Jahrhundert v. Chr. Für eine umfangreiche und detaillierte Studie zu dieser Epoche und ihren Texten siehe Sallaberger, 1999.

[9] Siehe Deimel, 1909, 109; Allotte de la Fuÿe, 1915, 52; Dunham, 1986, 33.

[10] Siehe Nissen / Damerow / Englund, 1991, 110; Quillien, 2003.

[11] Für weitere Studien zu den neusumerischen Feldplänen mit vielen Beispielen siehe z.B. Liverani, 1990 mit Rezension von Maekawa, 1992; Nissen / Damerow / Englund, 1991, 106–110; Friberg, 2007, 137–146.

Äquivalentwert.[12] Der Gesamtwert einer Warenlieferung wird dann im Gerste-Äquivalent angegeben. Die Texte folgen einem regelhaften Schema, sowohl im Hinblick auf die Anordnung der Produkte[13] wie auch im Bezug auf die rechentechnische Gliederung.[14] Im Hinblick auf die Ausführlichkeit der Darstellung gibt es gewisse Freiheiten, ähnlich wie in den mathematischen Aufgabentexten: In manchen Texten werden mehr Zwischenschritte explizit notiert als in anderen. Die umfangreicheren dieser Texte sind strukturell recht komplex.[15] Eine schematische Analyse eines solchen Texts zeigt Abbildung 1.

⋮			
7′)	ŠU.NIGIN$_2$ 8.4.1.0 **gur**	Insgesamt (wovon?)	8.4.1.0
8′)	**še-bala-bi** 8.4.1.0	Dafür Gerste-Aufschlag	8.4.1.0
9′)	ŠU.NIGIN$_2$ 0.1.0.0 **inda$_3$** GIŠ.AŠ	Insgesamt **inda$_3$** GIŠ.AŠ	0.1.0.0
	še-bala-bi 0.1.0.0	Dafür Gerste-Aufschlag	0.1.0.0
10′)	ŠU.NIGIN$_2$ 1.3.3.8 **sila$_3$ inda$_3$ saga$_{10}$**	Insgesamt **inda$_3$ saga$_{10}$**	1.3.3.8
11′)	**igi-5-g̃al$_2$-bi** 0.1.4.3$\frac{1}{2}$ **sila$_3$** 06 **gig̃$_4$ gur**	Davon ein Fünftel	0.1.4.3▲36
12′)	ŠU.NIGIN$_2$ 3.1.1.8 **sila$_3$ inda$_3$** DU	Insgesamt **inda$_3$** DU	3.1.1.8
13′)	$\tilde{5}$.3.3.9$\frac{1}{2}$ **sila$_3$** 06 **gig̃$_4$**	Zwischensumme	$\tilde{5}$.3.3.9▲36
14′)	**igi-$\tilde{15}$-g̃al$_2$-bi** 0.1.5.4$\frac{2}{3}$ **sila$_3$** 02 **gig̃$_4$**	Davon ein Fünfzehntel	0.1.5.4▲42
15′)	ŠU.NIGIN$_2$ 02 35.3.1$^?$.0$\frac{1}{3}$ [**sila$_3$** …]	Insgesamt […]	02 35.3.1.0▲2...
16′)	**še-bi** 03 03.0.2.4 ⟨**sila$_3$**⟩ 12 **gig̃$_4$ gur**	$\sum$	03 03.0.2.4▲12
17′)	**ša$_3$-bi-ta**		
18′)	3.2.3.0 **inda$_3$** GIŠ.AŠ	**inda$_3$** GIŠ.AŠ	3.2.3.0
19′)	1.2.2.8 **sila$_3$ inda$_3$ zi$_3$**-KAL	**inda$_3$ zi$_3$**-KAL	1.2.2.8
20′)	**še-bala-bi** 4.4.5.8 **sila$_3$**	Dafür Gerste-Aufschlag	4.4.5.8
21′)	01 03.4.2.5 **sila$_3$** ⟨**inda$_3$**⟩ **saga$_{10}$ gur**	**inda$_3$ saga$_{10}$**	01 03.4.2.5
22′)	**igi-5-g̃al$_2$-bi** 12.3.5.3 ⟨**sila$_3$**⟩	Davon ein Fünftel	12.3.5.3
23′)	01 18.2.4.1$\frac{2}{3}$ **sila$_3$ inda$_3$** DU	**inda$_3$** DU	01 18.2.4.1▲40
24′)	02 $\tilde{45}$.0.5.5$\frac{2}{3}$ **sila$_3$**	Zwischensumme	02 $\tilde{45}$.0.5.5▲40
25′)	**igi-15-g̃al$_2$-bi** 11.0.0.$\tilde{3}\frac{2}{3}$ **sila$_3$** 02 **gig̃$_4$**	Davon ein Fünfzehntel	11.0.0.$\tilde{3}$▲42
26′)	6.3.0.0 **dabin gur**	**dabin**	6.3.0.0
	LEERZEILE		
27′)	[ŠU.NIGIN$_2$$^?$] ⌜03⌝ [02].3.5.9$\frac{1}{3}$ **sila$_3$**	$\sum$	03 02.3.5.9▲20

Abbildung 1: Transliteration, Übersetzung und schematische Darstellung der Wertumrechnungen in dem neusumerischen Verwaltungstext FLP 800 (Sigrist u.a., 1984, Nr. 236).
In dem gezeigten Textabschnitt werden verschiedene Brotsorten (**inda$_3$** = „Brot“) sowie Standard-Gerstemehl (**dabin**) auf verschiedene Weise in die Basis-Verrechnungseinheit Gerste (**še**) umgerechnet. Der erste Abschnitt verhandelt Wareneingänge, der zweite Warenausgänge.
Darstellung aus Brunke 2011a, 79.

---

[12] Beispielsweise ist „gewöhnliches Brot“ oder „gewöhnliches Bier“ soviel wert wie dieselbe Menge (im Hohlmaß) Gerste, Bulghur (o.ä.) soviel wie die anderthalbfache Menge Gerste, und Weizen soviel wie die doppelte Menge Gerste.

[13] Sortiert nach Gattung, innerhalb einer Gattung nach absteigendem Gerste-Äquivalentwert.

[14] Beispielsweise werden verschiedene Produkte mit gleichem Gerste-Äquivalentwert nicht einzeln umgerechnet, sondern ihre Mengen addiert und dann die Summe umgerechnet.

[15] Für ausführliche Betrachtungen zu diesen Umrechnungen siehe Brunke, 2011a, 9–22, 79–85 und die Literatur dort (S. 9).

1.2 Mathematische Regeln

Es erweist sich als zweckmäßig, bei den mathematischen Regeln zwischen *Grundregeln* und *abgeleiteten Regeln* zu unterscheiden.[16] Die Begriffe sollen wie folgt verstanden werden:

1. Mathematische *Grundregeln* (Grundtatsachen) sind unmittelbar als richtig (gültig, wahr) erkannte oder auch einfach vorausgesetzte/angenommene/unterstellte Tatsachen (in heutiger Sprechweise etwa „Axiome")[17] sowie (ggf. sekundär) getroffene Übereinkünfte bzw. Festsetzungen.[18]

2. *Abgeleitete Regeln* sind aus Grundregeln oder aus anderen (einfacheren) abgeleiteten Regeln abgeleitet, folgen also aus ihnen durch mathematisches Schließen.[19] Abgeleitete Regeln können sehr unterschiedlich komplex sein, je

---

[16a] Ob eine eindeutige Zuordnung zu einer der beiden Kategorien im Einzelfall tatsächlich möglich ist, hängt natürlich wesentlich von unserem jeweiligen Kenntnisstand ab, was aber für die hier angestellten grundsätzlichen Überlegungen keine Rolle spielt.

[16b] Von den mathematischen Regeln strikt zu unterscheiden sind Formulierungs- oder Codierungskonventionen für Regeln (insbesondere für die komplexen Regeln, etwa die Lösungsalgorithmen in den Aufgabentexten), d.h. etablierte, aber keineswegs absolut verbindliche Formen der sprachlichen und methodischen Darstellung einer Regel (z.B. eines Lösungsverfahrens, aber auch von einfachen Regeln, etwa in Gestalt bestimmter Formate für Koeffizientenlisten).

[17] Ein Beispiel hierfür ist die *Additivität des Maßes*, d.h. die Vorstellung, dass sich die Größenwerte, die man etwa Streckenstücken, Flächenstücken oder Körpern zuordnet (also Längen, Flächeninhalte, Rauminhalte), in dem Sinne additiv verhalten, dass etwa die Länge eines (überschneidungsfrei!) aus zwei oder mehreren Teilstreckenstücken zusammengesetzten Streckenstücks oder Streckenzugs gleich ist der Summe der Längen der Teilstreckenstücke (analog für Flächenstücke und Flächeninhalte bzw. Körper und Rauminhalte). Analoges gilt für Gewichte. Diese gewissermaßen „natürliche" Vorstellung, die die gesamte Geometrie grundlegend prägt – und die vermutlich allen Kulturen eigen war, die gemessen und/oder gewogen haben –, folgt nicht aus einfacheren oder grundlegenderen Tatsachen oder Einsichten, sondern dürfte unmittelbar aus der alltäglichen Erfahrung heraus als gültig bzw. wahr angesehen worden sein. (Das hier Gesagte gilt ebenso für die *Isotonie des Maßes*, d.h. die Vorstellung, dass der Größenwert, der einem Streckenstück [Flächenstück, …] zugeordnet ist, kleiner oder gleich ist demjenigen Größenwert, der einem Streckenstück [Flächenstück, …] zugeordnet ist, in dem es vollständig enthalten ist.) Heute ist diese *Additivität des Maßes* eines der Axiome des als *Maßtheorie* bezeichneten Teilgebietes der modernen Mathematik.

[18] Beispielsweise ist die Festlegung des Einheitsflächenstücks als dasjenige Quadrat, dessen Kanten die Länge des Einheitslängenstücks haben – und damit letztlich die Koppelung der Flächen- an die Längenmessung – eine solche Übereinkunft. Aus ihr und der Additivität des Maßes (vgl. Fußnote 17) folgt z.B. die abgeleitete Regel (siehe unten), dass der Flächeninhalt eines Rechtecks als Produkt der beiden Seitenlängen zu berechnen ist und weiters die Verfahren zur Berechnung der Flächeninhalte anderer geradlinig begrenzter Flächenstücke (vgl. Brunke, 2011b, 114–116; auch Brunke, 2012b, 9–12). Ein weiteres Beispiel für eine solche Übereinkunft/Festsetzung ist möglicherweise die Bestimmung des Flächeninhalts eines Kreises als U212, wobei U der Kreisumfang ist, was der Festsetzung dessen, was wir „π" nennen, auf den Wert 3, der dann freilich (als Resultat einer Übereinkunft/Festsetzung) nicht einfach nur eine Näherung ist (siehe Brunke, 2011b).

[19] Damit soll nicht angedeutet werden, dass es genau definierte Schlussregeln gegeben habe. Die Herleitung solch abgeleiteter Regeln – von denen uns in der Regel nicht bekannt ist, wie man auf sie gekommen ist, wie also der Schlussfolgerungsprozess ausgesehen hat

nachdem, ob sie direkt aus den Grundregeln abgeleitet sind[20] oder mehrerer oder gar vieler Teil- bzw. Zwischenschritte bedürfen, wie beispielsweise die komplexen Algorithmen zur Lösung quadratischer Gleichungssysteme, von Feldteilungsproblemen etc. Letztere sind es, die aufgrund ihres dann auch differenzierteren sprachlichen Niederschlags (in den Aufgabentexten) in den anderen Beiträgen dieses Bandes vorzugsweise behandelt werden.

Als Regel*system* kann man eine Gruppe thematisch/inhaltlich zusammengehöriger oder aufeinander bezogener Regeln verstehen.[21] Ein solcher Aufeinander-Bezug kann ggf. wieder als (übergeordnete, Meta-) Regel begriffen werden, was aber hier nicht weiter verfolgt wird.[22]

Neben die „eigentlichen" mathematischen Regeln könnte man als *Methodenregeln/Schlussregeln* die beiden grundlegenden Herleitungsprinzipien Mittelung und Analogiebildung[23] (und ggf. weitere) stellen.[24]

– mag im Einzelfall durchaus rein intuitiv erfolgt sein. In jedem Fall aber müssen sie aus den Grundregeln und anderen, bereits früher aufgefundenen abgeleiteten Regeln hervorgegangen sein. Dabei scheint es, dass sich zwei wichtige Schluss- bzw. Herleitungsmethoden identifizieren lassen: das der *Mittelung* und das der *Analogiebildung* (siehe unten).

[20] Ein Beispiel sind die Regeln zur Berechnung der Flächeninhalte von Rechtecken und anderer geradlinig begrenzter Flächenstücke (siehe Fußnote 18), wie etwa von Dreiecken, Trapezen, regulären Fünf-, Sechs-, und Siebenecken etc.

[21] Und nicht etwa eine Abfolge von nacheinander angewandten Regeln, z.B. innerhalb des Algorithmus zur Lösung einer Aufgabe. Diese ist kein Regelsystem, sondern eine Regel.

[22] Beispiele für Regelsysteme wären demnach etwa

1. die Regeln zur Berechnung der Flächeninhalte von regulärem Fünf-, Sechs-, Siebeneck aus der Seitenlänge; die Meta-Regel wäre dann das Prinzip der Approximation der n-Ecke durch einen Kreis (Vogel, 1959, 69–70), die auch für andere Werte von n anwendbar ist und analoge, bislang allerdings im Textbefund nicht nachgewiesene Regeln liefert,
2. das System der Wertumrechnungen in den administrativen Texten (siehe oben).

Auch eine „parameterabhängige" Regel kann als Spezialfall eines Regelsystems begriffen werden, z.B. das allgemein formulierte quadratische Gleichungssystem mit $n \geq 2$ Unbekannten in BM 13901, Nr. 18 (siehe unten).

[23] Vgl. Fußnote 19.

[24] Beispielsweise kommt das Prinzip Analogiebildung bei der Ableitung der Regel zur Ermittlung des Rauminhalts eines (planparallelen) Kegelstumpfs als Produkt aus seiner Höhe und dem Mittelwert der Flächeninhalte von Boden- und Deckfläche (BM 85194, Vs. iii 23–30 [Neugebauer, MKT I, 176]) zur Anwendung, und zwar als Analogiebildung zur Regel für die Berechnung des Flächeninhalts eines Trapezes (Produkt aus dem Mittelwert der Längen der beiden parallelen Seiten und der Höhe). Das Prinzip der Mittelung bei der Ableitung der Regel zur Berechnung der Rauminhalts einer Rampe mit trapezförmigen Querschnitten variabler Böschung als Produkt aus dem Mittelwert der kleinsten und der größten Höhe, dem Mittelwert der Mittelwerte der vorderen und der hinteren parallelen Trapezseiten, und der Länge: BM 85194, Vs. i 1–12 (Neugebauer, MKT I, 165; Brunke, 2012b, 18–21). Zwar sind diese Regeln nach heutigem Verständnis falsch, aber da sie durch Anwendung dieser grundlegenden Schlussregeln abgeleitet wurden, kann man sie durchaus als im Rahmen des Mesopotamischen mathematischen Denkens „intrinsisch richtig" ansehen. Möglicherweise ist auch die Regel zur Ermittlung des Flächeninhalts eines unregelmäßigen Vierecks als Produkt der Mittelwerte der Längen einander gegenüberliegender Seiten das Resultat einer Analogiebildung zum Trapez; für andere mögliche Ursprünge dieser Regel siehe Damerow, 2001, 258 f., 282–284 und Brunke, 2015, 5–7.

Es scheint, dass das Konzept der unmittelbar als gültig erkannten oder angenommenen Grundtatsachen („Axiome") in gewisser Weise mit dem des überpositiven Rechts im Sinne (nicht verschriftlichter) rechtlicher Fundamentalien vergleichbar ist. In diesem Sinne schlage ich folgende Entsprechung zwischen mathematischen und rechtlichen Regeln vor:[25]

Grundregeln/Grundtatsachen (ohne Festsetzungen)	$\longleftrightarrow$	natürliches/überpositives Recht
Festsetzungen und abgeleitete Regeln	$\longleftrightarrow$	positives Recht

2. Manifestation und Gültigkeitsanspruch

Im Folgenden geht es um die Frage, auf welche Weise sich mathematische Regeln im Textbefund manifestieren und welcher Zusammenhang zwischen Ausdruck und (dem Maß an) Normgültigkeit besteht. In diesem Zusammenhang ist es von entscheidender Bedeutung, dass etwas (z.B. eine Aussage darüber, wie etwas ist oder sein kann bzw. soll) nicht bereits aufgrund des ihr innewohnenden Geltungsanspruchs (also dadurch, dass es als solche postuliert und ggf. explizit niedergeschrieben ist) eine Regel ist, sondern erst dadurch, dass dieser Geltungsanspruch (und damit der Regelcharakter von etwas) innerhalb der diesbezüglich relevanten Gruppe von Personen allgemein anerkannt wird; und dass eine Regel erst dadurch zur *Norm* wird (d.h. Normgültigkeit besitzt), wenn sie im „mathematischen Alltag", in der täglichen einschlägigen Praxis tatsächlich angewandt wird, und zwar (zumindest fast) ausschließlich (vgl. Abschnitt 1.1 oben), also wiederum durch die *allgemeine Anerkennung*, diesmal als Norm.[26] Entsprechend ist die Normgültigkeit einer Regel für uns erst dann erkennbar, wenn Textbefund (oder anderer gleichwertiger Befund) *aus der Praxis* vorliegt, der ihre (zumindest fast) ständige und ausschließliche Verwendung in einem bestimmten Kontext belegt. Damit kann dann aber auch eine mathematische Regel und ggf. ihre Normgültigkeit sogar dann als solche erkennbar sein, wenn sie nirgendwo explizit als solche formuliert ist (implizite Regel),[27] sofern nur hinreichende Evidenz für ihre (fast) ständige und ausschließliche Verwendung vorliegt.

---

[25] Gemeint ist mit der vorgeschlagenen Entsprechung das Folgende: Es gibt rechtliche Grundregeln oder Grundtatsachen (Fundamentalien), wie z.B., dass man nicht ohne Grund jemanden aus der eigenen Gemeinschaft töten darf. Daraus abgeleitet sind die vom Menschen festgelegten Gesetze (positives Recht), die z.B. regeln, was passiert, wenn jemand gegen die Grundregeln verstößt, also etwa jemanden (ohne hinreichenden Grund) tötet. Natürlich sind diese Gesetze nicht abgeleitet im Sinne einer mathematischen oder logischen Deduktion, sie sind aber die *Konsequenz* aus der Existenz der Grundregel. Das oben als „Methodenregeln/Schlussregeln" bezeichnete Ableitungsprinzip könnten z.B. das Gerechtigkeitsempfinden, göttliche Vorgaben o.ä. sein. Dass die Grundregeln nirgendwo explizit notiert sind, haben sie mit den mathematischen Grundregeln gemein (siehe unten).

[26] Vgl. hierzu Yuri Manins entsprechende Ausführungen zum Thema Beweis: „A proof becomes a proof only after the social act of 'accepting it as a proof.'" (Manin, 2010, 45).

[27] Natürlich sind die Kategorien „implizit" und „explizit" das Resultat der Sicht von heute auf den Textbefund und damit abhängig von der Überlieferungslage bzw. vom Überlieferungszufall.

Wichtig ist nun, dass der *sprachliche Ausdruck* oder gar dessen genaue grammatikalische Ausprägung dabei *a priori* unerheblich ist.[28] Erheblich und die Anerkennung als geltende Norm massiv unterstreichend ist es allerdings, wenn (a) im

---

[28a] Dies sei deshalb betont, weil in der Diskussion der Projektgruppe vor allem der sprachliche Ausdruck in Gesetzestexten und mathematischen *Aufgaben*texten im Mittelpunkt steht, der aufgrund von deren Natur als prozedurale Texte Ähnlichkeiten aufweist: erstens im Aufbau (algorithmische Struktur [siehe Ritter, 2004]; bei mathematischen Lösungsverfahren mit rückbezüglichen und verweisenden Elementen), und zweitens in der Verwendung bestimmter grammatikalischer Formen (im Fall der babylonischen mathematischen Aufgabentexte Fokus auf Imperativ und Präsens). Entsprechendes findet man auch in den altbabylonischen Kochrezepten (Bottéro, 1995). In diesem Zusammenhang ist Wert auf die Feststellung zu legen, dass flektierte Verbformen im Präsens oder Imperativ in den babylonischen mathematischen Aufgabentexten keineswegs die einzigen Ausdrucksmittel zur Formulierung der einzelnen Lösungsschritte/Anweisungen sind. Häufig finden sich stattdessen

1. Nominalformen sumerischer Verben („Partizipien“), z.B. in BM 85194 (Neugebauer, MKT I, 142–193; Neugebauer, 1935b, Tafeln 5, 6), Rs. i 21–24: **igi** 36 … **du$_8$-a** 01 40 *ta-mar*; 01 40 *a-na* 36 *i-ši* 01 *ta-mar*; 01 **ĝar-ra**; 25 … *a-na* 36 *i-ši* 15 *ta-mar*; 15 *i-na* 01 **ba-z[i]** 45 *ta-mar* …; 15 *a-na* 01 **tah-ha** 01 15 *ta-mar* „Das Inverse von 36 … gebildet (Partizip), 01 40 siehst du ; 01 40 mit 36 multipliziere (Imperativ), 01 siehst du ; 01 hingesetzt (d.h. niedergeschrieben, Partizip); 25 … mit 36 multipliziere (Imperativ), 15 siehst du ; 15 wird von 01 abgezogen (flektiert, unpersönlich), 45 siehst du …; 15 zu 01 hinzugefügt (Partizip), 01 15 siehst du“.
2. oder auch überhaupt keine Verben. So z.B. sehr oft Minimal-Nominalsätze wie 20 **u$_3$** 20 ; 40 oder auch 20 **u$_3$** 20 ; 06 40 (wie in BM 13901, Aufgabe 18, Zeilen 41–42 im ersten Textbeispiel von Abschnitt 3); in diesem Fall also so verkürzt, dass erst durch den „Comment“ (40 bzw. 06 40) klar wird, ob mit **u$_3$** „und“ Addieren oder Multiplizieren gemeint ist. Auch das Ziehen einer Quadratwurzel wird m.W. nie durch eine Verbform ausgedrückt, sondern immer durch einen sumerischen Nominalsatz, wie z.B. 10 25-**e** 25 **ib$_2$-sa$_2$** „aus 625 ist 25 die Quadratwurzel“ in BM 13901, Aufgabe 9, Zeile 7 im zweiten Textbeispiel von Abschnitt 3.

Es ist klar, dass diese Schritte von demjenigen, der den Algorithmus anwendet, durchzuführen sind, da sie Bestandteil des Lösungsverfahrens sind; dennoch werden sie nicht als Anweisungen (Imperativ oder Präsens) formuliert, sondern als Feststellungen („die Wurzel aus 625 ist 25“). Nicht selten wird die „Anweisung“ zur Durchführung einer Operation auch durch eine Frage, gefolgt von einem Nominalsatz, ausgedrückt. So z.B. BM 96957 + VAT 6598 (Robson, 1999, 231–244), Rs. i 28–29: … 01 40 *ta-mar* **en-nam ib$_2$-sa$_2$** 10 **ib$_2$-sa$_2$** „… 01 40 (= 100) siehst du. Was ist die Quadratwurzel? 10 ist die Quadratwurzel“. So auch regelmäßig, wenn das Inverse einer sexagesimal irregulären Zahl benötigt wird, z.B. BM 13901, Aufgabe 10 (Vs. ii 11–18), Zeilen 15–16, wo 21 15 00 (= 76500) durch 01 25 (= 85) geteilt werden soll: **igi** 01 25 *u$_2$-la ip-pa-ṭa-ar mi-nam a-na* 01 25 *lu-uš-ku-un ša* 21 15 *i-na-di-nam* „Das Inverse von 01 25 (= 85) kann nicht gelöst/gefunden werden (nämlich in einer Reziprokenliste; vgl. Beispiel 1 in Fußnote 5). Was soll ich zu 01 25 setzen (d.h. dazu multiplizieren), was 21 15 00 (= 76500) ergibt?“ (Die Antwort, 15 00 [= 900], wird nicht eigens genannt, sondern sofort im nächsten Schritt weiterverarbeitet: 15-**e** 30 **ib$_2$-sa$_2$** „aus 15 00 [= 900] ist 30 die Quadratwurzel“). Bleibt zu erwähnen, dass sich bisweilen natürlich auch Prekativformen sumerischer Verben finden, z.B. in dem von einzelnen akkadischen Wörtern abgesehen rein sumerisch geschriebenen Text Straßburg 367 (Frank, 1928, Text 10), Vs. 7–8: 01 **u$_3$** 03 **he$_2$-ĝar** ; 01 **u$_3$** 03 **ĝar-ĝar** 04; „01 und 03 sollen addiert werden ; 01 und 03 addiert: 04“. Dies findet sich in akkadischen und sumerischen Gesetzestexten meines Wissens nicht.

Falle der Existenz sprachlichen Ausdrucks dieser immer derselbe ist, oder (b) im Falle völligen Fehlens von sprachlichem Ausdruck (z.B. in den neusumerischen Feldplänen, siehe oben), die nicht-sprachliche formale Erscheinung immer dieselbe ist; in jedem Fall also die Regelhaftigkeit des Erscheinungsbildes, die Existenz eines einheitlichen Musters der Darstellung. Dies ist administrativen Texten und z.B. Prozessurkunden gemeinsam.

Es scheint, dass sich ein Zusammenhang feststellen lässt zwischen der Komplexität einer Regel, ihrem sprachlichen Ausdruck bzw. ihrer Explizitheit, und dem Maß an Normgültigkeit. Während die „Axiome“ unter den Grundregeln und möglicherweise auch die Festsetzungen (Abschnitt 1.2) niemals explizit als Regeln formuliert sind,[29] sind die abgeleiteten Regeln teils explizit als Regeln formuliert (z.B. durch Angabe der relevanten Größen in den Koeffizientenlisten, wie im Fall der Regeln zur Berechnung der Flächeninhalte regulärer Polygone), teils nur implizit (durch Anwendung in Aufgabentexten oder auch administrativen Texten, letzteres z.B. im Fall der Regel zur Berechnung des Flächeninhalts eines allgemeinen [irregulären] Vierecks).[30] Die komplexen abgeleiteten Regeln

---

[28b] So ist etwa die Phrase „5: Koeffizient des Kreises“ (z.B. 05 **igi-gub** *ša*$_3$ **gur**$_2$ oder 05 **igi-gub** *ki-pa-tim* o.ä.; für Belegstellen siehe Robson, 1999, 34–35) in einer Koeffizientenliste gleichwertig mit der Anweisung „multipliziere das Umfangsquadrat (eines Kreises) mit 5, um den Flächeninhalt zu erhalten“ in einem Aufgabentext (z.B. Böhl, 1821, 13–14 [Leemans, 1951]: 15 *a-na* 05 **igi-gub-ba [gur**$_2$**]**//*i-ši* 01 15 **iri gibil**$_4$ *ta-mar* „15 [= das im vorangehenden Schritt ermittelte Quadrat des Kreisumfangs] mit 05, dem Koeffizienten [des Kreises]//multipliziere! 01 15, die neue Stadt [hier der gesuchte Flächeninhalt des Kreises] siehst du.“) Erstere ist eine implizite Aussage darüber, wie man aus dem Umfang eines Kreises seinen Flächeninhalt berechnet – hier wird die Regel nicht als Anweisung formuliert, sondern über das Wort **igi-gub** als Regel kenntlich gemacht –, zweitere eine explizite. Ersteres setzt die Kenntnis der Bedeutung des Koeffizienten 5 im vorliegenden Kontext voraus, letzteres nicht unbedingt. Bisweilen, aber keineswegs immer, wird in einem Aufgabentext eine solche Größe wie in diesem Beispiel die 5, ausdrücklich als Koeffizient angesprochen (so wie in dem Beispiel Böhl, 1821 oben). Man kann wohl sagen, dass die Regel in den Koeffizientenlisten formuliert und in den Aufgabentexten angewandt wird, womit das Auftreten hinreichend vieler derartiger Verwendungen in Aufgabentexten als Beleg für die Normgültigkeit der Regel herangezogen werden kann.

[29a] Beispielsweise ist die Regel von der Additivität des Maßes nur implizit im Textbefund greifbar, dies allerdings wegen ihrer fundamentalen Bedeutung reichlich. So unter anderem in den aus ihr folgenden (abgeleiteten) Regeln zur Berechnung der Rechtecksfläche und anderer geradlinig begrenzter Flächenstücke. Z. B. des regulären Fünf-, Sechs- und Siebenecks in der Koeffizientenliste TMS 3 (Bruins / Rutten, 1961, Text 3, 26–28): 01 40 **igi-gub** *ša*$_3$ **saĝ**-5//02 37 30 **igi-gub** *ša*$_3$ **saĝ**-6//03 41 **igi-gub** *ša*$_3$ **saĝ**-7 „01 ▲ 40: Koeffizient des Fünf-Seits//02 ▲ 37 30: Koeffizient des Sechs-Seits//03 ▲ 41: Koeffizient des Sieben-Seits“ (für die Interpretation siehe Vogel, 1959, 69–70; Robson, 1999, 48–50; vgl. Fußnote 18). Ferner in graphischen Abbildungen, die die Zerlegung einer Figur zum Zweck der Berechnung ihres Flächeninhaltes als Summe der Teilflächenstücke zeigen (z.B. für das reguläre Sechs- und Siebeneck in TMS 2 [Bruins / Rutten, 1961, Text 2]; Transliteration z.B. in Friberg, 2007, 218), und in den neusumerischen Feldplänen (siehe oben).

[29b] Dasselbe gilt für die „Methodenregeln/Schlussregeln“ (siehe Ende von Abschnitt 1.2). Auch hier ist die Evidenz rein implizit, etwa im Falle der Ableitung der Regel für die Berechnung des Rauminhalts eines Kegelstumpfes durch Analogieschluss durch die „Einsortierung“ der fraglichen Aufgabe in einen Kontext mit Trapezflächenberechnungen (vgl. Fußnote 24).

[30] Beachte aber Fußnote 27!

finden sich immer explizit ausformuliert in den Lösungsalgorithmen der Aufgabentexte. Charakteristisch (wenn auch nicht zwingend) für sie sind Rückbezüge und verweisende Elemente (gewissermaßen als „Variablenersatz").[31]

Die Grundregeln sind in der Regel zwingende Normen (d.h. als *allein*gültig anerkannt), da per „fundamentaler Einsicht" oder Festlegung (diese wiederum wohl in der Regel aus empirischem Befund gewonnen) etabliert, so z.B. die geometrischen Koeffizienten und Materialkonstanten in den Koeffizientenlisten, Arbeitspensa (in Koeffizientenlisten und administrativen Texten) und Wertäquivalenzen (in administrativen Texten).[32] Dagegen sind die komplexeren abgeleiteten Regeln, also z.B. Lösungsverfahren zu mathematischen Problemstellungen, freier. Es handelt sich damit eher um Lösungs*möglichkeiten* als um zwingende Vorgaben, siehe das Beispiel in Abschnitt 3 unten. Das scheint mir ein wesentlicher inhaltlicher Unterschied zu rechtlichen Regeln/Rechtsnormen zu sein, der bei Fixierung auf den sprachlichen Ausdruck völlig untergeht.

Zusammenfassend sind die beiden wesentlichen Thesen der obigen Ausführungen, dass

1. mathematische Regeln bzw. ihre Etablierung als Normen durch Kontexte erfolgen können/kann, die nicht im eigentlichen Sinne sprachlich sind, zumindest nicht in erster Linie, sondern z.B. durch (nichtsprachliche) regelhaft wiederkehrende *formale Strukturen*, also durch Form statt durch sprachlichen Ausdruck. Beispiele sind die altbabylonischen Koeffizientenlisten, die Wertäquivalenz-Umrechnungen von Getreideprodukten in die Grundeinheit Gerste in den neusumerischen Wirtschaftsurkunden, und – als Evidenz „völlig nichtsprachlicher Regelsysteme" – die neusumerischen Feldpläne;
2. dort, wo mathematische Regeln vermittels sprachlicher Elemente formuliert werden (Lösungsverfahren in den Aufgabentexten), sie (trotz der häufigen Verwendung von Imperativen) in vielen Fällen nicht als bindend oder zwingend zu verstehen sind, sondern als jeweils eine von ggf. mehreren Möglichkeiten, was sie von rechtlichen Regeln wesentlich unterscheiden dürfte. Es liegt in der Natur der Sache, dass der zwingende Charakter einer Regel mit zunehmender Komplexität abnimmt. Als besonders augenfälliges Beispiel werden unten (Abschnitt 3) zwei konzeptionell völlig verschiedene Lösungsverfahren ein und derselben Aufgabe (auf derselben Tafel) vorgestellt.

---

[31] Vgl. beispielsweise Ritter, 1998.

[32] Davon unberührt ist die (sanktionierte) Möglichkeit der Bereitstellung und Verwendung einfacherer Werte oder von Werten reduzierter Genauigkeit, die die praktische Anwendung vereinfachen. So gibt es ein Beispiel für gerundete Werte bei den Wertäquivalenzumrechnungen, nämlich für das Produkt **babir**$_2$ **saga**$_{10}$ („gutes Bierbrot, guter Sauerteig o.ä.", eine Zutat beim Bierbrauen): Neben dem regelhaften exakten Wert $1\frac{39}{60}$ finden sich (selten) die mithilfe der benachbarten sexagesimal-regulären Zähler genäherten Werte $1\frac{3}{5}$ (= $1\frac{36}{60}$) und $1\frac{2}{3}$ (=$1\frac{40}{60}$; siehe Brunke, 2011a, 17–18, Bemerkung 2.12). Im Bereich der geometrischen Koeffizienten sind hier beispielsweise die beiden (verschieden genauen) Approximationen für den Wert von $\sqrt{2}$ in den Koeffizientenlisten zu nennen. Vgl. Brunke 2017, 21 Anmerkung 35 mit weiteren Belegen. (Die beiden Werte können als der zweite und der gerundete dritte Schritt des „babylonischen Wurzelalgorithmus" zum Startwert 1 interpretiert werden [siehe Neugebauer / Sachs, 1945, 42].)

3. Beispiel: Quadratische Gleichungssysteme

Das angekündigte Beispiel für den nicht-zwingenden Charakter komplexer abgeleiteter Regeln sind zwei Aufgaben zu – in moderner Terminologie – quadratischen Gleichungssystemen auf der altbabylonischen Sammeltafel BM 13901. Es handelt sich um zwei verschiedene, sogar konzeptionell komplementäre Lösungswege (Vervielfachung vs. Teilung einer charakteristischen Figur bzw. Größe) für dasselbe mathematische Problem. Die erste der beiden betrachteten Aufgaben ist BM 13901, Nr. 18 (Rs. i 39–49):[33]

39) **a-ša**$_3$ *ša-la-aš mi-it-ha-ra-ti-ia ak-mur-ma* 23 20
40) *mi-it-har-tum* **ugu** *mi-it-har-tim* 10 *i-te-er*
41) 10 *ša i-te-ru a-na* 01 *ta-na-ši* 10 *a-na* 02 *ta-na-ši* 20 **u**$_3$ 20
42) 06 40-**e** 10 **u**$_3$ 10 *tu-uš-ta-kal* 01 40 *a-na* 06 40 *tu-ṣa-ab* 08 20
43) *lib*$_3$ *-ba* 23 20 *ta-na-sa*$_3$ *-ah-ma* 15 *a-na* 03 *mi-it-ha-ra-*[*ti*]
44) *ta-na-ši 45 ta-la-pa-at 10* **u**$_3$ *20 ta-ka-mar-ma*
45) 30 **u**$_3$ 30 *tu-uš-ta-kal* 15 *a-na* 45 *tu-ṣa-ab-ma*
46) 01-**e** 01 **ib**$_2$**-sa**$_2$ 30 *ša tu-uš-ta-ki-lu ta-na-sa*$_3$ *-ah-ma* 30 *ta-la-pa-at*
47) **igi**-03 *mi-it-ha-ra-ti* 20 *a-na* 30 *ta-na-ši* 10 *mi-it-har-tum*
48) 10 *a-na* 10 *tu-ṣa-ab-ma* 20 *mi-it-har-tum* **ki**-2 10 *a-na* 20
49) *tu-ṣa-ab-ma* 30 *mi-it-har-tum* **ki**-3

Die nachstehende Übersetzung folgt nicht der Zeileneinteilung des Akkadischen Texts, die sich (wie in diesen Texten üblich) nicht an einer durch die einzelnen mathematischen Schritte bzw. Operationen gegebenen inhaltlichen Gliederung orientiert, sondern gewissermaßen als „Spaghetti-Code" daherkommt. Stattdessen wird die Übersetzung jedes einzelnen Schrittes in einer eigenen Zeile gegeben, die mit den Buchstaben A bis T bezeichnet sind. Ergänzungen und Erläuterungen, die das Verständnis der sehr knapp gehaltenen Ausführungen[34] erleichtern sollen, sind in Klammern gesetzt. Die Sexagesimalzahlen des Originals sind in Dezimalzahlen umgerechnet.[35]

[33] Die Tafel wurde zuerst von Thureau-Dangin, 1936a und Thureau-Dangin, 1936b, 83 f. untersucht und nochmals in Thureau-Dangin, 1938, 1–10. Eine Neubearbeitung des Textes mit detaillierten Analysen und Kommentaren gibt Neugebauer, 1937, 1–14. Die hier betrachtete Aufgabe Rs. i 39–49 wird auch von Høyrup, 2002, 108–110 behandelt.

[34] So fehlt zum Beispiel sogar die Frage nach den gesuchten Größen.

[35a] Zwei Bemerkungen zur Übersetzung. (1) Der Verständlichkeit halber verwendet die Übersetzung moderne Terminologie und lässt die spezielle Art des Akkadischen Ausdrucks für bestimmte mathematische Operationen unberücksichtigt, z.B. dass „abziehen" wörtlich als „herausreißen" wiederzugeben wäre oder dass es verschiedene kontextabhängige Wörter für „addieren" und „multiplizieren" gibt. Für die grundlegenden Untersuchungen zu derartigen Fragen des sprachlichen Ausdrucks in den mathematischen Texten siehe Høyrup, 1990 und Høyrup, 2002, sowie für eine Extremform einer Wort-für-Wort-Übersetzung unseres Textbeispiels Høyrup, 2002, 108 f. (2) In Zeile 47 gibt der Text das „Inverse von 3 (, der Anzahl der) Quadrate(n)" (Schritt Q) als 20 an, was als $\frac{20}{60}$ (= $\frac{1}{3}$) zu interpretieren und in der Übersetzung auch so wiedergegeben ist. Es folgt aus den Besonderheiten der in den babylonischen mathematischen Texten verwendeten relativen Positionsnotation der Zahlen, dass beispielsweise die Zahlen 20, $20 \cdot \frac{1}{60}$ und $20 \cdot 60$ auf dieselbe Art, nämlich einfach als „20" notiert werden. Siehe zum Beispiel Friberg, 1987–90, 533–537.

A: Ich habe die Flächen meiner drei Quadrate addiert und 1400 (ist das Ergebnis).
B: Quadratseite überragt Quadratseite um 10.
C: (Diese) 10, die übersteht, nimmst du einmal.
D: Du nimmst (diese) 10 zweimal.
E: (Die resultierende) 20 und (die resultierende) 20 (multipliziert, ergeben) 400.
F: Du multiplizierst 10 (aus Schritt C) und 10 (aus Schritt C).
G: Du addierst (die resultierende) 100 zu (der) 400 (aus Schritt E).
H: Du ziehst (die resultierende) 500 von 1400 (der Summe der drei Quadrate) ab
I: und multiplizierst (die resultierende) 900 mit drei (, der Anzahl der) Qua drate(n).
J: Du schreibst (die resultierende) 2700 hin
K: Du addierst 10 (aus Schritt C) und 20 (aus Schritt D)
L: und multiplizierst (die resultierende) 30 und (die resultierende) 30.
M: Du addierst (die resultierende) 900 zu 2700 (aus Zeile J)
N: und die Quadratwurzel aus (der resultierenden) 3600 ist 60.
O: (Von dieser 60) ziehst du die 30, die du (in Schritt L) quadriert hast, ab
P: und schreibst (die resultierende) 30 hin.
Q: Das Inverse von 3 (, der Anzahl der) Quadrate(n), $\frac{20}{60}$, multiplizierst du mit (der) 30 (aus Zeile P).
R: (Die resultierende) 10 ist die (erste) Quadratseite.
S: Du addierst 10 (gegeben in Zeile B) zu 10 (aus Schritt R) und (die resultie rende) 20 ist die zweite Quadratseite.
T: Du addierst 10 (gegeben in Zeile B) zu 20 (aus Schritt S) und (die resultie rende) 30 ist die dritte Quadratseite.

Gegeben sind also drei Quadrate unbekannter Größe sowie die Information, dass sich die Seitenlängen um je 10 unterscheiden und dass die Summe ihrer Flächen 1400 beträgt. Gesucht sind die Seitenlängen der drei Quadrate. In moderner Ausdrucksweise geht es also um die Lösung eines Systems von drei Gleichungen, nämlich

---

[35b] Es ist ein charakteristisches Merkmal vieler mathematischer Aufgabentexte, dass die Aufgabenstellung in der ersten Person Singular erfolgt und die Lösung an eine zweite Person Singular (maskulin) gerichtet ist. Die einzelnen Lösungsschritte werden entweder als Anweisungen im Präsens (wie in diesem Textbeispiel ausschließlich) oder Imperativ formuliert oder unpersönlich durch Nominalformen („Partizipien") sumerischer Verben oder durch reine Nominalsätze (vgl. Fußnote 28a). Ebenso kann eine Aufgabenstellung unpersönlich eingeleitet werden: z.B. BM 96957 + VAT 6598 (Robson, 1999, 231–244), Rs. i 25: *šum-ma* **ka**$_2$ 40 **kuš**$_3$ **sukud** 41 15 *ṣi*$_2$*-li-ip-tum* **dagal en-nam** „Wenn ein Tor (gegeben ist), 40 Ellen die Höhe, 41 15 die Diagonale. Die Breite ist was?" (die Angabe der Höhe ist fehlerhaft, gemeint sind 00 ▲ 40 **nindan** = 8 Ellen). Dabei kann auch bereits in der Aufgabenstellung die zweite Person direkt angesprochen werden, z.B. BM 85194, Vs. ii 19–20: **bad**$_3$ 01$^{\check{s}u}$ **uš** 30 *mu-hu* 01 *sa*$_3$*-sum*$_2$ 06 **sukud sahar-hi-a**; *a-na* 1 **lu**$_2$ **uš** *pu-lu-uk* „Eine Mauer: 01 00 die Länge, 00 ▲ 30 die Oberseite, 01 die Basis, 06 die Höhe. Volumen. Für einen Mann grenze (anteilig) die Länge ab" (die Mauer hat trapezförmigen Querschnitt; Oberseite und Basis sind die beiden parallelen Seiten dieses Trapezes). Der Schüler wird also aufgefordert, das Volumen und den anteiligen Abschnitt eines Arbeiters daran (aufgrund eines Arbeitspensums) zu ermitteln.

$$
\begin{aligned}
&(i) \quad x^2 + y^2 + z^2 = A \\
&(ii) \quad y = x + b \\
&(iii) \quad z = y + b
\end{aligned}
\tag{1}
$$

in drei Unbekannten (den Seitenlängen) x, y, z, hier mit den konkreten Zahlenwerten $A = 1400$ für die Gesamtfläche und $b = 10$ für die Differenzen zwischen den Seitenlängen.[36] Es ist wichtig zu bemerken, dass die Richtigkeit des Lösungsverfahrens von den konkreten Zahlenwerten (1400 und 10) nicht abhängt, sondern ganz allgemein gilt, wie man an der geometrischen Erläuterung unten sehen kann. Auch ist beachtenswert, dass (wie in solchen Aufgaben häufig) Längen- und Flächenangaben ohne Maßeinheiten, sondern unterschiedslos als reine Sexagesimalzahlen angegeben werden, was ein recht hohes Maß an Abstraktion anzeigt.

Der Verdeutlichung des Lösungsverfahrens soll eine graphische Interpretation dienen, in der die einzelnen Schritte durch Zerlegung, Beschneidung und Neuzusammensetzung von geometrischen Figuren erfolgen.[37] Die gezeigten Figuren sind nicht maßstabstreu im Hinblick auf die im Text gegebenen Zahlenwerte, um zu verdeutlichen, dass die Richtigkeit des Verfahrens von diesen konkreten Werten nicht abhängt.

Die Gesamtfläche, also die Summe der drei Quadratflächen, lässt sich wie folgt darstellen. In der Abbildung rechts sind die „Überschüsse“ des zweiten und dritten Quadrates gegenüber dem ersten in verschiedenen Graustufen wiedergegeben:

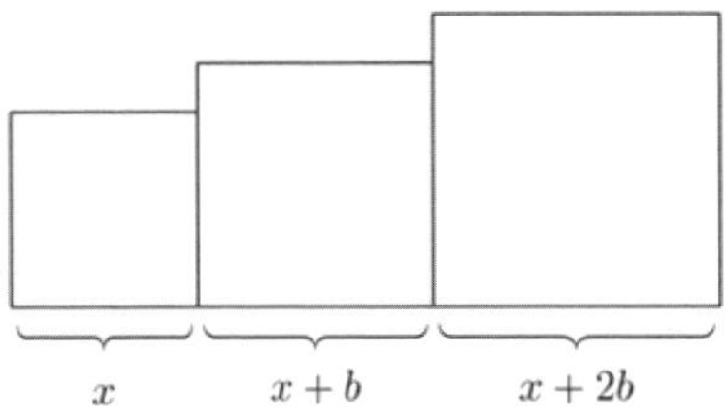

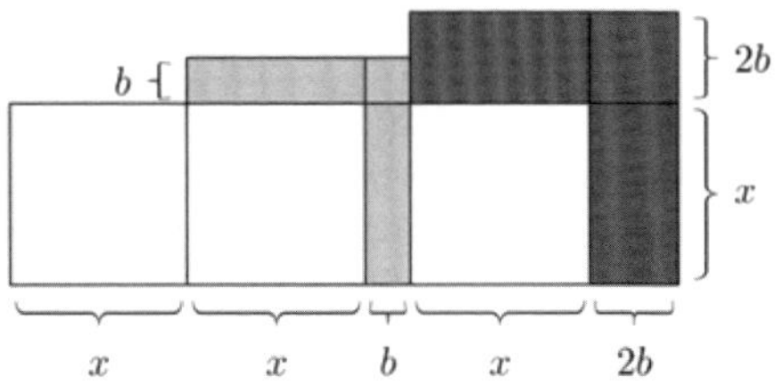

[36] Beachte, dass die Gleichungen *(ii)* und *(iii)*, also $y = x + b$ und $z = y + b$ aus der Aufgabenstellung „Quadratseite überragt Quadratseite um 10“ noch gar nicht hervorgehen. Denkbar wäre hier auch z.B. $z = y = x + b$. Dass tatsächlich das oben genannte Gleichungssystem gemeint ist, folgt erst aus dem Lösungsverfahren und ganz explizit aus den Zeilen S und T.

[37] Die Erkenntnis, dass die Lösungsmethoden derartiger algebraischer Aufgabenstellungen auf „cut-and-paste geometric operations“ zurückgehen, ist Jens Høyrup zu verdanken. Für eine ausführliche Darstellung mit vielen Beispielen siehe etwa Høyrup, 2002 und Høyrup, 2010. Ob es tatsächlich genau die im Folgenden vorgestellten Figuren waren, anhand dener man die Aufgabe gelöst oder möglicherweise die Aufgabenstellung auch konstruiert hat, bleibt offen, da der Text selbst ja keine Diagramme enthält und auch keine Angaben zu einem etwaigen „Umschichten“ von Figuren oder Teilen davon macht.

In Schritt H werden die zwei kleinen Quadrate (mit den Seitenlängen b und $2b$) aus den rechten oberen Ecken des zweiten und dritten Quadrates entfernt:

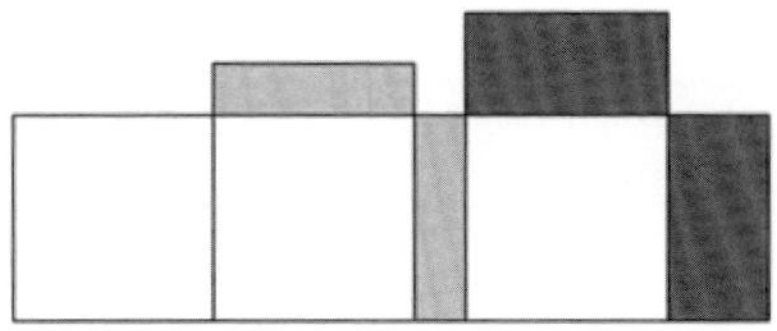

Die verbleibenden Teile der Figur können folgendermaßen umgeordnet werden:

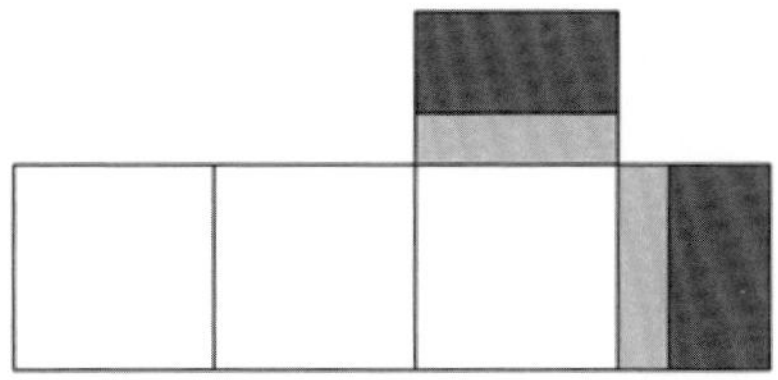

In Schritt I wird diese Figur dreimal genommen. Das Ergebnis kann folgendermaßen angeordnet werden:

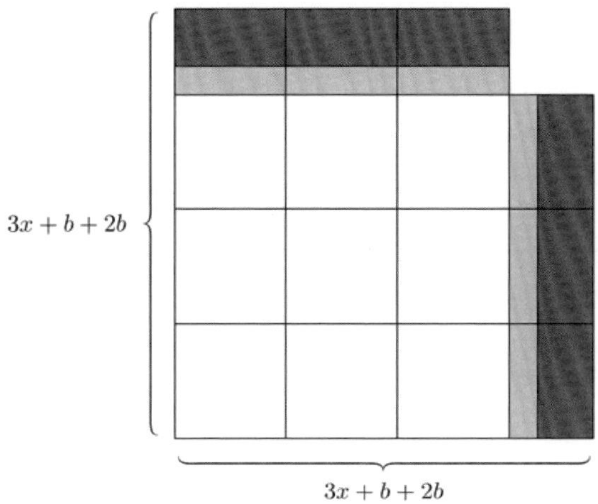

Die Addition eines Quadrates der Seitenlänge $b + 2b$ (Schritt M) liefert ein vollständiges Quadrat der Seitenlänge $3x + b + 2b$:

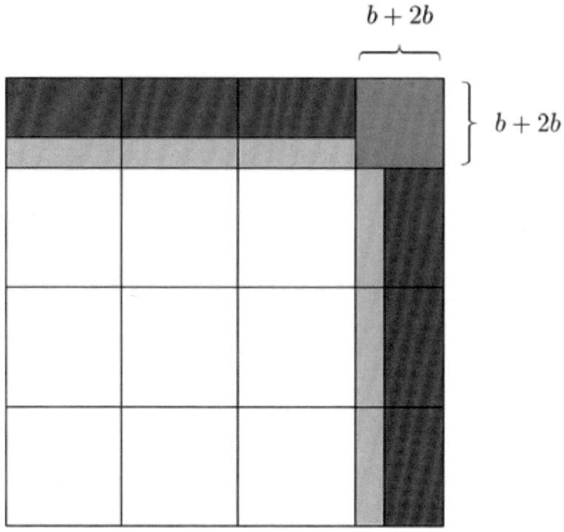

Ziehen der Wurzel aus diesem Quadrat (Schritt N) liefert seine Seitenlänge, $3 + b + 2b$. Durch Subtraktion von $b + 2b$ (Schritt O) erhält man $3x$ und als dessen dritten Teil (Schritt Q) schließlich x, die kleinste der drei gesuchten Seitenlängen. Sukzessive Addition von b, dem Überschuss von y gegenüber x und von z gegenüber y, (Schritte S und T) liefern die Seitenlängen des zweiten und dritten Quadrates, y und z.

Wichtig ist nun, dass die Zahl 3, mit der bzw. ihrem Inversen Zwischenergebnisse multipliziert werden (Schritte I und Q), im Text explizit als „(Anzahl der) Quadrate" (Zeilen 43 und 47: 3 *mitharāti*) angesprochen wird, was darauf hindeutet, dass man um die Verallgemeinerbarkeit des Verfahrens auf analoge Probleme mit anderen Anzahlen von Quadraten wusste, in denen für diese „(Anzahl der) Quadrate" dann der entsprechende Wert anzusetzen wäre.[38] Im Fall von n Quadraten ist also das Gleichungssystem

$$\begin{aligned} \textstyle\sum_{i=1}^{n} x_i^2 &= A \\ x_{i+1} &= x_i + b \quad \text{für} \quad i \in \{1, \ldots, n-1\} \end{aligned} \tag{2}$$

zu lösen.[39] Für eine graphische Darstellung analog der oben gegebenen für den Fall $n = 4$ siehe Anhang A. Insbesondere funktioniert das Verfahren aber auch für den Fall lediglich zweier Quadrate (also $n = 2$), wie die folgenden Abbildungen analog zu oben veranschaulichen.

[38] Oder eher, dass die vorliegende Aufgabe eine von vielen möglichen analogen Problemstellungen mit beliebigen Anzahlen von Quadraten ist. Diese Einsicht geht auf Neugebauer, 1937, 13 zurück, der feststellt, dass „aus der ganzen Formulierung deutlich hervorgeht, dass hier der Fall von drei Unbekannten nur als Spezialfall einer analogen Aufgabe … für eine beliebige Anzahl n von Unbekannten angesehen wurde." Also liegt hier ein gewissermaßen durch n, die Anzahl der Quadrate, parametrisiertes System von Aufgaben vor, weshalb das angegebene Lösungsverfahren als (parametrisiertes oder parameterabhängiges) Regelsystem angesprochen werden kann (vgl. Fußnote 22).

[39] Vgl. Neugebauer, 1937, 13.

Die zwei Quadrate:

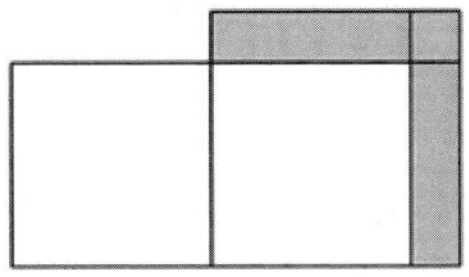

Entfernen des kleinen Quadrats in der rechten oberen Ecke des zweiten Quadrats:

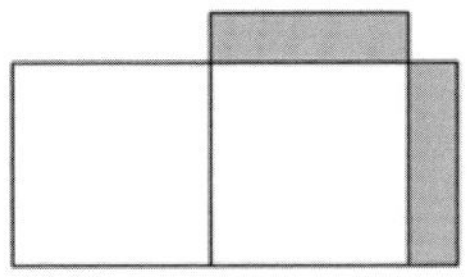

Die Figur wird zweimal (der Anzahl der Quadrate) genommen und das Ergebnis umgeordnet:

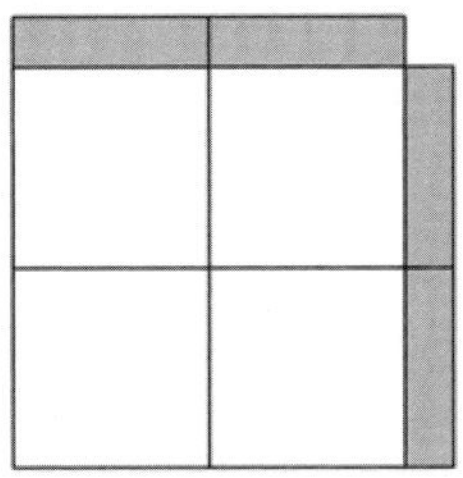

Das Resultat wird zu einem vollständigen Quadrat ergänzt:

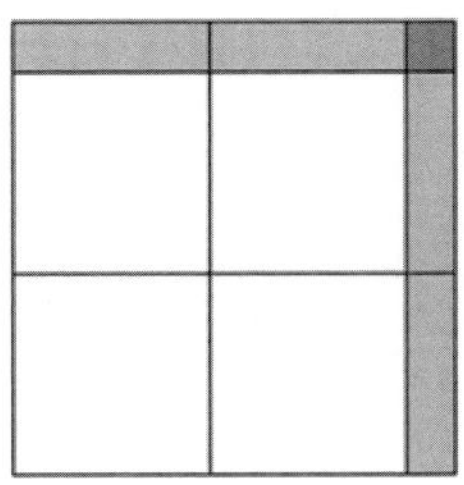

Anschließend wird aus diesem vollständigen Quadrat die Wurzel gezogen und analog zu oben die beiden Seitenlängen berechnet.

Allerdings wird in einem anderen Abschnitt *auf derselben Tafel* ein völlig anderes, in gewisser Weise sogar konzeptionell entgegengesetztes Verfahren zur Lösung genau dieses Problems für den Fall von zwei Quadraten angewandt:[40]

BM 13901, Nr. 9 (Vs. ii 3–10).[41]

3: *a-ša₃ ši-ta mi-it-ha-ra-ti-ia ak-mur-ma* 21 40
4: *mi-it-har-tum ugu mi-it-har-tim 10 i-te-er*

---

[40] Bemerkenswerterweise findet sich hier keine Angabe der Art „2, (die Anzahl der) Quadrate"; und tatsächlich lässt sich dieses Verfahren nicht auf den Fall von mehr als zwei Quadraten verallgemeinern oder übertragen. Der Grund, dieses Verfahren dem allgemeingültigen vorzuziehen, mag darin bestanden haben, dass es einfacher ist.

[41] Vgl. Brunke, 2015, 11–12.

5: *ba-ma-at* 21 40 *te-he-pi-ma* 10 50 *ta-la-pa-at*
6: *ba-ma-at* 10 *te-he-pi* 05 *u₃* 05 *tu-uš-ta-kal*
7: 25 *lib₃-bi* 10 50 *ta-na-sa₃-ah-ma* 10 25-**e** 25 *ib₂-sa₂*
8: 25 *a-di ši-ni-šu ta-la-pa-at* 05 *ša tu-uš-ta-ki-lu*
9: *a-na* 25 *iš-te-en tu-ṣa-ab-ma* 30 *mi-it-har-tum*
10: 05 *lib₃ -bi* 25 *ša-ni-im ta-na-sa₃-ah-ma 209mi-it-har-tum ša-ni-tum*

A: Ich habe die Flächen meiner zwei Quadrate addiert und 1300 (ist das Ergebnis).
B: Quadratseite überragt Quadratseite um 10.
C: Du brichst die Hälfte von 1300 (aus Zeile A) ab
D: und schreibst (die resultierende) 650 hin.
E: Du brichst die Hälfte von 10 (aus Zeile B) ab.
F: Du multiplizierst (die resultierende) 5 und (die resultierende) 5.
G: Du reißt (die resultierende) 25 aus 650 (aus Zeile D) heraus.
H: (Aus der resultierenden) 625 (ist) 25 (die) Quadratwurzel
I: Du schreibst (diese) 25 zweimal hin.
J: Du addierst die 5, die du (in Schritt F) quadriert hast, zu der einen 25 (aus Zeile I)
K: und (die resultierende) 30 ist (die erste) Quadratseite.
L: Du ziehst (die) 5 (die du in Schritt F quadriert hast) von der zweiten 25 (aus Zeile I) ab
M: und (die resultierende) 20 ist die zweite Quadratseite

Es geht also um das Gleichungssystem

$$\begin{aligned} &(i) \quad x^2 + y^2 = A \\ &(ii) \quad y = x+b \end{aligned} \tag{3}$$

diesmal mit den konkreten Zahlenwerten $A = 1300$ und $b = 10$. Es folgt die graphische Veranschaulichung dieses Verfahrens.[42]

Der „Überschuss"(grau) des zweiten (größeren) Quadrates gegenüber dem ersten besteht aus den zwei hellgrauen rechteckigen Streifen der Dicke *b* (und der Länge *x*) und dem kleinen dunkelgrauen Quadrat mit Kantenlänge *b*:

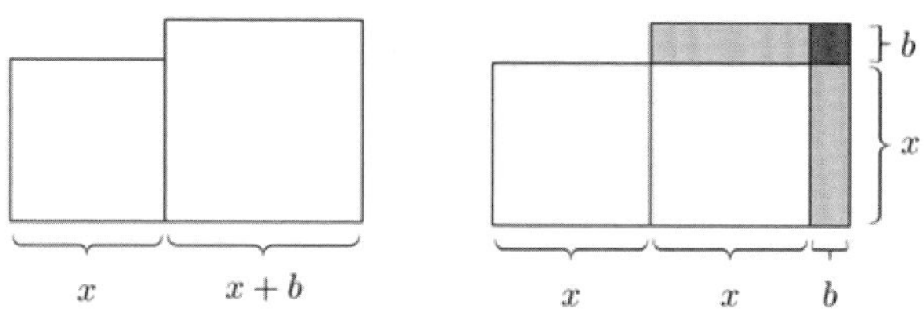

Die Gesamtfigur (bzw. deren Fläche) kann halbiert werden („du brichst die Hälfte von *A* ab", Zeile C), indem eines der beiden (gleichgroßen) weißen Quadrate, die Hälfte eines jeden der beiden hellgrauen Streifen und zwei Viertel des kleinen dunkelgrauen Quadrats entfernt werden.

[42] Für eine andere diagrammatische Interpretation siehe Høyrup, 2002, 68–70.

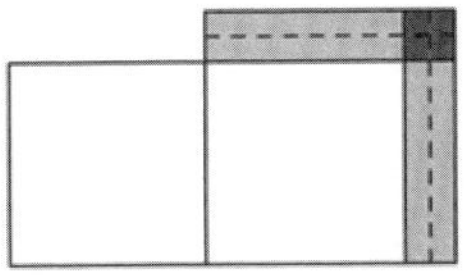

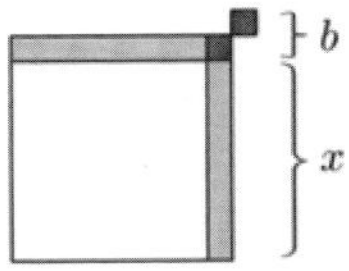

Jedes der beiden verbleibenden dunkelgrauen Teilquadrate hat die Seitenlänge $\frac{b}{2}$ (im konkreten Zahlenbeispiel also 5) und damit den Flächeninhalt $(\frac{b}{2})^2$ (im konkreten Zahlenbeispiel also 25). In Schritt G wird eines von ihnen entfernt („du reißt 25 aus 650 heraus"), z.B. das Äußere. Es verbleibt ein Quadrat der Seitenlänge $x + \frac{b}{2}$:

Ziehen der Quadratwurzel daraus (Schritt H) liefert die Seitenlänge, $x + \frac{b}{2}$. Dieses Zwischenergebnis wird „zweimal hingeschrieben" (Schritt I) und anschließend zwei verschiedenen Operationen unterzogen: Addition von $\frac{b}{2}$ (Schritt J) liefert $x + b$, die Seitenlänge des größeren Quadrates (Zeile K); Subtraktion von $\frac{b}{2}$ (Schritt L) hingegen liefert x, die Seitenlänge des kleineren Quadrates (Zeile M).

Anhang: Vier Quadrate

Im Folgenden soll die Verallgemeinerbarkeit des in BM 13901, Aufgabe 18 (siehe Abschnitt 3) für den konkreten Fall $n = 3$ ausgeführten Verfahrens zur Lösung des Gleichungssystems (2) (Seite 98) auf beliebige Werte für n durch völlig analoge Behandlung des Falles $n = 4$, also des Gleichungssystems

$$\begin{array}{rl} (i) & x^2 + y^2 + z^2 + w^2 = A \\ (ii) & y = x + b \\ (iii) & z = y + b \\ (iv) & w = z + b \end{array}$$

in den jetzt vier Unbekannten (Seitenlängen) x, y, z, w illustriert werden.[43] Für die Gesamtfläche der vier Quadrate und die Differenzen zwischen den Seitenlängen werden diesmal willkürlich die Werte $A = 5400$ und $b = 10$ gewählt. Ein hypothetischer, analog zu BM 13901, Nr. 18 formulierter Aufgabentext könnte beispielsweise folgendermaßen lauten:

A: Ich habe die Flächen meiner vier Quadrate addiert und 5400 (ist das Ergebnis).
B: Quadratseite überragt Quadratseite um 10.
C: (Diese) 10, die übersteht, nimmst du einmal.

[43] Die entsprechenden Ausführungen beispielsweise für die Fälle $n = 5$ oder $n = 6$ seien – um eine in der modernen mathematischen Literatur beliebte Phrase zu missbrauchen – der Leserin/dem Leser zur Übung überlassen.

D: Du nimmst (diese) 10 zweimal.
E: Du nimmst (diese) 10 dreimal.
F: (Die resultierende) 30 und (die resultierende) 30 (multipliziert ergeben) 900.
G Du multiplizierst 20 (aus Schritt D) und 20 (aus Schritt D).
H: Du addierst (die resultierende) 400 zu (der) 900 (aus Schritt F).
I: Du multiplizierst 10 (aus Schritt C) und 10 (aus Schritt C).
J: Du addierst (die resultierende) 100 zu 1300 (Resultat aus Schritt H).
K: Du ziehst (die resultierende) 1400 von 5400 (der Summe der vier Quadrate) ab
L: und multiplizierst (die resultierende) 4000 mit vier (der Anzahl der) Quadrate(n).
M: Du schreibst (die resultierende) 16000 hin.
N: Du addierst 10 (aus Schritt C) und 20 (aus Schritt D) und 30 (aus Schritt E)
O: und multiplizierst (die resultierende) 60 und (die resultierende) 60.
P: Du addierst (die resultierende) 3600 zu 16000 (aus Zeile M)
Q: und die Quadratwurzel aus (der resultierenden) 19600 ist 140.
R: (Von dieser 140) ziehst du die 60, die du (in Schritt O) quadriert hast, ab
S: und schreibst (die resultierende) 80 hin.
T: Das Inverse von 4 (, der Anzahl der) Quadrate(n), 1560, multiplizierst du mit (der) 80 (aus Zeile S).
U: (Die resultierende) 20 ist die (erste) Quadratseite.
V: Du addierst 10 (gegeben in Zeile B) zu 20 (aus Schritt U) und (die resul tierende) 30 ist die zweite Quadratseite.
W: Du addierst 10 (gegeben in Zeile B) zu 30 (aus Schritt V) und (die resul tierende) 40 ist die dritte Quadratseite.
X: Du addierst 10 (gegeben in Zeile B) zu 40 (aus Schritt W) und (die resul tierende) 50 ist die vierte Quadratseite.

Die Gesamtfläche wird analog zu oben folgendermaßen dargestellt, rechts mit den Überschüssen des zweiten, dritten und vierten Quadrates gegenüber dem ersten in verschiedenen Graustufen:

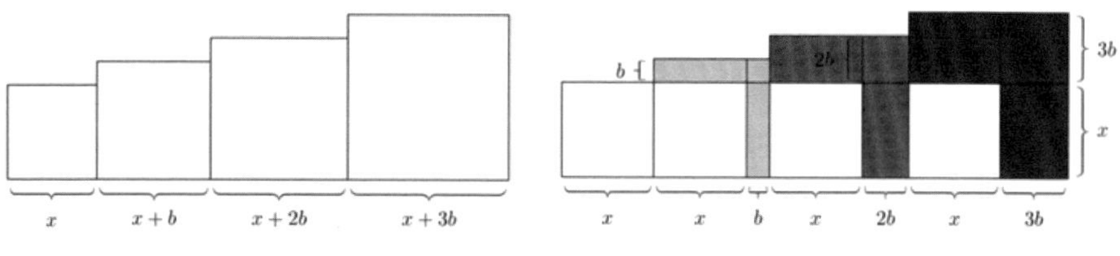

In Schritt K werden die drei kleinen Quadrate (mit den Seitenlängen b, $2b$ und $2b$) aus den rechten oberen Ecken des zweiten, dritten und vierten Quadrates entfernt:

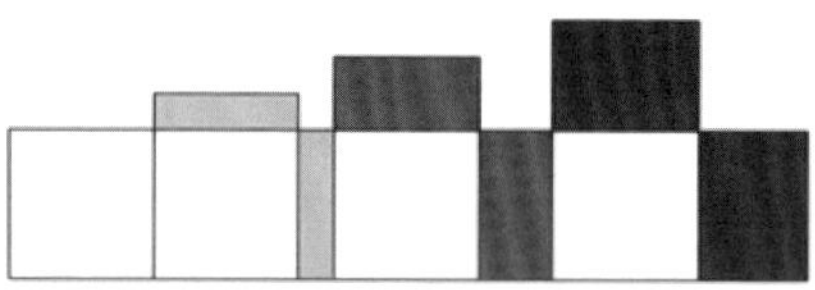

Die verbleibenden Teile der Figur können folgendermaßen umgeordnet werden:

In Schritt L wird diese Figur viermal genommen. Das Ergebnis kann folgendermaßen angeordnet werden:

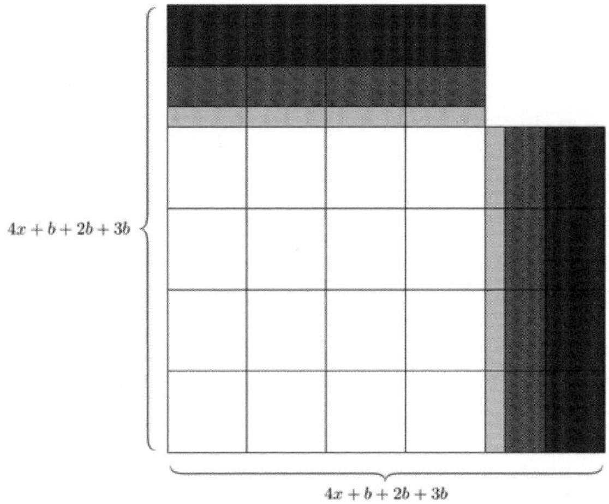

Die Addition eines Quadrates der Seitenlänge $b + 2b + 3b$ (Schritt P) liefert ein vollständiges Quadrat der Seitenlänge $3x + b + 2b + 3b$:

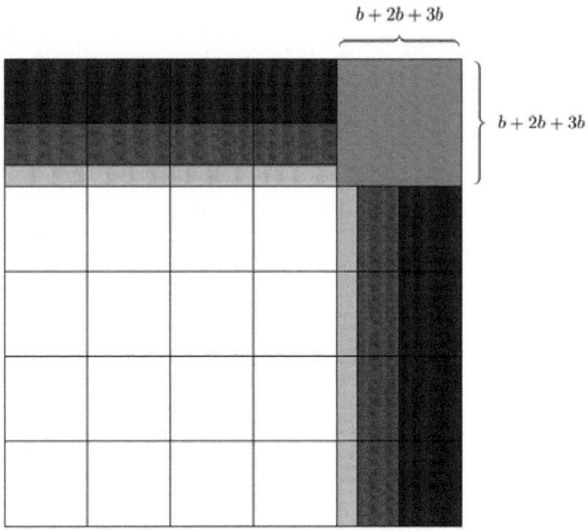

Ziehen der Wurzel aus diesem Quadrat (Schritt Q) liefert seine Seitenlänge, $3x + b + 2b + 3b$. Durch Subtraktion von $b + 2b + 3b$ (Schritt R) erhält man $4x$ und als dessen vierten Teil (Schritt T) schließlich x, die kleinste der vier gesuchten Seitenlängen. Sukzessive Addition von b, dem Überschuss von y gegenüber x, von z

gegenüber *y*, und von *w* gegenüber *z* (Schritte V, W und X) liefern die Seitenlängen des zweiten, dritten und vierten Quadrates, *y*, *z* und *w*.

Abkürzungs- und Literaturverzeichnis

A = Tafeln aus der Sammlung des Oriental Institutes, University of Chicago.
BM = British Museum, London.
CBS = University Museum, Philadelphia (Catalogue of the Babylonian Section).
FLP = Siglum Free Library of Phildadelphia.
HS = Hilprecht Sammlung, Jena.
Ist.T. = Siglum des Arkeoloji Muzesi, Istanbul.
MKT I–III = Neugebauer, Otto, 1935–37: *Mathematische Keilschrifttexte* I–III (Quellen und Studien zur Geschichte der Mathematik, Astronomie und Physik, Abt. A, Bd. 3). Berlin: Springer. (MKT I = Text, 1935; MKT II = Register, Glossar, Nachträge, Tafeln, 1935; MKT III = Ergänzungsheft, 1937).
MLC = Morgan Library Collection; Siglum der Yale Babylonian Collection, New Haven.
TMS = *Textes Mathémathiques de Suse.*
VAT = Vorderasiatische Abteilung Tontafeln, Siglum des Vorderasiatischen Museums, Berlin.

Allotte de la Fuÿe, François-Maurice, 1915. „Un cadastre de Djokha". *Revue d'Assyriologie* 12, 47–54.

Bottéro, Jean, 1995. *Textes culinaires Mésopotamiens* (Mesopotamian Civilisations 6). Winona Lake: Eisenbrauns.

Bruins, Evert M. / Marguerite Rutten, 1961. *Textes Mathémathiques de Suse* (Mémoires de la Mission Archéologique en Iran 34). Paris: Paul Geuthner.

Brunke, Hagan, 2011a. *Essen in Sumer. Metrologie, Herstellung und Terminologie nach Zeugnis der Ur III-zeitlichen Wirtschaftsurkunden.* München: Herbert Utz.

— 2011b. „Überlegungen zur babylonischen Kreisrechnung". *Zeitschrift für Assyriologie und Vorderasiatische Archäologie* 101, 113–126.

— 2012a. „Ein neuer Ur III-zeitlicher Feldplan". In: Sabine Ecklin / Catherine Mittermayer (Hg.) *Altorientalische Studien zu Ehren von Pascal Attinger* (Orbis Biblicus et Orientalis 256). Fribourg: Academic Press/Göttingen: Vandenhoeck & Ruprecht, 39–63.

— 2012b. „On Mesopotamian Measure Theory". In: Mark Geller / Klaus Geus (Hg.) *Productive Errors: Scientific Concepts in Antiquity.* Berlin: Max-Planck-Institut für Wissenschaftsgeschichte, 9–22.

— 2015. „Überlegungen zu Raumerfassung und Flächenrechnung in Mesopotamien". *eTopoi. Journal for Ancient Studies* 4, 1–17. (http://journal.topoi.org/index.php/etopoi/article/view/195/223)

— 2017. „Zur Frage von Ausdruck und Normgültigkeit mathematischer Regeln in Mesopotamien". *Cuneiform Digital Library Preprints* 11, 18.12.2017. (http://cdli.ucla.edu/?q=cuneiform-digital-library-preprints)

Clay, Albert T., 1923. *Epic Hymns, Omens and Other Texts* (Babylonian Records in the Library of J. Pierpont Morgan 4). New Haven: Yale University Press.

Damerow, Peter, 2001. „Kannten die Babylonier den Satz von Pythagoras?“. In: Jens Høyrup / Peter Damerow. *Changing Views on Ancient Near Eastern Mathematics* (Berliner Beiträge zum vorderen Orient 19). Berlin: Dietrich Reimer, 219–310.

Deimel, Anton, 1909. „Studien zu CT I, III, V, VII, IX und X“. *Zeitschrift für Assyriologie und Vorderasiatische Archäologie* 22, 17–53.

Delaporte, Louis, 1911. „Document Mathémathique de l'époque des Rois d'Our“. *Revue d'Assyriologie* 8, 131–133.

Dunham, Sally, 1986. „Sumerian Words for Foundation“. *Revue d'Assyriologie* 80, 31–64.

Frank, Carl, 1928. *Straßburger Keilschrifttexte in sumerischer und babylonischer Sprache*. Berlin/Leipzig: Walter de Gruyter & Co.

Friberg, Jöran, 1987–90. „Mathematik“. In: Dietz-Otto Edzard (Hg.) *Reallexikon der Assyriologie und Vorderasiatischen Archäologie* 7. Berlin / New York: De Gruyter.

— 2007. *A Remarkable Collection of Babylonian Mathematical Texts* (Manuscripts in the Schøyen Collection: Cuneiform Texts I). New York: Springer.

Hilprecht, Hermann Vollrat, 1906. *Mathematical, Metrological and Chronological Tablets from the Temple Library of Nippur* (The Babylonian Expedition of the University of Pennsylvania 20.1). Philadelphia: Department of Archaeology, University of Pennsylvania.

Høyrup, Jens, 1990. „Algebra and Naive Geometry. An Investigation of Some Basic Aspects of Old Babylonian Mathematical Thought I“. *Altorientalische Forschungen* 17, 27–69.

— 2002. *Lengths, Widths, Surfaces. A Portrait of Old Babylonian Algebra and its Kin*. New York / Berlin / Heidelberg: Springer.

— 2010. *L'Algèbre au temps de Babylone. Quand les mathématiques s'écrivaient sur de l'argile*. Paris: Vuibert, Adapt-SNES éditions.

Kilmer, Anne D., 1960. „Two New Lists of Key Numbers for Mathematical Operations“. *Orientalia Nova Series* 29, 273–308.

Leemans, Wilhelmus F., 1951. „Un texte vieux-bab ylonien concernant des cercles concentriques“. *Compte Rendu de la Rencontre Assyriologique Internationale* 2, 31–35.

Legrain, Léon, 1922. *The University Museum Publications of the Babylonian Section. Bd. 13: Historical Fragments*. Philadelphia: The University Museum.

Liverani, Mario, 1990. „The Shape of Neo-Sumerian Fields“. *Bulletin on Sumerian Agriculture* 5, 147–186.

Maekawa, Kazuya, 1992. Rezension zu Liverani, 1990. *Acta Sumerologica* 14, 407–423.

Manin, Yuri I., 2010. *A Course in Mathematical Logic for Mathematicians* (Graduate Texts in Mathematics 53). New York: Springer. (2. Auflage).

Nemet-Nejat, Karen R., 1993. *Cuneiform Mathematical Texts as a Reflection of Everyday Life in Mesopotamia* (American Oriental Series 75). New Haven: American Oriental Society.

Neugebauer, Otto, 1969. *Vorlesungen über Geschichte der antiken mathematischen Wissenschaften; Erster Band: Vorgriechische Mathematik*. Berlin / Heidelberg / New York: Springer.

Neugebauer, Otto, / Abraham J. Sachs, 1945. *Mathematical Cuneiform Texts* (American Oriental Series 29). New Haven: American Oriental Society and American Schools of Oriental Research.

Nissen, Hans J. / Peter Damerow / Robert K. Englund, 1991. *Frühe Schrift und Techniken der Wirtschaftsverwaltung im alten Vorderen Orient. Informationsspeicherung und -verarbeitung vor 5000 Jahren*. Hildesheim: Franzbecker / Berlin: Max-Planck-Institut für Bildungsforschung. 2. Auflage.

Proust, Christine, 2007. *Tablettes mathématiques de Nippur* (Varia Anatolica 18). Paris: De Boccard Edition-Diffusion.

Quillien, Jacques, 2003. „Deux cadastres de l'époque d'Ur III". *Revue d'histoire des mathématiques* 9, 9–31.

Ritter, Jim, 2004. "Reading Strasbourg 368: A Thrice-Told Tale". In: Karine Chemla (ed.) *History of Science, History of Text* (Boston Studies in the Philosophy of Science 238). Dordrecht: Springer, 177–200.

Robson, Eleanor, 1999. *Mesopotamian Mathematics, 2100–1600 BC. Technical Constants in Bureaucracy and Education* (Oxford Editions of Cuneiform Texts 14). Oxford: Clarendon Press.

— 2008. *Mathematics in Ancient Iraq*. Princeton: Princeton University Press.

Sallaberger, Walther, 1999. „*Ur III-Zeit*". In: Pascal Attinger / Markus Wäfler (Hg.) *Mesopotamien. Akkade-Zeit und Ur III-Zeit* (Orbis Biblicus et Orientalis 160/3). Freiburg, Schweiz: Universitätsverlag/Göttingen: Vandenhoeck & Ruprecht, 121–414.

Sigrist, Marcel / David I. Owen / Gordon D.Young, 1984. *The John Frederick Lewis Collection, Part II* (Materiali per il vocabolario neosumerico 13). Roma: Multigrafica Editrice.

Thureau-Dangin, François, 1936a. „L'équation du deuxième degré dans la mathématique babylonienne". *Revue d'Assyriologie* 33, 27–48.

— 1936b. „Textes mathématiques babyloniens". *Revue d'Assyriologie* 33, 65–84.

— 1938. *Textes Mathématiques Babyloniens*. Leiden: E. J. Brill.

Vogel, Kurt, 1959. *Vorgriechische Mathematik II. Die Mathematik der Babylonier* (Mathematische Studienhefte für den mathematischen Unterricht an höheren Schulen 2). Hannover: Hermann Schroedel / Paderborn: Ferdinand Schöningh.

Hethitische Landschenkungsurkunden: Normative Ausgestaltung und praktische Geltung königlicher Schenkungsverfügungen

Daliah Bawanypeck

Volkert Haas in memoriam
1936–2019

Abstract ... 107
1 Die hethitischen Rechtstexte ... 108
1.1 Vorbemerkungen ... 108
1.2 Die hethitische Rechtssammlung ... 110
1.3 Die hethitischen Landschenkungsurkunden ... 117
2 Die normative Ausgestaltung der Landschenkungsurkunden ... 118
2.1 Das äußere Erscheinungsbild der Tafeln ... 118
2.2 Das Formular ... 119
2.2.1 Einleitungsformel ... 120
2.2.2 Schenkungsformel und Schenkungsgegenstand ... 121
2.2.3 Vindikationsklausel ... 123
2.2.4 Veränderungsverbot ... 123
2.2.5 Ort der Urkundenausfertigung, Schreiber und Zeugen ... 124
3 Die praktische Geltung der königlichen Schenkungsverfügungen ... 124
4 Normativität und Dauerhaftigkeit ... 128
5 Fazit ... 133
Abkürzungs- und Literaturverzeichnis ... 134

Abstract

Das Projekt „Die Normativität formaler Ordnungen und Prozeduren in der Antike – Mathematische und rechtliche Regelsysteme im Vergleich“ basiert auf der Annahme, dass Systeme von Rechtsnormen und mathematische Regelsysteme formale Ordnungen sind, die hinsichtlich Aufbau und Anwendung von Meta-Normen geprägt sind, innere Kohärenz besitzen und auf Problemlösungen zielen. Hethitische Landschenkungsurkunden bilden ein Korpus von Rechtstexten, das ein hohes Maß an normativer Ausgestaltung aufweist, die sich sowohl in der Formelhaftigkeit des Formulars als auch in der äußeren Gestalt der Tontafeln zeigt. Im Folgenden wird die Rechtspraxis der Landschenkungen betrachtet und sondiert, ob sich Anhaltspunkte bieten für einen Zusammenhang zwischen der Normativität der Urkunden und dem Wunsch der hethitischen Herrscher, ihren Schenkungsverfügungen (und damit verbundenen politischen Intentionen) dauerhafte Geltung zu verleihen.

1. Die hethitischen Rechtstexte

Der folgende Beitrag befasst sich mit der normativen Ausgestaltung und praktischen Geltung hethitischer Rechtstexte. Als Quellenkorpus wurden die Landschenkungsurkunden hethitischer Könige aus der Zeit des älteren Hethiterreiches ausgewählt, da sie sowohl durch ihren Aufbau und Inhalt als auch aufgrund der hervorragenden Textedition von Christel Rüster und Gernot Wilhelm[1] einen guten Zugang zum Untersuchungsthema gewähren.

1.1 Vorbemerkungen

Das hethitische Reich existierte vom 17. Jahrhundert bis gegen 1180 v. Chr.[2] auf dem Gebiet der heutigen Türkei. Ab der Mitte des 14. Jahrhunderts war es eine Großmacht, deren Herrschaftsbereich sich auch auf weite Teile Syriens erstreckte. Die Hethiter nannten ihr Reich KUR ^{URU}*Ḫatti* „Hatti-Land", ein Name, der sich auf die Hattier, eine bereits vor den Hethitern in Zentralanatolien ansässige Population, bezieht. Ihre Sprache nannten sie *nešili* „nesisch" nach der altanatolischen Stadt Neša/Kaneš, dem heutigen Kültepe. Unsere Begriffe „Hethiter" und „hethitisch" sind auf Martin Luthers Übertragung des hebräischen Ethnikons Ḫittîm aus dem Alten Testament zurückzuführen, das eigentlich die Einwohner der in Nordsyrien gelegenen späthethitischen (luwischen) Kleinstaaten des 1. Jahrtausends v. Chr. bezeichnet.[3]

Die Schriftzeugnisse der Hethiter sind durch zwei verschiedene Schriftsysteme überliefert: Die hethitische Keilschrift, die ab dem 16. Jahrhundert überwiegend auf Tontafeln tradiert ist und auch zur Aufzeichnung weiterer Sprachen genutzt wurde, sowie eine anatolische Hieroglyphenschrift, deren Ursprung vermutlich auf die Wende vom 3. zum 2. Jahrtausend zurückgeht[4] und die ausschließlich die luwische Sprache wiedergibt. Sie ist ab dem 14. Jahrhundert auf Stein- und Felsinschriften sowie auch auf Siegeln bzw. Siegelabdrücken belegt und existierte – anders als die hethitische Keilschrift – nach dem Untergang des hethitischen Reiches in den späthethitischen Kleinstaaten weiter. Ein Großteil der Keilschriftfunde, etwa 30.000 Tontafeln und -fragmente, kommt aus den Archiven der hethitischen Hauptstadt Ḫattuša (Boğazköy, heutzutage Boğazkale), die ungefähr 150 km östlich von Ankara liegt. Neben hethitischen Texten enthalten die Keilschriftarchive auch Niederschriften in Akkadisch, Sumerisch, Luwisch, Hurritisch, Palaisch und Hattisch.

Die Keilschrift wurde im 16. Jahrhundert als Mittel der Machtausübung unter dem hethitischen Herrscher Ḫattusili I., der Schreiber aus Nordsyrien/Obermesopotamien verpflichtete, in Anatolien eingeführt. Anfänglich war der Anwendungsbereich der nur in Akkadisch geschriebenen Schrift auf diplomatische

---

[1] Rüster / Wilhelm, 2012; siehe dazu auch den Rezensionsartikel von Beckman, 2015.

[2] Im Folgenden beziehen sich alle Daten ohne weitere Angabe auf die vorchristliche Zeit. Die Jahreszahlen sind nur als annähernde Werte zu verstehen und folgen der in der Hethitologie gebräuchlichen kurzen Chronologie, nach der die Eroberung Babylons durch Muršili I. im Jahr 1531 stattfand.

[3] Cancik, 2002.

[4] Dazu grundlegend Waal, 2012.

Zwecke und sehr wenige interne Angelegenheiten begrenzt.[5] Im ausgehenden 15. Jahrhundert ist ein Anwachsen der schreiberischen Aktivitäten zu verzeichnen, das wohl mit der Herrschaft Telipinus verbunden werden kann.[6] Spätestens ab dieser Zeit wurden Texte, die sich mit internen Angelegenheiten des hethitischen Staates befassen, auch auf Hethitisch überliefert. Unter Tutḫaliya I./II. (gegen 1420) kam das Akkadische für derartige Texte gänzlich außer Gebrauch.

Die hethitischen Textzeugnisse werden drei Sprachstufen zugewiesen: Althethitisch (ca. 1600–1500), Mittelhethitisch (bis Šuppiluliuma I., ca. 1350) und Junghethitisch (bis zum Untergang des Großreiches gegen 1180).

Anders als in Mesopotamien sind in den hethitischen Archiven keine rein mathematischen Texte anzutreffen. Es gibt jedoch eine Reihe von buchhalterischen Verwaltungstexten, in erster Linie Listen mit Bestandsaufnahmen von Personen, Ortschaften und Feldern (CTH 230–239) sowie Inventare (CTH 240–246[7], 503–504[8]) und Empfangsbescheinigungen (CTH 247). Sie wurden ganz überwiegend in der hethitischen Hauptstadt gefunden, hinzu kommen einige Texte aus Maşat, Ugarit, Emar und Tell Afis sowie vereinzelte Texte aus Ortaköy, Kayalıpinar und Oymaağaç. Die Gesamtzahl ist außergewöhnlich gering: Boris Alexandrov, der einen kurzen Überblick über die Buchhaltungstexte aus Ḫattuša bietet, geht davon aus, dass sie nur 3% der dort gefundenen Texte ausmachen.[9] Listen von Feldern und Kataster (CTH 239) dienten möglicherweise als Register für die Zuteilung von Saatgut oder die Bestimmung von steuerrelevanten Felderträgen.[10] Der topographische Text KBo 62.5 (CTH 230), der markante landschaftliche Merkmale in der Umgebung der Stadt Šaššūna beschreibt, könnte das Gebiet zum Zwecke von Steuererhebungen oder für eine Landschenkung näher bestimmt haben.[11] Inventare sind häufig nach Materialien (Metalle, Textilien etc.) bzw. Verpackungen und ihren Inhalten geordnet, wobei es sich um Rohstoffe oder bereits verarbeitete Produkte handeln kann. Durch Angaben zu Herkunft und Menge der Ware, Empfänger, Ort und Art der Aufbewahrung sowie den Verwendungszweck gewähren sie Einblicke in den Ablauf von Warenverwaltungsprozessen.[12]

Die Listen aus Ḫattuša sind vorwiegend in die junghethitische Zeit zu datieren und stammen – sofern ihre Fundorte bekannt sind – aus den Magazinräumen des Haupttheiligtums Tempel 1, dem vermutlichen Zentrum der ökonomischen

---

[5] Einen Überblick über die Situation bietet van den Hout, 2009b, besonders 87–94; siehe auch van den Hout, 2009a, 28–33.

[6] Dazu detailliert van den Hout, 2012a, 76–80.

[7] Košak, 1982.

[8] Zur Zuordnung von CTH 503 und 504 zu dieser Gruppe siehe Waal, 2015, 246 mit Anmerkung 734.

[9] Alexandrov, 2016, 3. Zu den hier interessierenden Fundorten der administrativen Texte (Magazinräume des Tempels 1, „Haus am Hang", Archive auf der Königsburg Büyükkale) siehe die Synopse von Waal, 2015, 4–8; dazu beispielsweise auch van den Hout, 2006, 84–87.

[10] Van den Hout, 2006, 84.

[11] Lorenz / Rieken, 2007, 485.

[12] Siegelová, 1986.

Verwaltung sowie aus dem „Haus am Hang“.[13] In der Großreichszeit gab es im Haus am Hang ein Skriptorium[14], das funktionell mit den Magazinräumen des Tempel 1 verbunden war.[15] Im südwestlichen Teil des Tempelkomplexes befand sich das É.GIŠ.KIN.TI (wörtlich „Haus der Handwerker“), wo in der späten Großreichszeit ebenfalls ein Skriptorium untergebracht war.[16] Vereinzelte ältere Verwaltungslisten wurden an anderen Stellen gefunden.

Die Inventare und Empfangsbestätigungen aus Ḫattuša stammen aus der junghethitischen Zeit und kommen überwiegend aus den Archivräumen der Königsburg Büyükkale sowie aus dem Bereich des Tempels 1. Zudem ist es wahrscheinlich, dass etliche Fragmente von Inventartexten, deren Fundorte nicht bekannt sind, aus dem Haus am Hang kommen.[17] Auf Büyükkale ist eine Häufung von Inventaren in Gebäude D, dem „Siegeldepot“, zu beobachten, wo auch etliche Landschenkungsurkunden und gesiegelte Tonbullen gefunden wurden.[18]

Da die buchhalterischen Keilschrifttafeln in der Regel keine Kolophone enthalten, in denen der Schreiber genannt wird[19], und Holztafeln, auf denen die alltägliche Buchhaltung vermutlich mit Tinte in anatolischer Hieroglyphenschrift aufgezeichnet wurde[20], nicht erhalten sind, wissen wir kaum etwas über die Ausbildung und Organisation der Verwaltungsschreiber.

1.2 Die hethitische Rechtssammlung

Im Hethiterreich gingen die Menschen davon aus, dass ihr Wohlergehen und das Gedeihen des Landes in erster Linie von der Gunst der Götter gegenüber König und Königshaus sowie der Einhaltung der göttlichen Ordnung abhängen würden.[21] Verstöße gegen diese Ordnung führten zur Erzürnung der Götter, die versöhnt werden mussten, um das Ungleichgewicht wieder ins Lot zu bringen. Sofern rechtliche Verstöße die göttliche Ordnung störten, konnten Strafen zur Aussöhnung beitragen. Unter den „tausend Göttern des Hatti-Landes[22]“ ist der Son-

---

[13] Sämtliche Angaben zu Fundorten und Datierungen der in diesem Beitrag aufgeführten Texte sind Silvin Košaks online-Datenbank *Konkordanz der hethitischen Keilschrifttafeln* des Hethitologie Portals Mainz entnommen: S. Košak, hethiter.net/: hetkonk (v. 1.95).

[14] Zur Definition des Begriffes und den Tätigkeiten, die dort durchgeführt wurden, siehe Torri, 2009, 209 mit Anmerkung 12.

[15] Torri, 2009, 209; dieselbe, 2010, 384.

[16] Gordin, 2010; derselbe, 2015, 13. Zum Bedeutungswechsel bei der hethitischen Verwendung des Sumerogramms É.GIŠ.KIN.TI siehe Weeden, 2011, 85–90.

[17] Torri, 2016.

[18] Die Siegelungen aus den Grabungen bis 1938 wurden von Güterbock bearbeitet und in zwei Bänden (SBo I, 1940; SBo II, 1942) vorgelegt.

[19] Zum hethitischen Kolophon siehe Waal, 2015, 139–172; zu Kolophonen auf buchhalterischen Tafeln ebenda, 173–174 und 244–249.

[20] Dazu ausführlich Waal, 2011.
Die Beurkundung von Getreidevorräten auf Holztafeln ist in § 54'a der Instruktionen des Arnuwanda I. an die Grenzpostengouverneure (CTH 261.1=Miller, 2013, Nr. 17, S. 212–237, hier 232–235.) dokumentiert. Zur Datierung dieses Belegs siehe Miller, 2011, 200 f.

[21] Vgl. van den Hout, 1998, 1; Bawanypeck, 2005, 12.

[22] So lautet die Bezeichnung, die etliche Keilschrifttexte für das hethitische Pantheon verwenden.

nengott des Himmels – als der, der alles sieht – derjenige, der für Recht und Gesetz sorgt.[23] Nach hethitischer Sicht wird der König vom obersten Gott, dem Wettergott, zur Herrschaft über das Land eingesetzt, das in göttlichem Eigentum steht. Dafür genießt er den Schutz der Götter und erhält seine Legitimation gegenüber der Bevölkerung.[24] Als Verwalter des hethitischen Staates ist der König für das gedeihliche Leben im Land verantwortlich und verfügt neben politischer, militärischer und religiöser Macht auch über juristische Autorität.[25] Als oberster Richter[26] untersteht er lediglich den Göttern, denen gegenüber er die Wahrung der göttlichen Ordnung durch rechtliche Mittel – also gerechte Rechtsetzung und Rechtsprechung – zu verantworten hat.[27]

Die Hauptquelle für unsere Kenntnisse des hethitischen Rechts bildet eine Rechtssammlung, die üblicherweise als „Hethitische Gesetze" (HG) bezeichnet wird.[28] Es handelt sich um eine Zusammenstellung von zweihundert Paragraphen, aufgeteilt in zwei Serien, die jeweils nach den Anfangsworten ihrer ersten rechtlichen Regelung benannt sind: Serie A „Wenn ein Mann"[29] (CTH 291, §§ 1–100) fängt mit Tötungsdelikten und Körperverletzungen an, Serie B „Wenn ein Weinstock"[30] (CTH 292, §§ 101–200) beginnt mit Regelungen zum Schutz landwirtschaftlicher Güter und enthält auch Vorschriften zu Löhnen, Preisen und Tarifen.[31]

Die Sammlung liegt in zahlreichen Keilschriftkopien vor, die in hethitischer Sprache verfasst sind. Serie A ist auf 27 Textvertretern überliefert, Serie B auf 37.[32] Die meisten Tafeln sind in die junghethitische Zeit zu datieren, einige zeigen spätjunghethitischen Duktus. Daneben sind alt- und mittelhethitische Exem-

---

[23] Dies ergibt sich aus CTH 372 § 1–8, einer hethitischen Hymne an den Sonnengott, die auch babylonische Motive enthält, siehe Singer, 2002, 30 f. (eine englische Übersetzung der Hymne findet sich ebendort, 36–40); vgl. auch Haas, 1994, 141.

[24] IBoT 1.30 Vs. 1–8, eine Übersetzung der Passage bietet Haas, 1994, 189 f.; siehe auch Beckman, 1995, 530.

[25] Ähnlich Beckman, 1995, 532 f.

[26] Güterbock, 1997 (1954), 229; Hoffner, 1997, 4; derselbe, 2006, 93 f.

[27] Dies zeigt sich auch in dem königlichen Titel [d]UTU-*ŠI* „meine Sonne" (üblicherweise mit „Majestät" übersetzt), der sich auf den Sonnengott als Richter bezieht, vgl. Hoffner, 1995, 563.

[28] Bei Verweisen auf diese Rechtssammlung wird im Folgenden auf die Edition von Hoffner, 1997 Bezug genommen.

[29] Der nicht erhaltene Beginn der Serie A ist durch den Kolophon KBo 6.6 iv 1 überliefert.

[30] Der Anfang von Serie B ist durch den Kolophon auf der Rückseite der Tafel KBo 6.13 gesichert.

[31] Hoffner, 1997, 13–15 gewährt einen tabellarischen Überblick über die thematische Anordnung der Paragraphen. Dort finden sich auch einige kurze Bemerkungen zur Gliederungssystematik der hethitischen Gesetze. Haase, 2004, 49 charakterisiert die Systematik bezüglich der Zusammenstellung der Tatbestände, der sozialen Abstufungen (Stellung von Personen) und Rechtsfolgen als „Prinzip der Anordnung nach abnehmender Bewertung". Mit den Gliederungsprinzipien des Codex Ur-Namma befasst sich der Beitrag von Hans Neumann in diesem Band.

[32] Vgl. die Konkordanz bei Hoffner, 1997, 160–164; siehe auch die Abfragen zu CTH 291 und 292 (http://www.hethport.uni-wuerzburg.de/hetkonk/hetkonk_abfrage.php; Zugriff am 26.07.2020) bei S. Košak, hethiter.net/: hetkonk (v. 1.994).

plare vorhanden. Die Rechtssammlung wurde während der gesamten Existenzzeit des Hethiterreiches überliefert, niedergeschrieben und in der Hauptstadt Ḫattuša aufbewahrt. Sofern die Fundorte bekannt sind, stammen die Tafeln überwiegend aus den Magazinräumen des Tempels 1. Hinzu kommen einige Tafeln von der Königsburg Büyükkale, insbesondere dem Archivgebäude A.

Die Abfassung der Rechtssammlung lässt sich in mindestens drei Phasen einteilen.[33] Einige Paragraphen weisen explizit auf Unterschiede zwischen alter und neuer Rechtspraxis hin. Die alten Regelungen sind durch das Adverb *karū* „früher" gekennzeichnet, das auf die mündlich übermittelte zentralanatolische Rechtstradition vor dem 17./16. Jahrhundert verweist. Diese Regelungen werden den neuen Vorschriften, die ab dem Einsetzen der hethitischen Schriftüberlieferung im 16. Jahrhundert aufgezeichnet wurden[34], mit der Wendung *kinun=a* „aber jetzt" gegenübergestellt. Die Reformen betreffen in der Regel das Strafmaß (Ersatz körperlicher Bestrafungen durch Geldstrafen, Minderung der Geldbeträge[35]). In §§ 9, 25 HG wird ein nicht namentlich genannter König als Urheber dieser Reformen angeführt. Der Kolophon KBo 6.6 iv 1–2 weist die zweite Tafel der Serie A „Wenn ein Mann" als die Rechtssammlung des Vaters der Majestät aus, wobei nicht sicher ist, um welchen althethitischen Herrscher es sich handelt. Möglicherweise ist die älteste geschriebene Version in die Zeit des Telipinu (etwa 1510–1490) zu datieren.[36] Die nächste Redaktionsphase lässt sich an kleineren Änderungen zwischen den alt- und junghethitischen Kopien erkennen. Die erste Serie wird zudem durch den junghethitischen Paralleltext KBo 6.4 modifiziert.[37]

Die Paragraphen verfügen über einen regelhaften Stil. Sie sind fast alle in kasuistischer Form abgefasst[38] und in formalisierte Konditionalsätze mit Protasis (hier Tatbestand) und Apodosis (Rechtsfolge) eingekleidet. Beide sind im Präsens formuliert, wobei die Apodosis mit „wird" bzw. „soll" zu übersetzen ist[39],

---

[33] Hoffner, 1997, 5–7; Güterbock, 1997 (1954), 231. Ausführliche chronologische Erläuterungen zu den Textzeugen bietet Hoffner, 1997, 229–264. Mit der diachronen Entwicklung einiger Regelungen der hethitischen Rechtssammlung befasst sich Jauß, 2015.

[34] Der Zeitpunkt ergibt sich daraus, dass Paragraphen mit solchen Reformen bereits auf den althethitischen Textvertretern anzutreffen sind.

[35] Einen Überblick über die Herabsetzungen der Strafen bietet Hoffner, 1997, Tabelle 1, S. 6. Die Sanktionsprinzipien der hethitischen Rechtssammlung werden ausführlich von Christiansen, 2015 erörtert.

[36] Vgl. Güterbock, 1997 (1954), 231; Hoffner in Roth, 1997, 214; Hoffner, 1997, 229 f.; zu dieser Thematik auch van den Hout, 2012a, 78. Eine frühere Datierung nehmen z.B. Singer 2001, 289 f. und Archi 2010, 42 f. an, die die Verschriftung Ḫattušili I. zuweisen möchten.

[37] Siehe dazu die jeweiligen Passagen im Kommentar bei Hoffner, 1997, 165–191. Jauß, 2015, 202 geht davon aus, dass die hethitische Rechtssammlung durch den Paralleltext eine umfassende Überarbeitung erhielt.

[38] Zur Syntax der Rechtssammlung siehe Hoffner, 1997, 11–13. Die Syntax des Codex Ur-Namma behandelt Hans Neumann in diesem Band.

[39] Hoffner / Melchert, 2008, 420: „By far the most common type of conditional clause in Hittite is the simple future (open or fulfillable) condition, attested especially in the laws, in omen texts, in instructions, and in treaties".

z.B. im Paralleltext § V (KBo 6.4 i 14–15): „If anyone blinds a free man in a quarrel, he shall pay 40 shekels of silver“.[40] Wenn die Regelungen zu Löhnen, Preisen und Tarifen konditional ausgedrückt sind, bezieht sich der Bedingungssatz auf das Kauf- oder Mietobjekt bzw. die Arbeitsleistung, der folgende Hauptsatz auf den zu zahlenden Betrag, wie das Beispiel aus § 152 HG zeigt: „If anyone rents a horse, a mule or an ass, he shall pay one shekel of silver for one month“.[41]

Mit der konditionalen Form benutzt die hethitische Rechtssammlung dieselbe Satzstruktur wie die mesopotamischen Codizes. In der Protasis entspricht die hethitische Konjunktion *takku* „wenn“ dem sumerischen tukumbi bzw. dem akkadischen *šumma*. Wenn eine untergeordnete Voraussetzung vorliegt, die den Tatbestand eingrenzt oder präzisiert, wird anstelle von *takku* die hethitische Konjunktion *mān* „wenn“ verwendet, z.B. im Paralleltext § VII (KBo 6.4 i 18–19): „If (*takku*) anyone knocks a free man’s tooth – if (*mān*) he knocks out 2 or 3 teeth – he shall pay 12 shekels of silver“.[42]

In Mesopotamien treten prozedural strukturierte Konditionalsätze nicht nur in paradigmatischen Fallsammlungen („*procedural texts*“) mit rechtlichem Inhalt auf, sondern auch in medizinisch-diagnostischen und divinatorischen Kompendien. Der gemeinsame kasuistische Aufbau weist darauf hin, dass diese Wissenstexte einer gemeinsamen Kategorie angehören, für die Jim Ritter den Begriff „*rational practice texts*“ eingeführt hat.[43] Gemäß Hans Neumann sind diese Texte in mesopotamischer Vorstellung durch eine „Gesetzmäßigkeit des Weltgefüges“ verbunden, die durch Kausalität charakterisiert ist.[44] In hethitischen Texten sind derartig formalisierte Konditionalsätze außerhalb der Gesetze ebenfalls in medizinischen[45] und divinatorischen[46] Kompendien anzutreffen, wobei die Beispiele aus Abfassungen in mesopotamischer Tradition stammen.

Der rechtliche Charakter der hethitischen Rechtssammlung ist unklar.[47] Die Regelungen sind auf Tontafeln überliefert – eine Stele, die auf eine öffentliche Aufstellung hindeuten könnte, gibt es nicht. Anders als die mesopotamischen Codizes (Codex Ur-Namma, Codex Lipit-Eštar, Codex Ešnunna sowie der Codex Ḫammurapi) ist die hethitische Rechtssammlung weder mit Prolog noch

---

[40] Übersetzt gemäß Hoffner, 1997, 21.
[41] Hoffner, 1997, 124.
[42] Hoffner, 1997, 22.
[43] Ritter, 2004; derselbe, 2010; sowie in seinem Beitrag in diesem Band, S. 8.
[44] Neumann, 2008, 38 mit Anmerkung 7; siehe auch seinen Beitrag in diesem Band, S. 66. Fincke, 2006–2007 sieht die Verbindung in einer zugrunde liegenden Rechtsverbindlichkeit, da Omina und diagnostische Texte göttliche Gesetze der Divination seien.
[45] Beispielsweise in KUB 44.63+KUB 8.83 iii 8'–21'. Eine Übersetzung bietet Klinger, 2010, 179–181.
[46] Zum Beispiel in KBo 13.34, einer Sammlung von Geburtsomina. Der Text wurde von Riemschneider, 1970, 26–39 bearbeitet.
[47] Güterbock, 1997 (1954), 231; dazu kürzlich auch Jauß, 2015, 183 mit Literatur in Anmerkung 1. Zum kontrovers diskutierten Gesetzescharakter altorientalischer Rechtssammlungen siehe z.B. Hans Neumann in diesem Band, S. 63 f. sowie Neumann, 2004, 72 f. mit Anmerkung 6 f.

Epilog[48] versehen und enthält daher keinen ausdrücklichen Hinweis darauf, dass der Herrscher von göttlicher Seite beauftragt wurde, Recht und Gerechtigkeit im Land zu etablieren. Da der König aber für die Gewährleistung der göttlichen Ordnung verantwortlich war (s.o. S. 110 f.), gehörte die Festsetzung von Recht und Gerechtigkeit implizit zu den Aufgaben, die ihm die Götter übertragen hatten. Die lange Überlieferungszeit, das Vorhandensein zahlreicher Textvertreter und die unterschiedlichen Redaktionsphasen deuten darauf hin, dass die Rechtssammlung im Rahmen der Schreiberausbildung tradiert wurde. Dies schließt jedoch keineswegs aus, dass es sich bei dem Inhalt der Regelungen um die Wiedergabe geltenden Rechts handelte. Der Wortlaut des Kolophons KBo 6.6 iv 1–2 („Zweite Tafel. Vollständig. ‚Wenn ein Mann.‘ (Das) des Vaters der Majestät.“) verweist wahrscheinlich darauf, dass der Vater des aktuellen Herrschers – wohl als dessen Vorgänger – die Niederschrift veranlasst oder genehmigt hatte. Auch die in §§ 9, 25 HG anzutreffende Zuschreibung eines Königs als Urheber rechtlicher Reformen spricht dafür, dass die Rechtssammlung nicht nur als Erzeugnis der Gelehrsamkeit gebildeter Schreiber anzusehen ist. Auf die tatsächliche Anwendung der rechtlichen Regelungen deutet auch die Gegenüberstellung früherer und geltender Rechtspraxis hin. Zudem ist in § 55 HG ein Rechtsfall geschildert, der von einem namentlich nicht genannten „Vater des Königs“ entschieden wurde (dazu ausführlicher auf S. 126 f.).

Die hethitische Rechtssammlung enthält vielfach Vorschriften, die Zahlenwerte betreffen oder sich auf normierte Werte beziehen. Hierzu zählen Gewichte, Qualitäten, Preise und Maße. Es gibt Wert- bzw. Äquivalentangaben in Silberschekeln für Waren (Stoffe, Öle, domestizierte Tiere und deren Produkte), aber auch Aussagen über den Wert ausgebildeter Handwerker. Weitere Zahlenwerte beziehen sich auf Löhne von Ärzten sowie auf monatliche Mieten, die für menschliche und tierische Arbeitskraft zu leisten sind (wie Erntearbeiter/-innen, Pflugrinder, Pferde, Maultiere und Esel). Auch Straf- oder Schadensersatzzahlungen für Totschlag, Körperverletzungen und Diebstahl werden in Silberschekeln angegeben.[49]

Bestimmungen zur Regulierung von Preisen und der Festsetzung von Maßen und Gewichten finden sich auch in CTH 269, einem königlichen Erlass über soziale und wirtschaftliche Reformen.[50] Der fragmentarisch erhaltene Text ist wohl in der althethitischen oder frühen mittelhethitischen Zeit verfasst worden.[51] §§ 3'–4' listen frühere Preise für verschiedene Waren (Textilien, Schafe, Lederschuhe, Wein und Bier) auf und stellen sie den neuen gegenüber. Die Äquivalente sind jeweils in Silberschekeln angegeben. Die nur schlecht erhaltenen §§ 5'–6' betreffen Regelungen zu Maßen und Gewichten, die wohl während der Regierungszeit des nicht namentlich genannten Vaters des Königs festgesetzt wurden. Die spätere Erwähnung von „Bestechungen“ und „armen Menschen“

---

[48] Zu den Prologen und Epilogen der altorientalischen Rechtssammlungen siehe Neumann, 2008, 38 f.; Pfeifer, 2012, 20 f.

[49] Vgl. Hoffner, 1997, Tabellen 2–4, S. 7–11.

[50] Dazu zuletzt Miller, 2013, Nr. 5, S. 122–125.

[51] Miller, 2013, 122.

deutet darauf hin, dass die Reformen in den Kontext der Wiederherstellung sozialer Gerechtigkeit zu stellen sind.[52]

Die Verknüpfung von rechtlichen Regelungen und Zahlenwerten bezeugt, dass sich die mathematische und metrologische Ausbildung bei den Hethitern nicht auf Schreiber beschränkte, die im Bereich der Warenverwaltung eingesetzt wurden. Der junge Paralleltext KBo 6.4 wurde von Ḫanikkuili, dem Sohn des NU.^{GIŠ}[KIRI$_6$], Enkel des Oberschreibers Ziti geschrieben.[53] Dieser Name lässt darauf schließen, dass die Rechtssammlung von Schreibern aufgezeichnet wurde, die für Traditionstexte zuständig waren,[54] denn aus drei weiteren Kolophonen[55] geht hervor, dass er auch mit Themen aus dem kultisch-religiösen Bereich betraut war. Er fertigte Kopien von Ritualen an, die den Expertinnen Anniwiyani und Maštigga zugeschrieben wurden und erstellte anlässlich der Thronfolge des Tuthaliya IV. eine neue Version des Inthronisationsrituals für Tutḫaliya I/II. Dass sich seine editorische Tätigkeit nicht auf kultisch-religiöse Texte beschränkte, belegt die Tafel KBo 6.4, die eine Überarbeitung der vorherigen Versionen der Rechtssammlung enthält.[56]

Auffällig ist, dass gerade die rechtlichen Regelungen, die Zahlenwerte betreffen, diachronen Änderungen unterworfen sind.[57] In den Bestimmungen, in denen der Herrscher frühere körperliche Strafen in Geldstrafen umwandeln lässt oder neue Normen zur Regulierung wirtschaftlicher Angelegenheiten mittels mathematischer bzw. metrologischer Richtwerte festsetzt, könnte die Mathematik den Zweck haben, Gerechtigkeit[58] oder soziale Ordnung zu garantieren.

Folgende Beispiele belegen die Milderung archaischer Strafen, die vermutlich die zentralanatolische Rechtspraxis vor der althethitischen Zeit widerspiegelten, wobei körperliche Züchtigung bis hin zum Tod durch Geldstrafe ersetzt werden konnte:

§§ 91, 92 HG[59] betreffen den Diebstahl von Bienen. Früher wurde der Dieb Bienenstichen, die auch seinen Tod verursachen konnten, ausgesetzt.[60] Jetzt (d.h. zum Zeitpunkt der schriftlichen Überlieferung im 16. Jahrhundert) erhält er eine Geldstrafe, die je nach der Schwere des Vergehens – Entwendung mehrerer Schwärme, eines Schwarms, eines leeren Bienenstocks – zwischen sechs und drei Silberschekeln liegt.

---

[52] Vgl. auch Miller, 2013, 123.

[53] Zu dieser Schreiberfamilie siehe kürzlich Gordin, 2015, 179–185.

[54] Guido Pfeifer geht in seinem Beitrag im vorliegenden Band auf die mesopotamische Schreiberausbildung und das Entstehen der Rechtssammlungen in diesem Kontext ein (S. 48); dazu auch Neumann, 2004, 74 f. mit Anmerkung 12 f.

[55] VBoT 24 iv 38 (CTH 393); KBo 12.105 iv 6' (CTH 404); KBo 10.34 iv 16 (CTH 700).

[56] Vgl. Jauß, 2015, 202.

[57] Hoffner, 1997, 5–7 bespricht einige Modifikationen und mögliche Gründe für die Reformen.

[58] Grundlegend zum Konzept der Gerechtigkeit im Alten Orient siehe Pfeifer, 2012. Zur Festsetzung von Tarifen und Zinssätzen als Ausdruck sozialer Gerechtigkeit siehe ebenda, 26 f.

[59] Englische Übersetzung in Hoffner, 1997, 90 f.

[60] Dazu zuletzt Christiansen, 2015, 44 f.

§ 121 HG[61] ist zu entnehmen, dass der Dieb eines Pfluges früher mittels Pflug und Ochsen zu Tode gebracht wurde (vgl. § 166 HG[62]). Jetzt genügt eine Geldstrafe, die sich auch nach dem sozialen Status des Diebes richtet: für den Sklaven sind nur drei Schekel zu entrichten, während der Freie sechs Schekel zu zahlen hat.

In einigen Regelungen wird die Höhe von Geld- und Sachstrafen um bis zu 50% herabgesetzt.[63] Da die reduzierten Geldstrafen nicht dem reinen Wert des Schadens entsprechen, sondern diesen erheblich übersteigen, bleibt der Strafcharakter deutlich erhalten. Es handelt sich daher nicht um eine Verschiebung vom Hauptzweck Strafe zu reiner Kompensation des Geschädigten.

So mindert sich gemäß § 57 HG[64] beim Diebstahl eines Bullen die Strafe um die Hälfte: statt 30 Rindern sind nur noch 15 Rinder (je fünf zweijährige und einjährige Tiere sowie fünf frisch entwöhnte Kälber) zu leisten. Nach den Preisangaben in § 178 HG[65] beträgt der Wert eines Bullen zehn Schekel, einer Kuh sieben Schekel, eines einjährigen Rindes fünf Schekel und eines entwöhnten Kalbes vier Schekel.

Anscheinend stand dem Palast bei der Zahlung von Geldstrafen manchmal ein eigener Anteil zu. Die Minderung der Strafe um diesen Anteil könnte auf die Herstellung von „Gerechtigkeit", im Sinne von „Sozialverträglichkeit", durch Verzicht des Königs auf diese Zahlungen hinweisen:

In § 9 HG[66] wird die für Körperverletzung zu zahlende Strafe um 50% von sechs auf drei Schekel gemindert. Die Hälfte der Summe ging ursprünglich an die geschädigte Partei, die andere Hälfte war an den König zu zahlen. Im Rahmen der Reform bleibt der Anteil, den der Geschädigte erhält, gleich. Der König verzichtet auf seinen Anteil, was zu der Minderung um die Hälfte führt. Ein solcher Verzicht des Palastes ist auch in § 25 HG[67] explizit erwähnt. Unklar ist, ob sich der Verzicht des Palastes stillschweigend auf alle mit Geldstrafe zu ahndenden Fälle bezieht, bei denen dem Palast ursprünglich die Hälfte der Zahlung zustand, oder ob es sich bei §§ 9, 25 um Ausnahmetatbestände handelt. Eine vergleichbare Regelung, die ebenfalls in die althethitische Zeit zu datieren ist, findet sich im Telipinu-Erlass (CTH 19), der sowohl in Hethitisch als auch in Akkadisch (nur fragmentarisch erhalten) überliefert ist.[68] Dort heißt es in Rs. iv 27/19'–29/21': Und die Angelegenheit des Blutes ist folgendermaßen: „Wer eine Bluttat begeht, (dem geschieht), was des Blutes Herr sagt. Wenn er sagt: ‚Er soll sterben!', dann soll er sterben. Wenn er aber sagt: ‚Er soll Ersatz leisten, dann soll er Ersatz leisten.' Dem König aber (soll) er dabei nichts (leisten)."[69] Telipi-

[61] Hoffner, 1997, 110 f.
[62] Hoffner, 1997, 133 f., 203; dazu auch Christiansen, 2015, 42.
[63] Die betreffenden Regelungen und den jeweiligen Prozentsatz der Minderungen hat Hoffner, 1997 in Tabelle 1, S. 6 aufgeführt.
[64] Hoffner, 1997, 68 f.
[65] Hoffner, 1997, 142.
[66] Hoffner, 1997, 22 f.
[67] Hoffner, 1997, 33 f.
[68] Bearbeitet von Inge Hoffmann, 1984.
[69] Übersetzung nach Hoffmann, 1984, 53.

nus Erlass enthält eine ganze Anzahl politischer und rechtlicher Reformen. Neben der berühmten Thronfolgeregelung (Vs. ii 36–39) geht es um die Bestrafung von Gewaltdelikten gegenüber der königlichen Familie (Vs. ii 40–73) und die Einführung administrativer und steuerlicher Neuerungen (Rs. iii 1–54, der Kontext ist schlecht erhalten). Die vierte Kolumne bietet juristische Anweisungen, wie z.B. bei Bluttat und Zauberei zu verfahren ist (vgl. z.B. die zitierte Passage). Anders als in der hethitischen Rechtssammlung sind diese nicht in normativem Stil verfasst.

KBo 6.4, die junghethitische Parallelversion der Rechtssammlung, enthält in einigen Regelungen zur Körperverletzung Modifikationen hinsichtlich der Sanktionshöhe. Diese beziehen sich auf das vorsätzliche bzw. fahrlässige Handeln des Täters oder nehmen die Schwere der Tatfolge in den Blick.[70] So wird gemäß § V[71] die fahrlässige Verletzung, die zur Erblindung eines freien Mannes führt, mit der Zahlung von 20 Silberschekeln geahndet, während die absichtliche Verletzung im Kampf eine Zahlung von 40 Schekeln bedingt. Gemäß § VI[72] wird dasselbe Prinzip auch auf die Verletzung von Sklaven angewendet, wobei der halbierte Betrag – 10 bzw. 20 Schekel – auf dem sozialen Status des Verletzten beruht. Die Schwere der Körperverletzung spielt in §§ X, XI[73] eine Rolle. Die Körperverletzung an Arm bzw. Bein eines Freien wird mit 10 Schekeln geahndet, führt das Delikt zu fortdauernder Behinderung, sind 20 Schekel zu leisten; für entsprechende Verletzungen von Sklaven ist wiederum jeweils die Hälfte zu zahlen. Die stärkere Sanktionierung von Vorsatztaten und Taten, die zu bleibenden Schäden führten, könnte darauf gründen, dass durch die Reform eine Bestrafung im Einklang mit der sozialen Ordnung erzielt werden sollte. In Betracht kommt aber auch, dass in der Parallelversion die Tatbestände differenzierter ausformuliert wurden, so dass – vorher nicht explizit niedergeschriebene – Varianten auftreten.

1.3 Die hethitischen Landschenkungsurkunden

Hethitische Landschenkungsurkunden (LSU) sind gesiegelte Tontafeln, auf denen königliche Schenkungen von Grundeigentum (landwirtschaftliche Flächen einschließlich Bauten, Personal und Vieh) an hohe Funktionäre oder auch Institutionen verzeichnet sind. Diese Rechtsurkunden haben den Zweck „den Besitz des vom König verliehenen Grund und Bodens unter Rechtsschutz zu stellen".[74]

Bislang sind 91 hethitische Landschenkungsurkunden bekannt.[75] Nur zwei von ihnen wurden außerhalb von Ḫattuša – in Inandik (LSU 1) und dem weit ent-

[70] Dazu kürzlich auch Jauß, 2015, 198 f.
[71] Hoffner, 1997, 21.
[72] Hoffner, 1997, 22.
[73] Hoffner, 1997, 25, 26.
[74] Riemschneider, 1958, 328. Zum Terminus „Landschenkungsurkunde" siehe Rüster / Wilhelm, 2012, 35. Da die Urkunden Nr. 1, 3 und 28 keine LSU in engerem Sinne sind, stellt Beckman, 2015, 258 auf folgende Gemeinsamkeit ab: „… that each matter is decided by or undertaken by the king and that real estate almost always plays some role in the business".
[75] Vgl. Rüster / Wilhelm, 2012, Konkordanz Nr. 1, S. 25–27. Im Folgenden werden die Landschenkungsurkunden nach den dort vergebenen Nummern bezeichnet. Abgesehen von den Landschenkungsurkunden sind in Ḫattuša lediglich Fragmente von acht weiteren

fernten Tarsus (LSU 21) – gefunden. Die Landschenkungsurkunden aus Ḫattuša wurden in verschiedenen Archiven aufbewahrt: 23 stammen aus dem Bereich der Königsburg Büyükkale (davon 7 aus Gebäude D, dem „Siegeldepot"[76]), 11 oder 12 kommen aus dem Gebiet des Tempels 1 und seiner Magazinräume, weitere 10 wurden im Bereich von Tempel 8 in der Oberstadt entdeckt. Mit 28 Urkunden bildet das Archiv des Westbaus des Nişantepe den Hauptfundort der Tafeln, die entweder aus Raum 3 oder aus dem Schuttgeröll des Hangschnitts kommen. Ursprünglich wurden sie im darüber liegenden Stockwerk aufbewahrt und sind während des zerstörenden Brandes nach unten gestürzt. Die Landschenkungsurkunden wurden im Westbau – als einzige Tontafeln – zusammen mit über 3000 gesiegelten Tonbullen hethitischer Herrscher und Funktionäre gefunden.[77]

Der Gebrauch von Landschenkungsurkunden ist nur in der Vorgroßreichszeit belegt. Sie treten etwa an der Wende vom 16. zum 15. Jahrhundert erstmals auf und bleiben bis ins 14. Jahrhundert gebräuchlich. Die ältesten Exemplare stammen aus der Regierungszeit des Telipinu (1510–1490), eine wurde eventuell kurz davor – vielleicht unter seinem Vater Ammuna – verfasst.[78] Die jüngste bekannte Urkunde verzeichnet eine Schenkung des Königspaares Arnuwanda I. (etwa 1400–1375) und Ašmunikkal an die Frau Kuwatalla (LSU 91), die als Ritualexpertin aus der Textgruppe CTH 760 gut bekannt ist. Landschenkungen bleiben – wie sich aus großreichszeitlichen Texten ergibt – zwar in der Folgezeit weiterhin üblich, junghethitische Urkunden sind jedoch nicht gefunden worden.

2. Die normative Ausgestaltung der Landschenkungsurkunden

Die hethitischen Landschenkungsurkunden zeichnen sich durch eine stark ausgeprägte Normativität aus, die sich sowohl an äußeren Faktoren als auch an ihrem Formular festmachen lässt. Hinzu kommen textinterne Standardisierungen wie z.B. die Einhaltung fester Reihenfolgen bei Aufzählungen.

2.1 Das äußere Erscheinungsbild der Tafeln

Ihr auffällig normiertes Erscheinungsbild weist die Texte aus Ḫattuša, Inandik und Tarsus auf den ersten Blick als Landschenkungsurkunden aus. Die einkolumnigen Tafeln sind auf der Vorderseite stark nach außen gewölbt, in der Mitte befindet sich ein Siegelabdruck, der durch Ritzlinien vom Text getrennt ist.[79] Im Inneren der Tafel waren – heute nicht mehr erhaltene – Schnüre fächerförmig eingebettet, die unten an einem durch Ritzlinien eingefassten Schnurloch zusammentrafen und dort nach außen traten. An diesen Schnüren waren höchstwahrscheinlich Tonbullen mit Siegelungen angebracht.[80]

---

mit Stempelsiegeln versehenen Tontafeln gefunden worden, darunter zwei Staatsverträge; dazu ausführlich Balza, 2012.

[76] Vgl. S. 110 mit Anmerkung 18.

[77] Bawanypeck, 2006, 109 f.

[78] Rüster / Wilhelm, 2012, 35, 51.

[79] Siehe z.B. Neve, 1993, S. 33 Abb. 83 und S. 60, Abb. 163.

[80] Zur Siegelpraxis hethitischer Tontafeln aus Ḫattuša, Ras Šamra/Ugarit und Meskene/Emar siehe Herbordt, 2005, 26–32; insbesondere zur Siegelung der Landschenkungsurkunden ebenda, 27 f. und 38 Abb. a.

2.2 Das Formular

Die Landschenkungsurkunden folgen einem akkadischen Formular, das in Altbabylonisch verfasst ist und in das individuelle Angaben zur Agrarlandschaft und Topographie auf hethitisch eingefügt sind. Nur die jüngste Urkunde (LSU Nr. 91) ist hethitisch-sprachig konzipiert, wobei die traditionellen juristischen Elemente des Urkundenformulars weiterhin in Akkadisch geschrieben sind.[81] Spätestens ab dem ausgehenden 15. Jahrhundert wurden auch andere Texte, die sich mit internen Angelegenheiten des hethitischen Staates befassen, in Hethitisch überliefert (siehe oben S. 108 f.).

Von den 91 Landschenkungsurkunden sind 15 komplett erhalten.[82] Sie bezeugen, dass das Formular dieser Textgattung fünf obligatorische Elemente umfasst, die stets in derselben Reihenfolge auftreten: Einleitungsformel (EF), Schenkungsformel (SF), Vindikationsklausel (VK), Veränderungsverbot (VV) sowie die Nennung von Ausstellungsort, Schreiber und Zeugen (OSZ). Die Einleitungsformel beginnt entweder auf dem oberen Tafelrand oder auf der ersten Zeile der Vorderseite. Alle Siegelungen befinden sich auf der gewölbten Mitte der Vorderseite.

Die restlichen 76 Landschenkungsurkunden sind mehr oder weniger vollständig. Den besser erhaltenen Stücken lässt sich klar entnehmen, dass auch auf ihnen die Reihenfolge der fünf Elemente des Urkundenformulars gewahrt ist und der Siegelabdruck sich an der zu erwartenden Stelle befindet. Dies stützt die Annahme, dass die Anwendung des stark normierten Formulars auf allen hethitischen Landschenkungsurkunden zu erwarten ist. Die Größe der Tafeln hängt von der Schilderung des Schenkungsgegenstandes ab, da die Beschreibung der zu übertragenden landwirtschaftliche Flächen einschließlich Bauten, Personal und Vieh vom Umfang der Schenkung bedingt wird.

Die nachstehende Tabelle gibt einen Überblick über das Vorhandensein der Formularbestandteile und Siegelungen auf den Urkunden. Die Angabe „✓" zeigt an, dass zumindest ein Teil des jeweiligen Elements des Urkundenformulars erhalten ist.

LSU Nr.	EF	SF	VK	VV	OSZ	Siegel
1, 5, 7, 11, 12, 22, 26, 28, 29, 30, 40, 41, 46, 47, 91	✓	✓	✓	✓	✓	✓
42	✓	✓	✓	ø	✓	✓
9	✓	✓	✓	ø	ø	✓
44	✓	✓	ø	✓	✓	ø
21	✓	✓	ø	ø	ø	✓
23, 48, 59	✓	✓	ø	ø	✓	ø
67, 81	✓	✓	ø	ø	ø	ø

[81] Die Sprache der Landschenkungsurkunden wird bei Rüster / Wilhelm, 2012, 72–73 detailliert behandelt.

[82] LSU 1, 5, 7, 11, 12, 22, 26, 28, 29, 30, 40, 41, 46, 47, 91.

64	✓	∅	∅	∅	✓	∅
3, 4, 6, 14, 31, 34	∅	✓	✓	✓	✓	✓
13, 18, 62	∅	✓	✓	✓	✓	∅
39	∅	✓	✓	✓	∅	✓
8, 50, 51, 58, 84	∅	✓	✓	✓	∅	∅
52	∅	✓	✓	∅	∅	∅
60	∅	✓	∅	✓	✓	∅
71	∅	✓	∅	∅	✓	∅
10, 15, 16, 24, 32, 33, 35, 53, 54, 76, 77, 78, 83	∅	✓	∅	∅	∅	✓[83]
20, 25, 65, 66, 68, 69, 70, 72, 73, 74, 75, 79, 80, 82, 85, 86, 87	∅	✓	∅	∅	∅	∅
17	∅	∅	✓	✓	✓	✓
55, 56	∅	∅	✓	✓	∅	∅
57	∅	∅	✓	∅	∅	∅
19, 36, 37, 43, 63	∅	∅	∅	✓	✓	∅
88	∅	∅	∅	✓	∅	∅
2, 38, 45, 61	∅	∅	∅	∅	✓	∅
27, 49, 89, 90	∅	∅	∅	∅	∅	✓

Tabelle 1: Erhaltungszustand der 91 LSU (Formular und Siegelungen).

Die einzelnen Elemente des Urkundenformulars werden im Folgenden eingehender betrachtet.

2.2.1 Einleitungsformel

Die Einleitungsformel der Landschenkungsurkunden lautet: $^{\mathrm{NA4}}$KIŠIB *tabarna* LUGAL.GAL „Siegel des Tabarna, des Großkönigs".[84] Eine Ausnahme bildet lediglich die jüngste Urkunde des Arnuwanda I. (1400–1375) und seiner Gemahlin Ašmunikkal. Beide waren auf dem oberen Tafelrand namentlich genannt, wobei der Titel Großkönig und der Name der Königin noch erhalten sind. Diese Urkunde trägt auch das gemeinsame digraphische Siegel des Königspaares.[85] Die anderen Urkunden sind mit Tabarna-Siegeln versehen, deren akkadische Inschrift folgendermaßen lautet: „Siegel des Tabarna, des Großkönigs, wer (es) vertauscht, wird sterben" bzw. „Siegel des Tabarna, des Großkönigs KN, wer sein Wort vertauscht, wird sterben".[86]

[83] Auf sechs LSU ist die Siegelung erkennbar, aber das Siegelbild zerstört.

[84] Rüster / Wilhelm, 2012, 35: „Die alt- und mittelbabylonische Verwendungsweise von = *kunukkum*/$^{\mathrm{NA4}}$KIŠIB erlaubt aber auch die Übersetzung ‚gesiegelte Urkunde des Tabarna, des Großkönigs', …".

[85] Rüster / Wilhelm, 2012, 48 (Siegel Nr. 13).

[86] Im Einzelnen zu den Siegeln und ihren Inschriften siehe den Katalog bei Rüster / Wilhelm, 2012, 41–48.

Obwohl die Einleitungsformel lediglich den königlichen Titel Tabarna enthält, lassen sich etliche Landschenkungsurkunden anhand ihrer Siegelabdrücke Königen zuweisen, die etwa zwischen 1500 und 1400 regierten. In chronologischer Reihenfolge handelt es sich um Alluwamna (LSU 26–27; Siegel 7), Ḫantili (LSU 28–35; Siegel 8), Zidanza II. (LSU 39; Siegel 9), Taḫurwaili (LSU 89; Siegel 10), Ḫuzziya II. (LSU 40–42; Siegel 11) und Muwatalli I. (LSU 46–47; Siegel 12). Von Arnuwandas direktem Vorgänger Tutḫaliya I./II. ist keine Landschenkungsurkunde erhalten.

16 Landschenkungsurkunden wurden mit anonymen Tabarna-Siegeln von sechs verschiedenen Siegelstöcken gesiegelt.[87] Nach Rüster / Wilhelm, 2012, S. 49–51 sind LSU 3–20 aus stilistischen und prosopographischen Gründen in die Regierungszeit des Telipinu zu datieren. LSU 1 aus Inandik sowie die mit demselben Siegel versehene LSU 2 stammen vermutlich aus seinen Anfangsjahren oder wurden kurz davor ausgestellt. LSU 22–24 gehören in Telipinus späte Regierungsphase oder an den Beginn der Herrschaft seines Nachfolgers Alluwamna. Theo van den Hout möchte auch diese Urkunden Telipinu zuweisen, da er davon ausgeht, dass die Namensnennung auf den Siegeln notwendig war, um die Transaktionen der Könige zu unterscheiden.[88] Jedenfalls bilden die Tafeln mit den anonymen Tabarna-Siegeln die älteste Gruppe unter den Landschenkungsurkunden.

2.2.2 Schenkungsformel und Schenkungsgegenstand

Die Schenkungsformel setzt sich aus der Beschreibung des Schenkungsgegenstands und der darauf folgenden normierten Schilderung der königlichen Schenkung, der sog. *našûm-nadānum*-Formel[89], zusammen. Letztere lautet gewöhnlich: LUGAL.GAL *išši*[90]*-ma ana* PN … ARAD-*di-šu ana* NÍG.BA-*su iddin* „Der Großkönig hat (es) genommen und dem PN …, seinem Diener, zum Geschenk gegeben.“ Wenn der König eine Schenkung an die Institution „Haus von Ḫattuša in der Stadt Šarišša“ tätigt (LSU 4, 5, 7), wird das akkadische Verb *šakanu* benutzt: LUGAL.GAL *išši-ma ana* É ^{URU}*Ḫattuša* ^{URU}*Šariššai iškun* „Der Großkönig hat (es) genommen und dem Haus von Ḫattuša in Šarišša zugewiesen.“

Der Umfang der Schenkung wird im Anschluss an die Einleitungsformel bekannt gegeben. Übertragungsgegenstand können Ländereien des Palastes oder seiner Institutionen samt dazugehörigen Anwesen inklusive Personal, zusätzlichen Arbeitskräften sowie Vieh[91] sein. Die Größe und Art des Grundbesitzes

[87] Im Katalog Siegel Nr. 1–6.

[88] Van den Hout, 2012a, 77.

[89] Nach Rüster / Wilhelm, 2012, 36 wird *našûm* im Akkadischen üblicherweise nicht in Bezug auf Immobilien verwendet. Vorliegend gibt es das hethitische Verb *šarā da-* „aufnehmen“ wieder, das in Kopplungen (hier: *našûm* … *nadānum* „aufnehmen … geben“) gerne benutzt wird.

[90] Bei LSU 12 und 26 wird stattdessen das Verb *leqûm* „nehmen“ verwendet.

[91] Vieh wird in LSU 91 im Anschluss an das Personal aufgelistet, wobei nach Gattung, Geschlecht und Alter differenziert wird. Eine Liste der aufgeführten Tiere bieten Rüster / Wilhelm, 2012, 242.

und das Zubehör werden in standardisierter Form beschrieben, die Abfolge ist verbindlich festgelegt.

Bei den Angaben zur Grundstücksfläche ist zu beachten, dass das Verhältnis des hethitischen Maß- und Gewichtssystems zum babylonischen und assyrischen System unklar ist. Einige mesopotamische Termini wurden übernommen, ohne jedoch denselben Inhalt zu haben; d.h. die Hethiter vergaben dafür eigene Werte. Außerdem gab es von der mesopotamischen Terminologie unabhängige Maßeinheiten. Inwieweit hattischer oder hurritischer Einfluss auf die hethitische Metrologie bestand, ist unklar.[92] In den Landschenkungsurkunden wird die Größe der Grundstücke mit dem hethitischen Flächenmaß *kapunu* und seiner Untereinheit IKU sowie mit Ellen (Sumerisch KÙŠ, Akkadisch ${}^{\text{GIŠ}}$*gipeššarannu*, Hethitisch *gipeššar*) angegeben. Im altbabylonischen Flächenmaßsystem ist ein IKU 3600 m^2 groß.[93] Aufgrund der größten Untereinheitensumme von 27 IKU (vgl. LSU 22 Zeile 57; LSU 4 Zeile 6) müsste ein *kapunu* mehr als 972 ha (also fast 10 km^2) umfassen, wenn man dem IKU den babylonischen Wert zugrunde legt. In LSU 7 Zeile 7 würde demnach Sommerweide im Umfang von etwa 350 km^2 (35 *kapunu*) übertragen.

Die Aufzählung der landwirtschaftlichen Liegenschaften erfolgt in einer festen Reihenfolge. An erster Stelle stehen die Felder (A.ŠÀ) und ihre jeweilige Größe. Sie können durch Angaben zu Nutzungsart, Besitzern und Lage näher spezifiziert werden.[94] Dann wird das Weideland aufgelistet (Ú.SAL und *alaleššar*), gefolgt von Gemüsegärten (${}^{\text{GIŠ}}$MÚ.SAR)[95] und Baumpflanzungen, d.h. Wald (${}^{\text{GIŠ}}$TIR[96]), Obst- (${}^{\text{GIŠ}}$KIRI$_6$) und Weingärten (${}^{\text{GIŠ}}$KIRI$_6$.GEŠTIN) sowie Dreschplätzen (KISLAḪ) mit den spezifischen Größenangaben.

Wird mit dem Grundbesitz auch das dazugehörige Personal übertragen, kann die Auflistung Einblicke in die gesellschaftliche Ordnung und das soziale Ansehen im hethitischen Staat gewähren.[97] Zunächst wird gesagt, um wessen Anwe-

[92] Van den Hout, 1987–1990, 517.

[93] Vgl. Klengel, 1975, 192 f.; van den Hout, 1987–1990, 522.

[94] Einen ausführlichen Überblick zu den Ackerflächen bietet die Tabelle bei Rüster / Wilhelm, 2012, 78–82. Die Angaben können auch detaillierte topographische Lagebeschreibungen enthalten (z.B. LSU 10: vom *ḫuwaši*-Stein … bis zum Berg …; LSU 34: … an der Straße nach …; LSU 39: … des Flusses/am Fluss …, … am Weg nach …, … vor dem Berg …, … oberhalb des Weingartens …; LSU 40: … hinter dem Dreschplatz, … links vom Weg, … am Weg rechts, an den kalten Wassern, … bei der Quelle von …). Königliche Landschenkungen sind auch auf den babylonischen Kudurru-Inschriften belegt, die grundlegend von Susanne Paulus, 2014 untersucht und ausgewertet wurden. Auch diese enthalten Lagebeschreibungen, die dazu dienen, das Land grob zu lokalisieren. Genannt werden der Fluss bzw. Kanal, an dem die Ländereien sich befinden, die Provinz, zu der das Land gehörte und die Feldflur, der gewöhnlich der Name einer Ortschaft beigefügt ist. Dazu kommen Beschreibungen der Grundstücksseiten mit Nennung der benachbarten Anwesen und Flussläufe, manche Kudurrus enthalten auch standardisierte Lageskizzen; vgl. Paulus, 2014, 82–84. Zum Formular der Kudurrus siehe ebenda, 71–78.

[95] Die Gemüsegärten werden manchmal erst nach den Baumpflanzungen aufgeführt.

[96] Zuweilen sind die Baumsorten oder die Anzahl der Bäume angegeben.

[97] Die gesellschaftliche Ordnung spiegelt sich auch in der Systematik der hethitischen Rechtssammlung, wo ebenfalls soziale Abstufungen erkennbar sind (siehe oben S. 111 mit Anmerkung 31; S. 117).

sen es sich handelt. Dann wird die Anzahl der Personen angegeben, wobei nach sozialer Wertigkeit, Geschlecht und Alter klassifiziert wird: Mann, Knabe, männlicher Säugling, Frau, Mädchen, weiblicher Säugling, alter Mann, alte Frau, Blinder, Blinde, (blinder männlicher Säugling), blinder weiblicher Säugling, Sklave und Sklavin.[98] Bei umfangreichen Aufzählungen von Grundbesitz und Personal können auch Summen gebildet werden, vgl. z.B. LSU 22 Zeile 48: „17 Anwesen. 61 Männer. Insgesamt 257 Männer, Frauen, Kinder, 177 Sklaven." Zusätzliche Arbeitskräfte werden als „einzelne (Person)" (Akkadisch *ēdēnû*) bezeichnet. Zunächst wird ihre Gesamtzahl aufgelistet, dann werden sie in der üblichen Reihenfolge klassifiziert und zudem namentlich genannt (z.B. LSU 22 Zeilen 49–56).

2.2.3 Vindikationsklausel

Mit der Vindikationsklausel wird sowohl dem Empfänger der Landschenkungsurkunde als auch seinen Nachkommen zukünftige Rechtssicherheit garantiert. Die Ausdehnung der Vindikationsformel auf Söhne und Enkel enthält das Recht zur Vererbung des durch die Urkunde verliehenen Besitzes.[99] Die standardisierte Formel lautet: *urram šēram ana* PN … *mamman lā iraggum* „In Zukunft darf (dies) dem PN niemand streitig machen" oder *urram šēram ana* PN *ana* DUMU.DUMU-*ri-šu* … *mamman lā iraggum* „In alle Zukunft soll den Söhnen und Enkeln des NN niemand (dieses) streitig machen".

Eine Ausnahme bildet LSU Nr. 3 Rs. 15', die eine frühere Landschenkung – die bereits Gegenstand zweier Prozesse war – an den Begünstigten bestätigt und erneute Klagen abweist: *urram šēram awīlum ana awīlim lā irragum* „In Zukunft darf einer gegen den anderen nicht gerichtlich klagen". Diese Urkunde wird auf S. 124–128 ausführlich behandelt.

2.2.4 Veränderungsverbot

Die Gültigkeit der in den Landschenkungsurkunden niedergelegten Transaktionen wird durch ein Veränderungsverbot bekräftigt, das mit einer tödlichen Strafandrohung versehen ist: *awāt tabarna* LUGAL.GAL *ša* AN.BAR *ša lā nadīam ša lā šebērim ša ušpaḫḫu* SAG.DU-*su inakkisū* „Das Wort des Tabarna, des Großkönigs, (ist) aus Eisen, (es ist) nicht zu verwerfen, nicht zu zerbrechen. Wer (es) verändert, dessen Kopf wird man abschlagen". Sinn der Formel ist es, die Tafel vor Fälschung oder Vernichtung zu schützen. Dieses Veränderungsverbot korrespondiert mit den akkadischen Inschriften der Tabarna-Siegel, mit denen die Landschenkungsurkunden gesiegelt werden.

---

[98] Vgl. die Tabelle zu LSU 15 bei Rüster / Wilhelm, 2012, 131–133. Auf den babylonischen Kudurrus werden zur Schenkung gehörige Personen nur ausnahmsweise aufgelistet; dazu Paulus, 2014, 90 f.

[99] Rüster / Wilhelm, 2012, 36.

2.2.5 Ort der Urkundenausfertigung, Schreiber und Zeugen

Die Landschenkungsurkunden schließen damit, dass der Schreiber angibt in welchem Ort und vor welchen Zeugen er die Urkunde ausgestellt hat: *ṭuppam anniam ina* ^{URU}ON *ana pani* $^{m}Z_1$ ... $^{m}Z_x$ ^{m}S DUB.SAR *išṭur* „Diese Tafel hat in der Stadt ON vor den Zeugen Z_1, Z_2 usw. der Schreiber S geschrieben". Die Zeugen werden namentlich und mit ihren Ämtern aufgeführt. Ein Beispiel bietet LSU 12[100] Zeilen 21–26: „Diese Tafel hat in Ḫattuša vor Ḫappuwaššu, dem Obersten der Palastbediensteten, vor Marakui, dem *uriyanni*, vor Zidanni, dem Obersten der Weinschenken, Ḫutarli, der Schreiber, geschrieben".

3. Die praktische Geltung der königlichen Schenkungsverfügungen

Einen Einblick in die Rechtspraxis der königlichen Landschenkungen gewährt LSU 3[101] aus dem Westbau-Archiv in Ḫattuša. Das Dokument ist keine Landschenkungsurkunde im eigentlichen Sinn, sondern eine Art Prozessurkunde, die eine frühere Landschenkung durch den Vater des Königs an den Vorsteher Inar bestätigt und vor zukünftigen Klagen schützen soll. LSU 3 trägt den Abdruck eines anonymen Tabarnasiegels.

Laut Vs. 2–5 hatte der Vater des Königs, der wie auch der König selbst nicht namentlich genannt ist, dem Inar Ländereien in Zitalkišwa zum Geschenk gegeben. Die Bezeichnung als Oberster (sum. GAL, wörtlich „Großer") weist Inar als hochrangigen Würdenträger aus, auch wenn der Name der ihm unterstehenden Berufsgruppe nicht erhalten ist.

Vs. 6–16 berichten von einem früheren Prozess gegen Inar, der in Ḫattuša vor dem Vater des Königs stattgefunden hatte. Eine Gruppe von Priestern und Palastbediensteten, mit denen Inar verwandtschaftlich oder geschäftlich verbunden war[102], hatten Anspruch auf Miteigentum an 30 *kapunu* des Feldes erhoben. Nach vierjähriger Prozessdauer hatte der Vater des Königs die Ansprüche der Kläger zurückgewiesen und die 30 *kapunu* Feld dem Inar erneut übertragen.

Vs. 17–27 schildern einen weiteren Prozess gegen Inar, der im fünften Jahr vor dem Großkönig in Ḫattuša stattfand. Diesmal bestritten die Kläger, dass 20 IKU hinter dem Dreschplatz liegende Feldfläche zu den 30 *kapunu* gehören würden, die der Vater des Königs dem Inar übertragen hatte. Der Großkönig wies die Ansprüche der Kläger ebenfalls zurück und übertrug die 30 *kapunu* Feld ein weiteres Mal dem Inar. Zudem verlieh er ihm das Amt des „Holztafelschreibers des Hauses von Ḫattuša" in der Stadt Šarišša.

In Vs. 28–Rs. 14' werden die verliehenen Ländereien näher spezifiziert. Die Auflistung erfolgt in der bekannten normierten Reihenfolge. Abschließend wird all dies als „Eigentum?[103] der Stadt (Ḫattuša) in Zitalkišwa" bezeichnet. Dieses

[100] Rüster / Wilhelm, 2012, 120 f.

[101] Rüster / Wilhelm, 2012, 92–97.

[102] Vgl. den Kommentar zu LÚ ḪA.LA bei Rüster / Wilhelm, 2012, 96.

[103] Rüster / Wilhelm, 2012, 95, 111 übersetzen *ešzi-* c. mit „Besitz?". Nach HW² E, 127 f. handelt es sich um ein Substantiv unbekannter Bedeutung, das irgendeine Beziehung zum König hat. In den Belegen ist es gemeinsam mit Häusern und Gut des Königs genannt. Da Inar die Ländereien zwar nutzen, nicht aber übertragen darf, wurde hier als Übersetzung von *ešzi-* der Terminus „Eigentum?" (hier der Stadt Ḫattuša) gewählt.

wurde dem Inar anscheinend als eine Art „Lehen" verliehen, an dem königliches Obereigentum fortbestand. Daher konnten die Geschäftspartner und deren Verwandte aus ihren Beziehungen zu Inar keine Ansprüche auf das Land ableiten.[104]

Durch die Ausstellung der LSU 3 bestätigt der Herrscher das Urteil seines Vaters, bekräftigt somit die Gültigkeit der früheren Transaktion und stellt diese durch ein ausdrückliches Verbot, gegen das Urteil vorzugehen, unter speziellen Schutz. Die Formulierung „In Zukunft darf einer gegen den anderen nicht gerichtlich klagen" weicht vom gängigen Wortlaut der Vindikationsklauseln ab. Die Urkunde ist sehr wahrscheinlich in die Regierungszeit des Telipinu zu datieren.[105] Demgemäß erfolgte die ursprüngliche Landschenkung durch seinen Vater, Ammuna[106], in dessen Regierungszeit dann auch der erste Prozess stattgefunden haben müsste. Der Telipinu-Erlass (siehe oben S. 116 f.) erwähnt in KBo 3.1 ii 23 einen Obersten der Mundschenke namens Inar.[107] Dieser gehörte zu einer Gruppe von hochrangigen Würdenträgern, die gegen Telipinu intrigiert hatten und dafür bestraft wurden.[108] Falls es sich um denselben Inar wie in LSU 3 handelt, müsste die Urkunde vor diesem Ereignis ausgestellt worden sein.

Im Folgenden werden einige Regelungen aus der hethitischen Rechtssammlung herangezogen, die weitere Einblicke in die Rechtspraxis der Landvergabe und damit verbundener Obligationen geben können. Selbst wenn nicht genau zu sagen ist, ob die Verschriftung der Rechtssammlung in der althethitischen Zeit tatsächlich in die Regierungszeit des Telipinu fällt[109], erfolgte sie sicherlich zu einem Zeitpunkt, der nicht stark von dem der Ausstellung der LSU 3 abweicht. Da keine Anzeichen für eine Reform der Landvergabe und damit einhergehender Regelungen erkennbar sind, können die Rechtssammlung und die Landschenkungsurkunden im Hinblick auf das damals praktizierte Recht gemeinsam betrachtet werden.

Das hethitische Land war Eigentum des Palastes, der es unter der Auflage von Dienst- und Aufgabenleistungen (*šahhan* und *luzzi-*) an andere Nutzer vergab.[110] Der auch in Landschenkungsurkunden und der hethitischen Rechtssammlung auftretende akkadische Begriff *ilku*(*m*), der eine Pflichtleistung für Landzuteilung bezeichnet, wird meist mit Hethitisch *šaḫḫan* gleichgesetzt.[111] Zusätzlich zu diesen Lehensdiensten gab es ^{GIŠ}TUKUL-Leistungen, die an den Besitz von ^{GIŠ}TUKUL-Feldern gebunden waren.[112] Feldbesitz ist auch für Tempel und Gemeinden belegt.[113]

104 Rüster / Wilhelm, 2012, 97.

105 Rüster / Wilhelm, 2012, 49 f., 94 f.; van den Hout, 2012a, 77; siehe dazu bereits S. 120 f.

106 Vgl. Klengel, 1999, 79.

107 Rüster / Wilhelm, 2012, 94 f.

108 KBo 3.1 ii 20–30; siehe Hoffmann, 1984, 30–33.

109 Siehe dazu bereits S. 112 mit Literatur in Anmerkung 36.

110 Klengel, 2006, 3; siehe auch Céntola, 2017, 196 f. mit Anmerkung 5.

111 Vgl. CHD Š/1, S. 3.

112 Dazu ausführlich Beal, 1988.

113 Klengel, 2006, 3.

Eine Vorschrift aus der Rechtssammlung befasst sich explizit mit königlichen Landschenkungen. Sie ordnet die Freistellung der Begünstigten von *šahhan-* und *luzzi-*Diensten an.

> § 47A HG[114]: If anyone holds land as a royal grant, [he shall] not [have to render] *šahhan-* and *luzzi-*services. Furthermore, the king shall provide him with food at royal expense.

§§ 40, 41 HG regeln die Sicherung von Ansprüchen, die sich aus der Übernahme von Land ergeben, für das Lehensdienste zu leisten sind. Da dazu auch *šahhan-*Dienste gehören, handelt es sich bei der Bereitstellung des Landes nicht um Landschenkungen.

> § 40 HG[115]: If a man who has a TUKUL-obligation disappears, and a man owing *ILKU-*services is assigned (in his place), the man owing *ILKU-*services shall say: „This is my TUKUL-obligation, and this (other) is my obligation for *šaḫḫan-*services." He shall secure for him a sealed deed (*anda šittariezzi*[116]) concerning the land of the man having a TUKUL-obligation, he shall both hold the TUKUL-obligation and perform the *šaḫḫan-*services. But if he refuses the TUKUL-obligation …

> § 41 HG[117]: If a man owing *ILKU-*services disappears, and a man having a TUKUL-obligation is assigned (in his place), the man having the TUKUL-obligation shall say: „This is my TUKUL-obligation, and this (other) is my obligation for *šaḫḫan-*services." He shall secure for him a sealed deed (*anda šittariezzi*) concerning the land of the man owing *šaḫḫan-*services. He shall hold the TUKUL-obligation and perform the *šaḫḫan-*services. But if he refuses (to do) the *šaḫḫan-*services …

Mit Leistungspflichten aus Landbesitz befasst sich auch § 55 HG, eine Regelung, die aufgrund ihrer narrativen Formulierung von der normativen Struktur der anderen Vorschriften in der Rechtssammlung abweicht und eine Entscheidung durch den Vater des Königs schildert.[118] Wenn man mit Hoffner davon ausgeht, dass die Rechtssammlung erstmals unter Telipinu verschriftet wurde, würde es sich – ebenso wie in LSU 3 – bei dem Vater des Königs um Ammuna handeln.[119]

---

[114] Übersetzung gemäß Hoffner, 1997, 56; althethitische Fassung in KBo 6.2 ii 43–44.

[115] Übersetzung gemäß Hoffner, 1997, 47; althethitische Fassung in KBo 6.2+KBo 19.2 ii 18–22.

[116] Hoffner, 1997, 298 gibt für *anda ši(ya)ttariya* die Bedeutung „to secure a sealed deed" an; CHD Š3, 345 übersetzt „to have (something) recorded on a sealed document". Das hethitische Verb für „siegeln" ist *šai-*, *šiye-* („to impress (with a seal), to seal", CHD Š1, 15–17), **šiyatar* bezeichnet sowohl das Siegel als auch die Siegelung („a seal", „seal impression, sealing", CHD Š3, 341 f.); hierzu auch van den Hout 2007, 340.

[117] Übersetzung gemäß Hoffner, 1997, 50; althethitische Fassung in KBo 6.2+KBo 19.2 ii 23–26.

[118] Im Zusammenhang mit dem narrativen Charakter dieser Regelung erwägt van den Hout, 2012a, 78, dass die althethitische Palastchronik (CTH 8) mit ihrer Anekdotensammlung eine frühe Form von Gesetzgebung widerspiegeln könnte.

[119] Hoffner in Roth 1997, 214. Dagegen wendet sich z.B. Singer 2001, 89. Er und die Autoren, die er in Anmerkung 5 nennt, gehen davon aus, dass sich die Bezeichnung „Vater des Königs" (*ABI* LUGAL) in althethitischem Kontext ausschließlich auf Ḫattu-

§ 55 HG[120]: When (a delegation of) Hittites, men owing *šaḫḫan*-services, came, they did reverence to the father of the king, and said: „No one pays us a wage. They refuse us (saying): ‚You are men required to perform your jobs as a *šaḫḫan*-service!'" The Father of the king [stepped] into the assembly and instructed(?) them under his seal: „You too must perform (*šaḫḫan*-services) just like your colleagues."

§§ 40, 41 HG verlangen eine gesiegelte Urkunde zur Sicherung von Ansprüchen, die sich aus der Übernahme von Land gegen Lehensdienste ergeben. Dies lässt darauf schließen, dass bei jeglicher Vergabe von Land durch den Palast die Ausstellung solcher Urkunden gängige Praxis war. Daher ist auch bei königlichen Landschenkungen anzunehmen, dass jeweils zwei gesiegelte Urkunden ausgestellt wurden: eine Tontafel, die in den Archiven des Palastes verblieb, und ein Exemplar, das dem Begünstigten übergeben wurde.[121] Mit diesem konnte er seine Ansprüche im Prozess geltend machen.

Aus KUB 13.2 iii 31–23, einem Ausschnitt aus den Instruktionen des Arnuwanda I. für die Provinzgouverneure (*BĒL MADGALTI*, CTH 261), ergibt sich, dass neben gesiegelten Tontafeln auch gesiegelte Holztafeln zu Beweiszwecken im Prozess zugelassen waren: *mān DĪNU=ma kuiš* GIŠ.ḪUR *tuppiaz šiyan udai nu auriyaš EN-aš DĪNAM* SIG$_5$-*in ḫannau.* Das CHD übersetzt diese Passage folgendermaßen: „But if someone brings a lawcase, (namely) a wood tablet (taken) from a clay tablet (and) sealed, let the governor of a border province judge the case well".[122] Danach würde die Holztafel eine Kopie von einer Tontafel darstellen. Nach der Übersetzung von Willemijn Waal wurde entweder eine Tontafel oder eine Holztafel ausgestellt: „But if someone brings a case on a wooden tablet (or) a (clay) tablet, sealed, let border commander judge the case well."[123] Sie geht davon aus, dass im Hethiterreich zwei Schrifttraditionen nebeneinander existierten: Die auf Tontafeln überlieferte hethitische Keilschrift, die als Schrift der Herrschenden für die Zwecke des Palastes benutzt wurde, sowie die anatolische Hieroglyphenschrift, die in luwischer Sprache mit Tinte auf Holztafeln notiert wurde.[124] Die Existenz von – heute nicht mehr erhaltenen – Holztafeln ist durch ihre Erwähnung in etlichen Keilschrifttexten gesichert. Neben o.g. gesiegelten Rechtsdokumenten handelt es sich um religiöse Texte (oft aus dem luwisch-sprachigen Kizzuwatna), administrative bzw. buchhalterische Vorgänge, geschäftliche Transaktionen und private Korrespondenz.[125] Auch der Beruf des Holztafelschreibers (^{LÚ}DUB.SAR.GIŠ) ist gut belegt.[126] Für

šili I. bezieht und der politischen Legitimation seines Adoptivsohns Muršili I. diente; vgl. auch Archi 2010, 42 f.

120 Übersetzung gemäß Hoffner, 1997, 67 f.; althethitische Fassung in KBo 6.2 iii 16–20.

121 Vgl. auch Singer 2013, Spalte 7.

122 CHD Š1, 16 f.. Zu dieser Passage auch Miller, 2013, 51.

123 Waal, 2011, 27.

124 Die Argumente sind ausführlich in Waal, 2011 dargestellt. Welcher Schrifttyp und welche Sprache auf den Holztafeln Verwendung fanden, wird kontrovers diskutiert, siehe dazu auch Singer 2013, Spalte 6 mit Anmerkung 14 und die Literaturangaben bei Miller, 2013, 51.

125 Vgl. Waal, 2011, 25–28.

126 Anders van den Hout, 2010, der vermutet, dass es sich bei den $^{\text{LÚ.MEŠ}}$DUB.SAR. GIŠ um Magazinverwalter handelt und GIŠ als Abkürzung für hölzerne Kisten zur Aufbewahrung der gelagerten Güter steht.

die Textstelle über die beiden gesiegelten Dokumente, die zu Beweiszwecken verwendet werden, nimmt Waal an, dass die explizite Erwähnung des Materials wegen der Verwendung unterschiedlicher Schriften und Sprachen bedeutsam ist.[127]

Es ist davon auszugehen, dass Inar zum Beweis seines Anspruchs vom Vater des Königs eine gesiegelte Urkunde erhalten hatte, welche die Schenkung in ihren Einzelheiten dokumentierte. Diese hatte er zum Beweis seines Anspruchs im Prozess vorzulegen. Ebenso müsste er aufgrund des zweiten Prozesses ein gesiegeltes, mit LSU 3 inhaltsgleiches, Dokument erhalten haben. Offen bleibt, ob es sich um Tontafelkopien von den Urkunden handelte, die im Palast aufbewahrt wurden, oder ob ihm Holztafeln ausgehändigt wurden. Da der Großkönig dem Inar das Amt des „Holztafelschreibers des Hauses von Ḫattuša in der Stadt Šarišša" verliehen hatte, scheint der Gebrauch solcher Tafeln im Verwaltungskontext bereits in dieser frühen Periode üblich gewesen zu sein (wobei zu dieser Zeit die anatolische Hieroglyphenschrift vielleicht auch zur Wiedergabe der hethitischen Sprache benutzt wurde[128]). Möglicherweise wurden sie zeitgleich auch schon für gerichtliche Zwecke benutzt.

4. Normativität und Dauerhaftigkeit

Im Folgenden wird erörtert, ob ein Zusammenhang zwischen der starken Normierung der Landschenkungsurkunden und dem Bestreben der hethitischen Könige nach Dauerhaftigkeit ihrer Verfügungen bestehen könnte.

Um die Tafel und damit die königliche Verfügung vor Vernichtung oder Fälschung zu schützen, enthalten alle Landschenkungsurkunden die Bekräftigungsformel mit dem Veränderungsverbot: „Das Wort des Tabarna, des Großkönigs (ist) aus Eisen, (es ist) nicht zu verwerfen, nicht zu zerbrechen. Wer (es) verändert, dessen Kopf wird man abschlagen". Landschenkungsurkunden aus der Großreichszeit (etwa 1350–1180 v. Chr.) sind zwar nicht bekannt, die Formel ist aber – ebenfalls in akkadischer Sprache – auch in anderen großreichszeitlichen Texten belegt.[129] Dort fehlt jedoch der Teil mit dem Eisen. So heißt es im Staatsvertrag des Muwattalli II. mit Talmi-Šarrumma von Aleppo: „Das Wort des Tabarna, des Großkönigs, (es ist) nicht zu verwerfen, nicht zu zerbrechen. Wer (es) verändert wird sterben."[130] Und im Dekret des Ḫattušili III. über die Befreiung des *ḫekur* des Pirwa von Abgaben steht: „Das Wort des Tabarna Ḫattušili, des Großkönigs, (es) ist nicht zu verwerfen, nicht zu zerbrechen".[131]

Auf den Landschenkungsurkunden wird das Verbot zusätzlich durch den Abdruck eines Tabarna-Siegels in der Mitte der Urkunde verstärkt. Tabarna-Siegel sind reine Keilschriftsiegel, deren Inschriften sich auf das gesiegelte Schriftstück, also die Urkunde, beziehen: „Siegel des Tabarna, des Großkönigs, wer

[127] Waal, 2011, 27.
[128] Vgl. Waal, 2012, 310.
[129] Rüster / Wilhelm, 2012, 37.
[130] KBo 1.6 Vs. 6–7 (CTH 75).
[131] KBo 6.28 Rs. 28–29 (CTH 88).

(es) vertauscht, wird sterben“ oder „Siegel des Tabarna, des Großkönigs, wer sein Wort vertauscht, wird sterben“. Die Todesandrohung für den Fall der Abänderung des gesiegelten Dokuments stellt eine Verkürzung des Veränderungsverbots der Landschenkungsurkunden dar[132], die Bezug auf die Autorität der Tafel nimmt.[133] Auf den älteren Tabarna-Siegeln (Siegel 1–6), die vielleicht alle Telipinu zuzuweisen sind (siehe oben S. 120 f.), wird der Königsname nicht genannt.[134] Auf den Siegeln von Alluwamna bis Muwatalli I. (Siegel 7–12) wird der Name zusammen mit den Königstiteln Tabarna und LUGAL.GAL aufgeführt, die Reihenfolge kann variieren.[135] Die Verwendung von Siegeln des Tabarna-Typs gerät nach Muwatalli I. außer Gebrauch. Die jüngste bislang bekannte Landschenkungsurkunde LSU Nr. 91 enthält zwar die Bekräftigungsformel mit dem Veränderungsverbot, ist aber mit einem digraphischen Gemeinschaftssiegel von Arnuwanda I. und Ašmunikkal gesiegelt, dessen Inschrift die Genealogie des Königspaares enthält.[136] Dieses Siegel bezieht sich somit nicht auf die Tafel und ihren Inhalt. Auch auf den Abdrücken von reinen Keilschriftsiegeln, die Einzelsiegel des Arnuwanda[137] und der Ašmunikkal[138] darstellen, enthalten die Inschriften kein Veränderungsverbot. Festzustellen ist, dass es in dieser Zeit zu generellen Änderungen der Siegeldarstellungen und Legenden kommt, die dann unter Šuppiluliuma I. zur Einführung der sogenannten Aediculasiegel führen.

Gemäß der Bekräftigungsformel der Landschenkungsurkunden ist das Wort des Großkönigs aus Eisen und nicht zu zerbrechen. Durch die Anspielung auf die Härte und Beständigkeit des Metalls wird das Streben nach Dauerhaftigkeit der königlichen Verfügung ausgedrückt.

Aus Eisen (Hethitisch *ḫapalki*, Sumerisch AN.BAR) werden in Anatolien wichtige Herrschaftsgegenstände angefertigt, da dieses Haltbarkeit und besondere Qualität symbolisiert. Im historiographischen Text des anatolischen Fürsten Anitta (CTH 1) sind ein Thron und ein Szepter aus diesem Material belegt: „Als ich […] in den Kampf zog, [brachte] der Mann von Purušḫanda Geschenke zu mir, und zwar brachte er mir einen Thron aus Eisen und ein Szepter aus Eisen als Geschenk.“[139] Anitta trägt nach militärischen Erfolgen nicht mehr nur den Titel Fürst (Akkadisch *rubā'um*), sondern auch Großfürst (*rubā'um rabūm*) und bezeichnet sich im Anitta-Text erstmals als LUGAL.GAL[140] (Großkönig). Damit benutzt er einen Titel, der wenig später für die hethitischen Könige üblich wird. Die weiteren Belege für die Verwendung von Eisen kommen aus dem kultisch-religiösen Bereich: Einen Thron aus Eisen stellt sich die Göttin Kam-

[132] Bawanypeck in Herbordt / Bawanypeck / Hawkins, 2011, 65.
[133] Vgl. van den Hout, 2012a, 77–78 mit Anmerkung 22.
[134] Vgl. den Siegelkatalog in Rüster / Wilhelm, 2012, 41–44.
[135] Vgl. den Siegelkatalog in Rüster / Wilhelm, 2012, 44–48.
[136] Siegel Nr. 13 in Rüster / Wilhelm, 2012, 48.
[137] SBo I Nr. 76, S. 44, 69.
[138] SBo I Nr. 77, S. 44, 69; Herbordt / Bawanypeck / Hawkins, 2011, Kat. 3, Tafel 1 Abb. 3.1; dazu Bawanypeck, ebenda S. 66 mit Anmerkung 257, S. 109.
[139] KBo 3.22 Rs. 73–75; die Übersetzung folgt Neu, 1974, 15.
[140] KBo 3.22 Vs. 41.

rušepa in dem Ritual CTH 441 hin (KUB 12.26 ii 3) und gemäß KBo 56.107 Zeile 3, dem kleinen Fragment eines Festrituals, gibt man dem König einen Lituus aus Eisen.

Eine Tafel aus Eisen ist im Zusammenhang mit einer Landschenkung im Vertrag des Tutḫaliya IV. mit Ulmitešub (Kuruntiya) von Tarḫuntašša genannt. Dort wird demjenigen, der die Worte der Tafel ändert, die Bestrafung mit dem Tod angedroht: (KBo 50.60+KUB 40.69+KBo 4.10 Rs. 21–27)[141]

> Und was ich, Meine Majestät[142], dem Ulmitešub, König von Tarḫuntašša, gegeben habe, welche Grenze ich ihm gesetzt habe und was ich nachher ihm gegeben habe, das habe ich auf einer Tafel aus Eisen eingeritzt, und das soll in Zukunft der Nachkommenschaft des Ulmitešub keiner wegnehmen, und keiner soll (es) ihm anfechten. Der König soll es sich nicht nehmen, auch seinem Sohn soll er es (später) nicht geben, und einer anderen Nachkommenschaft soll man es nicht geben. In Zukunft sollen die Herrschaft von Tarḫuntašša nur Nachkommen des Ulmitešub innehaben. Wer aber ihm Not bereitet und ihm Land wegnimmt oder auch ein einziges Wort dieser Tafel verdreht, den (und) seine Nachkommenschaft sollen der Wettergott, König des Himmels, die Sonnengöttin von Arinna, Herrin der Länder von Ḫatti, Šarruma, Sohn des Wettergottes, Ištar (und) die 1000 Götter dieser Tafel aus dem atti-Lande völlig vernichten!

Es ist bekannt, dass hethitische Staatsverträge auf Metalltafeln niedergeschrieben werden konnten. Der Staatsvertrag („Friedensvertrag") zwischen Ḫattušili III. und Ramses II. wurde Ramses von einer hethitischen Delegation auf einer silbernen Tafel vorgelegt. Tontafelfragmente der akkadischen Fassung des Vertragstextes, die als Grundlage für den Text der Silbertafel gedient haben dürften, wurden in Boğazköy gefunden.[143] Die einzige bekannte erhaltene Metalltafel ist die Bronzetafel aus Boğazköy (Bo 86/299)[144], auf der ein weiterer Staatsvertrag des Tutḫaliya IV. mit Kuruntiya von Tarḫuntašša niedergelegt ist. Auch dieser Vertrag enthält einen Passus, mit welchem demjenigen, der (auch nur) ein einziges Wort dieser Tafel ändert, der Tod durch die Eidgötter angedroht wird (Bo 86/299 iv 15–29[145]). Das Material der Tafel findet in diesem Passus allerdings keine Erwähnung. Da auch die Tontafelkopien der sonstigen hethitischen Staatsverträge keine textinternen Verweise auf das Material der Originaltafel enthalten, könnte die Verwendung einer eisernen Tafel für den Ulmitešub-Vertrag eine auf die Ewigkeit bezogene Besonderheit dargestellt haben, die ausdrücklicher Erwähnung bedurfte.

In Bezug auf die Landschenkungsurkunden heißt das, dass sie das Rechtsgeschäft durch die Dauerhaftigkeit symbolisierende Festigkeit des königlichen Wortes schützen, das die Autorität der Tafel begründet. Hier zeigt sich ein kon-

---

[141] Übersetzung nach van den Hout, 1995, 47, 49.

[142] Wörtlich: Sonne.

[143] Vgl. Klengel, 2002, 78–83; ausführlich zu diesem Vertrag zuletzt Jauß, 2018 (zur Quellenlage insbesondere S. 24–28).

[144] Bearbeitet von Otten, 1988.

[145] Otten, 1988, 27.

zeptioneller Unterschied zu mesopotamischen Landschenkungsurkunden, die die Transaktionen durch göttlichen Beistand sichern. Bei den Kudurrus geschieht das entweder durch Schutzklauseln, die mit göttlichen Fluchandrohungen versehen sind oder durch das Göttersymbol selbst.[146] In den Landschenkungsurkunden neuassyrischer Könige wird der Wortlaut der Urkunden durch die Anrufung verschiedener Gottheiten unter Schutz gestellt.[147]

Für den Wunsch nach dauerhafter Geltung der königlichen Worte ist auch der Zeitpunkt bedeutsam, an dem die hethitischen Landschenkungsurkunden erstmalig auftreten. Die Zunahme der Schreibertätigkeiten im ausgehenden 15. Jahrhundert (vielleicht auch das Einsetzen hethitisch-sprachiger Texte) könnte einhergehen mit den „Bemühungen Telipinus, Schrift und schriftliche Dokumente in erhöhtem Maß als Verwaltungsinstrument einzusetzen und ihnen eine eigene Autorität zuzumessen".[148] Telipinus Regierung war vom Streben nach Stabilisierung der politischen Verhältnisse geprägt. Auf ihn sind eine ganze Reihe außen- und innenpolitischer Neuerungen zurückzuführen.[149] Sein Vertrag mit Išputaḫšu von Kizzuwatna (CTH 21) stellt das älteste Schriftexemplar eines internationalen Vertrages dar, das von einem hethitischen Herrscher geschlossen wurde. Die innenpolitischen Beweggründe für politische und rechtliche Reformen sind im Telipinu-Erlass[150] (CTH 19), der wie der Išputaḫšu-Vertrag in Akkadisch und Hethitisch überliefert ist, ausführlich geschildert. Seit etlichen Generationen hatte es Kämpfe um den hethitischen Thron gegeben. Auch Telipinus Vater und Brüder waren im Zuge dieser Kämpfe von hochrangigen Funktionären des Königshofs, meist Mitgliedern des erweiterten Kreises der königlichen Familie, ermordet worden. Mit der neuen Thronfolgeregelung wollte der Herrscher solche Streitigkeiten zukünftig verhindern. Zur Befriedung der politischen Verhältnisse sollten sicherlich auch die rechtlichen Regelungen (Bestrafung von Mitgliedern der Königsfamilie und hohen Würdenträgern bei Gewalttaten; Strafen für Bluttaten und Zauberei) beitragen. Die Abgabenreform, die auch die Verwaltung des Landes tangiert zu haben scheint, könnte dem Streben nach innerpolitischer Stabilität durch Schaffung sozialer Gerechtigkeit gedient haben.

Telipinu ging davon aus, mit seinem Erlass ein normatives Werk geschaffen zu haben, das „in alle Zukunft"[151], d.h. über seine Lebensspanne hinaus, gelten sollte. Zur Umsetzung seiner Ziele stützte er sich auch auf die Autorität, die der Tontafel selbst beigemessen wurde.[152] Dies wird durch seine Forderung nach deren Konsultation (CTH 19 Vs. ii 46-48) belegt: „Ferner, wer auch immer König wird und Böses gegen Bruder (oder) Schwester plant – ihr aber (seid) sein *pankuš* (beratende Versammlung[153]). Sagt ihm wahrheitsgemäß: Siehe diese Angelegenheit des Blutes aus der Tafel."

---

[146] Vgl. Paulus, 2014, 10; zum Formular der Kudurrus siehe ebenda, 71–78.

[147] SAA 12, XXI–XXXI; 1–64.

[148] Van den Hout, 2012a, 79.

[149] Vgl. van den Hout, 2012a, 76–80.

[150] Siehe dazu auch S. 116.

[151] CTH 19 Vs. ii 40 (Hoffmann, 1984, 33).

[152] Vgl. auch van den Hout, 2012a, 78.

[153] Vgl. CHD P, 91 „the totality of the king's retinue as an advisory and admonitary body".

Ab Telipinu war es bei den hethitischen Königen gängige Praxis, sich der Gunst der Großen des Reiches durch Landschenkungen zu versichern. Die Würdenträger mussten die königlichen Verfügungen auch zukünftig beachten, denn die Kontrolle über den Landbesitz ist ein Machtfaktor, den das hethitische Herrscherhaus sicherlich nicht aus der Hand geben wollte. Daher wurden die Landschenkungsurkunden als Dokumente konzipiert, die das Rechtsgeschäft durch die Autorität schützten, welche die Tafel selbst verkörperte. Das geschah explizit durch das Veränderungsverbot und die Inschriften der Tabarna-Siegel, und implizit durch das stark normierte äußere Erscheinungsbild der Tafeln[154]. Das strenge Formular der Urkunden dürfte zusätzlichen Schutz vor Fälschungen geboten haben, zudem ermöglichte die feste Reihenfolge der verschiedenen Kategorien landwirtschaftlichen Grundbesitzes eine Übersicht über die verliehenen Ländereien.

Ein weiteres Indiz für das Streben nach Dauerhaftigkeit der königlichen Verfügungen könnte die lange Archivierung von Landschenkungsurkunden im Westbau und dem sog. Siegeldepot D bieten. In beiden Gebäuden wurden sie gemeinsam mit gesiegelten Tonbullen über einen Zeitraum verwahrt, der vom 15. Jahrhundert bis zum Ende der Großreichszeit (ca. 1180) reicht.[155] Wie oben dargestellt, ist davon auszugehen, dass über jede Landschenkung zwei Urkunden ausgestellt wurden: Eine für die offiziellen Archive und eine für den jeweils Begünstigten, die dieser zu Beweiszwecken behielt. Bei den Urkunden aus der hethitischen Hauptstadt dürfte es sich um die Exemplare handeln, die staatlicherseits aufbewahrt wurden. Als Verwaltungsdokumente gehören sie zu den Texten, die nicht kopiert[156] und in der Regel nur über einen Zeitraum von 1–2 Generationen aufgehoben wurden.[157] Dass die vorgroßreichszeitlichen Landschenkungsurkunden bei der Pflege der Archive nicht ausgesondert wurden, spricht für die Bedeutung, die ihrem Inhalt hinsichtlich der Kontrolle über die Landvergabe zugemessen wurde. Solange eine Landschenkung gültig war, wurden die Dokumente aufgehoben. Möglicherweise enthielten die Urkunden zudem Informationen, welche für die Zusammenfassung zurückliegender Ereignisse (z.B. für die historischen Einleitungen der Staatsverträge[158] oder bei der Schilderung von Taten der einzelnen Herrscher) bedeutsam sein konnten.

Für die Großreichszeit sind zwar königliche Landschenkungen (z.B. CTH 224, 225), aber keine diesbezüglichen Urkunden und auch keine Tabarna-Siegel belegt. Die jüngste bekannte Landschenkungsurkunde, die aus der Regierungszeit des Arnuwanda I. stammt, unterscheidet sich hinsichtlich Sprache und Siegel von allen älteren Urkunden. Auffällig ist, dass im Westbau – wo neben 28 Landschenkungsurkunden etwa 3400 gesiegelte Tonbullen hethitischer Herrscher und

---

[154] So auch van den Hout, 2012b, 42: „… laid down on specially formatted tablets, these charters must have been a powerful tool in buying the allegiance of the nation's elite."
[155] Vgl. Bawanypeck, 2006, 109–116.
[156] Vgl. van den Hout, 2002, 864.
[157] Van den Hout, 2002, 870.
[158] Für die Konsultation von Landschenkungsurkunden bei der Erstellung von Staatsverträgen könnte das Auftreten des Veränderungsverbots in CTH 675.A (Talmi-Šarruma-Vertrag) sprechen, siehe dazu Devecchi, 2010, 5 f.

Funktionäre aufbewahrt wurden – das Aussetzen der Urkunden mit dem Auftreten neuer Siegeltypen auf den Tonbullen einhergeht.[159] Es ist möglich, dass die Bullen an Holztafeln (bzw. Dossiers mit Holztafeln) befestigt waren, die bei der Zerstörung des Westbaus durch Brand vernichtet wurden.[160] Die chronologische Abfolge der Landschenkungsurkunden und gesiegelten Tonbullen im Westbau und Siegeldepot D könnte darauf deuten, dass die Tondokumente durch gesiegelte bzw. mit Siegeln versehene Urkunden aus Holz abgelöst wurden.[161] Davon ausgehend, dass im Hethiter-zeitlichen Anatolien mit Tinte beschriftete Holztafeln (und nicht aufklappbare Holztafeln, die mit Wachs beschichtet waren) benutzt wurden, läge auch hier ein Schriftträger vor, der geeignet ist, längere Zeiträume zu überdauern.[162]

5. Fazit

Anhand der hethitischen Rechtstexte lassen sich verschiedene Möglichkeiten aufzeigen, wie durch Normativität Gültigkeit und Autorität erzeugt werden können. Die hethitische Rechtssammlung und die Landschenkungsurkunden stellen formale Ordnungen dar, die eine innere Kohärenz aufweisen (beispielsweise die Relation der Strafen in Bezug auf die Art der Delikte oder das Verhältnis von Strafe und sozialer Stellung des Geschädigten; die Verwendung einheitlicher Terminologie) und geeignet sind, konkrete Probleme zu lösen. Bei beiden besteht ein Zusammenhang zwischen der Geltung der Texte und der Autorität, die ihnen beigemessen wird. Die Methoden, mit denen Autorität generiert wird, unterscheiden sich jedoch voneinander.

Die Rechtssammlung ist auf Tontafeln aus den Archiven Ḫattušas überliefert, die sich äußerlich nicht von den anderen dort aufbewahrten Tafeln unterscheiden. Hinweise darauf, dass die Rechtsnormen – wie in Mesopotamien oder dem antiken Griechenland – auch auf steinernen Stelen niedergeschrieben waren, gibt es nicht. Daher basiert die Autorität der Rechtssammlung nicht auf äußeren Umständen wie der Gestaltung des Schriftträgers, Monumentalität oder Publizität durch öffentliche Aufstellung. Die besondere sprachliche Ausgestaltung in kasuistischer Form, eingekleidet in formalisierte Konditionalsätze mit Tatbestand und Rechtsfolge, stellt einen inneren Faktor für die Gültigkeit der Regelungen dar. Hier benutzt die hethitische Rechtssammlung dieselbe Satzstruktur wie die mesopotamischen Codizes sowie die paradigmatischen Fallsammlungen aus dem medizinisch-diagnostischen und divinatorischen Bereich, die eine gemeinsame Kategorie von Wissenstexten bilden. Die Regelungen sind (bis auf eine

---

159 Vgl. Bawanypeck, 2006, besonders 111 f.

160 Herbordt, 2005, 36–39. Zur Fundsituation siehe Herbordt in Herbordt / Bawanypeck / Hawkins, 2011, 7–10.
Die Funktion des Westbaus und die Art der Objekte, die mit den Bullen ausgestattet waren, werden kontrovers diskutiert. Gegen die These der Lagerung von Holztafeln wenden sich z.B. van den Hout, 2007, 341–343; van den Hout, 2012b; Mora 2012, die eher von einem Warenverwaltungskontext (z.B. Registrierung von Luxusgütern für Mitglieder der königlichen Familie) ausgehen.

161 Siehe auch Marazzi 2007, 467; Singer 2013, Spalte 7 geht davon aus, dass beide Gebäude als „royal (crown) land registry“ fungierten.

162 Waal, 2011, 28–30.

Ausnahme in § 55 HG) unpersönlich formuliert, was dazu dienen könnte, ihrer Geltung eine Dauerhaftigkeit zu verleihen, die von persönlicher Autorität unabhängig ist.[163] Da die hethitische Rechtssammlung – anders als die mesopotamischen Codizes – keinen Prolog und Epilog hat, enthält sie auch keinen sonstigen Hinweis auf den königlichen Gesetzgeber und seinen göttlichen Auftrag. Die Autorität, die ihr beigemessen wird, lässt sich auch daran erkennen, dass sie von der althethitischen Zeit bis zum Ende des Hethiterreiches nicht nur tradiert sondern auch aktualisiert wurde.

Die Autorität der Landschenkungsurkunden wird durch das Aussehen der Tafel und ihren formelhaften Inhalt generiert. Der Abdruck des königlichen Siegels mitten auf der Vorderseite ließ die Autorität des Königs erkennen, die durch die Tafel und ihr Aussehen verkörpert wurde. Ihre spezielle Gestaltung identifizierte die Urkunden auf den ersten Blick als königliche Verfügungen, die dem Begünstigten zukünftige Rechtssicherheit garantierten. Die Formelhaftigkeit der Sprache sollte dauerhafte Gültigkeit bedingen[164], die besonders in Zeiten politischen Umbruchs wichtig ist. Das erste Auftreten von Landschenkungsurkunden in Zeiten des Strebens nach politischer Stabilität fügt sich hier gut ein. Das Veränderungsverbot und die Inschrift des Tabarna-Siegels sind abweichend vom sonstigen Text im Präsens/Futur geschrieben, wodurch die dauerhafte Wirkung besonders betont wird. Die Autorität der Landschenkungsurkunden speist sich auch aus dem Text heraus, der auf den König verweist, dessen Wort nicht verändert werden darf, wobei auf den Symbolwert des Materials Eisen verwiesen wird. Die Verwendung des akkadischen Formulars ist wahrscheinlich nicht nur auf das hohe Alter der Landschenkungsurkunden zurückzuführen, denn von der hethitischen Rechtssammlung existiert keine akkadische Fassung. Hier dürfte auch das Prestige der akkadischen Sprache eine Rolle gespielt haben, das den Urkunden eine zusätzliche Autorität verliehen haben könnte.

Abkürzungs- und Literaturverzeichnis

CHD = *The Hittite Dictionary of the Oriental Institute of the University of Chicago* (Chicago, 1980 ff.).

CTH = *Catalogue des Textes Hittites*: Emil Laroche, fortgeführt von Silvin Košak und Gerfrid G. W. Müller; S. Košak – G.G.W. Müller – S. Görke – Ch. Steitler, hethiter.net/: Catalog (2020-01-27) (http://www.hethport.uni-wuerzburg.de/CTH).

hetkonk = Silvin Košak, *Konkordanz der hethitischen Keilschrifttafeln* = S. Košak, hethiter.net/: hetkonk (v. 1.994) (http://www.hethport.uni-wuerzburg.de/hetkonk).

HG = Hetihitische Gesetze.

HW^2 E = Friedrich, Johannes / Annelies Kammenhuber, 1988. *Hethitisches Wörterbuch* Band II: E, Heidelberg: Universitätsverlag Winter, (2. völlig neu bearbeitete Auflage).

---

[163] Vgl. dazu Markus Asper in diesem Band (S. 216).

[164] Vgl. auch den Beitrag von Katelijn Vandorpe und Valérie Wyns in diesem Band.

IBoT 1 = Bozkurt. Hatice / Muazzez I. Çiğ, 1944. *Istanbul Arkeoloji Müzelerinde Bulunan Boğazköy Tabletleri* 1, Ankara: Türk Tarih Kurumu Basımevi.
KBo = *Keilschrifttexte aus Boghazköi* (Leipzig / Berlin, 1916 ff.).
KUB = *Keilschrifturkunden aus Boghazköi* (Berlin, 1921 ff.).
LSU = Landschenkungsurkunden.
SAA 12 = Kataja, Laura / Robert M. Whiting, 1995. *Grants, Decrees and Gifts of the Neo-Assyrian Period* (State Archives of Assyria 12). Helsinki: Helsinki University Press.
SBo I = Güterbock, Hans G., 1940. *Siegel aus Boghazköy* I. *Die Königssiegel der Grabungen bis 1938* (Archiv für Orientforschung Beiheft 5). Berlin, im Selbstverlag des Herausgebers.
SBo II = Güterbock, Hans G., 1942. *Siegel aus Boghazköy* II. *Die Königssiegel von 1939 und die übrigen Hieroglyphensiegel* (Archiv für Orientforschung Beiheft 7). Berlin, im Selbstverlag des Herausgebers.

Alexandrov, Boris, 2016. „Accounting texts from Boğazköy in current Hittitological research“. *Comptabilités* [En ligne] 8, 1–14. (https://comptabilites. revues.org/2010).
Archi, Alfonso, 2010. „When did the Hittites Begin to Write in Hittite?“. In: Yoram Cohen / Amir Gilan / Jared Miller (Hg.) *Pax Hethitica: Studies on the Hittites and their Neighbours in Honour of Itamar Singer* (Studien zu den Boğazköy-Texten 51). Wiesbaden: Harrassowitz, 37–46.
Balza, Maria E., 2012. „Sealed Tablets from Ḫattuša“. In: Maria E. Balza / Mauro Giorgeri / Clelia Mora (Hg.) *Archivi, depositi, magazzini presso gli ittiti* (Studia Mediterranea 23). Genova: Italian University Press, 77–110.
Bawanypeck, Daliah, 2005. *Die Rituale der Auguren* (Texte der Hethiter 25). Heidelberg: Universitätsverlag Winter.
— 2006. „Die hethitischen Königssiegel vom Westbau des Nişantepe in Boğazköy-Ḫattuša“. In: Dirk P. Mielke / Ulf-Dietrich Schoop / Jürgen Seeher (Hg.) *Strukturierung und Datierung in der hethitischen Archäologie* (BYZAS 4) Istanbul: Ege Yayınlari, 109–123.
Beal, Richard H., 1988. „The ^{GIŠ}TUKUL-institution in Second Millennium Hatti“. *Altorientalische Forschungen* 15, 269–305.
Beckman, Gary, 1995. „Royal Ideology and State Administration in Hittite Anatolia“. In: Jack M. Sasson et al. (Hg.) *Civilizations of the Ancient Near East* I. New York: Charles Scribner's Sons, 529–554.
— 2015. Rezensionsartikel zu Christel Rüster / Gernot Wilhelm, 2012. *Zeitschrift für Assyriologie und Vorderasiatische Archäologie* 105, 258–259.
Cancik, Hubert, 2002. „Das ganze Land Ḥet – Hethiter und die luwischen Staaten in der Bibel“. In: Kunst- und Ausstellungshalle der Bundesrepublik Deutschland GmbH (Hg.) *Die Hethiter und ihr Reich*: *Das Volk der 1000 Götter* (Ausstellungskatalog). Darmstadt: Wissenschaftliche Buchgesellschaft, 30–33.
Céntola, Francisco, 2017. „Royal Justice or Realpolitik? The Diviner Zū-Baʿla and the Hittites once again“. *Antiguo Oriente* 15, 195–221.
Christiansen, Birgit, 2015. „‚Früher war er ein von Bienen Zerstochener. Jetzt aber gibt er 6 Schekel Silber‘: Sanktionen und Sanktionsprinzipien in der He-

thitischen Rechtssammlung". *Zeitschrift für Altorientalische und Biblische Rechtsgeschichte* 21, 31–101.

Devecchi, Elena, 2010. „We are all descendants of Šuppiluliuma, Great King". *Die Welt des Orients* 40, 1–27.

Fincke, Jeanette C., 2006–2007. „Omina, die göttlichen ‚Gesetze' der Divination". *Jaarbericht Ex Oriente Lux* 40, 131–147.

Gordin, Shai, 2010. „Scriptoria in Late Empire Period Ḫattusa: The Case of the É GIŠ.KIN.TI". In: Yoram Cohen / Amir Gilan / Jared Miller (Hg.) *Pax Hethitica: Studies on the Hittites and their Neighbours in Honour of Itamar Singer* (Studien zu den Boğazköy-Texten 51). Wiesbaden: Harrassowitz, 158–177.

— 2015. *Hittite Scribal Circles: Scholarly Tradition and Writing Habits* (Studien zu den Boğazköy-Texten 59). Wiesbaden: Harrassowitz.

Güterbock, Hans G., 1997 (1954). „Authority and Law in the Hittite Kingdom". *Assyriological Studies* 26, 229–232. [Reprint aus: *Journal of the American Society Supplement* 17 (1954) 16–24].

Haas, Volkert, 1994. *Geschichte der Hethitischen Religion* (Handbuch der Orientalistik, Abteilung I Band 15). Leiden / New York / Köln: Brill.

Haase, Richard, 2004. „Zum Ordnungsdenken der hethitischen Juristen". *Welt des Orients* 34, 40–49.

Herbordt, Suzanne, 2005. *Die Prinzen- und Beamtensiegel der hethitischen Großreichszeit auf Tonbullen aus dem Nişantepe-Archiv in Hattusa* (Boğazköy–Ḫattuša 19). Mainz: Philipp von Zabern.

Herbordt, Suzanne / Daliah Bawanypeck / J. David Hawkins, 2011. *Die Siegel der Großkönige und Großköniginnen auf Tonbullen aus dem Nişantepe-Archiv in Hattusa* (Boğazköy–Ḫattuša 23). Mainz: Philipp von Zabern.

Hoffmann, Inge, 1984. *Der Erlass Telipinus* (Texte der Hethiter 11). Heidelberg: Universitätsverlag Winter.

Hoffner, Harry A., 1995. „Legal and Social Institutions of Hittite Anatolia". In: Jack M. Sasson et al. (Hg.) *Civilizations of the Ancient Near East* I. New York: Charles Scribner's Sons, 555–569.

— 1997. *The Laws of the Hittites. A Critical Edition* (Documenta et Monumenta Orientis Antiqui 23). Leiden / New York / Köln: Brill.

— 2006. „Prozeß (Process). B. Bei den Hethitern". In: Michael P. Streck (Hg.) *Reallexikon der Assyriologie und Vorderasiatischen Archäologie* 11. Berlin / New York: De Gruyter, 2006–2008, 91–98.

Hoffner, Harry A. / H. Craig Mechert, 2008. *A Grammar of the Hittite Language* I (Languages oft he Ancient Near East 1) Winona Lake: Eisenbrauns.

Jauß, Steffen M., 2015. „Kasuistik – Systematik – Reflexion über Recht. Eine diachrone Betrachtung der Rechtstechnik in den Hethitischen Rechtssätzen". *Zeitschrift für Altorientalische und Biblische Rechtsgeschichte* 21, 185–206.

— 2018. „Zur Konzeption des Vertrages zwischen Pharao Ramses II. und Großkönig Ḫattušili III. (1259 v. Chr.)". *Zeitschrift der Savigny-Stiftung für Rechtsgeschichte* 153, 21–75.

Klengel, Horst, 1975. „Zur ökonomischen Funktion der hethitischen Tempel". *Studi Miceni ed Egeo-Anatolici* 16, 181–200.

— 1999. *Geschichte des Hethitischen Reiches* (Handbuch der Orientalistik, Abteilung I Band 34). Leiden / Boston / Köln: Brill.

— 2002. *Hattuschili und Ramses. Hethiter und Ägypter – ihr langer Weg zum Frieden*. Mainz: Philipp von Zabern.

— 2006. „Studien zur hethitischen Wirtschaft, 2: Feld- und Gartenbau". *Altorientalische Forschungen* 33, 3–31.

Klinger, Jörg, 2010. „II. Texte der Hethiter". In: Bernd Janowski / Daniel Schwemer (Hg.) *Texte zur Heilkunde* (Texte aus der Umwelt des Alten Testaments Neue Folge 5). Gütersloh: Gütersloher Verlagshaus, 177–187.

Košak, Silvin, 1982. *Hittite Inventory Texts (CTH 241-250)* (Texte der Hethiter 10). Heidelberg: Universitätsverlag Carl Winter.

Lorenz, Jürgen / Elisabeth Rieken, 2007. „Auf dem Weg der Stadt *Šāššūna* …". In: Detlev Groddek / Marina Zorman (Hg.) *Tabularia Hethaeorum. Hethitologische Beiträge. Silvin Košak zum 65. Geburtstag* (Dresdner Beiträge zur Hethitologie 25). Wiesbaden: Harrassowitz, 467–486.

Marazzi, Massimiliano, 2007. „Sigilli, Sigillature e Tavolette di Legno: Alcune Considerazioni Alla Luce di Nuovi Dati". In: Metin Alparslan / Meltem M. Doğan Alparslan / Hasan Peker (Hg.) *Vita. Festschrift in Honor of Belkıs Dinçol and Ali Dinçol*. Istanbul: Ege Yayınları, 465–474.

Miller, Jared L., 2011. „Die hethitischen Dienstanweisungen. Zwischen normativer Vorschrift und Traditionsliteratur". In: Manfred Hutter / Sylvia Hutter–Braunsar (Hg.) *Hethitische Literatur: Überlieferungsprozesse, Textstrukturen, Ausdrucksformen und Nachwirken* (Alter Orient und Altes Testament 391). Münster: Ugarit-Verlag, 193–205.

— 2013. *Royal Hittite* Instructions *and Related Administrative Texts* (Writings from the Ancient World 31). Atlanta: Society of Biblical Literature.

Mora, Clelia, 2012. „The enigma of the ‚Westbau' depot in Ḫattuša's Upper City", in: Maria E. Balza / Mauro Giorgeri / Clelia Mora (Hg.) *Archivi, depositi, magazzini presso gli ittiti* (Studia Mediterranea 23). Genova: Italian University Press, 59–76.

Neu, Erich, 1974. *Der Anitta-Text* (Studien zu den Boğazköy-Texten 18). Wiesbaden: Harrassowitz.

Neumann, Hans, 2004. „Prozeßführung im Edubba'a". *Zeitschrift für Altorientalische und Biblische Rechtsgeschichte* 10, 71–92.

— 2008. „Göttliche Gerechtigkeit und menschliche Verantwortung im alten Mesopotamien". In: Heinz Barta / Robert Rollinger / Martin Lang (Hg.) *Recht und Religion. Menschliche und göttliche Gerechtigkeitsvorstellungen in den antiken Welten*. Wiesbaden: Harrassowitz, 37–48.

Neve, Peter, 1993. *Ḫattuša – Stadt der Götter und Tempel*. Mainz: Philipp von Zabern.

Otten, Heinrich, 1988. *Die Bronzetafel aus Boğazköy. Ein Staatsvertrag Tutḫalijas IV.* (Studien zu den Boğazköy-Texten Beiheft 1). Wiesbaden: Harrassowitz.

Paulus, Susanne, 2014. *Die babylonischen Kudurru-Inschriften von der kassitischen bis zur frühneubabylonischen Zeit* (Alter Orient und Altes Testament 51). Münster: Ugarit-Verlag.

Pfeifer, Guido, 2012. „Gerechtigkeit aus der Perspektive der altorientalischen Rechtsgeschichte." In: Markus Witte (Hg.) *Gerechtigkeit* (Themen der Theologie 6). Tübingen: Mohr Siebeck, 15–35.

Riemschneider, Kaspar K., 1958. „Die hethitischen Landschenkungsurkunden". *Mitteilungen des Instituts für Orientforschung* 6, 321–381.

— 1970. *Babylonische Geburtsomina in hethitischer Übersetzung* (Studien zu den Boğazkoy-Texten 9). Wiesbaden: Harrassowitz.

Ritter, Jim, 2004. „Reading Strasbourg 368: A Thrice-Told Tale." In: Karine Chemla (Hg.) *History of Science, History of Text* (Boston Studies in the Philosophy of Science, 238). Dordrecht: Springer Verlag, 177–200.

— 2010. „Translating Rational-Practice Texts." In: Annette Imhausen / Tanja Pommerening (Hg.) *Writings of Early Scholars in the Ancient Near East, Egypt, Rome, and Greece: Translating Ancient Scientific Texts*. Berlin: De Gruyter, 349–383.

Roth, Martha T. 1997. *Law Collections from Mesopotamia and Asia Minor* (Writings from the Ancient World 6). Atlanta, Georgia: Scholar's Press.

Rüster, Christel / Gernot Wilhelm, 2012. *Landschenkungsurkunden hethitischer Könige* (Studien zu den Boğazköy-Texten Beiheft 4). Wiesbaden: Harrassowitz.

Siegelová, Jana, 1986. *Hethitische Verwaltungspraxis im Lichte der Wirtschafts- und Inventardokumente* (Band 1–3). Prag: Národni Muzeum v Praze.

Singer, Itamar, 2001. Rezensionsartikel zu Harry A. Hoffner, 1997. *Journal of Near Eastern Studies 60*, 286–289.

— 2002. *Hittite Prayers* (Writings from the Ancient World 11). Atlanta, Georgia: Society of Biblical Literature.

— 2013. „The ‚Royal Land Registry' in Hattuša and its Seal Impressions" (Rezensionsartikel zu Suzanne Herbordt / Daliah Bawanypeck / J. David Hawkins, 2011). *Bibliotheca Orientalis* 70, Spalte 5–16.

Torri, Giulia, 2009. „The Old Hittite Textual Tradition in the ‚Haus am Hang'". In: Franca Pecchioli Daddi / Giulia Torri / Carlo Corti (Hg.) *Central-North Anatolia in the Hittite Period – New Perspectives in Light of Recent Research. Acts of the International Conference held at the University of Florence (7-9 February 2007)* (Studia Asiana 5). Rom: Herder, 207–222.

— 2010. „The Scribal School of the Lower City of Hattuša and the Beginning of the Career of Anuwanza, Court Dignitary and Lord of Nerik". In: Maria G. Biga / Mario Liverani (Hg.) *Ana turri gimilli. Studi dedicati al Padre Werner R. Meyer, S.J.* Rom: Dipartimento di Scienze Storiche, 383–396.

— 2016. „The Goldsmith Zuzu(l)li and the Find-spots of Inventory Texts from Ḫattuša". *Altorientalische Forschungen* 43, 147–156.

van den Hout, Theo P. J., 1987–90. „Maße und Gewichte. Bei den Hethitern". In: Dietz Otto Edzard (Hg.) *Reallexikon der Assyriologie und Vorderasiatischen Archäologie* 7. Berlin / New York: De Gruyter, 517–527.

— 1995. *Der Ulmitešub-Vertrag* (Studien zu den Boğazköy-Texten 38). Wiesbaden: Harrassowitz.

— 1998. *The Purity of Kingship. An Edition of CTH 569 and Related Hittite Oracle Inquiries of Tutḫaliya IV* (Documenta et Monumenta Orientis Antiqui 25). Leiden / Boston / Köln: Brill.

— 2002. „Another View of Hittite Literature“, in: Stephano de Martino / Franca Pecchioli Daddi (Hg.) *Anatolia Antica. Studi in Memoria di Fiorella Imparati* (Eothen 11). Firenze: LoGisma, 857–878.

— 2006. „Administration in the Reign of Tutḫaliya IV and the Later Years of the Hittite Empire“. In: Theo P. J. van den Hout (Hg.) *The Life and Times of Hattušili III and Tutḫaliya IV – Proceedings of a Symposium held in Honour of J. de Roos, 12–13 December 2003*. Leiden: NINO, 77–106.

— 2007. „Seals and Sealing Practices in Hatti-Land: Remarks à propos the Seal Impressions from the *Westbau* in Ḫattuša“, *Journal of the American Oriental Society* 127 (2007), 339–348.

— 2009a. „A Century of Hittite Text Dating and the Origins of the Hittite Cuneiform Script“, *Incontri Linguistici* 32, 11–35.

— 2009b. „Reflections on the Origins and Development of the Hittite Tablet Collections in Ḫattuša and Their Consequences for the Rise of Hittite Literacy“. In: Franca Pecchioli Daddi / Giulia Torri / Carlo Corti (Hg.) *Central-North Anatolia in the Hittite Period – New Perspectives in Light of Recent Research. Acts of the International Conference held at the University of Florence (7-9 February 2007)* (Studia Asiana 5). Rom: Herder, 71–96.

— 2010. „^{LÚ}DUB.SAR.GIŠ = ‚Clerk?‘“. *Orientalia Nova Series* 79.2, 255–267.

— 2012a. „Die Rolle der Schrift in einer Geschichte der frühen hethitischen Staatsverwaltung“, in: Gernot Wilhelm (Hg.) *Organization, Representation, and Symbols of Power in the Ancient Near East*. Winona Lakes, Indiana: Eisenbrauns, 73–84.

— 2012b. „Administration and Writing in Hittite Society“. In: Maria E. Balza / Mauro Giorgeri / Clelia Mora (Hg.) *Archivi, depositi, magazzini presso gli ittiti* (Studia Mediterranea 23). Genova: Italian University Press, 41–57.

Waal, Willemijn, 2011. „They wrote on wood. The case for a hieroglyphic scribal tradition on wooden writing boards in Hittite Anatolia“. *Anatolian Studies* 61, 21–34.

— 2012. „Writing in Anatolia: The Origins of the Anatolian Hieroglyphs and the Introductions of the Cuneiform Script“. *Altorientalische Forschungen 39*, 287–315.

— 2015. *Hittite Diplomatics: Studies in Ancient Document Format and Record Management* (Studien zu den Boğazköy-Texten 57). Wiesbaden: Harrassowitz.

Weeden, Mark, 2011. *Hittite Logograms and Hittite Scholarship* (Studien zu den Boğazköy-Texten 54). Wiesbaden: Harrassowitz.

Normative Structures in Texts from the Contexts of Mathematics, Justice, and Law in Pharaonic Egypt

Annette Imhausen

Abstract 141
1 Introduction: Questions and available sources 141
2 Normative structures in mathematical and legal sources 143
2.1 Mathematical sources 143
2.2 Legal sources 148
3 Mathematics and Justice: The evidence from *Teachings* 157
4 Conclusions 160
Abbreviations and references 161

Abstract

The contribution looks at normative orders of ancient Egyptian mathematical texts and sources from the context of law. The mathematical problem texts show a set of distinct formal features, which are used, with some variations in the extant sources. One significant feature of their grammar is the use of a specific verb form indicating a necessary consequence. This form is not found (prominently) within collections of law that can be found in ancient Egypt only from the time of the later New Kingdom onwards. However, these texts, also show some formal features. In addition, a strong link between mathematics and the idea of justice can be found in some of the wisdom teachings that can be considered the background of Egyptian legal concepts.

1. Introduction: Questions and available sources

As was described in more detail in the introduction to this volume, a number of structural parallels can be found between mathematical and legal texts from various periods of time. Other contributions in this volume present impressive evidence from Mesopotamia as well as from demotic Egypt, and ancient Greece. At first glance, this connection between the areas of mathematics and legal affairs results from general characteristics and aims that are integral or at least ideally attributed to both areas. Thus, on a naive level, e.g. to the intuition of a modern reader, both areas are connected to neutrality (and impartiality): the result of a mathematical problem is not changed by any hopes or wishes but can be obtained by using the appropriate mathematical procedure, just like the outcome of a legal dispute is meant to be dependent only on the legal rules of a given culture.

Mesopotamia and Egypt are the earliest cultures that developed writing systems and notations for numbers, which were then used by their respective rulers to administer the country. Both, writing and numbers were aides for the rulers to structure and control the available resources. In addition, they were also used to establish and structure formal systems, which lent them normative influence within the formation of these early cultures. Both, Mesopotamia and Egypt used lists and paradigmatic examples to structure bodies of knowledge.[1] These bodies of knowledge express explicitly and implicitly elements of their underlying normative orders, e.g. expressing the royal control of work through standardizing work-loads by means of quantifying amounts of produce that was to be delivered in a given period of time. However, despite these general correspondences between Egypt and Mesopotamia, several differences have resulted in bodies of knowledge that are characteristic for the respective culture. Thus, the Old Babylonian mathematical texts from Mesopotamia comprise a variety of types (problem-texts, table-texts, coefficient lists, catalogues of problems, students' rough work, and model-contracts) whereas the mathematical knowledge of ancient Egypt (extant in sources from the Middle Kingdom and Second Intermediate Period) presents itself largely as a collection of tables and problems only.[2] Similarly, Mesopotamia has left us with evidence of legal codici starting from the end of the third millennium (cf. the contributions by Hans Neumann and Jim Ritter in this volume) whereas Egypt did not until at least the later part of the New Kingdom (and even then the available evidence has prompted some modern scholars to argue *that* and *why* ancient Egypt did not have legal codes).[3]

The aim of this chapter is an analysis of the available evidence for mathematical and legal practices and concepts from Egypt during the Middle and New Kingdoms and their interplay. An analysis of the extant mathematical problems (dating, as mentioned earlier from the Middle Kingdom and Second Intermediate Period) reveals that they are not simply randomly collected accumulations of various problems that were tackled, but rather that they are ordered compilations in which groups with similar or related problems and procedures can be discerned.[4] For the legal side of the paper, evidence for at least the existence of laws, as well as their examples (from the New Kingdom) will be analyzed. In addition, to establish a connection of the areas of mathematics and law in ancient Egypt, evidence of other sources to secure justice through referring to mathematical structures will be invoked.[5]

---

[1] For ancient Egypt, cf. Deicher / Maroko, 2015; for Mesopotamia see Cancik-Kirschbaum, 2015; Taylor, 2007 and Veldhuis, 2014 for lexical knowledge as well as Robson, 2003 for mathematical knowledge. For the racially incriminated terminus technicus of „Listenwissenschaft" which has not yet vanished even in more recent literature cf. Hilgert, 2009. Generally, cf. also Ecco, 2009.

[2] On the types of Old Babylonian mathematical texts and their content see Robson, 1999, 6–15.

[3] Many works on legal knowledge in ancient Egypt begin by pointing out the lack of law codicis, e.g. Allam, 2012, 129; Assmann, 1994, 61, 62, 66; Lippert, 2008, 9, 32; Müller-Wollermann, 2004, 23. Cf. also Lorton, 1977, 5.

[4] For an analysis of such groups of mathematical problems cf. Imhausen, 2003.

[5] For this compare also the contributions of Mark Depauw, Jim Ritter and Guido Pfeifer in this volume.

2. Normative structures in mathematical and legal sources

2.1 Mathematical sources

Ancient Egypt is among the first cultures that have left us with mathematical texts, i.e. texts that describe procedures by which mathematical problems were solved. Within ancient Egypt, mathematics was developed to solve the practical needs of administration. The mathematical texts that survive were probably used to teach scribes, i.e. Egyptian administrators, the mathematics that they needed in their daily work lives. The designation 'scribe' indicates the most significant ability those persons needed to have, i.e. the ability to read and write, which, as I have argued elsewhere, also meant the ability to be proficient with numbers.[6] However, as can be deduced from accounts, depictions of scribes in tombs and some of those tombs as well, there was a variety of hierarchies, with probably a larger number of persons with limited ability in literacy and numeracy who would work in basic administration (and simply execute procedures they were taught) and a small number of high level scribes who would create texts and be the superiors of their lower level colleagues. Nevertheless, even the high-ranking scribes chose a form of statuary in their tombs called scribal statue, that would represent them in reading or writing a papyrus roll.[7]

Due to the association of mathematics with administration, a daily life activity that was located in the towns and cities of Egypt along the Nile, only few mathematical texts from ancient Egypt are still extant.[8] The hieratic sources include eight sources among which only one larger text, the Rhind mathematical papyrus, is of good quality and provides a corpus of some 70 problems. Among the other mathematical papyri, the Moscow Papyrus and the Lahun mathematical fragments also hold significant places.[9] The Moscow papyrus holds 25 problems, of which the first three are too damaged to determine more than a probable type of problem. In addition, unlike the problems of the Rhind papyrus, those of the Moscow papyrus were not arranged in groups of problems according to their content but seem to be written down in no apparent order. The Moscow papyrus also holds two duplicate problems in numbers 8 (identical with problem no. 5) and 13 (identical with problem no. 9). However, among the problems of the Moscow papyrus are two of the most interesting for historians of mathematics, problem no. 10 about the area of a curved surface and problem no. 14 about the volume of a truncated pyramid. The Lahun mathematical fragments are also noteworthy because they are the only Egyptian mathematical papyri with a known provenance, that of the pyramid town of Sesostris II. They contain apart from few problems the second instance of the 2/n table[10] (the other coming from the Rhind papyrus) as well as the second instance of a title of a mathematical text (much shorter than that of the Rhind papyrus).

---

[6] For the role of numeracy and metrology in scribal work cf. Loffet, 2001 and the various examples in Pommerening, 2005.

[7] For this type of statue cf. Allon, 2019 and Scott, 1989.

[8] For an overview of sources and editions cf. Imhausen, 2016, 63–69.

[9] The remaining sources are the Mathematical leather roll, the Cairo Wooden boards, the Berlin Papyrus, and two ostraca.

[10] The 2/n table is the most fundamental table for Egyptian fraction reckoning. Cf. Imhausen, 2016, 93–96 for a more detailed explanation and references to further literature.

As Jim Ritter has done with the example of one Mesopotamian mathematical problem, it may be helpful to look at the structure of the Egyptian mathematical texts to analyse general characteristics of their formal structure.[11] However, looking at and comparing the Rhind, Moscow and Lahun papyri quickly reveals that while there are some features that can be found in all three sources (and may be used to identify an Egyptian mathematical text based on formal basis), there are also individual features of each of these sources, as shall be illustrated using problem 50 of the Rhind papyrus and comparing it with problem 17 of the Moscow papyrus and the problem of the Lahun fragment UC 32134A.

Problem 50 of the Rhind papyrus calculates the area of a circle. The hieratic text is written to be read from right to left, using red ink to highlight the beginning of the problem.[12] The transliteration (written from left to right) imitates the arrangement of the problem found in the hieratic text while the translation arranges the text according to its logical steps. Red ink in the original papyrus is rendered as bold print in the transliteration and translation. Fractions, which are always unit fractions in Egyptian mathematics, are indicated by an overbar over the number that designates the denominator. Line numbers in raised capitals are provided to help navigating transliteration and translation.

Papyrus Rhind, problem 50

Transliteration

[1] ***tp n jr.t*** *3ḥ.t dbn n ḫt 9*
[2] *ptj rḫ.t.f m 3ḥ.t ḫbj.ḫr.k* $\overline{9}$*.f m 1*
[3] *d3.t m 8 jrj.ḫr.k w3ḥ-tp m 8 zp 8*
[4] *ḫpr.ḫr.f m 64 rḫ.t.f pw m 3ḥ.t 64*

[5] *jr.t mj ḫpr* (ḫt 9)

[6] .	*9*		
[7] $\overline{9}$	*1*		
[8] *ḫb.t ḫnt.f d3.t 8*			
[9] .	*8*	[11] *4*	*32*
[10] *2*	*10*	[12] *8*	*64*

[13] *rḫ.t.f m 3ḥ.t*
[14] *64*

Translation

[1] **Method of calculating** a circular area of 9 *ḫt*.
[2] What is its amount as area?
You shall subtract its $\overline{9}$ as 1. [3] The remainder is 8.
You shall multiply 8 times 8. [4] It shall result as 64.
It is its amount as area: 64.

[5] Method how it results (ḫt 9)

[6] .	9
[7] $\overline{9}$	1

[8] Subtracting from it, remainder: 8.

[9] .	8
[10] 2	16
[11] 4	32
[12] 8	64

[13] Its amount as area [14] is 64.

---

[11] Ritter, 2010 and 2004.

[12] A photo of the problem can be found in Robins / Shute, 1987, plate 16.

The problem calculates the area of a circle of given diameter.[13] The text of the problem is structured into several parts that can be distinguished by their grammar and by the use of a number of key words:

1. Title and given datum
The problem begins with a heading that announces the type of the problem (calculation of the area of a circle) and the respective data (in our example the only datum is the length of the diameter). This is usually introduced by a genitive construction 'method of calculating …' (*tp n jr.t*). The data may also be introduced in a separate section after the title of the problem which is introduced by the phrase 'if you are told …' (*mj ḏd n.k*).[14] This section may (as in our example) end with an explicit question for what should be calculated, however, this may also be assumed as self-evident from the statement of problem and its data.[15]

2. Procedure
After the data have been announced, the procedure is indicated that will solve the given problem. The beginning of the procedure may be signaled by a key word like *sšm.t.f* or *jr.t mj ḫpr*, or, as in this example, simply begin with the first instruction. The procedure consists of a sequence of instructions and intermediate results. The instructions use either the imperative or, as in our example, a specific verb form called *sḏm.ḫr.f* (or varying between both). The *sḏm.ḫr.f* is also used to indicate the results. In our example, an adverbial sentence is used to indicate the result of the first instruction.

3. Indication of the result
The final result is indicated with a noun phrase.

4. Written calculations
Many problems of the Rhind papyrus also include numerical sections, in which the calculations that are mentioned in the procedure are carried out in writing. These can be placed either directly after the respective instruction, or, as in our example at the end of the text in a separate section. This section is headed in our example by the phrase 'Method how it results' (*jr.t mj ḫpr*). The written calculations consist of purely numerical schemes.

Some of these characteristic elements can also be found in the problems of the Moscow papyrus as the example of problem 17 from the Moscow Papyrus illustrates.[16] The text of Papyrus Moscow is also written in hieratic, using red ink to indicate the beginnings of a new problem for problems 1–16, but otherwise written in black ink only. The text of the Moscow papyrus is written on a papyrus that is almost as long as the Rhind papyrus but has only a quarter of its height. The text is written in columns that run from the top to the bottom of the papyrus. A

[13] For the Egyptian procedure cf. Imhausen, 2009, 787–789.

[14] The first problem in the Rhind papyrus where this construction can be found is problem 49. It is also found in problems 51, 52, 61b, 62, 64, 72, 77 and 78. Problem 68 begins with *jr ḏd n.k zš* (without initial *tp n*…).

[15] As for example in problem 26 and elsewhere.

[16] For the hieratic text (black-and-white photograph) cf. Struve, 1930, Columns XXXIII–XXXIV.

new problem is usually marked by beginning a new column.[17] Problem 17 calculates the base and height (called 'length' and 'width' in the text of the problem – i.e. they are the sides surrounding the right angle, and the triangle is conceived of as a rectangle divided diagonally into two identical right triangles) of a right triangle of given area and relation of base and height.

Papyrus Moscow, problem 17

Transliteration

[1] *tp n jr.t spd.t*
[2] *mj ḏd n.k spd.t n.t 20 m ꜣḥ.t.s*
[3] *jr dj.t.k ḥr ꜣw dj.n.k* $\overline{3}$ $\overline{15}$ *jw.f ḥr wsḫ*
[4] *jrj.ḫr.k qꜣb.k 20 ḫpr.ḫr 40*
[5] *jrj.ḫr.k jrj.k* $\overline{3}$ $\overline{15}$ *r gm.t 1 ḫpr.ḫr zp 2* $\overline{2}$
[6] *jrj.ḫr.k jrj.k 40 zp 2* $\overline{2}$ *ḫpr.ḫr 100 jrj.ḫr.k. jrj.k qnb.t.s*
[7] *ḫpr.ḫr 10 mk 10 pw m ꜣw jrj.ḫr.k jrj.k* $\overline{3}$ $\overline{15}$
[8] *n 10 ḫpr.ḫr 4 mk 4 pw ḥr wsḫ*
[9] *gmj.k nfr*

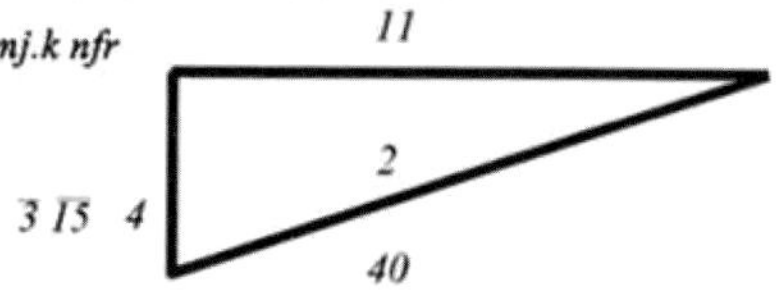

. 40
\2 80
\\$\overline{2}$ 20 *dmḏ 100 qnb.t 10*

Translation

[1] Method of calculating a triangle
[2] If you are told: a triangle of 20 as its area,
[3] concerning your giving as length is that which you have given $\overline{3}$ $\overline{15}$ of as being the width.
[4] You shall double 20. 40 shall result.
[5] You shall divide 1 by $\overline{3}$ $\overline{15}$. 2 $\overline{2}$ times shall result.
[6] You shall calculate 40 times 2 $\overline{2}$. 100 shall result.
You shall calculate its root. [7] 10 shall result.
Behold, it is 10 as length.
You shall calculate $\overline{3}$ $\overline{15}$ [8] of 10. 4 shall result.
Behold, it is 4 as width.
[9] What has been found by you is correct.

Again, several sections of the text of the problem can be distinguished. In this case, the title and indication of the data are given separately. This is followed by the procedure. Instructions and indication of intermediate results in this case both use exclusively the *sḏm.ḫr.f*. The instructions use a periphrastic construction with *jrj*, the indication of the results use *ḫpr*. The final results (length and width) are (like in the problem from the Rhind Papyrus) indicated in separate statements. These are then followed by the phrase 'What has been found by you is correct', which presumably served to mark the end of a problem.[18] The text of the problem is followed by a sketch with annotations and a set of calculations underneath.

The third example is found in the second column of Lahun fragment UC 32162.[19] The fragment has a vertical written title for the whole composition in the first

[17] The only exception is the beginning of problem 13.
[18] The phrase is found consistently at the end of almost all problems of the Moscow Papyrus. It is not found in any of the problems of the Rhind Papyrus.
[19] The hieratic text (colour photograph) can be found on the CD of Collier / Quirke, 2004.

column, and contains a second problem in its third column. The problem found in the second column is again concerned with the calculation of areas. A large rectangle, presumably indicated by the length of its sides (40 and 3) shall be divided into 10 smaller rectangles with a given ratio of their sides of 3/4 to 1.

UC 32162 Column II

Transliteration

1 ***tp*** [- - - -] ***r*** [- -]
2 [-]*w*? *m* [- - -] *10* [- -]
3 *ꜣw*? *n pꜣ* [- - -]*nw*? [- -]
4 *jrj.ẖr.k pꜣ* ***40*** *zp 3*
5 *ẖpr.t jm pw* ***120*** *jrj.ẖr.k*
6 $\overline{\textbf{10}}$ *n* [*120*] *ẖpr.t jm pw* ***12***
7 *jrj.ẖr.k pꜣ* $\overline{\textbf{2}}$ $\overline{\textbf{4}}$ *r gm.t wꜥ*
8 *ẖpr.t jm pw zp* ***1*** $\overline{\textbf{3}}$ *jrj.ẖr.k*
9 *pꜣ* ***12*** *zp* ***1*** $\overline{\textbf{3}}$ *ẖpr.t jm pw* ***16***
10 *jrj.ẖr.k qnb.t.f m* ***4*** *jrj.ẖr.k*
11 $\overline{\textbf{2}}$ $\overline{\textbf{4}}$ *n 4 ẖpr.t jm pw* ***3***
12 *ẖpr.t jm pw ḥꜣy.t.f* ***10*** *n.t mḥ* ***4*** *r* ***3***

Translation

1 **Method [- - - -] by [- -]**
2 [-] as [- - -] 10 [- -]
3 The length of this [- - -] ? [- -]
4 You shall calculate this **40** times 3. 5 That which shall result is **120**.
You shall calculate 6 $\overline{\textbf{10}}$ of [**120**]. That which shall result is **12**.
7 You shall divide 1 by this $\overline{\textbf{2}}$ $\overline{\textbf{4}}$. 8 That which shall result is **1** $\overline{\textbf{3}}$ times.
You shall calculate 9 this **12** times **1** $\overline{\textbf{3}}$. That which shall result is **16**.
10 You shall calculate its root as **4**.
You shall calculate 11 $\overline{\textbf{2}}$ $\overline{\textbf{4}}$ of **4**. That which shall result is **3**.
12 That which shall result is **10** of its rectangles of **4** cubits by **3** cubits.

The title of the problem is indicated in red ink – as are all but two of the numerical values that appear during the procedure (this can also be found in the other problem on this fragment but in no other of the known mathematical texts). The instructions use the *sḏm.ẖr.f* throughout. The indication of intermediate results uses the verb *ẖpr*, but not in the for of the *sḏm.ẖr.f* but as *ẖpr.t jm pw*, which can also be found regularly in Lahun fragment UC32134A.

The three examples given above illustrate the extent of regularities and varieties in the formal structure of Egyptian mathematical texts. Most mathematical texts show some of the variety of available formal features. There are key phrases to indicate certain sections of the mathematical text, however, they do not have to be used in each problem. The highlighting with red ink may be used to indicate the beginning of a problem (or not – as in a number of problems of the Moscow papyrus) as well as other sections (like, rather unusually, almost all of the numerical values of the Lahun fragment). Rough work (i.e. the carrying out of the calculations that are detailed in the instructions) may be added directly after the respective instruction, or in a separate section at the end, or not at all. Despite this variation, however, an underlying formal order of Egyptian mathematical texts can still be determined. Thus the choices that were made in writing a mathematical texts could choose, but only from a „given“ set of choices.

The grammatical feature that is common in all procedures of the mathematical texts is the use of imperatives and the form called *sḏm.ḫr.f*. While imperatives are used (as one might expect) in a wide variety of texts, the *sḏm.ḫr.f* is the characteristic verb form for mathematical texts. It also appears in medical texts, but there much fewer in number and in combination with another verb form, the *sḏm.jn.f*. Within the procedures of the mathematical texts, the *sḏm.ḫr.f* is used to announce the result of arithmetic operations and in the instructions. From its occurences in the mathematical and medical texts and the few other occurences as well, Egyptologists have agreed that the form serves the function to express a certain necessity in an action, which results from something preceding.[20] The usage within the announcement of the results of mathematical operations is obvious – if a mathematical operation is carried out (correctly), it will necessarily lead to a predictable result, e.g. adding 5 and 7 will always yield 12. It is interesting, then, to notice that the *sḏm.ḫr.f* is also used regularly within the instructions of the procedure, thus indicating their normative character. If the scribe wants to solve the given problem he must follow the indicated operations in the order that is prescribed by the procedure. Thus, the mathematical side of ancient Egyptian texts provides with the *sḏm.ḫr.f* (which is most prominent in the mathematical texts) a specific verb form to express the normativity inherent in mathematical operations (and their results). At the same time, it must be noted, however, that the existence of this verb form does not make it the sole form used in mathematical procedures. As the examples indicated above illustrate, the instructions may also use the imperative (and do so on a regular basis) and the indication of the (intermediate) results may also use other constructions than the *sḏm.ḫr.f* (although one has to admit that it is found there a lot).[21]

2.2 Legal sources

The normative framework of Egyptian legal concepts and practices is expressed by the Egyptian term *mꜣꜥt*.[22] This term comprises the idea, that there is a certain perfect order of the cosmos and everything in it. Thus the term *mꜣꜥt* is closely linked or may express ideas of truth, order and justice.[23] From the idea of a perfect

---

[20] Allen, 2014, 297 stresses the necessity that the form expresses without reference to a prior statement. On the *sḏm.ḫr.f* cf. most recently Pommerening, (2014, 13–15 with a focus on the medical texts. General discussions of this form can be found in Junge, 1972; Vernus, 1990, and Polis, 2005.

[21] For a more detailed analysis of formal features in Egyptian mathematical texts see Imhausen, 2014. There, the number of attestations of imperatives and *sḏm.ḫr.f* is compared based on the existing texts, which results for the Moscow Papyrus in imperative: *sḏm.ḫr.f* = 1:15 (approximately), and even in the Rhind Papyrus, which also has few further forms, in 1:3 (approximately).

[22] For monographs on *mꜣꜥt* cf. Assmann, 2006; Lichtheim, 1992, and Menu, 2005; a shorter description of the concept can be found in Assmann, 2011. For an introduction of the concept of *mꜣꜥt* and its repercussions for Egyptian legal concepts cf. Lippert, 2008, 2–4. For a description of the emergence of legal concepts and its relation to *mꜣꜥt* cf. van Blerk, 2018.

[23] Assmann, 2006, 17.

order of the cosmos then follow certain codes of conduct. Every Egyptian was supposed to adhere to the respective rules in his or her daily life, as was summarized by Jan Assmann as follows:

> Das ägyptische Wort Maat bezieht sich auf semantische Felder, die wir im Deutschen mit Recht, Gerechtigkeit, Richtigkeit, Wahrheit, Ordnung umschreiben können. Ma'at ist eine regulative Idee, an der sich sowohl die Rechtsprechung der Richter als auch die Unterweisung der sogenannten Weisheitslehrer orientieren soll. Ma'at ist also der Oberbegriff aller Gesetze und Vorschriften, nach denen sich die Richter bei der Rechtsprechung, die Priester bei der Kultausübung, die Beamten bei der Verwaltung und – dieser Punkt ist entscheidend – jeder Ägypter in einer verantwortlichen Lebensführung zu richten habe.[24]

Extant *Teachings* (with settings from the Old Kingdom on) provide explicit evidence for these rules for specific members of higher levels of Egyptian society, like scribes (*The Loyalist Teaching*, *The Teaching of Khety*, *The Instruction of Any* and *The Instruction of Amenemope*), viziers (*The Instruction addressed to Kagemni* and *The Teaching of Ptahhotep*), princes (*The Instruction of Prince Hardjedef*) or even kings (*The Teaching for King Merikare, The Teaching of King Amenemhat*).[25] This type of text and its relation to mathematics will be analysed in detail in a later section of this chapter.

The obvious textual counterpart for a direct comparison with the mathematical texts would be a collection of laws of some sort, providing a (structured) assortment of individual laws that detail a procedure how to deal with specific offenses including their respective punishments. For Mesopotamia, a good number of mathematical texts exist from the Old Babylonian Period, and the Codex Ḫammurapi provides a good-size contemporary source text for the textual evidence of legal concepts.[26] Thus Jim Ritter has shown similarities (as well as differences) in philological structures of Old Babylonian mathematical problem texts and the texts of the law code of Ḫammurapi.[27]

For Egypt, however, the source situation is rather different. The earliest mathematical texts originate from the Middle Kingdom (2055–1650 BCE), which is contemporary to the Mesopotamian Old Babylonian period. Attestation of individual laws, much less of collections of them, are not extant from that time.[28]

---

[24] Assmann, 2000, 185. (My) English translation of the quote: "The Egyptian word *maat* refers to semantic fields that we paraphrase in German as law, justice, rightness, truth, order. *Maat* is a regulative concept that is meant to guide jurisdiction of judges as well as the instructions of the wisdom teachers. Thus *maat* is the superordinate concept of all laws and rules that must be obeyed by judges in jurisdiction, priests in the execution of cult practices, officials in administration, and – this aspect is crucial – each Egyptian who is living responsibly."

[25] For translations of these texts cf. Parkinson, 1997 and Lichtheim, 1975 and 1976.

[26] On the *Codex Ḫammurapi* cf. Jim Ritter and Guido Pfeifer in this volume.

[27] Cf. Ritter, 2004 and the contribution by Jim Ritter in this volume.

[28] Jasnow, 2003, 255 and Lippert, 2008, 32. Even the most promising collection of papyri from the Middle Kingdom, the Lahun Papyri, which have contributed essential documents for mathematics and medicine, has only a smallish selection of legal documents that mostly

Nevertheless there is at least indirect evidence for their existence from literary texts (*The admonitions of Ipuwer* and *The Teaching for King Merikare*) and administrative papyri (most notably Papyrus Brooklyn 35.1446 rto).[29] The respective passages in *The admonitions of Ipuwer* and the *Teaching for King Merikare* read:

> "O, but the laws of the Stronghold
> are thrown outside;
> but they walk on them in the public places;
> wretches are breaking them up in the streets."[30]

> "Make your great ones great, so that they will enact your laws!"[31]

The passage in *The Teaching for King Merikare* indicates that the king apparently did issue laws (as is exemplified for the New Kingdom by the stela of Horemheb). *The admonitions of Ipuwer* refer to the existence of a collection of laws that are apparently not in use during a time of crisis. The stronghold, that *The admonitions of Ipuwer* refers to, was an institution linked to the administration of labor duty.[32] It is from this same context that further indirect evidence for the existence of laws originates in some passages of Papyrus Brooklyn 35.1446, which dates to the later Middle Kingdom. Papyrus Brooklyn 35.1446 contains seven texts that may not all be related to each other: a register of fugitives, a copy of a letter, two copies of royal decrees, two lists of servants and a deed of conveyance. [33] The main text of the recto is the list of fugitives, which details "seventy-six residents of southern Upper-Egypt who appear to have absconded without completing or to avoid performing services required of them by the state", as well as instructions for the respective prison that would be responsible for their punishment.[34] The instructions to the prison include references to specific laws, e.g. "The law pertaining to those who desert" (line 10) or "The law pertaining to one who deliberately deserts for six months (or more)" (lines 55–56).[35] While none of the laws are cited beyond

---

consists of specfic deeds as well as some fragmentary texts (cf. Collier / Quirke, 2004, 99–123) – but unfortunately no legal code of any kind. For a brief overview of sources including laws cf. Lippert, 2012 (http://digital2.library.ucla.edu/viewItem.do?ark =21198/zz002bzzgj; accessed June 6th 2019). One should keep in mind that the search for law-codes maybe something that as such was not an independent part of Egyptian law. If one were to attempt an emic perspective, it becomes apparent that the Egyptian word *hp,* sometimes translated as 'law' includes more than we would associate with it from a modern perspective, cf. Philip-Stépħan, 2008, 14 and Mark Depauw in this volume.

[29] Jasnow, 2003, 255–256 and Lippert, 2008, 32. The lack of extant sources has led to speculations about reasons why there might not have been law-codes in Egypt, e.g. Assmann, 1994. Assmann, 1994, 63 f. explicitly separates the royal decrees (which contain at least some wordings of 'laws' and the repercussions for their transgressions) in another category. Based on the extant texts from the New Kingdom, however, and the indirect evidence cited above, it may also be the vagaries of preservation that has led to the lack of sources of this kind.

[30] *The admonitions of Ipuwer* 6.9–10, translation: Parkinson, 1997, 177.

[31] *Teaching for King Merikare*, E42, translation: Parkinson, 1997, 219.

[32] Parkinson, 1997, 194, note 50.

[33] Quirke, 1990, 128 f.

[34] Hayes, 1955, 19.

[35] Hayes, 1955, 47 f.

the reference to their titles, these alone might be considered sufficient evidence to indicate the existence of collections of laws – however, since none of them are extant, there are no sources that could be used for a comparison with the mathematical texts.

The earliest extant 'collection' of something like laws, that is a normative order of a code of conduct including consequences for those that do not follow these rules, is found on a stela with a text known as *The Great Edict of Horemheb*, originates from the end of the 18th Dynasty (1550–1295 BCE) – that is, the end of the first part of the New Kingdom.[36] Because of its content and the (at least nominal) royal authorship the edict of Horemheb is classified, together with several similar texts, in Egyptological literature as a *royal criminal law decree*.[37] The analysis of Arlette David includes six later texts that also belong to this group, of which the Nauri Decree from the times of Seti I (1294–1279 BCE) is the most complete extant source.[38]

Horemhebs reign (1323–1295 BCE) followed the aftermath of the Amarna Period under Akhenaten (1352–1336). The text on his stela presumably was intended to display the efforts that Horemheb took in order to reorganize the country. This reorganization included not only building projects at the old temples and maybe the systematic destruction of the city of Amarna, but also legal measures to terminate various kinds of abuses by officials who apparently used the power of their offices to gain personal advantages, e.g. by requisitioning resources for their private use.[39]

The stela of Horemheb, which was placed in the temple of Karnak, is rather deteriorated.[40] As far as a reconstruction is possible, the text on the stela included a prologue and an epilogue as well as ten paragraphs of laws and an administrative section.[41] Kruchten, who provided the most recent detailed analysis only uses the

---

[36] The edition of the stela can be found in Kruchten, 1981. Cf. also Gnirs, 1998; Helck, 1955 and Pflüger, 1946.

[37] For an analysis of such texts see David, 2006. Royal decrees are extant from the Old Kingdom on. They contain information about the organization of temples in terms of resources. Like the decrees cited above, they include rules and punitive measures should these rules be offended, cf. Lippert, 2008, 20 f. For English translations of several examples of such decrees cf. Strudwick, 2005, 97–127. From the Middle Kingdom only few royal decrees are extant, cf. Lippert, 2008, 38 f.

[38] David, 2006, 18.

[39] Van Dijk, 2000, 293.

[40] Wolfgang Helck described the stela as follows: "Am 10. Pylon in Karnak vor der nördlichen Wand des westlichen Turmes, steht der Rest einer hohen Sandsteinstele, an ihrer Vorderseite sowie an den beiden Schmalseiten beschrieben. Sie ist von der Zeit schwer mitgenommen worden: in ihrem oberen Teil blieb nur ein nach oben immer schmaler werdender Rest am (vom Betrachter gesehenen) rechten Rand erhalten; die Endzeilen der rechten Schmalseite sind mit Teilen der Stelenrückseite abgebrochen und liegen z. T. verstreut in der Umgebung der Stele herum, vermischt mit den Bruchstücken anderer Inschriften der Ramessidenzeit. Zudem hat die aus dem Boden aufsteigende Feuchtigkeit den unteren Teil der Stele zerfressen und unleserlich gemacht." (Helck, 1955, 109).

[41] As with all ancient law codes, there has been some discussion on its actual "Sitz im Leben"; cf. Gladić, 2018, 223 (https://ubt.opus.hbz-nrw.de/opus45-ubtr/frontdoor/ deliver /index/docId/829/file/Dissertation_Gladic.pdf; accessed September 15th 2019).

first seven laws in his analysis, because the others are too fragmentary.[42] Despite the poor state of the text, there are apparent regularities, which was also pointed out by Kruchten.[43] There is a consistent structure of each of the paragraphs, which can be followed with the example of the third law:[44]

m mjtt	Likewise,
wnn nꜣ n sḏm(-ʿš) n ʿ.t ḥnk.t pr-ʿꜣ	if the attendants of the storehouse of pharaoh,
ʿnḫ wḏꜣ snb	may he live, prosper and be healthy
ḥr šm.t ḥr kfʿ m pꜣ dmj	go and seize objects in the town
r ṯꜣj kṯ m-ʿ nꜣ n nmḥw	in order to take the *kṯ*-plant from the *nmḥw*-workers
mtw nꜣ n sḏm-ʿš n ʿ.t ḥnkt n pr-ʿꜣ	and the attendants of the storehouse of pharaoh,
ʿnḫ wḏꜣ snb	may he live, prosper and be healthy
ḥr jṯ.t pꜣ ḥm tꜣ ḥm.t n ʿnḫ nb n pꜣ mšʿ	take the slave (male or female)
n rmṯ nb	of a simple soldier or of anybody
n pꜣ tꜣ r ḏr.f	of the whole land
ḥnʿ s.t ḥr nḥmw ḥr hrw 6 ḥr hrw 7	and take them for six days or for seven days
jw bw rḫ.tw šm.t m-dj-sn m wsṯn	and they cannot leave unhindered
r ntj ḫn pw n ḥꜣw pꜣj	Regarding that matter: this is an abuse.
m rdj jr.tw	Don't let it be done.
m mjtt gr.t	Likewise,
ḫr jr sḏm-ʿš nb n ʿ.t ḥnkt pr-ʿꜣ	concerning every attendant of the storehouse of pharaoh
ʿnḫ wḏꜣ snb	may he live, prosper and be healthy
ntj jw.tw r sḏm r ḏd	of whom one shall hear with the words:
st ḥr kfʿ r ṯꜣj kṯ grw	"They seize to take *kṯ*-plants."
ḥnʿ ntj kjj jj.t r smj r ḏd	and of whom another reports with the words:
jṯ(w) pꜣj.j ḥm tꜣj.j ḥm.t ḥr hrw 6 ḥr hrw 7	"My slave (male or female) was taken for 6 days or for 7 days."
jr.tw hp r.f	One shall execute the law against him
m zwꜣ fnḏ.f djw m ṯꜣrw	by hacking off his nose after he is taken to Tjaru (Sile).

[42] Kruchten, 1981, 10.
[43] Kruchten 1981, 10–12.
[44] On the regularities of the phrasings of decrees see also Pflüger, 1946, 260.

The law begins with the description of the abuse (which in the examples of the stela is perpetrated by men who work for pharaoh and abuse the power that is invested in them through this position), which is stated as something that is happening. This abuse is then explicitly labeled as being wrong, followed by its prohibition, this should not be done. Then follows the description of a potential abuse that is described in exactly the same words as the initial abuse; that is the situation is repeated but this time indicated as something that might happen, and be reported, this description provides the protasis to the following apodosis, the penalty that would then be inflicted on the transgressor.

Similar to the structure of the mathematical texts, the individual sections use specific grammatical constructions. Since the mathematical texts were written in Middle Egyptian, while the language of the stela is Late Egyptian, a comparison of the grammatical structures is not straightforward, but must take the two stages of the language into account. Despite of this, the normativity inherent to the text of the laws of Horemheb is expressed as a negative imperative, which is similar to the expression of normativity in mathematical procedures by the use of the imperative within the mathematical texts. However, it is also quite obvious, that the text of *The Great Edict of Horemheb* does not allow us to match the Egyptian collection of laws as closely with the mathematical procedures as it is possible in the Mesopotamian example. The conclusion based on the comparison above remains on a rather general level: Both are formally structured compositions that show some similarities. However, even more similarities could be found in the Egyptian material rather easily between mathematical and medical procedures.

Another text that includes a collection of laws is the Nauri-Decree which was written in the fourth year of Seti I. (1294–1279 BCE). The text consists of 128 lines written on a sandstone rock at Nauri, 35 km north of the third cataract.[45] The top of the stela depicts Seti I. presenting an offering to a group of gods headed by Amun (cf. figure 1). The king is standing in front of the gods and holds a figure of a seated goddess *M3ˁt* in his left hand. The top of the stela of Horemheb showed the king in front of Amun with a similar posture of his arms, however, his hands (and what may have been in them) are not extant.

Figure 1: Top of the stela with the Nauri Decree
(Griffith 1927: plate xxxix)

[45] Griffith, 1927, 193; Iskander / Rohim, 2016, 182.

The text of the stela then begins with date and titles of the king followed by a description of the king and his approval by the gods.[46] This is followed by a detailed description of the donations of the king for the domain of Abydos, which are also the focus of the following decree.[47] The stela ends with an epilogue in which Seti I dedicates his works to Osiris.

The section of the actual decree that is found in between consists of individual examples of transgressions and their respective punishment. Similar to the Decree of Horemheb, the text shows the usage of specific expressions that are used to structure the individual sections of the law texts.

Based on the (grammatical) structure of the text, the individual concerns that are addressed in the examples of the decree can be divided in three sections, as will be exemplified by the beginning of the decree followed by examples from the list of its concerns and the sections that refer to this:[48]

jw wḏ.n ḥm.f rdj.t ḥn.tw	His Majesty has commanded
tꜣ ḥwt nt ḥḥw m rnpwt	that the temple of Millions of Years,
nsw-bjt,	of the King of Upper and Lower Egypt,
Mn-mꜣꜥt-Rꜥ	Menmaatre,
ib-hrw m ꜣbdt	the heart is content in Abydos,
ḥr mw ḥr tꜣ	be regulated upon water and upon land,
ẖt spꜣwt Šmꜥw Mḥw	throughout the nomes of Upper and Lower Egypt:
r tm djt	so as not to allow
(...)	(...)
r tm rdjt	so as not to allow
(...)	(...)
r tm [rdjt]	so as not [to allow]
(...)	(...)
r tm rdjt	so as not to allow
šnꜥ.tw jmw.sn ḥr mw jn šnꜥj nb	the detaining of their boat upon the water by any policeman;
r tm rdjt	so as not to allow
tht.tw r ꜣḥwt nb n tꜣ ḥwt Mn-mꜣꜥt-Rꜥ ib-hrw m ꜣbdt m sḫt [...].sn jn ꜥs-nsw nb ḥrt-pḏt nb rwḏ nb n pr rwḏ n pr-nsw [rmṯ] h<ꜣ>b m wpwt r Kš	a transgression against any field of the temple of Menmaatre, the heart is content in Abydos, in the country, their [...] by any Viceroy, any troop commander, any agent of the house or agent of the palace of the King, or [a person] sent on business to Kush;

[46] For a more detailed analysis of the structure of the text cf. Maderna-Sieben, 2018, 70–72 and 229–264, for a philological analysis cf. David. 2006, 17–107. The legal section is discussed in Edgerton, 1947.

[47] Maderna-Sieben, 2018, 71.

[48] The transcription and translation given here are based on Davies, 1997 and David, 2006. Cf. also Edgerton, 1947.

r tm djt (...)	so as not to allow (…)
r tm rdjt *th.tw r wḥꜥw nb n tꜣ ḥwt nt ḥḥw m rnpwt n nsw-bjt Mn-mꜣꜥt-Rꜥ ỉb-hrw m ꜣbdt ḥr sšw.f n grg ḥr mw.f n ḥꜣmw ḥr sẖt r nwt n.f*	so as not to allow a transgression against a fowler of this temple of Millions of Years, of the King of Upper and Lower Egypt, Menmaatre, the heart is content in Abydos, in his hunting nests upon his water of fishing and upon the marshland to annoy (?) him;
r tm djt (...)	so as not to allow (…)
r tm djt (...)	so as not to allow (…)
wpw-ḥr wnn.sn ẖwj mkj *jw s nb jm.sn ḥr jrt ḥnt.f jr.t <m> [t]ꜣ ḥwt nt ḥḥw m*	But they shall be guarded and protected every man amongst them doing his services which are done [in the] temple
rnpwt n nsw-bjt Mn-mꜣꜥt-Rꜥ ỉb-hrw m ꜣbdt	of Millions of Years of the King of Upper and Lower Egypt, Menmaatre, the heart is content in Abydos.
jw nn rdjt ḏꜣj.tw tꜣ r.sn jn sꜣ-nsw n Kš nb ḥrj-pḏt nb srw nbw kḏn nb ḥrj-jḥw nb ṯꜣj srjt nb wꜥw nb n mꜥs rmṯ nb hꜣb m wpwt r Kš	They shall not be interfered with by any Viceroy of Kush, any troop commander, any nobleman, any charioteer, any chief of stables, any standard bearer, any soldier of the army or any person sent on business to Kush.
jn (=jr) sꜣ-nsw n Kš nb ḥry-pḏt nb (…)	As for any Viceroy of Kush, any troop commander, (…)
jr.tw hpw r.f m (…)	One shall execute the law against him (…)
ẖr jr sꜣ-nsw nb ḥrj-pḏt nb ḥꜣtj-ꜥ nb rwḏ nb sr nb rmṯ nb hꜣb m wpwt r Kš	Now as for any Viceroy, any troop commander, any nomarch, any agent, any nobleman or any person sent on business to Kush
ntj jw.f [r] šnꜥ jmw nb n tꜣ ḥwt Mn-mꜣꜥt-Rꜥ ỉb-hrw m ꜣbdt	who will detain any boat oft he temple of Menmaatre, the heart is content in Abydos,
m mjtt jmw nb n rwḏ nb n pr pn	or likewise any boat of any agent of this house,
mtw.f mnj.f m wꜥ n hrw wꜥtj r ḏd	and will moor it for a single day, saying:
jw.j r jṯꜣ.f m nḥm r [wp]wt nb n pr-ꜥꜣ ꜥnḫ wḏꜣ snb jm.f	"I will take it away from him by force for any [busi]ness of Pharaoh, may he live, prosper and be healthy."

jr.tw hpw r.f m [*ḥwt.f*] *m sḫ 200 wbnw sd 5 m-dj šd bꜣkw n pꜣ jmw m-dj.f, m hrw nb ntj jw.f r jr.f mnj ddjw r tꜣ ḥwt Mn-mꜣꜥt-Rꜥ ib-hrw m ꜣb*[*d*]*t*	One shall execute the law against him by [beating him] with 200 blows, and 5 open wounds, and exacting the work of the boat from him, for every day that he will moor (it), (it) being given to the temple of Menmaatre, the heart is content in Aby[d]os.
ḫr-jr sr nb jmj-r ꜣḥwt nb n pr pn ꜥꜣmj skꜣ nb rwḏ nb	Now as for any nobleman, any overseer of the fields of this house, any Asiatic(?) of the ploughing, or any agent
ntj iw.f r tht r tꜣš n ꜣḥwt n tꜣ ḥwt Mn-mꜣꜥt-Rꜥ ib-hrw m ꜣbdt r smnmn tꜣšw.sn	who will infringe against the border of the fields of the temple of Menmaatre, the heart is content in Abydos, in order) to shift their boundaries –
jr.tw hpw r.f m swꜣ fnḏ.f msḏrwj.f<j> ddjw r ꜥḥwtj m tꜣ ḥwt Mn-mꜣꜥt-Rꜥ ib-hrw m ꜣbdt	One shall execute the law against him by cutting off his nose and his ears and (he) being placed as a field laborer in the temple of Menmaatre, the heart is content in Abydos.
m mjtt rmṯ nb	Likewise, any person,
ntj m tꜣ r-ḏr.f	who is in the entire land and
ntj	who shall attack any fowler of the temple of Menmaatre, the heart is content in Abydos, in his hunting fields or his fishing ponds –
jr.tw hpw r.f m ḥwt.f m sḫ 100 wbnw sd 5	One shall execute the law against him by beating him with 100 blows and 5 open wounds.
(...)	(...)

At the beginning it is indicated who and/or what is intended to be protected by the order of king Seti I., namely his temple in Abydos, and specific details about the protection (or rather details about the actions that consider infringements) are listed. The introductory phrase used in detailing the infringements is *r tm* (*r*)*djt* 'so as not to allow'. This list of actions that are not allowed is followed by a statement of protection including details of those protected, namely, everyone who 'is doing his services' in the temple at Abydos, and those that they are protected from, i.e. the viceroy of Kush or other officials. Unlike the text of *The Great Edict of Horemheb*, the transgressions are not repeated and stated as transgressions. However, then follows, like in *The Great Edict of Horemheb*, the description of potential infringements (that repeat with some variations to the introductory description of the transgressions) as protasis to the following apodosis, the penalty that will be inflicted on a transgressor. Here, the same phrase that was used in *The Great Edict of Horemheb* is used: *jr.tw hpw r.f* 'One shall execute the law against him'.

Another parallel between legal and mathematical texts from ancient Egypt (in which they differ somewhat from Mesopotamia) are the variations found within the key-phrases used to structure the respective texts.[49] Thus while there are key words as well as key phrases to indicate the beginning or ending of a specific section of the text, these words and phrases are used with a certain degree of freedom. However, as with the degree of variations found within the mathematical texts, the legal texts also are composed using a certain repertoire of phrases and key words.

Concerning the comparison between the textual evidence from Egypt and Mesopotamia, one possible explanation for their difference in the legal texts may be found in the concept of *mꜣꜥ.t* that was described at the beginning of the section on legal sources. While the Egyptians were obviously aware that in the course of events things might happen that were not according to the rules, the idea was that this should (and would) not happen on a regular basis. Transgressions against *mꜣꜥ.t* should be extraordinary exceptions to the general rule, which might also explain the wordiness of the phrasings of the individual laws on the stela of Horemheb. In addition, this might explain the absence of the Middle Egyptian *sḏm.ḫr.f* within this type of texts.[50] The *sḏm.ḫr.f* is used to describe normative sequences. Transgressions against *mꜣꜥ.t*, however, were conceptualized outside of this framework.[51]

In addition to the admittedly rather general formal similarities of ancient Egyptian mathematical and legal documents that were detailed above, there is one further feature that provides a link between these two domains, namely their setting within the ancient Egyptian culture. Both areas were aspects of the domain of administration, and were apparently not separated off with exclusively mathematical or judicial experts.[52] Just as officials judged cases, the mathematical training that happened seemed to have been part of the administrative training. This observation then provides the transition to another group of texts, namely the *Teachings* mentioned earlier.

3. Mathematics and Justice: The evidence from *Teachings*

The invention and practice of mathematics in ancient Egypt was closely linked to Egypt's administrational needs. Thus, the invention of the number system can be shown to probably have happened at the same time as the invention of writing and to have been prompted by the need of an emerging elite to control their goods. In the further development, mathematics became a key-tool for the king and his administrative body to organize and control produce and people.

---

[49] The use of these variations renders the task of a formal analysis more complicated, as has in the past been expressed by frustrated comments, like the one from Gardiner, 1952, 24: "…, I feel sure that the clauses were drafted with the carelessness characteristic of Pharaonic scribes."

[50] Although one might argue in the cases of the Decree of Horemheb and the Nauri Decree that the *sḏm.ḫr.f* is absent because of the later stages of the language, the Brooklyn Papyrus from the Middle Kingdom uses the same phrase to indicate the resulting punishment as the later texts.

[51] Cf. also Quack, 2002, which details that there were aspects in Egyptian culture that were consciously omitted from the written testimony.

[52] Cf. the role of the scribe within the realm of jurisdiction in Deir el-Medina as detailed in Allam, 2012, 131 and 137.

This control was also subject to the concept of *mꜣˁ.t* – mathematical control was supposed to be just. It should be kept in mind, however, that justice in ancient Egypt did not entail general equality. Rather depending on ones specific position within Egyptian society, respective rules for conduct were presupposed. Justice did imply a certain rationality and order (or protection against arbitrariness), which is where mathematics comes into play. Mathematics was used in Egyptian administration not only to control, but also to ensure justice, e.g. by avoiding unequal treatment of people through setting mathematical quantities for the produce they are expected to deliver.[53] The basic idea of the combination of mathematics and justice is that there are just distributions of goods, in which everybody receives his proper share (This does not necessarily mean that just shares are the same, however, it entails that differences must be implicitly or explicitly justified.). This is also the underlying concept of two types of justice which were established by Aristotle, namely in Book V, section 4 of his *Nicomachean Ethics*. Two mathematical terms can be used to describe two kinds of justice: arithmetical justice and geometrical justice. Arithmetical justice (which is based on arithmetical proportions) aims to compensate injust inequalities. Geometrical justice (based on geometrical proportions) aims to give to each his proper (i.e. proportional) share. And again, through using these mathematical proportions, the sizes of shares in a distribution become determinable and are taken out of the realm of arbitrariness, because identical situations will lead (through the use of mathematics) to identical results. My argument is, that one of the uses of mathematics in ancient Egypt was that of a tool to establish the framework of numerical values that would ensure justice in those areas that were ruled by this set of numerical values. While the general idea of this usage of mathematics may be grasped indirectly as early as the Old Kingdom, it becomes apparent in the genre of *Teachings*, texts that were created from the Middle Kingdom on. The most obvious association of justice and mathematics can be found in a composition from the late New Kingdom.

Teachings are a well attested genre in Egyptian literature.[54] The extant examples have settings from the Old Kingdom on, however the date of their composition probably only begins with the Middle Kingdom. Among the oldest teachings is *The Teaching of Ptahhotep* (set in the Old Kingdom, but probably written during the 12th dynasty, i.e. the Middle Kingdom), where a few general references to the idea of 'one's rightful part' can be found in e.g. in the 5th maxim:[55]

---

[53] Obviously the setting of a numerical quantity is only part of achieving a just system. Setting the quantity ensures, as indicated in the text above an equal treatment according to that numerical value. In order to achieve justice, the size of that value needs to be agreed on as being „reasonable". The actual setting of the numerical values was the responsibility of the king – certain literary texts and depictions in tombs seem to hint that the prescribed amounts to deliver were probably not easily achieved by those who had to produce them. A similar phenomenon is documented in Mesopotamia, where the set values regularly led into debt, which was then counteracted at certain intervals by amnesties, cf. Pfeifer, 2012, 22.

[54] Cf. Allen, 2007, 392 f., Parkinson, 2002, 235–241 and Parkinson, 2009, 126.

[55] The transliteration and translation follow: http://www.ucl.ac.uk/museums-static/digitalegypt/literature/ptahhotep.html.

If you are among leaders
and you command the condition of the multitude,
seek yourself every effective moment,
so that your condition is without fault.

Maat is great, and (its) keenness enduring.
It has not been overturned since the time of Osiris
The one who overlooks (its) laws is punished;
that is what is overlooked by the sight of the greedy.

It is the small-minded that seizes riches,
but crime never managed to land its rewards,
the one who says 'I snare for myself'
does not say 'I snare for my needs'.

When the end comes, Maat endures
and a man will say 'that is the property of my father'.

The issue of just distribution is raised in the second paragraph – life according to Maat is directly juxtaposed with that of a greedy person, i.e. somebody who tries to obtain for himself more than his just share. This is relevant for all aspects of life and all kinds of goods. Two later sections (19th and 20 maxims) of *The Teaching of Ptahhotep* also refer to greed, and while the reference from maxim 19 is rather general again, the sentence from maxim 20 explicitly refers to the distribution of goods:

> "**Don't be greedy over a share,** do not be jealous of what is not your due".

Much more numerous, and equally much more precise, concerning the link between mathematics and justice is *The Instruction of Amenemope*.[56] The composition probably dates to the end of dynasty 20 or the beginning of the 21st dynasty.[57] Ignoring the references given within the context of Amenemope's self-presentation, there are 43 lines that refer to mathematical practices, e.g. lines 1–4 from the chapter 6 (VII: 12–15):

Do not move the markers on the borders of fields,
Nor shift the position of the measuring rod.
Do not be greedy for a cubit of land,
Nor encroach on the boundaries of a widow.

Where *The Teaching of Ptahhotep* had general warnings against 'greed' and 'wanting more than one's righful share', the references found in *The Instruction of Amenemope* give specific references warning against manipulations in the execution of

[56] These are (cited according to column and line from Papyrus BM 10474, which has 28 columns of 18–23 lines): [I: 15, 16, 19; II: 1, 2, 3, 4, 5, 6 – all part of the self-presentation of Amenemope]; IV: 4; VI: 14, 15; VII: 12, 13, 14, 15, 16, 17; VIII: 9, 10, 11, 12; XIV: 5, 6; XV: 20, 21; XVI: 3, 4; XVII: 18, 19, 20, 21; XVIII: 4, 15, 16, 17, 18, 19, 20, 21, 22, 23; XIX: 2, 3, 4, 5, 6, 7, 8, 9 and XXI: 17, 19.

[57] The most recent edition is Laisney, 2007. See also Black, 2002. On the date of Papyrus BM 10474 see also Verhoeven, 2001, 290–303. An English translation can be found in Lichtheim, 1976, 146–163.

measuring procedures that result in the numeric data that are considered to be just. Boundary stones and measuring rod determine the size of fields in order to calculate their area and the revenue expected from them. Even the greed, which is (like in *The Teaching of Ptahhotep*) explicitly warned against, is specified numerically, one should not 'be greedy for a cubit of land'. *The Instruction of Amenemope* includes specific requests for carrying out measuring processes correctly: The measuring of fields is detailed in chapter 6 (as described above). The allocation of goods is described in chapter 5 (temple rations), chapter 11 (rations of a poor man) and chapter 20 (property to its owner). The correct notation of (numerical) written data is the topic of chapter 13. The rightful handling of scales, weights and measuring vessels is delineated in chapters 16 and 17.

As the text of the example from chapter 6 indicates, the references to metro-mathematical practices in *The Instruction of Amenemope* show a development in terms of the responsibility of scribes concerning Maat. While *The Teaching of Ptahhotep* instructed its reader not to be greedy for more than one's rightful share, *The Instruction of Amenemope* takes the responsibility further – the scribe also has to ensure that the measuring operations that determine numerical values are carried out correctly, i.e. that the measuring tools that are used to establish the amounts are not falsified.

The analysis of the entire corpus of extant teachings has yielded only few further references. No reference to mathematics/measuring and justice is made in *The Instruction of Any* or *The Loyalist Instruction*.[58] However, in *The Teaching of King Amenemhet*, at least a general reference to the (mathematical) administration of fields and the success from it is given:

"I was one who increased the grain,
(For I was) favored by Nepri;
Hapy gave me honor on every field,
so that none hungered during my years, / none thirsted therein.
Men took their ease through what I had done
And recounted legends about me,
For I ordered everything in its proper place."[59]

4. Conclusions

Despite the absence of the wealth of sources that is extant from Mesopotamia, the available material does provide us with a picture how mathematics was used in legal contexts in Egypt. Despite the presumably similar reasons for linking these two areas in Egypt and Mesopotamia (as well as in later times and other places), e.g. the attempt to achieve justice through avoiding arbitrariness, thus using the basic mathematical feature of measuring and quantifying, the picture that emerges for Egypt is different from that found in Mesopotamia.

Based on the basic concept of *mꜣꜥt*, and thus the idea that wrongdoing should be eliminated, and at best, not occur at all, the philological instrument of the *sḏm.ḫr.f* that for a modern reader seems so obviously suited to express the legal

[58] For a comparison of the content of these teachings cf. Verhoeven, 2009.
[59] Translation from Simpson, 2003, 169.

consequences of wrongdoing may not have been used in the Egyptian texts. The evidence, on which this claim is based, is admittedly thin – one could argue that the actual law texts date from the New Kingdom, and in Late Egyptian, the *sḏm.ḫr.f* was not used. Or, that the evidence for extant collections of laws is to little to make any claims. Be that as it may, it is striking, how much care is taken in the Stela of Horemheb to describe the rightful state first, and then to detail the transgression, emphasizing its non-*mꜣꜥt*-state followed by the respective punishment.

The idea of measuring in quantifying also has a prominent place within the Egyptian concept of justice, as can be seen in the teachings with examples from *The Teaching of Ptahhotep* and *The Instruction of Amenemope*. In addition, the judgement of the dead presents further evidence for the concurrence of mathematics and justice in ancient Egypt. In order to prove worthy for the afterlife, the deceased had to pass judgement of his way of life. In order to be successful, the deceased first had to recite sins that he did not commit during his lifetime. Then his heart was weighed on a balance against a feather, a symbol of the goddess *Mꜣꜥt*. If the balance showed equilibrium between the heart and the feather, the judgement was passed successfully and the dead would be presented to Osiris. It is the mathematical operation of weighing that ensures a just judgement of the deceased.

Abbreviations and references

UC = Collection London, University College, Petrie Museum
http://www.ucl.ac.uk/museums-static/digitalegypt/literature/ptahhotep.html.

Allam, Schafik, 2012. "Strafrechtliches im pharaonischen Ägypten". In: Robert Rollinger / Martin Lang / Heinz Barta (eds.) *Strafe und Strafrecht in den antiken Welten. Unter Berücksichtigung von Todesstrafe, Hinrichtung und peinlicher Befragung* (Philippika. Marburger altertumskundliche Abhandlungen 51). Wiesbaden: Harrassowitz, 129–145.

Allen, James P., 2007. "Literature". In: Toby Wilkinson (ed.): *The Egyptian World*. London and New York: Routledge, 388–398.

Allen, James P., 2014. *Middle Egyptian. An Introduction to the Language and Culture of Hieroglyphs*. Cambridge: Cambridge University Press. (3rd edition).

Allon, Niv, 2019: *Writing, Violence, and the Military: Images of Literacy in Eighteenth Dynasty Egypt (1550–1295 BCE)*. Oxford: Oxford University Press.

Assmann, Jan, 1994. "Zur Verschriftung rechtlicher und sozialer Normen im Alten Ägypten". In: Hans-Joachim Gehrke (ed.) *Rechtskodifizierung und soziale Normen im interkulturellen Vergleich* (ScriptOralia 66). Tübingen: Günter Narr, 63–85.

— 2000. *Herrschaft und Heil. Politische Theologie in Altägypten, Israel und Europa*. Darmstadt: Wissenschaftliche Buchgesellschaft.

— 2006. *Ma'at. Gerechtigkeit und Unsterblichkeit im Alten Ägypten*. München: C.H. Beck.

— 2011. "Altägyptische Weisheit". In: Helmut Schwier (ed.): *Zwischen Torheit und Weisheit*. Heidelberg: Winter-Verlag, 221–235.

Black, James R., 2002. *The Instruction of Amenemope. A Critical Edition and Commentary. Prolegomenon and Prologue*. Dissertation. University of Wisconsin-Madison.

Blerk, Nicolaas Johannes van, 2018. "The Emergence of Law in Ancient Egypt. The Role of *MAAT*". *Fundamina* 24, 69–88.

Cancik-Kirschbaum, Eva, 2015. "Stabilität, Change Management und Iteration. Listenwissenschaft in Mesopotamien." In: Eva Cancik-Kirschbaum / Anita Traninger (eds.): *Wissen in Bewegung. Institution – Iteration – Transfer*. Wiesbaden: Harrassowitz, 289–305.

Collier, Mark / Stephen Quirke, 2004. *The UCL Lahun Papyri: Religious, Literary, Legal, Mathematical and Medical* (BAR International Series 1209). Oxford: Archaeopress.

David, Arlette, 2006. *Syntactic and Lexico-Semantic Aspects of the Legal Register in Ramesside Royal Decrees* (Göttinger Orientforschungen IV. Reihe Ägypten 38). Wiesbaden: Harrassowitz.

Davies, Benedict G., 1997. *Egyptian Historical Inscriptions of the Nineteenth Dynasty* (Documenta Mundi: Aegyptica 2). Jonsered: Paul Åströms förlag.

Deicher, Susanne / Erik Maroko (eds.), 2015. *Die Liste: Ordnungen von Dingen und Menschen in Ägypten* (Ancient Egyptian design, contemporary design history and anthropolgy of design 1). Berlin: Kadmos.

van Dijk, Jacobus, 2000. "The Amarna Period and the Later New Kingdom". In: Ian Shaw (ed.): *The Oxford History of Ancient Egypt*. Oxford: Oxford University Press, 272–313.

Ecco, Umberto, 2009. *The Infinity of Lists: An Illustrated Essay*. New York: Rizzoli.

Edgerton, William F., 1947. "The Nauri Decree of Seti I: A Translation and Analysis of the Legal Portion". *Journal of Near Eastern Studies* 6, 219–230.

Gardiner, Alan H., 1952. "Some Reflections on the Nauri Decree". *Journal of Egyptian Archaeology* 38, 24–33.

Gladić, Domagoj A., 2018. *Das Dekret von Memphis (196 v. Chr.). Kommentar und Auswertung*. Inauguraldissertation Universität Trier. (https://ubt.opus.hbz-nrw.de/opus45-ubtr/frontdoor/deliver/index/docId/829/file/Dissertation_Gladic.pdf.?)

Gnirs, Andrea, 1998. "Haremhab – ein Staatsreformator? Neue Betrachtungen zum Haremhab-Dekret". *Studien zur Altägyptischen Kultur* 16, 83–110.

Griffith, Francis L., 1927. "The Abydos Decree of Seit I at Nauri". *Journal of Egyptian Archaeology* 13, 193–208.

Hayes, William C., 1955. *A Papyrus of the Late Middle Kingdom in the Brooklyn Museum (Papyrus Brooklyn 35.1446)* (Wilbour Monographs V). New York: The Brooklyn Museum.

Helck, Wolfgang. 1955. "Das Dekret des Königs Haremheb". *Zeitschrift für Ägyptische Sprache und Altertumskunde* 80, 109–136.

Hilgert, Markus, 2009. "Of 'Listenwissenschaft' and 'Epistemic Things'. Conceptual Approaches to Ancient Mesopotamian Epistemic Practices". *Journal for General Philosophy of Science 40*, 277–309.

Imhausen, Annette, 2003. *Ägyptische Algorithmen. Eine Untersuchung zu den mittelägyptischen mathematischen Aufgabentexten* (Ägyptologische Abhandlungen 65). Wiesbaden: Harrassowitz.

— 2009. “Traditions and myths in the historiography of Egyptian mathematics”. In: Eleanor Robson and Jacqueline Stedall (eds.) *The Oxford handbook of The History of Mathematics*. Oxford: Oxford University Press, 781–800.

— 2014. “Normative structures in ancient Egyptian mathematical texts”. In: Daliah Bawanypeck / Annette Imhausen (eds.) *Traditions of Written Knowledge in Ancient Egypt and Mesopotamia* (Alter Orient und Altes Testament 403). Münster: Ugarit Verlag, 153–187.

— 2016. *Mathematics in Ancient Egypt. A contextual history*. Princeton: Princeton University Press.

Iskander, John M. / Afifi Rohim, 2016. “A Ramesside Royal Decree from Memphis”. *Zeitschrift für Ägyptische Sprache und Altertumskunde* 143, 177–193.

Jasnow, Richard, 2003. “Egypt: Middle Kingdom and Second Intermediate Period”. In: Raymond Westbrook (ed.): *A history of Ancient Near Eastern Law*. Volume 1 (Handbuch der Orientalistik, Abteilung I Band 72). Leiden / Boston: Brill, 255–288.

Junge, Friedrich, 1972. “Zur Funktion des *sḏm.ḫr.f*”. *Journal of Egyptian Archaeology* 58, 133–139.

Kruchten, Jean-Marie, 1981. *Le décret d'Horemheb. Traduction, commentaire épigraphique, philologique et institutionnel*. Bruxelles: Editions de l'Université de Bruxelles.

Laisney, Vincent Pierre-Michel, 2007. *L'Enseignement d'Amenemope* (Studia Pohl 16). Rome: Pontifical Biblical Institute.

Lichtheim, Miriam, 1975. *Ancient Egyptian Literature. Volume I: The Old and Middle Kingdoms*. Los Angeles: University of California Press.

— 1976: *Ancient Egyptian Literature. Volume II: The New Kingdom*. Los Angeles: University of California Press.

— 1992. *Maat in Egyptian Autobiographies and Related Studies* (Orbis Biblicus et Orientalis 120). Freiburg, Switzerland / Göttingen, Germany: Universitätsverlag / Vandenhoeck Ruprecht.

Lippert, Sandra, 2008. *Einführung in die altägyptische Rechtsgeschichte* (Einführungen und Quellentexte zur Ägyptologie 5). Münster: LIT Verlag.

— 2012. “Law (Definitions and Codifications)”. In: Willeke Wendrich (ed.): *UCLA Encyclopedia of Egyptology*. Los Angeles (http://digital2.library.ucla.edu/viewItem.do?ark=21198/zz002bzzgj).

Loffet, Henri, 2001. *Les Scribes comptables, les mesureurs de cereales et de fruits, les metreurs-arpenteurs et les peseurs de* l'Égypte *(de l'époque thinite à la 21. dyn.)*, Lille: Atelier National de Reproduction des Theses.

Lorton, David, 1977. “The Treatment of Criminals in Ancient Egypt: Through the New Kingdom”. *Journal of the Economic and Social History of the Orient* 20, 2–64.

Maderna-Sieben, Claudia, 2018. *Königseulogien der frühen Ramessidenzeit: Politische Propaganda im Dienst der Legitimierung einer neuen Dynastie*. Heidelberg: Propylaeum.

Menu, Bernadette, 2005. *Maât. L'ordre juste du monde*. Paris: Editions Michalon.

Müller-Wollermann, Renate, 2004. *Vergehen und Strafen. Zur Sanktionierung abweichenden Verhaltens im Alten Ägypten*. Leiden / Boston: Brill.

Parkinson, Richard B., 1997. *The Tale of Sinuhe and Other Ancient Egyptian Poems 1940–1640 BC*. Oxford: Oxford University Press.

— 2002. *Poetry and Culture in Middle Kingdom Egypt. A Dark Side to Perfection*. London / New York: Continuum.

— 2009. *Reading Ancient Egyptian Poetry: Among Other Histories*. Malden, MA: Wiley-Blackwell.

Pfeifer, Guido, 2012. "Gerechtigkeit aus der Perspektive der altorientalischen Rechtsgeschichte". In: Markus Witte (ed.): *Gerechtigkeit*. Tübingen: Mohr Siebeck, 15–35.

Pflüger, Kurt, 1946. "The Edict of King Haremhab". *Journal of Near Eastern Studies* 5, 260–276.

Philip-Stephan, Alexandra, 2008. *Dire le droit en Égypte pharaonique : Contribution à l'étude des structures et mécanismes juridictionnels jusqu'au nouvel empire*. Brussels: Safran.

Polis, Stéphane, 2005. "Les formes «contingentes» en Égyptien ancien: une catégorisation en question". In: Christian Cannuyer (ed.) *La langue dans tous ses états* (Acta Orientalia Belgica 18). Bruxelles: Société Belge d'Études Orientales, 301–322.

Pommerening, Tanja, 2005. *Die altägyptischen Hohlmaße* (Studien zur altägyptischen Kultur, Beihefte 10). Hamburg: Helmut Buske.

— 2014. "Die *šsꜣw*-Lehrtexte der heilkundlichen Literatur des Alten Ägypten. Traditionen und Textgeschichte". In: Daliah Bawanypeck / Annette Imhausen (eds.) *Traditions of Written Knowledge in Ancient Egypt and Mesopotamia* (Alter Orient und Altes Testament 403). Münster: Ugarit Verlag, 7–46.

Quack, Joachim, 2002. "Explizite Aufzeichnungsmeidung im Alten Ägypten". *Lingua Aegyptia* 10, 339–342.

Quirke, Stephen, 1990. *The Administration of Egypt in the Late Middle Kingdom. The Hieratic Documents*. New Malden: SIA Publishing.

Ritter, Jim, 2004. "Reading Strasbourg 368: A Thrice-Told Tale". In: Karine Chemla (ed.) *History of Science, History of Text* (Boston Studies in the Philosophy of Science 238). Dordrecht: Springer, 177–200.

— 2010. "Translating rational practice texts". In: Annette Imhausen / Tanja Pommerening (eds.), *Writings of Early Scholars in the Ancient Near East, Egypt, Rome, and Greece* (Beiträge zur Altertumskunde 286). Berlin / New York: De Gruyter, 349–383.

Robins, Gay / Carles Shute, 1987. *The Rhind Mathematical Papyrus. An Ancient Egyptian Text*. London: British Museum.

Robson, Eleanor, 1999: *Mesopotamian Mathematics, 2100–1600 BC. Technical Constants in Bureaucracy and Education*. Oxford: Clarendon Press.

— 2003. "Tables and Tabular Formatting in Sumer, Babylonia, and Assyria, 2500–50 BCE". In: Martin Campbell-Kelly / Mary Croarken / Raymond Flood / Eleanore Robson (eds.): *The History of Mathematical Tables. From Sumer to Spreadsheets*. Oxford: Oxford University Press, 18–47.

Scott, Garry, 1989. *The History and Development of the Ancient Egyptian Scribe Statue*. Yale University. Unpublished PhD dissertation.

Simpson, William Kelly (ed.), 2003. *The Literature of Ancient Egypt. An Anthology of Stories, Instructions, Stelae, Autobiographies, and Poetry*. New Haven / London: Yale University Press.

Strudwick, Nigel C., 2005. *Texts from the Pyramid Age* (Writings from the Ancient World 16). Atlanta: Society of Biblical Literature.

Struve, Wasili W., 1930. *Mathematischer Papyrus des Staatlichen Museums der Schönen Künste in Moskau* (Quellen und Studien zur Geschichte der Mathematik, Abteilung A: Quellen: 1). Berlin: Springer.

Taylor, Jon, 2007. "Babylonian Lists of Words and Signs". In: Gwendolyn Leick (ed.) *The Babylonian World*. New York: Routledge, 432–443.

Veldhuis, Niek, 2014. *History of the Cuneiform Lexical Tradition* (Guides to the Mesopotamian Textual Record 6). Münster: Ugarit.

Verhoeven, Ursula, 2001. *Untersuchungen zur späthieratischen Buchschrift* (Orientalia Lovaniensia Analecta 99). Leuven: Peeters.

— 2009. "Von der 'Loyalistischen Lehre' zur 'Lehre des Kairsu'. Eine neue Textquelle in Assiut und deren Auswirkungen". *Zeitschrift für ägyptische Sprache und Altertumskunde* 136/1, 87–98.

Vernus, Pascal, 1990. *Future at Issue. Tense, Mood and Aspect in Middle Egyptian: Studies in Syntax and Semantics* (Yale Egyptological Studies 4). New Haven: Yale Egyptological Seminar.

How to Express Normativity in Demotic. The Mathematical and Legal Manuals in Context

Mark Depauw

Abstract ... 167
1 Preliminaries ... 168
1.1 What is normativity? ... 168
1.2 What is Demotic? ... 168
1.3 Normativity in Demotic: where and how? ... 168
2 Substantive or procedural: the term *hp* ... 169
2.1 'Law' ... 169
2.2 'Rules' ... 170
2.3 'Verdict' ... 170
2.4 'Legal claim', 'right' ... 171
2.5 'Custom' ... 172
2.6 'Rite' ... 172
2.7 'Justice' ... 172
3 Other expressions to normativity in Demotic ... 173
3.1 Non-scientific texts: letters, petitions, decrees, … ... 173
3.2 Scientific (not mathematical) texts ... 175
3.3 Mathematical texts ... 176
3.4 Legal texts ... 177
4 Conclusion ... 178
Abbreviations and references ... 178

Abstract

Explicit references to the norm as the way things should be and should be done are not omnipresent in Egyptian sources in Demotic, a stage of the indigenous language and script flourishing between roughly 650 BC and AD 200.

The standard term to refer to this concept seems to be *hp*, which depending on the context can be translated as law, justice, legal claim or even rite. In letters and petitions, it is sometimes said that the addressee 'knows what to do', i.e. act on the plaintiffs behalf. It is sometimes also said that some actions are 'fitting' by means of the verb *pḥ*. The so-called habitual (or aorist – *ḫr sḏm=f*), the tense one expects to be used for statements answering to the norm, is in fact rather rare in general. Instead, scientific works dealing with mathematics or other fields normally takes a more practical stance, and refer to concrete actions to be performed. Only in legal texts is the habitual more common.

1. Preliminaries

1.1 What is normativity?

Starting from the Wikipedia page 'Normative',[1] normativity can be roughly defined as the principle that there is a standard, 'correct' way of acting. The norm is the way things should be and should be done. As there is a substantive and a procedural component to every action, normativity can focus on moral or on practical aspects. Philosophy by its nature does the former, and defines normative statements as claims about how things should or ought to be. Law, on the other hand, deals with the latter, and legal norms specify the way things should be done. Similarly, for mathematics, the 'Truth' (an Egyptian could call it Ma'at) is pre-existent, and emphasis also seems to be on the procedure, on how to obtain the correct result.

1.2 What is Demotic?

Demotic is a stage of the ancient Egyptian script and language, used between roughly the seventh century BC and the fifth century AD. Most documents date to the 3rd and 2nd century BC. With the 1st century BC suffering from a general lack of evidence in any language, it is hard to see how common Demotic was for everyday use then. There are good arguments, however, to believe that the sudden disappearance of Demotic contracts and receipts in the course of the 1st century AD is the result of a deliberate Roman policy. This does not mean, however, that Egyptian disappeared altogether. Demotic (and its brother Hieratic, an older cursive script) lived on in literary and scholarly texts, and was still used in funerary and other religious contexts. That ancient Egyptian lived on as a spoken language is clear from its re-emergence in the fourth century AD as Coptic, now using the Greek alphabet.[2]

1.3 Normativity in Demotic: where and how?

Demotic is thus used for a broad range of genres, and several of these are relevant for our topic today, normativity. Moral ('philosophical') normativity can especially be found in wisdom texts, where the proper state of the world and the proper way to act is described in aphorisms. It also appears in more narrative texts or private letters where individuals occasionally express thoughts about desired behaviour from a moral point of view. In the so-called sacerdotal decrees, finally, attention also goes to the way things should be, but combine this with more practical matters about the implementation of new legislation. They thus form a nice transition to procedural ('legal') normativity, which is formulated in texts such as law manuals, mathematical and other scientific texts, and tangentially also in legal documents.

---

[1] https://en.wikipedia.org/wiki/Normative (consulted 15 Sep 2016).

[2] Depauw, 2012.

2. Substantive or procedural: the term *hp*

When discussing normativity in Demotic, an important term is *hp*. It is notoriously difficult to translate, and seems to cover both substantive and procedural aspects.[3] A survey of its use is not only interesting to get an idea of what types of normativity are expressed in Demotic sources, but also to see how these are formulated.

2.1 'Law'

A first translation of *hp* is 'law', both in the general sense of the legal system in place, as in a concrete formulation for a specific aspect. A first example is found in a petition:

> *ỉn=w s n=y r ỉr pꜣy=f wꜣḥ r-ẖ nꜣ nty sẖ (n) pꜣ hp tw=y ỉn=w nꜣ nty sẖ (n) nꜣ hp.w ẖr-r.r=w ỉw=f sẖ n pꜣ ỉpt mḥ-8 pꜣ hp (n) Kmy nty ỉw=w ḏd n=f n pꜣ ꜥ.wy (n) wrr ỉn-nꜣ.w wpy.t ẖpr (n) ḏbꜣ ꜥ.wy k.t-ẖe.t nkt \pꜣ bnr/ n pꜣ bꜣk nty sẖ n pꜣ hp mḥ-6 pꜣ nty mḥṯ̭ n.ỉm=f bw ỉr=w rg=f n-ḏr.ṯ̭=f šꜥ.tw=w ḏrꜥ tꜣ wpy*
>
> They brought it to me to formulate an answer to it according to what is written in the *law*. I let them bring what is written in the *law* concerning it, while it is written in the eighth table (?) of the *law* of Egypt which is called 'prison': if a trial is taking place about a house or other things *except* (*added later*) for a slave, which is written in the sixth *law*, the one who is holding it, it is not seized from his hand until the judgement is written down.
>
> P. BM 10591 (= TM 53822),[4] Vo, col. 3 lines 15–19, translation of Baetens / Depauw 2015.

In this case the concrete normative statement, introduced – as so often in the casuistic law system – by a conditional sentence, employs a negative habitual (also called 'aorist'): *bw ỉr=w rg=f* 'it is not seized' or 'one does not (normally) seize it'.

Other examples of concrete formulations of laws occurs in a copy of the legal verdict in a case dealing with marriage and inheritance:

> *ỉw=f sẖ n pꜣ hp n ḥꜣ.t-sp 21.t ḏd i.ỉr rmt ḥms ỉrm s-ḥm.t (...) mtw=f ḥms ỉrm ky s-ḥm.t (...) mtw pꜣ rmt rn=f mwt nꜣy=f nkt.w i.ỉr-ẖr di=w s n nꜣ ẖrd.ṯ̭.w n tꜣ ḥm.t ḥꜣ.t*
>
> ... while it is written in the *law* of year 21: "If a man marries a woman (...) and [after divorce] he marries another woman (...), when the man dies, his property is wont to be given to the children of the first wife."
>
> P. Siut p. 3–12 BM 15091 Ro [B] (= TM 43343), col. 1 lines 17–20.

---

[3] Nims, 1948.

[4] The TM number identifies the text in question: please use www.trismegistos.org/text/1234 to find TM 1234.

Here again the habitual is used, now affirmatively in a second tense construction stressing the adverbial part of the sentence: *i.ir-ẖr di=w* 'is wont to be given' or 'one (normally) gives it'.

And:

> *in-n3.w rmt i.ir sẖ s ꜥnḫ n s-ḥm.t* (...) *mtw=f di.t nkt mtw=f n ky rmt* (...) *bw-ir=w w ꜥb n=f bw-ir-w di.t mḥ=f n-im=w*
>
> If a man makes a document of endowment for a woman (…), and he sells property belonging to him to another man (…), the property shall not be clear (in title) to him and he shall not be given fulfillment therein.
>
> P. Siut p. 3–12 BM 15091 Ro [B] (= TM 43343), col. 10 lines 7–9.

This *bw-ir=w wꜥb* 'shall not be clear' or 'one shall not (normally) clear it' is another example of the negative habitual.

2.2 'Rules'

The word *hp* is also used in documents listing desired and undesired behaviour of members of a guild. Here 'rules' seems to a better translation for the plural *hp.w*.

> *ḫ n3 hp.w r-mtr* (...) *r.r=w r ir=w*
>
> Copy of the *rules* which (the members) have agreed to observe
>
> *iw=n f3y ꜥq yš ḥm3* (...) [*mtw=n*] *di ḥḏ qt 1*
>
> We will bring rations, resin, salt, … (…) and we will give one kite …
>
> P. Lille Dem. 1 29 (= TM 2784), lines 2–6.

In this case the (third) future of the first person plural is used to express what should be done: *iw=n* (*r*) *f3y* 'we will bring'. That this is a normative statement rather than just a plain expression of future is not only clear from the context, but also from the fact that it is continued by a conjunctive: *mtw=n di* 'and we will give'.

There are even fines for those who act incongruously:

> *p3 rmt n-im=n nty iw=f st3.ṯ=f r tm ir r ẖ md.t nb.t nty ḥry* (...), *p3y=f qns* (...) *iw=n m-s3=f r di.t ir=f r ẖ md.t nb.t nty ḥry n3 ssw.w nty ḥry n ḥtr iwtj mn*
>
> The one among us who will turn his back to not act according to all that is written above (…), his fine: (…). We will have a claim on him to cause that he acts according to everything above on the days written above, by force and without delay.
>
> P. Lille Dem. 1 29 (= TM 2784), lines 26–28.

2.3 'Verdict'

In combination with the verb *ir* 'to do, to make', *hp* can also refer to the result of a legal procedure, in which case 'verdict' seems an appropriate translation.

p3 rmt n-im=n nty iw=f r smy m-s3 ir n=f p3 hp r-r=w ẖn p3 ʿ.wy

The man among us who complains further after the *verdict* in regard to them has been made for him in the (chapter) house, …

P. Cairo 2 30605 (= TM 2774), lines 19–20.

2.4 'Legal claim', 'right'

In other contexts, especially in contracts of sale or similar transactions, *hp* refers to a 'legal claim':

tw=y wy.k r p3 hp n t3 ʿ3 km (…)iw iwiw(=y) r.r=k ḏd ir-šwṱ r-ḏb3 ḥḏ p3 i. ir=y

I am far from *the legal claim* to the black she-ass … concerning which I came against you, saying: "Selling her for specie payment is that which I did."

P. Hou 8 (= TM 46432), lines 2–3.

tw=y wy.w r-r=k p3 hp n3 nkt.w r-iwiw=y r-r=k r-ḏb3=w ḏd ir=k n=y rd n-im=w n p3 ʿ.wy n Pkry

I am far from you concerning *the legal claim* to the things for which I came against you, saying: "You were for me representative of them in the house of …"

P. Teos 12 (= TM 44654), lines 3–7.

mn mtw=y hp wpy md nb p3 t3 i.ir-n=t n rn=f ṯ3y p3 hrw r-ḥry

There is not owing to me *a legal claim*, a judgment, or anything in the world from you in its name from today onward

P. Glanville p. 4–9 BM 10522 (= TM 43759), line 3.

Hp also occurs in divorce documents, where a similar translation as 'right' seems fitting:

ẖ3ʿ=y ṱ=t tw=y wy.k r-ḥr=t n hp ḥm.t mn mtw=y md nb p3 t3 i.ir-n=t rn p3 hp ḥm.t ṯ3y p3 hrw r ḥry

I have abandoned you as wife. I am far from you in regard to *right* of wife. There is not owing to me anything in the world from you in the name of *right* of wife from today onward.

P. Reich p. 43–46 BM 10074 (= TM 2722), line 2.

In these contexts, *hp* seems to refer to statutorily expected behaviour resulting from a legal procedure such as sale or marriage. Compare also the following passage from a marriage contract:

iw=y ir n=t p3 sẖ ḏb3 ḥḏ nty ḥry tw=t m-s3=y p3 hp p3 sẖ sʿnẖ ḥḏ 21 r-ir=y n=t mtw=y ir n=t p3y=f hp ḥnʿ p3 hp p3 sẖ ḏb3-ḥḏ nty ḥry mḥ sẖ 2 iw=y ir n=t p3y=w hp

> Since I have made for you the document of sale, you have a claim upon me for the *right* of the document of endowment of 21 (deben) of silver which I made for you; I am to do for you its *right* together with the *right* of the document of sale, making two documents; I will do for you their *right*.
>
> P. Eheverträge p. 164–166 no. 8 Z (= TM 43277), line 4.

Here the document itself stands for the legal procedure connected with the transfer.

2.5 'Custom'

In some cases, *hp* does not really refer to concrete legislation or rights conferred through procedures conforming with that legislation, but rather to a more substantive sense of what is proper. When in the so-called First Setne-story pharaoh wonders whether a brother-sister marriage is desirable for his children Ihweret and Naneferkaptah, *hp* in all likelihood does not refer to positive law, but rather to natural law:

> *iw=f ḫpr iw mn mtw=y šr m-sꜣ šr 2 in pꜣ hp di.t ḥms wꜥ irm wꜥ n-im=w*
>
> If it happens that I have only two children, is it then *done/law* to let them marry one another?
>
> Setne I (= TM 55857), col. 3 lines 1–2.

Pharaoh adds that he much prefers to give each of them in marriage to the offspring of generals, so that his family will be numerous. But intriguingly, the story continues in an unexpected way. When the time of the marriages arrives, the princess is sad that she cannot marry her brother. The king summons her and says: "Ihweret, have you written to me foolishly: 'May I be married to my brother Nanaferkaptah'? I (Ihweret) answered: 'May I be married out to the son of a general, and my brother to the daughter of a general, so that our family will be numerous'. I laughed, and Pharaoh laughed."

2.6 'Rite'

This aspect of propriety also comes to the fore in more religious contexts, where a translation as 'rite' seems fit.

> *wꜣḥ=f iy r rsy r šwn irm=y wꜣḥ=f gšpi. ṯ=y wꜣḥ=f ir pꜣ hp n Ỉs.t*
>
> He came south to Syene with me; he re-examined me; he did the *rite* of Isis.
>
> Graff. Dodec. Philae 417 (= TM 51872), line 4.

2.7 'Justice'

Finally, in some contexts 'justice' seems to be the most appropriate translation. Thus a wisdom texts uses *hp* to refer to what could be called 'divine justice':

> *mtw=f pꜣ nty di pꜣ hp md-mꜣꜥ.t iw mn wpy.t*

He [god] is the one who gives *justice* and righteousness without judgment (in a trial?)

P. Insinger (= TM 55918), col. 31 line 15.

Hp is thus a very broad term, referring to the way things should be and should be done. Ideally, these two fall together: law (*hp*) is justice (*hp*), and legal claims (*hp*) emanate from legal proceedings (*hp*) that are proper (*hp*) and correct (*hp*), just as rites (*hp*) should be performed in the right way (*hp*) to do what should be and has always been done (*hp*).

3. Other expressions to normativity in Demotic

In the above, some attention was given to how normativity is expressed in Demotic sources explicitly mentioning *hp*. Of course there are other contexts in which people formulate what they think should be done, and I will now look at whether similar constructions are used there.

3.1 Non-scientific texts: letters, petitions, decrees, …

In letters, both private and official, requesting specific action by the addressee or third parties is a very common feature, often even the sole purpose of writing. According to the hierarchy of the correspondents, plain unmitigated imperatives can be used, or the request can be softened by polite formulae such as 'it would be nice if …', 'may one do me this favour: …', or 'may one order to …'.[5] As a rule, however, the action desired is very concrete and in a very concrete context, i.e. not based on general principles. It does not surprise therefore that there are only few explicit references to the norm.

One such reference may well be *pꜣ sḥn nfr st ỉr-rḫ s*, which occurs 14 times in Demotic letters. Although the expression has been interpreted in different ways, the most likely translation is '(may) you know the right thing to do'. This explains why it also occurs in oracle questions, where the local god is asked for advice on which path of action to take, or in tenders for farming a tax, where individuals want the officials to assign the monopoly of a tax or trade to them.[6]

But really the most common way in which the norm is made explicit in petitions, letters and related genres is by using the verb *pḥ*, which literally means 'to arrive' but of which impersonal forms can be used idiomatically as 'to be fitting'. Consider the following examples,[7] where infinitives are used as complements to *pḥ* 'to be fitting':

st pḥ n dỉ,t ỉr=n pꜣ hrw ỉ(w)=n swr ḥq,t m-bꜣḥ Ỉmn n Tꜣy=w-ḏy

It is fitting to cause that we pass this day drinking beer before Amun of Teudjoi

P. Rylands 9 (= TM 47388), col. 9, lines 6–7.

---

[5] Depauw, 2006, 260–269.

[6] Depauw, 2006, 231–235.

[7] The examples were found through a search in the Demotische Textdatenbank (DTD, G. Vittmann), accessible in the Thesaurus Linguae Aegyptiae (TLA): http://aaew.bbaw.de/tla (accessed 15 Sep 2016).

ỉn ỉw=s pḥ r dỉ,t ẖdb Ỉmn pꜣ sp n nꜣy ẖr.w

Would it be fitting to cause Amun to kill the rest of these young men?

P. Rylands 9 (= TM 47388), col. 12, line 17.

pꜣ sẖ pꜣ nty-ỉw=s pḥ r.r=f dỉ.t ꜥfẖ (n-)dr. ṱ=f

The scribe is the one whom *it is fitting* for him to give an oath in his hand

P. Berlin P 13537 (= TM 44206), line 22.

pꜣ smt n nꜣy bw-ỉr=s pḥ n ỉr=w n mr-šn

This kind of men, *it does not do* to make them lesonis

P. Berlin P 13540 (= TM 46470), line 3.

pꜣ smt n pꜣy pꜣ nty-ỉw=s pḥ n ỉr=f n mr-šn

This kind of man, *what fits is* to make him lesonis

P. Berlin P 13540 (= TM 46470), lines 5–6.

In the penultimate example the negative habitual *bw-ỉr=s pḥ* is used, probably because it is a more general, almost axiomatic statement. The last example, on the other hand, uses the relative first present *pꜣ nty-ỉw=s pḥ*, as this is the concrete application of the norm.

That this distinction should not be pushed too far, however, is clear from a similar combination of negative habitual *bw-ỉr=s pḥ* and affirmative first present *st pḥ*, where both are concrete:

bw-ỉr=s pḥ šsp smy (...) *st pḥ dỉ,t mḥ* (...)

It is not fitting to accept a complaint (… [from party A]). *It is fitting* to cause that (… [party B]) gets ownership

P. Siut p. 3–12 BM 15091 Ro [B] (= TM 43343), col. 10, lines 10–11.

In normative texts such as the Codex Hermopolis and the Canopos Decree, the relative clause *pꜣ nty-ỉw=s pḥ* is used in combination with other tenses:

<nꜣ>? nty pḥ r dỉ,t st n=f ẖr dỉ=w st

What is fitting to give to him, *they should give* it to him

Codex Hermopolis (= TM 48855), col. 8 line 33.

mtw=w ỉr pꜣ ḥb (n)-rn=f šꜥ hrw 5 (...) ỉrm pꜣ sp md,t nty pḥ n ỉr=w

And they will celebrate the feast in question for five days (…) together with all the things that are fitting to do

Cairo CG 22186, Kom el-Hisn (= TM 6378), lines 10–11.

r dỉ,t ẖpr=f ꜥn n ỉr pꜣ nty pḥ n wš nb r-ẖ tꜣ ẖ,t nty-ỉw tꜣ p,t smn ḥr-ꜣt. ṱ={w}=<s> n pꜣ-hrw

To cause that it happens *that one does* what is fitting in every moment, according to the way in which the sky is fixed above today

Cairo CG 22187, Tanis (= TM 55659), line 39.

In the first case the habitual *ḫr di=w* is used, although it is a concrete application of the norm. In the second the first present *n3 wʿb šʿš* expresses what is customary and fitting. And in the third and final attestation, 'what is fitting' is the object of the infinitive *ỉr* 'to do'. Interesting there is the comparison with the fixed presence of the sky, stressing how normative the action really is.

This can be compared to two passages from the well-known sacerdotal decrees, in which *pḥ* is used together with a reference to *hp* 'custom'.

> *ỉrm p3 sp md(.t) nty pḥ ỉw ỉr=w n=w n hp*
>
> (…) and the rest of the things that are fitting to do for them according to custom (*hp* !)
>
> Synodal decree Alexandria (= TM 129851), line 30.
>
> *n3 md,t-pḥ.w nty pḥ n n3 ỉrpy.w* (...) *ỉr=f smn=w ḥr p3y=w gy r-ḫ p3 hp*
>
> 'The honours that are fitting for the temples (…) he confirmed them as they were, according to custom (*hp* !)'
>
> Rosettana (= TM 8809), line 19.

3.2 Scientific (not mathematical) texts

Are the patterns used in scientific texts comparable? At first sight not. To describe the actions to be undertaken by the magician, the Magical Papyrus of London and Leiden (= TM 55955), a handbook with spells for all kinds of magic, uses the second tense *i.ỉr=k sḏm* and the continuative conjunctive *mtw=k sḏm*, in the second person. Although the second tense is notoriously difficult to interpret,[8] it seems likely that here it is used as an injunctive 'you should …'.[9]
To describe the actions of the mummifier, the Apis Embalming Ritual (= TM 56081) uses *ỉw=f sḏm*. Although this is interpreted and translated as a present by the editor, it is occasionally continued by a conjunctive *mtw=f sḏm*,[10] which suggests that a third future is an alternative and perhaps more attractive interpretation.

Of course, many of these texts were copied from older models in hieratic and with more archaic grammar. This will have had repercussions on the use of tenses, as is also suggested by P. Vienna D 6257 (= TM 55973), a medical handbook. As a recent study points out,[11] the texts uses the infinitive for the recipes, but also the (third) future second person *ỉw=k sḏm*, and the conjunctive, also in the third person plural *mtw=w sḏm*.

Finally, divinatory texts such as the astrological handbook P. Berlin 15683 (= TM 55959) also employ the third person (third) future *ỉw=f r sḏm*, but the tense here may be connected to the fact that these works inherently refer to the future.

---

[8] Widmer, 1999.
[9] It is as also translated in this way in Johnson, 1986.
[10] See Vos, 1993, 353.
[11] Hoffmann, 2013, 27–28.

3.3 Mathematical texts

And so we have arrived at the texts on which this project focuses: mathematical and legal texts. To start with the former, it should be stressed that these are relatively rare in Demotic. The main text is the set of some 40 problems preserved on the verso of the Legal Code (the so-called Codex of Hermopolis or P. Cairo JdE 89127ff Vo = TM 55975). Other, shorter texts, are of similar structure and contents.[12]

As expected in the casuistic tradition, the problems are always concrete, with concrete solutions. Only in a single case, a general rule seems to be formulated. The order of the problems is more or less logical, and certainly not completely arbitrary:[13]

division: 1–3
logical progression of series of fractions: 4–6
impact of changes in width and height on area (and vice versa): 7–12, 14–18
progressively halving fractions: 23
triangular calculations with shift of basis pole: 24–31
relation between area and sides (or diameter) of land: 32–38
relation between height and other dimensions: 39–40
unclear: 13, 19–22 (interest?)

The structure of the individual problems is more or less fixed. Often a generalizing title is provided at the start, e.g. 'the things you (should) know about X'. Then follows the question itself, often introduced by *iw=w ḏd n=k* 'they will say to you', sometimes followed by a plain imperative. More often, however, it takes the form of an interrogative sentence, with *iẖ* + infinitive, e.g. *iẖ mḥ=w* 'what to fill them?' (problem 4 line 1), or most commonly with *iẖ* + equative sentence with relative form, e.g. *iẖ pꜣ nty iw=f wꜣḥ r pꜣy=s ṯs* 'what is that which should be added to its height?' (problem 12, line 13). The solution is often introduced by *pꜣ gy ir=f* 'the way to do it', as a rule followed by *iw=k ḏd* 'you will say'. The consecutive steps to be taken towards the solution are phrased as further (third) futures or as imperatives.[14] The result is often just plain *r* 'which makes'. The verification, finally, is introduced by *r di.t rẖ=k s* 'to cause that you know it'.

As in other scientific texts, the habitual is rare, and occurs in the following contexts (these attestations of *ẖr* seem to be part of verbal forms rather than particles):

- for an approximative (and intermediate) solution (in 3)
- for an intermediate result (in 8–10)
- to introduce a question (in 34, 37, 39)
- in a description, as a step-up to the problem (in 35, 38, 40)
- for the first step of the solution (in 10, 36)
- as a transition to the next step (42 l. 7 and 43 l. 23)

[12] Parker, 1972.

[13] The numbers are those of Parker, 1972.

[14] The imperative *my* here is not to be interpreted as an optative, but translates 'cause that'.

In many of these cases, a translation as 'now' and an interpretation as a transition to a next step seems better than the expected 'usually'. Perhaps this usage can be reconciled with viewing the habitual as expressing a necessary, inevitable action. In any case the paucity of attestations in comparison to earlier mathematical texts (see Annette Imhausen in this volume) is remarkable.

3.4 Legal texts

Finally, the legal texts. Again, there are relatively few of them extant. The most important one is the already mentioned Legal Code of Hermopolis, on the recto of the mathematical text discussed above (P. Cairo JdE 89127ff Ro = TM 48855). Its nature is still debated, although most now agree that it is a law collection rather than a private manual. It is neatly ordered with sections and titles, and consists of conditional sentences with an apodosis in the third future or in the habitual tense:

> *ỉn-n3.w rmt sẖt ʿ.wy r tm di.t qt=w s* (...) *ỉw=f smy r t3ti ḏd* (...)
>
> If a man impedes that one builds it (...), he will file a complaint with the vizier saying …
>
> P. Cairo JdE 89127ff Ro (= TM 48855), col. 7 line 29.
>
> *ỉn-n3.w nb n p3 ʿ.wy ḏd my di=f n=y n3 ḥḏ.w i.ir ỉr sp n swn p3y(=y) ʿ.wy ẖr di=w di=f st n=f* (...)
>
> If the owner of the house says: "Let him give to me the money that has remained unpaid of the price of my house", one should cause that he gives it to him.
>
> P. Cairo JdE 89127ff Ro (= TM 48855), col. 7 line 3.

Other legal texts seem of a slightly different nature. The best preserved example is P. Berlin 23757 Ro (= TM 56178), which contains less concrete legal problems, with equally more abstract solutions. It may well be a didactic compendium rather than a collection of laws, and thus a better parallel for the mathematical texts than the Legal Code.

The more didactic legal texts are structured as problems with a solution. The problem is generally structured as a question, mostly taking the form *iẖ* + equative sentence with relative form. Occasionally quotes from laws or case descriptions precede the question. The solution is almost always introduced by *p3y=f w3ẖ* 'its answer', and formulated in an objective way.[15]

Normative statements in legal texts are similar to those in mathematical texts: common are equative (or 'nominal') sentences and third futures, not only expressing objective future ('you will') but also expressing the norm ('you shall'). A major difference, however, is the very frequent use of the habitual *ẖr sḏm=f* echoing the frequent attestation of the *sḏm. ẖr.f* in earlier legal texts. It expresses general validity and habitude, but also normativity as 'should' or 'can'. Also, legal texts tend to use second tenses more often than mathematical texts, both as a condition or to stress the adverbial element in the sentence.

---

[15] Lippert, 2004, 131–143.

4. Conclusion

Explicit references to the norm, the right way of doing things that are right, are found in several types of texts in Demotic. The term *hp* seems to express the norm, and references to it abound in Demotic sources. It is the way things should be and should be done. Ideally, these two fall together: law (*hp*) is justice (*hp*), and legal claims (*hp*) emanate from legal proceedings (*hp*) that are proper (*hp*) and correct (*hp*), just as rites (*hp*) should be performed in the right way (*hp*) to do what should be and has always been done (*hp*).

But how does Demotic express that actions are according to *hp*, i.e. the right thing to do in a right way? In letters and petitions, a not uncommon expression is *p3 sḥn nfr st ỉr-rḫ s* '(may) you know the right thing to do', an implicit appeal to decide in the sender's or applicant's favour. Another way to appeal to the norm is by using the verb *pḥ* 'to be fitting', which is in some cases even directly connected to *hp*. The so-called habitual tense (*ḫr sḏm=f*) can be found in connection with these references to the norm, but its use is irregular at best. Scientific texts other than mathematical handbooks almost never use this habitual, nor do they seem to refer to the norm in an explicit way. The right course of action is simply described by a present or future tense. Mathematical handbooks are very similar, and tend to use the future tense to describe the different steps to come to a correct solution. The habitual occurs occasionally, but not always where it is expected. In legal texts, on the other hand, the habitual is very common, here in combination with the third future so typical of mathematical and other scientific texts.

In all, the specificity of legal texts lies in their referring to a moral norm, a customary and correct way of doing things according to what is fitting (*p3 nty-ỉw=s pḥ*), according to custom and law (*hp*). The frequent use of the habitual may well be related to this, although this tense should be studied in more detail to determine its precise meaning. In scientific texts, on the other hand, the correct course of action is described without explicit reference to the norm. The veracity of natural laws is evident through the application of rules, but these seem to be presented as positive rather than normative.

Abbreviations and references

The abbreviations for text editions found in this article mostly follow the standard of the Trismegistos database (http://www. trismegistos.org), which are largely based on the Demotic Berichtigungsliste (S. Vleeming). The TM number refers to the number to be used to retrieve the text, e.g. www.trismegistos.org/text/56178.

Baetens, Gert / Mark Depauw, 2015. "The legal advice of Totoes in the Siut archive (P. BM 10591, verso, col. I–III)". *Journal of Egyptian Archaeology* 101, 197–215.

Depauw, Mark, 2006. *The Demotic Letter. A Study of Epistolographic Scribal Traditions against their Intra- and Intercultural Background* (Demotische Studien 14). Sommerhausen: Gisela Zauzich Verlag.

— 2012. “Language Use, Literacy, and Bilingualism”. In: Christina Riggs (ed.) *Oxford Handbook of Roman Egypt*. Oxford: Oxford University Press, 493–506.

Hoffmann, Friedhelm, 2013. “Die Verwendung hieratischer Zeichen in demotischen medizinischen Texten”. In: Sven P. Vleeming (ed.) *Aspects of Demotic Orthography. Acts of an International Colloquium held in Trier, 8 November 2010* (Studia Demotica 11). Leuven: Peeters, 25–39.

Johnson, Janet H., 1986. “PDM xiv. 1–1227”. In: Hans Dieter Betz (ed.) *The Greek Magical Papyri in Translation, including the Demotic Spells*. Chicago / London: University of Chicago Press, 195–251.

Lippert, Sandra, 2004. *Ein demotisches juristisches Lehrbuch. Untersuchungen zu Papyrus Berlin P 23757 rto* (Ägyptologische Abhandlungen 66). Wiesbaden: Harrassowitz.

Nims, Charles F., 1948. “The Term HP, ‘Law, Right’, in Demotic”. *Journal of Near Eastern Studies* 7, 243–260.

Parker, Richard A., 1972. *Demotic Mathematical Papyri* (Brown Egyptological Studies 7). London: Brown University Press.

Vos, René L., 1993. *The Apis Embalming Ritual: P. Vindob. 3873* (Orientalia Lovaniensia Analecta 50). Leuven: Peeters.

Widmer, Ghislaine, 1999. “Emphasizing and Non-Emphasizing Second Tenses in the ‘Myth of the Sun's Eye’”. *Journal of Egyptian Archaeology* 85, 165–188.

Normative Texts in Ptolemaic Egypt[1]

Katelijn Vandorpe and Valérie Wyns

Abstract ... 181
1 Preliminaries ... 181
2 Extra-textual normative elements ... 185
3 Textual normative elements: explicit reference to the authority and the authoritative character of the text ... 187
4 Textual normative elements: abstraction, coherence and linguistic characteristics ... 188
5 Illustration of normative texts from Ptolemaic Egypt: the Codex Hermopolis (Demotic, Egyptian Law) and the Revenue Laws (Greek, royal law) ... 189
5.1 Demotic Codex Hermopolis (P. Mattha and Donker Van Heel 1990) ... 189
5.2 The Revenue Laws (P. Rev.) (Col. 1–22) ... 191
6 Conclusions ... 192
Abbreviations and references ... 193

Abstract

After Alexander had liberated Egypt from the Persian dominion and the new dynasty of the Ptolemies had been founded, many Greeks emigrated to the Nile country. Although Greek was the language of the ruling class, Egyptian remained an important legal language. The range of normative texts became diverse, going from royal ordinances, civil codes of Greek poleis, Egyptian priestly decrees, Egyptian law codes, rules of associations and non-legal normative texts of a scientific or ethical nature. They all show a high level of abstraction and coherence. The extra-textual and textual normative elements of these text types are discussed and two examples (the Codex Hermopolis and the Revenue Laws) illustrate the principles of normative texts in Ptolemaic Egypt.

1. Preliminaries

The arrival of Alexander the Great in Egypt and his consecutive proclamation as pharaoh in 332 BC marked the end of the second Persian rule of the Nile country and the start of Hellenistic Egypt. After the death of Alexander, his general Ptolemy ascended to the throne, first as satrap, in 306 BC as pharaoh. The Ptole-

[1] The authors would like to thank Nico Dogaer for sharing his expertise on the Revenue Laws.

maic dynasty would rule Egypt for almost 300 years, its last queen the famous Cleopatra VII.[2]

Although Greek was the language of the new ruling class, Egyptian Demotic remained an important administrative and legal language throughout Egypt. The first Ptolemy generally left the existing bureaucracy intact, and although his son Ptolemy II introduced an administrative reform, much of the Pharaonic bureaucratic hierarchy was continued. The new rulers did not replace the existing laws of the country, but introduced both Greek and royal law alongside it, the latter taking precedence over all. Traditional Egyptian law courts, composed of *laokritai* or Egyptian priests, were complemented, amongst others, by the courts of the *chrematistai*, appointed by the crown to pass judgment in fiscal and civic cases over all population groups. The Ptolemaic dynasty never compiled a comprehensive law book, possibly deliberately to facilitate the functioning of the several law traditions alongside each other. Hence officials, lawyers and priests made compilations of law excerpts for consultation, which today provide us with most of our information on the functioning of the legal system of Ptolemaic Egypt.[3]

The corpus of normative texts originating from Ptolemaic Egypt is quite extensive. Climate characteristics provided excellent circumstances for the preservation of papyrus – a medium otherwise prone to swift deterioration – in buildings, dumps or even in mummy cartonnage[4] or mummified crocodiles stuffed with old papers. A large number of papyri and papyrus archives has thus survived to present day.[5] They convey information about a large number of aspects of Egyptian daily life, including law and legislation. Officials, priests and laymen collected and archived letters, tax receipts, a variety of contracts and other pieces of documentation that held some use for them. Among these papers, copies of royal ordinances, law excerpts and other legal texts can be found, possibly because the owner wished to make use of them during a trial or other legal proceedings. Another source of information are the royal, priestly and honorary decrees, carved into stone for eternity and often displayed in temple areas.

The range of texts in Ptolemaic Egypt having a normative character is diverse, consisting of legal and non-legal normative texts. Language and character of the texts depend on the authorities that promulgated them and the target audience. In what follows, we differentiate between six main types of normative texts.

(1) Legal normative texts issued by the king or his direct representatives include royal ordinances (general *prostagmata* applicable to all subjects or large groups; we do not include epistolary ordinances with once-only orders). The Ptolemaic kings also authorized laws (*nomoi*), revisions of laws (*diorthomata*), and 'regis-

[2] For a general introduction to the Ptolemaic period, see Vandorpe, 2010.

[3] For an introduction to Egyptian law, see Lippert, 2008. For an introduction to law in Ptolemaic Egypt, see Seidl, 1962. For a source book of law in Greco-Roman Egypt, including general introductions, see Keenan / Manning / Yiftach-Firanko, 2014.

[4] Disused papyrus was often recycled for the fabrication of mummy cases or mummy decoration such as collars.

[5] For the papyrus texts, see the Trismegistos database https://www.trismegistos.org, for the papyrus archives, see https://www.trismegistos.org/arch/index.php.

ters' (*diagrammata*, e.g. of taxable property). A coherent collection of fiscal rules is found in the so-called Revenue Laws (P. Rev.) by Ptolemy II. Royal law took precedence over all other law traditions present in Egypt, as attested in a papyrus from 226 BC.[6] The several law traditions that operated at the same time in the Ptolemaic kingdom, could only be applied if they did not conflict with royal law. When neither royal law nor the *politikoi nomoi* provided judges and other legal professionals with guidelines, they were to rely on *gnome dikaiotatè*, or the 'most equitable opinion', in other words, use common sense.

(2) Normative texts inspired by Greek tradition were issued by the highest authorities of Greek *poleis*. Ptolemaic Egypt harboured only three such city states, Naukratis, a pre-Ptolemaic foundation, Alexandria, founded by Alexander the Great, and Ptolemais in Upper Egypt, founded by Ptolemy I. Textual sources from these *poleis* are scarce due to urban development in later times, a moist climate or lack of excavations. A third-century BC civil code is attested for Alexandria by P. Hal. 1 which contains excerpts from the laws governing the city state, such as its city law (*politikos nomos*).[7] This collection of Alexandrian laws, discovered in the Apollonopolite nome in Upper Egypt, was composed by or for an unknown lawyer who wanted to present them in court. For the city of Ptolemais, several decrees or *psephismata* (including honorary decrees, which can be prescriptive and durative) are attested, usually issued by the *boulè* and the *dèmos* of the *polis*, comparable to the Greek decrees of classical Greece and the Hellenistic world.[8]

(3) Egyptian and bilingual normative texts were issued by the priestly class, among these the priestly synodal decrees in honour of the king(s) written in two languages (Greek and Egyptian), but in three scripts (Greek, Demotic and hieroglyphs), e.g. the Canopus (237 BC) and Rosettana (196 BC) decrees;[9] it has been argued by Clarysse[10] that the Greek text was at the base of the Egyptian versions and not vice versa. Priests were also responsible for the redaction of rituals in honour of the gods (descriptive and durative) and of the rules for cult guilds (prescriptive and durative for members of the association).

(4) Laws originating from the Egyptian legal tradition, known as the 'laws of the *chora* (country-side)', continued to be applied by the Egyptian population and law professionals even after the Greek-Macedonian government had been installed. They were passed down by the Egyptian clergy, to which Egyptian notaries, judges (*laokritai*) and teachers belonged who applied or taught these laws. The continuation of Egyptian legal practice was sanctioned and even encouraged by the Ptolemaic dynasty.

---

[6] P. Petrie III 21g (= Mitt. Chr. 21) + P. Gur. 2 (= Sel. Pap. II 256; CPJud. I 19).

[7] For an English translation of part of P. Hal. 1, see Bagnall / Derow, 2004, no. 124; see also Fraser, 1972, 93–131.

[8] See Vallet, 2015.

[9] The oldest priestly decree is the recently discovered trilingual decree of Alexandria from 243 BC, see El-Masry / Altenmüller / Thissen, 2012.

[10] Clarysse, 1999.

The most important piece of evidence is the Codex of Hermopolis (P. Mattha),[11] best described as a legal manual, written in Demotic. The Codex was found in the Middle-Egyptian city of Hermopolis (modern Tuna el-Gebel) in 1938–1939. Its verso presents a collection of mathematical problems.[12] There is probably no direct connection between the manual and the mathematical texts, but, as priests could act both as judges and teachers, it is not peculiar that they appear on the same papyrus.[13] What was the purpose of the legal manual? It may have been a collection of juridical practices in casuistic form or a codification of priestly common law under Ptolemy II, but for these the composition does not seem general enough. The manuscript is rather a juridical handbook with procedures to be applied to various complex cases, probably guidelines for priestly, Egyptian judges in native courts. For paleographical and other reasons, the collection dates from the early third century BC, but at least part of the book might be traced back to an original of the eighth century BC under Pharaoh Bocchoris (Bakenranef, 24th Dynasty).[14] Some parts of the text have been translated: A Greek copy originating from Oxyrhynchus dates to the second half of the second century AD (P. Oxy. XLVI 3285 Vo).[15] Consequently, for several centuries from the eighth century BC until the second century AD, the same manual has been used by Egyptian priests in the native courts, probably all over Egypt. Fragments of other manuals dating from the same period are extant.[16]

(5) Cult guilds, professional and artistic groups were also allowed to promulgate rules for their association with a durative character. Well-attested are cult rules of priestly associations, e.g. those from the temple of Horus of Edfu, which have been taken over by other associations, such as in the Fayum village Pisai (P. Assoc.) or the Greek rules of a Zeus-association (P. Lond. VII 2193). Cult rules are called *hp.w*, 'laws' or *p3 hp irm n3 md.w.t*, 'the law and clauses' in Demotic, νόμος in Greek. Members were supposed to heed the rules of their societies, and a wide array of possible punishments if they failed to do so has survived.[17] Rules and verdicts issued by the aforementioned guilds and associations were acknowledged by the other law traditions of Egypt, as attested by the judgment by the *laokritai* on members of a professional guild in P. BM 10591 ro, col. VI.3.[18]

---

[11] P. Mattha (with English translation) contains corrections by George R. Hughes, brought together with later corrections by e.g. Pieter W. Pestman in Donker Van Heel, 1990. For an introduction, German translation and notes, see Grunert, 1982. For a discussion of the structure of the text and other issues, see Grunert, 1983.

[12] Published in Parker, 1972.

[13] A search in the Trismegistos database renders no attestations of a similar combination of mathematics and law on the same papyrus.

[14] Pestman, 1983. See though also Markiewicz, 2008.

[15] Pestman, 1985. See also Donker Van Heel, 1990.

[16] E.g. P. Carlsberg 1 p. 96; 103–127; Lippert, 2003; Lippert, 2004, 21–117; P. Brooklyn Dem. 212.

[17] E.g. P. Lille Dem. 29; P. Cairo Dem. 30606; 30605; 31179; 30619; SB V 7835; P. Prag. Dem. 17.

[18] Thompson, 1934.

(6) Non-legal normative texts are never referred to as νόμος or *hp*, 'law', and the authority that issued them is not explicitly mentioned. Such is the case for mathematical texts, both Greek and Egyptian. They were, of course, composed by scientists, but who authorized them? Can we consider an abstract, scientific authority? The same goes for medical texts and Egyptian didactic literature. The latter provided a code of conduct in several settings, mainly under the guise of so-called 'wisdom texts'. These present a fictitious authority, such as a pharaoh or a vizier, in the introduction to the code of proper behavior, which is called *mtr.t*, '(ethical) instruction'. The advice is often presented as being told by a father to his son, as in the *Instruction of Anqscheshonqy*[19], which was probably composed under the early Ptolemies.[20]

As normative texts should have a durative character, we do not include prescriptive texts with once-only orders, such as orders by the king or officials to their subordinates as found e.g. on petitions and in several epistolary royal ordinances. In decrees, especially honorary decrees, both durative and once-only orders may be recorded, hence only the examples with a durative character are included, although text structure and linguistic elements are similar in both groups.

In this paper, we discuss extra-textual and textual elements that reflect the normative character in our corpus.[21] A distinction should be made between normative texts with a legal character (1–5) and those with a scientific/ethical character (6).

2. Extra-textual normative elements

A monumental and public nature has been suggested to be a characteristic of normative texts. In Greek and Roman society, not only publication, but also filing were essential steps for public and temple records to become normative. The Athenian Metroon was a kind of central archive where public records, written on perishable material, could be consulted by officials and interested parties. They were furthermore disseminated not only orally, which is important in a society with a low level of literacy, but also published on stone and even on bronze, serving a permanent purpose. The Aerarium and annex-Tabularium were Rome's counterpart of the Metroon in republican times. Laws and decrees, such as the *senatus consulta*, became valid and hence normative, only after they had been deposited in the Aerarium under the guardianship of Saturn. The archives could be consulted by magistrates only. Rome's public records were subsequently proclaimed by heralds and published on temporary wooden boards or on 'eternal' bronze. Greek and Roman public records on stone or bronze were set up in the most frequented or most visible places and were authoritative, as were the copies in the archives; hence legal copies could be made from them.[22]

---

[19] See Glanville, 1955; for an English translation see Lichtheim, 1983, 66–93.

[20] For an up-to-date list of Egyptian wisdom texts of the Ptolemaic period, see Wyns, 2017, 138–143, 164–171.

[21] Compare the inspirational article by Asper, 2004.

[22] Clarysse / Vandorpe, 2008.

For Hellenistic Egypt, information on the filing of normative public records is lacking, but must have existed given the elaborate system that existed for the filing of non-normative official and private documents. An exception to the gap in our knowledge are agreements (*synchoreseis*) drawn up after a trial, which were mandatorily deposited with the royal administration[23] and for which the parties of a law suit probably had to pay a tax.[24] Temple records of a normative nature were kept in the temple archives together with scientific, didactic, mathematical and cultic literature, as for instance in the library of the temple of Tebtynis from Roman Egypt,[25] or the above-mentioned manual of Egyptian laws known as the Codex Hermopolis, containing on its verso-side mathematical problems.

In Hellenistic Egypt, the publication of normative texts was common and was in line with Greek and Egyptian practice. Royal ordinances, decrees from the Greek *poleis* and priestly decrees were published on stone[26] and set up in public places. Priestly decrees honouring the king in the temple complexes of first, second and third rank were placed in their most visible place (Canopus) or alongside the statue of the king (Rosettana). Royal ordinances had to be published in the nome metropoleis and in the 'most significant places in the nome' (C. Ord. Ptol. 75). Most of the royal ordinances known to us today have mainly survived on the medium of papyrus. Published Ptolemaic royal ordinances with a confirmed found site origin mostly appear outside of Egypt, such as C. Ord. Ptol. 33 from the ruins of the gymnasion of the Ptolemaic garrison on Thera, and C. Ord. Ptol. 45–46, set up on the agora of the city of Cyrene. Only a small number of royal decrees in their published form survived to present day, possibly due to the perishable material they were painted on. Not all royal ordinances would have been published on a costly stone stele, especially those concerning a specific region or period of time. A request for the permission to display a royal decree on a white board or *leukoma* in front of a house is preserved in C. Ord. Ptol. 62, 62 descr. and 63.

The language in which the texts were published depended on the target audience. Royal ordinances applying to all subjects were ordained to be engraved in Greek and Egyptian Demotic script,[27] the priestly decrees in Greek, Demotic and hieroglyphic script, the city-state decrees only in Greek. The order for publication could be recorded in the law or decree itself (P. Rev., Canopus, Rosettana), or in an accompanying letter which was sometimes also published on stone (C. Ord. Ptol. 75–76). Hieroglyphic cultic texts (codified rituals) were sometimes engraved on the temple walls.

Some normative texts with a legal character are not mentioned in the preceding paragraph: Egyptian laws or rules of cult-guilds may have been published in a temple context, but this procedure is not documented up to now.

---

[23] E.g. P. Erbstreit (2017) 9=10; 13; 17=18.

[24] E.g. BGU VI 1213.1–2.

[25] Vandorpe / Clarysse / Verreth, 2015, 391–393; http://www.trismegistos.org/arch/detail.php?tm=537.

[26] Sometimes bronze was allowed, see the Canopus Decree.

[27] Lewis, 1993.

It is unlikely that scientific/ethical normative texts were made public in the same way as were laws and decrees. They were rather made 'public' through education. The Egyptian texts circulated and were taught within a temple context, as part of the scribal tradition that had existed since Pharaonic times. For the Greek mathematical texts, one can refer to Alexandria's Mouseion and to the Greek gymnasia that were erected all over the Egyptian country, which both preserved and taught Greek science.

3. Textual normative elements: explicit reference to the authority and the authoritative character of the text

Normative texts with a legal character from Hellenistic Egypt mention as a rule the responsible authority: the king or his high representatives, the priestly class or the *boulè* and *dèmos*. The authority is mentioned at the beginning of the text and the authoritative character of the text is explicitly referred to:

- The verb προστάσσω, 'to command, to ordain', in royal ordinances. In the late Ptolemaic period, the king confirmed the decision with his 'signature' at the end of the document in the form of the verbal expression γινέσθωι, 'make it happen', which was copied when the law was reproduced later on.[28]
- The verbal expression ἔδοξεν … , 'Have decided (the *boulè* and *dèmos*)', in city-states, e.g. Ptolemais, followed by a formula such as NN εἶπεν, 'NN said (i.e. proposed)', or πρυτανέων γώμη, 'proposition of the prytans' (e.g. OGIS 48).
- The expression ψήφισμα in priestly decrees, followed by a list of priests and εἶπαν, rendered in Demotic by *wt: … ḏd*, 'decree: (list of priests) said' (Canopus and Rosettana).
- The cult rules (*hp.w*, 'laws', or *pꜣ hp irm nꜣ md.w.t*, 'the law and the clauses') of the priestly association of for instance Pisai, are said to have been adopted (*mtj*) by the members of the association of the Horus temple and to have been approved by the members of the association of the temple in Pisai. Often the approval is said to have been taken 'all together' (*n wꜥ sp*). A representative chosen by the members can force them to keep to the rules (P. Assoc.). The Greek cult rules recorded in P. Lond. VII 2193 are called the νόμος ὃν ἔθεντο [κα]τὰ κοινὸν οἱ ἐκ τῆς τοῦ Διὸς Ὑψίστου συνόδου τοῦτον εἶναι κύριον, "law which those of the association of Zeus the Highest made in common, that it should be authoritative".

The prescriptive character is furthermore reflected by the use of infinitives (depending for instance on the verb προστάσσω), imperatives or future tenses in Greek texts. Demotic documents prefer future and second tenses or a specific quasi-normative tense, the *ḫr.sḏm=f*. The latter is in fact an aorist that expresses habitual action or a universal truth, and is often used parallel with present tense constructions.[29]

[28] E.g. the 'signature' of Cleopatra VII in P. Bingen 45; van Minnen, 2000.

[29] Johnson, 1991, 132–153; Simpson, 1996, 114–116, discussing different views on the use of the *ḫr.sḏm=f*.

Contrary to legal normative texts, scientific normative texts do not refer explicitly to an authority nor do they mention terms reflecting an obligation; the quasi-normative tense *ḫr.sḏm=f is* rarely found. Ethical normative texts on the other hand, introduce a fictitious authority in the introductory narrative. The abovementioned *Instruction of Anqsheshonqy*, for instance, is attributed to a priest of Re at Heliopolis, who was imprisoned because he had not informed the king about a conspiracy, and spent his days composing a code of conduct for his youngest son. In these ethical instructions the quasi-normative tense *ḫr.sḏm=f* is commonly found. Hence, the ethical/didactic texts seem to be a category in between the legal and non-legal normative texts.

4. Textual normative elements: abstraction, coherence and linguistic characteristics

Legal normative texts show a high abstraction level, as they in general, do not refer to individuals by name nor to specific situations. Exceptions are honorary decrees with a normative character. The priestly decrees of Canopus and Rosettana for instance, praise and thus name the king and list the specific reasons why the king should be honoured in the future on a permanent basis.

Legal normative texts also show a high level of abstraction and coherence regarding content. General rules are formulated, often followed by a (sometimes very long) series of possible exceptions or special cases. The Demotic Codex Hermopolis for instance, lists all possible occurrences in the event of a father dying without a will (section 5.1). Non-legal normative texts may also show a high level of abstraction and coherence, not only within one mathematical problem (presentation of the problem and solution), but also in larger compositions: the mathematical problems on the verso of the Codex Hermopolis have a well-organized presentation, 'developing from relatively simple arithmetic to plane geometry. The last, most complicated problem deals with calculating the volume of a pyramid'.[30]

The abstract character of legal normative texts is reflected by their language. Greek legal normative texts usually prefer the neutral infinitive and when an imperative or future tense is used, the third person singular (never the second person) is found. When reference is made to a person in conditional clauses, the indefinite pronoun τις is used. Demotic legal texts have the tenses in the third person as well, and *pꜣ rmt* ('the man') is the counterpart of Greek τις, while our expression 'person X/person Y' for example in 'person X, son of person Y' is rendered by *pꜣ mn sꜣ pꜣ mn*, 'So-and-so, son of So-and-so'. Demotic also likes to make use of the third person plural ('they will do ... '), which is the only way in Demotic to construct a passive voice. An exception are Demotic cult rules that, contrary to the Greek cult rules of P. Lond. VII 2193, formulate the obligations in the first person plural ('we shall ... '), due to the fact that the cult members impose the rules on themselves. So here, the authority and the people who undergo the authority are the same. Finally, non-legal normative texts which are taught within an educational context, prefer to use the second person.

[30] Depauw, 1997, 104.

Coherence is linguistically reflected in diction (by a limited word variation, for example 'make a public protest' is each time [in all 15 times] rendered by *ir šʿr* in the Codex Hermopolis) and syntactically (by the use of the same constructions for general rules and for conditional clauses without much variation, (last paragraph in sections 5.1 and 5.2). The coherence in longer law texts or in codifications may be strengthened by the layout, by using subtitles, sometimes rendered in larger or capital letters (see e.g. the Greek codes such as the Revenue Laws and the section on 'On planting, building and deep digging' in the civil code of Alexandria, P. Hal. 1, ll. 79–83), paragraph lines (see Greek laws and codes) or extra blank space before the start of a new (sub)case (see Demotic codes, such as the Codex Hermopolis). Coherence is also found in another respect: Greek or Egyptian laws, rules and decrees are quite uniform regarding text structure all over Egypt (see Greek decrees and Egyptian cult rules).

Only when translations are involved do practices differ. Parts of the Demotic Codex Hermopolis, for example, have been translated into Greek (section 1, p. 206 f.). Interestingly, the interpreter uses other linguistic patterns to 'translate' the normative character of the Demotic text than in texts that have originally been redacted in Greek. The orders expressed in Demotic by future and second tenses are rendered in Greek by a simple indicative praesens in the passive voice or by using the impersonal δεῖ or ἀναγκάζεται ('it is necessary to'), or προστάσσεται ('it is enjoined upon the man'). The variation in diction and the use of the praesens in the passive voice are otherwise not commonly found in Greek normative texts. Similarly, Greek normative texts that have been translated into Demotic, result in a deviant structure, diction and syntax (e.g. the priestly decrees, which follow the structure and vocabulary of the Greek honorary decrees).

5. Illustration of normative texts from Ptolemaic Egypt: the Codex Hermopolis (Demotic, Egyptian Law) and the Revenue Laws (Greek, royal law)

Unfortunately, no parallel laws treating the same subject from different law traditions in Egypt survive to this day. However, in order to illustrate the principles of normative texts in Ptolemaic Egypt, we have selected two representative examples: the aforementioned Codex Hermopolis representing the Egyptian law tradition, and the Revenue Laws as an example of royal legislation. Comparing the normative traditions that are illustrated by these examples is somewhat impeded by the different subjects that the documents cover. While the Codex Hermopolis concerns itself with family law, the Revenue Laws deal with state fiscal affairs.

5.1 Demotic Codex Hermopolis (P. Mattha and Donker Van Heel 1990)

The Codex Hermopolis has four large sections:[31] instructions listing possible problems concerning

[31] See Grunert, 1983, 157–163.

1. loans
2. lease
3. alimentation
4. property (real estate).

We discuss here in more detail part of the last section dealing with possible inheritance problems (col. VIII l. 30 – col. IX l. 26).[32] According to good Egyptian tradition, Egyptians divided their property in a deed of division: during his lifetime, the testator divided his belongings between his children, who then became joint owner of their part while the testator was alive, and full owner on his death. The Codex Hermopolis deals with all possible problems arising when a father leaves behind his real estate without such a deed of division.

Case-distinction:

General rule:
- If a man dies, without having ascribed shares of his property to his children while alive,
- *ORDER*: it is his eldest son who takes possession of the property.

Subcase 1:
- If the younger brothers claim their part,
- *five ORDERS*: the property is to be divided according to the list of children (male and female) drawn up by the eldest brother, etc.,
- *+ three SPECIAL CASES are added at the end.*

Subcase 2:
- If the younger brothers do not agree with the list of children drawn up by the eldest brother,
- *four ORDERS*: an oath is to be sworn by the eldest brother and the property is to be divided, etc.; an example of the oath is added;
- *SPECIAL CASE added at the end*: an analogous procedure for females.

Subcase 3:
- If a man dies possessing property while the property is already in the hands of his eldest son,
- *three SPECIAL CASES are added.*

Subcase 4:
- if a man has only daughters,
- ORDER: the property is to be divided among the daughters,
- *two SPECIAL CASES are added at the end.*

Subcase 5:
- if some property is in hands of a younger son, etc.,
- ORDER: an oath has to be sworn by the younger son and he can keep it; the consequences of swearing and not-swearing the oath are recorded,
- *a SPECIAL CASE is added at the end.*

---

[32] For this section, see now the new edition by P.W. Pestman, *La succession* ab intestat *d'après le manuel juridique (P. Mattha 8.20–9.26, 30 et 32)*, forthcoming as Pap. Lugd.Bat. XXVIII 3.

Subcase 6:

- if there is a deed for the eldest son only, *followed by one further condition*,
- ORDER: he can keep the property.

Subcase 7:

- If a man dies and he has (only) one house, and he did not write a title to it for a son of his, *followed by four further conditions*,
- ORDER: the money of the price of the house is to be divided among the children.

The general rule and each subcase are introduced by a blank space (except if recorded at the beginning of line) and by *in.nꜣ.w*, a conditional auxiliary, followed by a noun subject (never a pronoun) and a verb. The orders are usually rendered by a *ḫr-sḏm=f* (expressing a habitual action, also used to give instructions; negative form: *bw-ir= f sḏm*), in a minority of cases by a future tense or by a nominal sentence (*NN pꜣ nty* … , 'it is NN who … '). The verbs by which the orders are expressed, are put in the third person plural, which is a way in Egyptian to construct a passive, impersonal voice. The special cases are all introduced *by iw=f ḫpr r* ('if it happens'). The counterpart of our 'person X son of person Y' is rendered *pꜣ mn sꜣ pꜣ mn*, 'So-and-so, son of So-and-so'.

5.2 The Revenue Laws (P. Rev.) (Col. 1–22)

Since the Ptolemaic kings never intended to impose a unified code of law upon their subjects, the selection of an appropriate document for our study proves to be somewhat difficult. We eventually selected the Revenue Laws, which are labeled rather misleadingly, since the laws and ordinances recorded in the papyrus do not form one book of law, but are a collation of legal documents that were probably collected by a member of the royal administration as a reference work.[33] However, the separate texts can be differentiated quite clearly, and we have selected the first document, consisting of the 22 first columns of the papyrus. The document records rules concerning the auctioning of crown revenues and the tax-farming system.

The rules attested by our document chronologically treat the correct procedures to be followed by crown officials, tax-farmers and their associates. The described chronology runs as follows:

1. Auctioning of the different revenues
2. Relationship between outgoing and incoming tax-farmers
3. Conditions under which new tax-farmers and their associates entered office
4. Process of tax collection
5. Monthly and final balancing of accounts.

As an example, the process of balancing of accounts is elaborated further:

Case distinction:

General rule:

The local *oikonomos* is responsible for the balancing of tax accounts.

[33] See Bingen, 1978.

Subcase 1:

- Backpayments are exacted
- ORDER: the *oikonomos* is to apply a deviant system of credit.

Subcase 2:

- Occurrence of surplus or deficit
  - 3 possible scenarios are described
  - Each scenario is accompanied by an ORDER.

Subcase 3:

- Accounts are properly balanced
- ORDER: they are to be sealed, copied into the archive of the *oikonomos*, and sent to the *dioiketes* (minister of finances) for further examination.

Subcase 4:

- Expiration of taxation period
- *Special case*: Occurrence of final deficit or surplus
  - Deficit → ORDER
  - Surplus → ORDER.

Subcase 5:

- *Dioiketes* (the minister of finances) has finished his examination of the accounting books
  - *Special case*: A deficit is discovered
    - ORDER: the *oikonomos* pays the arrears within three days
      - If not: Penalty for non-compliance
    - Subcase: Tax farmers fail to balance accounts
      - Penalty
    - Subcase: *Oikonomos* fails to give account of sureties
      - Penalty.

The start of different sections of the text sometimes coincides with the start of a new column. A new section is generally accompanied by a heading in capital letters, but we cannot be certain this was always the case, since a considerable number of lines is lost. A blank space also precedes the start of a new section. The future tense is usually used to describe the expected protocol, while the imperative aorist expresses more direct orders, especially in the case of deviant scenarios and certainly in the description of penalties. All verbs are rendered in the third person, either singular or plural.

6. Conclusions

Ptolemaic normative texts originated from a wide variety of legal traditions, and could be composed in Greek and Egyptian Demotic, sometimes both versions published on the same medium. Normative texts, whether legal, scientific or ethical, show a high level of abstraction and coherence, reflected in diction, syntaxis and overall layout, except in the case of translation of Greek documents into Demotic and vice versa. In contrast to scientific/mathematical normative texts, normative texts with a legal character (laws, cult rules, etc.) explicitly refer to the responsible authority and the authoritative character is reflected by the use of (quasi-)normative tenses such as the *ḫr.sḏm=f* in Demotic. Their publication resembles Greek practice, appearing in the most prominent places of the community, which in the Egyptian context often translated into the temple enclosure. The Demotic ethical/didactic literature seems to be a category in between, introducing a fictitious authority and using regularly the quasi-normative tense *ḫr.sḏm=f.* Also, while both in legal and ethical/didactic texts people are prompted to a certain behavior in the third person, scientific/mathematical texts offer instructions in the second person. The Codex Hermopolis constitutes one of the few links between legal and mathematical texts, as the 'code' is written on the recto-side, mathematical problems on the verso of the same papyrus, which illustrates the integrated education in the Egyptian temple context.

Abbreviations and references

Sources

C. Ord. Ptol. = *Corpus des Ordonnances des Ptolémées*, Marie-Thérèse Lenger (ed.), 1980. Brussels: Palais des Académies. (2nd edition, corrected and updated).

I. Prose = André Bernand (ed.), 1992. *La prose sur pierre dans l'Egypte hellénistique et romaine*. Paris: Centre national de la recherche scientifique. (2 volumes)

OGIS = Dittenberger, Wilhelm, 1903–1905. *Orientis Graeci Inscriptiones Selectae*. Leipzig: S. Hirzel.

For abbreviations of papyrological sources (P., O., BGU., SB. etc.), see Oates, John F. et al., 2001. *Checklist of Greek, Latin, Demotic and Coptic Papyri, Ostraca and Tablets, 5th edition* (Bulletin of the American Society of Papyrologists, Supplement 9). New Haven, Conn.: American Society of Papyrologists. Regularly updated in the online version:
http://www.papyri.info/docs.checklist or see Trismegistos database: https://www.trismegistos.org/tm/.

Canopus decree:

Simpson, Robert S., 1996. *Demotic Grammar in the Ptolemaic Sacerdotal Decrees* (Griffith Institute Monographs). Oxford: Griffith Institute / Ashmolean Museum. Canopus H (p. 224–241) + I. Prose 8.

Spiegelberg, Wilhelm, 1922. *Der demotische Text der Priesterdekrete von Kanopus und Memphis (Rosettana)*, Heidelberg: C. Winter, 3–37.

English translation in: Austin, Michel M., 2006. *The Hellenistic World. From Alexander to the Roman Conquest. A Selection of Ancient Sources in Translation*. Cambridge: Cambridge University Press, no. 271. (2nd augmented edition).

Rosettana decree:

Simpson, Robert S., 1996. *Demotic Grammar in the Ptolemaic Sacerdotal Decrees* (Griffith Institute monographs). Oxford: Griffith Institute / Ashmolean Museum. Memphis Ros. (p. 258–271) + I. Prose 16

Spiegelberg, Wilhelm, 1922. *Der demotische Text der Priesterdekrete von Kanopus und Memphis (Rosettana)*, Heidelberg: C. Winter, 38–65.

English translation in Austin, Michel M., 2006. *The Hellenistic World. From Alexander to the Roman Conquest. A Selection of Ancient Sources in Translation.* Cambridge: Cambridge University Press, no. 283. (2nd augmented edition)

Secondary literature

Asper, Markus, 2004. "Law and Logic. Towards an Archaeology of Greek Abstract Reason". *Annali dell'Istituto Universitario Orientale di Napoli* 26, 73–94.

Bagnall, Roger S. / Peter Derow, 2004. *The Hellenistic Period: Historical Sources in Translation* (Blackwell Sourcebooks in Ancient History 1). Malden / Oxford: Blackwell. (2nd edition).

Bingen, Jean, 1978. *Le Papyrus Revenue Laws: Tradition grecque et adaption hellénistique* (Vorträge der Rheinisch-Westfälische Akademie der Wissenschaften G 231). Opladen: Westdeutscher Verlag.

Clarysse, Willy, 1999. "Ptolémées et temples". In: Dominique Valbelle / Jean Leclant (eds.) *Le décret de Memphis. Colloque de la Fondation Singer-Polignac à l'occasion de la célébration du bicentenaire de la découverte de la Pierre de Rosette, Paris 1er juin 1999.* Paris: DeBoccard, 41–62.

Clarysse, Willy, / Katelijn Vandorpe, 2008. "Information Technologies". In: John P. Oleson (ed.) *Oxford Handbook of Engineering and Technology in the Classical World.* Oxford: Oxford University Press, 726–733.

Depauw, Mark, 1997. *A Companion to Demotic Studies* (Papyrologica Bruxellensia 28). Bruxelles: Fondation égyptologique reine Élisabeth.

Donker Van Heel, Koenraad, 1990. *The Legal Manual of Hermopolis (P. Mattha). Text and Translation.* Leiden: Papyrologisch Instituut.

El-Masry, Yahia / Hartwig Altenmüller / Heinz-Josef Thissen (eds.), 2012. *Das Synodaldekret von Alexandria aus dem Jahre 243 v. Chr.* (Studien zur Altägyptischen Kultur Beihefte 11). Hamburg: Helmut Buske Verlag.

Fraser, Peter M., 1972. *Ptolemaic Alexandria,* volume 1. Oxford: Clarendon Press.

Glanville, Stephen R. K., 1955. *The Instructions of 'Onqscheshonqy* (British Museum Papyrus 10508). London: British Museum Publications.

Grunert, Stefan, 1982. *Der Kodex Hermopolis und ausgewählte private Rechtsurkunden aus dem Ptolemaïschen Ägypten.* Leipzig: Reclam.

Grunert, Stefan, 1983. "Der juristische Papyrus von Hermopolis – Kodex oder Kommentar?". *Altorientalische Forschungen* 10, 151–190.

Johnson, Janet H., 1991. *Thus wrote 'Onchsheshonqy: An Introductory Grammar of Demotic* (Studies in Ancient Oriental Civilization 45). Chicago: The Oriental Institute. (2nd edition).

Keenan, James G. / Joseph G. Manning / Uri Yiftach-Firanko (eds.), 2014. *Law and Legal Practice in Egypt from Alexander to the Arab Conquest. A Selection of Papyrological Sources in Translation, with Introductions and Commentary.* Cambridge: Cambridge University Press.

Lewis, Naphtali, 1993. "The Demise of the Demotic Document: When and Why". *Journal of Egyptian Archaeology* 79, 276–281.

Lichtheim, Miriam, 1983. *Late Egyptian Wisdom Literature in the International Context: A Study of Demotic Instructions* (Orbis Biblicus et Orientalis 52). Göttingen: Vandenhoeck & Ruprecht.

Lippert, Sandra L., 2003. "Die sogenannte Zivilprozessordnung: weitere Fragmente der Ägyptischen Gesetzessamlung". *The Journal of Juristic Papyrology* 33, 91–136.

— 2004. *Ein demotisches juristisches Lehrbuch. Untersuchungen zu Papyrus Berlin P 23757 recto* (Ägyptische Abhandlungen 66). Wiesbaden: Harrassowitz.

— 2008. *Einführung in die altägyptische Rechtsgeschichte* (Einführungen und Quellentexte zur Ägyptologie 5). Berlin: LIT.

Markiewicz, Tomasz, 2008. "Bocchoris the Lawgiver. Or was he really?". *Journal of Egyptian History* 1, 309–330.

Parker, Richard A., 1972. *Demotic Mathematical Papyri* (Brown Egyptological Studies 7). Providence: Brown University Press.

Pestman, Pieter W., 1983. "L'origine et l'extension d'un manuel de droit égyptien. Quelques réflexions à propos du soi-disant Code de Hermoupolis". *Journal of the Economic and Social History of the Orient* 26, 14–21.

— 1985. "Le manuel de droit égyptien de Hermoupolis. Les Passages transmis en démotique et en grec". In: Pieter W. Pestman (ed.) *Textes et études de papyrologie grecque, démotique et copte* (Papyrologica Lugduno-Batava 23). Leiden: Brill, 116–143.

— 2001. *La succession ab intestat d'après le manuel juridique (P. Mattha 8.20–9.26, 30 et 32)*, forthcoming as Pap.Lugd.Bat. XXVIII 3. Leiden: Brill.

Seidl, Erwin, 1962. *Ptolemäische Rechtsgeschichte* (Ägyptologische Forschungen 22). Glücksstadt et al.: Augustin. (2nd edition).

Simpson, Robert S., 1996. *Demotic Grammar in the Ptolemaic Sacerdotal Decrees* (Griffith Institute Monographs). Oxford: Griffith Institute.

Thompson, Herbert, 1934. *A family archive from Siut, from papyri in the British Museum, including an account of a trial before the Laocritae in the year B.C. 170*. Oxford: Oxford University Press.

Vallet, Matthieu, 2015. *Ptolémaïs en Haute-Égypte. Une cité grecque au cœur de la Thébaïde,* unpublished PhD, Paris 1, Panthéon-Sorbonne. http://univ-paris1.academia.edu/MatthieuVallet.

Vandorpe, Katelijn, 2010. "History. Ptolemaic period". In: Alan B. Lloyd (ed.) *The Blackwell Companion to Ancient Egypt. Volume* 1 (Blackwell Companions to the Ancient World). Malden: Wiley-Blackwell, 159–179.

Vandorpe, Katelijn / Willy Clarysse / Herbert Verreth, 2015. *Graeco-Roman archives from the Fayum* (Collectanea Hellenistica 6). Leuven / Paris: Peeters.

van Minnen, Peter, 2000. "An Official Act of Cleopatra (with a Subscription in her Own Hand)". *Ancient Society* 30, 29–34.

Wyns, Valérie, 2017. "The State Ideology of the Ptolemies: Origin and Influences". *Chronique d'Egypte* 92, 137–174.

On the Authority of Normative Texts. Inscriptional Law and Mathematical Literature in Ancient Greece[1]

Markus Asper

Abstract 197
1 Greek Inscriptional Law and Court Practices 197
2 Greek Mathematics 207
3 Comparative Remarks on Normative Order and Authority 215
References 216

Abstract

The paper throws a glance at the textual codification of normative orders in ancient Greece, choosing as a focus inscriptional law and two fields of mathematics, 'practical' computation and 'theoretical' geometry. In all three fields, the precise relation between the texts themselves and the respective normative order they represent is problematic. Since the normative orders themselves tend to remain implicit even in the 'codes', issues of primary justification and of how the texts trigger practices of deduction and application emerge. Concluding remarks settle upon cross-field authority-maintaining textual strategies.

Discourses of law and of theoretical mathematics, modern or ancient, provide ample illustration of how normative orders are set up and operate, notwithstanding the fact that their normativity regards rather different fields of concept and action. This paper attempts to compare the respective textual technologies of trust in these two fields while concentrating on ancient Greece. Due to the peculiar situation of ancient Greek literature and its widely lost contexts, however, I will have to focus primarily on material and textual representations of normativity. The question as to how the normative orders concerned emerged themselves will thus have to remain in the background.

1. Greek Inscriptional Law and Court Practices

Let me begin by briefly discussing early Greek inscriptional law, that is, the remnants of the laws of the Greek poleis until the fourth century BC. At which

[1] Thanks to Annette Imhausen for inviting me to speak at 'Normative Orders' and to the Frankfurt working group for discussion and sharing their research. Special thanks go to Markus Heim for help with the diagram illustrating Euclid, *Elem.* III 5. Work on this paper has greatly benefitted from academic leave in summer 2016 granted thanks to the generosity of TOPOI II.

time Greek city-states began to display law inscriptions at prominent public places, we do not know.[2] The oldest extant inscriptions date to the second half of the seventh century BC (from Tiryns in the Argolid and the Cretan poleis Dreros and, well-known, Gortyn), which is about the time-frame the ancient tradition allots to the first famous lawgivers, such as Zaleucus.[3] With the exception of Sparta, where an alternative concept governed the representation of normative orders, the oral ῥήτρα, inscriptional law is a common feature of early poleis all across the Greek world. Apart from the differences due to local dialects, alphabets and inscriptional style, the inscriptions exhibit significant similarities regarding their textual organization: Mostly, such laws consist of conditional periods. While most of the older inscriptions contain a single law each, the notion of a collection or 'code' is also well-known to the tradition (e.g., in the traditions about Solon), for which a few inscriptional examples are known, most strikingly the Gortyn inscription (fifth century BC), which apparently replaced an older one. It seems, thus, that inscriptional law is not only the oldest Greek prose genre; it is also the media of communication with the strongest possible involvement in public decision-making,[4] because all acts of communication involving the law directly affected the political-religious-economical structure of the community. Two modest examples will illustrate that; at the same time they will have to exemplify the structure and style of Greek inscriptional law. My first example is the oldest specimen of a Greek law inscription (from Dreros, Crete; approx. 650–600 BC):[5]

> Θιός ολοιον ἆδ' ἔϝαδε : πόλι· : ἐπεί κα κοσμήσει, : δέκα ϝετίον τὸν ἀϝτὸν : μὴ κοσμε̂ν· : αἰ δὲ κοσμησίε, : ὅ[π]ε δικακσίε, : ἀϝτὸν ὀπῆλεν : διπλεῖ κἀϝ̂τὸν ἄκρηστον : ἦμεν, : ἆς δόοι, : κὃτι κοσμησίε : μηδὲν ἤμην. *vac.* ▷◁ ὀμόται δὲ : κόσμος κοὶ δάμιοι : κοὶ : ἴκατι : οἱ τᾶς πόλ[ιο]ς.

> God ? … ?! The *polis* has decided the following: When someone is *kosmos*, for ten years the same man shall not be *kosmos* again. If he does become *kosmos*, whatever he decides as a judge, he shall owe the double and he shall be ineligible for office (ἄχρηστος), as long as he lives, and whatever he does as *kosmos* shall be null and void. The swearers shall be the *kosmos* (i.e., the board of all *kosmoi*) and the *damioi* and the Twenty of the city.[6]

---

[2] As is the case with other forms of early writing in Greece, inscriptional law is an acculturated form of public and, especially, elite communication (for Near Eastern background, see Hans Neumann in this volume (pp. 61–64), my feeble attempts in Asper 2004, 90; and especially Westbrook, 2015, esp. 59–69 and 181–193. Nonetheless, its sudden and wide dissemination must be due to its usefulness for certain structures of Greek archaic upper-class culture, especially the curtailing of intra-elite competition: see Hawke, 2011.

[3] For Zaleucus see Eusebius, *Chronics* volume 2, p. 86 ed. Schoene; for Cretan influence Ephorus, *Fragments* FGrHist 70 F 139 ed. Jacoby; cf. Archilochus, *Fragments* Fr. 232 ed. West. – In the following, all law texts are quoted from the edition of Koerner, 1993; the translations are mine, based on Koerner's where possible.

[4] Whatever 'public' means. Perhaps 'public' denotes precisely the space within which inscriptional law and communal decision-making resonates, as sketched out by Hölscher 1998 (cf. Gerhardt, 2012, 54–76 on τὸ κοινόν).

[5] Koerner, 1993, no. 90 = Meiggs / Lewis, 1969, no. 2, p. 2 f.

[6] All translations in this paper are my own.

The law's diction is clear and carefully crafted; the same holds for its inscription, despite the fact that the initial invocation was added later by the stonemason.[7] While historians debate its precise implications and its intent, it is evident that the law excludes the repeated tenure of being *kosmos*, presumably the most important magistrate, before ten years have passed. Quite clearly, behind the law there looms the concept of rotating offices and thus the norm of excluding the accumulation of political power in the hands of a single man, which are precisely the fundamentals of the Greek polis, understood as a carefully calibrated and institutionalized balance of power among a ruling elite. In archaic Gortyn, political decision-making is carried out by the polis herself ('the polis has decided … ') which delegates power to certain offices and committees, e.g. the *kosmos* or the 'Twenty of the polis'. The last provision of the law is obviously motivated by the concept of two or more political bodies controlling each other. It is quite fascinating that within these few lines and that early, almost the whole concept of the polis is already present in full. In addition to what the law actually says, even the monumental materiality of the law which was inscribed on a temple wall with unusual care (punctuation, clause-marker)[8] sends a message of authority. All contextual detail, e.g. information is suppressed as to when the law was ratified, who supported it, who was *archon/kosmos* at that time, against whom was it directed, which makes the law timeless and unconditionally valid, and thus adds to its monumentality. […]?

In order to demonstrate the genre's stable and quasi-international character, I choose as my second example a much later, actually fourth-century, law from a place that must have differed to a great extent from archaic Dreros, namely Demosthenes' Athens, and that focuses on a less noble matter than the rotation of public offices (quoted in Demosthenes, *Against Lacritus* (orat. 35) 51):

> Ἀργύριον δὲ μὴ ἐξεῖναι ἐκδοῦναι Ἀθηναίων καὶ τῶν μετοίκων τῶν Ἀθήνησι μετοικούντων μηδενί, μηδὲ ὧν οὗτοι κύριοί εἰσιν, εἰς ναῦν ἥτις ἂν μὴ μέλλῃ ἄξειν σῖτον Ἀθήναζε ... ἐὰν δέ τις ἐκδῷ παρὰ ταῦτα, εἶναι τὴν φάσιν καὶ τὴν ἀπογραφὴν τοῦ ἀργυρίου πρὸς τοὺς ἐπιμελητάς, καθάπερ τῆς νεὼς καὶ τοῦ σίτου εἴρηται, κατὰ ταὐτά. καὶ δίκη αὐτῷ μὴ ἔστω περὶ τοῦ ἀργυρίου, ὃ ἂν ἐκδῷ ἄλλοσέ ποι ἢ Ἀθήναζε, μηδὲ ἀρχὴ εἰσαγέτω περὶ τούτου μηδεμία.
>
> It shall not be allowed to Athenians and metics who live in Athens nor to those whose legal guardians they are, to issue a credit on a ship which is not supposed to bring cereals to Athens. … But if someone issues a credit against this (law), he shall be reported and there shall be a list of funds addressed to port authority, just as was said with respect to the ship and the cereals, exactly like that. And he shall not have the right to reclaim the credit in court, which he issued (for a ship going) elsewhere than to Athens, and no office shall introduce legal procedures on his behalf.

---

[7] See Meiggs / Lewis, 1969, 2 for θιοσολοιον.
[8] See plates no. 59, 1a and 1b in Jeffery, 1961.

Admittedly, the law quoted exists only as part of this speech, in which an unknown Athenian accuses a family of metics of having violated the law. The speech, however, adduces verbatim excerpts from a number of documents that are usually held to be genuine. The speaker quotes this law probably either from an inscription or from an intermediate source.

When we compare the two texts, we find parallel structures that apply just as well to the hundreds of law inscriptions and indirectly transmitted laws, all over the Greek world and well into Roman imperial times, and must thus be treated as generic markers. For this paper's argument, the following four are of importance:

(i) These texts assert a norm of action in the form of a conditional sequence of actions (conditional law). Aptly, Jim Ritter has labeled the structure 'sequential'.[9] The sequence's parts follow the pattern 'If someone/when someone/who carries out action x, sanction y has to be implemented.' The protasis can appear in strictly conditional, temporal or relative guise, the apodosis usually takes on the infinitive. In cases where action x is evident, that is, either by context or situation, the law has the form of an unconditional command, again usually expressed through infinitive; rarely, one finds prohibitive clauses or impersonal statements.[10] (ii) These laws are abstract, that is, they suppress social or legal context, and they keep the provisions strictly impersonal, that is, free from names, etc.[11] (iii) They are monumental and 'public', that is, located at places where centers of elite communication were institutionalized. (iv) They commit 'particular' norms to writing, i.e., the whole normative order of which the particular law is but a part, is not subject to that monumentalization.[12]

I suggest that observations two and three are two aspects of the same communal desire to make these norms work, that is, to invest them with validity and permanence. I assume that we should see such written regulations as the last step in a long process of public debate, which is finally and publicly settled only by the inscription's installment. The debate must have been often controversial, even disruptive. The monumentality of the inscription should thus be seen as an attempt to make it valid. Thus, its being abstract appears as the linguistic aspect of the same monumental character. Although the normative order of which the

---

[9] The principle of conditional law and the function of the single conditional period as the basic 'unit' in Greek law texts is one of the strongest reasons for the assumption that inscriptional Greek law was acculturated from Near Eastern practices of codifying law, because 'conditionality' is, among ancient Near Eastern cultures a dominant principle of textual organization not only in law, but also in omina texts, medicine and even mathematics: Cf. Asper 2004, 90; Asper, 2007, 378 f.; Hans Neumann (p. 66) and Jim Ritter (p. 8) in this volume.

[10] Prohibitive, e.g., Koerner, 1993, no. 53 (Krim, fifth century BC): μὴ χέσες ἱεροῦ. Impersonal, e.g. Koerner, 1993, no. 54 (Delos, fifth century BC): ξένῳ οὐχ ὁσίη ἐσι[έναι]. My impression is that unconditional law is more frequent with respect to sanctuaries. Cf. Asper, 2001, 94.

[11] Which is different in edicts (see Asper, 2001, 96).

[12] For a curiously similar phenomenon in Ancient Near Eastern law see Westbrook, 2015, 61: "Legal sources do not expound legal principles [...].".

single law is an upshot, remains implicit, quite early there emerge what I would like to term 'meta-laws' that attempt to regulate legal procedure rather than sanctionable social action in general. At Olympia, for example, the following *lex sacra* was inscribed at about 500 BC on a beautiful, but modestly sized bronze plaque found in the sanctuary of Zeus:[13]

> Τὸν δέ κα γραφέον, ὅ τι δοκέοι καλιτέρος ἔχεν πο<τ> τὸν θ<ε>όν, ἐξαγρέον κα<ὶ> ἐνποι · ν σὺν βολαῖ <π>εντακατίον ἀϝλανέος καὶ δάμοι πλεθύοντι δινάκοι· <δινά>κοι δέ κα <ἐ>ν τρίτον, αἴ τι ἐνποιοῖ αἴτ' ἐξαγρέοι.
>
> Of what is inscribed (i.e., the laws), how it will appear more agreeable to the god, may he change securely[14] deletions and additions in accordance with the council of the Five Hundred and the full assembly. He may change at the third time, whether he adds or deletes.

While details of content and phrasing remain a little opaque, it is uncontroversial that this is a law about how to change already existing law and thus, a norm that regulates how to deal with norms. In the context of early Greek provisions about changing existing law, this one strikes us as rather liberal.[15] The law assigns a special status to the laws it is about: they are summarized as 'what is written' (τὰ γραφέα). Obviously, the normative order in the background thus consists of different parts which one can identify, e.g., according to their different materiality. Probably we have to supply as a subtext that the community can change only 'what is inscribed', according to carefully determined procedure, while what is not inscribed, it cannot change. In this case, the provisions preceding this one on the same plaque regulate sanctions again defecation within the sanctuary and against judgments that contradict existing law. The concluding provision which is the one quoted above perhaps applies only to these preceding laws. At the end, the body of unwritten norms is probably quoted as τὰ πάτρια, the *mos maiorum*, as it were.[16] A modern observer might wonder why these rather specific regulations were committed to writing but not the more fundamental normative order the regulations are based upon? Perhaps the procedures of inscribing which implied several bodies of a polis' citizenry, were too time-and-cost expensive in order to put them to work at anything else but those provisions that were precarious. Viewed from that perspective, it seems only natural that inscription was reserved to what was subject to potential dissent and thus needed monumental stabilization. The view that one needs to primarily codify fundamentals and principles,

---

[13] See Jeffery, 1961, 408 and plate 42 no. 5; Koerner, 1993, no. 43.

[14] The meaning of ἀϝλανέος and δινάκοι remains unknown (note that the second occurrence of the latter term is almost entirely conjectural). Koerner's interpretation which I follow, depends ultimately upon Meister, 1882, 24. It is especially odd that the subject of action is not determined; second, the strange use of the optative, which is, as far as I can see, never used this way elsewhere in the Olympian corpus.

[15] Cf. Koerner, 1993, no. 29 (Argos, sixth century BC) and no. 47.9 ff. (Naupaktos, c. 500 BC) which threaten legal sanction against any attempt of trying to change written law.

[16] See Koerner, 1993, 119 who quotes from another bronze plaque of the same provenience and time (Jeffery, 1961, 408 and plate 42 no. 4).

that is, in our case the most general normative assumptions, a view that is central to modern discussions of axiomatic systems, uses writing merely as a vehicle towards improving the system's premises and over-all architecture. Under archaic conditions the system of the normative order itself was probably taken to be stable and beyond criticism, anyway. With respect to individual laws, however, "rationale Überzeugungsbildung unter Gleichen"[17] was probably not the model according to which we have to imagine those political agreements; rather, we have to imagine tough negotiations among several competing groups and teeth-grinding concessions of the weaker ones to the collective along the lines of rational-choice theory.[18] The conclusion thus becomes attractive that monumentalization by writing is not aiming at the normative order itself, which is supported by research on norms in ancient fields other than law.[19] Monumentality is, under such circumstances, meant to at the same time document and support the consensus. Inscribed, monumentalized law thus displays its authority which is based on the pertaining procedures carried out by legitimate agents. Inscription is probably merely the material proof for legitimation through public procedure.[20]

Many such texts have been collected since the days of Boeckh; constantly new ones are discovered and published. Despite their being quite different when it comes to detail, the four general features listed above apply to all of them. For the purposes of the present paper these texts function as index of a specific normative order and for the problematic relation of such an order to the codification of certain specific provisions. As to the normative order's precise extent and its supra-regional structures, we can only guess. Nonetheless, some features of the whole system are, I believe, fairly obvious:

(a) presence, distribution, impact: In the sixth to fourth centuries, i.e., the time-span in which most of the theoretical pre-Platonic work in Greece emerged, such texts were known to every Greek citizen and visible to every person present at

---

[17] Forst / Günther, 2010, 7.

[18] I understand 'Rational Choice' as a socio-economical theory that investigates the emergence of rational behavior from communal attempts to maximize benefits; see, e.g., Braun / Gautschi, 2011; Kunz, 2004.

[19] It may appear to contradict Assmann's claims concerning the textual basis of cultural memory (e.g. 2013, 91–97) that fundamental communal convictions are not primarily subject to monumentalization through writing. At least in early Greek discourse, however, it is precisely what is not written, which claims priority (cf., e.g., Andocides as quoted below and, most famously, Sophocles, *Antigone* v. 450–455; later, e.g. Demosthenes, *On the Crown* (or. 18) 275 ff.). As far as the early polis is concerned, writing becomes part of procedure and secondary normative provisions, while oral tradition appears to remain more authoritative (which explains, e.g., Plato's famous criticism of writing in *Phaedrus* 275 D 5 – E 5; see Asper, 2007, 149.).

[20] Luhmann, 1983, has coined the phrase and described the cultural pattern, but he restricts its coverage explicitly to modern societies (11). However, his chapter "Verfahren als soziales System" (38–53) applies directly to both early Greek law and mathematics (see below (2)). Luhmann's narrative of law's emergence as a development from archaic procedural mediation ("archaische[s] Schlichtungsverfahren") to law in early modern, i.e., differenciated, societies will probably not hold up to scrutiny (40), though.

these public sites (with the exception of Sparta).[21] About 1000 ancient *poleis* are known, today;[22] most if not all of them will have had such publicly inscribed law. While it is not credible that a majority of citizens were actually literate in archaic times, at least the members of the polis elite must have been familiar with the problem of codifying normative behavior in the face of multifarious social realities, that is, of providing abstract norms in a fixated medium, writing. For example, the former and actual *kosmoi* of Dreros and all elite citizens who might have had aspired to becoming *kosmos* one day, will have engaged in heated debate about the law quoted above itself and its precise wording. Once it was established, the courts of Dreros will have used it in argument, might have subjected it to exegesis later on, etc. The presence and importance of these texts as well as their constant use in civic procedure must have made them prominent models for communication about normative orders in general, but also for writing prose about abstract subjects in general.[23]

(b) form: In these inscriptional law texts we find some distinctive features, above all their impersonality. Most laws do not mention individuals or hint at certain situations, e.g., the problem that eventually led to the law or the individual who proposed it to the assembly. A certain tendency towards standardization corresponds with that impersonality: the syntax of law shows minimal variance; it provides a model for argument that either needs to establish or deny a connection between actual case and abstract conditional norm. It thus largely consists of conditionals and, less frequently, temporal clauses. In the Gortyn inscription (Crete, fifth century BC, Koerner, 1993, nos. 163–181), for example, we find about 170 such clauses. The norm itself uses infinitives or, more rarely, different forms of imperatives (see above). As far as we can tell, laws tend to restrict the use of synonyms, of course with a view to avoiding ambiguities. For example, the much-discussed Athenian law on homicide ('Drakon's law', sixth century BC, Koerner, 1993, no. 11, p. 27) chooses, from a vast array of possible words for 'kill' only one (κτείνειν). Where these features cross the line between functional determinant and aesthetic (stylistic) preference, for example when cross-references are concerned, one can diagnose a drive towards standardization, that is, the emergence of a language of authority. For a modern reader, these texts might appear to be almost painfully uniform;[24] for an ancient beholder, however, this was monumental language, the only one that was dignified to codify the consensus forever.

---

[21] Where Lycurgus allegedly has restricted law to oral tradition, which epigraphic data interestingly seems to support: cf. Plutarch, *Life of Lycurgus* 13.1–4 (47 ab); Whitley, 1997, 646–649.

[22] According to Hansen, 2004, 79.

[23] As I claim in Asper, 2004 and 2007, 173–196.

[24] At least at Athens, a standardized form of writing itself corresponds to the standardized text, the so-called 'στοιχηδόν style', which achieves aesthetic dignity *at the cost of* readability (see Asper, 2007, 130 f. note 258; and for epigraphical discussion, e.g., Jeffery, 1961, 73).

(c) Single law and body of laws: Most of the law inscriptions present single laws, often not more than one conditional period. Even the (few) extant law 'codes', that is, the large inscriptions that collect a greater number of single laws, mostly extant from Crete and attested for Athens, never address issues of coherence and systematicity.[25] The principles of organization, well-discussed by assyriologists with respect to Babylonian law codes, only implicitly betray notions of coherence, for example by grouping together similar topics or complementary provisions.[26] Above all, these texts never argue by recourse to fundamental norms. Such recourse, however, must have existed: it is quite prominent in slightly later Athenian literature (tragedy, oratory)[27] and there is no need to assume that sixth-century law courts heard speeches totally different content-wise from what a fifth-century Athenian was accustomed to. Therefore, we have to conclude that inscriptional law relates to the overarching normative order of which it is but a part, in a way similar as an apparatus of footnotes would relate to the main text or, perhaps more relevant, a commentary to an established, but slightly outdated classic, aiming mainly at explication and, possibly, actualization.

(d) Law as catalyzing and as reflecting logical practices: Groups may decide to settle dissent in various ways, e.g., by oracle, ordeal, decisions by charismatic authority or formalized debate about the relation of the actual case to any normative order. The last, which in Greece (and certainly elsewhere around the Mediterranean) took the form of searching for decision of any given case by discussing whether and which older, codified, abstract law would apply, thus entailing a good deal of exegesis. In daily court practice, this mode of settlement must have involved some forms of argument, which I would like to describe as logical practices. Put briefly,[28] the committee of lawgivers, by proceeding from individual cases, has to devise an abstract norm, put it into adequate language and fixate it according to a certain procedure as a normative rule of conduct.[29] The courts that work on the receiving side of the law, however, operate with codified law that has defined what is right sometimes for decades or even hundreds of years (as is the case with Drakon's law in fifth-century Athens). These courts and the opposing parties involved need to discuss whether the abstract text fits the actual, individual, case. The main logical structures of these operations we could conceptualize as 'induction' (lawgiver) and 'deduction' (court and litigants, modern theorists of law call this part 'subsum(p)tion').[30] These operations must have taken place thousands of times in the archaic poleis (and, as a matter of course, in Mesopotamian law systems as well).[31] Furthermore, since

[25] On systematicity see Asper, 2016, esp. 104–107.

[26] See Hans Neumann in this volume (p. 64 f.).

[27] See below and Thür, 2003, 201.

[28] See my more detailed argument in Asper 2004; 2007, 173 ff.

[29] For the relation of rule, norm and normative order see now Möllers, 2015, 180 f.

[30] See already Max Weber, 1980, 394 (orig. 1922). For 'subsum(p)tion' and modern concepts of logic in trial see Asper, 2001, 101 f.; Bung, 2004, 23–35 (the remainder of this fascinating book shows, however, that the problem is more complicated); Möllers, 2015, 180 note 107.

[31] The 'branching structures' which Jim Ritter has expounded so well with the help of flow-diagrams in this volume (pp. 19–28) clearly cater to the need for subsum(p)tion.

they were contested on both sides, especially on the one of deduction, the structures of argument itself, even if only in individual cases, must have come under scrutiny. Logical operations such as the distinction of cases and their exhaustion or *modus tollens*, which we know from early theoretical literature,[32] must have played a role in such court practices. The same holds for concepts such as 'terminology' or 'accuracy of language', because in law, the stakes were too high for sloppy language. Thus, what we see in fourth-century Attic oratory, that is constant debate about subsum(p)tion and induction applied to individual cases, we can take for granted, at least *in nuce* and on a minor scale, for any Greek polis as of the seventh century BC. The polis's peculiar 'public' space, whether or not historically unique, perhaps accelerates and radicalizes the emergence of such logical practices and their awareness considerably. It is, however, not the actual cause for their existence as such; far less, 'democracy'. These logical practices emerge because of pre-existent, abstract, and written law used in actual court proceedings, and should emerge wherever such form of law exists, independent of the community's overarching political system (I have to leave it to experts of ancient Near-Eastern cultures to decide whether or not these conditions would have been fulfilled).

(e) Law and primary justification: The notion of 'normative order' implies, I believe, a hierarchical structure of norms and procedures of justification that base more specific on more general norms and, ultimately, on something one might call normative principles the recourse to which would be primary justification.[33] A simple list of norms at the same level may well be a collection, but not yet an order, that is, a system of norms. Even normative bodies of low complexity, such as the Decalogue in *Exodus* 20, shows a certain tendency to begin with more fundamental norms that somehow add impulse to what follows. Even here, deduction somehow lurks in the back. Greek inscriptional law shows, albeit rarely, second-order rules and principles, but analogously to conditional law, always as isolated rules. Sixth-century Gortynian law knows, for example, the following provision (Koerner, 1993, no. 124, p. 373 f.):

> Πρόθεσιν : μήτ‛ ἀ[πο]δικάζαι : μήτ‛ ἀπομ[όσαι].
>
> You shall not contradict what is (inscribed in) public, neither by judgment nor by oath.

Judged by its materiality, this was obviously considered an important law, inscribed on a single stone with ample space and utmost care, phrased in brief, symmetrical colons and thus invested with authority. Admittedly, the meaning of πρόθεσις is not entirely clear, since the word has, as a compound of τίθημι, a notoriously wide spectrum of denotations.[34] I have translated it as 'what is (in-

[32] See Asper, 2004, 74–77 for examples.

[33] For a theoretical view of axiomatics in law, see Bung, 2004, 129–135.

[34] The only 'parallel' I can find is Aristotle, *Politics* VII 8, 1322 a 9 περὶ τὰς προθέσεις τῶν ἀναγεγραμμένων. While ἀναγεγραμμένα here means something as 'fine as written down (= recorded) in office', πρόθεσις seems to imply 'publication' (I have consulted Franz Susemihl, Franz F. Schwarz and Eckart Schütrumpf). Although I acknowledge the vast cultural gap between Aristotle and archaic Gortyn, this seems to be precisely the

scribed in) public'. Here, '(inscribed in) public' seems to function as a term more general than 'law'. It thus seems that this law regulates the hierarchy of potentially conflicting norms: abstract law, judgment in an individual trial and an involved party's oath. Probably, the last two are forms of settlement that precede the introduction of written law. The apodictic statement thus demonstrates how conflicts that are internal to the normative set are solved by systematization, which then becomes second-order discourse.

In later Athenian court-speeches such distinctions are well attested. The famous defense of Andocides, delivered when he was tried for impiety (ἀσέβεια) in 400 BC, quotes a remarkable sub-set of law (*On the Mysteries* 87):

> Καί μοι ἀνάγνωθι τοὺς νόμους.
> NOMOI. Ἀγράφῳ δὲ νόμῳ τὰς ἀρχὰς μὴ χρῆσθαι μηδὲ περὶ ἑνός. Ψήφισμα δὲ μηδὲν μήτε βουλῆς μήτε δήμου νόμου κυριώτερον εἶναι. Μηδὲ ἐπ' ἀνδρὶ νόμον ἐξεῖναι θεῖναι, ἐὰν μὴ τὸν αὐτὸν ἐπὶ πᾶσιν Ἀθηναίοις, ἐὰν μὴ ἑξακισχιλίοις δόξῃ κρύβδην ψηφιζομένοις.
>
> Please read out the laws!
> LAWS: Offices shall not use unwritten law and certainly not (law) about one individual. No decree, neither of the council nor of the assembly, shall be more valid than a law. Nor shall it be lawful to establish a law against one individual, if the same (law) does not hold for all Athenians alike and unless six thousand (citizens) decide by secret ballot.

The first sentence probably only means that a certain class of laws shall not be used by offices, before they have undergone a certain form of scrutiny. Clearly, the three laws quoted are all 'meta-norms', which structure the normative order by internal hierarchy and additional rules, thus trying to avoid conflicts of norms. In the Athenian court-system which must have been considerably more complex that the one operative in, say, Cretan Dreros, the codification of such meta-rules may have become useful or even necessary due to the increased number of laws and the increased frequency and intensity of debating internal contradictions.

Suffice it to say in preliminary conclusion that inscribed law in early Greece does usually not intend to codify a normative order as a whole, but rather reflects such an order. Cogent justification ('der logische Raum der Gründe') becomes explicit in court practice, especially in controversial argument and in second-order attempts at improving systematic coherence. Inscription means stabilization of a norm precisely by cutting off and suppressing the discussion that led to the norm, which, for us, has the unwelcome consequence that fundamental issues which will have cropped up in that discussion, usually remain implicit.

I move on to Greek mathematics, a field in which the search for 'normative order' acquires an epistemic perspective.

---

meaning that would fit our law (pace Koerner, 1993, 374), that is, πρόθεσις is a general term for what has been communally validated by 'publication' (through inscription) and includes laws, edicts, etc.

2. Greek Mathematics

Historiography of mathematics tends to focus on theoretical mathematics à la Archimedes and its predecessors back to Hippocrates of Chios in late fifth-century Athens. Such a perspective easily overlooks the existence of a wide-spread and well-differentiated tradition of practical mathematics in Greece.[35] Evidently, managers must have calculated costs, architects must have measured, officials must have assigned tax-rates, bankers will have computed interest, and geometers areas. As is the rule even with much later experts, they have become almost invisible to us as social entities; they have, however, left certain traces. The two groups we can still identify with some confidence are geometers and pebble arithmeticians. Recent discussions of these people, their procedures, and their relation to theoretical mathematics have left us with two or three widely accepted assumptions: First, practical mathematics in Greece continues and transforms much older traditions that go back to second-millennium scribal mathematics both in Babylon and Egypt. In this field as in many others, early archaic Greece appears as a Western outpost and off-shoot of an Eastern Mediterranean cultural 'koine' in the earlier first millennium BC. Second, part of what seems 'practical' at first, is in fact 'theoretical', for example calculations with impossible high numbers. Third, these traditions were astonishingly stable: with the help of single prominent problems or procedures that pop up in mathematical collections over the centuries, one can trace these traditions from Old-Babylonian times well into the early modern age. It is difficult to explain these findings unless one assumes a more or less stable, partly oral transmission of mathematical knowledge by migrating experts over three millennia and across all kinds of linguistic and cultural borders. Jens Høyrup, a historian of mathematics at Roskilde University has invested decades of work into the unearthing of missing links and the reconstruction of these traditions.[36] Clearly, in fifth- and fourth-century Greece there existed at least two parallel forms of mathematics side by side, one as part of a broadly settled and in itself differentiated culture of professional experts, the other one an elitist pursuit of abstract knowledge, close to the upper class and the centers of political power. It is not within this paper's scope, however, to further explore the dualism of these forms of mathematics;[37] rather, each of the two mathematical fields will be searched for their normative concepts.

To begin with practical mathematics: I have chosen two texts, both papyri now at Vienna, that concern themselves with the computation of areas and volumes. Although these texts originated in imperial Roman Egypt, both the knowledge itself and the form, in which it is presented, must be much older. We have to imagine this kind of textual knowledge[38] to be operative in, e.g., sixth-century Milet or early fifth-century Ephesus or Athens. This is how you should compute a given cube's volume (Papyrus Vindobonensis G 19996 r, first century AD):

[35] I have summed up the discussion in Asper 2003, 1–5; 2009, 108–114.
[36] See for example Høyrup, 1989; 2002.
[37] I have given an outline in Asper, 2009.
[38] For the concept of 'textual knowledge', see Asper, 2016 note 42.

Τῶ]ν δὲ λιθικῶν καὶ οἰκοδομι<κ>ῶν [τὰ στερεὰ μετ]ρήσεις ὅμοια τοῖς γεωμέτρου λόγοις ο[ὕτως·] ὁ λίθος· πάντοθεν ποδ(ῶν) ε‘ ποίησον τὰ ε‘ ἐπ[ὶ τὰ ε‘]· γί(νεται) κε‘· τοσούτου ἡ ἐπιφάνεια· ταῦτ‘ ἐπὶ τὰ ε‘ [τοῦ ὕψου]ς· γίνεται ρκε‘· τούτων ποδῶν ἔσται ὁ λίθος καὶ [κύϐος] καλεῖται.

Concerning stones and things needed to build a house, you will measure the volume according to the rules of the geometer as follows: the stone has 5 feet everywhere. Multiply 5 by 5! It is 25. That is the area of the surface. (Multiply) this 5 times concerning the height. It is 125. The stone will have so many feet and is called a cube.[39]

This little recipe-like structure is part of a *Rechenbuch* which collects 38 such paragraphs. They all exhibit the same structural and linguistic features. Of such collections, several fragmented papyri exist. I quote from a second one that focuses on the problem of how the circumference and the area of a given circle correlate (Papyrus Vindobonensis. G 26740, first century AD, again):[40]

ἔστ[ω] κύκλος, οὗ *ή* μὲν πε[ρί]μετρος σχοινίων [λ.] πόσων ἀρουρῶν ἐστ[ιν;] ὡς δεῖ ποιῆσαι. ποίησο*ν* τ*ὰ* σ(χοινία) λ ἐφ‘ ἑαυτ*ά*, γείνεται ϡ. τού*των* λαϐὲ τὸ ιϐ, *γεί*νονται [οε]; *τοσ*ούτων ἀρουρῶν ἐστιν ὁ κύκλος, ὡς *ὑπόκειται*.

Let there be a circle, the circumference of which is 30 *schoinia*. (An area) of how many *arourai* is he? How one has to multiply: Multiply the 30 *schoinia* by themselves; that is 900. Of those take $^{1}/_{12}$, that is 75. (An area) of so many *arourai* is the circle, as below.

Although the mathematical side of this text is well beyond the scope of this paper, let me briefly touch upon this little algorithm: Quite obviously, the recommended calculation operates without any approximation of Pi. If we assume that an aroura is simply the area of a square one side of which has the length of a schoinion,[41] the text provides a decent approximation. If the circle had, e.g., a circumference of 30 cm, the area would result in 75 cm^2; computed with Pi, we arrive at 71.62 cm^2. The procedure applies a coefficient (one twelfth of the square over the circumference), which transforms curvilinear to rectilinear forms and leaps from length to area. Thus, the algorithm effortlessly achieves the quadrature of the circle.[42] Furthermore, the text chooses a rather huge circle: Probably, the unit is the σχοινίον γεωμετρικόν, traditionally equivalent to 96 cubits (each c. 47.4 cm), i.e. roughly 45.50 m. Thus, a circle ensues with a circumference of 1.365 km and an area, according to our recipe-like text, of about 15.5 ha (= 155.269 m).[43] In other words, the textbook case has chosen an example

[39] Text from Gerstinger / Vogel, 1932; translation taken from Asper, 2009, 110.

[40] From Sijpestijn / Harrauer, 1985. Italics mark letters that remain ambiguous.

[41] Ancient metrologies are a slippery ground. I am not sure that my assumption is correct.

[42] On truth and practical standards see my work on the problematic notion of computational 'error' (Asper, 2012, esp. 48–54).

[43] In order to better visualize the area, I came across a farm in Austria (Ö-9241 Wernberg) which has exactly that area, is economically functional, and costs (at the time of

with dimensions that are not as easily grasped as a diagram on a textbook's page or my example with a circumference of 30 cm, but belongs to the field of surveying.[44]

Both texts have authority, because they represent an expert group's consensus, which establishes legitimate procedures. Whatever the group of experts does qua experts, produces truth. If the experts in charge compute areas according to these established procedures, then the procedure yields the correct result, regardless of what later times have to say about Pi (for the historian of science it is useless to ostentatiously compute the difference between 'their' and 'the' [i.e. modern, our] result, as I have done above).[45] These established procedures, however, are cast in normative frames: the first text refers to οἱ γεωμέτρου λόγοι, the second more abstractly describes the procedure as ὡς δεῖ ποιῆσαι ('how one must do/multiply it'). The second, impersonal form of the norm might convey an even greater claim to offering the correct procedure. The strong appeal to the reader emerges from the authority of setting out the correct method; typically, these texts offer a statement of closure. Both features play an essential role in the much older Babylonian and Egyptian traditions of this type. There is no justification beyond the reference to the canonicity of the rules applied. At first glance, these texts seem to give actual cases instead of general rules; a second one, however, reveals what we might call 'implicit abstraction': the algorithm operates with obviously pre-selected numbers; repetition and variation, however, will lead the reader to abstract cognition.

With respect to pebble-arithmeticians not one text has survived.[46] Some parts of their knowledge, however, became part of (Neo)Platonic number lore, unfortunately mainly those features of it that were less close to practical computation. In Nicomachus of Gerasa's influential *Introduction to Arithmetics*, for example, an attempt to collect the fundamentals of Platonist and Neo-Pythagorean arithmetics, one comes across many recipe-like instructions of how to produce certain classes of numbers. Often, terminology and even the lore itself betrays the pebble-arithmetician in the (historical) background. Quite famous is, e.g., the method of how to find prime numbers, which Nicomachus calls the 'sieve of Eratosthenes'[47] (Nicomachus, *Arithmetical Introduction* I 13.3 ff., p. 30 ff. ed. Hoche):

> ἔστι δὲ ὁ τρόπος τοῦ κοσκίνου τοιοῦτος· ἐκθέμενος τοὺς ἀπὸ τριάδος πάντας ἐφεξῆς περισσοὺς ὡς δυνατὸν μάλιστα ἐπὶ μήκιστον στίχον, ἀρξάμενος ἀπὸ τοῦ πρώτου ἐπισκοπῶ, τίνας οἷός τέ ἐστι μετρεῖν, καὶ εὑρίσκω δυνατὸν ὄντα τοὺς δύο μέσους παραλείποντας μετρεῖν, μέχρις

writing, i.e. Nov. 2015) 800.000 Euros. Presumably, such is the target domain of the knowledge that our ancient text transmits.

[44] Computed with Pi, the same circle has an area of only 14.8 ha, that is, it is smaller by 7.000 square meters. One wonders whether anyone benefits from such inaccuracies (perhaps fiscal authorities that assess taxes by areas?).

[45] That was my point in Asper, 2012, esp. 61–63.

[46] See Netz 2002a.

[47] See Asper, 2015, 50 ff.

οὗ ἂν προχωρεῖν ἐθέλωμεν, οὐχ ὡς ἔτυχε δὲ καὶ εἰκῇ μετροῦντα, ἀλλὰ τὸν μὲν πρώτως κείμενον, τουτέστι τὸν δύο μέσους ὑπερβαίνοντα κατὰ τὴν τοῦ πρωτίστου ἐν τῷ στίχῳ κειμένου ποσότητα μετρήσει, τουτέστι κατὰ τὴν ἑαυτοῦ· τρὶς γάρ· τὸν δ' ἀπ' ἐκείνου δύο διαλείποντα κατὰ τὴν τοῦ δευτέρου τεταγμένου· πεντάκις γάρ· τὸν δὲ περαιτέρω πάλιν δύο διαλείποντα κατὰ τὴν τοῦ τρίτου τεταγμένου· ἑπτάκις γάρ· τὸν δὲ ἔτι περαιτέρω ὑπὲρ δύο κείμενον κατὰ τὴν τοῦ τετάρτου τεταγμένου· ἐνάκις γάρ· καὶ ἐπ' ἄπειρον τῷ αὐτῷ τρόπῳ.
εἶτα μετὰ τοῦτον ἀπ' ἄλλης ἀρχῆς ἐπὶ τὸν δεύτερον ἐλθὼν σκοπῶ, τίνας οἱός τέ ἐστι μετρεῖν, καὶ εὑρίσκω πάντας τοὺς τετράδα δειλείποντας, ἀλλὰ τὸν μὲν πρῶτον κατὰ τὴν τοῦ ἐν τῷ στίχῳ πρώτου τεταγμένου ποσότητα· τρὶς γάρ·...

The way the sieve works is as follows: Beginning from three, I lay out all odd numbers in order, in a series as long as possible; I then begin with the first (i.e. three) and see, which numbers it can measure (i.e. divide); and I find that it can measure all numbers that leave two (numbers of the series) between them, as far as we wish to proceed. Not by chance, however, and without any rule it measures (these numbers), but the one that lies there first (in the series), this is, the one that leaves the two middle ones behind (i.e. nine), it will measure by the quantity of the one that lies there first in the series, this is, by itself, namely three times. And the number that is distant by two from this one (i.e. 15), it will measure by the one that has the place next to her in the series, namely by five. And then, again, the number that is two (numbers) farther away (i.e. 21), (it will measure) by the third place in the series, namely seven times; and then again (the number) that is two (numbers) farther away (i.e. 27), it will measure by the one that has the fourth position in the series, namely nine times. And in this same way (it will proceed) to the infinite.
Then, after this (number), from another starting-point I move on to the second number (in the series, i.e. 5) and see, which (numbers) it can measure; and I find that (it can measure) all (numbers) that leave four (numbers of the series) between, but the first (i.e. 15) by the quantity of that has the first position in the series, namely three times ...

The text is quite obviously meant to be read with pebbles on a tablet in front of the reader. The following little diagram will hopefully do, too (similar diagrammatic sketches adorn the margins of the leading manuscript of Nicomachus, a tenth-century codex now at Göttingen):

o o o o o o o o o o
o o o o

3 5 7 9 11 13 15 17 19 21
23 25 27 29

I have chosen this passage from many similar ones in order to provide an approximation to the epistemic style of pebble-arithmetics. The text describes arithmetical manipulations which lead to insights into properties of sets of numbers. These numbers, however, terminologically remain pebbles on a tablet that one can lay out (ἐκθέσθαι) in certain figures, that have spatial relations (τεταγμένος), etc. While reading Nicomachus, we are actually imagined by the author as looking at a tablet on which we move and count pebbles (the 'tablet', that is, a spatial structure which adds significance to the pebbles according to their actual position, is even reproduced in the manuscripts). The author's monologue is the one of the expert teaching pebble-arithmetics in personal interaction, at least on the levels of style and terminology.[48] However, despite the peculiar set-up, Nicomachus is clearly presenting 'theory', namely the way to an insight into prime-numbers by the intuition into rules of how to generate them. Any application of these numbers to problems of practical relevance remains off sight.

With respect to normative order we get the impression that Nicomachus' construction of authority does not rely on abstract justification, but on personal interaction which then leads the reader/disciple to intuition (interestingly, Eratosthenes' authority is moved to the background in favor of the ego-practitioner). It seems that intuition by practice is what this community cares for, not logical justification. I guess that the actual pebble-arithmeticians of the long history of the trade before Nicomachus were similar in this regard (the first abstract set of insights of these arithmeticians is usually identified as the 'doctrine of the even and the odd', i.e. as the 'source' of the ninth book of Euclid's *Elements*, to which there are indirect testimonies already in early fifth century BC).[49]

When we assume that these forms of conventional mathematics were widespread throughout the Greek world and provided the standard for mathematical procedural norms, the mathematics of Euclid and Archimedes, their (few) predecessors and successors, becomes even more remarkable.[50] Despite its social fragility, however, fourth-century Greek theoretical mathematics probably found a solution to the problem of how to justify and codify normative order and knowledge in general, which was taken up, adapted and further theorized by Plato and his successors, most of all by Aristotle, and thus became dominant. I have to restrict myself here to three aspects: deductivity, axiomatics, and standardization.

Deductive argument employs a consensual starting-point from which it proceeds by, again, an accepted set of rules in order to arrive at proof. Rules and even starting-points may remain implicit or taken to be evident. Greek theoretical mathematics exhibits such arguments in a mildly formalized manner. (Such forms of argument do not suddenly emerge at some place or time; in Greek liter-

---

[48] Geometrical terminology which contains many elements from practical mathematics, e.g. τείνω for the position of lines, which must be a surveyor's term, can also illustrate that terminologies are conservative, that is, prone to retaining elements from an obsolete social realm of a certain body of knowledge. While these elements obviously point to certain continuities, we wonder whether the conventionality of terminologies can add anything to normative stability.

[49] Whether Pythagorean or not: cf. Becker, 1936, 550 f.

[50] The social marginality of theoretical mathematics is aptly stressed by Netz in 1999a, 271–312 and in 2002b.

ature, we find them, applied in a casual way, for example in early historiography.) For matters of illustration, a brief and typical theorem-plus-diagram-and-proof from Euclid (*Elements* III 5, c. 300 BC) will be sufficient, I hope:

> Ἐὰν δύο κύκλοι τέμνωσιν ἀλλήλους, οὐκ ἔσται αὐτῶν τὸ αὐτὸ κέντρον. Δύο γὰρ κύκλοι οἱ ΑΒΓ, ΓΔΗ τεμνέτωσαν ἀλλήλους κατὰ τὰ Β, Γ σημεῖα. λέγω, ὅτι οὐκ ἔσται αὐτῶν τὸ αὐτὸ κέντρον. Εἰ γὰρ δυνατόν, ἔστω τὸ Ε, καὶ ἐπεζεύχθω ἡ ΕΓ, καὶ διήχθω ἡ ΕΖΗ, ὡς ἔτυχεν. καὶ ἐπεὶ τὸ Ε σημεῖον κέντρον ἐστὶ τοῦ ΑΒΓ κύκλου, ἴση ἐστὶν ἡ ΕΓ τῇ ΕΖ. πάλιν, ἐπεὶ τὸ Ε σημεῖον κέντρον ἐστὶ τοῦ ΓΔΗ κύκλου, ἴση ἐστὶν ἡ ΕΓ τῇ ΕΗ· ἐδείχθη δὲ ἡ ΕΓ καὶ τῇ ΕΖ ἴση· καὶ ἡ ΕΖ ἄρα τῇ ΕΗ ἐστιν ἴση ἡ ἐλάσσων τῇ μείζονι· ὅπερ ἐστὶν ἀδύνατον. οὐκ ἄρα τὸ Ε σημεῖον κέντρον ἐστὶ τῶν ΑΒΓ, ΓΔΗ κύκλων.
>
> Ἐὰν ἄρα δύο κύκλοι τέμνωσιν ἀλλήλους, οὐκ ἔστιν αὐτῶν τὸ αὐτὸ κέντρον· ὅπερ ἔδει δεῖξαι.

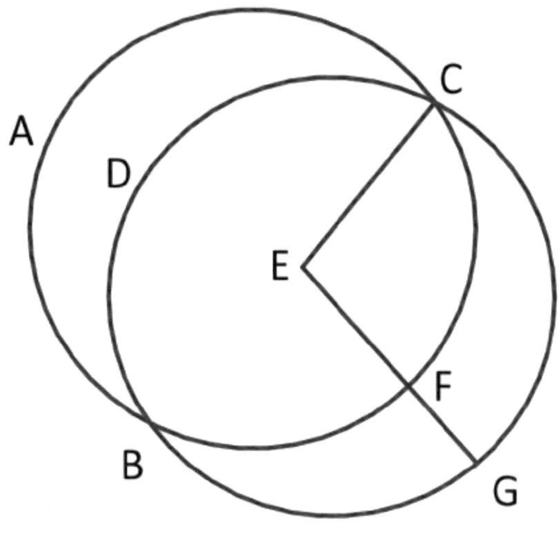

> If two circles cut each other, they will not have the same center. For let the two circles ABC, CDG cut each other in B, C. I claim that they will not have the same center. For if that were possible, let it be E and let there be connected EC and carried through EFG, just as it happens. And since E is the center of the circle ABC, EC is the same as EF. Again, since E is the center of the circle CDG, EC is the same as EG. And it was shown that EC and EF were the same. Therefore, EF is also the same as EG, the smaller (the same) as the bigger, which is impossible. Therefore, the point E is not the center of the circles ABC, CDG.
>
> If two circles cut each other, their center is not the same. Which was what had to be demonstrated.

The author sets out to demonstrate by formal proof what is almost evident to intuition, anyway. He assumes that the opposite is the case. Since this leads into contradiction and since only these two cases are possible, he has shown what he wanted to show. The proof's apparatus is quite remarkable, because it spends much effort on a modest result: a general statement introduces the structure, then the same statement follows, but specified with respect to a model case constructed by way of a lettered diagram, that provides evidence, in addition the proof proper and a general statement of closure again, that practically repeats the beginning statement. Both the impersonal style and the lettered diagram support transmission over gaps of space and time. The proof's deductive character remains rather implicit. Deduction rests on two axiomatic truths that had been stated in the beginning of book I: (1) As part of the definition of the circle, Euclid had stated that all radiuses in a given circle have the same length. Euclid untypically refers to that with the phrase "it was shown" (ἐδείχθη), which, however, in this context must mean that the two lines in question (EC, EF) have the same length as they both are demonstrably radiuses of the same circle. (2) The decisive argument, however, that EF and EG cannot have the same length ("which is impossible", ὅπερ ἐστὶν ἀδύνατον), follows directly from Axiom 8 ("The whole is bigger than the part."), which is not explicitly quoted here. And since it is impossible that there is a third option (the circles either have or do not have the same center), which means that one of the two must be true, the *reductio ad absurdum* of the one case is a valid method in order to demonstrate the other one. That way, the proposition becomes demonstrably true and one can use it for more complex demonstrations (which is probably the reason for demonstrating almost evident statements in the first place).

The second feature, axiomatics, has already been commented upon with respect to this actual proof. With respect to the whole body of theoretical mathematical literature and in marked contrast to law and even to early philosophy the central position of axiomatics warrants further attention, because it became paradigmatic for the way how theoretical systems can handle *den logischen Raum der Gründe*. When deduction had emerged as the most efficient method in theoretical mathematics, at some time, theoretical mathematicians began to collect all theorems and all primary starting-points. At Euclid's time, such collections (*stoikheia*) must have existed already for more than a century.[51] Mathematicians began to carefully set out their starting-points at the beginning of their argument (in a formalized manner, Euclid's Elements can illustrate that well; less formally, we see that Archimedes almost always lays bare the assumptions upon which his argument rests). Primary starting-points, that is, starting-points that are not themselves subject to proof, soon came into the focus of Platonic and Aristotelian theory.[52] The division of such axiomatic materials in three groups, as we find it at the beginning of *Elements* I, shows considerable overlap with what Aristotle has to say on starting-points in, e.g., his *Posterior Analytics* whose mathematical examples are taken from Euclid's predecessors.[53] Euclid's

[51] According to Eudemus in Proclus, the genre began with Hippocrates of Chios (c. 420 BC); see Asper, 2007, 109 f. The only argument of Hippocrates which we can analyze, heavily relies on deduction (ibid. 110–112), although it was not part of his *stoikheia*. For this proof, see Netz, 2004.

[52] For the division, see Hagan Brunke in this volume.

[53] E.g. *Posterior Analytics* I 10, 76 b 14 τὰ κοινὰ λεγόμενα ἀξιώματα; on mathematical examples in the Analytics see Berti, 1984.

manuscripts differentiate between three groups of axiomatic materials: definitions (e.g., I 2 “A line is length without width.”), postulates (e.g., I 2 “[Let it be postulated] that one can extend a limited straight line continuously in a straight way.”), and ‘common notions’ (i.e., I 2 “If same is added to same, the sums are the same.”). The urge to clarify and standardize the axiomatic material has thus even led to the classification of concepts, practices, and mathematical logic. With respect to these starting-points, an intense discussion among mathematicians and philosophers about starting-points ensued.[54]

I have already touched upon the notion of standardization (with respect to mathematical prose, the term is perhaps not entirely acceptable, but it covers well the most obvious textual feature that mathematics shares with laws). In Euclid and his peers we have the impression that structural and stylistic variation is kept minimal, to a certain extent perhaps due to pragmatic reasons; however, aesthetic considerations must have played a certain role, too.[55] The normative character of these texts shows in their intent to regulate and prescribe mathematical practices (most clearly in the postulates, which sketch out a normative pragmatics of geometrical construction, disguised as ‘starting-points’). Put briefly, these theoretical mathematicians state incessantly what it is to do mathematics – and what not (I believe that the second part of the message aims at practical mathematics).[56] With respect to practical mathematics, the group, perhaps somehow in ways comparable to those of later ‘guilds’, guaranteed the efficiency and the ‘rightness’ of the knowledge concerned; in other words, the normativity of their rules operates on a level of social pragmatics. Theoretical mathematicians moved their knowledge’s normativity into epistemic realms, and perhaps this is the decisive step that made their knowledge matter so much to philosophers.

While the mathematicians, in true Platonic vein, never admit that their pursuits are governed by complicated rules that are, at least, partly contingent upon motives external to mathematics, technicians are more liberal. Thus Heron, an imperial engineer and mathematician, states in the introduction to his *Geometrica*, a textbook of mathematical surveying tools, that he has to begin with defining ‘geometry’ in order to not be ‘barred from competition’ (*Geometrics*, praef. volume 4, p. 172 ed. Heiberg):

> ἵνα μὴ ἐξαγώνιοι γενώμεθα, εὔλογόν ἐστι τὸν ὅρον αὐτῆς εἰπεῖν.
>
> In order to not be disqualified, it is reasonable to first give its definition (i.e., the one of geometry).

The term ἐξαγώνιος which I have translated as ‘disqualified’, is exactly the Greek equivalent for not being able to participate in a competition. Heron thus

[54] Cf. Amphinomus as quoted in Proclus, *On Euclid's Elements* I, p. 202.9–12 ed. Friedlein.
[55] For example, the mathematical lexicon is almost free of synonyms; proofs consist usually of five parts that were described and named already in antiquity (see Proclus); certain classes of arguments are eschewed (e.g. *neusis*) and others favored (*abduction in absurdum*). For the mathematical lexicon see Netz 1999a, 89–167, for the components of Euclidian proof in Proclus, see Netz 1999b.
[56] See, e.g., Asper, 2009, 120–125.

openly acknowledges both the character of mathematics as a 'game' and, accordingly, that the rules are not exclusively determined by epistemic factors.

3. Comparative Remarks on Normative Order and Authority

Instead of normative orders as such I have presented some reflections of such orders in ancient Greek culture, concentrating on archaic inscriptional law and mathematical texts of two different traditions. The precise story of emergence of the preceding orders themselves remains, apart from scattered and isolated hints, mostly guesswork. By way of conclusion, I offer a few remarks on two clusters of concepts that have been pervasive throughout my argument: first, on the notion of 'normative order' with respect to the fields covered, second, on textual 'authority'.

(a) Coherence, abstraction, and deduction in normative orders: Is the notion of 'normative order' even appropriate, when we compare law and mathematics? I believe that it is, indeed. Without going too deeply into discussions about orders or systems a few words on the aspects of coherence, abstraction, and deduction in normative orders might be in place. As for coherence, inscriptional law (a body of rules of the type 'If someone does x, y must happen.') and procedural mathematics (a body of rules of the type 'If you wish to compute x, you have to perform steps y and z.') clearly have to be coherent, which means that these rules must somehow be in proportion to each other and cannot lead to contradictory results. In the body of law, e.g., fines must be proportionate (e.g., an oxen for my eye, a sheep for my slave's eye), terms must be handled consistently (e.g. homicide vs. murder), etc. Similarly, a body of mathematical procedural texts needs to use consistent terminology and cannot offer methods for solving the same problems that lead to different results. Both discourses, however, do not have an explicit notion of such systematic coherence. Theoretical Greek mathematics, on the other hand, more or less fulfils modern criteria of being 'systematic',[57] not least due to the fact that the modern philosophical notion of 'system' has been developed under indirect impact of Greek theoretical mathematics and its discussion by philosophers). The three fields allow for deductions: For theoretical mathematics, this is obvious. Inscriptional law has been designed precisely in order to apply a more general rule to the particular case ('subsum(p)-tion', see above); in such procedure, the verdict's justification is essentially deductive. The practical mathematician has learnt his examples as rules in which he inserts the numbers of a particular case. Searching for and applying the right rule is a process that works in a manner quite similar to jurisdiction. All three fields have produced collections or bodies of rules. Practices of collecting lead to systematization, that is, to the construction of abstract categories of rules, such as 'homicide law' or 'computation of curvilinear areas'. In addition, the collection needs to exhibit some internal structure, perhaps a hierarchical one (e.g., from most general to less general theorems). Last, in all three fields the claim to exhaustiveness will greatly add to the collection's authority.

[57] See Asper, 2016, 104 note 3 on consistency, exhaustiveness, connectiveness, simplicity, and manageability as features of 'systems'.

As for the justification of norms and rules, theoretical mathematics is, among the three realms, singular in making axiomatic justification explicit, to the degree of even formalizing it. In law, however, primary justification, understood as the center of normative order, does not become part of inscriptional law, because fundamental justification is consensual in the polis and thus does not need to be stabilized through monumental writing. Practical mathematics, however, is less interested in ultimate justification, because the work-flow itself is what matters,[58] not giving an account for why it works. Within the system of practical mathematics, the group's or the individual practitioner's personal authority, not abstract axiomatics, occupy the logical place of justification.

(b) Authority and text: The various representations of normative orders that have been the subject of this paper exhibit claims to authority in different ways. The texts of law and theoretical mathematics both opt for strict impersonality, the rules of the practical mathematicians for strong personal appeals to the reader. All three have developed different forms of standardization as a means to improve application/deduction and transportability. Law and theoretical mathematics intend to codify consensus in a way that extends communal acceptance to what is deduced in theory (mathematics) or practice (law). Apparently, the more monumental such a consensus, the more stable it is. Thus, costly public inscription of law and strictly regulated mathematical prose should be evaluated side by side as two forms of textual monumentality. In both forms, impersonality, even more: *Deagentivierung*, attempts to present the consensus as being independent from personal authority and thus valid even beyond time.[59] With respect to theoretical mathematics, the strategy has worked remarkably well. The authority of practical mathematical texts, on the other hand, has transferred all claims from the individual onto the group. These texts present themselves as 'collective statements',[60] remaining dependent upon the group of experts who are the acclaimed masters and authoritative guardians of legitimate procedure.

References

Editions of ancient authors

Andocides, *On the Mysteries*: Douglas M. Macdowell (ed.), 1962. *Andokides. On the Mysteries*. Oxford: Oxford University Press.

Archilochus, *Fragments*: Martin L. West (ed.), 1971. *Iambi et Elegi Graeci ante Alexandrum cantati.* Vol. I: *Archilochus, Hipponax, Theognidea*. Ed. alt, Oxford: Oxford University Press, 1–108.

Aristotle, *Politics*: David W. Ross (ed.), 1957. *Aristotelis Politica*. Oxford: Oxford University Press.

Aristotle, *Posterior Analytics*: David W. Ross (ed.), 1957. *Aristotle's Prior and Posterior Analytics*. Oxford: Oxford University Press.

Demosthenes, *Against Lacritus* (orat. 35): Mervin R. Dilts (ed.), 2008. *Demosthenis Orationes*, volume II 1. Oxford: Oxford: Oxford University Press.

[58] See Asper, 2012.

[59] Forrester, 1996, 14: "The marks of the successful Continental reform of the law were the ideal of the code with its erasure of history from the structure of the law […]".

[60] See Rosental, 2003, 624 ff., 639 ff.

Demosthenes, *On the Crown* (orat. 18): Mervin R. Dilts (ed.), 2002. *Demosthenis Orationes*, volume I. Oxford: Oxford University Press.

Ephorus, *Fragments*: Felix Jacoby (ed.), 1961. *Die Fragmente der griechischen Historiker*, II A: Nr. 64–105. Leiden: Brill, 37–109.

Euclid, *Elements*: Iohan L. Heiberg / Euangelos S. Stamatis (eds.), 1985. *Euclidis opera omnia*, volume I–V: Elementa. Leipzig: Teubner.

Eusebius, *Chronics*: Alfred Schoene (ed.), 1875. *Eusebi Chronicorum libri duo*. Berlin: Weidmann.

Hero, *Geometrics*: Iohan L. Heiberg (ed.), 1912. *Heron Alexandrinus, Opera*, volume IV. Leipzig: Teubner, 1912.

Nicomachus, *Arithmetical Introduction*: Richard Hoche (ed.), 1866. *Nicomachi Geraseni Pythagorei introductionis arithmeticae libri* II. Leipzig: Teubner.

Papyrus Vindobonensis G 19996 r: Hans Gerstinger / Kurt Vogel (eds.), 1932. "Eine stereometrische Aufgabensammlung in Papyrus Graecus Vindobonensis 19996". In: Hans Gerstinger (ed.) *Griechische literarische Papyri* I. (Mitteilungen aus der Papyrussammlung der Nationalbibliothek in Wien (Papyrus Erzherzog Rainer) Neue Serie 1). Wien: Österreichische Staatsdruckerei, 11–76.

Papyrus Vindobonensis G 26740: Pieter J. Sijpestijn / Hermann Harrauer (eds.), 1985. *Neue Texte aus dem antiken Unterricht* (Mitteilungen aus der Papyrussammlung der Nationalbibliothek in Wien (Papyrus Erzherzog Rainer) Neue Serie 15). Wien: Hollinek.

Plato, *Phaedrus*: Ioannes Burnet (ed.), 1901. *Platonis opera*, tom. II. Oxford: Oxford University Press.

Plutarch, *Life of Lycurgus*: Konrat Ziegler / Hans Gärtner (eds.), 1973. *Plutarchi vitae parallelae*, volume III 2. Stuttgart: Teubner.

Proclus, *On Euclid's Elements I*: Gottfried Friedlein (ed.) 1873. *Procli Diadochi In primum Euclidis elementorum librum commentarii*. Teubner: Leipzig, 1873.

Sophocles, *Antigone*: Hugh Lloyd-Jones / Nigel G. Wilson (eds.) *Sophoclis Fabulae*. Oxford: OUP, 1990.

Secondary Literature

Asper, Markus, 2001. "Stoicheia und Gesetze. Spekulationen zur Entstehung mathematischer Textformen in Griechenland". In: Jochen Althoff / Bernhard Herzhoff / Georg Wöhrle (eds.) *Antike Naturwissenschaft und ihre Rezeption* 11. Trier: Wissenschaftlicher Verlag Trier, 73–106.

— 2003. "Mathematik, Milieu, Text. Die frühgriechische(n) Mathematik(en) und ihr Umfeld". *Sudhoffs Archiv* 87, 1–31.

— 2004. "Law and Logic. Towards an Archaeology of Greek Abstract Reason". *Annali dell'università degli studi di Napoli "l'orientale"* 26, 73–94.

— 2007. *Griechische Wissenschaftstexte. Formen, Funktionen, Differenzierungsgeschichten*. Stuttgart: Steiner.

— 2009. "The Two Mathematical Cultures of Ancient Greece". In: Eleanor Robson / Jackie Stedall (eds.) *The Oxford Handbook of the History of Mathematics*. Oxford: Oxford University Press, 107–132.

— 2012. "'True' and 'False' Errors in Ancient (Greek) Computation". In: Klaus Geus / Mark Geller (eds.) *Productive Errors: Scientific Concepts in Antiquity* (Max Planck Institute for the History of Science. Preprint 430). Berlin: Max-Plank-Institut für Wissenschaftsgeschichte, 47–66.

— 2015. "(Some) Domains of Metaphor in Hellenistic Literature". In: Markus Witte / Sven Behnke (eds.) *The Metaphorical Use of Language in Deuterocanonical and Cognate Literature* (Deuterocanonical and Cognate Literature Yearbook 2014/15). Berlin: De Gruyter, 41–58.

— 2016. "On Systematicity. How to Write (Ancient Greek) Science". *Trends in Classics* 8, 103–122.

Assmann, Jan, 2013. *Das kulturelle Gedächtnis. Schrift, Erinnerung und politische Identität in frühen Hochkulturen*. München: Beck.

Becker, Otfried, 1936. "Die Lehre vom Geraden und Ungeraden im Neunten Buch der Euklidischen Elemente". *Quellen und Studien zur Geschichte der Mathematik, Astronomie und Physik, Abt. B: Studien* 3. Berlin: Springer, 533–553.

Berti, Enrico, 1984. "L'analisi geometrica della tradizione euclidea e l'analitica di Aristotele". In: Gabriele Giannantoni / Mario Vegetti (eds.) *La scienza ellenistica*. Napoli: Bibliopolis, 93–127.

Braun, Norman / Thomas Gautschi, 2011. *Rational-Choice-Theorie*. Weinheim: Beltz.

Bung, Jochen, 2004. *Subsumtion und Interpretation*. Baden-Baden: Nomos.

Forrester, John, 1996. "If p, then what? Thinking in Cases". *History of the Human Sciences* 9.3, 1–25.

Forst, Rainer / Klaus Günther, 2010. "Die Herausbildung normativer Ordnungen. Zur Idee eines interdisziplinären Forschungsprogramms". In: Rainer Forst / Klaus Günther (eds.) *Die Herausbildung normativer Ordnungen: Interdisziplinäre Perspektiven*. Frankfurt a. M.: Campus, 11–30.

Gerhardt, Volker, 2012. *Öffentlichkeit. Die politische Form des Bewusstseins*. München: Beck.

Hansen, Mogens H., 2004. *Polis. An Introduction to the Ancient Greek City-State*. Oxford: Oxford University Press.

Hawke, Jason, 2011. *Writing Authority: Elite Competition and Written Law in Early Greece*. DeKalb: Northern Illinois University Press.

Hölscher, Tonio, 1998. *Öffentliche Räume in frühen griechischen Städten*. Heidelberg: Universitätsverlag Winter.

Høyrup, Jens, 1989. "Sub-scientific mathematics: observations on a pre-modern phenomenon". *History of Science* 27, 63–87.

— 2002. *Lengths, Widths, Surfaces. A Portrait of Old Babylonian Algebra and Its Kin*. New York: Springer.

Jeffery, Lilian H., 1961. *The Local Scripts of Archaic Greece*. Oxford: Oxford University Press.

Koerner, Reinhard, 1993. *Inschriftliche Gesetzestexte der frühen griechischen Polis*. Köln: Böhlau.

Kunz, Volker, 2004. *Rational Choice*. Frankfurt a. M.: Campus.

Luhmann, Niklas, 1983. *Legitimation als Verfahren*. Frankfurt a. M.: Suhrkamp. (3. Auflage).

Meiggs, Russell / David Lewis, 1969. *A Selection of Greek Historical Inscriptions*. Oxford: Oxford University Press.

Meister, Richard, 1882. *Die griechischen Dialekte auf Grundlage von Ahrens' Werk*, volume 1. Göttingen: Vandenhoeck & Ruprecht.

Möllers, Christoph, 2015. *Die Möglichkeit der Normen. Über eine Praxis jenseits von Moralität und Kausalität*. Berlin: Suhrkamp.

Netz, Reviel, 1999a. *The Shaping of Deduction in Greek Mathematics*. Cambridge: Cambridge University Press.

— 1999b. "Proclus' Division of the Mathematical Proposition into Parts: How and Why Was It Formulated?". *Classical Quarterly* 49, 282–303.

— 2002a. "Counter Culture: Towards a history of Greek numeracy". *History of Science* 40, 321–352.

— 2002b. "Greek Mathematicians. A Group Picture". In: Christopher J. Tuplin / Tracey E. Rihll (eds.) *Science and Mathematics in Ancient Greek Culture*. Oxford: Oxford University Press, 196–216.

— 2004. "Eudemus of Rhodes, Hippocrates of Chios and the Earliest Form of a Greek Mathematical Text". *Centaurus* 46, 243–286.

Rosental, Claude, 2003. "Certifying Knowledge: The Sociology of a Logical Theorem in Artificial Intelligence". *American Sociological Review* 68, 623–644.

Thür, Gerhard, 2003. "Recht im antiken Griechenland". In: Ulrich Manthe (ed.) *Die Rechtskulturen der Antike. Vom Alten Orient bis zum Römischen Reich*. München: Beck, 191–238.

Weber, Max, 1980. *Wirtschaft und Gesellschaft. Grundriß der verstehenden Soziologie*. Tübingen: Mohr Siebeck. (5. Auflage).

Westbrook, Raymond, 2015. *Ex Oriente Lex. Near Eastern Influences on Ancient Greek and Roman Law*. Baltimore: Johns Hopkins University Press.

Whitley, John, 1997. "Cretan Laws and Cretan Literacy". *American Journal of Archaeology* 101, 635–661.

Überlegungen zu den Klagen strengen Rechts – *certum* und *incertum* als Leistungsgegenstand[1]

Peter Gröschler

Abstract 221
1 Das System von Klagen auf *certa pecunia*, *alia certa res* und *incertum* 222
2 Die Bedeutung des Systems des strengen Aktionenrechts im klassischen römischen Recht 226
2.1. Pflichtverletzung durch Unterlassen bei einer auf Geben (*dare*) gerichteten Verpflichtung 227
2.2. Schlechtleistung bei einer auf Geben einer bestimmten Sache (*certam rem dare*) gerichteten Verpflichtung 229
2.3. Festsetzung eines bestimmten Leistungsortes (*certus locus*) oder einer bestimmten Leistungszeit (*certus dies*) 231
2.4. Wahlschuld und Versprechen einer Leistung an einen Dritten ... 240
3 Zusammenfassung 246
Abkürzungs- und Literaturverzeichnis 247

Abstract

Den Ausgangspunkt des römischen Prozesses bildet die auf einen bestimmten Geldbetrag (*certa pecunia*) gerichtete Klage, bei der der Richter den Beklagten nur entweder in voller Höhe auf den eingeklagten Betrag verurteilen oder aber die Klage abweisen konnte. Es handelt sich dabei um eine Art von Ja-/Nein-Prozess, der im römischen Prozessrecht nie vollständig überwunden wurde. Freilich wurde im Laufe der Zeit der Ermessensspielraum des Richters erweitert, indem Klagen auf mengenmäßig oder individuell bestimmte Sachen (*aliae certae res*) eingeführt wurden, bei denen der Richter den Wert der Sachen schätzen muss. Schließlich ließ man auch Klagen auf einen unbestimmten Leistungsgegenstand (*incertum*) zu, also auf einen Leistungsgegenstand, der weder *certa pecunia* noch eine sonstige *certa res* ist, wie das z. B. bei der aus einem Tun bestehenden Werkleistung der Fall ist. Den Abschluss der Entwicklung bildet die Einführung der Klagen nach Treu und Glauben (*bonae fidei iudicia*), bei denen dem Richter ein denkbar weitgehender Entscheidungsspielraum zukommt. Gleichwohl waren auch die klassischen römischen Juristen, einschließlich der Spätklassiker, noch stark im überkommenen System der Klagen strengen Rechts verhaftet. Belege

[1] Der Beitrag ist in verkürzter Form auch erschienen in: *Scritti per Alessandro Corbino* III, 2016, 497–522.

dafür, dass *certum*-Schulden, also Schulden, die zu einer auf einen bestimmten Leistungsgegenstand (*certum*) gerichteten Klage führten, in einen unbestimmten Leistungsgegenstand (*incertum*) umdefiniert wurden, um dem Gläubiger die Vorteile der weiten Formel der *actio incerti ex stipulatu* zu verschaffen, lassen sich – soweit ersichtlich – nicht finden. Zu erklären ist das wohl nicht mit einem besonderen Konservativismus der römischen Juristen. Vielmehr steht zu vermuten, dass hierbei die Sonderrolle des förmlichen Schuldversprechens (*stipulatio*) ausschlaggebend war.

1. Das System von Klagen auf *certa pecunia*, *alia certa res* und *incertum*

Die römischen Juristen haben ihren Blick bekanntlich in erster Linie auf die praktische Durchsetzbarkeit von Rechten und Ansprüchen gerichtet. Man spricht daher vom „aktionenrechtlichen Denken" der römischen Juristen. Das, was wir heute im Anschluss an Windscheid[2] als materiell-rechtlichen Anspruch bezeichnen, wurde als prozessuale Klagemöglichkeit verstanden. Eine exakte Trennung zwischen materiellem Recht und Prozessrecht kannten die römischen Juristen noch nicht.[3] Das aktionenrechtliche Denken der römischen Juristen liegt darin begründet, dass im römischen Recht ein durchsetzbarer Anspruch nur dann vorlag, wenn der Prätor für den konkreten Fall eine Klagformel erteilte. Die Klagformeln waren im Edikt des Prätors im Grundsatz abschließend aufgelistet. Aufgrund der begrenzten Anzahl von Klagformeln sprechen wir auch von einem *numerus clausus* der anerkannten Schuldverhältnisse im römischen Recht.

Man kann das auch in anderen Bereichen des archaischen Rechts beobachten, für das noch das aus der sakralen Sphäre stammende Prinzip der „Wirkform" gilt, das heißt, dass ein Rechtsakt überhaupt nur durch seine Form existiert, die für ihn den wahren Geltungsgrund bildet.[4] Heute sprechen wir dagegen von einer „Zweckform"[5], weil sämtliche Formvorschriften des geltenden Rechts einen ganz bestimmten Zweck erfüllen, etwa einen Warnzweck, wie das z.B. beim Schriftformerfordernis für die Bürgschaftserklärung gemäß § 766 Satz 1 BGB der Fall ist. Ebenso wie die das Prinzip der „Wirkform" diente auch die formallogische Struktur des alten Prozessrechts, das nur Ja-/Nein-Entscheidungen kennt, dazu, die Sicherheit zu erhöhen. Zum Teil werden auch heute noch formallogische Strukturen des Rechts als Garant für die Verwirklichung der materiellen Gerechtigkeit angesehen. In gewissem Sinne ist auch das prozeduralistische Modell der Diskurstheorie des Rechts, wonach das Recht seine Legitimität aus den Formen der Kommunikation erlangt, in denen die Bürger ihre pri-

---

[2] Windscheid, 1856, 6: „Jemand hat eine Actio, heißt in die Sprache unserer Rechtsanschauung, für welche die gerichtliche Verfolgbarkeit erst die Consequenz des Rechtes ist, übersetzt: Jemand hat einen rechtlich anerkannten Anspruch."

[3] Zu den Ansätzen eines materiell-rechtlichen Verständnisses von *actio* bereits durch die römischen Juristen siehe Kaser, 1971, 224.

[4] Dulckeit, 1951, 161 f., 163; Kaser, 1949, 321–324; ders., 1971, 39 f. Siehe auch schon Savigny, 1850, 206–208 („formelle Contracte"); Jhering, 1898, 504–509.

[5] Siehe nur Flume, 1979, 244–246.

vate und staatsbürgerliche Autonomie verwirklichen können[6], ein moderner Versuch, materielle Gerechtigkeit durch einen formalen Ansatz zu schaffen.

Im römischen Prozessrecht wurde der Ausgangspunkt, nämlich der des Ja-/Nein-Prozesses, niemals vollständig überwunden. Die auf einen bestimmten Geldbetrag gerichtete Prozessbehauptung des Klägers, die bereits bei der *legis actio sacramento in personam* anzutreffen ist, taucht in abgewandelter Form wieder auf bei der durch die Zwölf Tafeln eingeführten Spruchformelklage durch Anforderung eines Privatrichters oder Schiedsrichters (*legis actio per iudicis arbitrive postulationem*), deren Klagbehauptung wie folgt lautet: „Ich behaupte, dass du mir aus einem Gelöbnis 10.000 Sesterze geben musst. Ich fordere dich auf, dies zuzugestehen oder zu leugnen." (*Ex sponsione te mihi x milia sestertia dare oportere aio: id postulo aias an neges.*)[7] Ganz ähnlich gestaltet ist die klägerische Behauptung bei der Spruchformelklage durch Terminsverkündung (*legis actio per condictionem*), die als jüngste Spruchformelklage durch eine *lex Silia* wohl Ende des 4. Jahrhunderts v. Chr., zunächst nur für Ansprüche auf *certa pecunia*, eingeführt worden ist: „Ich behaupte, dass du mir 10.000 Sesterze geben musst. Ich fordere dich auf, dies zuzugestehen oder zu bestreiten." (*Aio te mihi sestertium x milia dare oportere: id postulo aias an neges.*)[8] Der Richter konnte den Beklagten nur entweder auf den eingeklagten Betrag in voller Höhe verurteilen oder aber die Klage abweisen, was wiederum auf eine Ja-/Nein-Entscheidung hinausläuft.

Im Formularverfahren, das wohl auf die zweite Hälfte des 3. Jahrhundert v. Chr. zurückgeht[9], wurden die Klagen des alten Spruchformelverfahrens der Struktur nach übernommen. So ist etwa die Struktur des Spruchformelverfahrens bei der Klagformel der auf einen bestimmten Geldbetrag gerichteten Kondiktion (*condictio certae pecuniae*)[10], die die Nachfolgeklage zur *legis actio per condictionem* bildet, noch klar zu erkennen:

> Titius iudex esto. Si paret Numerium Negidium Aulo Agerio HS X milia dare oportere, qua de re agitur, iudex Numerium Negidium Aulo Agerio HS X milia condemnato, si non paret absolvito.[11]
>
> Titius soll Richter sein. Wenn es sich erweist, dass Numerius Negidius dem Aulus Agerius 10.000 Sesterze geben muss, worüber verhandelt wird, dann sollst du, Richter, den Numerius Negidius zugunsten des Aulus Agerius zu 10.000 Sesterzen verurteilen; wenn es sich nicht erweist, sollst du freisprechen.

---

[6] Hierzu Habermas, 1992, 493 [http://solomon.soth.alexanderstreet.com/cgi-bin/asp/philo/soth/getdoc.pl?S10023105-D000010 (aufgerufen am 31.8.2018)]. Siehe auch Alexy, 1991, 36 f., 399–403; Tschentscher, 2000, 119, 131.

[7] Gai. 4.17a.

[8] Gai. 4.17b, 19.

[9] Vgl. Kaser / Hackl, 1996, 153–157.

[10] Zum Begriff der Kondiktion (*condictio*) vgl. nur Gai. 4.5: *Appellantur autem in rem quidem actiones ‚vindicationes', in personam autem actiones, quibus ‚dari fierive oportere' intendimus, ‚condictiones'.* (Und zwar heißen die dinglichen Klagen ‚Vindikationen', die schuldrechtlichen Klagen aber, mit denen man beantragt, dass ‚etwas gegeben oder getan werden müsse', ‚Kondiktionen').

[11] Lenel, 1927, 237; Mantovani, 2002, 48.

Die Klage, die etwa beim Darlehen (*mutuum*) für den Anspruch des Darlehensgebers auf Rückzahlung zuständig war, war auf einen bestimmten Geldbetrag (*certa pecunia*) gerichtet, so dass es – ähnlich wie bereits im Spruchformelverfahren – zu einer Ja-/Nein-Entscheidung des Richters kam. Wurde vom Kläger zu viel eingeklagt, wurde die Klage insgesamt abgewiesen und der Kläger verlor seinen Anspruch im Regelfall endgültig.[12]

Durch die Zwölf Tafeln wurde der Entscheidungsspielraum des Richters erweitert. Mit der neu eingeführten Spruchformelklage durch Anforderung eines Richters oder Schiedsrichters (*legis actio per iudicis arbitrive postulationem*) konnte nun nicht mehr nur auf einen bestimmten Geldbetrag, sondern auch auf andere mengenmäßig oder individuell bestimmte Sachen (*aliae certae res*) geklagt werden.[13] Später, wohl immer noch vor Einführung des Formularverfahrens, wird auch die Spruchformelklage durch Terminsverkündung (*legis actio per condictionem*) durch eine *lex Calpurnia*, vermutlich aus dem 3. Jahrhundert v.Chr.[14], auf die Leistung von *aliae certae res* erweitert.[15] Soweit es um eine *alia certa res* geht, ist der Bereich des reinen Ja-/Nein-Prozesses überschritten. Der Richter muss, wenn er den Beklagten verurteilt, eine Schätzung des Streitgegenstandes vornehmen. Entsprechend dem Grundsatz der Geldkondemnation (*condemnatio pecuniaria*) musste eine Verurteilung nämlich stets auf einen Geldbetrag lauten. Zurückzuführen ist der Grundsatz der Geldkondemnation vermutlich auf den Übergang von einer Personal- zu einer Vermögenshaftung des Schuldners, die mit der Einschränkung oder Abschaffung der Schuldknechtschaft durch die *lex Poetelia* (326 v. Chr.) in Verbindung steht.[16] War etwa die Übereignung des Sklaven Stichus aufgrund eines förmlichen Schuldversprechens (*stipulatio*) geschuldet und klagte der Gläubiger gegen den Schuldner auf Vornahme der Übereignung, so genügte es nicht, wenn der Richter nur die Berechtigung der Forderung feststellte, was noch im Rahmen eines reinen Ja-/Nein-Prozesses möglich gewesen wäre. Der Richter musste vielmehr, um zu einer Geldverurteilung zu gelangen, den Wert des Sklaven schätzen. Darin liegt

---

[12] Gai. 4.53 f. (zur *pluris petitio re*).

[13] Unsicher ist, ob die Klage auch schon von vornherein auf einen unbestimmten Klagegegenstand (*incertum*) gerichtet sein konnte, zumal auch die *legis actio per condictionem* zwar seit der *lex Cornelia* auch auf eine andere *certa res* als einen bestimmten Geldbetrag (siehe Fn. 15), jedoch wohl nicht auf ein *incertum* gerichtet sein konnte; vgl. auch Knütel, 1976, 59 f. Gegen eine auf ein *incertum* gerichtete Spruchformelklage Broggini, 1957, 178–185; Pugliese, 1962, 338–342 Fn. 207 *bis* und 211; ders., 1963, 61 f. Anders Magdelain, 1980, 218 f. (= ders. 1990, 601 f.), im Hinblick auf Prob. Eins. 13 (Keil, 1864, 275): *T. M. D. F. O. te mihi dare facere oportere*, das sich aber auch auf das Formularverfahren beziehen kann; vgl. zum subjektiv stilisierten Vortrag des Klägers Gai. 4.2: *cum intendimus, dare facere praestare oportere;* 4.59: *Quod ego de te hominem Erotem emi.* Für eine frühe Klagemöglichkeit auf *incertum* aber auch Kaser, 1973, 206; ders., 1971, 170; Kaser / Hackl, 1996, 108–111 mit Fn. 8, 21.

[14] Behrends, 1974, 98 (zweite Hälfte des 3. Jahrhunderts v. Chr.). Kaser, 1971, 170, siedelt die *lex Calpurnia* im 2. Jahrhundert v. Chr. an, möglicherweise in Anlehnung an das sichere Datum der *lex Calpurnia repetundarum* (149 v. Chr.).

[15] Gai. 4.19: *de omni certa re.*

[16] Zur Bedeutung der *lex Poetelia* vgl. Kaser / Hackl, 1996, 145.

gegenüber dem reinen Ja-/Nein-Prozess eine wichtige Erweiterung des Entscheidungsspielraums des Richters. Im Formularverfahren entspricht dem die Klagformel der auf mengenmäßig oder individuell bestimmte Sachen gerichteten Kondiktion (*condictio certae rei* bzw. *condictio tritic*[*i*]*aria*)[17]:

> Titius iudex esto. Si paret Numerium Negidium Aulo Agerio hominem Stichum (tritici Alexandrini optimi modios centum) dare oportere, qua de re agitur, quanti ea res est, tantam pecuniam iudex Numerium Negidium Aulo Agerio condemnato, si non paret absolvito.[18]
>
> Titius soll Richter sein. Wenn es sich erweist, dass Numerius Negidius dem Aulus Agerius den Sklaven Stichus (100 Scheffel besten alexandrinischen Weizens) geben muss, worüber verhandelt wird, dann sollst du, Richter, den Numerius Negidius zugunsten des Aulus Agerius zu so viel Geld verurteilen, wie die Sache wert ist; wenn es sich nicht erweist, sollst du freisprechen.

Noch einen entscheidenden Schritt weiter geht die Zulassung von Klagen auf einen unbestimmten Leistungsgegenstand (*incertum*), mit anderen Worten: auf einen Leistungsgegenstand, der weder *certa pecunia* noch eine sonstige *certa res* ist. Sicher bezeugt ist eine derartige Klage im Rahmen des Formularverfahrens durch die auf einen unbestimmten Leistungsgegenstand gerichtete Klage aus förmlichem Versprechen (*actio incerti ex stipulatu*)[19]:

> Titius iudex esto. Quod Aulus Agerius de Numerio Negidio incertum stipulatus est, cuius rei dies fuit, quidquid ob eam rem Numerium Negidium Aulo Agerio dare facere oportet, eius iudex Numerium Negidium Aulo Agerio condemnato, si non paret absolvito.[20]
>
> Titius soll Richter sein. Da sich Aulus Agerius von Numerius Negidius eine unbestimmte Leistung hat versprechen lassen, die jetzt fällig geworden ist, was auch immer deswegen Numerius Negidius dem Aulus Agerius geben oder tun muss, zu dem sollst du, Richter, den Numerius Negidius zugunsten des Aulus Agerius verurteilen; wenn es sich nicht erweist, sollst du freisprechen.

Um einen derartigen unbestimmten Leistungsgegenstand geht es immer dann, wenn der Richter nicht einfach nur den Wert einer bestimmten Sache schätzen muss, sondern darüber hinausgehende Überlegungen anzustellen hat. Das ist etwa dann der Fall, wenn eine Werkleistung, z.B. der Bau eines Hauses, durch Stipulation versprochen wird. Hier geht es nicht um eine auf ein Geben (*dare*) gerichtete Verpflichtung, bei der Geld oder eine (zumindest mengenmäßig) bestimmte Sache übergeben und übereignet werden muss, sondern um eine viel

---

[17] Daneben gab es – zumindest in der Frühzeit des Formularverfahrens (vgl. aber auch Ulp. D. 45.1.51) – eine *actio certi ex stipulatu*, die als Nachfolgerin der *legis actio per iudicis arbitrive postulationem* anzusehen ist; Behrends, 1974, 105; Kaser, 1971, 542.

[18] Lenel, 1927, 240; Mantovani, 2002, 49.

[19] Die *condictio incerti* gehört dagegen erst dem klassischen Recht an; vgl. Kaser / Hackl, 1996, 111 Fn. 6; Kaser, 1971, 599 f.

[20] Gai. 4.136; hierzu Lenel, 1927, 240; Mantovani, 2002, 25.

komplexere, auf ein Tun (*facere*) gerichtete Verpflichtung, nämliche die Verpflichtung des Werkunternehmers zur Erstellung des versprochenen Werks. Dementsprechend ist die Klagformel sehr weit gefasst und richtet sich auf „was auch immer … geben oder tun muss" (*quidquid … dare facere oportet*), was für den Richter einen ganz erheblichen Ermessensspielraum mit sich bringt.

Vom Ausgangspunkt des Ja-/Nein-Prozesses mit seiner hohen Sicherheit und Klarheit sind wir hier schon sehr weit entfernt. Die Klageformel der *actio incerti ex stipulatu* muss im Gegenteil als hochgradig offen und unsicher bezeichnet werden. In der unbestimmten Klagformel liegt für den Kläger aber auch ein großer Vorteil: Da der Leistungsumfang durch die Klagformel nicht exakt bestimmt ist, kann und muss der Richter entscheiden, welche Aspekte von der vom Schuldner übernommenen Verpflichtung mit umfasst sind. Im Fall von Leistungsstörungen wie etwa dem Schuldnerverzug gibt es nur bei der auf „was auch immer … geben oder tun muss" (*quidquid … dare facere oportet*) gerichteten Klagformel eine Möglichkeit, den Schuldner über den Wert des eigentlichen Leistungsgegenstandes hinaus zu verurteilen. Bei einem reinen Ja-/Nein-Prozess ist ein solcher Ersatz etwa des Verzögerungsschadens von vornherein ausgeschlossen und auch dann, wenn die Klagformel auf einen bestimmten Leistungsgegenstand (*certum*) gerichtet ist, das heißt auf *certa pecunia* oder eine sonstige *certa res*, wird nur der Wert des geschuldeten Leistungsgegenstandes geschätzt; darüber hinausgehende Posten können nicht geltend gemacht werden.

2. Die Bedeutung des Systems des strengen Aktionenrechts im klassischen römischen Recht

Im römischen Recht richtete sich die Klagformel nach dem jeweiligen Leistungsgegenstand bzw. dem jeweiligen Vertragstyp und konnte nicht etwa frei gewählt werden.[21] So war beim Darlehen (*mutuum*) für den Anspruch des Darlehensgebers auf Rückzahlung die auf einen bestimmten Geldbetrag gerichtete Kondiktion (*condictio certae pecuniae*) – hier auch *actio certae creditae pecuniae* (Klage auf einen geschuldeten bestimmten Geldbetrag) genannt – zuständig, die ausschließlich auf die Rückzahlung des Darlehens gerichtet war. Schäden, die dem Gläubiger aus einer verzögerten Rückgewähr des Darlehensbetrags entstanden, konnten nicht geltend gemacht werden. Ebenso wenig konnten mit der *condictio certae pecuniae* Zinsen eingeklagt werden, weshalb diese, wie bei Geschäftsdarlehen üblich, förmlich durch *stipulatio* versprochen werden mussten. Insgesamt ist festzustellen, dass das System von Klagen auf *certa pecunia*, *alia certa res* und *incertum* ein sehr starres Gebilde darstellt, das zwar einerseits durch ein hohes Maß an Stringenz gekennzeichnet war, andererseits aber auch, gerade aufgrund der Starrheit, zu Ergebnissen führte, die nicht immer den heutigen, am Ziel der materiellen Gerechtigkeit orientierten Erwartungen genügen. Gerade was die Unterscheidung von *certum* und *incertum* betrifft, gibt es Erscheinungen, die nur durch die historische Entwicklung der Klagen von einem sehr engen (bei *certa pecunia*, *alia certa res*) hin zu einem weiten Streitgegenstand (bei einem *incertum*) erklärt werden können. Im Folgenden soll

[21] Vgl. statt aller Kaser, 1971, 492–94.

anhand einzelner Beispiele untersucht werden, inwiefern die römischen Juristen auch in der Zeit der Klassik noch an dem überkommenen System festhielten oder aber Ansätze zur Durchbrechung dieses Systems erkennbar sind.

2.1 Pflichtverletzung durch Unterlassen bei einer auf Geben (*dare*) gerichteten Verpflichtung

Besonders augenfällig ist die Beschränkung, die sich aus der engen Umschreibung des Klagegegenstands ergibt, bei einer auf Geben (*dare*) gerichteten Verpflichtung, die die Leistung eines konkreten Gegenstandes, z.B. eines individuell bestimmten Sklaven, zum Inhalt hat. Sowohl die auf eine bestimmte Sache gerichtete Kondiktion (*condictio certae rei*) als auch die auf eine bestimmte Sache gerichtete Testamentsklage (*actio certi ex testamento*)[22] waren hier jeweils auf eine Verpflichtung zum Geben (*dare oportere*) des geschuldeten Einzelgegenstandes gerichtet. Kaser spricht insofern von den Klagen „strengsten" Rechts.[23]

D. 45.1.91 pr., Paul. 17 ad Plaut.

Si servum stipulatus fuero et nulla mora intercedente servus decesserit: si quidem occidat eum promissor, expeditum est. sin autem neglegat infirmum, an teneri debeat promissor? considera[nti]b<im>us[24], utrum, quemadmodum in vindicatione hominis, si neglectus a possessore fuerit, culpae huius nomine tenetur possessor, ita et cum dari promisit, an culpa, quod ad stipulationem attinet, in faciendo accipienda sit, non in non faciendo. quod magis probandum est, quia qui dari promisit, ad dandum, non faciendum tenetur.

Ich habe mir einen Sklaven förmlich versprechen lassen und dieser ist ohne den Eintritt eines Verzugs gestorben: Wenn der Versprechende den Sklaven getötet hat, so ist der Fall klar. Wenn er ihn aber als Kranken vernachlässigt hat, muss dann der Versprechende haften? Wir werden in Betracht ziehen, ob – ebenso wie bei der bezüglich eines Sklaven erhobenen Eigentumsklage der Besitzer wegen Verschuldens haftet, wenn er den Sklaven vernachlässigt hat – auch der haftet, der zu geben versprochen hat, oder ob das Verschulden, soweit es das förmliche Versprechen betrifft, in einem Tun zu sehen ist, nicht in einem Unterlassen. Das ist als richtiger anzusehen, weil der, der zu geben versprochen hat, zum Geben und nicht zu einer sonstigen Leistung verpflichtet ist.

Da die stipulationsweise Verpflichtung zur Leistung eines individuell bestimmten Sklaven ausschließlich auf ein *dare* gerichtet war, gelangt der spätklassische Jurist Paulus noch zu dem Ergebnis, dass der Schuldner nur für eine durch positives Tun[25] herbeigeführte nachträgliche Unmöglichkeit hafte, also etwa dann,

---

[22] Auch die *actio ex testamento* wird sich ursprünglich ausschließlich auf ein *certum* gerichtet haben, ggf. zunächst nur auf *certa pecunia*; vgl. Honsell, 1987, 486.

[23] Kaser, 1971, 506.

[24] Lenel, 1889, I 1176 Fn. 2.

[25] Siehe auch PS. 5.7.4: *facto promissoris*.

wenn er den Sklaven durch eigenes aktives Handeln getötet hat. Dagegen führe eine – selbst vorsätzlich begangene – unterlassene Hilfeleistung, die zur Folge hat, dass der erkrankte Sklave stirbt, nicht zu einer Haftung des Schuldners, weil das auf eine bestimmte Sache gerichtete förmliche Versprechen (*stipulatio certae rei*) keine Verpflichtung zu einem Tun (*facere*) in Form der Veranlassung einer Behandlung des erkrankten Sklaven beinhalte.[26] Darauf, dass es hierüber immerhin eine Kontroverse unter den römischen Juristen gab, deutet zum einen die Argumentation Paulus' mit *magis probandum*[27], zum anderen auch der ausführliche Vergleich mit dem Vindikationsbeklagten hin, der im Rahmen der auf ein Herausgeben (*restituere*) abzielenden und auf „wieviel die Sache wert sein wird" (*quanti ea res erit*) lautenden Eigentumsklage (*rei vindicatio*) offenbar ab dem Zeitpunkt der Rechtshängigmachung (*litis contestatio*) auch für ein Unterlassen haftbar gemacht werden konnte.[28]

Die Befürwortung einer Fortsetzung der Verbindlichkeit (*perpetuatio obligationis*) nicht nur im Fall das aktiven Tuns, sondern bei einer durch Unterlassen herbeigeführten Unmöglichkeit der Leistung hätte für die *stipulatio certae rei* jedenfalls keinen gewagten dogmatischen Schritt bedeutet.[29] Das gilt in besonderem Maße angesichts des doch erheblichen Kunstgriffs, der in der bereits von den republikanischen Juristen[30] entwickelten *perpetuatio obligationis* selbst liegt[31], bei der die Weiterexistenz der in Wahrheit untergegangenen *certa res* fingiert wird[32]. Dass Paulus die vergleichsweise moderate Erweiterung auch auf Fälle des Unterlassens nicht vornimmt, ist überraschend und zugleich ein Beleg dafür, wie sehr auch Juristen der Spätklassik noch in den Kategorien des strengen Rechts verhaftet waren.[33] Einen möglichen Erklärungsansatz bietet Cannata, der die eingeschränkte Haftung des Stipulationsschuldners bei der *stipulatio certae rei* auf die Rechtsnatur der Stipulation als abstraktes, einseitig verpflichtendes Geschäft zurückführt, bei dem der vom Richter zu berücksichtigende Verpflichtungsumfang von den Parteien habe exakt formuliert werden müssen.[34]

---

[26] Zu Recht weist Cannata, 1966, 94–96, darauf hin, dass die Fälle des Nichttuns (*non facere*), die eine Haftung des Stipulationsschuldners ausschließen, wohl denkbar eng zu fassen waren. In der Tat ist in dem von Cannata herangezogenen Vergleichsfall des Verhungernlassens (*fame necare*), also dann, wenn der Stipulationsschuldner den Sklaven einsperrt und nicht mehr mit Nahrung versorgt (vgl. Gai. 3.219, Ulp. D. 9.2.9.2, 29.7, c), durchaus ein aktives Tun im Sinne eines *facere* zu sehen. Kaser, 1980, 95, stellt zusätzlich auf die Frage des Verschuldens ab und stellt fest, man habe bei Vernachlässigung eines Kranken (*neglegere infirmum*) als einem „passiven Verhalten ohne (oder mit nicht genügend deutlichem) Schuldbewusstsein" über die Haftung aus dem förmlichen Versprechen streiten können. Vgl. einschränkend auch MacCormack, 1973, 64.

[27] Vgl. Honsell, 1987, 235 Fn. 33.

[28] Zur *rei vindicatio* siehe Wimmer, 1995, 50.

[29] Für die Annahme, dass sich Paulus von der Position der republikanischen Juristen (*veteres*) zur *perpetuatio obligationis* sogar entfernt hätte (so Sargenti, 1954, 170), gibt es indes keinen Anlass.

[30] Paul. D. 45.1.91.3 (*veteres*).

[31] Kaser, 1980, 130, nennt die *perpetuatio obligationis* ein „vom strengen Aktionenrecht erzwungenes Hilfsmittel".

[32] Siehe Ulp. D. 45.1.82.1; PS. 5.7.4.

[33] Vgl. auch Kaser, 1980, 93, der von einer „etwas formalistischen Lösung" spricht.

[34] Cannata, 1966, 110–112.

2.2 Schlechtleistung bei einer auf Geben einer bestimmten Sache (*certam rem dare*) gerichteten Verpflichtung

Ein ähnliches Problem wie bei der Pflichtverletzung durch Unterlassen stellt sich bei auf Geben einer bestimmten Sache (*certam rem dare*) gerichteten Verpflichtungen im Fall der Schlechtleistung, also dann, wenn der Schuldner den Leistungsgegenstand zwar nicht zerstört, ihn aber verschlechtert bzw. sonst wissentlich mit einem Sach- oder Rechtsmangel behaftet oder unvollständig leistet. Hier müsste man bei einem strikten Verständnis der Verpflichtung zu dem Ergebnis kommen, dass der Schuldner durch die Leistung des verschlechterten bzw. mangelhaften Gegenstands seiner Übereignungspflicht als solcher vollständig nachgekommen ist. Da er nur zum Geben (*dare*) verpflichtet ist, würde er folglich für die bloße Verschlechterung des Leistungsgegenstands und für dessen Mangelhaftigkeit nicht haften. Im Fall der unvollständigen Leistung würde die auf eine Verpflichtung zum Geben einer bestimmten Sache (*certam rem dare oportere*) gerichtete Klage, die den Leistungsgegenstand in seiner Gesamtheit erfasst, bei strenger Betrachtung eine Zuvielforderung (*pluris petitio*) bedeuten, da ja der Schuldner zumindest teilweise bereits geleistet hat.

Das war offenbar, jedenfalls im Ausgangspunkt, noch die Sichtweise Labeos, der bei einer tatsächlichen oder rechtlichen Verschlechterung[35] des Leistungsgegenstands für den Rückgriff auf die Arglistklage (*actio de dolo*) plädiert, weil zumindest zweifelhaft sei, ob die Klage aus förmlichem Versprechen zur Verfügung stehe[36]:

> D. 4.3.7.3, Ulp. 11 ad ed.
>
> Non solum autem si alia actio non sit, sed et si dubitetur an alia sit, putat Labeo de dolo dandam actionem et adfert talem speciem. qui servum mihi debebat vel ex venditione vel ex stipulatu, venenum ei dedit et sic eum tradidit: vel fundum, et dum tradit, imposuit ei servitutem vel aedificia diruit, arbores excidit vel extirpavit: ait Labeo, sive cavit de dolo sive

[35] Cannata, 1966, 112 f. mit Fn. 107, will in dem von Labeo in D. 4.3.7.3 angeführten Beispiel der Übereignung eines vergifteten Sklaven keine Schlechtleistung annehmen, sondern geht von einer nach Erfüllung eintretenden Unmöglichkeit aus (mit der Folge, dass aufgrund des Erfüllungseintritts eine *perpetuatio obligationis* ausscheidet); ähnlich Albanese, 1961, 232 f., 235. Auch dann, wenn man einer derart strikten Trennung von Schlechtleistung und Unmöglichkeit folgen will, muss allerdings der Fall, dass der im Zeitpunkt der Übereignung vorhandene Defekt zum alsbaldigen Untergang des Leistungsgegenstands führt, der Schlechtleistung zumindest gleichgestellt werden. Das steht auch im Einklang mit fr. 7.3, wie die dort aufgeführten weiteren Beispiele zeigen: *vel fundum, et dum tradit, imposuit ei servitutem vel aedificia diruit, arbores excidit vel extirpavit* (oder [er schuldet] ein Grundstück und er hat dieses, bevor er es übergeben hat, mit einer Dienstbarkeit belastet oder Gebäude abgerissen, Bäume gefällt oder herausgerissen). Es geht hier eindeutig um Fälle der Schlechtleistung, die von Labeo bzw. Ulpian zusammen mit dem Fall des vergifteten Sklaven einer einheitlichen Lösung zugeführt werden.

[36] Labeo hat die Stipulationsklage nicht etwa „völlig abgelehnt“; so aber Kaser, 1980, 138.

> non, dandam in eum de dolo actionem, quoniam si cavit, dubium est, an competat ex stipulatu actio. sed est verius, si quidem de dolo cautum est, cessare actionem de dolo, quoniam est ex stipulatu actio: si non est cautum, in ex empto quidem actione cessat de dolo actio, quoniam est ex empto, in ex stipulatu de dolo actio necessaria est.[37]
>
> Aber nicht nur, wenn keine andere Klage gegeben ist, sondern auch dann, wenn zweifelhaft ist, ob eine andere Klage gegeben ist, müsse die Arglistklage erteilt werden, meint Labeo und führt folgenden Fall an: Jemand, der mir einen Sklaven entweder aus Kauf oder aus förmlichen Versprechen schuldete, gab ihm Gift und hat ihn in diesem Zustand übergeben; oder er schuldete ein Grundstück und hat dieses, bevor er es übergeben hat, mit einer Dienstbarkeit belastet oder Gebäude niedergerissen, Bäume gefällt oder herausgerissen. Labeo sagt, gegen ihn müsse die Arglistklage erteilt werden, gleichviel, ob er für Arglist Sicherheit geleistet hat oder nicht, weil es dann, wenn er Sicherheit gleistet hat, zweifelhaft ist, ob die Klage aus förmlichem Versprechen zusteht. Aber es ist richtiger, dass dann, wenn er für Arglist Sicherheit geleistet hat, die Arglistklage ausscheidet, weil die Klage aus dem förmlichen Versprechen gegeben ist. Wenn er keine Sicherheit geleistet hat, scheidet neben der Kaufklage die Arglistklage aus, weil ja die Kaufklage gegeben ist; neben der Klage aus förmlichem Verprechen ist aber die Arglistklage erforderlich.

Labeo hält hier die Klage aus förmlichem Versprechen selbst dann für zweifelhaft, wenn der Stipulationsschuldner ausdrücklich die Abwesenheit von Arglist versprochen hat (*cavit de dolo*). Arangio-Ruiz[38] formuliert das förmliche Versprechen mit Arglistklausel wie folgt: *spondes hominem Stichum dari dolumque malum huic rei abesse*? *spondeo*. (Gelobst du, den Sklaven Stichus zu geben und dass Arglist in dieser Sache fern sei? Ich gelobe es.) Diese Art der Verbindung des förmlichen Versprechens einer bestimmten Sache (*stipulatio certae rei*) mit der auf einen unbestimmten Leistungsgegenstand (*incertum*) gerichteten Arglistklausel, die ein Nichttun (*non facere*) im Sinne des Unterlassens jeden arglistigen Verhaltens zum Inhalt hat, war offenbar zur Zeit Labeos noch nicht allgemein anerkannt.[39] Womöglich stand dahinter das ursprüngliche Bestreben, im Bereich der strengrechtlichen Verbindlichkeiten keine Mischformen zu erzeugen.

Freier entscheiden dagegen die hoch- und spätklassischen Juristen, jedenfalls seit Julian, indem sie im Fall einer quantitativen oder qualitativen Schlechterfül-

---

[37] Auf die Frage, ob auch die Einbeziehung des Kaufs als klassisch anzusehen ist oder ob die Passagen „*vel ex venditione vel*" und „*in ex empto quidem … in ex stipulatu*" zu streichen sind, kommt es vorliegend ebenso wenig an wie darauf, ob im Hinblick auf die Übereignung des Grundstücks die *mancipatio* durch die *traditio* ersetzt worden ist; für entsprechende Textveränderungen etwa Arangio-Ruiz, 1958, 13; Voci, 1935, 50; Sargenti, 1954, 168 f. Entscheidend ist, dass im Schlusssatz jedenfalls die in den Worten „*si non est cautum,* […] *de dolo actio necessaria est*" enthaltene Stellungnahme Ulpians als klassisch anzusehen ist; vgl. Kaser, 1980, 138 Fn. 217.

[38] 1958, 14.

[39] Kaser, 1980, 128 Fn. 174.

lung einer auf *certam rem dare* gerichteten Verpflichtung dem Gläubiger die auf eine bestimmte Sache gerichtete Kondiktion (*condictio certae rei*) – bzw. die auf eine bestimmte Sache gerichtete Testamentsklage (*actio certi ex testamento*) – zubilligen, so als hätte der Schuldner noch überhaupt nicht geleistet.[40] Aufgrund der dem Schuldner anzulastenden Schlechtleistung kam es wohl ebenso wie im Fall der Unmöglichkeit der Leistung zu einer Fortsetzung der Verbindlichkeit (*perpetuatio obligationis*)[41], wobei der Schuldner im Rahmen des „wieviel die Sache wert ist“ (*quanti ea res est*) freilich nicht auf den vollen Betrag, sondern nur auf die in der Leistungsverkürzung liegende Wertdifferenz verurteilt wurde.[42]

Auffällig ist, dass Ulpian in fr. 7.3 für den Fall, dass der Stipulationsschuldner die Abwesenheit von Arglist nicht ausdrücklich versprochen hat (*si non est cautum*), noch mit Labeo in der Bewertung der Unsicherheit der *condictio certae rei* übereinstimmt, während er andernorts[43] gerade diese Klage befürwortet und insoweit offenbar keinen Rückgriff auf die *actio de dolo* für erforderlich hält. Das könnte so zu erklären sein, dass Ulpian – anders als bei einem ausdrücklichen Versprechen, nicht *dolos* zu handeln (Variante *si quidem de dolo cautum est*) – in der Variante *si non est cautum* die Zweifel Labeos zumindest noch für nachvollziehbar hält, obwohl er selbst dazu tendiert, auch in dieser zweiten Variante die *condictio certae rei* zu bejahen.

2.3 Festsetzung eines bestimmten Leistungsortes (*certus locus*) oder einer bestimmten Leistungszeit (*certus dies*)

Zu überlegen ist, ob für die Frage, ob es sich beim geschuldeten Leistungsgegenstand um eine *certa res* oder aber um ein *incertum* handelt, auch die Frage des Leistungsortes und der Leistungszeit von Bedeutung sein konnte.

In folgender Stelle geht es um die Festsetzung eines bestimmten Leistungsortes (*certus locus*), wobei sich diese Festsetzung auch auf die Leistungszeit auswirkte.

---

[40] Iul. D. 30.82 pr., 84.4; 46.3.33.1; Afr. D. 30.108.11; Ulp. / Marcell. D. 13.3.3 i.f.; Pap. D. 31.66.4; Scaev. D. 45.1.131.1. Siehe hierzu Kaser, 1933, 260 f.; ders., 1935, 96–99; ders., 1980, 137 f. Bei Pomp. D. 7.6.2 ist unsicher, ob das Vermächtnis eines Nießbrauchs (*legatum ususfructus*) als *certum* oder *incertum* eingestuft wurde; vgl. Kaser, 1935, 100; ders., 1980, 137; Medicus, 1962, 222–224.

[41] Zur *perpetuatio obligationis* siehe bei Fn. 29–32.

[42] Kaser, 1935, 99; ders., 1980, 138.

[43] Ulp. D. 46.3.27: *Etiam circa stipulationem et ex testamento actionem, si res tradita fuerit quae debebatur, quamdiu aliquid iuri rei deest, adhuc tamen ipsa res petenda est: ut puta possum fundum petere, licet mihi traditus sit, si ius quoddam cautionis supererit.* (Auch beim förmlichen Versprechen und bei der Klage aus Testament kann, auch wenn die Sache, die geschuldet war, übergeben worden ist, solange an der Sache rechtlich etwas fehlt, immer noch die Sache selbst gefordert werden. Zum Beispiel kann ich ein Grundstück fordern, auch wenn es mir übergeben worden ist, wenn noch irgendein Recht auf Sicherheitsleistung besteht.) Der Ausdruck „*possum fundum petere*“ zeigt, dass es Ulpian um die unveränderte *condictio certae rei* bzw. *actio ex testamento* geht.

D. 45.1.137.2, Ven. 1 stip.

Cum ita stipulatus sum ‚Ephesi dari?' inest tempus: quod autem accipi debeat, quaeritur. et magis est, ut totam eam rem ad iudicem, id est ad virum bonum remittamus, qui aestimet, quanto tempore diligens pater familias conficere possit, quod facturum se promiserit, ut qui Ephesi daturum se spoponderit, neque duplomate diebus ac noctibus et omni tempestate contempta iter continuare cogatur neque tam delicate progredi debeat, ut reprehensione dignus appareat, sed habita ratione temporis aetatis sexus valetudinis, cum id agat, ut mature perveniat, id est eodem tempore, quo plerique eiusdem condicionis homines solent pervenire.

eoque transacto, quamvis Romae remanserit nec possit Ephesi pecuniam dare, nihilo minus ei recte condicetur, vel quia per ipsum steterit, quo minus Ephesi daret, vel quoniam per alium Ephesi possit dari vel quia ubique potest solvere: nam et quod in diem debetur, ante solvi potest, licet peti non potest. quod si duplomate usus aut felici navigatione maturius quam quisque pervenerit Ephesum, confestim obligatus est, quia in eo, quod tempore atque facto finitum est, nullus est coniecturae locus.

Wenn ich mir folgendermaßen habe versprechen lassen: „dass in Ephesus gegeben wird?", liegt darin eine Zeitbestimmung. Es fragt sich aber, wie diese zu verstehen ist. Und es spricht mehr dafür, dass wir die ganze Angelegenheit dem Richter überlassen, das heißt einem redlichen Mann, damit dieser schätze, in welcher Zeit ein sorgfältiger Hausvater das vollbringen kann, was er zu tun versprochen hat, so dass der, der versprochen hat, etwas in Ephesus zu geben, weder gezwungen ist, mit kaiserlichem Geleitbrief Tag und Nacht und ohne Rücksicht auf jede Art von Witterung die Reise fortzusetzen, noch so vorsichtig dabei vorgehen darf, dass er tadelnswert erscheint, sondern unter Berücksichtigung von Zeit, Alter, Geschlecht und Gesundheit, indem er so handelt, dass er rechtzeitig ankommen, das heißt zu der Zeit, zu der die meisten Menschen in derselben Situation üblicherweise ankommen würden.

Wenn diese Zeit abgelaufen ist, kann gegen ihn, auch wenn er in Rom geblieben ist und nicht in Ephesus das Geld zahlen kann, trotzdem mit Recht geklagt werden, weil es entweder an ihm selbst lag, dass er nicht in Ephesus zahlte, oder weil er durch einen anderen in Ephesus hätte zahlen können oder weil er überall zahlen kann. Denn auch das, was auf Termin geschuldet wird, kann vorher geleistet werden, auch wenn es noch nicht gefordert werden kann. Wenn er also durch Gebrauch eines kaiserlichen Geleitbriefs oder aufgrund einer glücklich verlaufenen Schifffahrt früher als jeder andere nach Ephesus gelangt ist, ist er sofort verpflichtet, weil bei dem, was zeitlich oder tatsächlich beendet ist, keine Vermutung Platz greift.

Wer sich versprechen lässt, dass eine Leistung in Ephesus erbracht werde, räumt damit dem Schuldner stillschweigend eine angemessene Leistungszeit ein.[44] Venuleius beschäftigt sich im Fortgang der Stelle ausführlich mit der Frage,

[44] Vgl. auch Ulp. / Iul. D. 13.4.2.6; I. 3.15.5.

welche Leistungszeit in einem solchen Fall als angemessen anzusehen ist und welche Anstrengungen der Schuldner zu unternehmen hat, um die Leistung rechtzeitig am vereinbarten Ort erbringen zu können. Offenbar ging Venuleius selbst davon aus, dass der Schuldner hier nicht nur ein Geben (*dare*), sondern vielmehr auch ein Tun (*facere*) versprochen hat (*quod facturum se promiserit*).[45] Man könnte daher die Stipulation, eine *certa res* an einem bestimmten Ort zu leisten, durchaus als Versprechen eines *incertum* auffassen[46], weil sich der Versprechende implizit dazu verpflichtete, den Leistungsgegenstand (Geld oder eine *alia certa res*) in angemessener Zeit an den vereinbarten Ort zu schaffen, jedenfalls dann, wenn sich der geschuldete Gegenstand nicht schon vor Ort befindet. Der Aufwand einer Reise von Rom nach Ephesus war alles andere als gering, was sich auch in Venuleius' Überlegungen deutlich widerspiegelt. Es handelt sich daher nicht etwa um einen bloßen untergeordneten Nebenaspekt der Leistung.

Dennoch haben die römischen Juristen die Stipulation, Geld oder eine *alia certa res* an einem bestimmten Ort zu leisten, wohl in Wirklichkeit als Versprechen eines *certum* aufgefasst.[47] Das ergibt sich, jedenfalls was das Versprechen von *certa pecunia*[48] betrifft, aus dem Edikt *De eo quod certo loco dari oportet* (Über das, was an einem bestimmten Ort gegeben werden muss – D. 13.4). In diesem Edikt sah der Prätor eine sogenannte Ermessensklage (*actio arbitraria*)[49] vor,

---

[45] Arangio-Ruiz, 1958, 186, hält *quod facturum se promiserit* für „*comunque … fuori posto trattandosi di un'obbligazione in dando*", während er fr. 137.2 auf S. 188 dann doch zu den „*stipulazioni … in faciendo*" rechnet; vgl. auch S. 181: *stipulatio in dando*, bei der aber „*una particolare attività del debitore*" erforderlich wird. Den Ausdruck *quod facturum se promiserit* streicht auch noch Cannata, 1966, 100. Voci, 1990, 39 f., spricht von einer „*stipulatio che sia anche di facere*".

[46] So tatsächlich Honsell, 1987, 235 mit Fn. 34.

[47] Vgl. auch Cannata, 1966, 99, zu fr. 137.2: „*si tratta di una stipulatio in dando e non in faciendo*". Kritisch Talamanca, 1970, 174 Fn. 106.

[48] Vgl. Ulp. D. 13.4.2.1, 6: ‚*Ephesi decem dari*'. Für eine Beschränkung der *actio arbitraria* aus dem Edikt *De eo quod certo loco dari oportet* auf Geldschulden Kaser, 1971, 639; zustimmend noch Gröschler, 2007, 820 Fn. 65. Jedoch sprechen mehrere Quellenstellen dafür, dass das Edikt *De eo quod certo loco dari oportet* auch dann zur Anwendung kam, wenn es sich beim geschuldeten Leistungsgegenstand um eine *alia certa res* handelte: Gai. D. 13.4.3 (*vinum, oleum, frumentum*); Ulp. D. 13.4.2.2: *hominem dari stipulatus*; Paul. D. 13.4.5: *certo loco quid dare*; eod. 7.1: *Si tamen certo loco traditurum se quis stipulatus sit, hac actione utendum erit.* Zur Frage der Berücksichtigung des Ortsinteresses bei einer derartigen, auf eine *alia certa res* gerichteten Verpflichtung siehe sogleich.

[49] Gai. D. 13.4.3; Afr. D. 13.4.8; Ulp. D. 13.4.2 pr., 8; eod. 4.1; Paul. D. 13.4.5, eod. 7 pr., eod. 10; I. 4.6.33c; C. 3.18.1. Zu der sehr umstrittenen Frage, wie man sich die Formel der *actio arbitraria* vorzustellen hat, siehe ausführlich Pulitanò, 2009, 77–107, 131–167, 169–193, 342–347. Am plausibelsten (und einfachsten) erscheint es, dass etwa bei der *condictio certae pecuniae* die auf *sestertium x milia* lautende *condemnatio* durch eine solche auf *quanti ea res est* ersetzt wurde; vgl. Pulitanò, 2009, 166, 344; so auch schon Sacconi, 1977, 138; Medicus, 1962, 263 f.; Beseler, 1928, 326 f. (anders noch ders., 1907, 90–96); Arangio-Ruiz, 1912, 218 f. Dafür, dass es bei der Klage aus dem Edikt um eine eher behutsame Formelabwandlung ging, spricht auch die Bezeichnung als *utilis actio* in Gai. D. 13.4.1 i.f. Für eine wesentlich komplexere Formelfassung dagegen Lenel, 1927, 240–247; Mantovani, 2002, 49. Neben der Umstellung der *condemnatio* auf

damit die geschuldete Leistung auch an einem anderen Ort als dem eigentlich vereinbarten Leistungsort eingeklagt werden konnte. Dadurch wurde verhindert, dass sich der Versprechende seiner Verpflichtung entzog, indem er sich etwa dauerhaft vom Leistungsort fernhielt.[50] Der Richter musste im Rahmen seines Ermessens (*arbitrium*) bestimmen, welchen Wert die geschuldete Leistung am Klageort hatte. Das war erforderlich, weil das Urteil unter Berücksichtigung des Grundsatzes der Geldkondemnation nur auf Zahlung einer Geldsumme am Klageort, nicht dagegen auf Zahlung am Leistungsort gerichtet sein konnte. Wäre die auf Leistung *certo loco* gerichtete Stipulation als Versprechen eines *incertum* zu verstehen gewesen, hätte es nicht der Gewährung einer besonderen *actio arbitraria* bedurft. Das Ortsinteresse des Beklagten bzw. des Klägers hätte ohne weiteres im Rahmen der auf einen unbestimmten Leistungsgegenstand gerichteten Klage aus förmlichem Versprechen (*actio incerti ex stipulatu*) berücksichtigt werden können. Sinn und Zweck der *actio arbitraria* aus dem Edikt *De eo quod certo loco dari oportet* war es gerade, die Beschränktheit der Klagen „strengsten" Rechts[51] – die auf einen bestimmten Geldbetrag bzw. auf eine bestimmte Sache gerichteten Kondiktion (*condictio certae pecuniae* bzw. *certae rei*) – zumindest im Hinblick auf den Leistungsort zu überwinden.

Bei Verpflichtungen, die nicht auf *certa pecunia*, sondern auf eine sonstige *certa res* gerichtet waren, konnte der Richter das Ortsinteresse des Beklagten bzw. des Klägers, insbesondere den Mehr- oder Minderwert des Leistungsgegenstandes am Klageort gegenüber dem Wert am vereinbarten Leistungsort, ohne weiteres im Rahmen der auf „wieviel die Sache wert ist" (*quanti ea res est*) gerichteten Verurteilungsermächtigung (*condemnatio*) berücksichtigen, was insoweit der Grundform der *condictio certae rei* entspricht.[52] Damit der Richter das Ortsinteresse bei seinem *arbitrium* auch tatsächlich berücksichtigen konnte, musste er freilich entsprechend über den vereinbarten Leistungsort informiert werden. Das geschah wohl einfach dadurch, dass dieser Ort in der Klagbehauptung (*inten-*

---

quanti ea res est musste diese möglicherweise noch durch die Klausel „nach deinem Ermessen" (*arbitrio tuo*) ergänzt werden (vgl. Pulitanò, 2009, 165 f., 192 f., 346; Arangio-Ruiz, 1912, 216 f.), jedenfalls dann, wenn es nicht nur um den unterschiedlichen Wert der Leistung am Leistungs- bzw. am Klageort gehen sollte, sondern um ein darüber hinausgehendes subjektives Ortsinteresse. Auf diese Weise konnte der Gläubiger im Einklang mit Ulp. D. 13.4.2.8 auch Ersatz verlangen, wenn er aufgrund des Ausbleibens der Leistung am vereinbarten Ort an einen Dritten eine Vertragsstrafe leisten musste, es zum Verfall von Pfändern kam, die er einem Dritten gestellt hatte, oder wegen einer fälligen Steuerschuld ein ihm gehörender Gegenstand zwangsweise unter Wert veräußert worden ist. Insoweit für unecht hält fr. 2.8. jedoch Medicus, 1962, 22 mit Fn. 20; auch noch Kaser, 1935, 128 (anders aber ders., 1971, 501 Fn. 18: die Stelle habe „vielleicht einen echten Kern").

[50] Gai. D. 13.4.1.

[51] Siehe hierzu Fn. 23.

[52] Die Verurteilungsermächtigung (*condemnatio*) der *condictio certae rei* lautet: *quanti ea res est, tantam pecuniam iudex Numerium Negidium Aulo Agerio condemnato, si non paret absolvito* (dann sollst du, Richter, den Numerius Negidius zugunsten des Aulus Agerius zu so viel Geld verurteilen, wie die Sache wert ist; wenn es sich nicht erweist, sollst du freisprechen); siehe bei Fn. 18.

tio)[53] erwähnt wurde. Die Klagformel der *actio arbitraria* aus dem Edikt *De eo quod certo loco dari oportet* wird man sich daher bei einer stipulationsweise versprochenen *certa res* wie folgt vorstellen müssen[54]:

> Titius iudex esto. Si paret Numerium Negidium Aulo Agerio hominem Stichum Ephesi dare oportere, qua de re agitur, quanti ea res est, tantam pecuniam iudex Numerium Negidium Aulo Agerio (arbitrio tuo)[55] condemnato, si non paret absolvito.
>
> Titius soll Richter sein. Wenn es sich erweist, dass Numerius Negidius dem Aulus Agerius den Sklaven Stichus in Ephesus geben muss, worüber verhandelt wird, dann sollst du, Richter, den Numerius Negidius zugunsten des Aulus Agerius (nach deinem Ermessen) zu so viel Geld verurteilen, wie die Sache wert ist; wenn es sich nicht erweist, sollst du freisprechen.

Das entspricht der Klagformel mit Angabe bzw. Hinzufügung des Ortes (*commemoratio* bzw. *adiectio loci*), die indirekt in Gai. 4.53c[56] angesprochen ist. Da die *actio arbitraria* hier nur mit einer denkbar geringfügigen Formelabwandlung, nämlich der *adiectio loci* (und gegebenenfalls der Aufnahme der Klausel *arbitrio tuo*), verbunden war, darf es nicht verwundern, dass auf die Klage in den Quellen gelegentlich nur im Rahmen eines kurzen Annexes zur Grundklage hingewiesen wurde[57], auch ohne ausdrückliche Klarstellung, dass es insoweit um einen Anwendungsfall des Edikts *De eo quod certo loco dari oportet* geht.

Wurde die *certo loco* versprochene Leistung am vereinbarten Leistungsort eingeklagt, so führte bereits die unveränderte Grundform der *condictio certae pecuniae* bzw. *certae rei* zum zutreffenden Ergebnis, nämlich zur Verurteilung auf den am Leistungsort geschuldeten Geldbetrag bzw. auf den Wert der geschuldeten Sache am Leistungsort. Der Gläubiger konnte daher mit der unveränderten Grundform der Klage vorgehen (*pure petere*).[58]

---

[53] Die Klagbehauptung (*intentio*) der *condictio certae rei* lautet: *Si paret Numerium Negidium Aulo Agerio hominem Stichum* (*tritici Alexandrini optimi modios centum*) *dare oportere, qua de re agitur* (Wenn es sich erweist, dass Numerius Negidius dem Aulus Agerius den Sklaven Stichus (100 Scheffel besten alexandrinischen Weizens) geben muss, worüber verhandelt wird); siehe bei Fn. 18.

[54] Vgl. zur Klagformel der *actio arbitraria* auch Fn. 49.

[55] Zur Frage der Ergänzung der Klagformel durch die Klausel *arbitrio tuo* siehe Fn. 49 am Ende.

[56] Hierzu sogleich.

[57] So jeweils in Iul. D. 12.1.22: *si convenisset, ut certo loco redderetur, quanti eo loco esset*. Gai. D. 13.3.4: … *idemque iuris in loco esse, ut primum aestimatio sumatur eius loci, quo dari debuit*. In beiden Fällen ist anzunehmen, dass es um die Klage *adiecto loco* geht und damit um einen Anwendungsfall des Edikts *De eo quod certo loco dari oportet*. So auch Pulitanò, 2009, 145–147, 340 f; Sturm, 1977, 275. Anders Arangio-Ruiz, 1912, 131–133; Kaser, 1963, 175–177 (= ders. 1976, 293–295); ders., 1971, 639 mit Fn. 45; Amarelli, 1984, 121; Sacconi, 1977,136–138.

[58] Vgl. auch I. 4.6.33c: *si quis tamen Ephesi petat, id est eo loco petat quo ut sibi detur stipulatus est, pura actione recte agit: idque etiam praetor monstrat, scilicet quia utilitas solvendi salva est promissori*. (Doch wenn jemand in Ephesus klagt, das heißt an dem

Gai. 4.53c

Loco, veluti si, quod certo loco dari promissum est, id alio loco sine commemoratione eius loci petatur, veluti si a te stipulatus sim: ‚sestertia x milia Ephesi dare spondes?', deinde vero Romae pure hoc modo intendam: ‚Si paret te sestertia x milia ex stipulatu dare mihi oportere.' Plus enim petere ideo intellegor, quia utilitatem promissori adimo, quam, si Ephesi daret, habiturus esset. Ephesi tamen etiam pure potero petere, id est non adiecto loco.

Hinsichtlich des Ortes, zum Beispiel, wenn etwas, von dem die Leistung an einem bestimmten Ort versprochen ist, an einem anderen Ort ohne Angabe dieses Ortes eingeklagt wird, zum Beispiel, wenn ich mir von dir förmlich versprechen habe lassen: ‚Gelobst du, 10.000 Sesterze in Ephesus zu geben?', ich daraufhin aber in Rom den Klagantrag einfach folgendermaße stelle: ‚Wenn es sich erweist, dass du mir 10.000 Sesterze aus förmlichem Versprechen geben musst.' Denn begreiflicherweise klage ich deshalb zu viel ein, weil ich dem Versprechenden den Vorteil wegnehme, den er gehabt hätte, wenn er in Ephesus geben würde. Doch kann ich in Ephesus auch einfach klagen, das heißt ohne Hinzufügung des Ortes.

Gaius weist darauf hin, dass die Grundform der Klage ohne *adiectio loci*, wenn sie am vereinbarten Leistungsort angestrengt wurde, nicht zu einer Zuvielforderung hinsichtlich des Ortes (*pluris petitio loco*) führte, weil dem Versprechenden der Ortsvorteil nicht genommen wurde.

In fr. 137.2 ist wohl im zweiten Abschnitt mit „*nihilo minus ei recte condicetur* die *actio arbitraria*" aus dem Edikt *De eo quod certo loco dari oportet* angesprochen.[59] Auf den ersten Blick überraschend ist die Wendung im letzten Satz der Stelle: Wenn der Versprechende aufgrund glücklicher Umstände früher als zu erwarten in Ephesus eingetroffen ist, sei dieser verpflichtet, die Leistung sogleich zu erbringen (*confestim obligatus est*). Dahinter steht möglicherweise die spezielle Ausgestaltung der Stipulation, die im konkreten Fall etwa dahingehend lauten konnte, dass der Schuldner die Leistung zu erbringen hatte, „sobald er in Ephesus angekommen sein wird".

Die Überlegungen zu fr. 137.2 haben gezeigt, dass die Festsetzung eines bestimmten Leistungsortes (*certus locus*) offenbar nicht dazu führte, dass die geschuldete Leistung als *incertum* aufgefasst wurde, obwohl der Schuldner, der die Leistung von Geld oder einer *alia certa res* an einem bestimmten Ort verspricht, strenggenommen nicht nur ein *dare*, sondern auch ein *facere* schuldet. Vor diesem Hintergrund ist (*a maiore ad minus*) zu erwarten, dass auch die Festsetzung einer bestimmten Leistungszeit (*certus dies*) keinen Einfluss auf die Einordnung des Leistungsgegenstandes als *certum* oder *incertum* hatte.[60]

Ort, an dem er sich zu geben hat versprechen lassen, klagt er richtig mit der einfachen Klage. Und das gibt auch der Prätor zu erkennen, freilich weil dem Versprechenden der Vorteil in Bezug auf die Leistung erhalten bleibt.)

[59] Pulitanò, 2009, 342.

[60] Anders jedoch Platschek, 2013, 39 f.. Siehe hierzu unten bei Fn. 101.

Im Fall der Unmöglichkeit der Leistung einer beispielsweise aus Stipulation geschuldeten, individualisierten *certa res* kam es aufgrund der *condictio certae rei*, soweit die Voraussetzungen der Fortsetzung der Verbindlichkeit (*perpetuatio obligationis*)[61] erfüllt waren, ohne weiteres zur Verurteilung auf den Sachwert. Die folgende Pomponius-Stelle lässt sich daher problemlos den Schulden, bei denen eine bestimmte Sache zu geben ist („*certam rem dare*"-Schulden),[62] zuordnen.

> D. 45.1.33, Pomp. 24 ad Sab.
>
> Si Stichus certo die dari promissus ante diem moriatur, non tenetur promissor.
>
> Wenn versprochen worden ist, Stichus zu einem bestimmten Termin zu geben, und dieser vor dem Termin verstirbt, haftet der Versprechende nicht.

Im Umkehrschluss spricht die Stelle dafür, dass der Schuldner nach dem vereinbarten Leistungstermin aufgrund des hier wohl ohne Mahnung (*interpellatio*) eintretenden Verzugs[63] auch für den zufälligen Tod des Sklaven haftete[64]. Aufgrund der *perpetuatio obligationis* konnte der Gläubiger den Wert des Sklaven zum Zeitpunkt des Verzugseintritts verlangen[65] und war nicht – wie sonst – beschränkt auf die Geltendmachung des Werts zum Zeitpunkt der Rechtshängigmachung (*litis contestatio*).[66] Da der tote Sklave wertlos war, wäre es andernfalls im Ergebnis zu einem völligen Anspruchsausschluss gekommen.

Im Gegensatz zu den Fällen, in denen es um Wertersatz wegen Nichterbringung der Leistung geht, bereitet die Frage des Ersatzes eines Verzögerungsschadens erhebliche Schwierigkeiten.[67] Mit der *condictio certae rei*, die auf

---

[61] Zur *perpetuatio obligationis* siehe bei Fn. 29–32, 41.

[62] Kaser, 1980, 139.

[63] Zum Bezug von fr. 33 zur Regel „Der Termin mahnt anstelle des Menschen." (*dies interpellat pro homine*) vgl. Harke, 2005, 68. Offengelassen bei Jakobs, 1974, 53; Cannata, 1976, 924; Kaser, 1980, 114.

[64] Zur Zufallshaftung des Schuldners während des Verzugs vgl. auch Pomp. D. 45.1.23, Ulp. eod. 82.1. Hierzu Kaser, 1980, 139 f.

[65] Vgl. Pomp. D. 19.1.3.3 zur Verurteilung des Verkäufers (nach Wahl des Käufers) auf den jeweils höheren Wert der Kaufsache, den diese bei Verzugseintritts oder zum Zeitpunkt der *litis contestatio* hatte. Hierzu Honsell, 1969, 2–5; Kupisch, 1975, 8; Harke, 2005, 34 f., 110; Kaser / Knütel, 2014, 221 (§ 37 Rn. 9); Lohsse, 2007, 1321 mit Fn. 34. Dagegen bezieht Medicus, 1962, 31–34, die Wertbestimmung in fr. 3.3 auf den Zeitpunkt des Kaufabschlusses bzw. der Verurteilung.

[66] Afr. D. 17.1.37: (…) *aliter in stipulatione servatur: nam tunc id tempus spectatur quo agitur, nisi forte aut per promissorem steterit, quo minus sua die solveret, aut per creditorem, quo minus acciperet: etenim neutri eorum frustratio sua prodesse debet.* ((…) Anders wird es bei der Stipulation gehalten. Denn dann wird auf den Zeitpunkt abgestellt, zu dem geklagt wird, wenn es nicht etwa entweder am Versprechenden gelegen hat, dass er nicht am rechten Tag geleistet, oder am Gläubiger, dass er die Leistung nicht angenommen hat. Denn keinem der beiden darf die eigene Säumnis nützen.). Hierzu Harke, 2011, 44 f.

[67] Zur umstrittenen Frage, ob im Fall des Schuldnerverzugs (*mora debitoris*) regelmäßig auch der Verzögerungsschaden geschuldet war oder aber nur in Sonderfällen, siehe (für

„wieviel die Sache wert ist" (*quanti ea res est*) gerichtet ist und damit nur den Wert des Leistungsgegenstands erfasst, konnte ein Ersatz des Verzögerungsschadens nicht erreicht werden. Es stellt sich daher die Frage, ob die römischen Juristen aufgrund der Festsetzung der Leistungszeit dazu kamen, bei einem Versprechen der Leistung einer *certa res* eine *incertum*-Schuld anzunehmen, um auf diese Weise zur Anwendung der auf „was auch immer … geben oder tun muss" (*quidquid … dare facere oportet*) gerichteten *actio incerti ex stipulatu* zu gelangen.

Im Hinblick auf folgende Stelle wird dafür plädiert, dass die „Festsetzung einer bestimmten Leistungszeit das Versprechen zu einem *incertum* machte"[68], so dass es um einen Anwendungsfall einer Klage auf *incertum* gehe.[69]

> D. 45.1.114, Ulp. 17 ad Sab.[70]
>
> Si fundum certo die praestari stipuler et per promissorem steterit, quo minus ea die praestetur, consecuturum me, quanti mea intersit moram fact[i]<am>[71] non esse.
>
> Wenn ich mir habe förmlich versprechen lassen, dass ein Grundstück zu einem bestimmten Termin geleistet werde, und es am Versprechenden liegt, dass es an diesem Termin nicht geleistet wird, werde ich so viel erhalten, wie es meinem Interesse daran entspricht, dass es nicht zum Verzug gekommen wäre.

Der Schuldner hat versprochen, ein Grundstück, also eine bestimmte Sache (*certa res*), zu einem bestimmten Termin (*certo die*) zu leisten. Auf den ersten Blick könnte der Ausdruck „wie es meinem Interesse daran entspricht, dass es nicht zum Verzug gekommen wäre" (*quanti mea intersit moram factam non esse*) dafür sprechen, dass es hier um den Ersatz des Verzögerungsschadens geht[72], also etwa um den aufgrund einer verspäteten Leistung entgangenen Gewinn. Für einen derartigen Ersatz des Verzögerungsschadens wäre die auf „wieviel die Sache wert ist" (*quanti ea res est*) gerichtete *condictio certae rei* in der Tat ungeeignet gewesen. Allerdings ist der Ausdruck „*quanti mea intersit moram factam non esse*" trügerisch und darf nicht unbesehen mit einer Schadensbestimmung nach dem modernrechtlichen Interessenbegriff gleichgesetzt

---

weitgehenden Ersatz des Verzögerungsschadens) Honsell, 1969, 18 f., 168–173; ders., 1987, 247 mit Fn. 27; dagegen einschränkend Medicus, 1962, 28–44, 219–224; Kaser / Knütel, 2014, 221 (§ 37 Rn. 9); Lohsse, 2007, 1320–1322.

[68] Kaser, 1980, 114 f.; Medicus, 1962, 219 f. („*Leistung eines incertum*").

[69] Kaser, 1935, 87 mit Fn. 9, ordnet fr. 114 den „auf ‚*quidquid … oportet*'" lautenden *actiones incertae*" zu; ebenso Honsell, 1987, 247 mit Fn. 27 („Klagen auf *incertum*").

[70] Nach Lenel, 1889, II 1061, stammt fr. 114 aus einem Kommentarstück zum Inhalt des vermachten Nießbrauchs (*ususfructus legatus*). Daher nimmt Platschek, 2013, 39 Fn. 122, an, *fundum praestari* habe hier ursprünglich die „ermöglichte Ausübung eines Nießbrauchs" gemeint.

[71] Codex Secundus.

[72] So tatsächlich Cannata, 1976, 924: („*risarcimento dei danni per la tardatività della prestazione*"); Honsell, 1987, 247 mit Fn. 27; siehe auch schon Bruns, 1861, 63 (= ders., 1882, 251 f.).

werden.[73] Dass dem Gläubiger im hier behandelten Fall ein Verzögerungsschaden entstanden ist, wird in fr. 114 nicht mitgeteilt. Aufgrund der wenigen Angaben, die Ulpian macht (*et per promissorem steterit, quo minus ea die praestetur*), ist durchaus vorstellbar, dass es um einen schlichten Fall der Leistungsverzögerung geht, das heißt: Der Versprechende hatte, obwohl ihm das möglich gewesen wäre, zum vereinbarten Termin nicht geleistet, weshalb der Versprechensempfänger gegen ihn Klage aus dem förmlichen Versprechen erhob. Der Ausdruck „*quanti mea intersit moram factam non esse*" ist dann auf die Bestimmung des Grundstückswerts zu beziehen, in den der Versprechende zu verurteilen war. Nach Ulpian war das Interesse des Versprechensempfängers am Nichteintritt des Verzugs maßgeblich, was dazu führte, dass er vom Versprechenden den Grundstückswert bei Verzugseintritt verlangen konnte[74] und nicht etwa auf den Ersatz des Wertes zum Zeitpunkt der Rechtshängigmachung (*litis contestatio*) beschränkt war.[75] Damit löst sich in fr. 114 das Problem der Klage: Der Grundstückswert, auch bezogen auf den Zeitpunkt des Verzugseintritts, konnte ohne weiteres mit der auf *quanti ea res est* gerichteten *condictio certae rei* verfolgt werden. Damit besteht keine Notwendigkeit, die auf „dass ein Grundstück zu einem bestimmten Termin geleistet werde" (*fundum certo die praestari*) lautende Stipulation in eine *incertum*-Schuld umzudefinieren, wie es dagegen erforderlich gewesen wäre, wenn es in fr. 114 um den Ersatz eines Verzögerungsschadens gegangen wäre.

Das soeben geschilderte Verständnis von „*quanti mea intersit moram factam non esse*", nämlich im Sinne der Bestimmung des für die Berechnung des Grundstückswerts maßgeblichen Zeitpunkts, wird bestätigt durch folgende Afrikan-Stelle, in der es um das Vermächtnis des Nießbrauchs an einem Sklaven geht:

> D. 7.1.36.2, Afr. 5 quaest.
>
> Usus fructus servi Titio legatus est: cum per heredem staret, quo minus praestaretur, servus mortuus est: aliud dici non posse ait, quam in id obligatum esse heredem, quanti legatarii intersit moram factam non esse, ut scilicet ex eo tempore in diem, in quo servus sit mortuus, usus fructus aestimetur. Cui illud quoque consequens esse, ut si ipse Titius moriatur, similiter ex eo tempore, quo mora sit facta, in diem mortis aestimatio usus fructus heredi eius praestaretur.
>
> Titius ist der Nießbrauch an einem Sklaven vermacht. Während es am Erben lag, dass nicht geleistet wurde, ist der Sklave gestorben. Man könne, wie er meint, nichts anderes sagen, als dass der Erbe zu so viel verpflichtet sei, wie es dem Interesse des Vermächtnisnehmers, dass es nicht zum Verzug gekommen wäre, entspricht, so dass also der Nießbrauch von dem Zeitpunkt an bis zum Tag, an dem der Sklave gestorben ist, geschätzt

---

[73] Vgl. Medicus, 1962, 220.

[74] So auch Harke, 2005, 69.

[75] Zum Wahlrecht des Gläubigers hinsichtlich des Berechnungszeitpunkts bei der *mora debitoris* siehe bei Fn. 65 f.

werde. Dementsprechend sei es auch folgerichtig, dass dann, wenn Titius selbst stirbt, seinem Erben in ähnlicher Weise der Schätzwert des Nießbrauchs von dem Zeitpunkt an, in dem es zum Verzug gekommen war, bis zum Todestag geleistet werde.

Mit „wie es dem Interesse des Vermächtnisnehmers, dass es nicht zum Verzug gekommen wäre, entspricht" (*quanti legatarii intersit moram factam non esse*) ist ebenfalls der Wert des Leistungsgegenstandes gemeint, das heißt hier der zeitliche Wert des vermachten Nießbrauchs (*usus fructus aestimetur*), gerechnet vom Zeitpunkt des Verzugseintritts bis zum Tod des Sklaven, und nicht etwa ein Verzögerungsschaden.[76]

Insgesamt ist festzuhalten, dass wohl weder die Festsetzung eines bestimmten Leistungsortes (*certus locus*) noch einer bestimmten Leistungszeit (*certus dies*) einen Einfluss auf die Qualifikation des Leistungsgegenstandes als bestimmt oder unbestimmt (*certum* oder *incertum*) hatte. Insbesondere scheinen die römischen Juristen kein Bedürfnis gesehen zu haben, bei einem auf Leistung einer individualisierten *certa res* gerichteten Versprechen zu einer *incertum*-Schuld zu gelangen, um dem Gläubiger die mit „was auch immer … geben oder tun muss" (*quidquid … dare facere oportet*) weit gefasste *actio incerti ex stipulatu* zu eröffnen und ihm so etwa einen Anspruch auf Ersatz eines Verzögerungsschadens zu verschaffen. Auch hier lautet das Ergebnis, dass die althergebrachten Kategorien des strengen Rechts von den klassischen Juristen nicht durchbrochen wurden.

2.4 Wahlschuld und Versprechen einer Leistung an einen Dritten

Auf eine gewisse Flexibilität der römischen Juristen im Hinblick auf die Einordnung der versprochenen Leistung als bestimmt oder unbestimmt (*certum* oder *incertum*) könnte folgende Ulpianstelle zur Wahlschuld hindeuten.

> D.45.1.75.8, Ulp. 22 ad ed.
>
> Qui illud aut illud stipulatur, veluti ‚decem vel hominem Stichum', utrum certum an incertum deducat in obligationem, non immerito quaeritur: nam et res certae designantur et utra earum potius praestanda sit, in incerto est. sed utcumque is, qui sibi electionem constituit adiectis his verbis ‚utrum ego velim', potest videri certum stipulatus, cum ei liceat vel hominem tantum vel decem tantum intendere sibi dari oportere: qui vero sibi electionem non constituit, incertum stipulatur.
>
> Wenn sich jemand dieses oder jenes hat stipulieren lassen, z.B. ‚Zehn oder den Sklaven Stichus', fragt sich nicht ohne Grund, ob er etwas Bestimmtes oder etwas Unbestimmtes zum Gegenstand der Verbindlichkeit macht. Denn einerseits werden bestimmte Gegenstände bezeichnet, andererseits bleibt ungewiss, welcher davon wohl zu leisten ist. Jedoch kann jedenfalls von dem, der für sich ein Wahlrecht begründet hat durch Hinzufügung der Worte ‚welches von beiden ich will', annehmen, dass er

[76] Vgl. Medicus, 1962, 222 f.

sich etwas Bestimmtes hat stipulieren lassen. Wer für sich dagegen kein Wahlrecht begründet hat, lässt sich etwas Unbestimmtes stipulieren.

Ulpian wirft hier die Frage auf, ob die Alternative Versprechen von „zehn" (*decem*) – gemeint ist ein Geldbetrag von 10.000 Sesterzen – oder des Sklaven Stichus zu einer Verpflichtung gerichtet auf ein *certum* oder ein *incertum* führt. Die Akzentuierung der Frage mit „fragt sich nicht ohne Grund" (*non immerito quaeritur*) könnte auf einen Meinungsstreit unter den römischen Juristen hindeuten[77], was bedeuten würde, dass hier im Hinblick auf die Kategorien von *certum* und *incertum* eine gewisse Offenheit bestanden hätte. Andererseits kann „*non immerito quaeritur*", zusammen mit dem nachfolgenden *nam*-Satz (*nam et res certae designantur …*), auch einen bloßen explikativen Charakter haben: Ulpian weist darauf hin, dass die von ihm aufgeworfene Frage insofern berechtigt sei, als es sich bei den einzelnen Leistungsgegenständen (*decem*, *homo*) jeweils um ein *certum* handle. Im Folgenden kommt Ulpian dann zu einer eindeutigen Lösung: Je nachdem, ob das Wahlrecht dem Versprechensempfänger oder dem Versprechenden zustehe, handle es sich um eine Versprechen eines bestimmten oder aber unbestimmten Leistungsgegenstandes (*stipulatio certi* oder *incerti*), ohne dass insoweit ein Meinungsstreit ersichtlich wäre. Da sich ein Meinungsstreit auch nicht durch andere Quellenstellen mit abweichenden Stellungnahmen belegen lässt, spricht doch mehr dafür, in dem Ausdruck „*non immerito quaeritur*" und dem nachfolgenden *nam*-Satz nur eine einleitende Erläuterung für die sich anschließende differenzierende Lösung Ulpians zu sehen.

Insbesondere besteht kein Gegensatz zwischen der Lösung Ulpians in fr. 75.8 und den Ausführungen von Gaius zur Zuvielforderung hinsichtlich der Rechtslage (*pluris petitio causa*).[78]

Gai. 4.53d

Causa plus petitur, velut si quis in intentione tollat electionem debitoris, quam is habet obligationis iure, velut si quis ita stipulatus sit: ‚sestertia x milia aut hominem Stichum dare spondes?', deinde alterutrum eorum ex his petat; nam quamvis petat, quod minus est, plus tamen petere videtur, quia potest adversarius interdum facilius id praestare, quod non petitur. (…) Itaque sicut ipsa stipulatio concepta est, ita et intentio formulae concipi debet.

Hinsichtlich der Rechtslage wird zu viel eingeklagt, zum Beispiel, wenn jemand in der Klagbehauptung eine Wahlmöglichkeit des Schuldners wegnimmt, die dieser kraft seiner Verpflichtung hat, wenn zum Beispiel jemand folgendermaßen sich förmlich hat versprechen lassen: ‚Gelobst du, 10.000 Sesterze oder den Sklaven Stichus zu geben?', jetzt aber nur eins von diesen beiden einklagt; obwohl er nämlich weniger einklagt, klagt er dennoch, wie man annimmt, mehr ein, weil der Gegner unter Umständen das leichter leisten könnte, was nicht eingeklagt ist. (…)

[77] Vgl. Kaser, 1971, 494 Fn. 5: „Streitfrage".
[78] Apathy, 1971, 392 f.; Sacconi, 1977, 147.

Daher muss der Klagantrag in der Klageformel ebenso formuliert werden, wie das förmliche Versprechen selbst formuliert worden ist.

Gaius stellt fest, dass dem Gläubiger einer Wahlschuld mit Schuldnerwahl eine *pluris petitio* hinsichtlich der Rechtslage (*causa*) zur Last fällt, wenn er in der Klagbehauptung (*intentio*) das Wahlrecht des Schuldners übergeht. Als Beispiel nennt Gaius denselben Fall, den auch Ulpian in fr. 75.8 behandelt: Versprochen ist (mit Wahlrecht des Schuldners) ein Betrag von zehntausend Sesterzen oder der Sklave Stichus.[79] Wenn der Gläubiger hier nur einen der beiden Leistungsgegenstände einklagt, nimmt er dem Schuldner den in der Wahlmöglichkeit liegenden Vorteil.

Zum Teil wird vertreten, zwischen fr. 75.8 und Gai. 4.53d bestehe eine „Antinomie"[80], denn das von Gaius behandelte Problem einer *pluris petitio causa* sei ausgeschlossen, wenn man mit Ulpian aufgrund des Wahlrechts des Schuldners zu einem *incertum* und damit zu der auf einen unbestimmten Leistungsgegenstand gerichteten Klage aus förmlichem Versprechen (*actio incerti ex stipulatu*) gelange. Natürlich ist richtig, dass bei der *actio incerti ex stipulatu* aufgrund der weiten Klagbehauptung mit „was auch immer … geben oder tun muss" (*quidquid … dare facere oportet*) eine *pluris petitio* von vornherein nicht in Betracht kommt.[81] Aus der Stelle lässt sich aber nicht ableiten, dass Gaius hier das alternative Versprechen als Versprechen eines bestimmten Leistungsgegenstandes (*stipulatio certi*) eingeordnet und hierfür die Anwendbarkeit einer bestimmten Klagbehauptung (*intentio certa*) befürwortet hätte.[82] Gaius beschränkt sich im Gegenteil darauf, im Hinblick auf die damit verbundene *pluris petitio causa* davor zu warnen, nur einen der beiden (mit Schuldnerwahl) versprochenen Gegenstände einzuklagen, mit anderen Worten: Gaius warnt davor, die versprochenen 10.000 Sesterze isoliert mit der auf einen bestimmten Geldbetrag gerichteten Kondiktion (*condictio certae pecuniae*) oder aber den Sklaven Stichus isoliert mit der auf eine bestimmte Sache gerichteten Kondiktion (*condictio certae rei*) einzuklagen.

Gaius' Hinweis am Schluss von § 53d, dass die Klagbehauptung ebenso formuliert werden müsse, wie das förmliche Versprechen formuliert sei (*sicut ipsa stipulatio concepta est, ita et intentio formulae concipi debet*), ist so zu verstehen, dass die Klagbehauptung dem konkreten Versprechen Rechnung zu tragen hat.[83] Es besteht also keine Notwendigkeit, von einer *intentio* des Typs ‚*Si paret illud aut illud dare oportere*' (‚Wenn es sich erweist, dass dieses oder jenes

---

[79] Vgl. auch Paul. D. 2.14.27.6: *Sed si stipulatus decem aut Stichum de decem pactus sim et petam Stichum aut decem: exceptionem pacti in totum obstaturam.*

[80] So Sturm, 1977, 276. Einen Gegensatz zwischen Gaius und Ulpian nimmt auch Provera, 1955, 204–206, an.

[81] Vgl. Gai. 4.54: *Illud satis apparet in incertis formulis plus peti non posse*, … (Jenes ist hinreichend klar, dass man in unbestimmten Klagformeln nicht zu viel fordern kann, …).

[82] Sacconi, 1977, 147.

[83] Apathy, 1971, 393. Auch daraus, dass der Gläubiger in Paul. D. 2.14.27.6 (Fn. 79) den Sklaven Stichus oder *decem* einklagt (*petam Stichum aut decem*), lässt sich, wie Apathy zu Recht feststellt, nur schließen, dass „in der Klagformel der *actio incerti* der Inhalt der eingeklagten Stipulation … zumindest teilweise angeführt wurde" . Vgl. auch Ulp. D. 12.6.26.13: … *petique ab eo posse reliqua quinque aut Stichum.*

gegeben werden muss') auszugehen.[84] Aufgrund der zu großen zeitlichen Distanz zum Formularverfahren können auch nicht die Institutionen Justinians[85] zusammen mit der Theophilus-Paraphrase[86] als Belege für eine derartige Formelfassung angesehen werden. Gaius wird, nicht anders als Ulpian, bei einer Wahlschuld mit Wahlmöglichkeit des Schuldners die *actio incerti ex stipulatu* mit der auf *quidquid … dare facere oportet* gerichteten Klagbehauptung befürwortet haben.[87] Die Klagformel könnte etwa wie folgt gelautet haben:

> Titius iudex esto. Quod Aulus Agerius de Numerio Negidio sestertia x milia aut hominem Stichum stipulatus est, cuius rei dies fuit, quidquid ob eam rem Numerium Negidium Aulo Agerio dare facere oportet, eius iudex Numerium Negidium Aulo Agerio condemnato, si non paret absolvito.[88]

> Titius soll Richter sein. Da sich Aulus Agerius von Numerius Negidius 10.000 Sesterze oder den Sklaven Stichus hat versprechen lassen, was jetzt fällig geworden ist, was auch immer deswegen Numerius Negidius dem Aulus Agerius geben oder tun muss, zu dem sollst du, Richter, den Numerius Negidius zugunsten des Aulus Agerius verurteilen; wenn es sich nicht erweist, sollst du freisprechen.

Ein weiterer Aspekt, der hier noch betrachtet werden soll, ist das auf Leistung an einen Dritten gerichtete Versprechen in Form eines unechten Vertrags zugunsten Dritter.[89] In folgender Stelle wird ein alternatives Versprechen behandelt, bei dem sich der Gläubiger Zahlung eines Betrags an sich oder an einen Dritten hat versprechen lassen und das Wahlrecht dem Gläubiger zustehen sollte.

> D. 45.1.118.2, Pap. 27 quaest.

> ‚Decem mihi aut Titio, utrum ego velim, dare spondes?' ex eo, quod mihi dandum est, certi stipulatio est, ex eo, quod illi solvendum, incerti: finge mea interesse Titio potius quam mihi solvi, quoniam poenam promiseram, si Titio solutum non fuisset.

---

[84] So aber Sacconi, 1977, 147 f.; Grosso, 1966, 186 f.; Provera, 1955, 203.

[85] I. 4.6.33d: *qua de causa talis in ea re prodita est actio, ut quis intendat, hominem Stichum aut aureos decem sibi dari oportere, id est ut eodem modo peteret, quo stipulatus est.* (Deswegen ist in dieser Sache eine dahingehende Klage eingeführt worden, dass der jeweilige Kläger den Klangantrag stellt, dass ihm der Sklave Stichus oder zehn Goldmünzen gegeben werden müssen, das heißt, dass er in derselben Weise klagt, wie er sich hat versprechen lassen.)

[86] Theoph. 4.6.33d: ‚εἰ φαίνεται τὸν ἀντίδικον χρῆναι δοῦναι Στῖχον ἢ δέκα νομίσματα'. (‚Wenn es sich erweist, dass der Beklagte den Stichus oder 10.000 Geldstücke geben muss'.)

[87] Apathy, 1971, 393. Offengelassen bei Ziliotto, 2004, 22–24 Fn. 14.

[88] Zur Klagformel der *actio incerti ex stipulatu* vgl. Gai. 4.136; hierzu Lenel, 1927, 240; Mantovani, 2002, 25.

[89] Zur Wirksamkeit eines solchen Vertrags, wenn ein entsprechendes Eigeninteresse des Versprechensempfängers an der Leistung an den Dritten bestand, siehe Ankum, 1970, 21–29; zustimmend Kaser, 1986, 197 f.; Bayer, 1995, 12–16.

> ‚Versprichst du, mir oder Titius, welchen von beiden ich will, zehn zu geben?' Im Hinblick darauf, was mir zu geben ist, handelt es sich um eine Stipulation über etwas Bestimmtes, im Hinblick darauf, was jenem zu leisten ist, über etwas Unbestimmtes. Nimm etwa an, ich habe ein Interesse daran, dass eher Titius als mir geleistet werde, weil ich eine Vertragsstrafe für den Fall versprochen habe, dass Titius nicht geleistet würde.

Das Versprechen, „zehn" (*decem*) an den Versprechensempfänger (*ego*) zu zahlen, wird von Papinian als Versprechen eines bestimmten Leistungsgegenstandes (*stipulatio certi*) eingeordnet, dagegen das auf Zahlung an Titius gerichtete als Versprechen eines unbestimmten Leistungsgegenstandes (*stipulatio incerti*).

Das förmliche Versprechen, einem Dritten einen bestimmten Leistungsgegenstand (*certa pecunia* oder eine *alia certa res*) zu leisten, also ein Versprechen zugunsten eines Dritten (*stipulatio alteri*), gerichtet auf ein Geben (*dare*), konnte vom Versprechensempfänger nicht mit der auf einen bestimmten Geldbetrag gerichteten Kondiktion (*condictio certae pecuniae*) bzw. der auf eine bestimmte Sache gerichteten Kondiktion (*condictio certae rei*) mit Erfolg eingeklagt werden, weil diese Klagen eine Verpflichtung zum Geben (*dare oportere*) des Beklagten gerade gegenüber dem Kläger voraussetzten[90]: ‚*Si paret Numerium Negidium Aulo Agerio HS X milia dare oportere*' (‚Wenn es sich erweist, dass Numerius Negidius dem Aulus Agerius 10.000 Sesterze geben muss')[91] bzw. ‚*Si paret Numerium Negidium Aulo Agerio hominem Stichum dare oportere*' (‚Wenn es sich erweist, dass Numerius Negidius dem Aulus Agerius den Sklaven Stichus')[92]. Versprochen war aber bei einer *stipulatio alteri* nicht die Leistung an den Kläger, sondern an einen Dritten. Daher wird eine solche Stipulation in den Quellen als *inutilis* („unwirksam") bezeichnet.[93]

Anders verhält es sich allerdings, wenn der Versprechensempfänger ein Eigeninteresse an der Leistung an den Dritten hatte. Freilich konnte der Versprechensempfänger auch ein solches Eigeninteresse an einer Leistung an einen Dritten nicht mit der *condictio certae pecuniae* bzw. *certae rei* verfolgen, weil diese Klagen auf die Verurteilung in den versprochenen Geldbetrag oder auf „wieviel die Sache wert ist" (*quanti ea res est*), das heißt auf den Wert des Leistungsgegenstandes, gerichtet waren, so dass der Richter ein Interesse des Versprechensempfängers an der Leistung an einen Dritten nicht berücksichtigen konnte.[94] Die Berücksichtigung eines solchen Eigeninteresses ist nur im Rahmen der auf „was auch immer … geben oder tun muss" (*quidquid … dare facere oportet*) gerichteten *actio incerti ex stipulatu* denkbar. Genau das ist der Grund, warum Papinian in fr. 118.2 das förmliche Versprechen der Zahlung von „zehn" an Titius als Versprechen eines unbestimmten Leistungsgegenstandes (*incertum*) einordnet.[95] Aus der Sicht des Versprechensempfängers handelt es sich bei der Leis-

---

[90] Vgl. Ankum, 1970, 26; Kaser, 1986, 197 f.; Hallebeek, 2008, 10 f.
[91] Siehe bei Fn. 11.
[92] Siehe bei Fn. 18.
[93] Gai. 3.103; Paul. D. 45.1.126.2.
[94] Ankum, 1970, 26 f.
[95] Vgl. Ankum, 1970, 27; Kaser, 1986, 199.

tung eines *certum* an einen Dritten nicht um ein Geben (*dare*), sondern um eine sonstige Art der Leistung, also um ein Tun (*facere*)[96], und somit – was die Sicht des Versprechensempfängers betrifft – um einen unbestimmten Leistungsgegenstand. Das erforderliche Eigeninteresse des Versprechensempfängers an der Leistung an den Dritten konnte, wie der Schlusssatz der Stelle zeigt[97], darin liegen, dass er für den Fall, dass an den Dritten nicht gezahlt werde, die Leistung einer Vertragsstrafe versprochen hat.

Auch hier wird wieder deutlich, wie stark die klassischen römischen Juristen, in diesem Fall der Spätklassiker Papinian, dem System des strengen Rechts verhaftet waren. Die Einordnung des förmlichen Versprechens der Leistung an einen Dritten (*stipulatio alteri*) als Versprechen, das aus der Sicht des Versprechensempfängers auf einen unbestimmten Leistungsgegenstand (*incertum*) gerichtet war, bedeutet zwar insofern einen Fortschritt, als ursprünglich eine Klagmöglichkeit aus einem solchen Versprechen wohl gänzlich verneint worden ist.[98] Sie entspricht aber voll und ganz den Kategorien von *certum* und *incertum*[99], weshalb man Papinian nicht einen Systembruch zur Last legen kann[100]. Im Gegenteil belegt die Einordnung des Versprechens der Leistung von „zehn" an den Versprechensempfänger (*ego*) als Versprechen eines bestimmten Leistungsgegenstandes (*stipulatio certi*), dass es Papinian nicht darum geht, ein *certum* systemwidrig als *incertum* zu qualifizieren.

Freilich erscheint es aus moderner Sicht merkwürdig, dass dem Versprechensempfänger im Hinblick auf die Leistung, die an ihn selbst zu erbringen war, nur

---

[96] Vgl. auch Ulp. D. 45.1.38.21: *aut si quis, cum promisisset Titio fundum Maevium daturum aut, si is non dedisset, poenam se daturum, stipulatus a Maevio fuerit fundum Titio datu iri* (oder wenn jemand, nachdem er Titius versprochen hat, dass Mävius ihm sein Grundstück geben werde oder, wenn dieser es nicht geben würde, er Strafe leisten werde, sich von Mävius hat versprechen lassen, dass er das Grundstück dem Titius geben werde); eod. 38.23: *Unde et si procuratori meo dari stipulatus sum, stipulatio vires habebit: et si creditori meo, quia interest mea, ne vel poena committatur vel praedia distrahantur, quae pignori data erant* (Daher wird auch dann, wenn ich mir versprechen habe lassen, dass meinem Geschäftsführer gegeben werde, das förmliche Versprechen wirksam sein; ebenso, wenn ich mir versprechen haben lassen, dass meinem Gläubiger gegeben werden, weil ich ein Interesse daran habe, dass entweder nicht die Strafe verwirkt werde oder nicht die Grundstücke verkauft werden, die als Pfand gegeben waren.) [vgl. I. 3.19.20]; C. 8.38.3 pr.: … *alteri, cuius iuri subiectus non est, aliquid dari vel restitui, nisi sua intersit, nemo stipulari potest* (… kann sich niemand versprechen lassen, dass einem anderen, dessen Gewalt er nicht unterworfen ist, etwas gegeben oder herausgegeben werde, es sei denn, er hat ein eigenes Interesse daran). Hierzu Kaser, 1986, 200 f., 212 f.

[97] Gerke, 1957, 88 f., hält den Schlusssatz noch für unecht („erläuternde Glosse") und geht davon aus, dass auch der restliche Wortlaut der Stelle nicht von Papinian stamme. Dagegen ordnet Vážný, 1936, 264 f., immerhin die Unterscheidung zwischen *stipulatio certi* und *incerti* Papinian zu und hält nur den Schlusssatz für kompilatorisch.

[98] Vgl. Gai. 3.103; Ulp. D. 45.1.38.17. Zu fr. 38.17 siehe Kaser, 1986, 213 f. („verunglückte Reminiszenz an einen schon in der späten Klassik überwundenen Rechtszustand").

[99] Vgl. Harke, 2005, 45 Fn. 99, der zu Recht feststellt, in fr. 118.2 gehe es um „die schlichte Nichterfüllung einer Stipulation auf *incertum*".

[100] Ankum, 1970, 27, spricht von einer „infraction au système des actions".

die enge auf einen bestimmten Geldbetrag gerichtete Kondiktion (*condictio certae pecuniae*) bzw. die enge auf eine bestimmte Sache gerichtete Kondiktion (*condictio certae rei*) zustand, die nur zur einer Verurteilung des Versprechenden auf den zugesagten Geldbetrag oder den Wert des Leistungsgegenstandes führte, dagegen nicht geeignet war, ein darüber hinausgehendes Interesse (wie die vom Versprechensempfänger an einen Dritten zu leistende Vertragsstrafe oder den Verfall von Pfändern, die der Versprechensempfänger einem Dritten gestellt hatte) zu erfassen. Aus fr. 118.2 ergibt sich aber kein Indiz dafür, dass das Versprechen eines bestimmten Geldbetrags (*stipulatio certae pecuniae*), sofern es mit einem Leistungstermin versehen war, „nicht nur zur *actio certae creditae pecuniae*" führte, sondern es dem Gläubiger auch erlaubte, „sein Interesse mit der *actio* (*incerti*) *ex stipulatu* einzuklagen".[101] Im Gegenteil wird man die Stelle als Argument gerade gegen eine derartige Systemdurchbrechung werten müssen. Es bleibt daher dabei, dass der Gläubiger sich beim Versprechen eines *certum* nur durch die Aufnahme einer entsprechenden Strafklausel[102] vor Schäden schützen konnte, die über den versprochenen Geldbetrag bzw. den Wert des Leistungsgegenstandes hinausgingen.[103]

3. Zusammenfassung

Die Untersuchung hat gezeigt, dass auch die klassischen römischen Juristen, und zwar einschließlich der Spätklassiker, noch stark im überkommenen System der Klagen strengen Rechts verhaftet waren. Belege dafür, dass *certum*-Schulden, also Schulden, die zu einer auf einen bestimmten Leistungsgegenstand (*certum*) gerichteten Klage führten, in einen unbestimmten Leistungsgegenstand (*incertum*) umdefiniert oder uminterpretiert wurden, um dem Gläubiger die Vorteile der auf „was auch immer … geben oder tun muss" (*quidquid … dare facere oportet*) gerichteten weiten Formel der *actio incerti ex stipulatu*[104] zu verschaffen, lassen sich – soweit ersichtlich – nicht finden. Selbst naheliegende Möglichkeiten, etwa bei der Festlegung des Leistungsorts von einer Pflicht des Schuldners zu einem Tun (*facere*) auszugehen, wurden nicht genutzt. Die Gründe hierfür sind aus heutiger Sicht nicht mehr ohne weiteres fassbar, zumal der Beschränktheit der Klagen strengen Rechts eine größtmögliche Freiheit im Bereich der Klagen nach Treu und Glauben (*bonae fidei iudicia*)[105] gegenübersteht.

---

[101] So aber Platschek, 2013, 39 f., aufgrund folgender (spekulativen) Überlegung im Anschluss an fr. 118.2: „Kann etwas anderes gelten, wenn sich der Gläubiger die Leistung zu einem bestimmten Tag hätte versprechen lassen und wegen der Nichtleistung des Schuldners und dadurch bedingter mangelnder Liquidität des Gläubigers eine Vertragsstrafe zulasten des Gläubigers bei einem Dritten verfallen ist? Kann der Fall ‚ich brauche das Geld (sofort) bei Titius' anders gelöst werden als ‚ich brauche das Geld an den nächsten Kalenden'? Wir wollen es bezweifeln.".

[102] Siehe z.B. Paul. D. 45.1.85.6; hierzu Knütel, 1976, 84.

[103] Vgl. Rüfner, 2000, 45; Costa, 2011, 169.

[104] Siehe bei Fn. 20.

[105] Bei den auf Treu und Glauben abstellenden *bonae fidei iudicia*, zu denen beispielsweise die Kaufklage gehört, kommt dem Richter ein besonders weiter Ermessensspielraum zu, weil er das gesamte Schuldverhältnis auf der Grundlage von Treu und Glauben zu bewerten hat.

Fraglich bleibt, ob wir es hier mit einem Konservativismus der römischen Juristen zu tun haben. Eher leuchtet der bereits erwähnte Erklärungsansatz Cannatas ein, der auf die Sonderrolle der Stipulation als abstraktes, einseitig verpflichtendes Geschäft hinweist.[106] Immerhin galt für die Stipulation auch in anderer Hinsicht Besonderes: Die Anwendung der Regel „Über Unmögliches besteht keine Verbindlichkeit." (*inpossibilium nulla est obligatio*) auf die Stipulation hatte wohl, ebenso wie beim Verpflichtungsvermächtnis (*legatum per damnationem*), mit dem sakralrechtlichen Ursprung dieser Geschäfte oder zumindest deren streng formalem Charakter zu tun.[107] Eine sichere Erklärung wird sich aber auf der heute zur Verfügung stehenden Quellenbasis weder hierfür noch für unser Problem der *certum*-Schulden finden lassen.

Abkürzungs- und Literaturverzeichnis

Afr. = Afrikan
C. = Codex Iustinianus
D. = Digesta
fr. = fragmentum
Gai. = Gai institutiones
I. = Institutiones Iustiniani
Iul. = Julian
Marcell. = Marcellus
Pap. = Papinian
Paul. = Paulus
Plaut. = Plautius
Pomp. = Pomponius
Prob. Eins. = Marcus Valerius Probus, De litteris singularibus fragmenta (Codex Einsidlensis 326).
PS. = Pauli Sententiae
S. = Codex Secundus
Sab. = Sabinus
Scaev. = Scaevola
Theoph. = Theophili antecessoris paraphrasis institutionum
Ven. = Venuleius
Ulp. = Ulpian

Albanese, Bernardo, 1961. „La sussidiarietà dell'a. de dolo". *Annali del Seminario Giuridico. Università degli Studi di Palermo* 28, 173–322.

Alexy, Robert, 1991. *Theorie der juristischen Argumentation. Die Theorie des rationalen Diskurses als Theorie der juristischen Begründung*. Frankfurt a. M.: Suhrkamp. (2. Auflage).

Amarelli, Francesco, 1984. *Locus Solutionis. Contributo alla teoria del luogo dell'adempimento in diritto romano*. Mailand: Giuffrè.

Ankum, Hans, 1970. „Une nouvelle hypothèse sur l'origine de la règle ‚alteri dari stipulari nemo potest'". In: Yvette Lobin (Hg.) *Études offertes à Jean*

[106] Siehe bei Fn. 34.

[107] Vgl. Schermaier, 2007, 954 f.

Macqueron. Aix-en-Provence: Université d'Aix-Marseille. Faculté de Droit et des Sciences Economiques, 21–29.

Apathy, Peter, 1971. „Zur Abgrenzung von Novation und Bürgschaft". *Revue internationale des droits de l'antiquité, 3e Série* 18, 381–447.

Arangio-Ruiz, Vincenzo, 1912. „Studii formulari. I. De eo quod certo loco dari oportet". *Bulletino dell' Istituto di diritto* romano 25, 141–219.

— 1958. *Responsabilità contrattuale in diritto romano*. Neapel: Jovene. (Nachdruck der 2. Auflage).

Bayer, Walter, 1995. *Der Vertrag zugunsten Dritter. Neuere Dogmengeschichte – Anwendungsbereich – dogmatische Strukturen*. Tübingen: Mohr Siebeck.

Behrends, Okko, 1974. *Der Zwölftafelprozeß. Zur Geschichte des römischen Obligationenrechts*. Göttingen: Schwartz.

Beseler, Gerhard, 1907. *Das Edictum de eo quod certo loco. Eine rechtshistorische Untersuchung*. Leipzig: Deichert.

— 1928. „Romanistische Studien". *Tijdschrift voor Rechtsgeschiedenis* 8, 279–335.

Broggini, Gerardo, 1957. *Iudex arbiterve. Prolegomena zum officium des römischen Privatrichters*. Graz: Böhlau.

Bruns, Karl Georg, 1861. „Das constitutum debiti". *Zeitschrift für Rechtsgeschichte* 1, 28–130.

= ders., 1882. In: Ivo Bruns (Hg.), *Kleinere Schriften* I. Weimar: Böhlau, 221–312. (2 Bände).

Cannata, Carlo Augusto, 1966. „Appunti sulla impossibilità sopravvenuta e la ‚culpa debitoris' nelle obbligazioni da ‚stipulatio in dando'". *Studia et documenta historiae et iuris* 32, 63–113.

— 1976. „Mora (storia)". In: Francesco Calasso (Hg.) *Enciclopedia del Diritto Band* XXVI. Milano: Giuffrè, 921–934.

Costa, Paolo, 2011. „Pecunia constituta: ipotesi interpretative". *Studia et documenta historiae et iuris* 77, 129–256.

Dulckeit, Gerhard, 1951. „Zur Lehre vom Rechtsgeschäft im klassischen römischen Recht". In: Hans Niedermeyer / Werner Flume (Hg.) *Festschrift Fritz Schulz* Band I. Weimar: Böhlau, 148–190.

Flume, Werner, 1979. *Allgemeiner Teil des Bürgerlichen Rechts*. Zweiter Band. *Das Rechtsgeschäft*. Berlin: Springer. (3. Auflage).

Gerke, Theodor Joseph, 1957. „Geschichtliche Entwicklung der Bemessung der Ansprüche aus der lex Aquilia (mit einem vergleichenden Ausblick auf die geschichtliche Entwicklung der Ansprüche aus furtum)". *Studia et documenta historiae et iuris* 23, 61–118.

Gröschler, Peter, 2007. „§§ 269–272 BGB. Leistungsort und Leistungszeit". In: Mathias Schmoeckel / Joachim Rückert / Reinhard Zimmermann (Hg.) *Historisch-kritischer Kommentar zum BGB*. Band II. *Schuldrecht: Allgemeiner Teil. §§ 241–432. 1. Teilband: vor § 241–§ 304*. Tübingen: Mohr Siebeck, 808–830.

— 2016. „Überlegungen zu den Klagen strengen Rechts – certum und incertum als Leistungsgegenstand". In: Isabella Piro (Hg.) *Scritti per Alessandro Corbino*. Tricase: Libellula Edizioni, 497–522. (3 Bände).

Grosso, Giuseppe, 1966. *Obligazioni. Contenuto e requisiti della prestazione obligazioni alternative e generiche. Turin: Giappichelli*. (3. Auflage).

Habermas, Jürgen, 1992. *Faktizität und Geltung: Beiträge zur Diskurstheorie des Rechts und des demokratischen Rechtsstaats*. Frankfurt a. M.: Suhrkamp. http://solomon.soth.alexanderstreet.com/cgi-bin/asp/philo/soth/getdoc.pl?S10023105-D000010

Hallebeek, Jan, 2008. In: Jan Hallebeck / Harry Dondorp (Hg.) *Contracts for a third-party beneficiary. A Historical and Comparative Account*. Leiden: Martinus Nijhoff Publishers.

Harke, Jan Dirk, 2005. *Mora debitoris und mora creditoris im klassischen römischen Recht*. Berlin: Duncker und Humblot.

— 2011. „Das Vertragsrecht in Afrikans Quästionen". In: Jan Dirk Harke. (Hg.) *Africani quaestiones. Studien zur Geschichte und Dogmatik des Privatrechts*. Berlin: Springer, 37–52.

Honsell, Heinrich, 1969. *Quod interest im bonae-fidei-iudicium. Studien zum römischen Schadensersatzrecht*. München: C.H. Beck.

— 1987. In: Heinrich Honsell. / Theo Mayer-Maly / Walter Selb (Hg.) *Römisches Recht*. Berlin: Springer. (4. Auflage).

Jakobs, Horst Heinrich, 1974. „Culpa und interpellatio bei der mora debitoris nach klassischem Recht". *Tijdschrift voor Rechtsgeschiedenis* 42, 23–56.

Jhering, Rudolph von, 1898. *Geist des römischen Rechts auf den verschiedenen Stufen seiner Entwicklung. Zweiter Theil. Zweite Abtheilung*. Leipzig: Breitkopf und Härtel. (5. Auflage).

Kaser, Max, 1933. „Mora". In: Wilhelm Kroll (Hg.) *Paulys Realencyclopädie der classischen Altertumswissenschaft* Band XVI.1. Stuttgart: Metzler, 252-277.

— 1935. *Quanti ea res est. Studien zur Methode der Litisästimation im klassischen römischen Recht*. München: C.H. Beck.

— 1949. *Das altrömische ius. Studien zur Rechtsvorstellung und Rechtsgeschichte der Römer*. Göttingen: Vandenhoeck & Ruprecht.

— 1963. „‚Mutum' und ‚stipulatio'". In: Georgii S. Maridakis (Hg.) *Eranion in honorem Georgii S. Maridakis*. Vol. I. Athen: Facultas Iuris Universitatis Athenarum, 155–182.
= ders., 1976. *Ausgewählte Schriften* II, Neapel: Jovene, 271–300.

— 1971. *Das römische Privatrecht. Erster Abschnitt. Das altrömische, das vorklassische und klassische Recht*. München: C.H. Beck. (2. Auflage).

— 1973: „Die Stipulationsklausel ‚quanti ea res erit'". *Zeitschrift der Savigny-Stiftung für Rechtsgeschichte – Romanistische Abteilung* 90, 184–219.

— 1980. „Perpetuari obligationem". *Studia et documenta historiae et iuris* 46, 87–146.

— 1986. „Zur Interessebestimmung bei sog. unechten Verträgen zugunsten Dritter". In: Max Kaser, *Römische Rechtsquellen und angewandte Juristenmethode*. Köln: Böhlau, 197–214.

Kaser, Max / Karl Hackl, 1996. *Das römische Zivilprozeßrecht*. München: C.H. Beck. (2. Auflage).

Kaser, Max / Rolf Knütel, 2014. *Römisches Privatrecht. Ein Studienbuch*. München: C.H. Beck. (20. Auflage).

Keil, Heinrich (Hg.), 1864. *Grammatici latini*. Band IV. *Probi Donati Servii qui feruntur de Arte Grammatica Libri ex recensione Henrici Keilii*. Leipzig: Teubner.

Knütel, Rolf, 1976. *Stipulatio poenae. Studien zur römischen Vertragsstrafe.* Köln: Böhlau.

Kupisch, Berthold, 1975. „Id quod interest bei Nichterfüllung und Verzug des Verkäufers". *Tijdschrift voor Rechtsgeschiedenis* 43, 1–22.

Lenel, Otto (Hg.), 1889. *Palingenesia iuris civilis.* Leipzig: Tauchnitz. (2 Bände).

— 1927. *Das Edictum perpetuum. Ein Versuch zu seiner Wiederherstellung.* Leipzig: Tauchnitz. (3. Auflage).

Lohsse, Sebastian, 2007. „§§ 286–292 BGB. Verzug des Schuldners". In: Mathias Schmoeckel / Joachim Rückert / Reinhard Zimmermann (Hg.), *Historisch-kritischer Kommentar zum BGB.* Band II. *Schuldrecht: Allgemeiner Teil. §§ 241–432. 1. Teilband: vor § 241–§ 304.* Tübingen: Mohr Siebeck, 1312–1387.

MacCormack, Geoffrey, 1973. „Factum debitoris and culpa debitoris". *Tijdschrift voor Rechtsgeschiedenis* 41, 59–74.

Magdelain, André, 1980. „Aspectes arbitraux de la justice civile archaïque à Rome". *Revue internationale des droits de l'antiquité, 3e Série* 27, 205–281. = In: ders. (Hg.), 1990. *Ius imperium auctoritas, Études de droit romain* (Collection de l'École française de Rome 133). Rome: École française de Rome, 591–652.

Mantovani, Dario, 2002. *Le formule del processo privato romano. Per la didattica delle Istituzioni di dritto romano.* Padova: CEDAM. (2. Auflage).

Medicus, Dieter, 1962. *Id quod interest. Studien zum römischen Recht des Schadensersatzes.* Köln: Böhlau.

Platschek, Johannes, 2013. *Das Edikt De pecunia constituta. Die römische Erfüllungszusage und ihre Einbettung in den hellenistischen Kreditverkehr.* München: C.H. Beck.

Provera, Giuseppe, 1955. „Corrispondenze tra stipulatio ed intentio (Riflessioni su Gaio, 4, 53d)". *Annali della Facoltà Giuridica. Università degli Studi di Camerino* XXI.2, 197–216. (=http://www.ledonline.it/rivistadirittoromano/allegati/proveracorrispondenze.pdf).

Pugliese, Giovanni, 1962. *Il processo civile romano I, Le Legis Actiones* (Corso di Diritto Romano. Anno Accademico 1961–62). Rom: Edizioni Ricerche.

— 1963. *Il processo civile romano* II: *Il processo formulare. Tomo* I. Milano: A. Giuffrè.

Pulitanò, Francesca, 2009. *De eo quod certo loco. Studi dul luogo convenzionale dell'adempimento nel diritto romano.* Mailand: Giuffrè.

Rüfner, Thomas, 2000. *Vertretbare Sachen? Die Geschichte der res, quae pondere numero mensura constant.* Berlin: Duncker und Humblot.

Sacconi, Giuseppina, 1977. *La ‚pluris petition' nel processo formulare. Contributo allo studio dell'oggetto del processo.* Mailand: Giuffrè.

Sargenti, Manlio, 1954. „Problemi della responsabilità contrattuale". *Studia et documenta historiae et iuris* 20, 125–258.

Savigny, Friedrich Carl von, 1850. „Ueber den Literalcontract der Römer". In: Friedrich Carl von Savigny, *Vermischte Schriften* I. Berlin: Veit und Comp., 205–261.

Schermaier, Martin Josef, 2007. „§ 275 BGB. Ausschluss der Leistungspflicht". In: Mathias Schmoeckel / Joachim Rückert / Reinhard Zimmermann (Hg.), *Historisch-kritischer Kommentar zum BGB.* Band II. *Schuldrecht: Allgemeiner Teil. §§ 241–432. 1. Teilband: vor § 241–§ 304.* Tübingen: Mohr Siebeck, 941–1027.

Sturm, Fritz, 1977. „Rez. von Sacconi, Giuseppina. La ‚pluris petition' nel processo formulare. Contributo allo studio dell'oggetto del processo." *Rivista Internazionale di Diritto Romano e Antico* 28, 267–280.

Talamanca, Mario, 1970. „‚Alia causa' e ‚durior condicio' come limite dell'obbligazione dell' ‚adpromissor'". In: *Studi in onore di Giuseppe Grosso. Vol. III.* Turin: Giappichelli, 115–203.

Tschentscher, Axel, 2000. *Prozedurale Theorien der Gerechtigkeit: rationales Entscheiden, Diskursethik und prozedurales Recht.* Baden-Baden: Nomos.

Vážný, Jan, 1936. „Appunti alla dottrina classica die contratti a favore di terzi". In: *Studi in onore di Salvatore Riccobono nel XL anno del suo insegnamento. Vol. IV.* Palermo: Castiglia, 259–271.

Voci, Pasquale, 1935. „I limiti della responsabilità nell'adempimento di legati per damnationem e dei fedecommessi". *Studia et documenta historiae et iuris* 1, 48–72.

— 1990. „‚Diligentia',‚Custodia',‚Culpa'. I dati fondamentali". *Studia et documenta historiae et iuris* 56, 29–143.

Wieacker, Franz, 1988. Römische Rechtsgeschichte. Erster Abschnitt. Einleitung, Quellenkunde. Frühzeit und Republik. München: C.H. Beck.

Wimmer, Markus, 1995. *Besitz und Haftung des Vindikationsbeklagten* (Forschungen zum römischen Recht 41). Köln / Weimar / Wien: Böhlau.

Windscheid, Bernhard, 1856. *Die actio des römischen Civilrechts.* Düsseldorf: Buddeus.

Ziliotto, Paola, 2004. *Studi sulle obbligazioni alternative in diritto romano.* Padova: CEDAM.

Al-Shāfiʿī und Kelsen: Bestimmtheit, Wahrscheinlichkeit und Fehler(bewusstsein) in der formalen Rechtsordnung

Nahed Samour

Abstract 253
1 Einleitung: Systeme von Rechtsnormen als formale Ordnungen 254
2 Uṣūl al-fiqh: Über die Herausbildung des Formalen in der islamischen Rechtsordnung 257
2.1 Sammeln, Verschriftlichen, Fixieren: Das Formale als Überlieferungskette 257
2.2 Das Formale des Koran 257
2.3 Das Formale der Prophetensunna 260
2.4 Das Formale: Authentifizieren und Hierarchisieren 261
3 Bestimmtes und wahrscheinliches Wissen 263
3.1 Bestimmtheit (*qaṭʿ*) und Wahrscheinlichkeit (*ẓann*) als Rechtskategorien, Rechtsmetapher bei der Herausbildung formaler Ordnung 264
3.2 Die Bedeutung von Rechtsmetaphern für die formale Ordnung, in den Rechts- und Mathematikwissenschaften 265
4 Von formal zu formalistisch? 273
5 Schlussfolgerung 274
Literaturverzeichnis 275

Abstract

Bei der Herausbildung einer formalen Rechtsordnung unterschieden muslimische Juristen seit dem 2.–3./8.–9. Jahrhundert zwischen bestimmtem und wahrscheinlichem Wissen als juridischen Kategorien. Die Beschäftigung mit wahrscheinlichem Wissen eröffnete die Frage nach der Abgrenzung des Rechts von interessensgeleiteten Erwägungen – vergleichbar mit Hans Kelsen, dessen Anliegen es war, das Recht formal und damit politisch „rein" zu halten, eines der zentralen Anliegen in seiner „Reinen Rechtslehre" von 1934. Tatsächlich, anders als in Kelsens Erörterungen zum Positivismus, ging es den frühen muslimischen Juristen um die Frage, wie man das islamische Recht als formale Ordnung aus dem Material der religiösen Offenbarung herzuleiten hat. Vergleichbar mit Kelsens Ausführungen zu Normativität ging es jedoch in intensiver Kontroverse ebenfalls darum, wie man dabei menschliche, interessensgeleitete Elemente fernhalten kann, um das Recht als „göttlich" oder, mit Kelsen, als „rein" zu erhalten oder zu machen. Für die Unterscheidung zwischen bestimmtem und wahrscheinlichem Wissen wurde die Bestimmung der Gebetsrichtung (*qibla*) zur Rechtsmetapher, die auch für die Ordnungsfragen der mathematischen Wissenschaften von Bedeutung war. Als einer der ersten Rechtstheoretiker inkorporierte al-Shāfiʿī (gestorben 204/820, Fustāt, Ägypten) wahrscheinliches Wissen nach einem Verfahren der textorientierten Nachweise bzw. Hinweise (Singular *dalīl*, Plural *adillā*), und setzte sich dabei mit der Bedeutung von Fehlerbewusstsein und Fehler in der formalen Ordnung auseinander, die mit einem ordnungsrechtlichen Konsistenzanspruch in Einklang gebracht werden musste. Letztlich blieb der Errungenschaft des Formalen nicht aus, auch als „formalistisch" kritisiert zu werden.

1. Einleitung: Systeme von Rechtsnormen als formale Ordnungen

Das Herausarbeiten eines Ordnungssystems, das den Anspruch erhebt, hohe innere Kohärenz zu besitzen, deduktive Ableitungen zu ermöglichen und in ihrer Anwendung auf konkrete Probleme eindeutige Entscheidungen zu ermöglichen[1], ist keine Errungenschaft der Moderne.

Dennoch hat die Betonung der formalen Normenordnung, wie sie Hans Kelsen für die Rechtswissenschaften 1934 in seiner „Reinen Rechtslehre" formuliert hat, enorme nationale und internationale Resonanz gefunden.[2] So sehr, dass die Betonung des Formalen zu einem Spezifikum der europäischen Moderne stilisiert wurde.[3] Kelsen betonte, dass das Bestehen einer formalen Ordnung durch gewisse übergeordnete Normen geprägt wird, die den Aufbau und die Anwendung des Normen- bzw. Regelsystems leiten, und an deren Spitze eine (hypothetische) Grundnorm stünde.[4] Der Orientierung an einer solchen Grundnorm in einer Normenpyramide, liegt ein formales Verständnis von rechtlichen Ordnungen und Prozeduren zugrunde und dieses ermöglicht es, inhaltliche, zweckmäßige Fragen nach dem gerechten Recht auszuschließen, um damit die Rechtslehre von Interessens- und Machtgebundenheit rein zu halten. Kelsens Ziel war eine klare, formale Entscheidung zu ermöglichen, die nicht Spielball politischer Interessen ist.[5] Die formale Struktur sollte also vor der Politisierung des Rechts schützen.[6] In Kelsens Rechtstheorie ist das Recht von der Moral, und die Norm vom Faktum konsequent zu trennen, das Recht also als „ideologiekritischer Positivismus"[7] zu verstehen. Ein formales Verständnis von rechtlicher Ordnung

[1] Siehe Einleitung dieses Bandes.

[2] Kelsen, 1934; ders., 1960; ders., 1979.

[3] Zur Wirkkraft Kelsens sowie zur internationalen Kelsenforschung siehe Dreier, 1990. Zum Einfluss der Reinen Rechtslehre auf die Rechtstheorie in verschiedenen Ländern siehe Achterberg, 1978.

[4] Kelsen, 1960, 202.

[5] Baer, 2017, 29.

[6] Baer, 2017, 29 erinnert daran, dass Kelsen die Rechtswissenschaft formalisieren und „rein" halten wollte von der Ideologie eines aufkommenden Führerstaats des deutschen Nationalsozialismus, um das Recht vor nationalsozialistischem Volksgeist und Rassenlehre zu retten. Dazu insbesondere Kelsen 1922; derselbe 1928, beispielsweise 151–154, 253.

[7] Zur „Wiener Schule der Rechtstheorie" und ihrem Verständnis eines „ideologiekritischen Positivismus", siehe Jestaedt, 2008; Jestaedt, 2017, XXVI–XXVII, 3.

ist trotz der tatsächlich besonders systematisch formulierten und begründeten Position von Kelsen (als „radikalisierten Gedankengang“[8] von Kant gegen „bloß empirische Rechtslehre“[9]) jedoch keine *spezifisch* moderne und keine *spezifisch* europäische Perspektive. Diese Aussage wird im Folgenden anhand der Vorstellungen einer formalen islamischen Rechtsordnung begründet. Die Aussage ist vorab vor allem verbunden mit einer Einladung, rechtliche Ordnungen trotz ihrer gelegentlich inhaltlich sehr unterschiedlichen Ausgestaltung auf ihre „strukturierende Funktion bei der gesellschaftlichen Verankerung von Leitideen“[10] zu untersuchen, und damit Grundlagenfragen des Rechts und der „Rechtsordnung als Ganzes“[11] zu reflektieren. Recht wird hier in diesem Beitrag also als Strukturtheorie verstanden[12], und Hans Kelsen sowie Muḥammad al-Shāfiʿī werden hierfür herangezogen als prominente Vertreter für das Ordnungsrechtsdenken seit dem 20. Jahrhundert in Kontinentaleuropa (und darüber hinaus) sowie seit dem 9. Jahrhundert im islamischen Rechtskreis. Der Beitrag ist auch ein Versuch, die Reflexion über die Methoden der Rechtwissenschaft sowie das Verständnis ihrer Nachbardisziplinen zu überdenken. So empfahl der Wissenschaftsrat 2012: „Eine verstärkte Befassung mit den Grundlagenfächern erhöht die Chancen auf einen intensiveren wissenschaftlichen Austausch der Rechtswissenschaft mit den *geistes- und sozialwissenschaftlichen Nachbarfächern, mit denen sie ihre Methoden teilt.*“[13] Eine Auseinandersetzung mit frühen Formen formaler Ordnung lädt darüber hinaus dazu ein, die Rechtswissenschaft als Teil des Wissenschaftsdenkens mit den Ordnungswissenschaften zu sehen, wozu auch die Mathematik gehört. Die Frage nach der richtigen Gebetsausrichtung in ihrer juristischen, religiösen wie mathematischen, theoretischen wie praktischen, individuellen wie kollektiven Dimension bekräftigt hier die Orientierung an Ordnungswissenschaften anstelle der Unterscheidung in Geistes-, Sozial und Naturwissenschaften.

Ausgangspunkt dieser Betrachtung bleibt das Recht. Tatsächlich anders als bei Kelsen ging es frühen muslimischen Juristen im 2.–3./8–9. Jahrhundert um die Frage, wie man das islamische Recht als formale Ordnung aus dem Material der religiösen Offenbarung herzuleiten hat. Ähnlich zu Kelsens „Reiner Rechtslehre“ ging es jedoch in intensiver Kontroverse ebenfalls darum, wie man dabei menschliche, interessensgeleitete Elemente fernhalten kann, um das Recht als „göttlich“ oder, mit Kelsen, „rein“ zu erhalten oder zu machen. Der Drang nach Formalisierung erfolgte, wie zu Kelsens Zeiten, ebenfalls in höchst turbulenten Zeiten, denn das islamische Kalifat expandierte zu jener Zeit und seine territoriale Herrschaft erfasste eine multikonfessionelle und multiethnische Bevölkerung, die über eine gemeinsame Gesellschafts- und Rechtsordnung verbunden

---

[8] Naucke, 2005, 93.

[9] Kant, 1785, VI, 230. „Eine bloß empirische Rechtslehre ist (wie der hölzerne Kopf in Phädrus' Fabel) ein Kopf, der schön sein mag, nur Schade! daß er kein Gehirn hat.“

[10] Wissenschaftsrat, 2012, Drucksache 2558-12, 26.

[11] Wissenschaftsrat, 2012, Drucksache 2558-12, 26.

[12] Zur Rechtstheorie als analytischer Strukturtheorie des Rechts vgl. Jestaedt, 2000, 148, mit weiteren Nennungen; zu den Ursprüngen der europäischen juristischen Strukturtheorie, Funke, 2004.

[13] Wissenschaftsrat, 2012, Drucksache 2558-12, 36–37. Grimm, 1976.

werden musste, die zugleich demographische und geographische Heterogenität zuließ. Damit hatten sich islamische Juristen rasanten Wirkungen der Pluralisierung[14], aber auch den Versuchungen der Politisierung zu stellen.[15] Die juristischen Debatten der ersten Jahrhunderte der islamischen Rechtsgeschichte waren geprägt von einem Ringen um das Formale im Recht, den Positionen der „Anhänger der Tradition“ (*ahl al-ḥadīth*) und den „Anhängern der freien Meinung“ (*ahl al-ra'y*). Die „Anhänger der Tradition“ orientierten sich eng an Textpräzedenz, und zwar auch dort, wo der Text nicht gänzlich abgesichert war, aber doch Nachweise (*adillā*) lieferte, um nicht auf Gemeinwohlinteresse zurückgreifen zu müssen. Die „Anhänger der freien Meinung“ (*ahl al-ra'y*) bevorzugten eine Orientierung an Gemeinwohlinteressen, wenn Text als formales Element des Rechts nicht bestimmt oder bestimmbar genug erschien. Eine Vergleichbarkeit von Kelsens „Reiner Rechtslehre“ mit diesen Debatten der frühen islamischen Jurisprudenz, um juristische Leitideen und Leitbilder der Ordnung zu verstehen, erscheint daher sinnvoll, und wird hier nicht das erste Mal attestiert.[16]

Muḥammad Ibn Idrīs al-Shāfiʿī (gestorben 204/820, Fustāt, Ägypten) gilt als einer der ersten Begründer der islamischen Rechtstheorie (*uṣūl al-fiqh*).[17] In seiner grundlegenden Schrift *al-Risāla* (Die Abhandlung)[18] legte er erstmals die Quellen des Rechts theoretisch nieder und verdeutlichte die Ableitungsregeln (*istinbāt*). Dabei griff er auf die juristischen Debatten seiner Zeitgenossen zurück. Tatsächlich hat kein anderer Begründer der übrigen Rechtsschulen eine (heute noch existierende) Schrift zu diesem Thema hinterlassen, auch wenn es vor al-Shāfiʿī grundlegende Überlegungen zu den Arbeitsgrundlagen des Rechts gegeben hat, wenn auch nicht systematisch, umfassend und in einem Werk vereint.[19] Damit wurde er auch Namensgeber der Shāfiʾitischen Rechtsschule, einer der vier noch heute geltenden sunnitischen Rechtsschulen.[20]

Im Folgenden geht es um die Herleitung einer formalen Ordnung aus den Schriften des Rechtsgelehrten al-Shāfiʿī, dessen Rechtsgedanken formativ für das Werden der islamischen Ordnung wurden. In Abschnitt 2 gehe ich der Frage nach, wie *uṣūl al-fiqh*, „die Wurzeln der Rechtordnung“, als eine entstehende formale Ordnung verstanden werden können. Abschnitt 3 stellt die juridischen Kategorien von bestimmtem und wahrscheinlichem Wissen anhand einer Rechtsmetapher zur Gebetsausrichtung vor, die die Suche nach den Nachweisen oder Hinweisen (Plural *adillā*) für eine formale Ordnung versinnbildlicht und der Frage nach der formalen Ordnung eine für praktizierende Muslime hohe

[14] Ibn al-Muqaffaʿ, *Risālat al-ṣaḥab*.

[15] Zaman, 1997, 101.

[16] Siehe die knappe Anmerkung bei Zysow, 2013, 2.

[17] Über al-Shāfiʿī als „Master Architect“ siehe Coulson, 1964, 53–61. Kritisch zur Entstehung und Revision dieses Topos, siehe Hallaq, 1993.

[18] Ich verwende hier die gängige kritische Edition von Shākir, 1940. Diese nimmt zur Grundlage das sogenannte Rabīʿ Manuskript, benannt nach einem Schüler Shāfiʿīs und wohl auf das neunte oder womöglich zehnte Jahrhundert zurückgehend. Siehe Lowry, 2007, 7 Fn. 12.

[19] Krawietz, 2002, 66 f.

[20] Zu den bedeutenden Rechtsschulen, die historisch überlebten gehören die malikitische, hanafitische und hanbalitische.

Praxisrelevanz verleiht. Auch wird hier die Frage der erforderlichen Nachweise bei wahrscheinlichem Wissen und das Fehlerbewusstsein der Juristen in Anbetracht von wahrscheinlichem Wissen diskutiert. Abschließend wird der Schritt vom „Formalen" zum „Formalistischen" im Recht auf seine kritischen Auswirkungen beleuchtet.

2. Uṣūl al-fiqh: Über die Herausbildung des Formalen in der islamischen Rechtsordnung

Wie bildet sich eine formale Rechtsordnung heraus? Was macht das *Formale* aus? Die „Wurzeln der Rechtsfindung", arabisch *uṣūl al-fiqh*, beschäftigen sich mit Rechtsquellen und Rechtsfindungsinstrumenten. Sie haben ihren dokumentierten Anfang in den wachsenden Lernzirkeln in Mekka, Medina, Damaskus, Baghdad, Kufa und Basra (Irak) im zweiten Jahrhundert der islamischen Zeitordnung[21] (umgerechnet im achten Jahrhundert nach Christus). Sie ist die Beschäftigung mit den Grundlagen einer juristischen Ordnung, von denen alles abgeleitete Recht (*furūʿ*), wörtlich „die Äste", ausgehen soll. Muslimische Gelehrte standen vor der epochalen Herausforderung aus Text (*naṣṣ*), der als göttlich (*Qurʾān*) oder prophetisch (*Sunna*) legitimiert galt, eine Rechtsordnung herzustellen, die für Muslime allerorts und für alle Zeiten Verbindlichkeit herzustellen vermochte.

2.1 Sammeln, Verschriftlichen, Fixieren: Das Formale als Überlieferungskette

Die Herausforderungen, die die Bildung einer formalen Ordnung mit sich bringen, lassen sich an den Rechtsquellen nachzeichnen. Zunächst bestand die Aufgabe aus dem Sammeln, Verschriftlichen und Fixieren von allem, was Rechtleitung bot.[22]

2.2 Das Formale des Koran

Das betraf zunächst einmal den Koran selbst. Trotz, oder gerade wegen, einer Reihe von phonetischen, orthographischen und syntaktischen Varianten, die auf verschiedene Rezensionen zurückgehen und Kontroversen lieferten[23], entstand unter der Herrschaft des dritten Kalifen ʿUthmān (644–656) eine „kanonische" Textgestalt, die allen Muslimen gemein wurde und die der bei Gott „wohlverwahrten Tafel" (Koran 85:22) entsprach. Das Fixieren des Koran als Text muss dabei als Schlüsselmoment in der islamischen Geschichte gesehen werden.[24] War es aber auch ein Schlüsselmoment in der Herausbildung einer formalen Rechtsordnung? Es herrscht eine Kontroverse darüber, ob und wenn ja warum,

[21] Für Mekka siehe beispielsweise Motzki, 1991, 257.
[22] Ähnlicher Dreischritt auch in Sabra, 1987. Petra Schmidl, der ich für diesen Hinweis danke, unterteilt weitergehend die Astronomie in den vom Islam geprägten Gesellschaften in drei Schritte: 1. Sammeln, Verschriftlichen, Übersetzen, 2. Übernehmen, Anpassen, 3. Differenzieren, Kritisieren, Organisieren.
[23] Ein Überblick über muslimische und revisionistische Perspektiven zur Textgestalt des Koran, siehe Burton, 1977 sowie Burton, 2006.
[24] Hallaq, 2005, 33 f.

sich die frühen Juristen nur bedingt mit dem Koran als Rechtstext beschäftigt haben.[25] Tatsächlich lassen sich in den frühen *uṣūl*-Werken kaum detaillierte Auseinandersetzungen mit einzelnen Rechtsregeln des Koran nachweisen[26], womöglich weil dieser nicht in erster Linie legislativen Charakter hat und lediglich ca. 500 Verse rechtlichen Inhalt haben.[27] Al-Shāfiʿī hat sich relativ wenig dokumentierte Gedanken um den Koran gemacht[28], oder aber die Normativität des Koran als Grundnorm *vorausgesetzt*.[29] Ihn interessierte stattdessen die Frage nach dem Verhältnis von Prophetentraditionen (als Sunna, als Gesamtheit) und dem Koran (siehe unten). Viel bedeutsamer ist: Das Konstitutive für das Formale, oder für die Grundnorm, in der islamischen Rechtsordnung ist eine eindeutige Überlieferungskette. So auch für den Koran. Der Koran in seiner Gesamtheit, ganz gleich ob mündlich oder schriftlich fixiert, ist als Textbeleg (*naṣṣ*) dem Propheten in eben dieser Form offenbart worden.[30] Für al-Shāfiʿī heißt das: „Am Koran kann niemand auch nur einen Buchstaben bezweifeln."[31] Damit ist der Koran in seinem Bestand und seiner Überlieferung vom Propheten definitiv bestimmt (*qaṭʿī*). Da der Koran seine Adressaten vom Propheten ausgehend im Wege der ununterbrochenen Überlieferung (*tawātur)* erreichte, unterliegen alle seine Textbelege keinem Zweifel (*nuṣūṣ qaṭʿiyya al-thubūt*). So ist der Koran in all seinen Bestandteilen „definitiv hinsichtlich der Überlieferungskette (*qaṭʿī al-sanad*)". Anders jedoch in der Bedeutung des Koran, die in einigen Fällen durchaus wahrscheinlicher oder, hier besser, präsumtiver Natur sein kann.[32] Auch wenn der Koran somit in seinem materiellen Bestand absolut gesichert ist, liegen in ihm zwei Arten von rechtlicher Normativität vor, nämlich zum einen bestimmte, definitive Normativität und zum anderen wahrscheinliche, präsumti-

---

[25] Dass der Koran in den frühen islamischen Rechtswissenschaften keine zentrale Rolle gespielt hat, führte in der Orientalistik zu (anhaltenden) Spekulationen, vor allem Schacht, 1967, 2, 224 und später beispielsweise Powers, 1986, siehe auch zusammenfassend Burton, 1977, 351–361; Lowry, 2007, 42 und 207–215. Kritisch gegen Schachts Schlussfolgerungen als Übertreibungen, Motzki, 2001, 115–117 und 152–157.

[26] Dies könnte vergleichbar sein mit der Beobachtung von Markus Asper in diesem Band (S. 201 f.), wonach rechtliche Fundamentalien nicht verschriftet sind. Diese Beobachtung deckt sich einerseits mit Befunden in anderen rechtlichen und mathematischen Texten, in denen selbsterklärende und selbstverständliche Dinge nicht geregelt und aufgeschrieben sind (siehe in diesem Band Hagan Brunke, Mark Depauw, Peter Gröschler). Sie widerspricht aber andererseits ein Stück weit der These vom textgestützten kulturellen Gedächtnis (Jan Assmann). Dass Gründe nicht formuliert werden und dass dies daran liege, dass sie entweder als nicht wichtig oder als bekannt eingestuft wurden (S. 15), zielt in die gleiche Richtung. Ob eine Nicht-Verschriftung rechtlicher Fundamentalien charakteristisch ist für alle frühen Rechtsordnungen, bleibt erst einmal offen. Auch scheint, ob verschriftet wurde oder nicht, von der Textgruppe abzuhängen.

[27] Standardisierte Koran Ausgaben haben 6.236 Verse.

[28] Vertiefend zu Shāfiʿī's Auseinandersetzung mit dem Qur'ān, bei der die Bestimmtheit des Koran vorausgesetzt wird und es vor allem um das formale Verhältnis zur Sunna geht, siehe Lowry, 2007, 207–237.

[29] Kelsen, 1960, 197. „Die Grundnorm muss vorausgesetzt werden".

[30] Die definitive, bestimmte Überlieferung des Koran gilt als islamisch unwiderleglich. Diese Grundvoraussetzung, zu der Shāfiʿī schweigt, wird hier von Krawietz mit Verweis auf moderne Rechtsliteratur präzise zusammengeführt, Krawietz, 2002, 101.

[31] Al-Shāfiʿī, *Risāla*, 16.

[32] Krawietz, 2002, 101.

ve oder interpretationsfähige Normativität. *Dalāla qaṭʿiyya* bedeutet einen definitiven Nachweis (oder Hinweis), welcher keine andere als die intendierte Bedeutung zulässt, und damit eine eindeutige Entscheidung ermöglicht.[33] Es besteht kein Raum, im formalen Sinne auch kein Bedarf, für Rechtsfortbildung (*ijtihād*), denn es kann bezüglich des Textverständnisses zu keinem Unterschied in der Interpretation kommen. Als Beispiele solcher definitiven, bestimmten Norminhalte können angesehen werden die erbrechtlichen Regelungen in Sure 4:11[34], die Anweisungen in Sure 24:2 zur Sanktionierung von Ehebruch und außerehelichem Geschlechtsverkehr[35], und Sure 24:4 zur Sanktionierung der falschen Beschuldigung von Ehebruch und außerehelichem Geschlechtsverkehr[36]. Wegen des bestimmten (*qaṭʿī*) Charakters und seiner Rechtsfolgen, haben Juristen besonders hohe prozessuale Hürden für die Sanktionierung dieser im Koran verankerten Straftatbestände vorgenommen und damit diese Sanktion für weite Teile der islamischen Geschichte zu einer Norm der Abschreckung, denn der Umsetzung gemacht.[37] Tatsächlich bedeutet dies, dass es keine Diskussion darüber gab, *ob* Unzucht bestraft werden soll, sondern stattdessen, *wie* Unzucht überhaupt festgestellt werden kann, wenn vier glaubwürdige, also moralisch integre Zeugen schon gar nicht in die Privatsphäre anderer unerlaubt eintreten dürfen und darüber hinaus, nicht moralisch sein können, wenn sie den Geschlechtsakt selbst *konkret* bezeugen können sollen. Die Juristen haben die prozessrechtlichen Hürden für das Bezeugen der Unzucht so hoch gesetzt, dass weder ein glaubwürdiges Bezeugen und damit weder ein Urteil noch eine Sanktion mehr möglich ist. Für eine formale Ordnung bedeutet dies, dass die Grundnorm, hier das koranische Sanktionsrecht, aufrechterhalten wird (zur moralischen Abschreckung, um eine Ehe zu schützen) und gleichzeitig mit formalen Subsystemen, wie dem Strafprozessrecht, beeinflusst werden kann. Formale Systeme erlauben hier also ein hohes Maß der Steuerungsmöglichkeit.

Andere Verse im Koran sind hingegen in ihrem rechtlichen Bedeutungsgehalt als präsumtiv oder wahrscheinlich (*ẓannī*) eingeordnet worden, denn ihnen kommt mehr als eine Bedeutung zu. Als Beispiel kann angeführt werden Sure 2:228, wonach „geschiedene Frauen drei Perioden lang zu warten" haben,

---

[33] Krawietz, 2002, 110.

[34] Sure 4: 11: „Gott trägt euch für eure Kinder auf: Ein männliches bekommt denselben Teil wie zwei weibliche. Sind es Frauen, mehr als zwei, dann bekommen sie die zwei Drittel dessen, was er hinterlässt. Ist es nur eine, dann bekommt sie die Hälfte. Beide Eltern bekommen je ein Sechstel dessen, was er hinterlässt, wenn er ein Kind hat. Doch wenn er kein Kind hat und seine Eltern ihn beerben, dann bekommt seine Mutter ein Drittel. Hat er Brüder, dann bekommt seine Mutter ein Sechstel – nach Berücksichtigung einer von ihm hinterlassenen testamentarischen Verfügung oder einer Schuld. Eure Väter und eure Söhne – ihr wisst nicht, wer von ihnen euch im Nutzen näher steht. Eine Verpflichtung durch Gott! Gott ist wissend und weise". Übersetzt von Zirker, 2016.

[35] Sure 24:2: „Wenn eine Frau und ein Mann Unzucht begangen haben, dann gebt jedem von ihnen hundert Schläge. Keine Milde für sie soll euch ergreifen in Gottes Religion, falls ihr an Gott und den Jüngsten Tag glaubt. Bei ihrer Bestrafung soll eine Gruppe der Gläubigen als Zeugen anwesend sein". Übersetzt von Zirker, 2016.

[36] Sure 24:4: „ Die ehrbare Frauen beschuldigen, dann keine vier Zeugen bringen, die schlagt mit achtzig Schlägen! Nehmt nie mehr von ihnen Zeugnis an. Das sind Frevler!". Übersetzt von Zirker, 2016.

[37] Siehe Johansen, 1977; Rabb, 2015, 71–72.

bevor sie wieder eine Ehe schließen dürfen.[38] Unbestimmt war hier der Begriff „Periode“ (arab. *qurū'*), weil dies nicht nur „Menstruation“ heißen kann, wie die ḥanafitische Rechtsschule vertrat, sondern auch die *ṭuhr* Phase der Reinheit danach, so die shāfiʿitische Rechtsschule.[39] Für die Erhaltung der Unterhalts- und Erbansprüche eines Kindes gegenüber dem Vater, die Rechtmäßigkeit einer Ehe bzw. die Strafbarkeit wegen außerehelichen Geschlechtsverkehrs, war der rechtmäßige Beginn einer zweiten Ehe von Wichtigkeit.

2.3 Das Formale der Prophetensunna

Wesentlich kontroverser und herausfordernder verlief damals das Sammeln, Verschriftlichen und Fixieren der Ḥadīthe, der Aussprüche und Taten des Propheten, deren Gesamtheit die Sunna als normbildendes Verhalten bildet.[40] Die Quelle musste authentifizierbar sein und sich auf den Propheten (und anfänglich auch auf seine Gefährten) zurückführen lassen. Ein Ḥadīth hat meist die Form eines Augenzeugenberichts von einem Zeitgenossen, einem „Gefährten“ (*sāhib,* Plural *ashāb)* des Propheten. Vor dem Text steht grundsätzlich eine Überliefererkette (*isnād*) mit den Namen der mündlichen Überlieferer. Von Bedeutung ist das Wort „an“, also „auf Autorität von“, „auf Gewähr von“. Hiermit wurde in sprachlicher Regelmäßigkeit eine formale Struktur aufgebaut, die vor allem der Transparenz dienen sollte und damit die Zuverlässigkeit der Quelle nachvollziehbar machen sollte.[41]

Grundsätzlich galt, dass, je sicherer und authentischer eine Quelle war, desto höherrangiger galt sie im Rechtssystem. Als höchstes Maß an Authentizität galt eine nachvollziehbar ununterbrochene (*tawātir*) und weitverbreitete (*mashhūr*) Überliefererkette. Eine Aussage musste also immer im Ausgang auf den Prophe-

[38] Sure 2: 228: „Die geschiedenen Frauen warten ihrerseits drei Perioden ab, und ihnen ist es nicht erlaubt, dass sie verbergen, was Gott in ihrem Schoße schuf – sofern sie an Gott glauben und an den Jüngsten Tag. Ihre Männer sind voll dazu berechtigt, sie während dieser Zeit zurückzuholen, falls sie Aussöhnung wollen. Und den Frauen steht dasselbe zu, wozu sie ihrerseits nach Billigkeit verpflichtet sind. Die Männer stehen eine Stufe über ihnen. Gott ist mächtig und weise“. Übersetzung nach Bobzin, 2010.

[39] Zu dieser ḥanafitisch-shāfiʿitische Auseinandersetzung siehe Diskussion bei Krawietz, 2002, 110–111.

[40] Die Notwendigkeit der Authentifizierung von Hadithen kommt daher, dass der Prophet den Gefährten verboten haben soll, etwas anders als den Qur'ān schriftlich niederzulegen, damit der Qur'ān nicht mit etwas anderem vermischt wird. So hinderte er die Gefährten daran, die Sunna in einer von ihm autorisierten Weise niederzuschreiben, die damit auch die Authentizitätsfrage geklärt hätte. Trotz des Verbots wurde die Sunna von einzelnen Gefährten oder ihren Schülerinnen und Schülern nach dem Tod des Propheten aufgeschrieben, denn mit der offiziellen Redaktion des Qur'ān entfiel die Furcht davor, dass Qur'ān und Sunna durcheinander gebracht würden. Durch Auswendiglernen und mündliche Überlieferungen wurden zwischenzeitlich die Hadithe bewahrt. Zum dritten islamischen Jahrhundert entwickelten sich immer strengere Qualitätskriterien, die Anordnung erfolgte nach thematischen Aspekten, um juristischen Bedürfnissen gerecht zu werden. In diese Zeit fallen die Arbeiten der großen Hadith-Kompilatoren wie al-Bukhārī. Siehe Krawietz, 2002, 57–58.

[41] Beispiel einer *ḥadīth.* Überliefererkette (*isnād*): A überlieferte von B, der es gehört hatte von C: D hat mir überliefert, dass der Prophet gesagt hat: Text (*matn*): „Wer auf der Suche nach Wissen hinauszieht, der ist auf dem Wege Gottes, bis er heimkehrt.“

ten oder zumindest seine Gefährten und Gefährtinnen zurückzuführen sein und eine Kette von Überlieferern beinhalten. Meinungsstreit herrschte, wo dieses Höchstmaß nicht aufrechterhalten werden konnte und dann offen war, was mit dem defizitär übermittelten Informationsgehalt geschehen sollte. Zentral wurde die Frage, ob die Einzelüberlieferung (*khabar wāḥid*) als Teil der Sunna angesehen werden sollte, so al-Shāfiʿī[42], oder nicht, so die Anhänger der Ḥanafitischen Schule. Das war delikat, denn auch al-Shāfiʿī unterschied in Wissen, das Sicherheit erlaubt, und Wissen, das keine Sicherheit erlaubt und zählte hierzu den Einzelbericht (*khabar wāḥid*). Und die Frage nach deren Normativität war akut: Denn die islamische Jurisprudenz bezog sich vor allem auf Einzelberichte.[43] Für al-Shāfiʿī war es jedoch formaler und damit richtiger, eine Einzelüberlieferung als verbindlichen Teil der Sunna anzuerkennen anstelle des freien Rechtsdenkens (*ra'y*), wie es die Ḥanafitische Rechtsschule bevorzugte.[44] Al-Shāfiʿī warf den Ḥanafiten vor, den Prophetenüberlieferungen keinen Normvorrang einzuräumen, sich nicht ausschließlich am Propheten Mohammad zu orientieren, sondern auch an seinen Gefährten und Gefährtinnen. Damit würde nicht nur methodisch unsauber gearbeitet, sondern dies gefährde auch die „Reinheit" des Rechts, denn juristische Deutungsansprüche würden über die formale Herleitung des Rechts gestellt.[45]

2.4 Das Formale: Authentifizieren und Hierarchisieren

Zentrale Herausforderung für die muslimischen Juristen waren das Authentifizieren und Hierarchisieren der Rechtsquellen. Ein Verständnis für und ein Ringen um richtige und falsche bzw. fehlerhafte Quellen, Vorrangigkeit und Nachrangigkeit, Eigenständigkeit oder Komplementarität der Quellen wurde in den juristischen Abhandlungen zunehmend sichtbar. In der Eigenbegrifflichkeit des islamischen Rechts wurden diese Fragen mit den Erkenntnismethoden von bestimmt-wahrscheinlichen (*qaṭʿ-ẓann*)[46], allgemein-speziellen (*ʿamm–khāṣṣ*)[47], abrogierend-abrogierten (*naskḥ-mansūkh*)[48] und erklärenden Sätzen (*jumla tabyīn*)[49] verfolgt, um jegliche Möglichkeiten des Normwiderspruchs (*taʿāruḍ*) aufzulösen. Das Formale an dieser Ordnung lag maßgeblich in der Authentifizierung der Echtheit der Quellen, gefolgt von der Beschäftigung mit dem Inhalt

[42] Al-Shāfiʿī, *Risāla*, Abschnitt 1007–1086, S. 372–392; Abschnitt 1260–1261, S. 461; Abschnitt 1297, S. 468. Zum Stellenwert des Einzelberichts bei Al-Shāfiʿī siehe auch Lowry, 2007, 194.

[43] Hallaq, 2005, 74–75.

[44] Al-Shāfiʿī, *Risāla*, Abschnitt 1051, S. 384.

[45] Al-Shāfiʿī, *Kitāb al-jimāʿ*, Abschnitt 1–2, S. 11–12.

[46] Al-Shāfiʿī, *Risāla*, zur Bestimmtheit von Aussagen, die keinen Zweifel an ihrer Gewißheit haben (*qatʿ*), Abschnitt 1328–1329, S. 478; Abschnitt 616, S. 223, Abschnitt 99, S. 32, siehe auch die Ausführungen von Al-Salahat, *Malāmiḥ fiqh al-qatʿ wa al-zann ʿinda al-imām al-Shāfiʿī*, 2002, S. 82. Zur Methode der Ermittlung von Wahrscheinlichkeit (*zann*) und ihre verschiedenen Abstufungen der Wahrscheinlichkeit, Al- Shāfiʿī, *Risāla*, Abschnitt 557, S. 206–7, Abschnitt 588–589, S. 216, Abschnitt 1814, S. 599.

[47] Al-Shāfiʿī, *Risāla*, Abschnitt 179–235, S. 53–73.

[48] Al-Shāfiʿī, *Risāla*, Abschnitt 312–420, S. 106–146.

[49] Al-Shāfiʿī, *Risāla*, Abschnitt 421–568, S. 147–210.

der Quelle. Für die Überprüfung der Überlieferung wurden zwei formale Kriterien herausgearbeitet: Es wurde eine Überlieferungskette gefordert, die sowohl Transparenz über die Zurückführung auf den Propheten schaffen sollte (*isnād*) (x übermittelte auf Autorität von y, y übermittelte auf Autorität von z, etc.), als auch der Glaubwürdigkeit der Überlieferer diente, wofür Kriterien der Integrität (*ʿadāla*) aufgestellt wurden, beispielsweise Frömmigkeit und keine vorwerfbaren Handlungen (*fasād*).[50] Ein eigenes Genre etablierte sich, die „Wissenschaft von den Männern" (*kitāb al-rijāl*), Gelehrten-Biographien von z.T. erstaunlicher Detailliertheit, die trotz ihres grundlegenden Aussagewerts für die frühe islamische Rechtsgeschichte möglicherweise als „gossip"[51] überzeichnet wurden, jedoch wohl als Übertreibungen der Autoren gelten dürfen, um das Prestige der favorisierten Rechtsschule zu erhöhen.[52] Zwar erfolgte auch eine Prüfung der Glaubhaftigkeit des Inhalts (*matn*), die vor allem nach Plausibilitätsgründen erfolgte und die, vor allem *ex post*, nicht immer genügend priorisiert erschien. Aber der Grund hierin lag, vergleichbar mit Kelsen, darin, dass gerade die Prüfung der Überliefererkette, anders als der Inhalt, eine interessengeleitete Diskussion um Inhalt gerade vermeiden sollte[53], um das Recht davon „rein" zu halten. Das bedenkliche Verhältnis von Form zu Materie war auch ein Grund, warum etwas später die formale Ordnung unter einigen Gelehrten zu Recht auch als formalistisch diskutiert und kritisiert wurde (siehe unten). Mit den formalen Erfordernissen für die Entstehung der Überlieferungskette und die Glaubwürdigkeit der Überlieferer wurden zwei große Bausteine in der Herausbildung einer formalen Ordnung festgelegt. Damit wurde, vergleichbar mit Kelsen, ein Stufenbau der Rechtsordnung eingeführt, der die am sichersten überlieferte Quelle an die Spitze der Normhierarchie stellte und der alle weiteren Quellen folgten.[54] Die Unterscheidung zwischen einerseits der authentischen Überlieferung als Kriterium für das Formale und, andererseits einer Plausibilitätsprüfung des Inhalts, diente der Charakterisierung der Aussagen allein auf Grund der Form ihrer Echtheit, und damit als genuin islamisch. Grundsätzlich gesagt: Das Unterscheidungsmerkmal des „wie" überliefert wurde, wurde gegenüber dem „was" überliefert wurde priorisiert, um „menschlichen Interessenerwägungen" kein Einfallstor zu bieten. Es lässt sich damit also nicht überschätzen, wie zentral und viel diskutiert die Kriterien der Authentifizierung (der mündlich offenbarten oder tradierten, zunehmend verschriftlichten überlieferten Texte) und die

---

[50] Zum Begriff der Integrität (*ʿadāla*) als Voraussetzung glaubwürdiger Gelehrter, Ziadeh, 1990.

[51] Crone, 1980, 16–17.

[52] Siehe z.B. Melchert, 1997, 171.

[53] Brown, 2008.

[54] Kelsen bezeichnete als Stufenbau der Rechtsordnung, dass jede Rechtsnorm auf Ermächtigungsnormen beruhen muss um existent zu sein. Dabei steht die Ermächtigungsnorm, welche die Erzeugung von Rechtsnormen regelt, auf einer logisch höheren Ebene als die erzeugten Normen. Da jede Ermächtigungsnorm ihrerseits auf Ermächtigungsnormen beruhen muss, gibt es einen über mehrere Ebenen reichenden Geltungszusammenhang, den Stufenbau der Rechtsordnung. Diese für die Reine Rechtslehre grundlegende Konzeption wurde von Adolf Merkl entwickelt, vgl. insbesondere Merkl, 1923, 211 ff.; Lembke, 2009, 165–168.

Hierarchisierung der Quellen galten, um Verbindlichkeit im Recht, mithin also eine formale Ordnung, herzustellen. Diese Bemühung wurde zu einem der größten Bausteine des *uṣūl al-fiqh*.

Die Frage der Sunna war auch eine um die Verbindlichkeit und Einheitlichkeit im Recht als weiteres grundlegendes Element einer formalen Rechtsordnung.[55] In Angesicht des Politischen, der Expansion des Kalifats, war eine formale, geltende Rechtsordnung eine enorme Herausforderung. Über Kodifikation wurde formale Ordnung nicht hergestellt[56], auch wenn es schon im zweiten islamischen Jahrhundert eine politische Debatte zur Notwendigkeit hierzu gab, und Ibn Muqaffa' (gestorben ca. 139/756, Basra, Irak) als Sekretär des Kalifen Mansūr (gestorben 158/775, Nähe Mekka), eine Unüberschaubarkeit und Beliebigkeit des Rechts in den Weiten des Abbasidischen Reichs beklagte[57] und daher eine Ordnung für das gesamte Kalifat forderte.[58] Die Juristen jedoch lehnten eine Kodifikation zugunsten der schon früh pluralen Rechtsschulmeinungen ab. Die Herausbildung einer formalen Ordnung ging damit ohne eine Kodifikation vonstatten, doch wuchs die Einsicht, den Rechtspluralismus zunächst mit verstetigter Kompilation zunehmend durch gelehrte Kanonisierung regulieren zu können.[59]

3. Bestimmtes und wahrscheinliches Wissen

Mit dem formalen Ordnungsanspruch ist der Anspruch einer Einheit der Rechtsordnung formuliert: Das Rechtssystem müsse, wenn schon nicht lückenlos, so doch wenigstens widerspruchsfrei sein. Diese Überzeugung ist sowohl im frühen islamischen wie auch im modernen europäischen Rechtsdenken weit verbreitet, obwohl dies in einem eklatanten Widerspruch zum angewandten Recht stehen kann.[60] Kelsen erkannte die Möglichkeit der Widersprüche zwischen geltenden Rechtsnormen der gleichen Normstufe als Normenkonflikt an[61] und räumte ein, dass das Formale des Rechts nicht die Widersprüchlichkeit des Rechts zwangsläufig lösen kann. Normenkonflikte können nicht durch Logik, sondern nur durch Derogation gelöst werden, welche rechtlich vorgesehen sein muss, so Kelsen. Hier kann eine „vermutliche Rechtsgeltung“[62] entstehen. Die Widersprüchlichkeit einer Rechtsordnung entspringt ihr selbst, oder, wie Rechtswis-

---

[55] Zur Verbindlichkeit des Rechts: „Dass eine Norm gilt, bedeutet, dass sie verbindlich ist“. Geltungsgrund einer Norm kann nur eine anderen Norm sein, Kelsen, 1960, 196–197.

[56] Zu Fragen des Kodifizierungsgedanken als Aspekt einer formalen Ordnung, siehe Markus Asper in diesem Band.

[57] Das Abbasidische Reich erstreckte sich von Nordafrika bis Indien mit entsprechend heterogener Bevölkerung. Siehe Kennedy, 1981, 25; Gutas, 1998, 11.

[58] Ibn al-Muqaffaʿ, *Risālat al-ṣaḥab.*

[59] Zur Kanonisierung als „discursive shift“ in der Beziehung zwischen der muslimischen Gemeinschaft und ihrer autoritativen Texte, El Shamsy, 2013, 4.

[60] Eindrücklich zum rechtstheoretischen Fehlerkalkül der „verfassungskonformen Auslegung“ im bundesrepublikanischem deutschen Recht auf die Herausforderung einer „einheitlich geltenden Rechtsordnung“, Lembke, 2009,168, 185–212.

[61] Zu Widersprüchen Kelsen, 1979, 101 f., 168 f.

[62] Bei der „vermutlichen Rechtsgeltung“ kann die Nichtgeltung nicht aus dem Konflikt selbst folgen, Paulson, 1980, 489, 492–498, 505.

senschaftlerin Ulrike Lembke sagt, „Rechtsordnungen sind so widersprüchlich, wie sie selbst es zulassen. Das Ideal von der Einheit der Rechtsordnung muss sich durch deren geltende Regelungen korrigieren lassen“.[63]

Hier nun geht es darum, *uṣūl al-fiqh* („Die Wurzeln des Rechts“) als Versuch einer formalen Ordnung zu untersuchen, die die Unterscheidungen von bestimmtem Wissen (*ʿilm qaṭʿī*) und wahrscheinlichem Wissen (*ʿilm ẓannī*) zur epistemologischen Grundlage der Rechtsordnung macht. Diese Unterscheidung des Wissens in bestimmtes und wahrscheinliches, offenbart, dass die Möglichkeit des Widerspruchs, und gar des Fehlers, im/durch das Recht besteht. Was bedeuten diese Wissenskategorien für die Herausbildung einer formalen Ordnung? Die Metapher zur Ausrichtung der Gebetsrichtung diente der Rechtswissenschaft wie auch den mathematischen Wissenschaften schon früh als Ausgangspunkt für die Beschäftigung mit bestimmtem und wahrscheinlichem Wissen. Diese Rechtskategorien, die für sich genommen schon einen hohen Grad an Selbstreflexion aufzeigen, ermöglichen sodann eine Beschäftigung mit der Frage, welche Aufgabe wahrscheinliches Wissen für die Herausarbeitung der formalen islamischen Ordnung einnimmt. Wahrscheinliches und damit nicht sicheres Wissen lässt auch danach fragen, welche Rolle Fehler und das Bewusstsein um Fehler, bei der Herstellung einer formalen Ordnung einnehmen.[64] Wie verhalten sich Fehler(bewusstsein) und das Postulat von Kohärenz und Konsistenz einer formalen Ordnung? Wie wirkt sich ein Fehlerbewusstsein bei der Etablierung rechtlicher Kategorien zum Zeitpunkt ihrer Herausbildung aus? Lässt sich ein Fehlerbewusstsein mit Geltungsanspruch und Legitimation des Rechts vereinbaren? Diese Fragen setzen ein Rechtsverständnis voraus, das Fehler und Fehlentscheidung in der Rechtssystematik als Element wahr- und ernstnimmt. Die Fragen verschärfen sich – womöglich – in einer Rechtsordnung, die sich religiös legitimiert, und den Anspruch vertritt, auf göttlichem Recht begründet – und damit frei von Fehlern – und darüber hinaus universell zu sein. Abschließend geht es darum, wie frühe Juristen des islamischen Rechtssystems einen Anspruch auf Konsistenz erhoben, gleichwohl aber auch die Fehler(-haftigkeit) (*khaṭṭāʾ*) des Rechtssystems diskutierten.

3.1 Bestimmtheit (*qaṭʿ*) und Wahrscheinlichkeit (*ẓann*) als Rechtskategorien, Rechtsmetapher bei der Herausbildung formaler Ordnung

Dem islamischen Rechtsdenken wird eine hohe Selbstreflektion und eine epistemologisch intensive Auseinandersetzung mit sich selbst beschieden.[65] Dies schlägt sich nicht zuletzt in der Beschäftigung mit der Frage nieder, auf welches Wissen sich eine formale Ordnung stützen soll. Bei dieser konstitutiven Frage teilten sich die Rechtstheorien in diejenigen, die Bestimmtheit in allen Aspekten des Rechts verlangten, und diejenigen, die Wahrscheinlichkeit als Element des

[63] Lembke, 2009, 170.

[64] Zur Bedeutung von Fehlern in der europäischen Wissenschaftsgeschichte seit dem 18. Jahrhundert, Daston, 2001. Dass sich die Frage nach Fehler und Formaler Ordnung auch anderweitig aufdrängt, zeigen die Beiträge und Verweise von Markus Asper und Hagan Brunke in diesem Band, siehe auch Asper, 2012 und Brunke, 2012.

[65] Siehe beispielsweise Zysow, 2013, iii; Krawietz, 2002, VIII.

Rechts zuließen.[66] Es ist keine Kleinigkeit darauf zu verweisen, dass diejenigen Rechtsschulen, die Bestimmtheit in allen Einzelaspekten des Rechts forderten, historisch nicht überlebten.[67] Für diejenigen, die Wahrscheinlichkeit zuließen, wurde es brisant bei der Frage, welchen Stellenwert das wahrscheinliche Wissen für die Legitimierung von Analogie, für Verfahrensfragen zur Authentifizierung der Prophetentraditionen und für Interpretationsmöglichkeiten offenbarter Texte einnehmen sollte. Die Frage, warum sich die Unterscheidung in bestimmtes und wahrscheinliches Wissen überhaupt stellte und welchen Stellenwert die Unterscheidung bei der Herausbildung einer formalen Ordnung, und damit *uṣūl al-fiqh* hat, lässt sich an einer Rechtsmetapher erläutern.

3.2 Die Bedeutung von Rechtsmetaphern für die formale Ordnung, in den Rechts- und Mathematikwissenschaften

Die im Folgenden beschriebene Rechtsmetapher wurde zum Leitbild der gesamten islamischen Rechtstheorie und findet sich wieder in einer Vielzahl theoretischer Abhandlungen.[68] Sie zeigt, dass eine formale Ordnung auf Alltagsverständnisse und Bilder zurückgreift und diese in das Recht importiert.[69] Al-Shāfiʿī postulierte in seinem Werk *Kitāb jimāʿ al-ʿilm* („Gesamtheit [der Arten] des Wissens"), dass es Wissen von zweierlei Art gibt: Wissen, das Sicherheit erlaubt, und Wissen, das keine Sicherheit erlaubt, den Einzelbericht (*khabar wāḥid*), die Rechtsfortbildung (*ijtihād*) und, an anderer Stelle, die Analogie (*qiyās*).[70] Al-Shāfiʿī beschreibt zur Unterscheidung in bestimmtes und unbestimmtes, wahrscheinliches Wissen die Situation eines Gläubigen, der für die Ausrichtung des verpflichtenden Gebets die Richtung Mekka (*qiblā*) sucht.[71] Der Koran normiert die Pflicht mit dem Gesicht gen Heiliger Moschee (in Mekka) zu beten:

> Und von wo du auch herkommst, wende dein Gesicht in Richtung der heiligen Moschee. Und wo immer Du bist, wende Dein Gesicht in ihre Richtung. (2:150)

Diese Pflicht lässt sich als bestimmtes Wissen (*qaṭʿī*) qualifizieren, ist sie doch eindeutig in der Frage, dass das Gebet in Richtung der heiligen Moschee ausgerichtet werden muss. Der Textbeleg gilt als sicher, wenn seine Anwendungsmöglichkeit so begrenzt ist, dass eine mögliche Mehrdeutigkeit ausgeschlossen werden kann (*inqitāʿ al-iḥtimāl*).[72] Die Herausforderung liegt nun darin, die Gebetsrichtung zu bestimmen – ohne bestätigenden Blickkontakt, der Sicherheit gibt. Auch im Wissen, dass Mekka und die Heilige Moschee mit der *Kaʿba* existieren, auch wenn man womöglich nie dagewesen war, muss hier Wahrschein-

---

[66] Zysow, 2013. iii, 1.

[67] Zur ẓāhiri Schule, für die alle Überlieferungen Sicherheit voraussetzten und historisch nicht überlebte, siehe z.B. Zysow, 2013, 42–49, 152–157.

[68] El Shamsy, 2008, 14; Krawietz, 2002, 347.

[69] Grundlegend, wenn auch vor allem für den deutschen Rechtskreis, Esser, 1972.

[70] Siehe auch Calder, 1993, 224.

[71] Al-Shāfiʿī, *Kitāb al-jimāʿ*, 98, § 439–441, ebenfalls in Al-Shāfiʿī, *Risāla*, 104.

[72] Bukhārī, *Kashr al-asrār*, Band 1, 84; Siehe auch Zysow, 2013, 176, Fn. 7.

lichkeit herangezogen werden, um die konkrete Gebetsrichtung festzulegen. So schreibt al-Shāfiʿī in seinem Werk *Kitāb jimāʿ al-ʿilm* („Gesamtheit [der Arten] des Wissens"):

> Wie ist Deine Meinung, wenn wir auf Reisen sind und uns dort nicht auf die Gebetsrichtung einigen können, und ich es für wahrscheinlich halte, sie sei dort, und die anderen, sie sei da. Was ist dann unsere Pflicht? Wenn Du antwortest: „[Die Richtung] der *Kaʿba* [zu suchen"], dann hast Du recht. Selbst wenn die *Kaʿba* an ihrem tatsächlichen Ort eindeutig zu erkennen ist, so ist sie doch für diejenigen verborgen, die weit von ihr sind. Sie haben die Pflicht, alle Anstrengung auf die Ermittlung der Richtung, in der sie liegt, zu unternehmen, und zwar so genau ihnen das möglich ist und bis sich in ihrem Herzen durch Nachweise die Überzeugung bildet, dass sie sie wahrscheinlich ermittelt haben. Wenn sie so vorgehen, sind ihnen unterschiedliche Lösungen gestattet, und jeder hat die ihm obliegende Pflicht erfüllt, indem er selbständig nach der Wahrheit suchte (arab. *ijtihād*), die ihm verborgen war.[73]

Die Ermittlung der Gebetsrichtung dient als Sinnbild für die Ermittlung formaler Normativität: Einiges ist deutlich bestimmbar und sichtbar wie die *Kaʿba* für diejenigen, die in Mekka selbst sind. Anderes ist nicht sichtbar und muss aus Nachweisen oder Hinweisen erschlossen werden. Für al-Shāfiʿī sind diese Nachweise/ Hinweise vor allem in den Überlieferungen über den Propheten zu finden, die, als detaillierte Rechtsquelle, weitestgehend die Nachweise/ Hinweise bieten, um den Koran rechtlich lesen zu können. Die *qiblā* Metapher galt nunmehr als theoretische Rahmung für die Frage nach der Möglichkeit der Rechtsfortbildung (*ijtihād*) und der verbindlichen Rechtsbefolgung von Rechtsmethodik und der Rechtsprechung (*taqlīd*).[74] Dabei ging es zentral darum, gerade bei unsicherem Wissen eine kollektive Grundlage des Rechts zu schaffen, auf die nachfolgendes Recht gestützt werden kann. Auch das wahrscheinliche Recht muss überführt werden in eine Grundlage, die per rechtswissenschaftlicher Konvention nutzbar ist (wenn schon nicht sicher).

Die Suche nach der richtigen Gebetsausrichtung zeigt, dass es 1) eine Wahrheit gibt, 2) dass verbürgte Nachweise auf diese Wahrheit hinweisen, 3) dass es dennoch eine andere wirksame und gültige Entscheidung geben kann und 4) dass ein gewisses Maß an juristischer Meinungsverschiedenheit möglich und akzeptabel ist. Diese Form des Realismus demonstriert, dass es eine empirische und rechtliche Wahrheit gibt, aber sie womöglich nicht erkannt werden kann, und damit juristische Entscheidungen fehlbar sein können.[75] Al-Shāfiʿī zeigt, dass die Nachweise nach der richtigen Gebetsrichtung zu unterschiedlichen Ergebnissen führen können. Die Bemühungen um die richtigen Auslegungen der Nachweise müssen daher keineswegs zu dem einen Weg und der einen Lösung führen.

---

[73] Al-Shāfiʿī, *Kitāb al-jimāʿ*, Abschnitte 439–441, S. 98. Übersetzung angelehnt an Nagel, 2001, 209.

[74] El Shamsy, 2008, 15.

[75] Zu Fehlbarkeit und Fehlerbewusstsein in der shāfiʿitischen Rechtsschule, siehe El Shamsy, 2008, 15.

Nicht zufällig kommt der Ausrichtung des Gebets eine Bedeutung *par excellence* weit über die Rechtswissenschaft auch in der Mathematik, Astronomie und Astrologie zu.[76] Diese Wissenschaften haben als Ausgangspunkt das Erkenntnisinteresse, sowohl die örtliche als auch die zeitliche Ausrichtung des Gebetes berechnen zu müssen sowie darüber hinaus auch die Berechnung der Mondmonate für die Pflichtrituale des Fastenmonats und der zeitlich festgelegten Pilgerfahrt durchführen zu können. Ein konkretes Ausgangsproblem für alle Muslime, unabhängig von Ort und Zeit, wird damit zum Sinnbild für zwei Ordnungen, der juristischen und der mathematischen. Nicht ein abstraktes Theoriebild, sondern eine Frage, die für gläubige Musliminnen und Muslime tagtäglich von hoher Bedeutung ist, um sachgerecht das Gebet als Rechtspflicht (*farḍ*) vollziehen zu können, wird zum bildlichen und konkreten Grundstein für die Herstellung von (Ableitungs-)Regeln und Ordnung in den Rechts- und mathematischen Wissenschaften.[77] Mit Blick auf diese rituellen Rechtspflichten lassen sich die formalen Regeln der Mathematik und des Rechts ganz offensichtlich zusammenführen. Das Suchen nach der Gebetsrichtung, vielleicht mehr noch als das korrekte Finden, wird hier Ausgangspunkt zweier formaler Ordnungen, der juristischen und der mathematischen.[78] Und die große Hilfe liegt in den Nachweisen/Hinweisen (*dalīl,* Plural *adilla*) die es zu finden gilt.[79] Die Frage nach der richtigen Gebetsrichtung wird im Weiteren von Bedeutung sein: Wie ist sie zu bestimmen und wie ist eine Unsicherheit ihrer Bestimmung im Recht einzubauen, wenn statt bestimmtem Wissen (*ʿilm qatʿī*) lediglich wahrscheinliches Wissen (*ʿilm ẓannī*) vorliegt. Sollte die Muslimin dann ihrer Rechtspflicht, dem Gebet, nicht nachkommen, oder mit lediglich wahrscheinlichem Wissen ihrer Rechtspflicht womöglich ungenügend nachkommen? Schließlich ist ein Gebet in der offensichtlich falschen Richtung fehlerhaft und damit unwirksam (*fāsid*).[80] Weiter gedacht heißt dies: Wird die mögliche Fehlerhaftigkeit der Entscheidung

---

[76] Spezifischer zur Gebetsausrichtung (*qibla*) in der Mathematik, siehe auch Schmidl, 2007, insb. I, 75–78, 260–275 mit Kommentar in II, 578–599 (Ibn Rahiq, Hedjaz, 11. Jahrhundert) und I, 342–359 mit Kommentar in II, 637–699 (al-Farisi, Jemen, 13. Jahrhundert). King, 1999, insb. Kap. 2 mit einer Übersicht. Grundlegendes findet sich auch in King, 1979; King, 1987. Zur Bestimmung der Qibla und verschiedene Fallstudien mit volksastronomischen Methoden, siehe Schmidl, 1997; Schmidl, 1999; Schmidl, 2000; Schmidl / Herrera-Casais, 2008.

[77] Das Gebet gilt, wie auch andere Rechtsrituale, beispielsweise die Waschung vor dem Gebet, als individuelle Rechtspflicht. Diese Pflicht ist jedoch nicht justiziabel. Allein vor Gott ist das Gebet rechenschaftspflichtig. Das Gebet selbst ist an mehreren Stellen im Koran verankert. Nicht im Koran festgelegt ist die Anzahl von fünf Pflichtgebeten, die eindeutig nur in der Sunna überliefert ist. Zur Herleitung der Anzahl der (fünf) Gebete am Tag, al-Shāfiʿī, *Risāla*, Abschnitt 1336–1342, S. 480–481; Lowry, 2007, 219–223.

[78] Anders im Beitrag von Guido Pfeifer in diesem Band, bei dem die Rechtsmetapher *iudex non calculat* keine Berührungspunkte zwischen der Rechts- und Mathematikwissenschaft offenbart.

[79] Das *qiblā* Problem wird von den muslimischen Juristen als Rechtsfindungsproblem, nicht als Rechtsanwendungsproblem diskutiert.

[80] In der muslimischen Jurisprudenz wurde zudem intensiv darüber debattiert, wie viele Gebetsbeugungen (*rakʿas*) pro fünfmaligen Gebet zu verrichten seien. Zu dieser Debatte Lowry, 2007, 219–223.

in Kauf genommen, wenn beispielsweise die Nachweise/Hinweise für die richtige Antwort fehlerhaft gelesen werden? Tatsächlich wurde die mangelnde Richtigkeitsgewähr bei der Bestimmung der Gebetsausrichtung nach Mekka zu einer der großen Debatten in der islamischen Rechtstheorie.[81] Für die Rechtswissenschaft führt al-Shāfiʿī zur Herausforderung der Bestimmung der Gebetsausrichtung aus, dass die Menschheit durchaus in der Lage sei, hier eine Lösung zu schaffen:

> Er [Gott] schaffte Zeichen für sie, schaffte die Heilige Moschee für sie und ordnete an, in ihre Blickrichtung zu beten. Wenn sie in diese Blickrichtung beten, dann tun sie dies aufgrund dieser Zeichen, die Er für sie schaffte und mit Hilfe des Verstands (*ʿuqūl*), welcher Er ihnen gab, damit sie ihn nutzen zum Ableiten von Informationen von diesen Zeichen (*istadallū bihā ʿalā maʿrifat al-ʿalāmāt)*.[82]

Hier liegt also eine Anweisung für den Umgang mit Unbestimmtheit im Recht: Gott hat den Muslimen die Instrumente mitgegeben, um die Richtung nach Mekka ausfindig zu machen. Ebenso hat er den Juristen erlaubt, eine Antwort zu finden auf ein ansonsten unreguliertes juristisches Problem und, zumindest potentiell, eine tatsächlich korrekte Lösung abzuleiten. Für al-Shāfiʿī zeigt dies, dass in Situationen, die weder der Koran noch die Sunna explizit klären, Gott eine Methode bereitstellt (Ableitung, *istidlāl*), ein Instrument (den Verstand, *ʿaql,* Plural *ʿuqūl*) und relevante Informationen (Zeichen, *ʿalamāt*) zur Verfügung stellt. Zusammen führen diese zur Antwort.[83]

Ausgehend von bestimmtem Wissen bedarf es verbindlicher Verfahrensfragen im Umgang mit Nachweisen bzw. Hinweisen (*dalīl, adillā*), um mit wahrscheinlichem Wissen umzugehen. Al-Shāfiʿī ist zuversichtlich, dass der Umgang mit den Nachweisen die Lösung bringt:

> Kein Ereignis widerfährt einem Angehörigen der Religion Gottes, ohne dass sich im Buch Gottes Nachweise (*dalīl*) für den Weg der Rechtleitung diesbezüglich finden. (*laysat tanzilu bi-aḥad min ahl dīn allāh nāzila illā wa-fī kitāb allāh al-dalīl ʿalā sabīl al-hudā fīhā*).[84]

Die Suche nach den Nachweisen ist damit zentral für die Rechtleitung, und letztlich Rechtsordnung. Diese Nachweise zu sichten bedeutet auch, Verfahren hierfür zu entwickeln, die Konsistenz und Verbindlichkeit herstellen können, also eine formale Ordnung ermöglichen.

Die Frage nach dem Verfahren entwickelte sich zu einer der großen Richtungsstreitigkeiten in der frühen islamischen Rechtsgeschichte. Die Nachweise in der Sunna als Worte und Taten des Propheten zu suchen (und diese nicht zu verkennen und anderweitig zu suchen, wie es vor allem die ḥanafitischen Juris-

---

[81] Krawietz, 2002, 347.

[82] Al-Shāfiʿī, *Risāla*, Abschnitt 114, S. 38, er nennt diese Zeichen der Erkennbarkeit bayān. Übersetzung ins Englische, Lowry, 2007, 32–33.

[83] Lowry, 2007, 33.

[84] Al-Shāfiʿī, *Risāla*, Abschnitt 48, S. 20, übersetzt ins Englische, Lowry, 2007, 33.

ten taten bzw. ihnen vorgeworfen wurde) wär für al-Shāfiʿī maßgeblich. Tatsächlich lag eine der Herausforderungen für die Herstellung einer formalen Ordnung unter anderem in der scharf geführten Auseinandersetzung zwischen den „Anhängern der Tradition“[85] (*ahl al-ḥadīth*) und den „Anhängern der freien Meinung“ (*ahl al-ra'y*), die begleitet wurde durch die erhöhte Verbreitung der Überlieferungen von Ḥadīthen und das allseits bekannte Auftreten von Ḥadīth-Fälschungen sowie der Frage nach der Rolle von Gewohnheiten in der Rechtsordnung.[86]

Die Spannungslage zwischen den „Anhängern der Tradition“ und den „Anhängern der freien Meinung“ ist bezeichnend für das Streben nach einer formalen Rechtsordnung, wie auch für das Rechtsbewusstsein, dass das Postulat von Kohärenz und Konsistenz ganz maßgeblich von Authentifizierung wie auch Hierarchisierung geprägt sowie gefährdet ist. Für die „Anhänger der Tradition“ ging es darum, sich so eng wie möglich an den Bestand der übermittelten Tradition (über den Propheten und seine frühen Gefährten, *ṣaḥāba*) zu halten, und ihm Vorrang vor der freien Meinung (*ra'y*) zu geben, auch wenn die Authentizität der Tradition nicht gänzlich gesichert war, also auch wenn die Tradition nicht weit verbreitet war. Diese Vertreter waren zunächst und mit wachsendem Ruhm der Schule von Medina zuzuordnen. Sie standen den Anhängern der freien Meinung gegenüber, die dem Vorrang der Tradition nicht uneingeschränkt folgten, was womöglich auch damit zusammenhing, dass die überlieferten Traditionen (*Sunna*) nicht überall zeitgleich verbreitet wurden.[87] Daher mussten andere Rechtsüberlegungen angestellt werden, so wie sie für die Lernzirkel (den Vorläufern der Schulen) im Irak, insbesondere in Kufa, prominent wurden, darunter v.a. der Rückgriff auf die freie Meinung (*ra'y*). Hier wurde vertreten, dass die Bestimmungen des Offenbarungsrechts in ihrer Bedeutung rational zu erfassen sind, da sie auf den Menschen zu Gute kommenden, allgemeinen Interessen (*maṣāliḥ*) aufbauen und sich in einer jeweils nachvollziehbaren *ratio legis* ausdrücken, mit der Folge, dass widersprüchliche Ḥadīthe gelegentlich zurückgewiesen wurden. Häufig wiesen sie singuläre Traditionen (*akhbār āḥād*) zurück und gaben der Analogie (*qiyās*) ihnen gegenüber den Vorzug.[88] Es ist wichtig hervorzuheben, dass diese dogmatischen Positionen nicht als strenge Gegensätze gedacht wurden. Unter den Anhängern der Ḥadīthe gab es sicherlich auch solche, die sich des *ra'y* bedienten und umgekehrt unter den Irakern auch solche, die ihn ablehnten und sich enger am Ḥadīth orientierten.[89] Wichtig ist jedoch Folgendes: Die Rolle der Ḥadīthe für die Herausbildung einer formalen Rechtsordnung ist von enormer Bedeutung. Um dieser gerecht zu werden, wurde die

---

[85] Die Anhänger hier als Traditionalisten zu bezeichnen ist problematisch, wenn auch zur Konvention geworden aus der Übersetzung von Ḥadīth als „Tradition“ nicht weil die Ḥadīthe selbst eine Tradition etabliert hätten., Melchert, 1997, 2. Kritisch auch zur starren Gegenüberstellung in „Anhänger der Tradition“ und „Anhänger der freien Meinung“, weil die ersteren durchaus auch innovative Rechtsfortbildung betrieben und die letzteren ihre Rechtsmeinungen auch auf Hadithe stützten, Melchert, 1997, 2–7.

[86] Krawietz, 2002, 49.

[87] Krawietz, 2002, 51 mit Bezug zu Al-Ashqar, 1990, 77.

[88] Krawietz, 2002, 52.

[89] Krawietz , 2002, 53 mit weiteren Nachweisen.

Authentifizierung („Ist die Überlieferungskette glaubhaft und ihre Überlieferer glaubwürdig?") zu einer grundlegenden wissenschaftlichen Aufgabe, die sich auch ergänzender oder alternativer Überprüfungsmittel bediente.[90]

Besonderer Streitpunkt war, ob Normativität erzeugt werden darf, gestützt auf Hadith-Material, das nur über einen singulären Tradenten-Strang überliefert war (*khabar wāhid* bzw *ḥadīth āḥādī*), selbst wenn es von der Überlieferungsqualität her als korrekt (*saḥīḥ*) oder gut (*ḥasan*), oder gar schwach (*daʿīf*) eingestuft worden war? Ist die allgemeine Verbreitung (*shuhra*), wie dies Abū Ḥanīfa verlangte, eine Bedingung? Der bedeutende ḥanafitische Jurist Abū Yūsuf (gestorben 182/798 in Baghdad, Irak) sowie ein Großteil der ḥanafitischen Anhänger ließen besondere Strenge bei der Anerkennung von Ḥadīthen walten und akzeptierten sie nur, wenn sie ununterbrochen (*mutawātir)* oder zumindest weitverbreitet (*mashhūr)* waren.[91] Die Strenge in der Akzeptanz eines Ḥadīth führte dazu, dass ein fehlerhafter Ḥadīth sonst als Rechtsgrundlage ausschied und stattdessen die freie Meinung, an Gemeinwohlinteressen orientiert, als Quelle der Rechtsfindung Platz fand. Darf Analogie gegenüber dem Ḥadīth bevorzugt bzw. ihr der Vorzug gegeben werden gegenüber singulären Traditionen, wie Abū Yūsuf vorgeworfen wurde?[92]

Dies ist für al-Shāfiʿi eine Frage der Methode und damit auch, wieviel Raum für Interessen in einem göttlichen Recht, vermittelt durch den Propheten, eröffnet werden darf. Hier war al-Shāfiʿi eindeutig: „Wer vom Gesandten übernimmt, der übernimmt von Gott [selbst]."[93] D.h. auch eine formale Ordnung, die sich auf Gott bezieht, muss eng an den Ḥadīthen ausgerichtet sein. Auch folgendes Zitat zeigt, dass keine Beliebigkeit im Umgang mit Überlieferungen vorherrschen darf:

> Ich sagte zu einem [Diskutanten]: „Bedenke Deine Aussage, dass der Konsens (*ijmāʿ*)[94] auf [das Richtige] verweist! Wenn man Dir entgegenhält: ‚Zu dem, was wir vertreten, sei es einhellig, sei es mit unterschiedlichen Auffassungen, gehören [einerseits Fälle], in denen wir eine Überlieferung billigen, und [andererseits Fälle], in denen nach unserer Ansicht etwas [der Überlieferung] Gleichwertiges [als richtig] erwiesen ist, das von unseren Vorgängern stammt. Wir sind uns darüber einig, dass, sofern weder ein autoritativer Text noch eine Norm der Sunna gegeben sind, es erlaubt ist, einen Fall mit einem Analogieschluss (*qiyās*) zu lösen, selbst wenn dieser zu keiner einhelligen Ansicht führt', willst Du dann einmal die Nachrichten von [den Vorgängern] für ungültig erklären, deren Nachrichten und deren übereinstimmende Handlung nach Deiner Aussage beweiskräftig sind, ein anderes Mal sie aber bestätigen?' Bedenke auch, wie du antworten könntest, wenn jemand dir sagte: ‚Ich folge [den Vorgän-

[90] Brown, 2008, 150.
[91] Zur Diskussion der Ḥadīthe bei den Ḥanafiten, siehe Krawietz, 2002, 63–65.
[92] Krawietz, 2002, 65.
[93] Al-Shāfʿī, *Risāla*, Abschnitt 1309, S. 471.
[94] Womöglich ist hier der Konsens der zeitgenössischen Rechtsgelehrten gemeint, Al-Shāfʿī, *Risāla*, Abschnitt 351–355, S. 119–120.

gern], indem ich die Nachrichten des Zuverlässigen [über jene für richtig erkläre], selbst wenn es sich um Einzelberichte (*khabar wāhid*) handelt, und ich akzeptiere von [den Vorgängern] Analogieschlüsse in Fragen, über die keine Nachricht etwas aussagt, und gestehe zu, dass [die Vorgänger] dabei unterschiedliche Ergebnisse erzielten, in jedem Fall bin ich dann ihnen gefolgt', hat dieser dann nicht ein gewichtigeres Argument, kann er [nicht] behaupten, dass er den [Vorgängern] folge, lobt er sie [nicht] in schönerer Weise als du?"

„Diese Meinung also vertrittst Du?" „Ja!" bestätigte ich.[95]

Für al-Shāfiʿī stand fest, dass sich in den Überlieferungen der Nachweise in der Sunna zwar Fehler und Irrtümer eingeschlichen haben könnten, aber allein wegen dieser Möglichkeit dürfe man die Sunna nicht als Rechtsquelle ablehnen.[96] Al-Shāfiʿī war skeptisch, ob es den Juristen gelingen würde, die Überlieferungen einmal für gültig und einmal für ungültig zu erklären, und ob nicht doch eine Unsicherheit in der Methodik der Jurisprudenz bliebe, die einer formalen Ordnung im Wege stünde. Eine absolute Sicherheit würde niemals zu erreichen sein. Gesichtete Fehler in den Überlieferungen der Sunna gäben vielmehr Anlass, nach Nachweisen zu suchen, mit denen mit einem Analogieschluss das jeweilige Problem gelöst werden könne.[97] Dies verstand al-Shāfiʿī als einzig mögliche Rechtsfortbildung (*ijtihād*).

In dem Mühen um Rechtserkenntnis aus dem Formalen des Rechts selbst, und ohne Verweise auf andere Erkenntnismöglichkeiten, erklärt Kelsen seine reine Rechtslehre ähnlich:

> Wenn sie [d.h. diese Theorie] sich als „reine" Lehre vom Recht bezeichnet, so darum, weil sie nur eine auf das Recht gerichtete Erkenntnis sicherstellen und weil sie aus dieser Erkenntnis alles ausscheiden möchte, was nicht zu dem exakt als Recht bestimmten Gegenstand gehört. Das heißt: sie will die Rechtswissenschaft von allen ihr fremden Elementen befreien … In völlig kritikloser Weise hat sich Jurisprudenz mit Psychologie und Soziologie, mit Ethik und politischer Theorie vermengt.[98]

Für Kelsen hieß dies, dass das Recht nicht nach inhaltlich richtigem Recht suchen sollte, sondern nach den *erkennbaren* Formalelementen des Rechts.[99] Auch für al-Shāfiʿī war zentral die Erkennbarkeit, die Nachweise des Rechts, um eine formal einwandfreie Überlieferungskette in das Recht einzubeziehen bzw. Recht durch enge Nachweise mit Hilfe des Analogieschluss zu generieren. Hierzu sollte alles, was mit dem Propheten verknüpft werden kann, Teil des Rechts werden, als käme es von Gott selbst.

Al-Shāfiʿī ging es hier, wie Kelsen, um den Erzeugungsprozess von Recht. Es soll Recht sein, wenn die Erzeugung des Rechts in Ordnung war, also formalen Kriterien des Rechts entspricht. Hier sollte es keine Beliebigkeit geben: Bei

[95] Al-Shāfiʿī, *Risāla*, Abschnitt1309, S. 471. Übersetzung angelehnt an Nagel, 2001, 211.
[96] Al-Shāfiʿī, *Kitāb al-jimāʿ*, Abschnitt 317–319, S. 80.
[97] Al-Shāfiʿī, *Kitāb al-jimāʿ*, Abschnitt 105–109, S. 33.
[98] Kelsen, 1960, 1.
[99] Naucke, 2005, 207.

aller Unbestimmtheit, die ein Einzelbericht aufweist, erzeuge dieser nichtsdestotrotz Normativität.[100] Ähnlich ging es Kelsen um die Erzeugung des Rechts, nicht um den Inhalt. Damit Recht verbindlich sein konnte, musste man laut Kelsen nach der Norm fragen, die Erzeugung des Rechtssatzes zuließ, der Grundnorm also:

> … die vorausgesetzte Grundnorm [beinhaltet] nichts anderes als die Einsetzung eines normerzeugenden Tatbestandes, die Ermächtigung einer normsetzenden Autorität oder – was dasselbe bedeutet – eine Regel, die bestimmt, wie die generellen und individuellen Normen der auf dieser Grundnorm beruhenden Ordnung erzeugt werden sollen.[101]

Al-Shāfiʿī begreift das Recht als ein Korpus von Normen, die teils sichtbar und bestimmt (*qaṭʿī*), teils verborgen und wahrscheinlich (*ẓannī*) sind, der jedoch auch in den verborgenen Teilen möglichst genau befolgt werden muss. Daher könne einer Überlieferung, auch wenn sie vielfach nur von wenigen Personen bezeugt wird, nicht Normativität abgesprochen werden. Denn immerhin enthält auch die schwach bezeugte Überlieferung nützliche Hinweise auf die Art und Weise, in der die Juristen der frühen islamischen Geschichte Aufschluss über den verborgenen Teil des Gesetzes suchten.

Vergleichbar formal sieht es Kelsen:

> Fragt man nach dem Geltungsgrund einer zu einer bestimmten Rechtsordnung gehörenden Rechtsnorm, kann die Antwort nur in der Zurückführung auf die Grundnorm dieser Rechtsordnung, das heisst: in der Aussage bestehen, daß diese Norm der Grundnorm gemäß erzeugt wurde.[102]

Das Zurückführen auf die Grundnorm sieht al-Shāfiʿī im Zurückführen auf die Gemeinschaft, so sie doch eng an der Überlieferung festhält:

> Wer sagt, was die Gemeinschaft der Muslime sagt, der hält an ihrer Gemeinschaft fest. Wer dem widerspricht, was die Gemeinschaft sagt, der stellt sich gegen die Gemeinschaft, an der festzuhalten doch befohlen wurde [von Gott]. Fehler unterlaufen, wenn man sich spaltet. Der Gemeinschaft aber in ihrer Gesamtheit kann nie ein Fehler gegen eine Aussage des Korans, der Sunna oder einer Analogie unterlaufen, so Gott will.[103]

„Meine Gemeinschaft einigt sich nicht auf [Grundlage eines] Fehler[s].“[104] Gleichwohl diese Aussage als schwach (*daʿīf*) eingestuft wird, wird sie herangezogen, um zu überlegen, wie mit Unbestimmtem im Recht umgegangen wird, dabei ist der Gemeinschaft (*taqlīd*) zu folgen, auch wenn diese sich nicht alleine über eine Mehrheit konstituiert. Die Unfehlbarkeit der Gemeinschaft entspringt dem Fehlerbewusstsein. Die gelehrte Gemeinschaft kann zwar keine Sicherheit

---

[100] Al-Shāfiʿī, *Risāla*, Abschnitt 1051–1052, S. 384.
[101] Kelsen, 1960, 199.
[102] Kelsen, 1960, 202.
[103] Al-Shāfiʿī, *Risāla*, Abschnitt 1320, S. 475–476.
[104] Al-Tirmidhī, *Sunan al-Tirmidhī*, 466, Rn. 2167.

herstellen, aber doch eine Konvention begründen. Sie ist ein Versuch, die potentielle Fehlbarkeit von Quelle und Methodik durch die rechtswissenschaftlichen Methoden von Analogie und Konsens als Methode zu erheben.

Text ist wichtig für formale Ordnung, aber er allein reicht nicht. Al-Shāfiʿī wollte nicht, dass die Gemeinschaft den Text ersetzt, aber er hat auch erkannt, dass Text allein nicht ausreicht, auch wenn ausgeschlossen werden sollte, dass ohne oder gar gegen Textteile das Recht fortgeschrieben werden sollte. Für die muslimischen Juristen des 3./9. Jahrhunderts stellte sich letztlich bei der islamischen formalen Ordnung die Frage, wo die Grenzen der Analogie (*qiyās*) und Rechtsfortbildung (*ijtihād*) verliefen. Das Bewusstsein dafür, dass formale Ordnung nicht allein durch autoritativen Text hergestellt werden kann, machte die muslimischen Juristen sehr empfänglich für die Chancen und Grenzen menschlichen Räsonierens, das je nach Rechtsschule weiter oder enger, vor allem aber um die Methodik der Analogie (*qiyās*) diskutiert wurde – und das immer mit einem Fehlerbewusstsein einherging.[105] Des Weiteren wurde diskutiert, dass der Konsens (*ijmāʿ*) ein formales Mittel sein kann, um mit Unbestimmtheit im Text umzugehen, aber nicht, um Unbestimmtheit letztlich zu überwinden. Durch Konsens wird nicht Unbestimmtheit aufgelöst und in Bestimmtheit umgewandelt.

Letztlich haben die Juristen hier einen pragmatischen Standpunkt gefunden. Der Jurist und die Juristin schulden nicht mehr als das redliche Bemühen um das richtige Ergebnis: *Kullu mujtahid muṣīb* [106], „Wer Recht spricht, hat Recht“[107] oder „Jeder sich Mühende handelt richtig“.[108] Nach einer Überlieferung des Propheten soll der, dem auf der Suche nach Rechtsfindung das Richtige findet, zwei Löhne erhalten – derjenige dem dabei Fehler entstehen, erhalte dennoch für sein Bemühen einen Lohn.[109] Wahrscheinlichkeit als Plausibilität[110] sorgte für die genügende Stabilität im formalen System. Dort wo Bestimmtheit und Wahrscheinlichkeit festzulegen sind, dort herrscht auch die Möglichkeit der Fehler vor. Ein System, das die Kategorien von Bestimmtheit und Wahrscheinlichkeit zulässt, eröffnet einen weiten Beschäftigungsraum mit der Epistemologie des Wissens, und arbeitet mit einer Bewusstheit für Fehler, bei gleichzeitigem Anspruch auf Kohärenz. Bei Kelsen sollte die formale Struktur vor der Politisierung des Rechts schützen, bei al-Shāfiʿī sollte die formale Struktur vor der Vermenschlichung des Göttlichen schützen, und damit ebenfalls vor der Politisierung.

4. Von formal zu formalistisch?

Es blieb nicht aus, dass die große Vorliebe für Beschäftigung mit der Authentizität der Überlieferungen dazu führte, dass die Beschäftigung mit dem Inhalt gelegentlich zu kurz kam, oder man gar „formalistisch“ wurde, was jedoch auch

[105] Für das Fehlerbewusstsein der Richterschaft, Rebstock, 1999, 1–37.
[106] Van Ess, 1992, 153, 161: Man müsste also genauer übersetzen, „Wo immer jemand ein selbstständiges Urteil fällt, trifft er etwas Richtiges.“ Siehe auch Krawietz, 2002, 327ff; Johansen, 1999, insbes. 35 ff.
[107] In der Übersetzung von van Ess, 1992, 153, 161.
[108] In der Übersetzung von Rohe, 2009, 31.
[109] Zitiert bei Al-Shāfiʿī, *Risāla*, Abschnitt 1409, S. 494.
[110] Ich danke Hagan Brunke für diesen wertvollen Hinweis.

schon im 3.–4./9.–10. Jahrhundert kritisiert wurde.[111] Form schützte in diesen Fällen dann eben doch nicht vor Politisierung. Als Beispiel dient folgende Überlieferung, die auf den Propheten zurückgeführt wird: „Niemals wird das Volk zu Wohlstand gelangen, das seine Geschäfte einer Frau anvertraut!“ (*lam yafla*ḥ *qawmun wallaw ʿamruhum imra'a*). Prominent hat sich Fatima Mernissi mit dem „Werdegang“ dieser Überlieferung auseinandersetzt.[112] Dieser frauenfeindliche Ḥadīth, der in den kanonischen Ḥadīthsammlungen von al-Bukhārī (gestorben 256/870)[113] als *ṣaḥīḥ* (korrekt) gilt, wurde dennoch von Juristen wegen seines Inhalts kontrovers diskutiert und kritisch bis zum Teil ablehnend betrachtet.[114] Die Juristen konnten sich nicht über die Bedeutung einigen, die sie diesem Ḥadīth über die Frauen und die Politik beimessen sollten. Während einige die formal korrekte Erzeugung des Ḥadīth dazu brachte, Frauen von der politischen Entscheidungsgewalt auszuschließen, gab es auch andere, die dieses Argument (mit Blick auch auf die Rolle der frühen Frauen im Islam bzw. der unruhigen politischen Epoche der Entstehung des Ḥadīth) nicht stichhaltig und inhaltlich wenig überzeugend fanden. Dokumentiert wurde, dass auch solche Autoritäten wie Ṭabarī (gestorben 310/923, Bagdad, Irak) gegen den Ḥadīth Position bezogen. [115] Denn er fand, dass dieser Ḥadīth keine ausreichende Basis dafür stellte, um Frauen das Recht auf Teilhabe an Entscheidungen vorzuenthalten und ihren Ausschluss aus der Politik zu rechtfertigen. Die Kritik, dass das Formale zum Formalistischen werden kann, und damit gesellschaftliche Wirklichkeiten ausblende bzw. auch gesellschaftliche, politische, und ökonomische Notwendigkeiten der Veränderung zugunsten der Stabilisierung des Rechts(-apparats) hemme, hat auch Kelsens Reine Rechtslehre getroffen, dem eine „Entstofflichung und Entleerung“ des Rechts vorgeworfen wurde.[116] Damit bleibt die feine Linie zwischen den Vorteilen der formalen Lehre und den Lasten des formalistischen Rechts noch heute neuralgisch.

5. Schlussfolgerung

Die islamische Rechtsordnung ist ihrem Anspruch nach universell. Trotz – oder genau wegen – des universellen, göttlich untermauerten Anspruchs unterscheidet die islamische Rechtswissenschaft seit dem 3./9. Jahrhundert zwischen bestimmtem Wissen (*qaṭʿī*) und wahrscheinlichem Wissen (*ẓannī*) sowohl mit Bezug auf die Quellen als auch mit Bezug auf die Methoden des Rechts. Neben dem Aufbau einer formalen Ordnung kann auch das Fehlerbewusstsein als maßgeblich für das islamische Rechtsverständnis betrachtet werden. Das Fehlerbewusstsein gehörte nicht zu den Teilen der formalen Ordnung, die von den Juristen lamentiert wurden.[117] Anders als das akute Bewusstsein um Fehler und

---

[111] Brown, 2008.

[112] Mernissi, 1989, 49–61.

[113] Bukhārī, 1978, 226.

[114] Zu den einzelnen Positionen, siehe Ibn Ḥajar al-Asqalānī, Bd. XIII, 45–47; Mernissi, 1987, 61.

[115] Ibn Ḥajar al-Asqalānī, ohne Datum, 47.

[116] Zur Kritik der Reinen Rechtslehre siehe, Dreier, 1990, 519 ff.

[117] Lorraine Daston beschreibt, wie für die europäischen (Natur-)Wissenschaftler des 18. Jahrhunderts die Konfrontation mit grundlegenden Fehlern eine Epoche des Trauerns war. „For them, their epoch was one of grievous errors revealed as much as one of new

Fehlbarkeit, das seit dem 18. Jahrhundert als Errungenschaft der modernen europäischen Epistemologie gilt[118], gehörte diese Erkenntnis zu den Grundlagen des islamischen Ordnungsdenkens. Dies zeigt die Rechtsmetapher um die Gebetsausrichtung, *qibla*. Doch ist diese Rechtsmetapher für die Herausbildung der formalen Ordnung zu hinterfragen: Ergänzt es oder ersetzt es eine Argumentation[119], ob das Formale tatsächlich zu einem Erkennen des reineren oder göttlich sanktionierten Rechts verhilft? Während nicht in Zweifel gezogen werden kann, dass es Mekka und die dortige Heilige Moschee (*kaʿba*) tatsächlich gibt, besteht doch Anspannung darüber, ob, und wenn ja wo, es ein von Gott bestätigtes Recht gibt.[120] Gilt eine solche Frage auch für die Mathematik? Belastet das mathematisch-astronomisch-astrologische Vorgehen auch die Frage, ob es eine göttlich sanktionierte richtige Version gibt und ob diese jemals vollständig zur Kenntnis gebracht werden kann? Vielleicht liegt auch hier eine Gemeinsamkeit, nämlich die Orientierung an der praktischen Entscheidung und Rechtsgewinnung im Einzelfall.[121] Normativität kann, sie muss auf sozial-pragmatischer Ebene operieren.[122] Denn die Sicherheit, dass sich die ermittelte Entscheidung mit Gottes Willen deckt, wird nie gegeben sein, gleichwohl darf die Suche danach nicht aufgegeben werden[123] und wird im gemeinsamen Ringen einer Rechtsgemeinschaft erstritten: Ein Glücksfall für die Jurisprudenz und Demut und Ansporn für die Wissenschaft.

Literaturverzeichnis

Arabischsprachige Werke (Quellen und Editionen)

Bukhārī, ʿAbd al-ʿAzīz b. Aḥmad. 1394/1974. *Kashr al-asrār 'an uṣūl Fajhr al-Islām al-Bazdawī.* Istanbul. Neudruck Beirut: Dār al-kitāb al-ʿarabī. (4 Bände).

Bukhārī, Muḥammad b. Ismāʿīl, 1978. *Saḥīḥ* (Sammlung kanonischer Hadithe Band 4). Beirut: Dar al-Maʿrifa.

Ibn Muqaffa, ʿAbd Allāh, *al-Adab al-ṣaghīr wa'l-adab al-kabīr wa risālat al-ṣaḥabah.* Herausgegeben von Charles Pellat, 1976. *Ibn al-Muqaffa' (mort vers 140/757), "conseiller" du calife.* Paris: Maisonneuve et Larose.

Al-Shāfiʿī, Muḥammad ibn Idrīs, *Al-Risāla.* Būlāq: al-Maṭbaʿa al-Kubrā al-Amīrya, 1321 A.H. Herausgegeben von Aḥmad Muḥammad Shākir, 1940. Kairo: al-Ḥalabī.

Al-Shāfiʿī, Muḥammad ibn Idrīs, *Kitāb al-jimāʿ.* Herausgegeben von Aḥmad Muḥammad Shākir, 1940. Kairo: Matbaʿa al-Maʿārif.

knowledge discovered", Vortrag vom 8. Februar 2016 „Before Scientific Revolutions: Error and the Fear of Error" im Rahmen der Vorlesungsreihe „Errands" 2015–2016, https://www.ici-berlin.org/events/lorraine-daston-scientific-revolutions/.

[118] Ibid. „This acute consciousness of error and fallibility stamped modern epistemology ever since".

[119] Zu Leitbildern, die die Argumentation ersetzen, siehe Baer, 2004, 223, (249 f).

[120] Krawietz, 2002, 348.

[121] Krawietz, 2002, 349.

[122] Markus Asper in diesem Band.

[123] Calder, 1993, 243.

Al-Tirmidhī, Abū ʿĪsā Muḥammad ibn ʿĪsā as-Sulamī aḍ-Ḍarīr al-Būghī, *Sunan al-Tirmidhī* Babd 4. Herausgegeben von Atwa Ibrahim Awad. 1977. Beirut: Kitāb al-Fitan.

Sekundärliteratur

Achterberg, Norbert, 1978. *Der Einfluß der Reinen Rechtslehre auf die Rechtstheorie in verschiedenen Ländern* (Schriftenreihe des Hans Kelsen Instituts 2). Wien: Manz.

Al-Ashqar, Muḥammad Sulaymān 1990. *Tārīkh al-fiqh al-islāmī.* Blida, Algerien: Qaṣr al-Kitāb.

Asper, Markus, 2012. „‚True' and ‚False' Errors in Ancient (Greek) Computation". In Klaus Geus / Mark Geller (Hg.) *Productive Errors: Scientific Concepts in Antiquity* (Max Planck Institute for the History of Science. Preprint 430). Berlin: Max-Planck-Institut für Wissenschaftsgeschichte, 47–66.

Assmann, Jan, 2013. *Das kulturelle Gedächtnis. Schrift, Erinnerung und politische Identität in frühen Hochkulturen.* München: Beck.

Baer, Susanne, 2004. „Schlüsselbegriffe, Typen und Leitbilder". In: Eberhard Schmidt-Assmann / Wolfgang Hoffmann-Riem (Hg.) *Methoden der Verwaltungsrechtswissenschaft.* Baden-Baden: Nomos, 223–251.

— 2017. *Rechtssoziologie – Eine Einführung in die interdisziplinäre Rechtsforschung.* Baden-Baden: Nomos. (3. Auflage).

Bobzin, Hartmut, 2010. *Der Koran, Übersetzung.* München: Beck.

Brown, Jonathan A. C, 2008. „How we know early Hadīth Critics did *Matn* Criticism and why it's so hard to find". *Islamic Law and Society* 15/2, 143–184.

Brunke, Hagan, 2012. „On Mesopotamian Measure Theory". In Klaus Geus / Mark Geller (Hg.) *Productive Errors: Scientific Concepts in Antiquity* (Max Planck Institute for the History of Science. Preprint 430). Berlin: Max-Planck-Institut für Wissenschaftsgeschichte, 9–22.

Burton, John, 1977. *Collections of the Qur'ān.* Cambridge: Cambridge University Press.

— 2006. „Collection of the Qur'ān". In: Jane D. McAuliffe (Hg.) *The Encyclopaedia of the Qur'ān* 6. Leiden: Brill, 351–361.

Calder, Norman, 1993. *Studies in Early Muslim Jurisprudence.* Oxford: Clarendon Press.

Coulson, Noel J., 1964. *A History of Islamic law.* Edinburgh: University Press.

Crone, Patricia, 1980. *Slaves on Horses: the Evolution of the Islamic Polity.* Cambridge: Cambridge University Press.

Daston, Lorraine, 2001. „The Historicity of Science". In: Glenn W. Most (Hg.) *Historicization – Historisierung.* Göttingen: Vandenhoeck & Ruprecht, 201–221.

Dreier, Horst, 1990. *Rechtslehre, Staatssoziologie und Demokratie bei Hans Kelsen.* Baden-Baden: Nomos. (2. Auflage).

Ess, Josef van, 1992. *Theologie und Gesellschaft im 2. und 3. Jahrhundert Hidschra* Band 2. Berlin: Walter de Gruyter.

Esser, Josef, 1972. *Vorverständnis und Methodenwahl in der Rechtsfindung – Rationalitätsgrundlagen richterlicher Entscheidungspraxis*. Frankfurt a. M.: Athenäum-Fischer-Taschenbucherlag. (2. Auflage).

Funke, Andreas, 2004. *Allgemeine Rechtslehre als juristische Strukturtheorie: Entwicklung und gegenwärtige Bedeutung der Rechtstheorie um 1900*. Tübingen: Mohr Siebeck.

Grimm, Dieter (Hg.), 1976. *Rechtswissenschaft und Nachbarwissenschaften*. München: Beck. (2 Bände; 2. unveränderte Auflage).

Gutas, Dimitri, 1998. *Greek Thought, Arabic Culture. The Graeco-Arabic Translation Movement in Baghdad and Early 'Abbāsid Society (2nd–4th/ 8th–10th centuries)*. London: Routledge.

Hallaq, Wael B., 1993. „Was al-Shāfiʿī the Master Architect of Islamic Jurisprudence?“. *International Journal of Middle East Studies* 25/4, 587–605.

— 2005. *The Origins and Evolution of Islamic Law*. Cambridge: Cambridge University Press.

Ibn Ḥajar al-ʿAsqalānī, ohne Datum, *Fath al-Bārī bi Sharḥ Saḥīḥ Imām al-Bukhārī* Band 13. Kairo: al-Matbaʿa al-Bāhiya.

Jestaedt, Matthias, 2000. „Wie das Recht, so die Auslegung. Die Rolle der Rechtstheorie bei der Suche nach der juristischen Auslegungslehre“. *Zeitschrift für Öffentliches Recht* 55, 133–158.

— (Hg.), 2008. *Reine Rechtslehre: Einleitung in die rechtswissenschaftliche Problematik; Studienausgabe von Hans Kelsen der 1. Auflage von 1934. Herausgegeben und eingeleitet von Matthias Jestaedt*. Tübingen: Mohr Siebeck.

Jestaedt, Matthias, (Hg.) 2017. *Reine Rechtslehre. Mit einem Anhang: Das Problem der Gerechtigkeit, von Hans Kelsen. Studienausgabe der 2. Auflage 1960, unter Berücksichtigung von Kelsens Änderungen anlässlich der Übersetzungen ins Italienische 1966 herausgegeben und eingeleitet von Matthias Jestaedt*. Tübingen: Mohr Siebeck / Wien: Verlag Österreich.

Johansen, Baber, 1977. „Zum Prozessrecht der *uqubat*“. *Zeitschrift der Deutschen Morgenländischen Gesellschaft* Supplement III/1, 477–486.

— 1999. *Contingency in a Sacred Law: Legal and Ethical Norms in the Muslim Fiqh* (Studies in Islamic Law and Society 7). Leiden: Brill.

Kant, Immanuel, 1785. *Grundlegung der Metaphysik der Sitten,* Akademieausgabe Band 6.
https://korpora.zim.uni-duisburg-essen.de/Kant/aa06/230.html

Kelsen, Hans, 1922. *Der soziologische und der juristische Staatsbegriff: kritische Untersuchung des Verhältnisses von Staat und Recht*. Tübingen: Mohr. (1. Auflage).

— 1928. *Der soziologische und der juristische Staatsbegriff: kritische Untersuchung des Verhältnisses von Staat und Recht*. Tübingen: Mohr. (2. Auflage).

— 1934. *Reine Rechtslehre*. Leipzig: Deuticke. (1. Auflage).

— 1960. *Reine Rechtslehre*. Wien: Deuticke. (2. Auflage).

— 1979. *Allgemeine Theorie der Normen*. Kurt Ringhofer, / Robert Walter (Hg.) Im Auftrag des Kelsen Instituts aus dem Nachlass. Wien: Manz.

Kennedy, Hugh, 1981. *The Early Abbasid Caliphate: A Political History*. London/Totowa: Croom Helm/Barnes and Noble.

King, David A., 1979, „Kibla“. In: Peri J. Bearman, Thierry Bianquis, Clifford E. Bosworth, Emeri J. van Donzel, Wolfhart P. Heinrichs (Hg.) *The Encyclopaedia of Islam* 5. Leiden: Brill, 82–88.

— 1987. „Makka. iv. As centre of the world“. In: Peri J. Bearman, Thierry Bianquis, Clifford E. Bosworth, Emeri J. van Donzel, Wolfhart P. Heinrichs (Hg.) *The Encyclopaedia of Islam* 6. Leiden: Brill, 180–187. (2. Auflage).

— 1999. *World-Maps for Finding the Direction and Distance to Mecca – Innovation and Tradition in Islamic Science* (Islamic Philosophy, Theology and Science 36). Leiden: Brill.

Krawietz, Birgit, 2002. *Hierarchie der Rechtsquellen im tradierten sunnitischen Islam* (Schriften zur Rechtstheorie, Heft 208). Berlin: Duncker & Humblot.

Lembke, Ulrike, 2009. *Einheit aus Erkenntnis? – Zur Unzulässigkeit der verfassungskonformen Gesetzesauslegung als Methode der Normkompatibilisierung durch Interpretation* (Schriften zum öffentlichen Recht 1118). Berlin: Duncker & Humblot.

Lowry, Joseph E., 2007. *Early Islamic Legal Theory, The Risāla of Muḥammad ibn Idrīs al-Shāfiʿī* (Studies in Islamic Law and Society Vol. 30). Leiden: Brill.

Melchert, Christopher, 1997. *The Formation of the Sunni Schools of Law, 9th–10th Centuries C.E.* Leiden/New York: Brill.

Mernissi, Fatima, 1987. *The Veil and the Male Elite, A Feminist Interpretation of Women's Rights in Islam*, New York: Perseus Books. (1989 übersetzt ins Deutsche als *Der politische Harem – Mohammad und die Frauen*. Frankfurt/Main: Dağyeli. (1. Auflage).

Merkl, Adolf, 1923. *Die Lehre von der Rechtskraft entwickelt aus dem Rechtsbegriff – Eine rechtstheoretische Untersuchung* (Wiener staatswissenschaftliche Studien Bd. 15/2). Leipzig: Deuticke.

Motzki, Harald, 1991. *Die Anfänge der islamischen Jurisprudenz: Ihre Entwicklung in Mekka bis zur Mitte des 2./8. Jahrhunderts* (Abhandlungen für die Kunde des Morgenlandes 50/2). Stuttgart: Franz Steiner Verlag.

— 2001. *The Origins of Islamic Jurisprudence, Meccan Fiqh before the Classical Schools* (Islamic History and Civilisation 41). Leiden / Boston / Köln: Brill.

Nagel, Tilman, 2001. *Das islamische Recht: Eine Einführung*. Westhofen: WVA-Verlag.

Naucke, Wolfgang, 2005. *Rechtsphilosophische Grundbegriffe, begründet von Wolfgang Nauke und fortgeführt von Regina Harzer*. Neuwied: Luchterhand. (5. Auflage).

Paulson, Stanley L., 1980. „Zum Problem der Normenkonflikte“. *Archiv für Rechts- und Sozialphilosophie* 66, 487 –506.

Powers, David, 1986. *Studies in Qur'an and Ḥadīth*. Berkeley: University of California Press.

Rabb, Intisar, 2015. *Doubt's Benefits, Legal Maxims in Islamic Law, 7th–16th centuries*. Cambridge: Cambridge University Press.

Rebstock, Ulrich, 1999. „A Qadi's Errors“. *Islamic Law and Society* 6, 1–37.

Rohe, Mathias, 2009. *Das islamische Recht: Geschichte und Gegenwart*. München: Beck.

Sabra, Abdelhamid I., 1987. „The Appropriation and Subsequent Naturalization of Greek Science in Medieval Islam: A Preliminary Statement". *History of Science* 25, 223–243.

Al-Salahat, Sami, "Malāmiḥ fiqh al-qatʿ wa al-zann ʿinda al-imām al-Shāfiʿī", *Majallat al-Sharīʿa wa al-qanūn*, Nr. 17, Juni 2002, Universität Vereinigte Arabische Emirate, Abu Dhabi, 80–147. https://cl.uaeu.ac.ae/en/research/sljournal/journal_issues/issue17.pdf

Schacht, Joseph, 1967. *The Origins of Muhammadan Jurisprudence*. Oxford: Clarendon Press. (Revised Edition).

Schmidl, Petra G., 1997. „Two Early Arabic Sources on the Magnetic Compass (Revised Translation of a Master Thesis, Johann Wolfgang Goethe-Universität Frankfurt 1994)". *Journal of Arabic and Islamic Studies* 1, 81–132.

— 1999. „Zur Bestimmung der Qibla mittels der Winde". In: Peter Eisenhardt / Frank Linhard / Kaisar Petanides (Hg.) *Der Weg der Wahrheit. Aufsätze zur Einheit der Wissenschaftsgeschichte. Festgabe zum 60. Geburtstag von Walter G. Saltzer*. Hildesheim / New York: Georg Olms, 135–146.

— 2000. „Finding the Direction to Mecca with Folk Astronomical Methods: Qibla Schemes in a Medieval Yemeni Text by al-Farisi". In: César Esteban / Juan Antonio Belmonte (Hg.) *Astronomy and Cultural Diversity: Proceedings of the Conference „Oxford VI and SEAC (Société Européenne Pour L'astronomie Dans La Culture. Meeting) 99" held in Museo de la Ciencia y el Cosmos, La Laguna, June 1999*. Santa Cruz de Tenerife: Organismo Autónomo de Museos del Cabildo de Tenerife OACIM, 177–182.

— 2007. *Volkstümliche Astronomie im islamischen Mittelalter. Zur Bestimmung der Gebetszeiten und der Qibla bei al-Asbahi, Ibn Rahiq und al-Farisi* (Islamic Philosophy, Theology and Science 68). Leiden: Brill.

Schmidl, Petra G. / Herrera-Casais, Mónica, 2008. „The Earliest Known Schemes of Islamic Sacred Geography". In: Anna Akasoy / Wim Raven (Hg.) *Islamic thought in the Middle Ages. Studies in Text, Transmission and Translation, in Honour of Hans Daiber* (Islamic Philosophy, Theology and Science 75). Leiden / Boston: Brill, 275–300.

El Shamsy, Ahmed, 2008. „Rethinking ‚Taqlīd' in the Early Shāfiʿī School". *Journal of the American Oriental Society* Vol. 128/1, 1–23.

— 2013. *The Canonization of Islamic Law*. New York: Cambridge University Press.

Wissenschaftsrat, 2012. *Perspektiven der Rechtswissenschaft in Deutschland. Situation, Analysen, Empfehlungen*. Köln: Geschäftsstelle des Wissenschaftsrates.

Zaman, Muhammad Qasim, 1997. *Religion and Politics Under the Early ʿAbbasids. The Emergence of the Proto-Sunni Elite*. Leiden / New York / Köln: Brill.

Ziadeh, Farhat J., 1990. „Integrity (ʿAdālah) in Classical Islamic Law". In: Nicolas Heer (Hg.) *Islamic Law and Jurisprudence. Studies in Honor of Farhat J. Ziadeh*. Seattle/London: University of Washington Press, 73–93.

Zirker, Hans, 2016. *Der Koran (Übersetzung)*. Darmstadt: Wissenschaftliche Buchgesellschaft. (5. durchgesehene Auflage).

Zysow, Aaron, 2013. *The Economy of Certainty: An Introduction to the Typology of Islamic Legal Theory*. Atlanta, GA: Lockwood Press.

Indices

All index entries of the subject index are listed in English. Those entries that refer (also) to German contributions are indicated in German as well (English Word/German Word). If the entry only refers to German contributions, it is listed as English Word → German Word. German judicial expressions that do not have an English equivalent are included in German only and marked with an asterisk (*German Word).

Page numbers in *italics* refer to notes on that page.

Subject Index

abstraction/Abstraktion 2, 96, 181, 188, 192, 209, 215
Abydos 154–156
Aerarium (Rome) 185
Akkadian/Akkadisch 8 f., 12–14, 16, 25, 27, 29, 31, 43, 61 f., 65 f. *83*, *85*, *91*, 94, 108 f., 113, 116, 119–123, 125, 128–131, 134
*aktionenrechtliches Denken 222
Akhenaten 151
algorithm/Algorithmus 32–36, 38 f., 41 f., 83, 89, *91*, 208 f.
 arithmetic(al) operations 8, 32 f., 37, 40 f., 148
 control operations 32
 sub-algorithms 35–37, 41
Alexander the Great 181, 183
Alexandria 175, 183, 187, 189
Amun 153, 173 f.
Ammuna 118, 125 f.
Anatolia → Anatolien 108, 129, 133
aorist (habitual = grammatical form) 167, 169, 187, 192
Archimedes 207, 211, 213
Aristotle 158, *205*, 211, 213
Arnuwanda I *110*, 118, 120 f., 127, 129, 132
Ašmunikkal 118, 120, 129
Athens 199, *203*, 204, 207
authority/Autorität 2, 67, 111, 129–134, 185, 187 f., 192 f., 197, 199, 202–205, 209, 211, 215 f., 260, 262, 272, 274
Babylon 9, 47, 62, *108*, 207
Babylonia/Babylonien 29, 62
Babylonian/Babylonisch 11, 32, 56, 61–64, 85, *91*, *93*, *94*, *111*, 122, *123*, 204, 209
 Old Babylonian/Altbabylonisch 8–11, 25, *27*, *28*, 29 f., 32, 36 f., 41 f., 49, 55, 58, 61–65, *75*, 85, *91*, 93, 94, 119, *120*, 122, 142, 149, 207
basic arithmetical operations → Grundrechenarten 49, 55
capital penalty/Todesstrafe 24, 53, 67, 69, *70*, 73
casuistic/kasuistisch 3, *12*, 112 f., 133, 169, 176, 184
certificate form → Urkundenformular 119 f.
charge → Tarif 49, 55, *75*, 111, 113, *115*
claim/Anspruch, Forderung 2 f., *12*, 29, 58, *71*, 85, 124–128, 131, 161, 167, 170–173, 178, *202*, 209, 215 f., 222–224, 226, 240, 254, 263, 264, 273, 274
Cleopatra VII 182, *187*
code(x)/Codex *10*, 12, 15–17, 19 f., 28, *29*, 31, 48 f., 181, 183, 185, 189, 193, 197, 198, 210, *216*
 law code, legal code 2, 7–9, *12*, *13*, 29–32, *36*, 37, 41–43, 58,

142, *150*, *151*, 176, 181, 191, 204
Codex Ešnunna, Laws of Ešnunna (CE) 29, *55*, *62*, 65, 75, 113
Code/Laws of Ḫammurapi, Ḫammurapi law code, Codex Ḫammurapi, Codex Ḫammu-rāpi (CḪ) 3, 9, 25, 28 f., 31 f., 37, 41, 49–59, 62, 64 f., *67*, 68 f., 75, 113, 149
Codex (of) Hermopolis, Legal Code of Hermopolis 174, 176 f., 181, 184, 186, 188, 189, 190, 193
Codex Lipit-Eštar (CL) *62*, 113
Laws of Ur-namma → Codex Ur-namma (CU) 3, 61–67, 70, 71, 74, 75, *111*, *112*, 113
codification/Kodifikation 32, 158, 84, 189, 197, 202, 206, 263
cohabitation → Konkubinat 70
coherence/Kohärenz 1–3, 47, 49, 58, 107, 133, 181, 188, 189, 192, 204, 206, 215, 254, 264, 269, 273
collection/Fallsammlung, Kompendium 2, 113, 133, 215
law collection/Rechtssammlung 1–3, 47–49, *54*, 56 f., 61–64, *66*, *67*, 110, 113 f., *115*, 117, 133 f., 141, 149, 151, 161
mathematical collection 2, 207 f., 213
collective statement 216
computation/Berechnung 36, 86, *88* f., 92, 197, 207, 209, 215, 239, 267
computer (electronic) 37–39, 42
ENIAC 38–40
conditional clause (sentence)/ Konditionalsatz 12 f., 15, 66, 112 f., 133, 169, 177, 188 f.
conditionality *200*
consistency/Konsistenz 2, 49, 58, *215*, 264, 268 f.
custom 172, 175, 178
legal custom → Rechtsgewohnheit 58
definiteness → Bestimmtheit 253, *258*, *261*, 264 f., 273
Demotic 2, 4, 141, 167–169, 173, 176, 178, 182–189, 192, 193
Dreros 198 f., 203, 206
Egypt/Ägypten 1–4, 42, 141–143, 149, 150, 154–158, 160f., 169, 181–184, 186, 189, 207, 254, 256
Hellenistic Egypt 181, 186, 187
Pharaonic Egypt 141
Ptolemaic Egypt 3, 181–183, 189
Roman Egypt 186, 207
Egyptian/Ägyptisch 1, 3, 141, 143 f., *145*, 147–149, *150*, 153, 157 f., 161, 167 f., 181–187, 189, 190–193, 209
Ephesus 207, 232 f., 235 f.
epilogue/Epilog 10, 29, 53, 57–59, 62–64, 114, 134, 151, 154
*Ermessensklage (*actio arbitraria*) 233–236
Euclid *197*, 211–214
error awareness → Fehlerbewusstsein 254, 257, 264, *266*, 272–274
field/Feld 26, 50, 54, 65, 74, 75, 86, 109, 122, 124, 125, 154, 156, 159 f.
flow diagram 14–16, 18, 20 f., 23 f., 27, 32, 40, *204*
formalistic → formalistisch *228*, 254, 262, 273 f.
*Fortsetzung der Verbindlichkeit (*perpetuatio obligationis*) 228, *229*, 231, 237
fraction/Bruch(teil) 49–55, *85*, *143*, 144, 176
*Geldbetrag, bestimmter (*certa pecunia*) 221–226, *227*, 233–235, 242, 244, 246
geometrical/geometrisch 49 f., 55, *85*, 93, 96, 158, *211*, 214
geometry/Geometrie 50, *88*, 188, 199, 214
Gortyn 198 f., 203, *205*
Greece/Griechenland 2 f., 133, 141, 183, 197, *198*, 202, 204, 206, 207
Greek *1*, 4, *12*, 168, 181–189, 192 f., 197–202, 205–207, 211, 214 f.

hadith → Hadīth 260, 269 f., 274
Ḫammurapi, Ḫammu-rāpi 9–11, 29, 47, 49, 62 f.
handbook, manual 1, 40, 167 f., 175, 177 f., 184, 186
Ḫatti 29, 108, 110, 130
Ḫattuša 108–110, 112, 117 f., 121, 124, 128, 133
Ḫattusili I 108, *112*, *126 f.*
Ḫattušili III 128, 130
Hieratic 143–145, *146*, 168, 175
hierarchy/Hierarchie 53, 143, 173, 182, 206
Hippocrates 207, *213*
Hittite/Hethitisch 2, *54*, 66, 107–111, *112*, 113 f., 116–119, *121*, 122, 125, *126*, 127–134
Hittite laws → Hethitische Gesetze (HG) 111–116, 126 f., 134
homicide, murder/Mord 12, 14, 50, 65, *67*, 203, 215
Horemheb 150–154, 157, 161
injury → Körperverletzung 52, 65, 71–73, 111, 114, 116 f.
inscriptional law 197, 198, 203–205, 215 f.
Iraq → Irak 257, 263, 269 f., 274
*Ja-/Nein-Prozess 221, 223, 224–226
justice/Gerechtigkeit 3, 7, 9, 29, 57, 75, 114–116, 131, 141 f., 148 f., 157–161, 167, 172 f., 178, 222 f., 226
justification 16, 197, 205 f., 209, 211, 215 f.
*Klagen strengen Rechts 221, 246
Kush 154–156
land donations → Landschenkungsurkunden (LSU) 107 f., 110, 117–126, 128–134
Laokritai (Egyptian judges) 182–184
law/Recht, Gesetz 1–3, 7–25, *26*, 27–29, 37, 43, 47, 48, 56, 58, 59, 61, 63 f., 67, *68*, 70, *75*, 90, 111, *112*, 113 f., 123, 125, 141 f., 149–153, 155–157, 159, 167–169, 172 f., 177 f., 182–187, 189, 191 f., 197–206, 213–216, 221 f., *225*, *231* f., 253–257, 261–268, 270–275
law texts, legal texts/Rechtstexte *1*, 2, 8, 20, 29, 43, 49, 62, 107 f., 133, 141, 143, 154, 156 f., 161, 167, 176–178, 182, 188 f., *198*, *200*, 203, 258
legal metaphor → Rechtsmetapher 254, 256, 265, *267*, 275
legal practice/Rechtspraxis 58, 107, 112, 114 f., 124 f., 142, 148, 183
legislation /Gesetzgebung 64, *126*, 168, 172, 182, 189
legitimation/Legitimation 111, *127*, 202, 264
*Leistungsgegenstand 221, 225 f., 229, 231, 233 f., 238, 240–242, 244–246
  bestimmter (*certum*) 221 f., 226, *227*, *231*, 233, 236, 240–242, 244, 245 f., 247
  unbestimmter (*incertum*) 221 f., *224*, 225 f., 230 f., 233 f., 236, 238, 239–242, 244–246
*Leistungsort 231, 234–236, 246
  bestimmter (*certus locus*) 231, 236, 240
*Leistungszeit 231, 232 f., 238
  bestimmte (certus dies) 231, 236, 238, 240
letters 167 f., 173, 178, 182
-ma (role of) 13 f., 31, 37
maat/Ma'at, Maat 149, 159, 160, 168
magical papyrus 175
Marduk 29
marriage/Ehe 68, 70 f., 73, 169, 171 f., 259, 260
mathematical problem(s) 2–3, 7, 31, 34, 38, 42, 141–144, 184, 186, 188, 193
mathematical texts/ mathematische Texte *1*, 2, 8, 30–32, 36 f., 41 f., 49, 55, 58, *83*, 84, 87, *91*, *94* f., 109, 141–151, 153, 156 f., 168, 176–178, 184 f., 187, 192 f., 215 f., 258

mathematical problem texts 2, 8, 29–32, 36 f., 41–43, 84, 141 f., 149
mathematics/Mathematik 1–3, 8, *28*, 30, 38, 42 f., 47–49, 55–59, *84*, *88*, 115, 141–144, 149, 157–161, 167 f., *184*, 197, *200*, *202*, 206 f., 211, 213–216, 255, 267, 275
measure/Maß 49–51, 56, 83, 86, *88*, 90, 92, 114, 151
medical text(s) 8, *27*, *28*, 148, 185
medicine 8, 28, 17, *149*, *200*
Mekka 257, 263, 265, 266, 268, 275
Mesopotamia/Mesopotamien 1, 2 f., 7 f., 37, 42 f., 57, 62, *64*, 83, *84*, 109, 113, 122, 133, 141 f., 149, 156–158, 160
Mesopotamian/mesopotamisch 1–3, 7 f., 10, *29*, 37, 42, 43, *84*, *89*, 113, *115*, 122, 131, 133 f., 144, 149, 153
metrology/Metrologie 48, 122, *143*, 208
Metroon (Athens) 185
monumentality/Monumentalität *58*, 133, 199 f., 202, 216
Nicomachus 209f., 213
normative order(s)/normative Ordnung(en) 1 f., 141 f., 151, 197, 198, 200–206, 211, 215 f.
normativity/Normativität 1–3, 47 f., 64, 107, 118, 128, 133, 148, 153, 167–169, 173, 177, 197, 214, 255, 258 f., 261, 266, 270, 272, 275
norms, meta-morms → Normen, Meta-Normen 1, 7 f., 42 f., 47, *69*, 107, 115, 201–206, 216, 254, 272
  ethical norms (see legal codes)
  legal norms/Rechtsnormen 1, 54, 93, 107, 168, 200, 133, 154, 254, *262*, 263
  mathematical norms 211
  prescriptive norms (see mathematics)
number/Zahl 11, *25*, 28, 31–36, 40, *42*, 47, 49 f., *54* f., 58, *71*, *83*, *84*, *91*, *94*, 96, 98, 141–144, 148, *176*, 178, 207, 209–211, 215
numerical value/Zahlenwert 2, 3, 33, 36, 54, 96, 100, 114, 115, 147, 158, 160
omina texts/Omina *112*, *113*, 166, 200
(river) ordeal/(Fluss)Ordal 21, 70, *71*, 204
Osiris 154, 159, 161
petitions 167, 173 178, 185
Plato *202*, 211
permanence/Dauerhaftigkeit 107, 128–130, 132, 134, 200
Politikos nomos (city law) 183
priestly synodal decrees 183
probability → Wahrscheinlichkeit *69*, 253, *261*, 264–266, 273
procedures, procedural texts /Prozeduren 1 f., 31, 37, 42, 113, 107, 142, 168, 186, 254
  in law codes/legal procedures 1–3, 12, *36*, 149, 170–172, 184, 190 f., 199, 201–205, 215
    sequential 17
    conditional branching 20, 28
      parallel 25
      sequential 26
      simple 21
  in mathematics (see also algorithm) 1–3, 31 f., 141, 143, 145, 146–148, 153, 207–209, 211, 215 f.
  in medical texts 3, 8, 153
prohibition of modification → Veränderungsverbot 110, 123, 128 f., 132, 134
prologue/Prolog 10, 29, 50, 57, 62 f., 113 f., 134, 151
*Nachweis (*dalīl*) 254, 256 f., 259, 266–268, 271
Prostagmata (Ptolemaic ordinances) 182
Psephismata (decrees) 183
quran → Koran 257–259, 265–268, 272
Ramesses II → Ramses II. 130
rape → Vergewaltigung 65, 68 f., *72*
rational-choice theory 202

rational practice (texts) 8 f., 28 f., 37, 42 f.,113
(see also legal codes)
(see also mathematical problems)
reductio ad artem 43
Regelsysteme
mathematische 47, 57, 83, 107
rechtliche 47, 107
Revenue Laws 183, 189, 191
right *67*, 171–173, 178, 199, 204, 215
rite 167, 172 f., 178
robbery/Raub 19 f., 50, 65, 67,
Roman law → Römisches Recht 222, 226
römisches Prozessrecht 221, 223
rule/Regel, Regelung 1, 7f., 14–16, 28, 32, 64, 83–86, 88–90, 92–94, 111–117, 125 f., 131, 133, 141, 149, 151, 157 f., 170, 173, 176, 178, 181–184, 186–188, 189–192, 204, 205–211, 214–216, *237*, 247, 259, 264, 267, 272
*Sache 54f., 221, 225, 228, 231, 234 f., 238, 244
bestimmte (*certa res*) 221 f., 224–231, 233–235, 237 f., 240, 242, 244, 246
Šamaš 9
sanction/Sanktion 50–53, 55, 66–68, 200 f., 259
Scheil, Vincent 9, 11
*Schuldversprechen, förmliches (*stipulatio*) 222, 224–230, *231*, 233, 236–239, 242, 244 f.
Schwarzschild, Martin 38 f., 41
scribal education → Schreiberausbildung 47, 48, 63, 85, 114, *115*
scribe/Schreiber *10*, 36 f., 42, 108, 110, 114 f., 119, 124, 127 f., 143, 148 f., *157*, 160, 174
seal → Siegel 108, *110*, *118*, 119–121, 123 f., *126*, 128 f., 132–134
Seti I 151, 153 f., 146
slave/Sklave, Sklavin 22–25, 50, 52, 65, 68 f., 71–74, 116 f., 123, 152, 169, 215, 224, 225, 227–230, 235, 237, 239, 240–244
subsum(p)tion *28*, 204 f., 215
stereotyped character → Formelhaftigkeit 109, 134
Sumerian → Sumerisch, sumerisch 8, 43, 61–67, 83, *85*, 91, 95, 108, 113, 122, 129
systematicity 204
systematics → Systematik 47, 49, 56 f., 65, *111*, *122*
Tabularium (Rome) 185
talion → Talion 50–52, 55, 67
teachings 3, 141, 149, 157 f., 160 f.
Tebtynis temple library 186
Telipinu 109, 112, 118, 121, 125 f., 129, 131 f.
tenses, verbal (role of) 9, 12–14, 16–18, 20 f., 27 f., 31, 37
terminology/Terminologie 12, 48, 94, 122, 133, 205, 209, 211, 215
to be fitting 167, 173–175, 178
to collect/sammeln 182, 191, 202, 204, 208 f., 213, 215, 257, 260
to put into writing → verschriftlichen 257, 260
Ur-Namma 62 f., 75
unlawful detention → Freiheitsberaubung 65, 67 f.
*Vermögensstrafe 69
*Verpflichtung zu einem Geben (*dare*) 225, 227, 231, 233, 236, 244 f.
*Verpflichtung zu einem Tun (*facere*) 226, 228, 233, 236, 245 f.
*Versprechen einer Leistung an einen Dritten (*stipulatio alteri*) 240, 244 f.
von Neumann, John 38–40
*Wahlschuld 240, 242 f.
weight(s)/Gewicht(e) 50–55, 88, 114, 160
wisdom texts (Egyptian) (see also teachings) 168, 172, 185
validity claim → Geltungsanspruch 47f., 56, *58*, 85, 90, 264
verdict/Urteil 29, *56*, 125, 169–171, 184, 215, 234, 259, *273*
*Zuvielforderung (*pluris petitio*) *224*, 229, 236, 241 f.

Index of Texts

Ancient Near East

BM 13901 30–32, 34, 84, 89, *91*, 94, 99, 101
Bo 86/299 130
CTH 1 116, 129, 131
CTH 8 *126, 128*
CTH 19 116, 131
CTH 21 131
CTH 75 *128*
CTH 88 *128*
CTH 224 132
CTH 225 132
CTH 230 109
CTH 230–239 109
CTH 239 109
CTH 240–246 109
CTH 247 109
CTH 261 *110,* 127
CTH 269 114
CTH 291 111
CTH 292 111
CTH 372 *111*
CTH 393 *115*
CTH 404 *115*
CTH 441 130
CTH 503–504 109
CTH 675 *132*
CTH 700 *115*
CTH 760 118
HS 1883 *27,* 43
IBoT 1.30 *111*
KBo 1.6 *128*
KBo 3.1 125
KBo 3.22 *129*
KBo 6.2 *126–128*
KBo 6.4 112 f., 115
KBo 6.6 *111*, 112, 114
KBo 6.13 *111*
KBo 6.28 *128*
KBo 10.34 *115*
KBo 12.105 *115*
KBo 13.34 *113*
KBo 50.60+KUB 40.69+KBo 4.10 130
KBo 56.107 130
KBo 62.5 109
KUB 12.26 130
KUB 13.2 127
KUB 44.63+KUB 8.83 *113*
LSU 1 117, *119,* 121
LSU 2 121
LSU 3 121, *122*, 124–126, 128
LSU 4 121 f.
LSU 5 121
LSU 7 121 f.
LSU 10 *122*
LSU 11 119, 121
LSU 12 *121*
LSU 15 *123*
LSU 21 118
LSU 22 122 f.
LSU 22–24 121
LSU 26–27 121
LSU 28–35 121
LSU 34 *122*
LSU 39 121, *122*
LSU 40 *122*
LSU 40–42 121
LSU 46–47 121
LSU 89 121
LSU 91 118, *121*
VBoT 24 *115*

Classical World

Greek

Andocides, *On the Mysteries* 206
Archilochus, *Fragments* 198
Aristotle, *Nicomachean Ethics* *158*
Aristotle, *Politics* *205*
Aristotle, *Posterior Analytics* 213
Demosthenes, *Against Lacritus* 199
Demosthenes, *On the Crown* *202*
Ephorus, *Fragments* *198*
Euclid, *Elements* I 213, *214*
Euclid, *Elements* III 212
Eusebius, *Chronics* *198*
Heron, *Geometrics* 214
Koerner, 1993, no. 11 (Drakon's law) 203
Koerner, 1993, no. 29 *201*
Koerner, 1993, no. 43 *201*

Koerner, 1993, no. 47.9 *201*
Koerner, 1993, no. 90 *198*
Koerner, 1993, no. 124 205
Koerner, 1993, no. 163–183 (Gortyn inscription) 203
Nicomachus, *Arithmetical Introduction* 209
Plato, *Phaedrus* *202*
Plutarch, *Life of Lycurgus* *203*
Proclus, *On Euclid's Elements* I *214*
Sophocles, *Antigone* *202*

Latin

Cicero, *De iure civili in artem redigendo* *43*
Cicero, *De oratore* *43*
Codex Iustinianus
- 3.18.1 *233*
- 8.38.3 pr. *245*

Digesta
- 2.14.27.6 (Paul.) *242*
- 4.3.7.3 (Ulp. 11 ad ed.) 229
- 7.1 (Paul.) *233*
- 7.1.36.2 (Afr. 5 quaest.) 239
- 7.6.2 (Pomp.) *231*
- 9.2.9.2 (Ulp.) *228*
- 12.1.22 (Iul.) *235*
- 12.6.26.13 (Ulp.) *242*
- 13.3.3 i.f. (Marcell. / Ulp.) *231*
- 13.3.4 (Gai.) *235*
- 13.4 233
- 13.4.1 (Gai.) *233, 234*
- 13.4.1 (Ulp.) *233*
- 13.4.2 pr. (Ulp.) *233*
- 13.4.2.1 (Ulp.) *233*
- 13.4.2.2 (Ulp.) *233*
- 13.4.2.6 (Iul. / Ulp.) *232*
- 13.4.2.8 (Ulp.) *234*
- 13.4.3 (Gai.) *233*
- 13.4.5 (Paul.) *233*
- 13.4.7 pr. (Paul.) *233*
- 13.4.8 (Afr.) *233*
- 13.4.10 (Paul.) *233*
- 17.1.37 (Afr.) *237*
- 19.1.3.3 (Pomp.) *237*
- 29.7 (Ulp.) *228*
- 30.82 pr. (Iul.) *231*
- 30.108.11 (Afr.) *231*
- 31.66.4 (Pap.) *231*
- 45.1.23 (Pomp.) *237*
- 45.1.33 (Pomp. 24 ad Sab.) 237
- 45.1.38.17 (Ulp.) *245*
- 45.1.38.21 (Ulp.) *245*
- 45.1.38.23 (Ulp.) *245*
- 45.1.75.8 (Ulp. 22 ad ed.) 240
- 45.1.82.1 (Ulp.) *228*
- 45.1.85.6 (Paul.) 246
- 45.1.91 pr. (Paul. 17 ad Plaut.) 227
- 45.1.91.3 (Paul.) *228*
- 45.1.114 (Ulp. 17 ad Sab.) 238
- 45.1.118 (Pap. 27 quaest.) 243
- 45.1.126.2 (Paul.) *244*
- 45.1.131.1 (Scaev.) *231*
- 45.1.137.2 (Ven. 1 stip) 232
- 46.3.27 (Ulp.) *231*
- 46.3.33.1 (Iul.) *231*
- 82.1 (Ulp.) *228, 237*
- 84.4 (Iul.) *231*

Gai. Institutiones
- 3.103 *244 f.*
- 3.219 *228*
- 4.2 *224*
- 4.5 *223*
- 4.17 *223*
- 4.19 *224*
- 4.53 *224,* 235 f., 241 f.
- 4.54 242
- 4.59 *224*
- 4.136 *225, 243*

Institutiones Iustiniani
- 3.15.5 *232*
- 3.19.20 *245*
- 4.6.33 *233, 235, 243*

Pauli Sententiae
- 5.7.4 *227 f.*

Theophili antecessoris paraphrasis institutionum
- 4.6.33 *233, 235, 243*

Zwölf Tafeln 223 f.

Egypt

Apis Embalming Ritual 175
The Admonitions of Ipuwer 150
BGU VI 1213 186
Canopus decree 183, 186–188
C. Ord. Ptol. 33 186
C. Ord. Ptol. 45 186
C. Ord. Ptol. 46 186
C. Ord. Ptol. 62, 62 descr. 186
C. Ord. Ptol. 63 186
C. Ord. Ptol. 75 186
C. Ord. Ptol. 76 186
Demotic Graffiti of the Dodecaschoenus from the Temple of Isis on Philae Island 417 172
Great Edict of Horemheb 151, 153, 156
Instruction addressed to Kagemni 149
Instruction of Amenemope 149
Instruction of Anqscheshonqy 185
Instruction of Any 149, 160
Instruction of Prince Hardjedef 149
Loyalist Teaching 149
Magical Papyrus of London and Leiden 175
Mathematical Leather Roll (BM 10250) 143
Nauri Decree 151, 153, 157
P. Assoc. 184, 187
pBerlin 13537 174
pBerlin 13540 175
pBerlin 15683 175
pBerlin 23757 177
pBM 10057, 10058 (see pRhind, mathematical)
pBM 10074 (see pReich)
pBM 10474 *159*
pBM 10522 (see pGlanville)
pBM 10591 169, 178, 184
pBM 15091 (see pSiut)
pBrooklyn 35.1446 150
pCairo 2 30605 171
pCairo CG 22186 174
pCairo CG 22187 174
pCairo Demotic 30605 171, 184
pCairo Demotic 30606 *184*
pCairo Demotic 30619 *184*
pCairo Demotic 31179 *184*
pCairo JdE 89127 (Codex Hermopolis) 174, 176 f., 184, 186, 188–190, 193
pCarlsberg 1 184
pEheverträge no. 8 Z 172
pErbstreit (2017) 9=10; 13; 17=18 *186*
pGlanville (BM 10522) 171
pHalle 1 *183*
pHou 8 171
pInsinger 173
pLille Demotic 1 29 170
pLondon VII 2193 184, 187 f.
pMattha (Codex Hermopolis) 186, 189, *190*
pMoscow, mathematical (4676) 143–147
pOxyrhynchus XLVI 3285 184
pPrag Demotic 17 *184*
pPetrie III 21g +pGurob 2 *183*
pReich (BM 10074) 171
pRev (Revenue Laws) 186, 191
pRhind, mathematical (BM 10057, 10058) 143–146, *148*
pRylands 9 173 f.
pSiut (BM 15091) 169 f. 174
pTeos 12 171
pUC32134A 147
pUC32162 146
pVindob D(emotic) 6257 175
pVindob G(reek) 19996 207
pVindob G(reek) 26740 208
Rosettana decree 175, 183, 186–188
SB V 7835 184
Setne I *172*
Synodal decree Alexandria 175
Teaching for King Merikare 149 f.
Teaching of King Amenemhat 149
Teaching of Khety 149
Teaching of the Vizier Ptahhotep 149, 158–161

Muslim World

Al-Shāfiʿī, *al-Risāla* 263, 265–274
Al-Shāfiʿī, *Kitāb al-jimāʿ* 256, 258, *261, 265–268, 271 f.*, *273*, 275
Ibn al-Muqaffaʿ, *Risālat al-ṣaḥab* *256, 263*

Index of Akkadian, Arabic, Egyptian, Hittite, Greek, Latin, and Sumerian Words

Akkadian

awāt mīšarim 29
bašûm 27, 29, 31, 34
BĒL MADGALTI 127
dīnāt mīšarim 57
ēdēnû 123
GIŠ*gipeššarannu* 122
ḫabbātum 19
ibašši 26 f.
ikkiru 16
ilku(m) 125
inaddin 16
ilqû 16
iddâk 12, 14, 19, 21, 23
iddi 12–14, 21
iddinu 16
irtedī 22 f.
izzakar 22 f.
leqûm *121*
mimma 16
našûm *31, 121*
našûm … nadānum 121
redûm 22
rubā'um 129
rubā'um rabūm 129
šakanu 121
šamellûm 16
šū 14, 16, 19, 21–23, 26, 34, *73, 84,* 100, 121, 123
šumma 14, 16–19, *20,* 21–23, 25–28, 31, 66
šutākalum *31*
ubbir 12–14
uktīn 12–14, 21
zakārum 22

Arabic

akhbār āḥād 269
ahl al-ḥadīth 256, 269
ahl al-ra'y 256, 269
taʿārud 261
taqlīd 266, 272
tawātur 258
tawātir 260
jumla tabyīn 261
ḥadīth āḥādī 270
ḥasan 270
daʿīf 270
dalāla qaṭʿiyya 259
dalīl, adillā 268
ra'y 269
rakʿas 267
zann 261, 264
saḥāba 269
saḥīḥ 270, 274
sāhib, ashāb 260
Sunna 257 f., 260 f., 263, *267*, 268–272
shuhra 270
ṭuhr 260
ẓannī 259, 264, 267, 272, 274
ẓāhiri *265*
ʿadāla 262
ʿaql, ʿuqūl 268
ʿalamāt 268
ʿamm-khāṣṣ 261
ʿilm ẓannī 264, 267
ʿilm qaṭʿī 264, 267
farḍ 267
fasād 262
fāsid 267
furūʿ 257
qatʿ *261,* 264
qaṭʿ-ẓann 261
qaṭʿī 258f., 265, 272, 274,
qaṭʿī al-sanad 258
Qur'ān *260*
qurūʿ 260
qibla 254, 265 f., *267,* 275
qiblā 254, 265 f.
qiyās 265, 269 f., 273
kaʿba 265 f., 275

khabar wāḥid 261, 265, 270 f.
kitāb al-rijāl 262
lam yaflaḥ qawmun wallaw ʿamruhum imra'a 274
laysat tanzilu bi-aḥad min ahl dīn allāh nāzila illā wa-fī kitāb allāh al-dalīl ʿalā sabīl al-hudā fīhā 268
matn *260,* 262
mashhūr 260, 270
maṣāliḥ 269
mutawātir 270
naskḥ-mansūkh 261
naṣṣ 257f.
nuṣūṣ qaṭʿiyya al-thubūt 258
uṣūl al-fiqh 256f., 263f.
ijtihād 259, 265 f., 271, 273
ijmā 270, 273
istadallū bihā ʿalā maʿrifat al-ʿalāmāt 268
istidlāl 268
istinbāt 256
isnād 260, 262
inqitāʿ al-iḥtimāl 265

Egyptian

iw=w ḏd n=k 176
iw=f r sḏm 175
iw=f ḫpr r 191
iw=f sḏm 175
iw=n (r) fꜣy 170
iw=k sḏm 175
iw=k ḏd 176
in.nꜣ.w 191
ir 146 f., 169 f., 172, 174 f.
i.ir-ḫr di=w 169 f.
i.ir=k sḏm 175
ir.tw hpw r=f 155 f.
ir.t mj ḫpr 145
ir šʿr 189
ir ḏd n=k zš *145*
iḫ 176f.
iḫ pꜣ nty iw=f wꜣḥ r pꜣy=s ṯs 176
bw-ir=w wʿb 170
bw ir=w rg=f 169
bw-ir=f sḏm 191
bw-ir=s pḥ 174
pꜣy=f wꜣḥ 169, 177
pꜣ mn sꜣ pꜣ mn 188, 191
pꜣ nty 169, 172, 174, 191
pꜣ nty-iw=s pḥ 174
pꜣ rmt 169–171, 188
pꜣ hp irm nꜣ md.w.t 184, 187
pꜣ sḥn nfr st ir-rḫ s 173, 178
pꜣ gy ir=f 176
pḥ 167, 173–175, 178
mꜣʿt 148, 154–156, 160 f.
Mꜣʿt (goddess) 153, 161
mi ḏd n=k 145
mtj 187
mtw=w sḏm 175
mtw=f sḏm 175
mtw=n di 170
mtw=k sḏm 175
mtr.t 185
nꜣ wʿb šʿš 175
n wʿ sp 187
r 176
r tm (r)dit 156
r di.t rḫ=k s 176
hp *150,* 152, 168–173, 175, 178, 184 f., 187
ḫpr 145–147, 149, 172, 174, 191
ḫpr.t im pw 147
ḫr 152, 155 f., 176 f.
ḫr sḏm=f 167. 177 f., 187 f., 191, 193
ḫr di=w 169 f., 174f., 177
sšm.t=f 145
st pḥ 173 f.
sḏm.in=f 148
sḏm.ḫr=f 145, 147 f., 157, 160 f., 177
tp n ir.t 145

Hittite

alaleššar 122
anda šittariezzi 126
anda ši(ya)ttariya *126*
ešzi *124*
gipeššar 122
ḫapalki 129

ḫekur 128
kapunu 122, 124
karū 112
kinun=a 112
KUR ^{URU}*Ḫatti* 108
luzzi 125 f.
pankuš 131
šahhan 125–127
šarā da- *121*
takku 66, 113

Greek

ἀναγεγραμμένα *205*
ἀναγκάζεται 189
arourai 208
archon 199
ἀϝλανέος 201
ἄχρηστος 198
boulè 183, 187
γινέσθωι 187
gnome dikaiotatè 183
γραφέα 201
damioi 198
δεῖ 189, 208 f.
dèmos 183, 187
diagrammata 183
δινάκοι 201
dioiketes 192
diorthomata 182
ἐδείχθη 212 f.
ἔδοξεν 187
εἶπαν 187
εἶπεν 187
ἐκθέσθαι 211
θιοσολοιον *199*
κοινὰ λεγόμενα ἀξιώματα *213*
kosmos, kosmoi 198 f., 203
laokritai 182–184
leukoma 186
λόγοι: οἱ γεωμέτρου λόγοι 209
neusis *214*
nomos, nomoi 182
oikonomos 191 f.
ὅπερ ἐστὶν ἀδύνατον 212 f.
πάτρια 201
polis, poleis 181, 183, 186 f., 198 f., 201–205, 216
politikos nomo, politikoi nomoi 183
πρόθεσις 205, *206*
prostagmata 182
προστάσσεται 189
προστάσσω 187
πρυτανέων γώμη 187
psephismata 183
schoinia 208
stoikheia 213
synchoreseis 186
τείνω *211*
τεταγμένος 211
τις 188, 199,
chora 183
chrematistai 182
ψήφισμα 187, 206
ὡς δεῖ ποιῆσαι 208 f.

Latin

a maiore ad minus *236*
actio *222, 243*
actio arbitraria 233–236
actio certae creditae pecuniae 226, 246
actio certi ex stipulatu *225*
actio certi ex testamento 227, 231
actio de dolo 229, 231
actio ex testamento *227, 231*
actio incerti *242*
actio incerti ex stipulatu 222, 225 f., 234, 238, 240, 242–244
adiectio loci 235, 236
alia(e) certa(e) res 222–224, 226, 233, 236, 244
arbitrio tuo *234*, 235
arbitrium 234
bonae fidei iudicia 221, 246
cavit de dolo 229, 230
certam rem dare 229, 231, 237
certam rem dare oportere 229
certa pecunia 221–226, *227*, 233f., 244
certa res 221 f., 224–226, 228, 231, 233, 235–238, 240, 244
certo die 237–239
certo loco 233–236

certum 3, 222, 226 f., *231*, 233, 236, 240 f., 245–247
certus dies 231, 236, 240
certus locus 231, 236, 240
commemoratio loci 235
condemnatio *233*, 234
condemnatio pecuniaria 224
condictio *223*
condictio certae pecuniae 223, 226, *233*, 234 f., 242, 244, 246
condictio certae rei 225, 227, 231, 234, *235*, 237–239, 242, 244, 246
condictio incerti *225*
condictio tritic[i]aria 225
confestim obligatus est 232, 236
dare 223, *224*, 225–227, 229, 231–233, 235–238, 240–246
dare oportere 223, 225, 227, 229, 235, 243, 244
decem *233*, 240 f., *242*, 243 f.
facere 225 f., 228, 233, 236, 238, 240, 242–246
fame necare *228*
fundum certo die praestari 238 f.
fundum praestari *238*
homo 241
incertum 1, 3, 221 f., *224*, 225 f., 230 f., 233 f., 236, 238–246
inpossibilium nulla est obligatio 247
intentio *235*, 241 f.
intentio certa 242
interpellatio 237
inutilis 244
legatum per damnationem 247
legatum ususfructus *231*
legis actio per condictionem 223 f.
legis actio per iudicis arbitrive postulationem 223 f., *225*
legis actio sacramento in personam 223
litis contestatio 228, 237, 239
magis probandum *227*, 228
mora debitoris *237, 239*
mutuum 224, 226
nam et res certae designantur … 241
neglegere infirmum *228*
non facere *228*, 230
non immerito quaeritur 240 f.
numerus clausus 222
perpetuatio obligationis 228, *229*, 231, 237
pluris petitio *224*, 229, 236, 241 f.
pluris petitio causa 241 f.
pluris petitio loco 236
pluris petitio re *224*
pure petere 235
quanti ea res est/erit 225, 228, 231, *233*, 234 f., 238 f., 244
quanti mea/legatarii intersit moram factam non esse 238 f.
quidquid … dare facere oportet 238, 240, 242–244, 246
quod facturum se promiserit 232 f.
rei vindicatio 228
restituere 228
senatus consulta 185
si non est cautum 230 f.
si quidem de dolo cautum est 230 f.
stipulatio 222, 224, 226
stipulatio alteri 244, 245
stipulatio certae pecuniae 246
stipulatio certae rei 228, 230,
stipulatio certi 241 f., 244f .
stipulatio incerti 244
usus fructus aestimetur 239 f.
ususfructus legatus *238*
veteres 228

Sumerian

AN.BAR 123, 129
A.ŠÀ 122
dam-ĝuruš-a-da *71*
dumu-gi$_7$ *72*
é-dub-ba-a 48
en-nu[ĝ] 67
ereš-diĝir *70*
GAL 124
gaz 67
géme 72 f.
ĝuruš *68, 71*
ì-bíl-i-dè-eš *70*
ì-gaz-e-dam *67*

IKU 122, 124
^{GIŠ}KIRI$_6$ 122,
^{GIŠ}KIRI$_6$.GEŠTIN 122,
KISLAḪ 122
KÙŠ 122
lá *71*
lú-ra *71*
LUGAL.GAL 120 f., 123, 129
me-te-ni-ta *69*
^{GIŠ}MÚ.SAR 122
nam-érim-ta gur *74*
[nam-tag] dugud-bi [ḫé$^?$-Í]L$^?$-[e] *70*
ní-te-a-ni-ta *69*
nin 73
ra *73*, *91*, 94, 99
sa-gaz-šè – ak 67,
^{GIŠ}TIR 122
^{GIŠ}TUKUL 125,
tukumbi 66, 113
tuk[umbi á-su]ḫ *73*
Ú.SAL 122